T0364160

Law and Employment

**A National Bureau
of Economic Research
Conference Report**

Law and Employment
Lessons from Latin America and the Caribbean

Edited by **James J. Heckman and Carmen Pagés**

The University of Chicago Press

Chicago and London

JAMES J. HECKMAN is the Henry Schultz Distinguished Service Professor of Economics and of Social Sciences and director of the Economics Research Center and the Center for Social Program Evaluation at the University of Chicago, and a research associate of the National Bureau of Economic Research. He was awarded the Nobel Prize in Economics in 2000. CARMEN PAGÉS is a senior research economist in the research department of the Inter-American Development Bank.

The University of Chicago Press, Chicago 60637
The University of Chicago Press, Ltd., London
© 2004 by the National Bureau of Economic Research
All rights reserved. Published 2004
Printed in the United States of America
13 12 11 10 09 08 07 06 05 04   1 2 3 4 5
ISBN: 0-226-32282-3 (cloth)

Library of Congress Cataloging-in-Publication Data

Law and employment : lessons from Latin America and the
  Caribbean / edited by James Heckman and Carmen Pagés.
      p. cm. — (NBER conference report)
    ISBN 0-226-32282-3 (cloth : alk. paper)
      1. Labor market—Latin America. 2. Labor market—Caribbean
  Area. 3. Labor laws and legislation—Latin America. 4. Labor laws
  and legislation—Caribbean Area. I. Heckman, James J. (James
  Joseph) II. Pagés, Carmen. III. Series.

  HB5730.5.A6L38 2004
  331.1'098—dc22

                                                              2004047874

Relation of the Directors to the
Work and Publications of the
National Bureau of Economic Research

1. The object of the NBER is to ascertain and present to the economics profession, and to the public more generally, important economic facts and their interpretation in a scientific manner without policy recommendations. The Board of Directors is charged with the responsibility of ensuring that the work of the NBER is carried on in strict conformity with this object.

2. The President shall establish an internal review process to ensure that book manuscripts proposed for publication DO NOT contain policy recommendations. This shall apply both to the proceedings of conferences and to manuscripts by a single author or by one or more co-authors but shall not apply to authors of comments at NBER conferences who are not NBER affiliates.

3. No book manuscript reporting research shall be published by the NBER until the President has sent to each member of the Board a notice that a manuscript is recommended for publication and that in the President's opinion it is suitable for publication in accordance with the above principles of the NBER. Such notification will include a table of contents and an abstract or summary of the manuscript's content, a list of contributors if applicable, and a response form for use by Directors who desire a copy of the manuscript for review. Each manuscript shall contain a summary drawing attention to the nature and treatment of the problem studied and the main conclusions reached.

4. No volume shall be published until forty-five days have elapsed from the above notification of intention to publish it. During this period a copy shall be sent to any Director requesting it, and if any Director objects to publication on the grounds that the manuscript contains policy recommendations, the objection will be presented to the author(s) or editor(s). In case of dispute, all members of the Board shall be notified, and the President shall appoint an ad hoc committee of the Board to decide the matter; thirty days additional shall be granted for this purpose.

5. The President shall present annually to the Board a report describing the internal manuscript review process, any objections made by Directors before publication or by anyone after publication, any disputes about such matters, and how they were handled.

6. Publications of the NBER issued for informational purposes concerning the work of the Bureau, or issued to inform the public of the activities at the Bureau, including but not limited to the NBER Digest and Reporter, shall be consistent with the object stated in paragraph 1. They shall contain a specific disclaimer noting that they have not passed through the review procedures required in this resolution. The Executive Committee of the Board is charged with the review of all such publications from time to time.

7. NBER working papers and manuscripts distributed on the Bureau's web site are not deemed to be publications for the purpose of this resolution, but they shall be consistent with the object stated in paragraph 1. Working papers shall contain a specific disclaimer noting that they have not passed through the review procedures required in this resolution. The NBER's web site shall contain a similar disclaimer. The President shall establish an internal review process to ensure that the working papers and the web site do not contain policy recommendations, and shall report annually to the Board on this process and any concerns raised in connection with it.

8. Unless otherwise determined by the Board or exempted by the terms of paragraphs 6 and 7, a copy of this resolution shall be printed in each NBER publication as described in paragraph 2 above.

Contents

Acknowledgments

We would like to acknowledge the support for this project from our two sponsoring organizations: the American Bar Foundation, and in particular its director Bryant Garth, and the Inter-American Development Bank through the Latin American Research Network Program, coordinated by Norelis Betancour. Without their aid this project would not have been possible. Special thanks also go to Raquel Gomez, who provided continuous assistance in coordinating the research teams.

We also thank three outside reviewers for a close reading of all of the essays in the book. We explicitly acknowledge the helpful commentary of Giuseppe Bertola and John Donohue, as well as the helpful comments of two anonymous reviewers. We are also indebted to Leticia Cuevas, who helped us to run a questionnaire on labor regulations to the Labor Ministries of Latin America, and to Matias Busso for his valuable research assistance.

Finally, this book would not have been possible without the patient work of John Smith at IADB, who edited the chapters of this book in their working paper stage, and the close editorial support of Jennifer Boobar, Greg Orlowski, and Adam Zanolini at the University of Chicago.

Introduction

James J. Heckman and Carmen Pagés

I.1 Introduction

This book uses microdata from diverse Latin American and Caribbean
countries to investigate the impact of regulation on their labor markets.
Common methodologies are applied to extract empirical regularities from
the region. Latin America and the Caribbean are of interest in their own
right. But for several reasons, the lessons learned from studies of these labor markets have much greater generality.

The shifts in the policy regimes experienced in the region are dramatic
by the Organization for Economic Cooperation and Development
(OECD) standards, and many of these regime shifts are exogenous. This
large and exogenous variation provides identifying power not available to
analysts studying regulation in Europe and North America. Given the evidence on the comparability of labor demand functions around the world
summarized in Hamermesh (1993 and chap. 11 in this volume), lessons
about the impact of regulation learned from Latin American labor markets
apply more generally.

The studies in this volume are based on microdata. Use of such data
avoids reliance on fragile country aggregate statistics that have been the

James Heckman is the Henry Schultz Distinguished Service Professor of Economics and
of Social Sciences, director of the Center for Social Program Evaluation at the University of
Chicago, and a research associate of the National Bureau of Economic Research. Carmen
Pagés is a senior research economist in the research department of the Inter-American Development Bank.

We thank Ricardo Avelino, Giuseppe Bertola, John Donohue, David Bravo, Fernanda
Ruiz, Jagadeesh Sividasan, Sergio Urzua, and two anonymous referees for helpful comments.
Heckman's contribution to this work was supported by the American Bar Foundation. The
views expressed in this paper are those of the authors and not necessarily those of the Inter-
American Development Bank or its board of directors.

1

main source of information used to study European regulation (see, e.g., the evidence summarized in Nickell and Layard 1999). Countries have diverse economic regions and agents, and aggregation over these regions and their economic agents masks this diversity. In this chapter, we show the sensitivity of estimates of the impact of regulation obtained from conventional pooled time series cross sections of countries to alternative choices of samples and models, although a few important empirical regularities established at the microlevel hold up in macrodata. Our analysis builds the case for doing disaggregated analyses of the type reported in this book.

The evidence presented here challenges one prevailing view that labor market regulations affect only the distribution of labor incomes and have minor effects on efficiency.[1] The results presented in this volume suggest that mandated benefits reduce employment and that job security regulations have a substantial impact on the distribution of employment and on turnover rates. The most adverse impact of regulation is on youth, marginal workers, and unskilled workers. Insiders and entrenched workers gain from regulation, but outsiders suffer. As a consequence, job security regulations promote inequality among demographic groups. Most of the individual country studies demonstrate that regulations promoting job security reduce covered worker exit rates out of employment and out of unemployment, and on balance reduce employment.

This introductory essay has three main goals: (1) It summarizes the main lessons to be drawn from the studies assembled here; (2) It places the Latin American and Caribbean (LAC) regulatory burden in an international context by comparing the level and changes in LAC labor regulation policies with those in OECD countries, as well as providing some historical context about the origins of this regulation; and (3) It updates the work of Heckman and Pagés (2000) with an expanded sample and better measures of regulation, providing a cross-country time-series analysis of the impact of regulation on employment and unemployment. We quantify the cost of regulation in LAC and OECD regions. The fragility of the macro-based estimates documented in our paper suggests one reason why relatively little is known about the impact of regulations in Europe, despite an abundance of cross-country time series papers analyzing policies in that region. However, the macro time series literature does produce some empirical regularities. The methods used to analyze the microevidence presented in this book should be extended to produce more convincing evidence of the impacts of regulations on employment in the OECD region.[2]

This chapter proceeds in the following way. Section I.2 provides background on Latin American economic and labor market performance. Sec-

---

1. Freeman (2000) and Nickell and Layard (1999), among others, adopt this view.
2. See, however, the studies of Abowd et al. (1997), Abowd, Kramarz, and Margolis (1999), Abowd et al. (2000), Machin and Stewart (1996), Kugler, Jimeno, and Hernanz (2002), and others, who use microdata to investigate the impact of regulation in Europe.

tion I.3 presents some basic facts about regulation in LAC and compares LAC with OECD countries both in terms of the level and composition of labor cost and in terms of the labor market reforms experienced in the region. Section I.4 summarizes the main lessons from the essays presented in this book. Section I.5 updates Heckman and Pagés (2000) and uses the cost measures derived in section I.3 to examine the impacts of labor regulation on Latin American and OECD employment and unemployment rates. Section I.6 concludes and makes suggestions for future work on regulation in Latin American and OECD labor markets. We first present some background on Latin America and the nature of labor market regulation in the region.

I.2   Latin American Economic and Labor Market Performance

Latin American economic performance has been quite disappointing. Since 1970, growth of income per capita has been just over 1 percent per year, higher than in Africa or the Middle East, but much lower than in Asia or in the developed countries (figure 1). Up to the 1980s, trade policies heavily protected Latin American economies from foreign competition. There was a substantial degree of intervention by the state in the economy. The collapse of most economies during that decade due to growing fiscal and monetary imbalances led many countries to implement large structural reforms towards the end of the 1980s and early 1990s. Macroeconomic stabilization policies reduced fiscal deficits and brought inflation under control. Sweeping, fast-paced trade reforms lowered substantial tariff barriers on manufactured goods. Governments undertook fiscal reforms, lifted control over financial markets, and privatized most state-owned firms. Some countries also embarked on labor reforms described in the next section. While growth rates in the 1990s were higher than they were during the 1980s, the rates of growth in this period still fell short of those attained in other parts of the world.

Among the countries covered in this volume (Argentina, Brazil, Chile, Colombia, Peru, Uruguay, Barbados, Jamaica, and Trinidad and Tobago), Chile was the best performer, with an average growth rate of gross domestic product (GDP) of 4.8 during the period 1980–2001 (see table 1). Argentina and Trinidad and Tobago experienced the lowest average growth during the past two decades, despite high average growth rates during the nineties.

In spite of this weak economic performance, GDP per capita (purchasing power parity [PPP] US$ adjusted) levels in Latin American countries are higher than those of other developing regions. According to the World Bank Development Indicators, in 2001 the average GDP per capita in the Latin America and the Caribbean region was $7,050, considerably higher than that of East Asia and the Pacific ($4,233), Central and Eastern Europe ($6,598), South Asia ($2,730), Sub-Saharan Africa ($1,831) or the

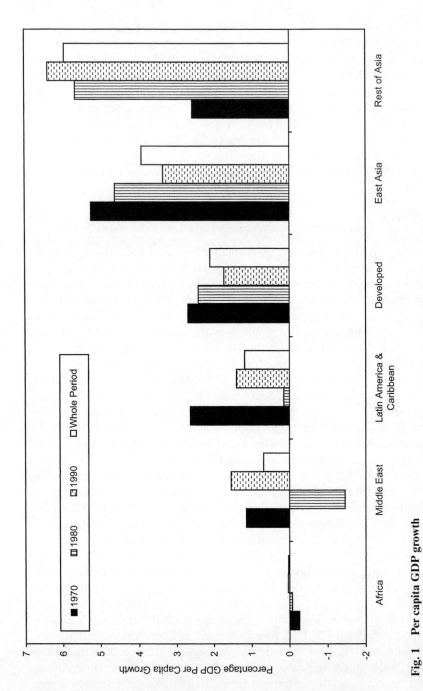

Fig. 1 Per capita GDP growth

Source: IADB calculations based on World Development Indicators (World Bank 2001).

Note: Averages are GDP weighted.

Table 1   Latin American and Caribbean Economic Performance Indicators

Country	GDP per Capita, 2001 (PPP US$) (1)	Human Development Index (HDI) Value, 2001 (2)	GDP Growth, 1980–2001 (3)	Employment Growth, 1980–1999 (4)	Female Labor Force Participation Growth, 1980–1999 (5)	Average Urban Unemployment Rate, 1980–2000 (6)
Argentina	11,320	0.849	1.132	1.16	1.12	9.30
Brazil	7,360	0.777	2.488	2.72	2.11	5.62
Chile	9,190	0.831	4.814	2.63	2.17	10.09
Colombia	7,040	0.779	3.089	3.23	3.56	12.10
Peru	4,570	0.775	1.553	3.52	2.27	8.03
Uruguay	8,400	0.834	1.795	1.43	2.37	10.62
Barbados	15,560	0.888	1.173	1.28	1.30	15.77
Jamaica	3,720	0.757	1.557	1.60	0.89	19.40
Trinidad and Tobago	9,100	0.802	0.108	0.78	1.30	15.85
Average	8,470	0.810	1.970	2.04	1.90	

Sources: Columns (1), (3), and (5) World Development Indicators (World Bank 2001); column (2) United Nations (2001); columns (4) and (6) Economic Commission for Latin America and the Caribbean (ECLAC 2001) and International Labour Organization (ILO 2002).

Notes: Column (3) is measured in local currency at constant prices; in column (6) the Caribbean rates are not comparable to Latin American rates because they are computed with a different methodology.

Arab States ($5,038). Similarly, the regional Human Development Index computed by the United Nations for LAC (0.77) was almost as high as in Central and Eastern Europe (0.78) and higher than in any other region except for the OECD (0.90). Among the countries whose labor markets are analyzed in this volume, Barbados and Argentina exhibited the highest income per capita and human development indexes, while Jamaica and Peru rank the lowest among the countries, both in per capita income and in human development (see table 1).

While GDP growth rates were not high, during the period 1980–1999 employment rates grew in the nine countries studied here. The highest growth rates were recorded in Colombia and Peru, countries that also experienced fast growth in female labor force participation. In contrast, average employment growth rates were low in Trinidad and Tobago and in Argentina. According to the International Labor Organization (ILO) and the Economic Commission for Latin America and the Caribbean (ECLAC) data, average urban unemployment rates during the 1980s and 1990s exceeded 8 percent in all countries analyzed in this book except for Brazil. Unemployment comparisons should be treated cautiously because they are not strictly comparable. For instance, in the Caribbean countries the unemployment rates include discouraged workers (those who drop out of the labor force), while such workers are excluded in the Latin American countries, which compute unemployment rates according to more traditional definitions.[3] Many have remarked that the high level of regulation of economic activity in the region accounts for problems in the labor markets in the region, and the essays assembled here shed light on this conjecture.

I.3   Labor Market Regulations and Institutions in Latin America and the Caribbean

This section sketches the history of labor market regulation in the region and describes and quantifies the regulatory environment in Latin America and the Caribbean. It compares the level of regulation and pace of regulatory reform in LAC countries and OECD countries. When it is credible to do so, we also make an effort to quantify the monetary costs (as a percentage of wages) of full compliance with regulations without discussing whether costs are borne by workers or firms. We discuss this issue more extensively in sections I.4 and I.5.

I.3.1   Regulations Governing Individual Contracts

Throughout Latin America, labor codes determine the types of contracts, the lengths of trial periods, and the conditions of part-time work.

---

3. That is, they only include persons who are available for work and who are taking specific steps to search for a job.

Regulations favor full-time, indefinite contracts over part-time, fixed-term or temporary contracts. As a form of worker protection, labor codes mandate a minimum advance notice period prior to termination, specify which causes are considered justified causes for dismissal, and establish compensation to be awarded to workers depending on the reason for the termination. In contrast, temporary contracts can be terminated at no cost, provided that the duration of the contract has expired. To prevent firms from exclusively hiring workers under temporary contracts, in most countries the use of such arrangements is severely restricted. Labor codes also limit trial periods—that is, the period of time during which a firm can test and dismiss a worker at no cost if his or her performance is considered unsatisfactory.

Although most OECD countries began regulating their labor markets when they had attained relatively high income per capita, Latin America and other developing countries started regulating their markets much earlier in the development process (Lindauer 1999). The first regulations date from the beginning of the twentieth century. The motivation for these regulations was the perceived need to protect the welfare of workers against the excessive power of employers, and to insure workers against the risk of job loss and income insecurity (Lindauer 1999). The Mexican Constitution of 1917 articulated the principle that protecting workers was one of the duties of the state. By the 1930s and 1940s, most countries had a labor code. The belief that each new reform should only strengthen the set of warranties and benefits awarded from previous laws became widespread. For many years, successive reforms expanded the protection that the law afforded to workers. There was little examination of the question of whether such regulations would affect economic performance. However, until the 1980s most countries in the LAC region were isolated and their industries heavily protected. Labor regulations were one way of distributing the rents from protection among covered workers and employers. Regulations are a low-cost way (from the point of government fiscal authorities) of providing social insurance to protect workers. The weak fiscal systems in place in the region together with the low level of income, and a tradition of tax evasion, corruption, and noncompliance made the social insurance schemes used in more developed countries prohibitively costly.

Military rule often led to deregulation of labor markets. Unions were frequent targets, as much for political as for economic reasons. The political and economic environment in LAC changed substantially in the 1980s and 1990s. Most countries restored democracy after long periods of military rule. These political changes bred some labor reforms—first, to restore union activity, which had been made illegal in many military regimes and, second, to reach a new social pact. In Chile, Brazil, and the Dominican Republic, at the beginning of the 1990s and later in Nicaragua in 1996, these reforms produced more protective labor regulations.

A new constitution was enacted in 1988 in Brazil as part of the process of redemocratization during the second half of the 1980s (see Barros and Corseuil, chap. 5 in this volume). This new constitution revised labor regulations that had been in place since the 1940s. The new constitution reduced the maximum working hours per week from forty-eight to forty-four hours; reduced the maximum number of hours for a continuous work shift from eight to six hours; increased the minimum overtime premium from 20 percent to 50 percent; increased maternity leave from three to four months; and increased the value of paid vacations from 1/3 to at least 4/3 of the normal monthly wage. The new constitution also modified the mandatory individual saving accounts system created in 1966. Prior to the reforms, the law required employers to deposit 8 percent of employees' wages into a worker-owned account. In case of a firm-initiated separation, workers could withdraw the accumulated funds (plus the interest rate). In addition, if a firm initiated a separation, it had to pay a penalty equivalent to 10 percent of the amount accumulated in the account. As part of the 1988 reform, this penalty was increased to 40 percent, considerably increasing the cost of dismissing a worker.

In the case of Chile, the 1990 reform introduced with the return to democracy reestablished some of the protection to workers that had been eliminated during the military regime. Under the dictatorship, union activity had been severely restricted and some benefits, such as indemnities for dismissal, had been substantially reduced.[4] In 1990, the new law increased maximum indemnities from five to eleven months of pay. It also reintroduced the need for firms to prove just cause for dismissal, although unlike the case in other countries, the new law considered the economic needs of the firm a just cause.

While in some countries lawmakers were busy increasing legal protection for workers, the economic environment was changing substantially. The deep economic crisis that ensued with the debt crisis of the early 1980s called into question the protectionist model. The relatively good performance of the Chilean economy, which in the mid-1970s opened to trade and introduced many promarket reforms, spawned imitators all across Latin America. By the second half of the 1980s and the early 1990s, most countries had drastically reduced tariffs on imports. The new openness to international trade increased the demand for labor market flexibility. It was argued that without sweeping labor market reforms, Latin American economies would not be able to compete internationally. This was the main motivation behind the reforms that introduced temporary contracts in Argentina, Colombia, Ecuador, Nicaragua, and Peru and that reduced the cost of dismissing workers with indefinite contracts in Colombia (1990)

---

4. See Montenegro and Pagés, chap. 7 in this volume.

and Peru (1991). Temporary and fixed-term contracts were introduced in Argentina in 1991, and their role was expanded in 1995 (see Hopenhayn, chap. 9 in this volume). These changes were influenced by similar reforms in Spain during the 1980s. Special fixed-term duration employment promotion contracts could be awarded to unemployed workers and to workers younger than twenty-five and older than forty years old. For some types of contracts, severance pay was reduced by 100 percent. However, these contracts were eliminated in 1998, when the share of persons working under these arrangements had increased substantially. Ecuador, Peru, and Colombia also lifted restrictions on the use of these types of programs in the early 1990s. In Peru, the number of workers hired under these contracts increased enormously. In Brazil, the use of such contracts has been liberalized since 1998.

The 1991 reforms in Peru reduced the cost of dismissing workers hired under indefinite contracts. During 1971–1991, workers who had completed trial periods were granted permanent job security. If a firm dismissed a worker and could not prove just cause in labor courts, the worker could choose between being reinstated in his or her job or receiving a severance payment of three months' wages per year of work (with a maximum of twelve months pay). In practice, because workers could always ask to be reinstated and then settle for a higher severance pay, the mandatory amount was a lower bound of the firing cost. See Saavedra and Torero (chap. 2 in this volume).

Beginning in 1991, workers hired after that year could be dismissed at will upon payment of a severance benefit. In addition, just cause clauses were extended to allow the dismissal of workers who did not perform up to expectations. The severance pay schedule was reduced from three months' wages to one month's wage for every year of tenure for workers with more than one year in the firm, with a minimum of three months' wages and a maximum of twelve. The 1993 constitution replaced the right of workers to a permanent job with the right of firms to dismiss workers. In July 1995, a second wave of labor reforms simplified the severance payment to one month per year of work, up to a maximum of twelve months, and the two-tier severance system was eliminated. These modifications substantially reduced the cost of dismissing workers. However, in November 1996 the severance payments rule was increased again to one and one-half months' wages per year of work, with an unaltered maximum cap of twelve wages.

In Colombia, the 1990 labor reforms liberalized many aspects of labor regulation. Besides regulations introducing the use of temporary contracts, the most important changes were those in the *Cesantias,* or severance pay that firms owed to workers at the end of the work relationship, regardless of the cause or the party that initiated separation. Prior to the reforms, employers were mandated to pay severance of one month per year at the time of the separation based on the salary at the separation. Workers could obtain advanced payments against their benefits. Such withdrawals were credited against the severance pay due to workers at the end of the labor relationship in nominal terms as of the date of the withdrawal. High rates of inflation increased the costs of such schemes to employers. After the reform, the withdrawals were credited in real terms, substantially reducing costs for firms. In addition, the reforms eliminated the right to reinstatement for workers with more than ten years of tenure. Offsetting these cost-reducing features, the reforms increased the cost of indemnities for dismissal.

Panama (1995) and Venezuela (1997) also undertook labor reforms with the goal of increasing labor market flexibility while preserving some form of protection to workers. In both countries, reforms increased mandatory pay in case of separation but considerably reduced the additional amount that firms had to pay in case of a firm-initiated dismissal.

In contrast to Latin American regulation, in the Caribbean a mixture of legislation, common law doctrines, custom, and policy characterizes the institutional context. At the beginning of the twentieth century, in all countries of that region, regulation of the labor market was based on common law rather than on the civil law tradition predominant in Latin America (see Downes, Mamingi, and Antoine, chap. 10 in this volume). While in some countries, like Barbados, most aspects of labor relation are still left to the courts to determine; in others, such as in Trinidad and Tobago, the enactment of different regulations has progressively increased the level of statutory protection to workers. In Barbados (1973), Trinidad and Tobago (1974), and Jamaica (1985), labor reforms instituted mandatory severance pay, although, as shown in the next section, at levels that are much lower than those prevalent in Latin America.

I.3.2   Payroll Contributions and Other Mandatory Benefits

As in most industrial countries, in LAC many social protection programs, such as old-age pensions, public health systems, unemployment subsidies, and family allowances are funded from payroll contributions. In addition, regulations mandate other employee-paid benefits such as occupational health and safety provisions, maternity and sick leave, overtime pay, and vacations.

Unlike changes in labor codes that tend to be infrequent events, changes in the level of contributions to these programs occur often. In addition, during the 1990s, many countries implemented reforms, which transformed pay-as-you-go systems into full or partial capitalization systems. One of the advantages of such schemes is that they tend to increase the link between contributions and benefits. However, at the same time, many countries, most noticeably Colombia, El Salvador, Mexico, Uruguay, and Brazil, increased the level of payroll taxes to reduce the actuarial imbalances present in their social security systems. Below, we quantify the levels and changes in these contributions across Latin America and OECD countries.

I.3.3   Collective Bargaining

Unions in Latin America tend to be firm- or sector-based and weak. In most cases, the state intervenes in union registration and accreditation as well as in the process of collective bargaining. The state authorizes only certain unions to have representation authority (Argentina, Mexico, Peru, and Brazil), and intervenes in the resolution of conflicts and the arbitration process (Argentina and Mexico). Only in Brazil and Argentina is collective bargaining highly centralized at the sector level, while in Nicaragua and Colombia, sector-level bargaining coexists with firm-based negotiation. In Mexico, collective bargaining takes place at the firm level, but a high level of centralization is achieved through a strong corporatist structure and through union discipline (O'Connell 1999). In contrast, unions are stronger, and collective bargaining tends to be national or sector-based in OECD countries, with the exception of Canada, New Zealand, the United Kingdom, and the United States.

According to data from ILO (1997–1998), union density as a percentage of nonagricultural employment is higher in Brazil, Mexico, Argentina, and Nicaragua and smaller in the rest of the Latin American countries. Union affiliation tends to be higher in countries where collective bargaining is more centralized. Overall, union density is lower in Latin America (14.7) than in industrial countries (36.6).[5] There are also large differences in coverage rates. Thus, while collective bargaining agreements in countries such as Spain, France, and Greece, which are negotiated by a minority, are extended to almost all employees, in Latin American countries this is generally not the case. As a result, coverage rates in Latin America tend to be much lower than those observed in OECD countries with similar affiliation rates.

The influence that collective bargaining exerts on wage and employment conditions, measured by affiliation rates, is declining over time. Thus, LAC countries share a trend that has been well documented for OECD countries. Affiliation rates have declined in all of the countries of the region.[6] This decline has been especially large in Mexico, Argentina, Venezuela, Costa Rica, and Uruguay. In this volume, we only present estimates for Uruguay on the impact of unionization on employment. Cassoni, Allen,

---

5. ILO data corresponds to the mid-1990s. The comparison between LAC and industrial countries reflects the difference between unweighted regional averages. The average for industrial countries includes the following countries: France, Spain, United States, Greece, Germany, Italy, United Kingdom, Denmark, Belgium, Finland, Iceland, Ireland, Sweden, and Canada.

6. The ILO data for 1985 and 1993 indicates that union affiliation increased in Chile during that period. Yet, data from a later period indicates that union affiliation has been declining since 1993.

and Labadie (chap. 8 in this volume) estimate a strong adverse impact of unionism on employment in Uruguay. The evidence for other Latin American countries is still too sparse.

I.3.4   Minimum Wages

Minimum wages are widely used in Latin America to increase the wages of the poorest workers. Figure 2 (taken from Maloney and Nuñez Mendez,

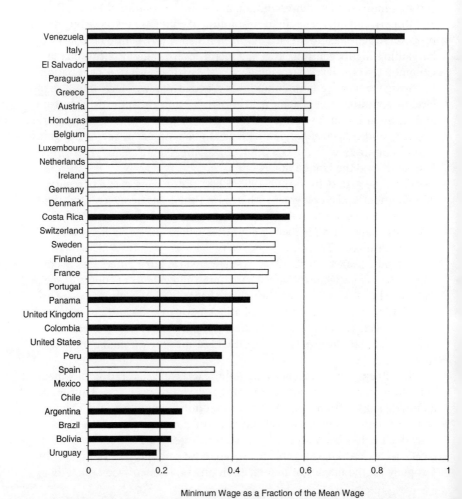

Fig. 2   Minimum wage/mean wage in OECD countries and in Latin America

Source: Maloney and Nuñez Mendez (chap. 1 in this volume).

Notes: Minimum wages from Dolado et al. (1996), for one year within the range 1991 and 1995. Minimum wages for Latin America are from 1995 or 1996, except Argentina (1998), Bolivia (1997), Brazil (1998), Colombia (1998), Honduras (1999), Mexico (1999), and Uruguay (1998).

chap. 1 in this volume) ranks various Latin American and OECD countries by their minimum wage, standardized by the mean wage.[7] While some Latin American countries appear in the lower range of this distribution—most notably Uruguay, Bolivia, Brazil, Argentina, Chile and Mexico—others, such as Venezuela, El Salvador, Paraguay, and Honduras, have very high minimum to average minimum wages by OECD standards. These high levels suggest that minimum wages are likely to be binding, and, as a result, to reduce employment and to retard downward wage movements in the presence of adverse demand shocks.

Data on enforcement of the minimum wage is incomplete. However, some evidence available for workers between twenty-five and forty years old suggests that about 10 percent of wage employees in that age range earn salaries below the minimum wage (see table 2). In some countries, such as Mexico, Uruguay, Bolivia, and Argentina, the proportion below the minimum in this age range is very small. In other countries, such as Colombia, minimum to average wages are high but a large proportion of the labor force in the twenty-five to forty age range earns wages below the statutory minimum. Whether the adverse effect of a high level of minimum wages is offset by substantial noncompliance remains an open empirical question.

I.3.5   What Motivates Reforms?

In studying the effect of reforms in the labor market it is important to examine what factors initiate these relatively infrequent episodes. It could be argued that labor market outcomes are driven by the same events that drive the reforms and not by the labor reforms themselves. Panels A–F of figure 3 (for Latin America) and panels G–I of figure 3 (for the Caribbean) plot GDP growth rates and unemployment rates for the countries covered in the individual country studies of this volume during the period 1980–2000. They also plot major episodes of labor reform (marked with a continuous line if a liberalization of the labor market occurred and a dotted line if the reforms increased protection to workers).[8] In addition, these figures mark episodes of major tariff reductions (double line) or the end of military regimes and the return to democracy (discontinuous line).

In Argentina, Colombia, Peru, and Uruguay, reforms that liberalized the labor market occurred within one or two years before or after major reductions in tariffs and were part of efforts to liberalize economies and increase the participation of the market in the production and allocation of goods and services. In Chile and Brazil, reforms that increased the legal

7. The observations are from the early 1990s for the OECD countries and from the mid- and late 1990s for LAC. Data from OECD were obtained from Dolado et al. (1996), data from LAC comes from IADB (1998–1999) and Maloney and Nuñez Mendez (chap. 1 in this volume).

8. Only major changes in labor codes or other major government interventions in the labor market are included. Changes in social security contributions or payroll taxes, as well as changes in the level of minimum wages—which occur quite frequently—are not included.

Table 2   Compliance with Regulations

| Country | % of Workers with Mandatory Social Security Programs | | % of Workers 25–40 Years Old with Net Earnings Below Minimum Wage |
	% of Total Employment (Mean 1990s)	% of Wage Employment (Mean 1990s)	Noncompliance with Minimum Wages (End 1990s)
Average Latin America[a]	42.76	60.05	10.06
Argentina	48.45	66.56	3.11
Bolivia (1999)	26.36	38.56	1.11
Brazil	48.18	64.04	5.80
Chile	64.47	77.45	7.3
Colombia (1999)	46.13	66.77	26.9
Costa Rica	65.92	74.61	15.7
Dominican Republic (1998)	29.08	49.40	n.a.
Ecuador (1995)	30.94	43.02	n.a.
El Salvador (1998)	33.49	50.04	3.6
Mexico	52.53	67.96	0.5
Panama (2001)	55.66	74.50	14.8
Paraguay (1995)	16.70	30.66	n.a.
Peru	17.99	51.90	23.5
Uruguay	74.12	93.12	0.5
Venezuela (1998)	31.37	52.22	17.9

Source: IADB (2004), based on individual country household surveys.

Notes: Percentage of workers between fifteen and sixty-four that are affiliated to social security. Time series data for the 1990s is incomplete; the mean was computed when data included three or more years spread over three periods: early (1990–1993), mid (1994–1997), and late (1998–2001). Noncompliance with minimum wage refers to employees between twenty-five and forty years old working more than thirty hours. Figures for this variable date from the late nineties. N.a. denotes not available.

[a]Unweighted average.

protection of workers occurred in the context of a transition to democracy. In all of these episodes it could be argued that labor reforms were exogenous to the economic system because they were driven either by a new economic philosophy or by profound transformations in political regimes, although one could counter that these political transitions were facilitated by economic developments. Some reforms and transformations are clearly driven by changes in economic activity. There is evidence that many reforms tend to occur around periods of negative economic growth. In the countries and periods analyzed in this volume, there have been at least fifteen episodes of reform. Out of these fifteen, six episodes of reform occurred in years in which GDP had declined the year before. However, four of those reforms increased the legal protection to workers, and two liberalized the labor market.

Overall, there is no empirical relationship between labor reforms and labor market outcomes driven by economic performance. Our cross-country

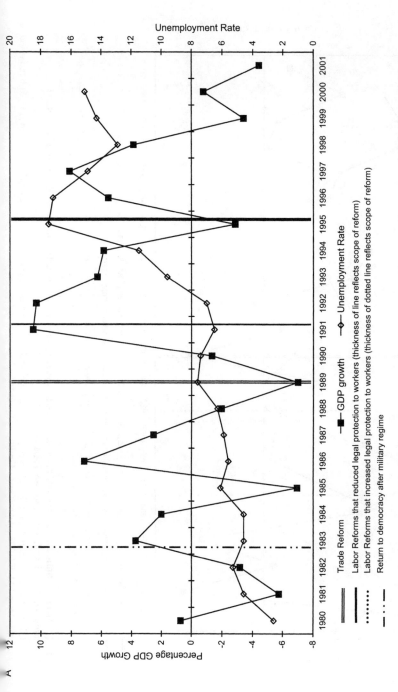

Fig. 3 Economic and trade labor reforms: *A*, Argentina; *B*, Brazil; *C*, Chile; *D*, Colombia; *E*, Peru; *F*, Uruguay; *G*, Barbados; *H*, Jamaica; *I*, Trinidad and Tobago

Sources: GDP growth rate from World Bank Development Indicators (2000), unemployment rates from ECLAC (2001) and ILO (2002), Period of trade reforms from IADB (1996), year of end of military regime from Nohlen (1993).

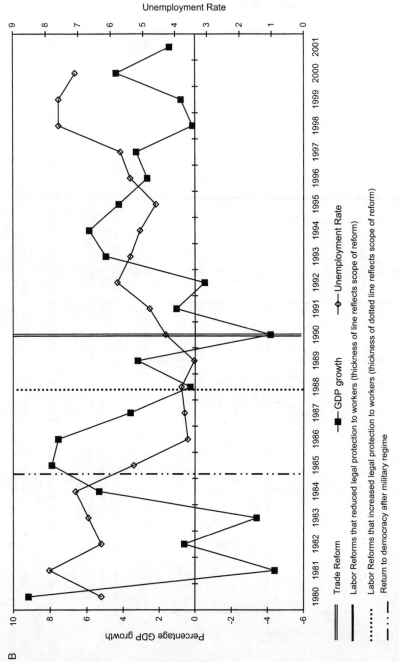

Fig. 3 **(cont.) Economic and trade labor reforms:** *A,* **Argentina;** *B,* **Brazil;** *C,* **Chile;** *D,* **Colombia;** *E,* **Peru;** *F,* **Uruguay;** *G,* **Barbados;** *H,* **Jamaica;** *I,* **Trinidad and Tobago**

Sources: GDP growth rate from World Bank Development Indicators (2000), unemployment rates from ECLAC (2001) and ILO (2002), Period of trade reforms from IADB (1996), year of end of military regime from Nohlen (1993).

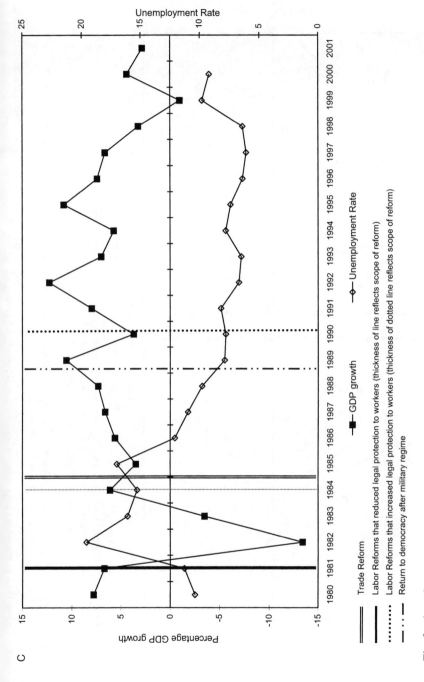

Fig. 3 (cont.)

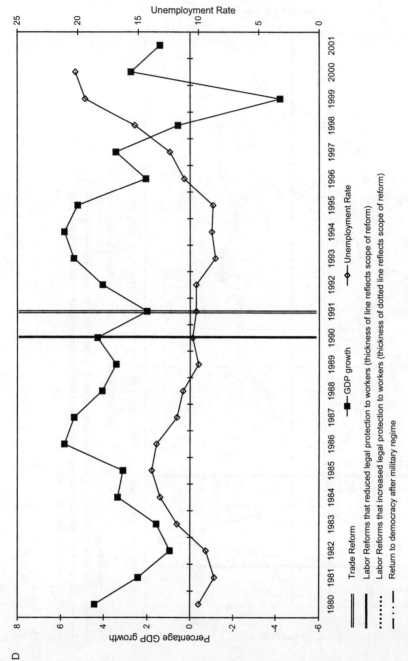

Fig. 3 (cont.) Economic and trade labor reforms: *A,* **Argentina;** *B,* **Brazil;** *C,* **Chile;** *D,* **Colombia;** *E,* **Peru;** *F,* **Uruguay;** *G,* **Barbados;** *H,* **Jamaica;** *I,* **Trinidad and Tobago**

Sources: GDP growth rate from World Bank Development Indicators (2000), unemployment rates from ECLAC (2001) and ILO (2002), Period of trade reforms from IADB (1996), year of end of military regime from Nohlen (1993)

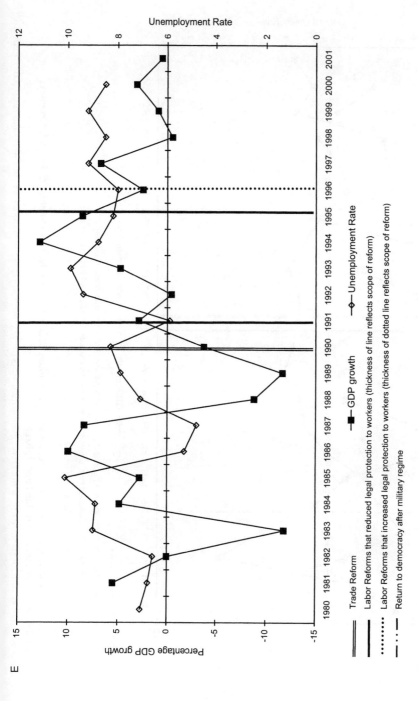

Fig. 3 (cont.)

E

Unemployment Rate

Percentage GDP growth

— Trade Reform

—■— GDP growth   —◇— Unemployment Rate

‖ Labor Reforms that reduced legal protection to workers (thickness of line reflects scope of reform)

········ Labor Reforms that increased legal protection to workers (thickness of dotted line reflects scope of reform)

—··— Return to democracy after military regime

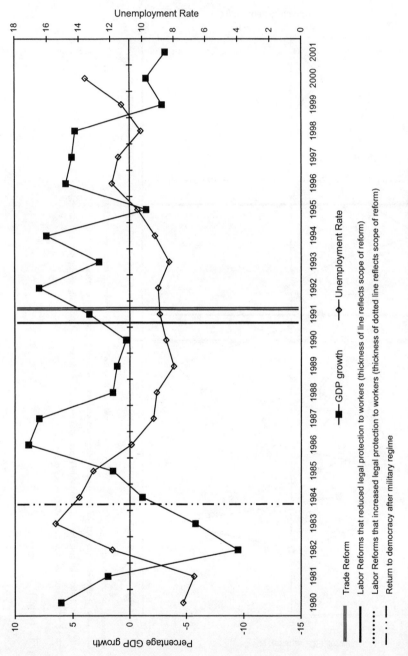

Fig. 3 (cont.) Economic and trade labor reforms: *A*, Argentina; *B*, Brazil; *C*, Chile; *D*, Colombia; *E*, Peru; *F*, Uruguay; *G*, Barbados; *H*, Jamaica; *I*, Trinidad and Tobago

Sources: GDP growth rate from World Bank Development Indicators (2000), unemployment rates from ECLAC (2001) and ILO (2002), Period of

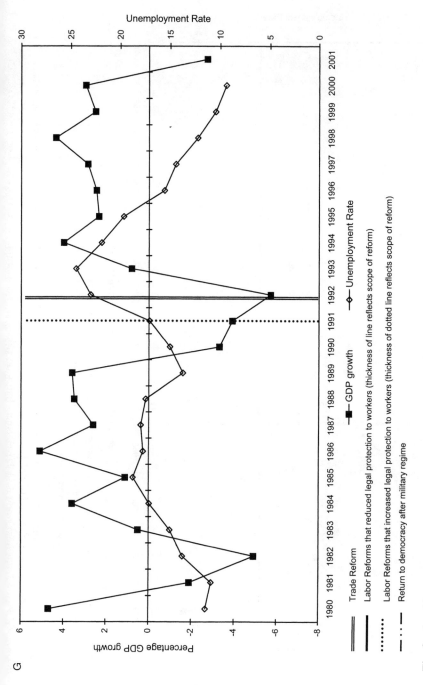

G

Fig. 3 (cont.)

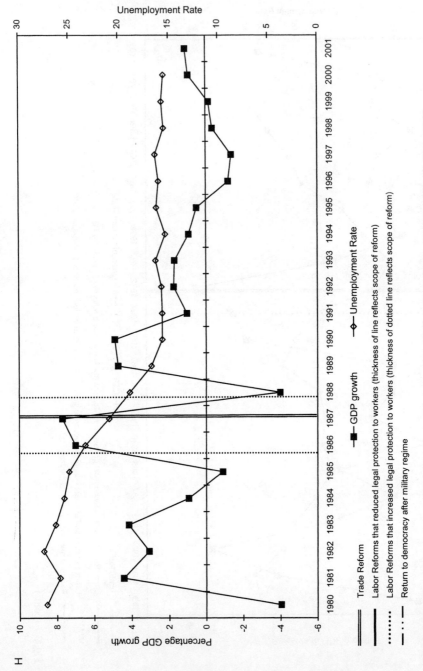

Fig. 3 (cont.) Economic and trade labor reforms: *A*, Argentina; *B*, Brazil; *C*, Chile; *D*, Colombia; *E*, Peru; *F*, Uruguay; *G*, Barbados; *H*, Jamaica; *I*, Trinidad and Tobago

Sources: GDP growth rate from World Bank Development Indicators (2000), unemployment rates from ECLAC (2001) and ILO (2002), Period of

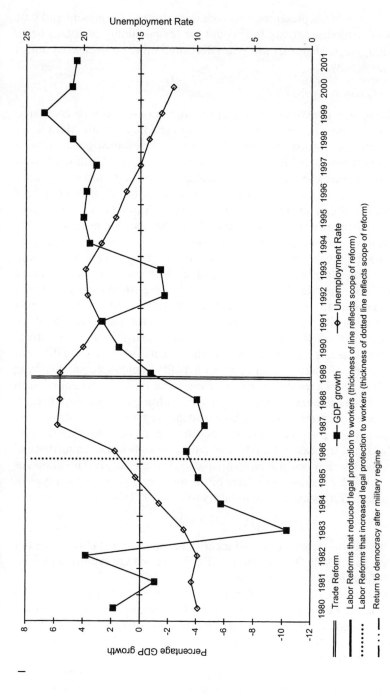

Fig. 3 (cont.)

time series analysis presented in this chapter controls for present and past levels of economic activity to account for the possibility of endogeneity. The disaggregated studies use year effects and other strategies to control for endogeneity.

I.3.6   Quantifying the Cost of Regulation

This section constructs measures of labor laws that can be compared across countries and time (see also Heckman and Pagés 2000). Many studies that summarize institutional data across countries construct qualitative indices that rank variables across countries. For instance, Grubb and Wells (1993) construct a series of indicators of employment protection by ranking different aspects of job protection across countries and averaging these different rankings in one summary indicator. Although such measures summarize many complex institutional features, they are not comparable over time. A second group of studies constructs measures that aggregate institutional aspects of the labor market by assigning to each country and year a value in a certain range, for instance, between zero and one. These measures summarize a large number of interesting aspects and are comparable across time. However, they can also be quite arbitrary because it is difficult to justify any assigned numerical values for qualitative variables, and because it is difficult to compare one measure against another. Moreover, the measures are very sensitive to the weights assigned to the different components of these measures. From a policy standpoint, summarizing many features of a regulatory system in one indicator makes it impossible to distinguish which components, if any, have an adverse effect on employment.

We take a different route by constructing measures of the direct cost (measured as a fraction of average monthly wages) of complying with labor laws. These measures can be compared not only across countries and over time, but they can also be compared against each other. This allows us to quantify, for instance, the share of the total costs given by each type of regulation. Our measure of mandatory total costs (TC) of regulations is

$$TC = SSP + JS.$$

It is the sum of the cost of social security payments (SSP) plus the cost of abiding by job security provisions (JS). These costs are expressed as fractions of the average monthly wage.

This measure of the cost of regulation omits some important components of labor cost. For example, the costs of abiding by certain laws are hard to quantify and are omitted. One example of laws whose costs are difficult to quantify is the prohibition against dismissing workers in bad times. In addition, this measure does not include the cost of regulating the length of the standard workweek and overtime work. It does not include the cost of complying with minimum wage laws or other income floors. We do not include regulations on temporary labor contracts. Although these regulations are likely to have effects on employment and unemployment, we choose to exclude them because comparable data on the share of the labor force affected by these regulations across time and countries are difficult to obtain. We leave the quantification of these features of regulations for future work.

There is one major conceptual problem with this index. It does not distinguish between static and dynamic aspects of the cost of labor. Job security affects both components of costs by raising the total cost of labor and by increasing the cost of adjusting labor. Social security costs affect the unit cost of labor without affecting dynamic costs of labor. Our index of total cost is not a measure of the price of labor facing firms at different stages of the business cycle. We develop this point below and in appendix B.

Quantifying Job Security Provisions

Our index includes, in job security legislation, those provisions of the law that increase the cost of dismissing a worker for economic reasons.[9] Across countries, termination laws require firms to incur at least five types of costs: administrative procedures, advance notification, indemnities for dismissal, seniority pay, and the legal costs of a trial if workers contest dismissals. Administrative procedures require the firm to notify and seek approval by labor unions or the Ministry of Labor to extend the period between layoff decisions and the actual occurrence of layoffs. They may also involve long negotiations to place workers in alternative jobs. The period of advance notification should also be included in the computation of labor costs because in many countries, laws allow firms to choose between providing advance notice or paying a compensation equivalent to the wages for the corresponding period. Moreover, since productivity declines substantially after notice, advance notification should be considered as a part of dismissal costs even when firms choose to notify workers in advance. Therefore, we assume that employees do not work at full productivity levels after notification.[10] In most countries, mandatory advance notice periods increase with tenure, and in others they are higher for white-collar than for blue-collar workers.

Most Latin American and OECD countries mandate indemnities in cases of firm-initiated dismissal. In general, indemnities are based on multiples of the most recent wage and the years of service. Some countries calculate the amount of mandatory indemnities based on whether the dismissal is deemed just or unjust or whether the worker is blue collar or white

9. In most countries, the law does not mandate compensation for dismissal if the separation is due to employees' misdemeanors. However, if such behavior cannot be proved, the worker has to be compensated at the regular legal rate.

10. There is some evidence that advance notice stimulates on-the-job search during the notification period (Addison and Portugal 1992), which suggests a reduction in the effort devoted to work.

collar. In contrast, seniority pay is only mandated in a few Latin American countries in which the law requires employers to make a payment upon termination of the work relationship, regardless of the cause or party initiating the separation. In these countries, firms initiating dismissal are required to pay both indemnities *and* seniority pay. In some countries, this payment is deposited as a regular contribution to the worker's individual savings account. In these countries, workers can withdraw principal and interest from their account upon separation. In other countries, seniority pay is determined as a given amount that has to be paid to the worker upon termination of the work relationship.[11] Finally, firms can incur considerable additional costs if workers contest dismissal in courts. If judges rule in favor of workers, firms not only have to pay indemnities, but also the workers' foregone wages during trial.

To compute the monetary cost of labor laws, we improve on the job security measures developed in Heckman and Pagés (2000) in three ways. First, we expand our previous database to include the 1980s in all OECD countries. This expansion of the data set allows us to capture some additional labor reforms in OECD countries not previously captured. Second, we revise and correct some of our previous data on advance notice and indemnities for a number of countries to better capture the actual cost of the law (see appendix A for a complete description of the methodology and assumptions involved). Finally, we include the cost of seniority pay in our measure of job security, which we did not include in our previous work.

Our measure of the cost of job security, JS_{jt}, for country j at time t is constructed from the following formula:

$$(1) \quad JS_{jt} = \sum_{i=1}^{T} \beta^i \delta^{i-1} (1 - \delta)(b_{j,t+i})$$

$$+ \sum_{i=1}^{T} \beta^i \delta^{i-1} (1 - \delta)[a_j \cdot y_{j,t+i^{jc}} + (1 - a_j) \cdot y_{j,t+i^{uc}}] + \sum_{i=0}^{T} \beta^i c_{j,t+i}$$

$$= AN_{j,t} + ID_{j,t} + SenP_{j,t},$$

where δ is the probability of a worker remaining in a job in a period, β is the discount factor, i denotes tenure at the firm, and T is the maximum tenure that a worker can attain in a firm, which is assumed to be twenty years ($T = 20$). The expression is broken down into three terms corresponding to advanced notice costs ($AN_{j,t}$), indemnity costs ($ID_{j,t}$), and seniority pay ($SenP_{j,t}$). The first term in expression (1) is the discounted cost of future advance notice, weighted by the probability that a worker will be dismissed, after one, two, three, and so on periods at the firm, where $b_{j,t+i}$ is the advance notice to a worker who has been i years at a firm measured in

---

11. For an extensive description of job security measures, see OECD (1993, 1999) for OECD countries and IADB (1996) for Latin America.

monthly wages. The second term in expression (1) is the discounted cost of future indemnities, weighted by the probability of dismissal after i periods at the firm. In this expression, a_j denotes the probability that the economic difficulties of the firm are considered a just cause of dismissal, while $y_{j,t+i}^{jc}$ ($y_{j,t+i}^{uc}$) is the mandated indemnity in case of just cause (unjust cause) dismissal, again measured in monthly wages. Finally, the third term in expression (1) captures the cost of seniority pay, and $c_{j,t+i}$ denotes contributions to a worker's savings account measured in monthly wages.[12] We assume a common discount and dismissal rate of 8 and 12 percent, respectively, across countries. The choice of the discount rate is based on the historical returns of an internationally diversified portfolio. Our choice of the turnover rate is motivated by the concern that turnover rates are affected by the legislation in countries with job security provisions and by the lack of the turnover data for most countries of the sample. We use a benchmark turnover rate from the United States, a country with lower job security costs than any country in our LAC sample. Evidence on turnover rates for Latin America is scant. However, evidence for a few countries for which job reallocation rates can be computed suggest that turnover rates in Latin America are within the ranges observed in the United States and other developed countries (Inter-American Development Bank [IADB] 2004). The choice of this benchmark is clearly a rough way to avoid endogeneity problems. To assign values to the discounted future payments of advance notice, indemnities and seniority pay, we use the information contained in tables A.1 and A.2 in appendix A. When regulations mandate different provisions for white-collar and blue-collar workers, we take the unweighted average for the two types of workers.

By construction, our job security measures give a higher weight to dismissal costs that may arise soon after a worker is hired because they are discounted less at the time of hiring, while they discount more firing costs that arise further in the future. Our measure captures the expected average cost. Consequently, it does not measure the true marginal labor cost, which is state contingent, nor does it distinguish dynamic from static costs, as we have previously noted. We discuss these issues further in appendix B.

Quantifying the Cost of Social Security

To quantify the cost of social security regulations and payroll taxation, we gather data on mandatory payroll contributions to old age, disability and death, sickness and maternity, work injury, unemployment insurance, and family allowances programs. Because the nominal incidence of the contributions (whether they fall on the employer or the employee) is irrel-

---

12. In two countries, the law mandates seniority pay, but this is not capitalized in individual savings accounts. See appendix A for a description of this case.

evant in measuring total social cost (although it is not irrelevant for the study of labor demand), we add both contributions as a percentage of wages. To quantify the cost of social security provisions in a way that is comparable to the cost of job security, we compute the expected cost of social security provisions (SSP) at the time of hiring as

$$SSP_{jt} = \sum_{i=0}^{T} \beta^i (ss^e_{j,t+i} + ss^w_{j,t+i}),$$

where $ss^e_{j,t+i}$ and $ss^w_{j,t+i}$ are, respectively, the costs of payroll taxes paid by the employer and the worker expressed as a percent of wages, and β is the discount rate.[13]

I.3.7   The Cost of Labor Laws across Countries

Table 3 summarizes our measures of the cost associated with different labor regulation regimes. In the first three columns, we summarize the cost of abiding by employment protection laws at the end of the 1990s. We generate these indices for all countries in all years for which we have data. Table 3 only reports those values for the last year of our sample. Column (1) summarizes the cost of giving advance notice to workers. In the Latin American countries, the typical required advance notice is a month or the equivalent to 0.63 monthly wages in expected value terms. Bolivia stands out as the country that requires one of the longer advance notice periods (1.77 months in expected terms), while Peru and Uruguay require no advance notice. Mandatory advance notice provisions tend to be more stringent in OECD countries. Many OECD countries mandate fairly long advance notice periods, particularly for skilled workers. In addition, in most countries, advance notice periods increase with seniority. In Belgium, for instance, the mandatory advance notice for skilled workers with ten years of seniority is nine months, while for workers with twenty years of seniority it is fifteen months. In Sweden, all workers with ten years of seniority are entitled to an advance notice period of five months, whereas for a worker with twenty years of seniority, the mandatory advance notice period is six months. The fact that Belgium and Sweden have very similar values in table 3 reflects the fact that in Belgium very high advance notice only applies to skilled workers, whereas in Sweden it applies to all workers. It also reflects the fact that our measure heavily discounts costs that are expected to occur far in the future. On average, mandated advance notice periods are significantly longer in OECD countries than in the LAC sample.

The second column displays the cost of indemnities for dismissal. Within the LAC sample, Colombia, Peru, Ecuador, Bolivia, El Salvador, and

---

13. We obtain the information on these contributions from the series *Social Security Programs Throughout the World*, edited by the United States Social Security Administration (1983–1999).

Table 3   Measures of Labor Market Regulations (end of 1990s)

Country	Year (1)	Advance Notice (EPV) (2)	Indemnities for Dismissal (EPV) (3)	Seniority Pay (EPV) (4)	Social Security Contributions (EPV) (1) + (2) + (3) + (4)	Total Cost (EPV)	Social Security Contributions as % of Total Costs	Social Security Contributions (% wage)
Australia	1999	0.73	0.99	0.00	1.95	3.67	53.04	0.02
Austria	1999	0.85	0.94	0.00	58.29	60.07	97.03	0.45
Belgium	1999	1.73	0.00	0.00	40.17	41.89	95.87	0.31
Canada	1999	0.60	0.19	0.00	18.56	19.35	95.93	0.14
Denmark	1999	1.73	0.04	0.00	n.a.	1.77	—	—
Finland	1999	1.61	0.00	0.00	35.62	37.23	95.67	0.27
France	1999	0.98	0.36	0.00	64.77	66.11	97.97	0.50
Germany	1999	1.14	0.00	0.00	53.48	54.63	97.91	0.41
Greece	1999	0.00	1.34	0.00	46.54	47.88	97.20	0.36
Hungary	1999	0.87	0.73	0.00	65.56	67.15	97.63	0.51
Ireland	1999	0.45	0.58	0.00	24.67	25.70	95.99	0.19
Italy	1999	0.60	2.63	0.00	91.53	94.76	96.60	0.71
Japan	1999	0.59	0.00	0.00	36.36	36.95	98.40	0.28
Korea	1999	0.59	2.99	0.00	18.08	21.66	83.49	0.14
The Netherlands	1999	0.88	0.00	0.00	84.99	85.87	98.97	0.65
New Zealand	1999	0.22	0.00	0.00	0.00	0.22	0.00	0.00
Norway	1999	0.88	0.00	0.00	28.43	29.31	97.00	0.22
Poland	1999	1.22	0.00	0.00	60.48	61.70	98.02	0.47
Portugal	1999	1.18	3.30	0.00	49.01	53.49	91.63	0.38
Spain	1999	0.59	2.58	0.00	49.43	52.60	93.98	0.38
Sweden	1999	1.79	0.00	0.00	28.86	30.65	94.16	0.22
Switzerland	1999	1.25	0.00	0.00	19.26	20.51	93.92	0.15
Turkey	1999	0.99	2.99	0.00	44.79	48.76	91.85	0.35
United Kingdom	1999	0.71	0.72	0.00	28.82	30.25	95.27	0.22
United States	1999	0.00	0.00	0.00	23.56	23.56	100.00	0.18
Average OECD	1999	0.89	0.82	0.00	40.55	42.25	95.97	0.31

(*continued*)

Table 3 (continued)

Country	Year (1)	Advance Notice (EPV) (2)	Indemnities for Dismissal (EPV) (3)	Seniority Pay (EPV) (4)	Social Security Contributions (EPV) (1) + (2) + (3) + (4)	Total Cost (EPV)	Social Security Contributions as % of Total Costs	Social Security Contributions (% wage)
Argentina	1999	0.80	2.20	0.00	44.49	47.48	93.69	0.34
Bolivia	1999	1.77	2.99	0.00	31.16	35.91	86.76	0.24
Brazil	1999	0.59	2.45	9.82	37.65	50.51	74.53	0.29
Chile	1999	0.59	2.79	0.00	27.20	30.58	88.95	0.21
Colombia	1999	0.30	3.49	9.82	38.75	52.35	74.01	0.30
Costa Rica	1999	1.05	2.60	0.00	35.05	38.69	90.58	0.27
Dominican Rep.	1999	0.59	2.16	0.00	16.23	18.97	85.52	0.13
Ecuador	1999	0.59	3.30	9.82	22.85	36.56	62.50	0.18
El Salvador	1999	0.06	2.99	0.00	27.26	30.31	89.94	0.21
Honduras	1999	0.59	2.94	0.00	13.63	17.16	79.43	0.11
Jamaica	1999	0.59	1.41	0.00	6.49	8.49	76.47	0.05
Mexico	1999	0.59	2.57	0.00	29.50	32.66	90.33	0.23
Nicaragua	1999	0.59	1.97	0.00	19.47	22.04	88.37	0.15
Panama	1999	0.59	2.09	0.75	15.19	18.62	81.58	0.12
Paraguay	1999	0.68	1.49	0.00	27.26	29.43	92.63	0.21
Peru	1999	0.00	3.80	9.82	27.26	40.88	66.69	0.21
Trinidad and Tobago	1999	1.18	1.33	0.00	10.90	13.41	81.31	0.08
Uruguay	1999	0.00	2.23	0.00	52.58	54.81	95.93	0.41
Venezuela	1999	0.93	2.03	5.97	18.43	27.36	67.37	0.14
Average Latin America		0.63	2.46	2.42	26.39	31.91	82.45	0.20

Source: Authors' calculations based on OECD (1999), Grubbs and Wells (1993), U.S. Social Security Administration (1983–1999), and Ministries of Labor in Latin America and the Caribbean.

Note: EPV denotes Expected Present Discounted Value. Dashes indicate missing value.

Honduras stand out as countries where the cost of abiding by these regulations is the highest. In the sample of OECD countries, Portugal, Turkey, Korea, Italy, and Spain are the ones where indemnities for dismissal laws are more costly (in terms of expected monthly wages), while a number of countries, including Belgium, Finland, Germany, Japan, Netherlands, New Zealand, Norway, Poland, Sweden, Switzerland, and the United States do not mandate indemnities for dismissal. Comparing the two regional samples, it is clear that, on average, compensation for dismissal is three times larger in LAC than in the OECD countries, despite the much lower level of income in the LAC region.

The third column refers to seniority pay. This additional payment is mandatory in only six Latin American countries, but the estimated expected discounted costs are large when this feature is present. In Colombia, Brazil, Ecuador, and Peru, employers are required to deposit about one month of pay every year to workers' individual savings accounts. Over the life of a worker, this provision is expected to cost about ten monthly wages in these four countries. Once advance notice, compensation for dismissal, and severance pay are added, we find that the cost of job security provisions is much higher in the poorer LAC region than in the richer OECD sample.

The fourth column reports the expected costs of complying with social security laws. Compared to the costs of employment security, social security costs are very large and therefore constitute the lion's share of the total costs of labor laws. In Argentina, for example, expected discounted costs of social security are 44.5 months of pay, while in many OECD countries these costs are even larger. In the average Latin American country, social security payments amount to 82 percent of the total costs of labor laws. This percentage is even larger in OECD countries where, on average, they reach 96 percent of the total regulatory costs.

Once all the costs are aggregated, labor laws impose a much larger cost in OECD countries. However, the composition of these costs is quite different. While the typical Latin American country mandates shorter advance notice periods and lower social security contributions than the average OECD country, job security provisions are substantially higher in LAC.

Latin American and Caribbean countries have a higher burden of regulations that affect adjustment processes in the labor market. European countries have a higher burden of payroll taxation that affects labor demand but not labor adjustment. Both regions have a much higher burden of labor costs than North America.

Exploring the relationship between income per capita and social protection across countries, it is clear that job security provisions are strategies of low-income regions. Figure 4 graphs regression relationships for each of our measures of labor cost on GDP per capita (PPP adjusted) and GDP squared. Across countries, advance notice costs tend to increase with income; seniority pay and indemnities for dismissal decline with country in-

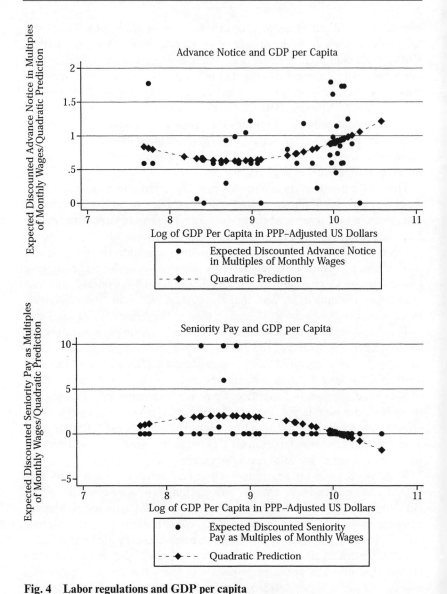

Fig. 4   Labor regulations and GDP per capita
Sources: Authors' calculations based on labor force statistics, OECD; World Bank (2000); and Ministries of Labor in Latin America and the Caribbean.

come. Social security contributions follow an inverted U-shape pattern in income. They tend to increase with income in the Latin American sample and reach a maximum in medium-income countries, while they tend to decline with income within the sample of upper-income countries. Regulation is an inferior good. It is the response of poor countries to the demand for worker security. By imposing a mandate on firms, central governments

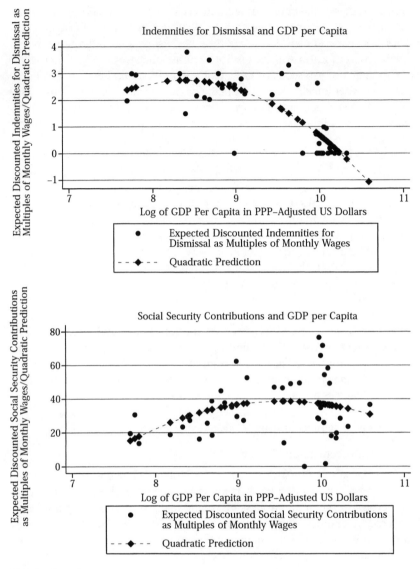

Fig. 4   (cont.)

avoid the direct fiscal cost of financing social safety nets, albeit at the cost of affecting their labor market performance.

We next examine the evolution of these measures over time. Since the early 1980s there have been few reforms in job security provisions in Latin America and even fewer in OECD countries. Social security contributions have changed more, but even they seldom change drastically. This lack of variability, particularly in job security provisions, poses a challenge for empirical studies of the impact of regulations. Figure 5 shows the level and the changes in job security since the late 1980s across Latin American countries. The general view that there have been important reductions in dismissal costs in Latin America is not accurate once we aggregate across all components of job security. Only Colombia, Panama, Peru, and Venezuela have experienced a reduction in the costs of terminating indefinite contracts. In Venezuela and Panama, the reduction in indemnities has been partly offset by increases in the costs of severance pay. Our measures reveal that Brazil, the Dominican Republic, Chile, and Nicaragua undertook reforms that increased the cost of dismissal. Assembling Latin American and OECD events, there are thirteen episodes in which job security provisions were changed. Nine of these episodes occurred in Latin America, and four occurred in the OECD sample. Figure 6 shows the percentage change in advance notice and indemnities for dismissal in the countries that have experienced reforms. It makes clear that changes in job security costs have been substantial in Latin America relative to the OECD sample. The enormous variation in the Latin American region and the exogeneity of some of the reforms is the reason why we think that the study of Latin American labor markets can inform further analyses of the impacts of regulation in economies around the world.

Figure 7 reports social security contributions (measured in expected discounted cost terms) at the beginning and at the end of the 1990s for Latin American countries. There have been important changes during the last decade. In many countries, social security contributions increased during the 1990s as a consequence of pension reforms and population aging. Yet, in some countries, most significantly in Argentina, social security contributions were reduced during the decade.

I.3.8   Enforcement and Informality

The measures summarized in table 3 calculate de jure cost of regulations, assuming that firms and workers abide by the text of the law. In practice, however, enforcement is at best weak, and many workers end up not being covered by mandatory regulations. Such workers are often referred to as informal workers. Given the difficulties in measuring the extent of informality, different approaches have been followed in the literature. Some authors follow the traditional ILO approach of classifying as informal those workers who are either self-employed, work for firms with five or less employees, work as unpaid family help, or are employed as domestic workers. Although some of these workers may be receiving the benefits prescribed by the law, there tends to be a high correlation between being in any of these categories of employment and not being covered by labor laws. Other authors use a more direct measure of informality, computing the percentage of workers who are affiliated with social security programs or have a formal labor contract. All authors in this volume use a "benefits" definition of

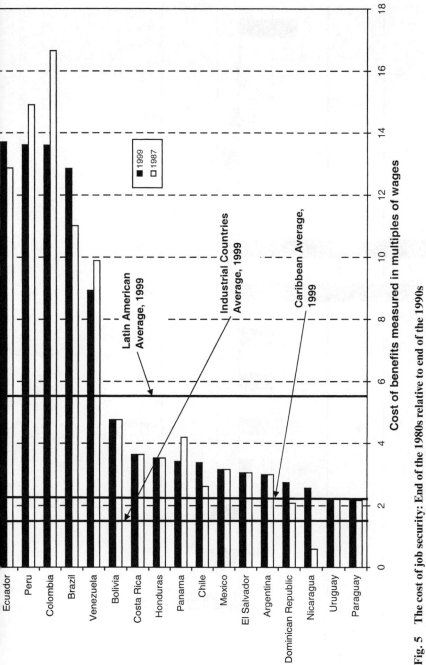

Fig. 5 The cost of job security: End of the 1980s relative to end of the 1990s

Source: Ministries of Labor of Latin America and the Caribbean.

Note: Cost of job security includes advance notice + indemnities for dismissal + seniority pay.

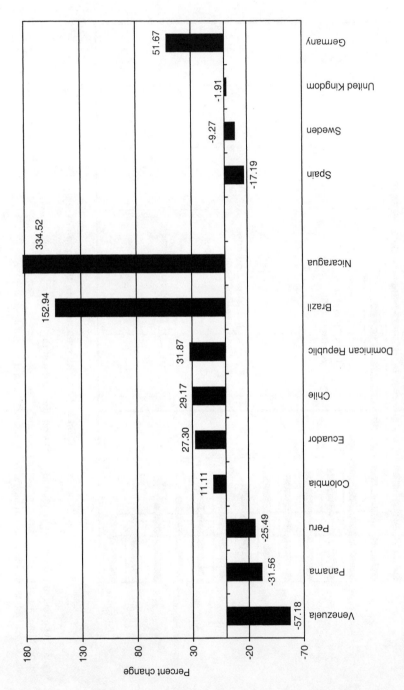

Fig. 6   Percent change in advance notice and indemnities for dismissal: 1990s relative to 1980s

Source: Ministries of Labor in Latin America and the Caribbean.

Note: Percentage change of the cost of providing advance notice and indemnities for dismissal as a consequence of labor market reforms. Seniority pay not included.

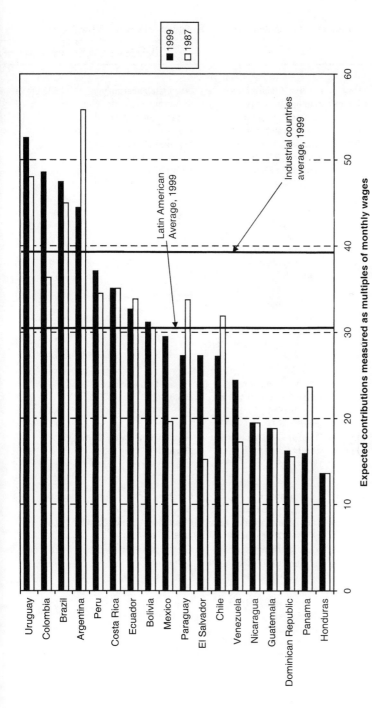

Fig. 7 Social security contributions, expected present value of payments after twenty years of employment

Source: United States Department of Social Security (1983–1999), Ministry of Labor in Latin America and the Caribbean.

Note: Includes the cost of seniority pay as well.

Table 4   **Estimates of Long-Run Constant-Output Labor Demand Elasticity**

Study	Data	Description	Wage Elasticity
	A. Latin America		
Mondino and Montoya (chap. 6 in this volume)	Panel of establishments; manufacturing; 1990–1996; quarterly; Argentina	No capital; instruments for output and wages; from dynamic labor demand	[−.353, −.94]
Saavedra and Torero (chap. 2 in this volume)	Panel of establishments; firms with more than 10 workers; 1986–1996; bimonthly; Peru	No capital; instruments for output; Labor costs includes legislative costs; static labor demand	−.19
Fajnzylber and Maloney (2000)	Panel of establishments; yearly; various countries		
	Chile (1981–1986):		
	White collar		−0.214
	Blue collar		−0.373
	Colombia (1990–1991):		
	White collar		−0.26
	Blue collar		−0.489
	Mexico (1986–1990):		
	White collar		−0.128
	Blue collar		−0.203
Roberts and Skoufias (1997)	Panel of manufacturing data; 1981–1987; Colombia		
	Skilled		−0.42
	Unskilled		−0.65
Cassoni, Allen, and Labadie (chap. 8 in this volume)	2-digit manufacturing; 1975–1997; Uruguay	No capital; system of equations	
	1975–1984		−0.69
	1985–1997		−0.22
Cárdenas and Bernal (chap. 4 in this volume)	Panel of 92 manufacturing sectors 4 digit CIIU; 1978–1995	No capital; dynamic labor demand	−1.43
	B. Rest of the World		
Waud (1968)	2-digit manufacturing; 1954–1964; quarterly; U.S.	Capital	−1.03
De Pelsmacker (1984)	5 auto manufacturing firms; 1976–1982; Belgium	Capital, labor prices, production workers	−0.44
Field and Grebenstein (1980)	10 2-digit manufacturing industry; 1971; U.S.	Capital and energy prices included	−0.51
Denny, Fuss, and Waverman (1981)	2-digit manufacturing; annual	Capital and energy prices	
	Canada: 1962–1975		−0.46
	U.S.: 1948–1971		−0.56
Wylie (1990)	Four 2-digit manufacturing; annual; 1900–1929; U.S.		−0.52

informality, except for the study by Maloney and Nuñez Mendez (chap. 1 in this volume), which follows the ILO convention.

Measured by the extent of compliance with social security regulations in Latin America, noncompliance is substantial. According to IADB (2004), only 42.7 percent of all workers and 60 percent of all wage employees are contributing to such programs (see table 2). Among the countries covered in the individual studies of this volume, compliance as percentage of total employment is the highest in Chile and Uruguay and the lowest in Peru. Compliance tends to be higher among skilled workers, among workers employed in larger firms, and in the manufacturing and high-paying finance and business services sectors. In these latter sectors, the effect of regulations should be easier to detect. Compliance is higher when the burden of regulation is lower.

I.4   The Impact of Labor Market Regulations

This section summarizes the studies of the impact of labor market regulations that are presented in this volume and places them in the context of the literature on more economically developed countries. We distinguish between policies that alter employment levels (generating static costs) from policies that affect employment flows (generating dynamic transition costs). The essays contained in this book present evidence on both types of policies. We also report findings on the effects of temporary contracts and minimum wages.

I.4.1   A Static Labor Demand-Labor Supply Analysis

A convenient starting point from which to assess the impact of labor market regulations on employment levels is the standard neoclassical labor demand-labor supply framework. If mandatory legislation increases labor costs, economic theory predicts that a move up the labor demand function produces a fall in employment. The slope of the labor demand schedule provides a good measure of the policy-induced change in employment when governments or trade unions set labor costs administratively. The standard theory is silent about the effects of the regulation on unemployment because it depends on whether the displaced workers drop out of the labor force or attempt to seek new jobs.

Table 4 summarizes estimates of constant-output labor demand elasticities for Latin America. As noted by Hamermesh (chap. 11 in this volume), these estimates are comparable to those estimated for other countries.[14] Al-

---

14. A more comprehensive measure of the impact of regulations on employment is given by the total elasticity, which includes the possible scale effects of an increase in regulation including the entry and exit of firms due to changes in labor costs. Unfortunately, there is very little empirical evidence in this book regarding the magnitude of the total elasticity, although studies by Hopenhayn and Rogerson (1993) and Nicoletti and Scarpetta (2003) suggest that entry and exit decisions are an important component of the response to regulation.

though labor demand studies abound, we focus on those studies that use disaggregated industry or individual firm data to infer the labor demand parameters, because models fit on such data produces more reliable estimates of underlying production parameters than models fit on data at higher levels of aggregation (Hamermesh 1993). Comparisons across types of workers indicate that labor demand elasticities are larger for blue-collar than for white-collar workers, suggesting a lower impact of regulations on the employment rates of the latter. Estimates of labor demand for Latin America tend to be somewhat lower than those obtained for other countries of the world, especially those estimated for Peru and Mexico. (See the estimates from industrial countries in the lower panel of the table.) Nonetheless, all estimates are between 0 and –1.5, and most of them cluster between –0.2 and –0.6, well within the range for worldwide estimates reported by Hamermesh (1993) for output-constant labor demand elasticities.[15] This range of estimates implies that a 10 percent increase in labor costs will result in a sizable decline in employment, between 2 percent and 6 percent.

The preceding analysis assumes that the cost of regulations is entirely paid by employers. However, when the supply of labor is not perfectly elastic, part of the increase in labor costs will be compensated by lower wages, reducing the disemployment effect of the regulations. Alternatively, workers may not perceive the cost of regulation as a tax, because higher contributions pay for improved job benefits, which are valued. In this case, workers will be willing to pay for this benefit, reducing their wage demands. This wage offset would also contribute to lessening the impact of regulations on employment.

How likely is it that the costs of labor market regulations are shifted to workers in Latin America? Before reviewing the existing evidence, it is important to note important features of Latin American labor markets. First, high evasion implies that the relevant labor supply to the formal sector in developing countries is likely to be more elastic than in developed ones. Thus, if workers have access to similar jobs in both the formal and informal sectors, the possibilities of shifting costs to workers are lessened, resulting in a high elasticity of labor supply to formal-sector firms that comply with regulations. Second, as previously noted, in some countries minimum wages are quite high, both absolutely and in relation to the average wage, and this reduces the scope for wage shifts (see figure 2). Moreover, Maloney and Nuñez Mendez (chap. 1 in this volume) show piling up of workers at minimum wage levels, suggesting that compliance with the minimum wage is substantial even in the so-called "informal" sectors so that wage shifting will be attenuated in countries with a binding minimum

---

15. Hamermesh (1993) reports a range between –0.15 and –0.75 and an average estimate of –0.45.

wage that also affects the informal sector. Third, although most social security programs in the region are restricted to covered workers, and this tightens the link between contributions and benefits, the dismal financial condition of some social security systems and the high degree of discretion exercised by governments over the determination of benefits weaken this link. In this respect, the recent social security reforms aimed at privatizing pensions should strengthen the relationship between benefits and costs in many countries of the region.

Several empirical studies have attempted to measure the impact of mandatory benefits on employment rates. Gruber (1994) analyzes the effects of insurance for workplace injuries and mandated maternity benefits in the United States and finds that a large share of the cost is shifted to wages, with only minor disemployment effects. In contrast, Kaestner (1996) examines the effect of unemployment insurance contributions on the employment of U.S. youth and finds large disemployment effects and little wage shifting.

For developing countries, there is some evidence on the magnitude of wage shifts predating the studies collected in this volume. MacIsaac and Rama (1997) assess the fungibility of the cost of mandated benefits in Ecuador. In 1994, the year they study, Ecuador had one of the most cumbersome labor legislation regimes in Latin America. Beyond mandated contributions to social security programs, the law also mandated payment of thirteen-, fourteen-, fifteen-, and sixteen-month payments for separation at various times of the same year. MacIsaac and Rama's analysis suggests that while labor market regulations increase labor costs, part of the increase is shifted to workers in the form of lower base wages. Thus, for an average Ecuadorian worker, social security contributions and other mandated benefits amount to a large share of the base wage. However, workers whose employers comply with regulations earn on average only 18 percent more than workers at noncompliant firms. This difference is explained by a 39 percent reduction in the base earnings of workers in compliant firms. Interestingly, these reductions are not uniform across firms; they are smaller in larger firms and essentially zero in the public sector and in unionized firms.

Mondino and Montoya (chap. 6 in this volume) and Edwards and Cox-Edwards (1999) explore this topic for Argentina and Chile, respectively, by comparing wages of workers who have access to social security programs with wages of uncovered workers. In Argentina, Mondino and Montoya (chap. 6 in this volume) find that during the period 1975–1996, wages of noncovered workers were 8 percent higher than the wages of covered workers. Considering that employee-paid payroll contributions average 40 percent of the payroll, the share of contributions paid by workers is around 20 percent of total labor costs. In Chile, Edwards and Cox-Edwards (1999) find evidence of a larger wage shift. In 1994, cash wages for workers covered by mandatory pension, health, and life insurance were 14 percent lower than wages for noncovered workers. Since, in that year, social security contributions amounted to 20 percent of wages and were nominally paid by workers, their estimates suggest that about 70 percent of the cost of social security contributions were absorbed by workers, while the other 30 percent fell on employers. Gruber (1997) reports evidence of an even larger wage shift in the aftermath of the 1981 pension reform in Chile. The 1981 reform reduced employer-paid labor taxes and increased taxes paid by employees. In addition, the funding of some programs was shifted to general revenue. Using this tax change as a "natural experiment" and data on individual firms' payments in labor taxes and wages, he seeks to determine whether lower employer-paid labor taxes are associated with higher wages within a firm. His results suggest a full shift of payroll taxes to wages and no effect on employment.[16]

Marrufo (2001) examines the 1997 reform in Mexico, which, as in Chile, transformed the pay-as-you-go pension system into an individual retirement accounts (IRA) system. She finds evidence of substantial employment reallocation between noncovered and covered sectors, suggesting that the labor supply to covered sectors is fairly elastic. However, she also finds evidence of a wage shift in response to a reform that ties benefits to taxes collected. Decomposing the effect of the reforms into the effect of a tax reduction and the effect of tying benefits to contributions, she finds that increasing social security taxes reduces wages by 43 percent of the tax increase, while increasing benefits decreases wages by 57 percent of the value of benefits.

An important factor determining the extent of wage pass-through is whether minimum wages bind. Maloney and Nuñez Mendez (chap. 1 in this volume) document that the minimum wage binds in Colombia. This explains the weak pass-through effects reported by Cárdenas and Bernal (chap. 4 in this volume) for Colombia. At the same time, the minimum wage is less binding, and pass-through effects may be more substantial in Mexico and Chile, and this may explain the Marrufo (2001) and Gruber (1997) results.

All in all, the available evidence suggests that at least part of the cost of

16. Measuring the impact of such an "experiment" is complicated by many factors. (See the discussion in Edwards and Cox-Edwards 2000.) First, although payroll taxes declined, worker contributions increased. If measured wage payments by firms include employee contributions, then a decline in employer-paid taxes will be associated with higher measured wages due to higher employee-paid contributions. Second, measurement error in wages biases his estimates toward finding full shifting, as he reports. The quality of his instruments is questionable, and he is forced to make strong assumptions to circumvent a severe measurement error problem. Third, at a time when social security reform made work benefits more attractive, he estimates that wages were rising. The only way that wages can rise to match the decreased employer taxes in an environment with an improved link between employee contributions and benefits is if labor supply is perfectly inelastic to covered sector firms, which seems implausible.

nonwage benefits is passed on to workers in the form of lower wages, and, therefore, the employment cost of such programs will be lower than what is predicted by the elasticity of the labor demand. Combining wage-shift and labor demand estimates indicates that a 10 percent increase in non-wage labor costs can lead to a decline in employment rates ranging between 0.6 and 4.8 percent, with most of the evidence shaded toward the high end of this spectrum.

Given the significance of these estimates for policy decisions, it is important to estimate them as accurately as possible. In this regard, the room for improvement in the literature is still large. As they stand, they might overestimate or underestimate the true employment impact depending on which of the following two effects dominates. On the one hand, the reported estimates are based on constant-output labor demand elasticities, which do not consider the employment effects of regulations through a negative effect on the scale of production of existing firms and on entry and exit decisions of firms. From this perspective, the reported range of estimates provides a lower bound on the disemployment effects of regulation. Moreover, the estimates of the wage shift in MacIsaac and Rama (1997), Mondino and Montoya (chap. 6 in this volume), and Edwards and Cox-Edwards (1999) only include the cost of social security programs, but do not include the cost of other regulations such as job security or vacation time. Once the cost of these regulations is taken into account, the computed wage shift could be lower than what we report above, and, therefore, the estimated effects of those costs on employment would be larger.

On the other hand, studies comparing wages of covered and noncovered workers performed using a cross-section of workers, such as most of the ones discussed above, may underestimate wage shifts and overestimate employment costs. It is necessary to model selection into covered sectors. This is because unobserved personal characteristics correlated with social security affiliation might explain higher wages in covered sectors.[17] If this correlation is substantial, it will lead to an underestimation of wage differences between covered and uncovered workers, and hence reduce estimates of the fraction of wage costs shifted to workers. This concern highlights the importance of the Marrufo (2001) study because she controls for sectoral self-selection bias and still finds substantial evidence of wage shifting. If her selection adjustments to the Mexican data are typical of what would be found in other Latin American countries, the weight of the evidence in this book and the literature on firm entry in response to incentives suggest that the studies reported in this volume underestimate the disemployment effects of regulation.

17. For instance, if workers covered by social security programs also happen to be more productive, then they will also have higher wages. Yet, higher wages are explained by unobserved productivity and not by social security affiliation.

I.4.2 Job Security Provisions Alter Hiring and Firing Decisions

Regulations affecting transition costs are not adequately analyzed within a simple static labor demand–labor supply framework. Dismissal costs and other regulations not only increase labor costs, but also alter firms' firing and hiring decisions. The importance of dismissal costs in Latin America is clearly shown in figure 5. Where nonwage labor costs are low relative to those of OECD countries, dismissal costs tend to be very high. These costs make Latin American labor markets less flexible than OECD markets and likely impair productivity and adaptation to new technology and trade patterns as they do in Europe (see Heckman 2003). It is thus important to assess the impact, if any, that such policies have on the functioning of the labor market.

Theoretical Discussion

To analyze the full impact of job security provisions requires a more complex framework that encompasses dynamic decisions of firms. Bertola (1990) and Bentolila and Bertola (1990) develop dynamic partial-equilibrium models to assess how a firm's firing and hiring decisions are affected by dismissal costs. In the face of a given shock, the optimal employment policy of a firm involves one of three state-contingent responses: (1) dismissing workers, (2) hiring workers, or (3) doing nothing. Appendix B presents a simple two-period model of labor adjustment that summarizes the main ideas in this literature.

In the face of a negative shock and declining marginal value of labor, a firm might want to dismiss some workers. However, it faces a dismissal cost in most regulatory regimes in LAC. This cost has the effect of discouraging firms from adjusting their labor force, resulting in fewer dismissals than the number of dismissals that would occur in a scenario in the absence of such costs. Conversely, in the face of a positive shock, firms might want to hire additional workers but would take into account that it would be costly for some workers to be fired if future demand declined. This potential cost acts as a hiring cost, effectively reducing the creation of new jobs in a relatively healthy economy. The net result is lower employment rates in expansions, higher employment rates in recessions, and lower turnover rates as firms hire and fire fewer workers than they would in the absence of adjustment costs.

Adjustment costs produce a decline in employment variability associated with firing costs. The implication of these models for average employment is ambiguous. In particular, whether average employment rates increase or decline as a result of firing costs depends on whether over the cycle the decline in hiring rates more than compensates for the reduction in dismissals. Simulations reported in Bertola (1990) and Bentolila and Bertola (1990) suggest that average employment in a given firm is likely to increase when firing costs increase. However, these results are quite sensitive to different assumptions about the persistence of shocks, the elasticity of the labor demand, the magnitude of the discount rate, and the functional form of the production function. Less persistent shocks and lower discount rates produce larger negative effects of job security on employment because both factors reduce hiring relative to firing (Bentolila and Saint-Paul 1994; Bertola, 1992). Furthermore, a higher elasticity of the demand for goods implies a larger negative effect of job security on employment rates. In addition, when investment decisions are also considered, firing costs lower profits and discourage investment, increasing the likelihood that they reduce the demand for labor (Risager and Sorensen 1997).

The Bertola (1990) and Bentolila and Bertola (1990) analyses focus on employment rates in a "representative" firm without considering the impact of firing costs on the extensive margin, that is, on how firing costs affect the creation and destruction of firms. Hopenhayn and Rogerson (1993) develop a general equilibrium model based on the U.S. economy. The partial equilibrium framework of Bertola (1990) is embedded in their model as part of a general equilibrium framework in which jobs and firms are created and destroyed in every period in response to firm-specific shocks. In the context of their model, Hopenhayn and Rogerson (1993) find that increasing firing costs in the United States would lead to an increase in the average employment of existing firms as a consequence of the reduction in firings. However, they also find that such a policy would result in lower firm entry and lower job creation in newly created firms. These final two effects could potentially offset the increase in employment in existing firms, and they would thus reduce overall employment rates.

The recent literature has also emphasized the possible impact of job security regulations on the composition of employment. Kugler (chap. 3 in this volume) proposes a model in which job security regulations provide incentives for high turnover firms to operate in the informal sector. This decision would entail producing at a small, less efficient scale in order to remain inconspicuous to tax and labor authorities. In this framework, high job security costs paid by formal sector firms would likely increase informality rates. Pagés and Montenegro (1999) develop a model in which job security provisions, which depend on tenure, bias employment against young workers in favor of older ones. As severance pay increases with tenure, and tenure tends to increase with age, older workers become more costly to dismiss than younger ones. If wages do not adjust appropriately, negative shocks result in a disproportionate share of layoffs among young workers. Therefore, job security based on tenure results in lower employment rates for the young, relative to older, workers because it reduces hiring and increases layoffs for young workers. This effect has also been found in studies of European employment (Heckman 2003).

Finally, it is important to understand that not all components of dismissal costs may have the same effect on employment and unemployment rates. Thus, in principle, there is an important conceptual distinction between advance notice and indemnities, which are state contingent and affect the cost of adjustment to different states, and seniority pay provisions, which are paid in all states and do not affect transitions. The latter are more comparable to other nonwage costs such as vacation and other mandatory benefits.

The existing evidence regarding the impact of employment protection is abundant but inconclusive. Table 5 from Addison and Teixeira (2001) summarizes the current literature. While Addison and Grosso (1996), Grubb and Wells (1993), Lazear (1990), Heckman and Pagés (2000), Nickell (1997), and Nicoletti and Scarpetta (2001) find a negative relationship between job security provisions and employment, other studies, such as Addison, Teixeira, and Grosso (2000), (Organization for Economic Cooperation and Development [OECD] 1999), Garibaldi and Mauro (1999), and Freeman (2002) do not find evidence of such a relationship. The evidence on the effects of job security on unemployment is equally ambiguous. Some studies find a positive link between job security and unemployment (Addison and Grosso 1996; Elmeskov, Martin, and Scarpetta 1998; Lazear 1990), while others find no effect (Blanchard 1998; Heckman and Pagés 2000; Nickell 1997). Our own estimates at the end of this chapter give reasons for these mixed findings. All these studies are based on the analysis of aggregates of cross-country time series data with little variation in regulatory policies. The studies presented in this volume surmount some of these difficulties by studying episodes of major labor reform using large microdata sets. Using disaggregated data for single countries, Mondino and Montoya (chap. 6 in this volume) and Saavedra and Torero (chap. 2 in this volume) find a large negative relationship between employment protection and employment. The studies presented in this volume contribute substantially to a literature that analyzes the consequences of reforms. Recent studies for OECD countries using disaggregated data suggest a negative effect of job security regulations on employment. Autor, Donohue, and Schwab (2003) estimate the effects of recent common law wrongful discharge doctrines adopted by courts across states in the United States that limit employment at will. They find that the wrongful discharge doctrine has a negative impact on employment to population rates in state labor markets. Similarly, Kugler, Jimeno, and Hernanz (2002) find that in Spain a combination of a reduction in payroll taxes and the reduction of dismissal costs increased the employment of workers on permanent contracts. Finally, Acemoglu and Angrist (2001), and the earlier work of Deleire (2000), examine the effects of the Americans with Disabilities Act (ADA), which outlaws discrimination against the disabled in hiring, firing, and pay on the employment rate of workers with disabilities. The Acemoglu and Angrist findings and prior work by Deleire (2000) suggest that the passage of the act reduced employment for disabled workers.

Table 5   Effects of Employment Protection on Employment and Unemployment: Selected Studies

Study	Sample	EP Measure	Outcome Indicator(s)	Other Variables	Methodology	Finding
Lazear (1990)	20 countries; 1956–1984	Severance pay due blue-collar workers with 10 years of service; time-varying measure	Employment population ratio, unemployment rate, average hours worked per week	Quadratic time trend and, in some specifications, controls for population of working age and growth in per capita GDP (interacted with EP measure)	Pooled time-series/ cross-section estimates; selective corrections for fixed effects, random effects, and autocorrelation	In favored specifications, EP raises unemployment and reduces employment participation and hours.
Addison, Teixeira, and Grosso (2000)	As above	As above	As above	As above, but uses full Lazear specification	Fixed and random effects, with correction for autocorrelation, plus FGLS estimates	EP is statistically insignificant.
OECD (1993)	OECD 19 countries; 1979–1991	Severance pay and notice periods combined across blue- and white-collar workers; moment-in-time indicator	Long-term unemployment	UI benefit duration; ALMP expenditures divided by UI benefit expenditures	Pooled time-series/ cross-section estimation	EP has positive effects on jobless duration, especially in southern Europe.
Grubb and Wells (1993)	11 EU countries; 1989	Authors' own indicators of ORDW, RDSM, RFTC, and RTWA	Employment; self-employment; part-time work; temporary work; agency work	None	Simple cross-section regressions	ORDW reduces employment, increases self-employment, and reduces part-time work. RDSM (RFTC) increases (decreases) temporary work. RTWA but not RDSM reduces temporary agency work.

(continued)

Table 5 (continued)

Study	Sample	EP Measure	Outcome Indicator(s)	Other Variables	Methodology	Finding
Scarpetta (1996)	17 OECD countries; 1983–1993	OECD strictness ranking for regulation of dismissal averaged over regular and fixed-term contracts (OECD 1994, Table 6.7, panel B, col. 2)	Structural unemployment, plus separate regressions for youth unemployment, long-term unemployment, and nonemployment rates	ALMP calculated as expenditure on active measures per person relative to output per capita; summary index of UI benefits (OECD 1994, chapter 8); union density; union coordination, employer coordination, and their sum; centralization of collective bargaining; tax wedge; proxy for product market competition; real interest rates; output gap	Random effects, feasible generalized least squares (FGLS)	EP raises structural unemployment, with stronger effects for youth and long-term unemployment. EP increases nonemployment rate.
Elmeskov, Martin, and Scarpetta (1998)	19 OECD countries; 1983–1995	OECD (1994, table 6.7, panel B, col. 2) ranking, but modified to take account of changes since late 1980s; two-observation, time-varying indicator	Structural unemployment	ALMP (as above); UI benefits (as above); union density; dummies for the degree of coordination on the employer and union sides; dummies for degree of centralization of collective bargaining; tax wedge; output gap, minimum wage relative to aver-	Random effects, FGLS	EP raises structural unemployment but interaction effects are important. EP not statistically significant in either highly centralized/coordinated or decentralized bargaining regimes.

Study	Sample	Source	Dependent variables	Independent variables	Methods	Results
Nickell (1997)	20 OECD countries; 1983–1988 and 1989–1994	OECD (1996, table 6.7, panel B, col. 5) ranking; also use of labor standards measure covering in addition to EP working time, minimum wages, and employee representation rights (OECD, 1994, table 4.8, col. 6)	Employment-population ratio for whole working-age population and for prime-age males; Overall labor supply (defined as actual annual hours divided by normal annual hours multiplied by employment-population ratio); Log unemployment rate and component short- and long-term rates	UI benefit replacement rate; UI benefit duration in years; union density; union coverage index; sum of indices of union and employer coordination; instrument for ALMP expenditure; tax wedge; change in inflation	GLS random effects using two cross sections	EP reduces overall employment rate but not that of prime-age males. EP also reduces overall labor supply. For unemployment, EP effect is negative but statistically insignificant. EP reduces short-term unemployment and increases long-term unemployment. Coefficient estimate for worker labor standards variable is statistically insignificant in unemployment regression.
Nickell and Layard (1999)	As above	As above	As above, plus measures of labor and total factor productivity growth, 1976–1992	As above, plus owner-occupation rate as a negative proxy for geographic mobility	As above; OLS for analysis of productivity growth	As above; EP is positive and statistically significant in labor and total factor productivity equations, but effect vanishes with correction for initial productivity gap.

(continued)

Table 5 (continued)

Study	Sample	EP Measure	Outcome Indicator(s)	Other Variables	Methodology	Finding
OECD (1999)	19 OECD countries; 1985–1990, 1992–1997	OECD (1999, table 2.5) measures for late 1980s and late 1990s; Single overall indicator and also separate indicators for regular employment, temporary employment and collective dismissal; In some specifications further disaggregations for regular and temporary employment	Log unemployment rate, log employment-population ratio, and changes in unemployment and employment; For unemployment: separate rate results for prime-age males, youth, and low-skilled; For employment: separate results for prime-age males, youth, share of self-employment, share of temporary employment, and temporary employment, and share in youth employment	UI benefit replacement rate; UI benefit maximum duration; ALMP expenditures as percentage of GDP; degree of centralization of collective bargaining; degree of coordination of collective bargaining; trade union density; trade union coverage; tax wedge; output gap	Two-period panel estimated by random effects, GLS (changes in levels model estimated by OLS)	Irrespective of the form of the indicator, EP coefficient estimate is statistically insignificant for overall employment. It is positive and statistically significant for prime-age male unemployment (overall indicator only). For all other demographic groups EP is statistically insignificant. Further, changes in EP do not affect changes in unemployment for other than prime-age females, where the effect is negative and statistically significant (strictness of EP with respect to regular employment). For employment, the coefficient estimates for EP are negative but statistically insignificant for overall, prime-age female, youth, and temporary employment. Otherwise they are positive and in the case of self-employment statistically significant (overall EP measure and its regular employment variant). Further, changes in EP have statistically insignificant effects for overall employment and for all demographic groups. For self-employment and the share of temporary employment, some statistically significant negative effects are observed.

| Garibaldi and Mauro (1999) | 21 OECD countries; 1980–1998 | OECD (1994, table 6.5, panel B, col. 5) ranking; Moment-in-time measure | Average growth in total civilian employment | Average change in inflation; average total taxation as share of GDP; average payroll taxes as share of GDP; average UI benefit net replacement rate for an unemployed worker (OECD 1994, chapter 8); union density; index of the coordination collective bargaining; time dummies | Random effects, GLS: six-year averages of data (1980–1985, 1986–1991, 1992–1997) | There is a strong negative association between EP measure and employment growth in cross section (for 24 out of 27 cases), but in panel regressions the association is less precisely estimated and is statistically significant in one of five specifications only. |

(*continued*)

Table 5 (continued)

Study	Sample	EP Measure	Outcome Indicator(s)	Other Variables	Methodology	Finding
Nicoletti and Scarpetta (2001)	20 OECD countries; 1982–1998	Two indicators of the stringency of the regulatory apparatus: the first is EP per se, and is based on the time-varying OECD (1999, table 2.5) measure; the second is a measure of the degree of product model regulation and is both static (based on Nicoletti, Scarpetta, and Boylaud 1999) and time varying (based on the authors' evaluation of regulation and market conditions in seven energy and service industries, 1970–1998)	Nonagricultural employment rate	Public employment rate; tax wedge union density; dummy variables for high and intermediate coordination of bargaining based on a summary indicator combining centralization and coordination; UI benefit replacement rate composite measure (OECD 1994, chapter 8); and the output gap	Fixed effects without product market regulation indicator; random effects with static product market regulation indicators and two stage regression approach, the second state involving regression of fixed country effects on the static product market regulation indicator. Also fixed effects panel estimates with time-varying EP and product market indicators	In initial fixed effects specification, EP is associated with a statistically significant reduction in employment. When EP enters in interaction with the coordination of collective bargaining dummies, its effects are negative and statistically significant for both intermediate and high coordination. The same results are obtained for the random effects and second state regressions. In each case, the negative effect on employment is stronger in countries with an intermediate degree of coordination. The effect of the static product market regulation variable is statistically significant and negative. Finally, for the fixed effect panel regressions, EP is negative and statistically significant in the basic specification. In interactive form, however, the negative coefficient estimate for EP is only statistically significant for the intermediate coordination measure. In interaction with the coordination measure, the product market regulation variable is negative throughout, but is statistically significant for low and intermediate coordination.

| Di Tella and Mac-Culloch (1999) | 21 OECD countries; 1984–1990 | World Competitiveness Report data; indicator of flexibility (see text); Time-varying measure with five data points | Employment-population ratio; participation rate; unemployment rate; long-term unemployment rate; and average hours worked per week. For the first two variables, disaggregations by gender are provided. | UI benefit composite measure (OECD 1984, chapter 8), plus level of GDP. Selective results are also provided for a specification that includes union coverage, a dummy for decentralized collective bargaining, and degree of home ownership. | Random effects, least squares dummy variable (LSDV) with country fixed effects, LSDV with country and time fixed effects, and generalized method of moments (GMM) estimates for each outcome indicator. | Statistically significant positive association between flexibility indicator and overall employment population ratio across all specifications. By demographic group this effect is much stronger for females than for males. Parallel results are obtained for the participation rate. Some evidence that flexibility increases average hours worked. The association between flexibility and the unemployment rate is negative throughout but not always statistically significant. The results for long-term unemployment are less precisely estimated. |

(continued)

Table 5 (continued)

Study	Sample	EP Measure	Outcome Indicator(s)	Other Variables	Methodology	Finding
Heckman and Pagés (2000)	41 countries from LAC and OECD; 1980–1997 (max)	Authors' own cardinal measure based on severance pay, notice interval, and compensation for unfair dismissal (see text); Two-period time-varying measure	Employment: total, prime-age male, prime-age female, youth, and self-employment. Unemployment: total, prime-age male, prime-age female, youth, and share unemployed for more than 6 months.	Level of GDP, GDP growth, and two demographic controls, namely, female participation rate and proportion of the population aged 15–24 years	Pooled cross-section/time series, random effects, and fixed effects; results for full sample and separate samples of OECD and Latin-American nations.	EP effect is negative and statistically significant for total employment for each estimating procedure. Similar results obtained for males and youth—but not females—the impact of EP on male employment being half the total employment effect and the youth effect is almost double the average effect. EP effects for females and self employment vary widely across estimating procedure. The results for unemployment depend on methodology and there is no statistically significant effect of EP on longer-term unemployment. Disaggregation by broad national grouping reveals that employment effects of EP by demographic group are negative and mostly statistically significant. The exception is females in the Latin-American grouping. The effects on EP on unemployment are nearly always positive and stronger for the OECD grouping.

| Freeman (2002) | 23+ countries; 1970–1990 | Fraser Institute index of economic freedom (see text); time-varying measure with 6 data points | Level of log GDP per capita, log employment-population ratio, log GDP per employee, and unemployment rate; also changes in levels for the first three variables | Squared freedom index term (in some specifications); country dummies; time dummies | Cross section and "panel" estimates | Countries with a high degree of economic freedom have higher GDP per capita, high employment-population rates, high GDP per employee, and low unemployment—at least in terms of levels. With the exception of unemployment these results do not survive the inclusion of country fixed effects. Estimating GDP per capita in levels and change form for a sample of less developed countries produces statistically significant positive coefficient estimates for the freedom indicator in cross-section and panel estimates. |

(continued)

Table 5 (continued)

Study	Sample	EP Measure	Outcome Indicator(s)	Other Variables	Methodology	Finding
Blanchard and Wolfers (2000)	20 OECD countries; 1960–1999; 8 five-year averages of data	Static and time-varying measures; static measure taken from Nickell (1997); time-varying measure taken from Lazear (1990) and updated	National unemployment rates (i.e., non-standardized). Basic argument is that unemployment can be explained by shocks which interact with labor market institutions. Shocks are first modeled as common and unobservable and then as country specific.	Basic specification uses 7 (other) labor market institutions taken from Nickell (1997); alternative specification(s) uses two measures of UI benefits (authors' own calculations) that are deployed in fixed and time-varying form	Nonlinear least squares with time effects are interacted with fixed institutions/time-varying institutions; robustness checks offered; nonlinear least squares with country-specific observable shocks (total factor productivity grow, the real rate of interest, and a labor demand shift measure) that are interacted with all 8 labor market institutions; as before, estimates provided for fixed and time-varying institutions	Shock-EP interaction terms point to amplification of the effects of adverse shocks. Essentially the same is true for the remaining institutional variables with two exceptions. The exceptions are coordination of collective bargaining and active labor market policies, which ameliorate the effects of adverse shocks. In general, much weaker interaction effect and poorer fit when static EP (and UI) measures replaced by their time-varying counterparts.

Source: Addison and Teixeira (2001).

Notes: EP = employment protection; UI = unemployment insurance; ALMP = active labor market policy; ORDW = restrictions on overall employee work; RDSM = restriction on dismissal of regular workers; RFTC = restrictions on fixed-term contracts; RTWA = restrictions on temporary work agencies.

Empirical Evidence for Latin America and the Caribbean

The essays assembled in this volume assess the impact of job security regulation on employment and turnover rates in LAC and provide the first systematic evidence of its impact on the labor market. Several studies assess the impact of job security on turnover rates in the labor market. Changes in turnover are measured using changes in the duration of jobs (tenure), the duration of unemployment, and rates of exiting out of employment and unemployment.[18] Higher employment exit rates indicate more layoffs (or more quits), while higher exit rates out of unemployment and into formal jobs indicate higher job creation in the formal sector. Other studies examine the impact of job security on employment rates. The definition of employment used in the empirical studies varies, depending on the country being analyzed. In general, most studies focus on employment in large firms, although some also examine more aggregated measures of employment. In addition, a small group of studies also examine the impact of job security on the composition of employment. See table 6 for an overview of the empirical evidence for LAC presented in this volume.

Turnover Rates

As predicted by most theoretical models, the bulk of empirical evidence reported in this volume confirms that less-stringent job security tends to be associated with higher turnover and greater flexibility in the labor market. Kugler (chap. 3 in this volume) analyzes the impact of the 1990 labor market reforms in Colombia. She finds that a reduction in job security costs reduces average tenure and increases employment exit rates.[19] This decline is significantly larger in the formal sector, which is covered by the regulations, than in the uncovered or informal sector. In addition, the increase is greater in large firms than in the small ones. Her results show similar patterns within tradable and nontradable sectors, providing a clear indication that the decline in tenure cannot be attributed to contemporary trade reforms. The increasing use of temporary contracts explains only part of the increase in formal turnover rates because job stability also declined for workers employed at permanent jobs.[20]

Kugler also finds a decline in the average duration of unemployment

18. These studies estimate hazard rates. The hazard rate is defined as the rate at which a given spell of employment or unemployment ends in a given period conditional on having lasted a given period of time in the spell (e.g., one month, one year).

19. In this study tenure is measured by the duration of incomplete employment spells.

20. In her study, Kugler performs two types of analyses. First, she uses a difference-in-differences estimator to analyze whether changes in average duration of employment (unemployment) are significantly different in the formal and informal sectors. Second, she estimates an exponential duration model to control for changes in demographic covariates, pooling data from before and after the reform and using interaction terms to assess the differential impact on the formal and informal sectors.

Table 6 **Summary of Existing Evidence on the Impact of Job Security (JS) Costs in Latin America**

Study	Country	Data	Results
		A. Studies that Analyze Exit Rates Into and Out of Employment	
Kugler (chap. 3 in this volume)	Colombia	Household data	Decline in JS leads to reduction in employment and unemployment duration; some effect due to deregulation of temporary contracts but not all.
Saavedra and Torero (chap. 2 in this volume)	Peru	Household data	Lower JS leads to lower average tenure; higher decline in formal sector; hazard rates increase just at the end of probation period.
Barros and Corseuil (chap. 5 in this volume)	Brazil	Employment Surveys, administrative data, and household surveys	Hazard rates for short durations declined but hazard rates for longer durations increased after an increase in job security. No effects either on adjustment costs or wage elasticities.
Hopenhayn (chap. 9 in this volume)	Argentina	Household data Rotating Panel	Deregulation of temporary contracts leads to increase in hazard rates; hazard rates for short spells (1–3 months) increase by 40% and for 3–6 months spells by 10%.
		B. Studies that Analyze Average Employment and Unemployment	
Kugler (chap. 3 in this volume)	Colombia	Household data on employment	Decline in JS in 1990 brings a decline in unemployment rates. This is based on computing the net effect of changes in hazard rates, in and out of unemployment, induced by the reduction in JS.
Saavedra and Torero (chap. 2 in this volume)	Peru	Firm and sector level data; 1986–1997	They include a direct measure of JS regulations in labor demand function. They estimate a negative and statistically significant coefficient, which is larger (in absolute value) in the more regulated period.
Mondino and Montoya (chap. 6 in this volume)	Argentina	Panel of manufacturing firms; does not account for firm creation	As Saavedra and Torero (this volume), they include a direct measure of JS in labor demand. They also find a negative effect of JS on LD.

Table 6 (continued)

Study	Country	Data	Results
Barros and Corseuil (chap. 5 in this volume)	Brazil	Monthly establishment-level data; 1985–1998; manufacturing; firms employing 5 or more workers	Two step procedure: First, find parameters for labor demand (LD) function for every month; then see whether those parameters change with labor reforms and other development. They find no effect of JS on LD parameters.
Downes, Mamingi, and Antoine (chap. 10 in this volume)	Barbados Trinidad; Jamaica	Aggregated employment. Annual; covers large firms (>10 emp)	The effects of JS on employment are statistically insignificant and the signs are positive in some cases.
Pagés and Montenegro (1999)	Chile	Household data on employment; annual; 1960–1998	Not a significant effect of JS on aggregated employment but important effect on its composition.
Marquéz (1998)	Cross-country	Cross-section data for LAC and OECD countries	Rank indicator of JS; not significantly associated with lower employment once GDP per capita is accounted for.

C. Studies that Analyze the Composition of Employment

Study	Country	Data	Results
Marquéz (1998)	Cross-country	Cross-section data for LAC and OECD countries	Self-employment rates are positively associated with JS even after accounting for differences in GDP per capita.
Montenegro and Pagés (chap. 7 in this volume)	Chile	Household survey data; 1960–1998	Job security is associated with lower employment rates for young workers, female and unskilled workers, and higher employment for older and skilled workers.

after the reforms. In addition, exit rates out of unemployment increase more for workers who leave unemployment by going into the formal sector than they do for those who exit into informal jobs. As with average tenure, her results show quite similar patterns across sectors and a higher exit rate toward larger firms. Finally, only two-thirds of the increase in the rate of entry into unemployment can be attributed to higher use of temporary contracts. The rest is explained by increased exit rates into permanent jobs in the formal sector.

Saavedra and Torero (chap. 2 in this volume) conduct a similar study, evaluating the impact of the 1991 reform in Peru. Like the reform in Colombia, the 1991 Peruvian reform considerably reduced the cost of dismissing workers. Their analysis shows a consistent decline in average tenure from 1991 onward, suggesting higher exit rates from employment. As in the Kugler study, the decline is significantly more pronounced in the formal sector than it is in the informal sector. In addition, the tenure patterns were quite similar across economic sectors, suggesting that these findings cannot be explained by the trade reforms that took place in the early 1990s.

In contrast to these findings, Barros and Corseuil (chap. 5 in this volume) find little evidence that the substantial 1988 Brazilian Constitutional reform altered employment exit rates. In that year, the cost of dismissing workers was raised, and, therefore, a reduction in exit rates would be expected as a result. (Many other reforms were also put in place as well.) Their results indicate that aggregate employment exit rates decline in the formal sector relative to the informal sector for short employment spells (two years or less), but increase for longer spells. Their measured increase in exit rates for long spells could be driven by the special characteristics of the Brazilian system. In this system, employers contribute 8 percent of a worker's wage to the worker's individual account. In case of involuntary dismissal, the worker can claim the principal, the compounded interest rate, and a penalty paid by the firm, which in the 1988 reform was raised from 10 percent to 40 percent of principal plus interest. In the case of a voluntary quit, the worker receives nothing. This asymmetry in the treatment of termination induces workers to force dismissal or to collude with firms to obtain the funds accumulated in the account. It can be argued that the 1988 reform greatly increased the incentives to force dismissals, particularly for workers with longer tenures. This may explain the increase in exit rates for workers with longer employment spells.

These three studies use the informal sector as a control group unaffected by the reforms. Their credibility hinges on the validity of this assumption. Kugler shows that estimates based on formal-informal sector comparisons are likely to be biased. However, such comparisons are still valid under certain conditions—at least as tests of the null hypothesis of no effect of the reform.[21] When viewed as a whole, these studies provide evidence that dismissal costs and other employment protection mechanisms reduce worker reallocation in the labor market. Unfortunately, these studies do not identify whether reduced worker reallocation is due to reduced layoffs, lower quits, or a mix of both.

Some studies in this book assess the impact of regulations on the speed of adjustment using the length of the lag (the speed of adjustment) as an alternative measure of the constraints faced by firms. The intuition supporting this is based on the original work of Holt et al. (1960).

Let n_t^* be the optimal level of employment at date t determined by some implicit (usually static) theory. Let the cost of being out of equilibrium, c_t^0, be quadratic in deviations of current employment from optimal employment:

$$(2) \qquad c_t^0 = \gamma_0(n_t^* - n_t)^2 \qquad \gamma_0 > 0$$

The greater the discrepancy between employment at t and optimal employment, the greater the cost. There is also a cost of adjustment, c_t^a, which is also assumed to be quadratic in the adjustment from n_{t-1} to n_t:

$$(3) \qquad c_t^a = \gamma_a(n_t - n_{t-1})^2$$

Minimizing the sum of these costs produces an optimal labor demand n_t:

$$n_t = (1 - \lambda)n_t^* + \lambda n_{t-1},$$

where

$$\lambda = \frac{\gamma_a}{\gamma_a + \gamma_0}.$$

The greater the cost of adjustment, the bigger the value of λ. Abraham and Houseman (1993) and many others use this method to assess the effect of different regulatory regimes across countries on adjustment costs, while others interact λ with measures of regulations to assess whether the speed of adjustment increases or declines when the regulatory environment is changed. Cárdenas and Bernal (chap. 4 in this volume), Barros and Corseuil (chap. 5 in this volume) and Saavedra and Torero (chap. 2 in this volume) use this methodology to examine whether the speed of adjustment increased or declined after labor reforms. In the study of Saavedra and Torero, their estimated interaction term suggests that more stringent regu-

---

21. Kugler shows that lower severance pay may induce high-turnover informal firms to move to the formal sector. Assuming either no overlap in the distribution of turnover between covered and uncovered firms or that entry to the covered sector comes from the high-end— or at least from the end that is higher than the formal sector—this shift results in higher turnover in both the formal *and* the informal sector. Higher turnover in the informal sector biases the difference-in-differences estimator downward. Therefore, a positive estimate still provides substantial evidence of increased turnover in the formal sector.

lations reduce the speed of adjustment, particularly in the prereform period, when regulation was very stringent. In the other two studies, this methodology is unable to identify any changes in adjustment due to reforms. This is particularly relevant in the study of Cárdenas and Bernal on Colombia because other methodologies based on duration data (Kugler, chap. 3 in this volume) show clear effects of regulation on adjustment. Addison and Teixeira (2001) indicate that "none of the implementations of this (adjustment cost) model in core OECD countries were able to detect a discernible impact of job security regulations on the speed of employment adjustment." In the concluding section of this paper, we discuss why the lag coefficient is not a reliable measure of the regulatory costs, especially when applied to cross-country data.

Average Employment

The available evidence for LAC countries shows a consistent, although not always statistically significant, negative impact of job security provisions on average employment rates. Saavedra and Torero (chap. 2 in this volume) and Mondino and Montoya (chap. 6 in this volume) use firm-level panel data to estimate the impact of job security on employment in Peru and Argentina, respectively. Both studies estimate labor demand equations in which an explicit measure of job security appears on the right-hand side of the equation, and both find evidence that higher job security levels are associated with lower employment rates.[22] In the case of Peru, Saavedra and Torero find that the size of the impact of regulations is correlated with the magnitude of the regulations themselves. Thus, the impact is very high at the beginning of their sample (1987–1990), coinciding with a period of very high dismissal costs (see their table 4). Afterward, and coinciding with a period of deregulation, the magnitude of the estimated coefficient declines after a new increase in dismissal costs, only to increase again from 1995 onward. Their estimates for the long-run elasticities of severance pay are very large (in absolute value). Between 1987 and 1990, a 10 percent increase in dismissal costs is estimated to reduce long-run employment rates by 11 percent, keeping wages constant. In subsequent periods, the size of the effect becomes smaller but is still quite large in magnitude (between 3 and 6 percent). In Argentina, the estimated long-run elasticity of a 10 percent increase in dismissal costs is also between 3 and 6 percent.[23]

22. The data for the Peruvian study covers firms with more than ten employees in all sectors of the economy. The Argentinean study only covers manufacturing firms. Given the nature of these surveys, these studies analyze formal employment rather than employment as a whole. The data used in these two studies does not capture job creation by new firms, because both panels are based on a given balanced panel census of firms, which does not adjust for attrition.

23. The methodology used by these studies might lead to upward biased estimates of the elasticity of employment to job security. Thus, for example, Mondino and Montoya construct explicit measures of job security based on

Kugler (chap. 3 in this volume) computes the net impact of the Colombian 1991 labor reform on unemployment rates. Using unemployment and employment exit rate estimates before and after the reform, she finds that the reforms cause a decline in unemployment between 1.3 and 1.7 percentage points. Thus, as in Mondino and Montoya (chap. 6 in this volume) and Saavedra and Torero (chap. 2 in this volume), Kugler's estimates of the impact of deregulation indicate that the positive impact of reduced labor costs on hiring outweighs the negative impact of reduced severance costs on firing, resulting in a decline in unemployment rates.

Heckman and Pagés's (2000) analysis of cross-section time series aggregates also finds evidence of a negative impact of employment protection on employment. However, the evidence presented at the end of this chapter suggests that their results for Latin America are not robust, although their results for OECD Europe are robust. The fragility of their estimates for Latin America, based on aggregate data, suggests the value of using more disaggregated data in reaching sharp conclusions.

Other studies find negative, but statistically less precisely estimated, effects of job security on average employment rates. Pagés and Montenegro (1999) find that job security has a negative but statistically insignificant effect on overall wage-employment rates in Chile. Similarly, Marquéz (1998), using a cross-section sample of Latin American and OECD countries, finds a negative but insignificant coefficient of job security on aggregate employment rates. Table 6 summarizes the various estimates of job security on employment.

Downes, Mamingi, and Antoine (chap. 10 in this volume) also use aggregate time series data to examine changes in the labor demand associated with changes in the regulatory framework in three Caribbean countries. Their inconclusive results are typical of an entire literature. They use an indicator variable that measures periods with more or less stringent regulations. Their estimates do not capture changes in labor demand before and after the reform. However, as in the case in most of the OECD-based literature, their sample variation in regulations and institutions may be too limited and the level of aggregation too great to capture any effects of regulation on employment.

$$JS_{jt} = \delta_j T_{jt} P_{jt} SP_{jt},$$

where δ_j is the average layoff rate in sector j, T_{jt} is average tenure in sector j for a time period t, P_{jt} is the share of firms in sector j for time period t that are covered by regulations, and SP_{jt} is the mandatory severance pay in sector j, given average tenure T_{jt}. This measure provides variability across sectors and periods, and, therefore, it yields a more precise estimation of the impact of job security than before-after types of comparisons. Yet, such a measure may also be correlated with the error term in a labor demand equation because both layoffs and the tenure structure of a firm might be correlated with its employment level. However, robustness analyses reported in Mondino and Montoya suggest that not considering some of this variability still produces positive and statistically significant estimates for the coefficient of the job security measure.

The Composition of Employment

Economists have paid relatively more attention to studying the effects of job security on the level of employment and unemployment than to studying the effects of such policies on the distribution of jobs. However, a few studies shed some light on the impact of job security on the composition of employment in LAC. Marquéz (1998) constructs a ranking of the relative severity of labor market regulations (including workweek, contract, and other regulations besides job security provisions) for LAC and OECD countries and uses it to estimate the effects of job security on the formal and informal distribution of employment. He finds that across countries, more stringent regulations coincide with a larger percentage of self-employed workers. In a study of Chile, Montenegro and Pagés (chap. 7 in this volume) use repeated cross-section microdata spanning forty years of data and substantial variation in labor market policies. They control for year effects that are common across workers, as well as for the differential effects of the business cycle and other labor market policies on each demographic group. They find that more stringent job security measures reduce the employment rates of youth and the unskilled, while increasing the employment rates of older and skilled workers. Their results also suggest that job security regulations increase the self-employment of women and unskilled workers, relative to other demographic groups. This evidence is consistent with evidence in Bertola (2001) and Heckman (2003) that job security provisions protect the relatively privileged workers at the expense of the less advantaged ones. In a review of the recent OECD literature, relying on cross-country time series analysis, Addison and Teixeira (2001) reach similar conclusions, stating that while prime-age male employment rates have not been affected by job security provisions, the employment rates of other groups, most notably younger workers, have been affected.

I.4.3   Temporary Contracts

Hopenhayn (chap. 9 in this volume) discusses the impact of temporary contracts on the Argentine labor market. Such contracts were introduced following the Spanish model. He finds that these contracts induce an increase in hiring and a substitution away from long-term employment toward short-term employment. So, in the short run, these contracts remove one barrier from the labor market and make it more fluid. At the same time, they tend to promote turnover. Hopenhayn finds that the average hazard rate for the first three months out of employment increased by 30 percent and for tenure above three months by 10 percent. While temporary contracts promote fluidity, they reduce firm attachment and the incentive of firms to invest in workers. Alonso-Borrego and Aguirregabiria (1999) document that in Spanish labor markets, the effect of temporary contracts is to reduce investment in workers and hence to produce lower quality (less-skilled) workers in the long run.

I.4.4   Minimum Wages

Maloney and Nuñez Mendez (chap. 1 in this volume) present novel estimates of the impact of minimum wages on wage distributions and employment. Their evidence demonstrates convincingly that minimum wages are binding in many Latin American countries and have substantial effects on employment and wage distributions. An important finding in their analysis is that both covered and uncovered sectors ("formal" and "informal" sectors) respond in similar fashion to wage minimums. The informal sector does not show the downward wage flexibility that traditional models of labor market dualism predict. Another important finding is that minimum wages percolate much more widely across wage distributions in Latin America than they do in the United States. There are substantial effects of minimum wages on wages far up in the distribution of wages. Their study puts to rest the claim that minimum wages are innocuous, even in countries with large "informal" sectors.

Montenegro and Pagés (chap. 7 in this volume) study the effects of minimum wages on the distribution of employment in Chile. They find that, like job security provisions, minimum wages reduce the employment probabilities of the young and the unskilled, relative to older and more skilled workers. Not surprisingly, as suggested in other studies for developed countries, their results indicate that minimum wages are particularly binding for young unskilled workers. However, their results also indicate an adverse effect of the minimum wage on prime-age unskilled workers. Minimum wages adversely affect disadvantaged workers of all ages.

We next turn to a pooled time series cross-country study of the impact of regulation on employment. The fragility and sensitivity of the estimates for the Latin American region that we find highlight the benefits of the microdata analysis reported in this volume.

I.5   Evidence from a Cross-Section Time Series Sample of LAC and OECD Countries

In this section, we summarize and expand on some of the main results of our recent work, updating our earlier paper (Heckman and Pagés 2000). We use time series of cross sections of countries, and we exploit the substantial variability in labor laws in Latin America to estimate their effects on employment and unemployment. These studies serve to place the chapters in this volume within the broader context of a literature that almost exclusively focuses on time series of cross-section averages of countries. Unfortunately, few empirical regularities emerge when an honest sensitivity analysis is conducted. Nonetheless, a few robust regularities do appear. Payroll taxes reduce employment and (less robustly) in OECD countries, job security regulation reduces employment.

I.5.1   The Data

Labor market studies focusing on developing countries are hampered by serious data problems. Thus, labor market variables contained in most cross-country databases suffer from a lack of comparability and reliability. To overcome these problems, we construct a new data set that includes OECD and LAC countries. For OECD countries, we collect employment and unemployment data from the OECD statistics. For the Latin American sample, we directly construct the same indicators out of a large set of Latin American household surveys. See appendix A for a more detailed description of the employment and unemployment variables as well as the countries and years used to obtain the LAC data. Population variables are obtained from the United Nations (UN) population database while GDP measures are from the World Bank development indicators. To characterize labor market regulations, we use the set of measures summarized in table 4, defined for each year and country.

Our joint sample collects more than 400 data points from thirty-eight countries; twenty-three in the OECD and fifteen in the LAC. (Mexico is included in the Latin America sample although it belongs to the OECD.) We analyze country means and do not disaggregate further. The sample is an unbalanced panel covering the period 1983–1999. Table 7 reports summary statistics of our data for both our whole sample and for the subregional ones.[24] There are large differences between the OECD and the LAC samples. The GDP per capita measures tend to be substantially lower in the LAC than in the OECD region. Conversely, GDP growth is lower in the latter. Indemnities for dismissal and seniority pay are higher in Latin America than in OECD countries, while advance notice provisions and social security contributions are lower. There are important differences in labor market aggregates as well. On average, employment rates are higher in the LAC region than in OECD countries. The reverse is true for unemployment rates. The LAC region also displays a lower percentage of the working-age population in the twenty-five to fifty-four-year-old and the fifty-five to sixty-five-year-old brackets than OECD countries and a higher share of the population in the fifteen- to twenty-four-year-old age group. By constructing our own data set from individual household-level surveys, we are guaranteed that all of the labor market variables are comparable and reliable. One drawback of our data is that for the LAC sample, we only have a few time series observations per country (usually six or seven), and not necessarily from consecutive years.

Our objective is to relate our measures of regulations to employment

24. Table 7 reports the data used in the baseline specification (see also table 8, column [1]). In the specifications where regulations are entered one to one, the number of observations used is larger because we have more data on some regulations than on others. Restricting the sample size to be equal to the one used in the baseline specification does not alter any of the results.

Table 7   **Summary Statistics of Sample used in Baseline Regression**

Variable	Mean	Standard Deviation	Min.	Max.
A. Total Sample (N = 417)				
Employment/Population	54.92	7.16	36.90	76.89
Unemployment rate (*N* = 416)	7.82	4.33	0.50	23.80
Log GDP per capita PPP adjusted	9.43	0.63	7.35	10.37
GDP growth	2.92	2.77	−8.59	12.82
Share of working age pop. 25–54	0.62	0.03	0.51	0.68
Share of working age pop. 55–64	0.14	0.03	0.06	0.19
Social Security (% wage)	0.27	0.15	0.00	0.71
Advance notice[a]	0.82	0.48	0.00	1.97
Indemnities for dismissal[a]	1.27	1.40	0.00	5.97
Seniority pay[a]	0.65	2.35	0.00	9.82
Social Security[a]	35.65	19.13	0.00	91.53
B. Latin America (N = 88)				
Employment/Population	59.09	5.35	47.10	76.89
Unemployment rate	6.52	3.23	0.63	17.10
Log GDP per capita PPP adjusted	8.49	0.45	7.35	9.44
GDP growth	3.31	3.60	−8.59	12.82
Share of working age pop. 25–54	0.58	0.03	0.51	0.64
Share of working age pop. 55–64	0.09	0.02	0.06	0.16
Social Security (% wage)	0.23	0.08	0.10	0.42
Advance notice[a]	0.65	0.45	0.00	1.77
Indemnities for dismissal[a]	2.82	1.05	0.00	5.97
Seniority pay[a]	3.09	4.33	0.00	9.82
Social Security[a]	30.14	10.17	12.98	53.87
C. Industrial Countries Sample (N = 329)				
Employment/Population	53.81	7.17	36.90	68.60
Unemployment rate (*N* = 328)	8.17	4.52	0.50	23.80
Log GDP per capita PPP adjusted	9.68	0.38	8.50	10.37
GDP growth	2.81	2.50	−7.00	10.74
Share of working age pop. 25–54	0.62	0.03	0.57	0.68
Share of working age pop. 55–64	0.15	0.02	0.09	0.19
Social Security (% wage)	0.29	0.16	0.00	0.71
Advance notice[a]	0.87	0.48	0.00	1.97
Indemnities for dismissal	0.86	1.17	0.00	3.30
Seniority pay	0.00	0.00	0.00	0.00
Social Security[a]	37.12	20.65	0.00	91.53

[a]Regulatory variables measured in multiples of monthly wages.

and unemployment outcomes. Although we perform multivariate analyses, it is interesting to examine the bivariate relationship between regulations and employment. This is particularly easy for regulations such as job security provisions that, within our sample, change at most once or twice per country. In figures 8 and 9, we graph employment before and after reforms for countries that experienced job security reforms. The graphs for LAC should be interpreted with caution because they have been interpolated from incomplete time series data.

There is little evidence that reforms that reduced job security increased employment rates in Colombia. There is also not much evidence that reforms that increased job security had a deleterious effect on employment in Brazil, Chile, or Nicaragua. However, there is some evidence indicating that reforms that liberalized labor markets in Peru increased employment rates, while reforms that increased labor market rigidities reduced employment. For Germany, our data suggest that employment declined at a slower rate after a reform that increased job security, while in Spain and the United Kingdom the opposite seems to be true after liberalization. These figures suggest that periods of less stringent job security regulations coincide with higher employment rates in some countries, while the reverse is also true in other countries. The data presented in these figures, however, fail to control for contemporaneous changes in economic activity or other factors that could be correlated with employment and labor reforms. In the next section, we perform an empirical analysis in an attempt to control for contemporaneous effects that may be correlated with reforms, employment, and unemployment outcomes.

I.5.2   Methodology and Results

To relate labor market regulations to employment and unemployment outcomes, we estimate the following model:

$$Y_{it} = \alpha_i + \beta_1 X_{it} + \beta_2 g_{it} + \beta_3 \text{GDPPC}_{it} + \beta_4 Z_{it} + \varepsilon_{it},$$

where Y_{it} is a labor market variable (employment or unemployment) of country i at period t, α_i denotes a country fixed effect, X_{it} denotes a vector of employment regulation variables, g_{it}, and GDPPC_{it} denote GDP growth and (log of) GDP per capita, respectively, Z_{it} is a vector of demographic controls, and ε_{it} is a mean zero error.

Given the nature of the data with incomplete gaps, we decided not to average observations from a given period to control for business cycle effects, as is often done in OECD studies. Instead, we control for the state of the business cycle in a given year using GDP growth.[25] Although a large part

---

25. The GDP growth is obtained from the World Bank development indicators. It turns out that deleting or including this variable has no important effect on our empirical conclusions. Deleting or including GDP per capita (PPP adjusted) does not alter our results, either.

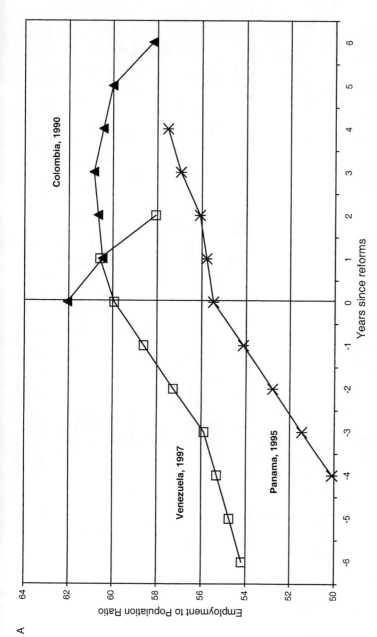

Fig. 8 *A,* Effect of job security reforms on employment: reforms that reduced job security; *B,* effect of job security reforms on employment: reforms that increased job security

Sources: A. Series constructed by authors from Household Survey data. See table A.4 for sources in each country; interpolated data.

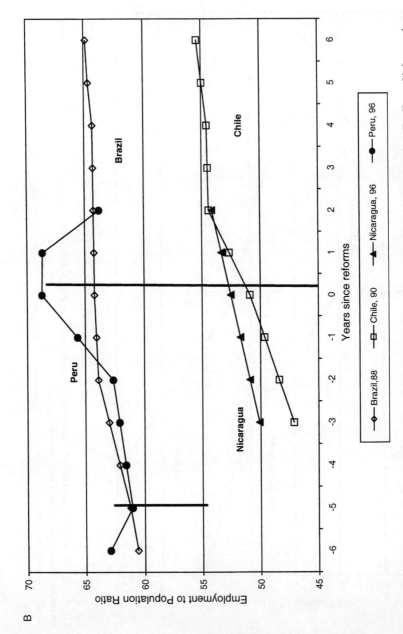

Fig. 8 (cont.) *A*, Effect of job security reforms on employment: reforms that reduced job security; *B*, effect of job security reforms on employment: reforms that increased job security

Sources: A. Series constructed by authors from Household Survey data. See table A.4 for sources in each country; interpolated data.

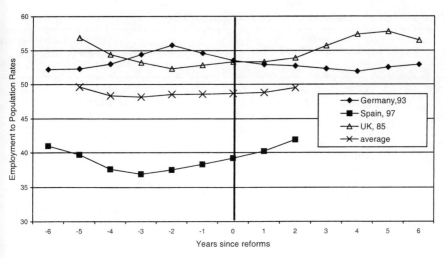

Fig. 9   The effect of job security reform on employment: Industrial countries
Source: Labor force statistics, OECD.

of our variation is cross sectional, we use fixed-effects estimates to control for unobserved variables that may be correlated with measures of regulation across countries. In addition, we control for demographic changes that may be correlated with employment and unemployment rates as well as regulatory variables that change over time. Finally, we use GDP per capita (adjusted by PPP) to control for differences in levels of country economic activity across years.[26] We estimate a reduced form model to investigate whether periods of high nonwage labor costs stemming from advance notice, indemnities for dismissal, severance pay, or social security contributions are associated with lower employment or higher unemployment rates. We thus estimate an average net effect of labor laws as they operate through intermediate variables, which we do not include in the regression. We do not estimate a theoretically more appropriate state-contingent labor demand specification because we lack the information on the firm-specific state of the product market confronting individual firms. Therefore, we only attempt to identify the effect of labor laws through their effect on expected (across labor market states) labor cost. This is a severe limitation. However, what we offer is an improvement over the existing literature on cross-country time series that does not quantify labor costs. Appendix B discusses conceptually more appropriate specifications of labor demand functions.

26. We control for GDP growth *and* GDP per capita (PPP adjusted) because we have few data points per country and they are not necessarily contiguous, so we cannot use the simple averaging method employed in OECD studies to control for business-cycle effects.

Table 8   Results for Employment to Population Rates

	Whole Sample					OECD Sample	Latin America Sample
	(1)	(2)	(3)	(4)	(5)	(6)	(7)
AN	13.938	12.400				13.755	16.637
	(15.959)	(16.841)				(14.564)	(15.420)
ID	1.161		−0.469			−2.577	0.330
	(0.897)		(0.730)			(1.196)**	(1.637)
SenP	3.292			1.837		n.a.	1.887
	(1.195)***			(0.213)***			(2.197)
SSC	−0.230				−0.191	−0.301	−0.187
	(0.081)***				(0.079)**	(0.102)***	(0.084)**
GDP growth	0.094	0.125	0.123	0.110	0.108	0.034	0.106
	(0.046)**	(0.050)**	(0.049)**	(0.042)***	(0.046)**	(0.050)	(0.072)
Log GDP per	2.318	−0.320	−0.451	0.834	3.122	1.828	11.639
capita	(1.277)	(1.044)	(1.079)	(2.253)	(2.260)	(1.334)	(8.152)
Share WAP							
25–54	17.584	29.171	33.259	22.143	16.534	12.112	9.126
	(16.750)	(16.608)	(18.135)	(21.704)	(23.535)	(19.197)	(70.273)
55–64	48.456	20.450	27.060	20.614	59.725	50.009	−197.99
	(35.685)	(27.018)	(27.465)	(26.721)	(33.501)	(35.553)	(317.709)
Constant	13.588	28.759	37.614	32.086	17.013	8.519	−40.525
	(17.743)	(18.736)	(13.754)***	(13.318)**	(13.165)	(31.305)	(55.759)
N	417	476	480	564	484	329	88
R^2	0.91	0.90	0.89	0.88	0.90	0.93	0.82
P-value F test[a]	0.00					0.04	0.00

Notes: Robust standard errors in parentheses. All specification includes country fixed effects. AN = advance notice; ID = indemnities dismissal; SenP = seniority pay; SSC = Social Security contribution; WAP = working age population; N = number of observations; n.a. = not applicable.
[a]P-value of test that all regulations are jointly equal to zero.
***Significant at the 1 percent level.
**Significant at the 5 percent level.

Table 8 displays our estimates for employment in the overall and regional samples. In these and subsequent results, we compute standard errors that are robust to heteroscedasticity. Throughout this analysis, we extend social security data to yearly frequencies because this information is only available biannually. We do so either by interpolating or by inputting each missing data value with the value from the former year. The results of our empirical analysis are robust across methods. Also, the results do not vary when we consider only the original biennial data. However, in this case, the number of available observations drops substantially.

The coefficients on GDP growth have the expected positive signs and are statistically significant for the overall sample. The coefficients on the demographic variables are positive, suggesting that countries with larger percentages of their working age population above age twenty-five tend to have higher employment rates. However, none of the coefficients on the demographic variables are statistically significant at conventional levels. A higher GDP per capita tends to coincide with higher employment to population rates. However, this estimated effect is not precisely determined.

Our main interest is on measuring the effect of the labor market regulations. We find that once we expand our sample to include a larger number of OECD and LAC countries, the strong negative effect on employment of indemnities for dismissal reported for the pooled sample in Heckman and Pagés (2000) disappears. This is somewhat surprising because not only do we expand the set of countries and periods for which we can construct the measure, but we also revise some of the variables used in our previous analysis to more accurately model the laws. We still estimate a negative, statistically significant coefficient for indemnities in the OECD specification, and this is an important contribution to the European debate on the impact of regulations. This evidence suggests a significant lack of robustness of the estimated effect of regulations that we explore in detail.

With regard to the rest of the regulations, we find a positive, although not statistically significant, coefficient on advance notice cost both in the joint and in the subregional samples. Because seniority pay regulations only exist in Latin America, we cannot identify the impact of these regulations in the OECD sample. However, we find positive coefficients for this variable both in the LAC and in the pooled sample. Moreover, the coefficient in the joint sample is statistically significant at the 5 percent level. The estimated coefficient suggests that an increase in payments equivalent to one month's pay (in expected present value) *increases* employment rates by 1.12 percentage points. One might argue that the strong association between contributions and benefits associated with these types of schemes contributes to an expansion of labor supply increasing overall employment rates. However, the coefficients on advance notice and on indemnities are also positive. In contrast to these results, our estimates suggest a negative effect of social security contributions on employment both in the joint and the subregional samples. (Recall that this is the total contribution of employers and workers.) This effect is statistically significant. According to our estimates, a reduction in the social security contributions from the OECD to the LAC average (see table 4) would increase employment by 3.25 percentage points for the coefficients from the joint sample or by 4.26 percentage points if the OECD coefficient is used (table 8, columns [1] and [6], respectively).

Because there is substantial correlation among our measures of labor market regulation, we also estimate specifications that include these measures one at a time.[27] The number of observations used in each regression

27. The correlation coefficient between advance notice, indemnities for dismissal, and seniority pay is between 0.15 and 0.21 (in absolute value) and statistically significant. Social security contributions are positively and significantly correlated with advance notice, but the correlation with the other measures is close to zero and not statistically significant.

varies because there are countries for which we do not have information for all the regulation measures. The results are unchanged if we restrict all regressions to have the same observations than the ones used in column (1). Adding the regulation measures separately tends to produce smaller coefficients for each of them, suggesting that there are important complementarities that are not captured by the one-at-a-time specifications. We strongly reject the hypothesis that the four measures are not jointly significant (last row, table 8) and therefore include them together in the remaining analysis.

Table 9 presents the estimates for unemployment. As for employment, indemnities for dismissal have a strong positive effect on unemployment in the OECD sample but no effect in the Latin America or the joint sample. The coefficient on advance notice is negative in the overall and OECD samples, but not in the LAC sample. However, the coefficient is not statistically significant in any sample. The coefficient on seniority pay is also

Table 9   Results for Unemployment

	Whole Sample					OECD Sample	Latin America Sample
	(1)	(2)	(3)	(4)	(5)	(6)	(7)
AN	−9.13	−7.29				−9.19	4.06
	(11.08)	(11.03)				(10.62)	(9.96)
ID	0.50		−0.01			3.00	0.43
	(1.00)		(0.40)			(1.01)***	(1.12)
SenP	0.79			0.21		n.a.	0.84
	(1.33)			(0.13)			(1.43)
SSC	0.18				0.13	0.22	0.15
	(0.07)**				(0.05)**	(0.09)**	(0.09)
GDP growth	−0.16	−0.19	−0.18	−0.18	−0.14	−0.13	−0.23
	(0.04)***	(0.05)***	(0.04)***	(0.05)***	(0.04)***	(0.05)**	(0.09)**
GDP per capita	−2.28	1.78	1.55	1.87	−1.47	−2.70	4.37
	(1.26)	(1.27)	(1.05)	(1.28)	(1.30)	(1.36)	(3.13)
Share WAP							
25–54	18.85	−2.72	−5.72	−4.27	17.19	25.20	−66.30
	(14.26)	(16.00)	(16.72)	(14.98)	(16.96)	(16.44)	(29.54)**
55–64	−7.35	6.69	2.17	−15.41	−14.69	−7.97	134.98
	(28.58)	(24.90)	(25.19)	(22.29)	(25.26)	(31.36)	(214.64)
Constant	23.01	1.13	−3.20	1.05	13.19	28.44	−16.54
	(13.02)	(12.88)	(9.99)	(7.40)	(7.63)	(23.31)	(34.32)
N	416	475	479	563	483	328	88
R^2	0.84	0.79	0.78	0.79	0.84	0.86	0.72
P-value F test	0.02					0.03	0.00

Note: See table 8. All specifications contain country fixed effects.

[a]P-value of test that all regulations are jointly equal to zero.

***Significant at the 1 percent level.

**Significant at the 5 percent level.

positive, suggesting that these schemes increase labor supply. However, the coefficient is not statistically significant. Finally, and consistent with our results on employment, we find that higher social security contributions are associated with higher levels of unemployment in the three samples considered. Our point estimates suggest that reducing social security contributions from the OECD to the LAC average reduces unemployment by 2.54 percentage points if we use the estimate for the joint sample or 3.11 percentage points if we use the OECD one. As with the case of employment, adding the regulatory measures one at a time produces smaller coefficients for each of the measures. As before, we reject the hypothesis that the coefficients of the four variables are jointly equal to zero, and, therefore, we will include them in the rest of the unemployment analysis.

Our results in tables 8 and 9 suggest that not all regulations have the same effect on employment and unemployment rates. Because all regulations are measured in multiples of monthly wages, we can compare the coefficients of the four regulations studied and assess whether they have similar effects. In table 10 we report the results of testing the hypothesis of equality of coefficients. We reject the null hypothesis of identical coefficients for the four measures in the employment, but not in the unemployment, specifications. Interestingly, we are also able to reject the hypothesis that social security payments exert the same effect on employment as seniority pay, despite the fact that both variables imply mandatory contributions defined as a fraction of wages. Perhaps because contributions to finance seniority pay are capitalized in individual accounts, the link between contributions and payments is strengthened, and this reduces or eliminates the "tax" effect. Instead, our results suggest that social security contributions tend to be perceived as taxes on labor and, therefore, reduce the demand of labor above and beyond a possible reduction in the supply of labor. Moreover, we reject the hypothesis that indemnities for dismissal and seniority pay have the same coefficient or that all components of job security (advance notice, indemnities for dismissal, and seniority pay) have the same coefficient. When we impose this (incorrect) constraint on the data, we obtain a positive but not statistically significant coefficient on job security regulations, while the coefficient on social security regulations remains negative and statistically significant.

Finally, although we reject the hypothesis that all four regulations have the same effect on employment, imposing this constraint yields a negative, statistically significant coefficient on employment and a positive, statistically significant coefficient on unemployment. Moreover, the size of the coefficients is very similar to the ones reported in tables 8 and 9 for social security. This is not surprising, because social security regulations constitute the lion's share of the total cost of regulations.

In summary, our results suggest that not all regulations have the same effect on employment rates. Thus, while social security contributions are

Table 10   Do all regulations have an equal effect?: Whole Sample

	Employment			Unemployment		
	(1)	(2)	(3)	(4)	(5)	(6)
AN + ID	−0.644			0.121		
	(0.651)			(0.342)		
SenP + SSC	−0.229			0.169		
	(0.081)**			(0.066)**		
AN + ID + SenP		0.492			0.226	
		(1.102)			(0.925)	
SSC		−0.230			0.169	
		(0.078)***			(0.066)**	
AN + ID + SenP			−0.231			0.169
+ SSC			(0.079)***			(0.066)**
GDP growth	0.089	0.090	0.089	−0.157	−0.157	−0.157
	(0.045)	(0.045)**	(0.045)	(0.040)***	(0.040)***	(0.040)**
Log(GDP) per capita	2.283	2.222	2.246	−2.276	−2.283	−2.281
PPP adjusted	(1.314)	(1.319)	(1.324)	(1.272)	(1.271)	(1.269)
% of WAP						
25–54	19.660	20.788	20.662	20.431	20.557	20.548
	(17.441)	(18.116)	(18.018)	(15.120)	(14.953)	(14.926)
55–64	56.924	57.644	58.367	−5.119	−5.007	−4.949
	(35.411)	(36.408)	(35.863)	(29.241)	(29.024)	(29.031)
Constant	27.194	23.669	25.604	15.621	15.285	15.438
	(13.367)	(13.226)	(13.741)	(10.285)	(10.434)	(9.910)
N	417	417	417	416	416	416
R^2	0.91	0.91	0.91	0.84	0.84	0.84
Test						
AN = ID[a]	0.42			0.39		
SenP = SSC	0.005			0.64		
AN = ID = SenP		0.00			0.49	
ID = SenP	0.00			0.39		
AN = ID = SenP = SSC			0.01			0.63

Notes: See table 8. All specifications contain country fixed effects. PPP = purchasing power parity US adjusted.

[a]*P*-values of the tests in this row and below.

***Significant at the 1 percent level.

**Significant at the 5 percent level.

negatively associated with employment (and positively associated with un-employment), the effect of job security measures on employment is ambiguous. While in the joint and LAC samples, advance notice and indemnities for dismissal have positive, although not statistically significant coefficients, the coefficient on indemnities in the OECD sample is negative and statistically significant at conventional levels. Seniority pay is positively associated with employment, and the coefficients on this variable are statistically significant in most specifications. We also reject the hypothesis that the coefficients on seniority pay and the coefficients on the rest of the components of job security are the same. These differences in results across regions, specifications, and samples, relative to our previous work, suggest a lack of robustness that we further explore. Before turning to a robustness analysis, we first consider the evidence on the shifting of the payroll tax.

Wage Shifts

What is the estimated wage pass-through implied by our coefficients on social security contributions? The social security effect is a robust finding of our aggregate country analysis and so is worth exploring further. Define α as the elasticity of employment with respect to the cost of labor. Assume that social security taxes are expressed as a percentage of wages. Writing labor demand as a function of wages inclusive of taxes in log linear form, we obtain

$$\ln \text{EMP(SS)} = \alpha \ln[W(\text{SS})(\text{SS})] + C,$$

where SS is the fraction of wages marked up by social security and $W(\text{SS})$ is the wage which depends on SS through equilibrium shifting effects, and C is a constant standing in for all other factors. Taking derivatives with respect to the SS markup, we obtain

$$\frac{\partial \ln \text{EMP(SS)}}{\partial \ln \text{SS}} = \alpha\left(\frac{\partial \ln W(\text{SS})}{\partial \ln (\text{SS})} + 1\right)$$

Solving for $\dfrac{\partial \ln W(\text{SS})}{\partial \ln \text{SS}}$, we obtain

$$\frac{\partial \ln W(\text{SS})}{\partial \ln \text{SS}} = \frac{1}{\alpha}\left(\frac{\partial \ln \text{EMP(SS)}}{\partial \ln \text{SS}} - \alpha\right).$$

To estimate the wage shift, we estimate $(\partial \ln \text{EMP(SS)})/(\partial \ln \text{SS})$ from a specification with the same control variables as the specification reported in table 8, column (1), but where the dependent variable is in logs, advance notice, indemnities for dismissal, and seniority pay are defined in logs, and social security contributions are defined as fractions of gross wages, and we use $\ln(\text{SS})$ as a regressor. Finally, the elasticity of labor demand to labor costs, α, is assumed to be within the ranges of estimates reported in table 4 and consistent with the estimates reported in these studies. With all of these elements, we obtain the estimates presented in table 11.[28]

We find that the elasticity of employment with respect to social security contributions is –0.7 for the whole sample, around –1 for the OECD sample and –0.447 for Latin America. This implies that increasing social

---

28. Hamermesh (1993) reports a range of elasticities between –0.15 and –0.7. We constrain wage effects of SS in table 11 to be nonpositive.

Table 11   Estimates of Wage Pass-Through for Different Labor
                  Demand Elasticities

	Labor Demand Elasticity	Whole Sample	OECD Sample	Latin American Sample
$\dfrac{\partial \ln \text{Emp}}{\partial \ln \text{SS}}$		−.702 (0.293)**	−1.048 (0.381)**	−.447 (0.270)
$\dfrac{\partial \ln W}{\partial \ln \text{SS}}$	−0.15	0	0	0
$\dfrac{\partial \ln W}{\partial \ln \text{SS}}$	−0.7	0	0	−.36
$\dfrac{\partial \ln W}{\partial \ln \text{SS}}$	−1.2	−.415	−.12	−.62

Notes: $\partial \ln \text{Emp}/\partial \ln \text{SS}$ is obtained from a regression in which the dependent variable is computed in logarithms and all regulatory variables are also computed in logs. The other control variables used in table 8 are used here. Social security contributions are defined as logarithms of the fraction of the contribution rate, that is we use ln(SS). Standard errors are in parentheses. The other three rows are obtained from the formula in the text, using alternative values of α, as shown in the first column of the table. When estimated effects on wages are positive, they are constrained to be zero.
**Significant at the 5 percent level.

security contributions by 10 percentage points will lower employment by 7 percent in the overall sample, 10 percent in the OECD and 4.5 percent in Latin America. These are large numbers. They also imply that for a large range of labor demand elasticities, the estimated pass-through is zero, particularly for the OECD sample. Thus, for a labor demand elasticity of −0.7, the pass-through is zero in OECD and 36 percent in Latin America. Although this larger pass-through in Latin America is at odds with the presumption of a very elastic labor supply to the formal sector, it is consistent with a much higher wage flexibility in Latin America than in industrial countries, due to greater inflation in the region (see IADB 2004). All in all, this evidence suggests that part of the cost of regulations is borne by workers but that social security contributions tend to be perceived as taxes on labor. Increasing social security taxes leads to substantial costs in terms of reductions in employment and increases in unemployment.

I.5.3   The Effect of Recent Social Security Reforms

Our negative coefficients on social security contributions suggest that the benefits associated with these contributions are valued at less than 100 percent of their cost. An interesting question is whether the recent wave of pension reforms in Latin America have contributed to strengthen the link between contributions and benefits as well as to increase the size of the wage pass-through. This is especially relevant because most reforms transformed pay-as-you-go systems into full or partial capitalization systems.

able 12   **The Effect of Pension Reforms on Employment and Unemployment**

	Employment			Unemployment		
	Whole Sample (1)	OECD Sample (2)	Latin American Sample (3)	Whole Sample (4)	OECD Sample (5)	Latin American Sample (6)
.N	14.080 (15.629)	13.755 (14.564)	1.184 (14.721)	−9.090 (11.011)	−9.195 (10.617)	17.297 (11.379)
O	1.286 (0.979)	−2.577 (1.196)**	0.087 (1.702)	0.470 (1.001)	3.005 (1.008)***	0.742 (1.089)
enP	3.480 (1.305)**	0.000 (0.000)	1.624 (2.299)	0.739 (1.332)	n.a.	1.247 (1.406)
SC	−0.243 (0.088)***	−0.301 (0.102)**	−0.168 (0.086)	0.173 (0.071)**	0.215 (0.098)**	0.118 (0.087)
SC · Reform	−0.138 (0.072)	0.000 (0.000)	−0.327 (0.134)**	0.124 (0.044)***	0.000 (0.000)	0.248 (0.109)**
eform	7.290 (3.174)**	0.000 (0.000)	10.665 (4.765)**	−4.349 (1.926)**	0.000 (0.000)	−7.234 (3.758)
DP growth	0.096 (0.048)	0.034 (0.050)	0.123 (0.084)	−0.164 (0.041)***	−0.130 (0.053)**	−0.239 (0.086)**
og GDP per capita	2.348 (1.227)	1.828 (1.334)	10.742 (7.643)	−2.336 (1.236)	−2.700 (1.355)	4.983 (3.292)
of WAP						
25–54	15.011 (16.884)	12.112 (19.197)	34.692 (69.954)	20.505 (14.199)	25.196 (16.442)	−93.257 (34.205)**
55–64	45.690 (35.828)	50.009 (35.553)	−449.346 (298.027)	−2.593 (28.761)	−7.975 (31.360)	365.975 (223.294)
onstant	15.044 (17.348)	8.519 (31.305)	1.087 (52.262)	20.739 (12.965)	28.443 (23.305)	−49.617 (36.657)
	417	329	88	416	328	88
²	0.92	0.93	0.84	0.84	0.86	0.76

otes: See table 8. See table A.1 for a definition of Reform variable.
**Significant at the 1 percent level.
*Significant at the 5 percent level.

To examine this possibility we create a dummy variable, Reform, which, for each country, takes the value of zero in the period prereform and 1 from the period of reform onward (see appendix A for a full description of the periods of reform). We add this variable and an interaction of reform with the cost of social security payments to our baseline specifications (tables 8 and 9 column [1]). Our results suggest contemporaneous positive effects of pension reforms on employment. (See table 12.) However, it is unclear whether this positive effect is associated with the reforms themselves or with other factors. Thus, we find a positive and statistically significant coefficient on the Reform variable, suggesting an increase in employment rates in the postreform period. However, the interaction term with social security reform is negative and statistically significant, indicating that social security taxes have larger disemployment effects after the reforms. This higher disincentive could be due to the mixed effects resulting from the transition to the new system. As workers move from the pay-as-you-go to the capitalization system, contributions to social security finance individual accounts and, in many instances, the pensions of those left in the old system. The contribution to fund the old system is likely to be viewed as a pure tax on employment.

I.5.4   Robustness

The results reported in this section are based on larger samples and depart substantially from those reported in Heckman and Pagés (2000).[29] Unfortunately, a lack of robustness to changes in specification or sample size is all too common in the cross-section time-series literature that uses aggregate data. Given this potential weakness, we investigate whether our new results are robust to changes in estimation method, measures of regulations, specification and sample size, as well as to the exclusion of outliers.

Given the limited variance of the job security variables, it is interesting to compare our fixed effects coefficients with the results obtained from estimating our main equation using random effects (RE; see table 13). We reject the hypothesis of consistency of the RE estimator for employment in the joint sample at 10 percent. The most substantial difference is the considerably smaller magnitude of the coefficient on indemnities for the OECD sample in the RE model. While in the OECD sample we still find a negative effect of indemnities on employment and a positive effect on unemployment, these effects are no longer statistically significant at conventional levels. The coefficient on advance notice is now positive and statistically significant in the employment regressions and negative and statistically significant in the unemployment regressions. The size and significance of the social security contribution coefficients are robust to the change in method of estimation.

In unreported results available upon request, we also examine whether our results are robust to alternative measurements of the cost of regulations that do not require assumptions about discount or layoff rates. Following Lazear (1990), we measure job security regulations as the mandatory amount (in multiples of monthly wages) that should be paid to a worker who is dismissed after ten years of tenure. A major disadvantage of this measure is that it only reflects job security in one point of the job security tenure schedule. In our samples, both his measure and our measure yield similar results.

---

29. We are greatly indebted to David Bravo and Sergio Urzua, who made us aware that adding Chile to the original sample used in Heckman and Pagés (2000) substantially changes our earlier conclusions.

Table 13   **Random Effect Estimates**

	Employment			Unemployment		
	Total Sample (1)	OECD Sample (2)	LAC Sample (3)	Total Sample (4)	OECD Sample (5)	LAC Sample (6)
N	4.142 (1.871)**	5.292 (1.986)***	1.417 (4.461)	−2.762 (1.278)**	−3.560 (1.733)**	−0.200 (1.997)
O	−0.250 (0.347)	−1.010 (0.809)	−0.358 (0.464)	0.027 (0.266)	0.326 (0.706)	−0.048 (0.298)
enP	0.899 (0.331)***	0.000 (0.000)	0.562 (0.438)	−0.074 (0.225)	0.000 (0.000)	0.009 (0.202)
SC	−0.221 (0.031)***	−0.259 (0.032)***	−0.164 (0.073)**	0.135 (0.023)***	0.153 (0.029)***	0.090 (0.050)
GDP growth	0.089 (0.046)	0.030 (0.051)	0.123 (0.097)	−0.157 (0.038)***	−0.133 (0.047)***	−0.205 (0.068)***
og GDP per capita (PPP)	2.292 (0.826)***	1.837 (0.784)**	8.931 (3.251)***	−2.117 (0.668)***	−2.606 (0.705)***	1.607 (1.869)
hare of WAP 25–54	17.462 (10.657)	8.760 (10.682)	21.529 (37.575)	21.471 (8.598)**	26.494 (9.616)***	−11.405 (22.081)
55–64	48.130 (20.842)**	34.748 (21.002)	−76.504 (75.751)	1.544 (16.411)	2.022 (18.910)	21.309 (40.005)
onstant	18.202 (6.616)***	31.222 (6.896)***	−19.363 (15.833)	12.749 (5.169)**	13.938 (6.160)**	−3.868 (9.823)
	417	329	88	416	328	88
ausman Test (P-value)	0.09	0.03	0.00	0.25	0.01	0.51
2	0.46	0.48	0.004	0.15	0.14	0.26

otes: See table 8 for explanations of abbreviations. Robust standard errors in parentheses. Columns (1) nd (4) include a dummy variable that identifies the region, and which takes the value equal to 1 if the untry is in Latin America and zero otherwise. PPP = purchasing power parity US$ adjusted; LAC = atin American and Caribbean.

**Significant at the 1 percent level.
*Significant at the 5 percent level.

We also assess the sensitivity of our results to the inclusion or exclusion of additional control variables such as year effects, region-specific year effects, time trends, and region-specific time trends. The results on the effect of social security contributions on employment and unemployment are very robust to changes in specification. Other results are less robust. For instance, in a specification with region-specific year-fixed effects, the coefficient on seniority pay is still positive, but it is no longer statistically significant at conventional levels. Adding or deleting either growth rates or GDP levels does not change our conclusions.

Important differences also arise when we assess the sensitivity of our baseline results to changes in sample size. In particular, we find that both the coefficients on advance notice provisions and indemnities for dismissal are sensitive to the inclusion/exclusion of some countries in the sample, while the coefficients on social security payments and seniority pay do not change. For instance, excluding Germany from the sample greatly increases the coefficient on advance notice in the baseline employment specification. Similarly, excluding Brazil or Peru changes the coefficient on indemnities for dismissal in the employment regressions.

Finally, we check whether our results are robust to the exclusion of outliers, which are defined as those observations for which the difference in the regression coefficient when the ith observation is included and when it is not, scaling the difference by the estimated standard error of the coefficient, is larger than $2/\sqrt{n}$ (Belsley, Kuh, and Welsch 1980). Our results confirm that there are no outliers that alter the coefficients for social security contributions. There are a few outliers that modify the coefficients on job security provisions (advance notice, indemnities, and seniority pay). However, they do not qualitatively alter our baseline results.

Taken as a whole, our results suggest that the negative (and statistically significant) association between social security contributions and employment, as well as a positive association between social security contributions and unemployment, is very robust to changes in estimation method, specification, regional sample, sample size, and outliers. The coefficients on our job security measures are much less robust. Thus, while the fixed effect (FE) estimates provide some evidence that in some OECD countries reducing indemnities results in higher employment rates, the evidence across countries provided by our RE estimates is less conclusive. One component of job security, seniority pay, is positively correlated with employment.

I.5.5 Endogeneity

It is often argued that labor reforms are put in place when labor market performance is poor. As demonstrated in the figure 3 plots, this is sometimes true for reforms in the LAC region. If a decline in employment rates (and an increase in unemployment rates) prompts a reduction in labor market regulations, then least squares estimates will be upward biased, potentially underestimating a negative relationship between job security or social security taxes and employment. Our baseline specification partly controls for the possibility of such reverse causality because the propensity for reform is partly captured by changes in the GDP or demographic conditions. Another source of concern is the timing of reforms. If labor reforms that liberalize the labor market are undertaken at particularly bad times, an estimated negative relationship between employment and regulations could just be the consequence of mean reversion.

In the results available on request, we address these issues in various ways. First, we attempt to control for differences in the propensity to reform at different points in time by including current and past GDP rates up

Table 14   **Correlation between Dependency Ratio and**
                      Social Security Contributions

	Social Security Payments (EPV)		
	Total	OECD	Latin America
Dependency ratio	112.10	102.38	283.6
	(14.65)***	(14.97)***	(133.30)***
Country fixed effects?	Yes	Yes	Yes
N	514	411	86
R^2	0.09	0.09	0.46

Notes: Dependency ratio computed as the ratio of the population 65 and older to the working age population (15–64). Robust standard errors in parentheses.
***Significant at the 1 percent level.

to five lags. Because, presumably, bad employment outcomes are strongly associated with poor GDP outcomes, the inclusion of this set of variables will control for the propensity to reform. Second, we control for the timing of reforms by interacting changes in regulatory variables with a variable that measures the distance (in years) between the current year and the last business-cycle trough. Finally, we directly address the problem of reverse causality by using the dependency ratio, defined as the ratio of the population aged sixty-five and older to the population in the working age (fifteen to sixty-four), as an instrument for social security contributions.[30] Our results suggest that controlling for either the propensity or the timing of reforms does not alter the conclusions of our analysis.[31]

Regarding our instrumental variable estimates, table 14 indicates that in the three samples considered, social security contributions increase with the dependency ratio. The average dependency ratio in our sample is 0.17, while OECD and LAC are 0.19 and 0.08, respectively. The coefficients in table 14 suggest that if the dependency ratio increases in 1 percentage point, expected discounted social security contributions increase in 1.12 months for the total sample, 1.02 for the OECD, and 2.83 for Latin America. Moreover, our instrumental variable estimates (table 15) suggest that there is a causal relation between changes in social security contributions and changes in employment and unemployment rates, at least in the overall and OECD sample. In these two samples, IV estimates produce larger coefficients than the FE regressions. Instead, the Latin America IV esti-

30. The source of this data is the United Nations Population Statistics (United Nations Population Fund 1988).
31. Another way to control for endogeneity is to use the information in the figure 3 sequence to break out episodes of reform that were not preceded by major downturns (or upturns) of the economy from other episodes and analyze the latter. The problem with this approach in our sample is that it uses up too many scarce degrees of freedom.

Table 15   Instrumental Variable Estimates

	Employment			Unemployment		
	Total	OECD	Latin America	Total	OECD	Latin America
AN	26.66	23.77	30.77	–15.72	–15.10	–12.73
	(16.26)	(13.51)	(24.61)	(11.29)	(10.01)	(19.86)
ID	–1.08	–7.15	2.33	1.73	5.80	–1.64
	(2.31)	(2.38)***	(3.71)	(1.68)	(1.94)***	(2.29)
SenP	–0.41	0.00	5.10	2.81	0.00	–2.55
	(3.56)	(0.00)	(5.42)	(2.50)	(0.00)	(3.22)
SSC	–1.37	–1.28	0.36	0.77	0.80	–0.47
	(0.78)*	(0.66)*	(0.58)	(0.48)	(0.45)*	(0.38)
N	404	321	83	404	321	83
R^2	0.70	0.79	0.70	0.67	0.74	0.33

Notes: All regressions include country fixed effects as well as GDP per capita (PPP adjusted), GDP growth, and the share of workers in working age population between twenty-five and fifty-four and fifty-five and sixty-four. We instrument Social Security contributions (measures in EPV) with the dependency ratio, computed as the ratio of the population sixty-five and older to the working age population (fifteen–sixty-four). Robust standard errors in parentheses. See table 8 for explanations of abbreviations.

***Significant at the 1 percent level.
*Significant at the 10 percent level.

mates yield coefficients with opposite signs to the ones obtained with the FE regressions. However, such coefficients are not statistically significant. The small number of observations available for Latin America is not sufficient to obtain precise IV estimates in this region.

I.5.6   Summary

Our analysis of pooled time series cross sections of countries underscores why the studies examining the impact of regulations in OECD countries based on such data have produced such ambiguous results. Lack of variation in the relevant policy measures and poor measures of regulation have hampered empirical analyses of the effect of regulations on labor market outcomes. To surmount these problems, we have expanded the number of countries comprising the LAC region, included more within-country variation, and improved the measures of regulation. Contrary to previously reported estimates, we have found little evidence of a systematic relationship between advance notice and indemnities for dismissal on employment or unemployment in our improved and expanded sample for Latin America. Estimates vary across countries, with some countries showing gains in employment after reducing job security and others showing little benefit to the employment rate or even employment reductions after such reforms, but no clear pattern emerges from the aggregates.

However, we find robust evidence that social security contributions are not fully shifted to workers. Payroll taxation tends to reduce employment and increase unemployment rates across samples and specifications. At the aggregate level, our analyses of reforms intended to increase the link between contributions and payments show mixed results.

I.6   Conclusions and Directions for Future Research

Summarizing an entire school of thought, Freeman (2000, 3) writes that "the institutional organization of the labor market has identifiable large effects on distribution, but modest hard-to-uncover effects on efficiency." This view is shared by many economists. However, the microevidence summarized in this volume suggests that mandated benefits and job security regulations have a substantial allocative impact both in Latin America and in OECD countries.

What policy lessons can be drawn from the essays in this volume? The evidence assembled in this volume suggests that labor market regulations are an inequality-increasing mechanism, because some workers benefit while many others are hurt. The benefits of programs funded with mandatory payroll contributions should be weighed against their costs in terms of employment. Funding such programs with general revenues does not necessarily reduce employment costs (see Nickell 1997), but strengthening the link between payments and benefits contributes to shifting the cost of such programs to workers, at least in the long run. Regulation acts unevenly across different groups in society. Young, uneducated, and rural workers are much less likely to enjoy coverage than older, skilled, and urban workers.

While the aggregate evidence on the effects of job security on the level of employment is inconclusive, the microstudies assembled here find a large and negative effect of job security on employment. Individual country studies based on microdata reduce the fragility and lack of robustness problems that pervade the cross section of countries' time series literature.

I.6.1   Lessons For Future Research

While these essays demonstrate that firms and workers respond to incentives in predictable ways and that regulation reduces employment and labor market turnover, more precise quantitative estimates would be desirable. We conclude with a discussion of the main areas in which future research could improve upon the current estimates.

Incidence of Payroll Taxes and General Equilibrium

Several essays in this volume take significant steps toward addressing whether workers accept lower wages if they receive mandated benefits. These estimates of incidence can be improved. Comparing the wages of covered and uncovered sectors to see if covered workers get lower wages, as in Cárdenas and Bernal (chap. 4 in this volume) and several other essays in this volume, fails to control for self-selection into these sectors, which several studies in this volume have documented to be important. The method fails to adjust for general equilibrium effects arising from induced entry and exit and the willingness of workers to purchase benefits by accepting reduced wages.

The most comprehensive approach to the incidence question is the analysis of Marrufo (2001), which finds that controlling for self-selection and accounting for general equilibrium effects substantially affects estimates of tax incidence, and difference-in-differences estimates understate the true extent of wage adjustment. As argued by Kugler, the simple difference-in-differences method is downward biased so that the estimates reported in this volume are conservative.

Dynamic Labor Demand

The empirical models of labor demand estimated by the authors in this volume are traditional static models and dynamic labor demand models based on the assumption of symmetric adjustment costs. They abstract from the asymmetries in labor demand that are produced by severance and indemnity systems. Appendix B sketches out the main ideas in the asymmetric demand literature using a two-period model. Alonso-Borrego and Aguirregabiria (1999) develop the econometrics needed to estimate such models, but the methods remain to be implemented on LAC data. Given that all of the labor demand models estimated in this book assume symmetric adjustment costs, it would be productive to rework these studies using more advanced methods. As previously noted, the inconclusive evidence on the effect of job security on firm adjustment dynamics may be an artifact of the symmetry assumption.

In this class of models, it would also be useful to account for general equilibrium effects of entry and exit of firms. Hopenhayn and Rogerson (1993) demonstrate that, in principle, accounting for general equilibrium effects can reverse the predictions of partial equilibrium models.

Accounting for Nonstationarity

All of the duration models used to determine the impacts of regulation on labor market turnover assume stationary environments. Any student of Latin America knows how poor that assumption is. The high volatility of economic outcomes in Latin America suggests that this assumption does not adequately characterize the region. Accounting for nonstationarity more systematically would improve econometric estimates of behavioral parameters for the region.

Accounting for the Effects of Regulation on Output

All of the labor demand studies estimate output-constant wage elasticities. Abstracting from the potentially important econometric problem of endogeneity of output, output-constant demand functions are more robust because they allow the analyst to abstract from product market adjustments to relative price changes. At the firm level, the output-constant effects of regulation understate the total effect of regulation if regulation raises the marginal cost of labor to the firm and costs cannot be shifted onto wages or other factor costs. The estimates reported here underestimate the full disemployment effects of deregulation in sectors adversely impacted. At the level of the national economy, the effects are more ambiguous because the burden of regulation may impact industries differently although it will still have efficiency losses by distorting sectoral allocations. In a closed economy, relative output prices adjust and will lead to an expansion of output in those sectors least impacted. So in those sectors, greater regulation may lead to greater employment. In an open economy facing world prices, when regulations are not accommodated by a downward adjustment of factor prices, regulation reduces output and accentuates reductions in employment.

A complete analysis of the impact of regulation would require accounting for both product market and factor market adjustments. The presumption is that a full account would produce disemployment effect of regulation on the overall economy, but not necessarily in each sector.

Notice, however, that even if wages adjust fully and there are no adverse effects of regulation on labor demand, regulation may still have substantial effects on the welfare of workers. If a job security mandate is offset by lower wages, worker welfare is not necessarily improved, at least not for all workers. It may be higher or lower depending on how much the mandate differs from what workers and firms would mutually agree upon in an unregulated environment.

Accounting for Serial Correlation

While most of the studies summarized in this volume measure the cost of regulations by elaborating direct monetary measures of their cost to employers, several authors use the length of the lag (the speed of adjustment) as an alternative measure of the cost of regulation facing the firm. The intuition supporting this is based on the original work of Holt et al. (1960), as previously described in section I.4.2.

In the simple model of equations (2) and (3), if we introduce an error term and an implicit theory of optimal employment as a function of the real wage, W_t, we obtain

$$(4) \qquad n_t^* = a + bW_t + \varepsilon_t, \qquad b \leq 0.$$

If ε_t is serially correlated, we obtain

$$(5) \qquad \varepsilon_t = \rho\varepsilon_{t-1} + u_t,$$

where u_t has zero mean and is independently and identically distributed, and ρ is the first-order serial correlation. Analysts obtain a high estimated value of λ (the coefficient on lagged labor) from a least squares estimation that does not correct for serial correlation because

(6) $\qquad n_t = (1 - \lambda)(a + bW_t) + \lambda n_{t-1} + (1 - \lambda)\varepsilon_t.$

If $1 < \lambda < 1$ and $\rho > 0$, ordinary least squares (OLS) estimates of λ are upward biased. An asymptotically unbiased estimator that accounts for this serial correlation is based on

(7) $\quad n_t = (1 - \lambda)(1 - \rho)a + (1 - \lambda)b(W_t - \rho W_{t-1}) + (\lambda + \rho)n_{t-1} - \lambda\rho n_{t-2}$

$\qquad + (1 - \lambda)u_t,$

which is derived from equation (6) by lagging it one period, solving for $(1 - \lambda)\varepsilon_{t-1}$, writing $\varepsilon_t = \rho\varepsilon_{t-1} + u_t$ in equation (6) and substituting for ε_{t-1}. This bias is especially important in making cross-country comparisons where serial correlation coefficients may differ greatly across economies. For studies of regulations in a single country, this bias will not affect estimates of the relative cost of different reforms if the serial correlation pattern is invariant across reforms. However, no meaning can be attached to the absolute value of the lag coefficient.

This conventional model assumes symmetric hiring and firing costs. Yet even in the original Holt et al. (1960) study, this assumption was only introduced as a mathematically simplifying one that was contrary to their evidence. A more accurate description of the data from Latin America and other regions is that there are substantial asymmetric adjustment costs.

A measurement model accounting for asymmetric adjustment costs requires a new econometric approach. In work available on request, we consider a model of asymmetric hiring and firing costs based on Hopenhayn and Rogerson (1993). The coefficient on lagged labor is not necessarily monotonic in the cost of labor regulations. This may account for the ambiguous evidence on the impact of regulation on the cost of adjustment obtained from the conventional estimates.[32]

I.6.2   Taking Stock

Although there is clearly room for improvement, the body of evidence summarized in this chapter and reported in this book demonstrates that regulation matters, that the choice of labor market institutions matters, and that further labor reforms offer the promise of promoting both efficiency and equity across demographic groups in Latin America. They demonstrate the power of microdata to answer important questions when the evidence from cross-country macro time series is ambiguous.

---

32. The intuition behind this result is simple. Different serial correlation-fixed cost pairs produce the same lagged employment coefficient. This is also possible in the simple model (6). So it is possible that a regime with higher labor transition costs is also one with lower serial correlation in shocks and so would display a lower estimated lag and a faster adjustment rate. See Barbarino and Heckman (2003).

Appendix A
Definitions and Sources of Variables Used in Section I.5

For the empirical analysis described in section I.5, we build an unbalanced panel data covering the period 1983–1999. Table A.3 describes the variables and their sources. Table A.4 describes the countries and the years covered in our sample.

Computation of Labor Market Regulation Measures

Advance Notice and Indemnities for Dismissal

OECD Countries

We gather information on advance notice and indemnities for dismissal for OECD countries from the OECD *Employment Outlook* table 2.A.2, "Required Notice and Severance Pay for Individual Dismissal" (1999, 94–96), which summarizes the "case of a regular employee with tenure beyond any trial period, dismissed on personal grounds or economic redundancy but without fault." For countries in which it is likely for individual dismissals to be considered "unjust" (measured as those countries to which the OECD gives a score of 2 or more in a 1–3 scale in table 2.A.4, 100)—that is, countries where a "transfer and or retraining to adapt to different work must be attempted prior to dismissal" and where "worker capability cannot be ground for dismissal"—we consider the information summarized in the table entitled "Compensation and Related Remedies Following Unjustified Dismissal." From this table we see that, for this subset of countries, in at least one country unjust dismissals carry a much higher penalty. This is the case of Spain. We make this contingency explicit by computing the expected severance pay by assigning a 1/2 probability that a dismissal will be considered unfair and will carry the higher severance pay that the law mandates in this event. We obtain information on labor reforms from table 2.1 (OECD 1999, 53), which describes the main changes in legislation since the mid-1980s. We also compare the information described in OECD (1999) with that presented in Grubb and Wells (1993). If they diverge, we take the information in the latter to be valid up to 1993, while we take the information presented in OECD (1999) to be valid from 1997 onward. For the years in between, the index has a missing value. There are only four countries where there are some divergences between the former and the latter source. This is the case of Denmark, Greece, Netherlands, and Sweden. Finally, in countries where the law prescribes different severance pay and advance notice for blue- and white-collar workers, we compute the cost of dismissal as the unweighted average for the two groups. For Hungary, Korea, New Zealand, and Turkey, the job security measures only take non-missing values from 1990 onward because we could not find legal information for former years. To construct our index, we do not consider upper monetary limits. In addition, we do not consider benefits that firms pay or unions can obtain for their workers that exceed the legal mandatory. Finally, we do not consider what workers can get in courts if they sue their employers.

The following are individual country notes. In Australia, we consider the severance pay awarded to workers dismissed for redundancy. For Canada, we take the maximum of the severance pay and advance notice mandated by the federal and the local jurisdiction. In Greece, for white-collar workers, advance notice can be waived if full severance pay is given. We thereby assume that firms pay in full to avoid paying additional advance notice. In Ireland, the awarded severance pay depends on the age of the worker. We assume that workers receive 0.18 monthly wages per year worked, which corresponds to the (unweighted) average of half of one week per year worked (workers under the age of forty-one) and one week per year worked (workers over the age of forty-one). In Norway, after ten years of tenure, notice period increases with age. To capture this effect, we have increased notice period from three months to four and five in the case of individuals of more than fifteen years of tenure. For Spain, we adjust the severance pay obtained in case of just dismissal by the fact that many dismissals are considered unjust. We therefore weigh mandatory dismissals in case of just and unjust causes by a probability of 1/2 for each event.

Latin America

We consider the legal information, summarized in tables A.1 and A.2, obtained from the Ministries of Labor of individual countries.

In Brazil, employers are required to deposit 8 percent of a workers' wage in individual workers' accounts, which accrue interest rates. In case of a firm initiated dismissal, firms are required to pay a worker severance pay that is a given fraction, φ, of what a worker owns in his individual account. The 1988 constitutional reform increased this share from 0.1 to 0.4 of the total amount in the fund. To compute the fraction of what is accrued in the individual fund, we assume that the interest rate equals the discount rate. Therefore, the indemnity is computed as

$$\text{Indemnities} = \sum_{i=1}^{T} \delta^{i-1}(1 - \delta)(i) \cdot \varphi,$$

where i denotes tenure at the firm, δ is the per period probability of survival (equal to 0.88), and T denotes the maximum tenure of a worker in a firm, which is assumed to be equal to twenty. In Honduras, Jamaica, Nicaragua, and Dominican Republic, a constant advance notice equal to one month is assumed. In Peru, there were reforms in job security in 1991, 1995, and

Table A.1   Legislation Concerning Termination of Indefinite Contracts in 1987 and 1999

Country	Date of Reform	Advance Notice 1987	Advance Notice 1999	Seniority Premium 1987	Seniority Premium 1999	Compensation if worker quits? 1987	Compensation if worker quits? 1999
Argentina	None	1–2 months	No changes	0	0	0	0
Bahamas	None	1/2–1 month	No changes	0	0	0	0
Barbados	None	Negotiable, in practice 1 month	No changes	0	0	0	0
Belize	None	1/2–1 month	No changes	0	0	$1/6x \cdot N$ if $N >10$	No changes
Bolivia	None	3 months	No changes	0	0	$1x \cdot N$ if $N \geq 5$	No changes
Brazil	1988	1 month	No changes	FUND (8% wage goes to FUND, plus interest rate)	No changes	0	0
Chile	1991	1 month	No changes	0	0	No	$1/2x \cdot N^a$ if $N \geq 7$
Colombia	1990	15 days	No changes	$x \cdot N$	FUND (8% wage + r)	$x \cdot N$	FUND (8% wage + r)
Costa Rica	None	1 month	No changes	0	0	0	0
Dominican Republic	1992	1/4–1 month	No changes	0	0	0	0
Ecuador	1991	1 month	No changes	FUND (8% wage + r)	No changes	FUND (8% wage + r)	No changes
El Salvador	1994	0–7 days	No changes	0	0	0	0
Guatemala	None	0	No changes	0	0	0	0
Guyana	1997	1/2 month	1 month if $N \geq 1$	0	0	0	0

(continued)

Table A.1 (continued)

Country	Date of Reform	Advance Notice 1987	Advance Notice 1999	Seniority Premium 1987	Seniority Premium 1999	Compensation if worker quits? 1987	Compensation if worker quits? 1999
Honduras	None	1 day–2 months	No changes	0	0	0	0
Jamaica	None	2–12 weeks	No changes	0	0	0	0
Mexico	None	0–1 month	No changes	0	0	0	0
Nicaragua	1996	1–2 months	0	0	0	0	$x \cdot N$ if $N = 1$–3; $3x \cdot N + 2/3x \cdot N$ if $N > 3$
Panama	1995	1 month	No changes	$1/4x \cdot N$ if $N \geq 10$	$1/4x \cdot N$	$1/4x \cdot N$ if $N \geq 10$	$1/4 \cdot x \cdot N$
Paraguay	None	1–2 months	No changes	0	0	0	0
Peru	1996, 1995, 1991	0	No changes	FUND (8% wage + r)	No changes	FUND (8% wage + r)	No changes
Suriname	None	1/4–6 months		0		0	0
Trinidad and Tobago	None	2 months		0	0	0	0
Uruguay	None	0	No changes	$x \cdot N$	No changes	0	0
Venezuela	1997	1/4–3 months	No changes	$x \cdot N$	$2x \cdot N$	$x \cdot N$	$2x \cdot N$

Source: Ministries of Labor in Latin America and the Caribbean.

Notes: FUND: A certain fraction of a worker's wage is deposit in an individual account every month. The principal plus the interest can be withdrawn by the worker upon dismissal and in some cases, upon voluntary separation. x = monthly wages; N = years of tenure; r = interest rate of fund.

[a] Workers can choose between getting an unconditional payment after seven years in the firm, or getting a higher indemnity in case of dismissal. Most workers opt for the latter.

Table A.2 Legislation Concerning Indemnities for Dismissal in 1987 and 1999

Country	Date of Reform	Compensation for Dismissal Due to Economic Reasons		To whom do the reforms apply?	Upper limit to compensation for dismissal?	
		1987	1999		1987	1999
Argentina	None	$2/3 \cdot N$, min 2 months	No changes		Max. lim. in x	No changes
Bahamas	None	Negotiable	No changes		No	No changes
Barbados	None	$0.41x \cdot N$ if $N \geq 2$	No changes		3.75 monthly salaries	No changes
Belize	None	$1/4x \cdot N$ if $N > 5$	No changes		Max. 42 weeks	No changes
Bolivia	None	$1x \cdot N$	No changes		No	No changes
Brazil	1988	$0.1 \cdot \text{FUND}$	$0.4 \cdot \text{FUND}$	All workers	No	No changes
Chile	1991	$1x \cdot N$	No changes	All workers	5 monthly salaries	11 monthly salaries
Colombia	1990	45 days $+ x \cdot N \cdot 0.5$ if $N < 5$ $x \cdot N \cdot 0.66$ if $N \geq 5$ and $N < 10$ $x \cdot N$ if $N \geq 10$	45 days $+ x \cdot N \cdot 0.5$ if $N < 5$ $x \cdot N \cdot 0.66$ if $N \geq 5$ and $N < 10$ $x \cdot N \cdot 1.33$ if $N \geq 10$	All workers	No	No changes
Costa Rica	None	$x \cdot N$	No changes		8 monthly salaries	No changes
Dominican Republic	1992	$1/2 \cdot x \cdot N$	$.67x \cdot N$ if $N = 1 - 4$ $.74x \cdot N$ if $N \geq 5$	New employees	No	No changes
Ecuador	1991	2 if $N \leq 2$ 4 if $N = 2$–5 6 if $N = 5$–20 12 if $N > 20$	3 if $N \leq 3$ $x \cdot N$ if $N > 3$	All workers	12 monthly salaries	25 monthly salaries
El Salvador	1994	$x \cdot N$; 0 if bankruptcy	$x \cdot N$; changes in max. x	All workers	Max. base wage $= 4$ min. wages	No changes
Guatemala	None	2 days-4 months if bankruptcy; $x \cdot N$ otherwise	No changes		No	No changes

(*continued*)

Table A.2 (continued)

Country	Date of Reform	Compensation for Dismissal Due to Economic Reasons		To whom do the reforms apply?	Upper limit to compensation for dismissal?	
		1987	1999		1987	1999
Guyana	1997	Negotiable in practice, 2 1/2 weeks per N	$1/4x \cdot N$ if $N = 1\text{--}5$; $1/2x \cdot N$ if $N = 5\text{--}10$	All workers	No	12 monthly salaries
Honduras	None	$x \cdot N$	No changes		15 monthly wages	No changes
Jamaica	None	$1/3x \cdot N$ if $x = 2\text{--}5$; $1/2x \cdot N$ if $x > 5$	No changes		No	No changes
Mexico	None	$2/3x \cdot N$ (min. $3 \cdot x$)	No changes		No	No changes
Nicaragua	1996	Negotiated in practice, $2x \cdot N$	$x \cdot N$ if $N = 1\text{--}3$; $3x \cdot N + 2/3x \cdot N$ if $N > 3$		No	5 monthly salaries
Panama	1995	$x \cdot N$ if $N \leq 1$; $3x$ if $N = 2$; $3x + 3/4x \cdot N$ if $=N > 2 < 10$; $9x + 1/4x \cdot N$ if $N \geq 10$	$3/4x \cdot N$ if $N < 10$; $7.5x + 1/4x \cdot N$ if $N \geq 10$	New employees	No	No changes
Paraguay	None	$1/2x \cdot N$	$1/2x \cdot N$		No	No changes
Peru	1996, 1995, 1991	$3x \cdot N$	$1.5 \cdot x \cdot N$	All workers	12 monthly salaries	No changes
Suriname	None	Negotiated	Negotiated		No	No changes
Trinidad	None	$1/3x \cdot N$ if $N = 1\text{--}4$; $1/2x \cdot N$ if $N > 5$	No changes		No	No changes
Uruguay	None	$x \cdot N$	No changes		6 monthly salaries	No changes
Venezuela	1997	$2/3\text{--}2x \cdot N$	$x \cdot N$	All workers	No	5 monthly salaries

Source: Ministries of Labor in Latin America and the Caribbean.

Notes: FUND: A certain fraction of a workers' wage is deposit in an individual account every month. The principal plus the interest can be withdrawn by the worker upon dismissal and in some cases, upon voluntary separation.

1996. Tables A.1 and A.2 only report the schedule as in 1990 and in 1999. See Saavedra and Torero (chap. 2 in this volume) for a more detailed description of the changes in the Peruvian labor code throughout the 1990s.

Seniority Pay

Seniority payments only exist in Latin America. There are two kinds. In Brazil, Colombia, Ecuador, and Peru, workers deposit 1/12 of their monthly wages in individual accounts. In this case, seniority pay is computed as

$$\text{SenP} = \sum_{i=0}^{T} \beta^i,$$

where $T = 20$. This reflects the discounted value of a stream of payments equivalent to one month of pay per year. For Colombia, Kugler (chap. 3 in this volume) reports that before the 1990 labor reform, workers were entitled to one month of salary per year of work as a seniority fund upon separation independent of the cause of separation. However, partial withdrawals were allowed and deducted in nominal terms from the final payment, implying a "double retroactivity" with an estimated cost of 35 percent of the total payments of seniority pay in the manufacturing sector. We therefore apply a surcharge of 35 percent to the legislated schedule for seniority pay during the period before 1990.

Instead, in Venezuela and Panama, labor codes mandate a mandatory seniority payment that is computed as multiples of the last wage per year of work. In those cases, seniority pay is computed as

$$\text{SenP} = \sum_{i=1}^{T} \delta^{i-1}(1 - \delta)(\alpha_j \cdot i),$$

where α_j denotes multiples of the last wage, and i denotes tenure at the firm. In Venezuela, the legal codes specified a seniority pay of one monthly wage per year of work ($\alpha_j = 1$). After the 1997, seniority pay was increased to two monthly wages per year of work ($\alpha_j = 2$). Notice that this formula assumes that the probability of worker turnover is identical to the probability of job turnover. Because, in general, worker turnover rates tend to be higher than job turnover rates, we also experimented with a probability of worker turnover equal to two times and three times the probability of job turnover. The cost of seniority pay declines with the rate of turnover (because the probability of surviving in the firm and obtaining larger amounts declines). Our estimated results are robust to different assumptions in the worker turnover rate.

Social Security Regulations

Information provided by *Social Security Programs Throughout the World* (United States Social Security Administration 1983–1999). Social

Table A.3   **Definitions and Sources of Variables Used in Section 5**

Variable	Source	Description
Employment/Population	OECD Statistics and Household Surveys Data from Latin America	OECD: Employment to population. Data refers to people 15 and over, but in some countries, data refers to people who are between 15 and 66 (Denmark), 15 and 74 (Finland, Hungary), 16 and 17 (Iceland, Norway), 16 and 64 (Sweden), or 16 and older (Spain, United Kingdom, United States). See the methodological notes of labor force statistics at www.oecd.org. National and/or European Labour Force Surveys are the main source for the Labor Force Statistics database. Latin America: Computed directly from Household Survey Data for the countries, years and sources listed in table A.4. Employment to population rate for workers 15–65. Are considered employed all workers that declared having a job in the week of reference. It also includes unpaid workers. National data except in Argentina, Bolivia, and Uruguay.
Unemployment	OECD Statistics and Household Surveys Data from Latin America	OECD: Unemployment rate of people 15–64. National and/or European Labour Force Surveys are the main source for the Labor Market Statistics indicator (LMSI) database, OECD. Latin America: Percent of the labor force 15–65 that did not work in the period of reference but are actively looking for a job. National data except in Argentina, Bolivia, and Uruguay.
GDP growth	World Bank Development Indicators (2001)	Annual percentage growth rate of GDP at market prices based on constant local currency. Aggregates are based on constant 1995 U.S. dollars. GDP measures the total output of goods and services for final use occurring within the domestic territory of a given country, regardless of the allocation to domestic and foreign claims.

Variable	Source	Description
GDP per capita, PPP (current international $)	World Bank Development Indicators (2001)	GDP per capita based on purchasing power parity (PPP). GDP PPP is gross domestic product converted to international dollars using purchasing power parity rates. An international dollar has the same purchasing power over GDP as the U.S. dollar in the United States. GDP measures the total output of goods and services for final use occurring within the domestic territory of a given country, regardless of the allocation to domestic and foreign claims.
Share of WAP 25–54	United Nations Population Fund (1998)	Share of working age population 15 to 64 that are between 25 to 54 years old
Share of WAP 55–64	United Nations Population Fund (1998)	Share of working age population 15 to 64 that are 55 or older
Advance notice (AN)	Own construction	Expected discounted cost of providing mandatory AN measured in multiples of monthly wages
Indemnities for dismissal (ID)	Own construction	Expected discounted cost of providing mandatory ID measured in multiples of monthly wages
Seniority pay (SenP)	Own construction	Expected discounted cost of providing SenP measured in multiples of monthly wages
Social Security contributions (SSC)	Own construction	Expected discounted cost of providing mandatory advance notice measured in multiples of monthly wages
Social Security contributions (ss)	U.S. Social Security Administration (1983–1999)	Per period cost of SSC measures as a percent of monthly wages

Table A.4 Countries and Years Included in Baseline Specification

Country	Years	N	Source of Employment and Unemployment Data
Argentina	1996, 1998, 1999	3	Encuesta Permanente de Hogares
Australia	1983–1999	17	Labor Force Statistics, OECD
Austria	1983–1999	17	Labor Force Statistics, OECD
Belgium	1983–1988	16	Labor Force Statistics, OECD
Bolivia	1986, 1990, 1993, 1995, 1996, 1997, 1999	7	Encuesta Continua de Hogares/Condiciones de Vida
Brazil	1983, 1986, 1988, 1992, 1993, 1995–1999	10	Pesquisa Nacional de Amostra de Domicilios
Canada	1983–1999	17	Labor Force Statistics, OECD
Chile	1987, 1990, 1992, 1994, 1996, 1998	6	Encuesta de Caracterización Socioecómica Nacional
Colombia	1990, 1991, 1993, 1995, 1996–1999	8	Encuesta Nacional de Hogares
Costa Rica	1981, 1985, 1987, 1989, 1991, 1993, 1995, 1997, 1998	9	Encuesta Nacional de Hogares
Dominican Rep.	1996, 1998	2	Encuesta Nacional de Fuerza de Trabajo
El Salvador	1995, 1997, 1998	3	Encuesta de Hogares de propósitos múltiples
Finland	1983–1999	17	Labor Force Statistics, OECD
France	1983–1999	17	Labor Force Statistics, OECD
Germany	1992–1999	8	Labor Force Statistics, OECD
Greece	1983–1993	11	Labor Force Statistics, OECD
Honduras	1989, 1992, 1996, 1997, 1998, 1999	6	Encuesta Permanente de Hogares de Propósitos Multiples
Ireland	1983–1999	17	Labor Force Statistics, OECD
Italy	1983–1999	17	Labor Force Statistics, OECD
Japan	1983–1999	17	Labor Force Statistics, OECD

Korea	1991–1999	9	Labor Force Statistics, OECD
México	1984, 1989, 1992, 1994, 1996, 1998	6	Encuesta Nacional de Ingreso Gasto de los Hogares
Netherlands	1983–1992, 1997	11	Labor Force Statistics, OECD
New Zealand	1991–1999	9	Labor Force Statistics, OECD
Nicaragua	1993, 1998	2	Encuesta Nacional de Hogares sobre Medición de Niveles de Vida
Norway	1983–1999	17	Labor Force Statistics, OECD
Panama	1991, 1995, 1997, 1998, 1999	5	Encuesta continua de Hogares
Paraguay	1995, 1998	2	Encuesta de Hogares
Peru	1985, 1991, 1994, 1996, 1997, 1998	6	Encuesta Nacional de Hogares sobre Medición de Niveles de Vida
Poland	1991–1998	8	Labor Force Statistics, OECD
Portugal	1983–1999	17	Labor Force Statistics, OECD
Spain	1983–1999	17	Labor Force Statistics, OECD
Sweden	1983–1999	17	Labor Force Statistics, OECD
Switzerland	1983–1999	17	Labor Force Statistics, OECD
Turkey	1991–1999	9	Labor Force Statistics, OECD
United Kingdom	1987–1999	13	Labor Force Statistics, OECD
United States	1983–1999	17	Labor Force Statistics, OECD
Uruguay	1989, 1992, 1995, 1997, 1998	5	Encuesta Continua de Hogares
Venezuela	1983, 1986, 1989, 1993, 1995, 1997–1999	8	Encuesta de Hogares por Muestra

Notes: See table 8 (col. [1]). Number of observations = 417.

security contributions include contributions by employers and employees to old age, disability and death, sickness and maternity, work injury, unemployment insurance, and family allowances programs. Because this information is only available biannually, we extend the data to yearly frequency in two alternative ways—by interpolating or by inputting each missing data value with the value in the former year. The results of our empirical analysis do not vary with the method used. The results also do not vary when we consider only the original biannual data.

For Argentina, we obtained direct information from the country. Rates apply to Buenos Aires. In all countries, we consider the rates applied to wage earners. We do not include contributions made by the government to fund social security programs. In cases where contributions differ across individuals, states, or industry risk, only one rate is chosen, and the choice varies somewhat across countries. However, the same criterion is used within countries across time. This somewhat reduces cross-country comparability but preserves across time comparability within countries.

Social Security Reform

The variable Reform takes a value of 1 after a country has implemented a social security reform that totally or partially replaces a pay-as-you-go system by an individual capitalization system. Based on social security reforms information summarized in Lora and Pagés (2000), this variable takes the value of 1 in Chile on and after 1981, in Colombia on and after 1994, in Argentina on and after 1994, in Uruguay on and after 1996, in Mexico and Bolivia on and after 1997, and in El Salvador on and after 1998.

Appendix B
Dynamic Demand Specifications

All of the papers on labor demand in this volume ignore the asymmetric nature of labor adjustment costs. In this appendix, we explore the consequences of this asymmetry on labor demand. The main conclusion is that static and dynamic costs of labor have separate effects on labor demand, and in general no scalar index adequately summarizes these costs. In order to specify labor demand functions in the presence of asymmetric hiring and firing costs, it is convenient to use a two-period model. Such a model is implicit in Kugler (chap. 3 in this volume). Let $f(\ell)$ denote output as a function of labor input ℓ. Let θ be a second period productivity shock. It is

We thank Jagadeesh Sivadasan for helpful comments on this appendix.

normalized against a first-period productivity shock of 1. We assume, for simplicity, that workers do not quit once they are hired.

Labor hired in period one is ℓ_1. Labor employed in period two is $\ell_2 = \ell_1 + \Delta$. Δ is thus the change in the stock of period-one labor. Spot wage W is assumed to be common in both periods, and is assumed to be exogenous to the firm. The cost of firing a worker is C. Offsetting this cost is the saving in wages. The cost of hiring a worker is the wage. Asymmetry arises when $C \neq 0$. Assume no discounting. Labor ℓ_1 is kept on in period two unless second-period demand shocks (θ) are sufficiently low. The firm maximizes profits

(B1) $f(\ell_1) - W\ell_1 + E[\theta f(\ell_1 + \Delta) - W(\ell_1 + \Delta) - C\text{Max}(-\Delta, 0)],$

where the first-period labor productivity is normalized to 1.

We assume that the support of θ is $(0, \infty)$ and that θ is an (absolutely continuous) random variable. If $\theta \geq 1$ with probability 1, the firm in the second period wants $\Delta \geq 0$. Labor productivity has increased when θ is bigger than its first-period value, which implicitly is set at 1.

The presence of second-period firing costs inhibits hiring in the first period. Thus, anticipating the possibility of an adverse shock in the second period, the firm hires less labor than it would hire in the first period in the absence of firing costs. If, for the sake of making an heuristic argument, we characterize the firm as myopically maximizing period-by-period profits, the firm acts as if the first-period productivity shock is less than 1 in making its first-period decisions and hires less labor than it would if there were no second-period firing costs. Letting $\bar{\theta}$ be the value of the "as if" first-period productivity shock, if $\theta > \bar{\theta}$ in period two, then $\theta f'(\ell_2) = W$ and $\ell_2 = [f']^{-1}(W/\theta) > \ell_1$.

If $\theta = \bar{\theta}$, the firm stays put at ℓ_1 so that $\ell_1 = \ell_2$ and $\Delta = 0$. If productivity is below $\bar{\theta}$, the firm may still keep its workforce at $\ell_1 = \ell_2$ because it is costly to fire labor. We now determine the lower bound on θ that gives rise to inaction. For a fixed ℓ_1, the two required conditions for inaction ($\Delta = 0$) are $\theta f'(\ell_1) < W$, so it pays in gross terms to get rid of a unit of ℓ_1, and $\theta f'(\ell_1) > W - C$, so it does not pay in net terms. Thus the inequalities determining the zone of inaction are (for a given ℓ_1)

$$W - C \leq \theta f'(\ell_1) \leq W.$$

The lower boundary θ^* is $(W - C)/(f'(\ell_1)) = \theta^*$. Holding ℓ_1 fixed, raising C lowers the threshold θ^*. Thus the zone of inaction for a given (ℓ_1, C) is $\theta^* \leq \theta \leq \bar{\theta}$, where $\bar{\theta} = W/(f'(\ell_1))$.

The first order condition for ℓ_1 is $f'(\ell_1) - W + E(\theta f'(\ell_1 + \Delta) - W) = 0$, where $\Delta = 0$ if $\theta^* \leq \theta \leq \bar{\theta}$, $\Delta < 0$ if $\theta < \theta^*$, and $\Delta > 0$ if $\theta > \bar{\theta}$. From concavity, ℓ_1 is decreasing in cost C. Intuitively, firms with high firing costs hold back on hiring ℓ_1. There is an option value of holding back on hiring

ℓ_1 to avoid the cost of firing unwanted second-period labor. In order to characterize ℓ_1, we must first characterize $\Delta(\ell_1)$.

Second-Period (Conditional on ℓ_1) Demand Functions

Letting Δ^- denote the reduction in the stock of labor and Δ^+ be the expansion of such stock, we obtain the first-order condition for Δ^- as

$$\theta f'(\ell_1 + \Delta^-) = W - C$$

or

$$\ell_1 + \Delta^- = (f')^{-1}\left(\frac{W - C}{\theta}\right).$$

Take ℓ_1 as given. Observe that if $0 < \theta < \theta^*, \Delta < 0$. Define $\varphi \equiv f'^{-1}$. Observe that from concavity $\varphi' < 0$. Then

$$\ell_1 + \Delta^- = \varphi\left(\frac{W - C}{\theta}\right).$$

Observe that at $\theta = \theta^*, \Delta^- = 0$. If $\theta > \overline{\theta}, \theta f'(\ell_1 + \Delta^+) = W$ and $(\ell_1 + \Delta^+) = \varphi(W/\theta)$. If $\theta^* < \theta < \overline{\theta}$, the firm operates at ℓ_1 and $\Delta = 0$. If $\theta < \theta^*, \theta f'(\ell_1 + \Delta^-) = W - C$ and $\ell_1 + \Delta^- = \varphi([W - C]/\theta)$. Define $g(\theta)$ as the density of θ. Given ℓ_1, expected demand in period two (averaged over the θ states) is, for a given firm,

$$E(\ell_2 \mid W, C, \ell_1) = \int_0^{\theta^*} \varphi\left(\frac{W - C}{\theta}\right) g(\theta) d\theta + \ell_1 \int_{\theta^*}^{\overline{\theta}} g(\theta) d\theta + \int_{\overline{\theta}}^{\infty} \varphi\left(\frac{W}{\theta}\right) g(\theta) d\theta.$$

Thus

$$\frac{\partial E(\ell_2 \mid W, C, \ell_1)}{\partial W} = \frac{\partial \theta^*}{\partial W} \varphi\left(\frac{W - C}{\theta^*}\right) g(\theta^*) + \int_0^{\theta^*} \frac{1}{\theta} \varphi'\left(\frac{W - C}{\theta^*}\right) g(\theta) d\theta$$

$$+ \int_{\overline{\theta}}^{\infty} \left(\frac{1}{\theta}\right) \varphi'\left(\frac{W}{\theta}\right) g(\theta) d\theta + \ell_1\left[\frac{\partial \overline{\theta}}{\partial W} g(\overline{\theta}) - \frac{\partial \theta^*}{\partial W} g(\theta^*)\right]$$

$$- \left(\frac{\partial \overline{\theta}}{\partial W}\right) \varphi\left(\frac{W}{\overline{\theta}}\right) g(\overline{\theta}),$$

$$\frac{\partial E(\ell_2 \mid W, C, \ell_1)}{\partial C} = \left(\frac{\partial \theta^*}{\partial C}\right) \varphi\left(\frac{W - C}{\theta^*}\right) g(\theta^*) - \int_0^{\theta^*} \frac{1}{\theta} \varphi'\left(\frac{W - C}{\theta}\right) g(\theta) d\theta$$

$$+ \ell_1\left[\frac{\partial \overline{\theta}}{\partial C} g(\overline{\theta}) - \frac{\partial \theta^*}{\partial C} g(\theta^*)\right] - \frac{\partial \overline{\theta}}{\partial C} \varphi\left(\frac{W}{\overline{\theta}}\right) g(\overline{\theta}).$$

Using the demand function, $\varphi([W - C]/\theta^*) = \ell_1$, and $\varphi(W/\overline{\theta}) = \ell_1$,

$$\frac{\partial E(\ell_2 \mid W, C, \ell_1)}{\partial W} = \int_0^{\theta^*} \frac{1}{\theta} \varphi'\left(\frac{W - C}{\theta}\right) g(\theta) d\theta + \int_{\overline{\theta}}^{\infty} \frac{1}{\theta} \varphi'\left(\frac{W}{\theta}\right) g(\theta) d\theta < 0,$$

and

$$\frac{\partial E(\ell_2 \,|\, W, C, \ell_1)}{\partial C} = -\int_0^{\theta^*} \frac{1}{\theta} \varphi'\left(\frac{W}{\theta}\right) g(\theta) d\theta > 0.$$

The positivity of this final expression arises from the fact that as C increases, the firm is more risk averse (θ^* falls) so that it is more likely that it hires labor in the second period.

If θ is iid across firms in period 2, and independently and identically distributed (i.i.d.) across time, then the mean conditional (on ℓ_1) labor demand function is not a direct function of $W + \Pr(0 < \theta < \theta^*)C$, which, in this simple framework, is the measure of labor cost used in Heckman and Pagés (2000) and in the empirical analysis of section I.5. In fact, the model predicts that

$$\frac{\partial E(\ell_2 \,|\, W, C, \ell_1)}{\partial W} + \frac{\partial E(\ell_2 \,|\, W, C, \ell_1)}{\partial C} < 0$$

so that $\partial E(\ell_2 \,|\, W, C, \ell_1)/\partial W$ is larger in absolute value than $\partial E(\ell_2 \,|\, W, C, \ell_1)/\partial C$, although they are of opposite signs.

This analysis suggests that empirical specifications of labor demand functions should use C and W separately. W corresponds to static costs as defined in the text. C corresponds to costs of adjustment. The OLS regressions of conditional (on ℓ_1) demand functions do not identify the standard substitution terms used in static demand analysis.

One way to avoid problems with direct estimation of labor demand functions is to estimate production functions. These can be used to derive the demand functions given fixed costs without directly estimating demand functions with fixed costs.

First-Period Demand Functions

These are obtained by substituting each state-contingent $\ell_2 = \ell_1 + \Delta$ demand function into expression (B1) and maximizing with respect to ℓ_1. As in the analysis of the second period demand function, $W + \Pr(0 < \theta < \theta^*)C$ is not an appropriate marginal price in any state. Substituting into expression (B1) and making the dependence of Δ^- and Δ^+ on W, C, ℓ_1 explicit, we obtain total profits (as perceived in the first period) as

$$f(\ell_1) - W\ell_1$$

$$+ \int_0^{\theta^*} \{\theta f[\ell_1 + \Delta^-(W, C, \ell_1, \theta)] - (W - C)\Delta^-(W, C, \ell_1) - W\ell_1\} g(\theta) d\theta$$

$$+ \int_{\theta^*}^{\bar{\theta}} [\theta f(\ell_1) - W\ell_1] g(\theta) d\theta$$

$$+ \int_{\bar{\theta}}^{\infty} \{\theta f[\ell_1 + \Delta^+(W, C, \ell_1)] - W[\ell_1 + \Delta^+(W, C, \ell_1)]\} g(\theta) d\theta.$$

Assuming an interior solution, and using the envelope theorem,

$$f'(\ell_1) - W + \int_0^{\theta^*} \{\theta f'[\ell_1 + \Delta^-(W, C, \ell_1, \theta)] - W\}g(\theta)d\theta$$
$$+ \int_{\theta^*}^{\bar{\theta}} [\theta f'(\ell_1) - W]g(\theta)d\theta = 0,$$

so the first period demand obtained as the solution to this equation ℓ is a function of W and C separately and not $W + \mathrm{Pr}(0 < \theta \le \theta^*)C$. Observe, trivially, that the ℓ_1 obtained as a solution of this first-order condition is lower than the ℓ_1 obtained when $C = 0$. This rationalizes our choice of $\bar{\theta} < 1$ in the heuristic solution outlined above.

References

Abowd, J., F. Kramarz, T. Lemieux, and D. Margolis. 1997. Minimum wages and youth employment in France and the United States. NBER Working Paper no. 6111. Cambridge, Mass.: National Bureau of Economic Research, July.

Abowd, J., F. Kramarz, and D. Margolis. 1999. Minimum wages and employment in France and the United States. NBER Working Paper no. 6996. Cambridge, Mass.: National Bureau of Economic Research, March.

Abowd, J., F. Kramarz, D. Margolis, and T. Phillippon. 2000. The tail of two countries: Minimum wages and employment in France and the United States. IZA Discussion Paper no. 203. Bonn, Germany: Institute for the Study of Labor.

Abraham, K., and S. Houseman. 1993. Job security and work force adjustment: How different are U.S. and Japanese Practices? In *Employment security and labor market behavior—Interdisciplinary approaches and international evidence,* ed. C. F. Buechtemann, 180–99. Ithaca, N.Y.: ILR Press.

Acemoglu, D., and J. Angrist. 2001. Consequences of employment protection? The case of the Americans with Disabilities Act. *Journal of Political Economy* 109 (5): 915–57.

Addison, J. T., and J. L. Grosso. 1996. Job security provisions and employment: Revised estimates. *Industrial Relations* 35 (4): 585–603.

Addison, J. T., and P. Portugal. 1992. Advance notice: From voluntary exchange to mandated benefits. *Industrial Relations* 31 (1): 159–78.

Addison, J. T., and P. Teixeira. 2001. The economics of employment protection. IZA Discussion Paper no. 381. Bonn, Germany: Institute for the Study of Labor, October.

Addison, J. T., P. Teixeira, and J. L. Grosso. 2000. The effect of dismissals protection on employment: More on a vexed theme. *Southern Economic Journal* 67: 105–22.

Alonso-Borrego, C., and V. Aguirregabiria. 1999. Labor contracts and flexibility: Evidence from a labor market reform in Spain. Universidad Carlos III de Madrid. Working Paper no. 99-27.

Autor, D. H., J. Donohue III, and S. Schwab. 2003. The costs of wrongful discharge laws. NBER Working Paper no. w9425. Cambridge, Mass.: National Bureau of Economic Research, January.

Barbarino, A., and J. J. Heckman. 2003. A framework for the study of the effects of labor market policies with asymmetric costs and entry and exit. University of Chicago, Department of Economics. Unpublished Manuscript.

Belsley, D. A., E. Kuh, and R. E. Welsch. 1980. *Regression diagnostics: Identifying influential data and sources of collinearity.* New York: Wiley.

Bentolila, S., and G. Bertola. 1990. Firing costs and labour demand: How bad is eurosclerosis? *Review of Economic Studies* 57:381–402.

Bentolila, S., and G. Saint-Paul. 1994. A model of labor demand with linear adjustment costs. *Labour Economics* 1:303–26.

Bertola, G. 1990. Job security, employment and wages. *European Economic Review* 34:851–86.

———. 1992. Labor turnover costs and average labor demand. *Journal of Labor Economics* 10 (4): 389–411.

———. 2001. Aggregate and disaggregated aspects of employment and unemployment. University of Torino, Department of Economics. Working Paper.

Blanchard, O. 1998. Thinking about unemployment. Paper presented at Paolo Baffi Lecture on Money and Finance. October, Rome, Italy.

Blanchard, O., and J. Wolfers. 2000. The role of shocks and institutions in the rise of European unemployment: The aggregate evidence. *Economic Journal* 11:1–33.

De Pelsmacker, P. 1984. Long-run and short-run demand for factors of production in the Belgian industry. In *Emploi-chomage: Modelisation et analyses quantitatives,* ed. D. Vitry and B. Marechal. Dijon, France: Librairie de la Université.

Deleire, T. 2000. The wage and employment effects of the Americans with Disabilities Act. *Journal of Human Resources* 35 (4): 693–715.

Denny, M., M. Fuss, and L. Waverman. 1981. Estimating the effects of diffusion of technological innovations in telecommunications: The production structure of Bell Canada. *Canadian Journal of Economics* 14:24–43.

Di Tella, R., and R. MacCulloch. 1999. The consequences of labor market flexibility: Panel evidence based on survey data. Harvard University, Harvard Business School. Unpublished Manuscript.

Dolado, J., F. Kramarz, S. Machin, A. Manning, D. Margolis, and C. Teulings. 1996. The economic impact of minimum wages in Europe. *Economic Policy* 23: 319–72.

Economic Commission for Latin America and the Caribbean (ECLAC). 2001. *Economic survey of Latin America and the Caribbean, 2000–2001.* Santiago, Chile: ECLAC.

Edwards, S., and A. Cox-Edwards. 1999. Social Security reform and labor markets: The case of Chile. University of California, Los Angeles; National Bureau of Economic Research; and California State University. Mimeograph.

———. 2000. Social Security reform and labor markets: The case of Chile. *Economic Development and Cultural Change* 50 (3): 465–89.

Elmeskov, J., J. P. Martin, and S. Scarpetta. 1998. Key lessons from labor market reforms: Evidence from OECD countries' experience. *Swedish Economic Policy Review* 5 (2): 207–52.

Fajnzylber, P., and W. F. Maloney. 2000. Labor demand and trade reform in Latin America. Universidade Federal de Minas Gerais and World Bank. Mimeograph.

Field, B., and C. Grebenstein. 1980. Capital energy substitution in U.S. manufacturing. *Review of Economics and Statistics* 70:654–59.

Freeman, R. B. 2000. Single peaked vs. diversified capitalism: The relation between economic institutions and outcomes. NBER Working Paper no. 7556. Cambridge, Mass.: National Bureau of Economic Research, February.

———. 2002. Institutional differences and economic performance among OECD countries. CEP Discussion Paper no. 557. London: Centre for Economic Performance, October.

Garibaldi, P., and P. Mauro. 1999. Deconstructing job creation. IMF Working Paper no. WP/99/109. Washington, D.C.: International Monetary Fund, August.

Grubb, D., and W. Wells. 1993. Employment regulation and patterns of work in EC countries. *OECD Economic Studies* 21 (winter): 7–58.

Gruber, J. 1994. The incidence of mandated maternity benefits. *American Economic Review* 84 (3): 622–41.

———. 1997. The incidence of payroll taxation: Evidence from Chile. *Journal of Labor Economics* 15 (3): S72–101.

Hamermesh, D. S. 1993. *Labor demand.* Princeton, N.J.: Princeton University Press.

Heckman, J. 2003. Flexibility, job creation and economic performance. In *Knowledge, information, and expectations in modern macroeconomics: In honor of Edmund S. Phelps,* ed. P. Aghion, R. Frydman, J. Stiglitz, and M. Woodford. Princeton, N.J.: Princeton University Press.

Heckman, J., and C. Pagés. 2000. The cost of job security regulation: Evidence from Latin American labor markets. *Economia: The Journal of the Latin American and Caribbean Economic Association* 1 (1): 109–54.

Holt, C. C., F. Modigliani, R. Muth, and H. Simon. 1960. *Planning production, inventories, and work force.* Englewood Cliffs, N.J.: Prentice Hall.

Hopenhayn, H., and R. Rogerson. 1993. Job turnover and policy evaluation: A general equilibrium analysis. *Journal of Political Economy* 101 (5): 915–38.

Inter-American Development Bank (IADB). 1996. *Making social services work.* Washington, D.C.: IADB.

Inter-American Development Bank (IADB). 1998–1999. *Facing up to inequality in Latin America.* Washington, D.C.: IADB.

Inter-American Development Bank (IADB). 2004. *Good jobs wanted: Labor markets in Latin America.* Washington, D.C.: IADB.

International Labour Organization (ILO). 1997–1998. *World labour report.* Geneva, Switzerland: ILO.

———. 2002. *Labour overview.* Lima, Peru: ILO.

Kaestner, R. 1996. The effect of government-mandated benefits on youth employment. *Industrial and Labor Relations Review* 50 (1): 122–42.

Kugler, A., J. F. Jimeno, and V. Hernanz. 2002. Employment consequences of restrictive permanent contracts: Evidence from Spanish labor market reforms. IZA Discussion Paper no. 657. Bonn, Germany: Institute for the Study of Labor, November.

Lazear, E. 1990. Job security provisions and employment. *Quarterly Journal of Economics* 105 (3): 699–726.

Lindauer, D. 1999. Labor market reforms and the poor. World Bank. Unpublished Manuscript. Available at http://www.worldbank.org/poverty/wdrpoverty/background/lindauer.pdf.

Lora, E., and C. Pagés. 2000. Hacia un envejecimiento responsable: Las reformas de los sistemsas pensionales América Latina. [Toward responsible aging: The reforms of the pension systems in Latin America]. *Cuadernos Económicos de I. C. E.* 65:283–324.

Machin, S., and M. Stewart. 1996. Trade unions and financial performance. *Oxford Economic Papers* 48:213–41.

MacIsaac, D., and M. Rama. 1997. Determinants of hourly earnings in Ecuador: The role of labor market regulations. *Journal of Labor Economics* 15: S136–65.

Marquéz, G. 1998. Protección al empleo y funcionamiento del mercado de trabajo: Una aproximación comparativ. [Employment protection and the performance of the labor market: A comparative approximation]. Inter-American Development Bank. Mimeograph.

Marrufo, G. 2001. The incidence of Social Security regulation: Evidence from the reform in Mexico. Ph.D. diss. University of Chicago.

Nickell, S. 1997. Unemployment and labor market rigidities: Europe versus North America. *Journal of Economic Perspectives* 11 (3): 55–74.

Nickell, S., and R. Layard. 1999. Labor market institutions and economic performance. In *Handbook of labor economics,* vol. 3C, ed. O. Ashenfelter and D. Card, 3029–84. New York: North-Holland.

Nicoletti, G., and S. Scarpetta. 2001. Interactions between product and labor market regulations: Do they affect unemployment? Evidence from OECD countries. Paper presented at the Bank of Portugal Conference, Labor Market Institutions and Economic Outcomes. 30 June, Cascais, Portugal.

———. 2003. Regulation, productivity and growth: OECD evidence. *Economic Policy* 36 (April): 10–72.

Nicoletti, G., S. Scarpetta, and O. Boylaud. 1999. Summary indicators of product market regulation with an extension to employment protection legislation. OECD Working Paper no. 226. Paris: Organization for Economic Cooperation and Development.

Nohlen, D. 1993. *Enciclopedia electoral Latinoamericana y del Caribe.* San Jose, Costa Rica: Instituto InterAmericano de Derechos Humanos.

O'Connell, L. 1999. Collective bargaining systems in six Latin American countries: Degrees of autonomy and decentralization. IADB Research Network Working Paper no. R-399. Washington, D.C.: Inter-American Development Bank.

Organization for Economic Cooperation and Development (OECD). 1993. *Employment Outlook.* Paris: OECD.

———. 1994. *The OECD jobs study: Facts, analysis, strategies.* Paris: OECD.

———. 1996. Employment adjustment, workers and unemployment. *OECD Economic Outlook,* 161–84. Paris: OECD, July.

———. 1999. Employment protection and labour market performance. *OECD Economic Outlook,* 49–132. Paris: OECD, June.

Pagés, C., and C. Montenegro. 1999. Job security and the age-composition of employment: Evidence from Chile. IADB Working Paper no. 398. Washington, D.C.: Inter-American Development Bank.

Risager, O., and J. R. Sorensen. 1997. On the effects of firing costs when investment is endogeneous: An extension of a model by Bertola. *European Economic Review* 41 (7): 1343–53.

Roberts, M. J., and E. Skoufias. 1997. The long-run demand for skilled and unskilled labor in Colombian manufacturing plants. *Review of Economics and Statistics* 79 (2): 330–34.

Scarpetta, S. 1996. Assessing the role of labour market policies and institutional settings on unemployment: A cross-country study. *OECD Economic Studies* 26: 43–98.

United Nations Development Programme (UNDP). 2001. *Human development report 2001: Making new technologies work for human development.* New York: UNDP.

United Nations Population Fund. 1998. *The state of world population 1988: The new generations.* New York: UNFPA.

United States Social Security Administration, Division of Research and Statistics. 1983–1999. *Social Security programs throughout the world.* Washington, D.C.: U.S. Dept. of Health and Human Services, Social Security Administration, Office of Research and Statistics.

Waud, R. 1968. Man-hour behavior in U.S. manufacturing: A neoclassical interpretation. *Journal of Political Economy* 76:407–27.

World Bank. 2001. *World development indicators.* CD-ROM. Washington, D.C.: World Bank.

Wylie, P. 1990. Scale-biased technological development in Canada's industrialization, 1900–1929. *Review of Economics and Statistics* 72:219–27.

1

Measuring the Impact of Minimum Wages
Evidence from Latin America

William F. Maloney and Jairo Nuñez Mendez

Minimum wages have again surfaced as a central issue in labor market policy in the region. In countries such as Mexico and Brazil, the real level of the minimum wage became so eroded over the 1980s that there is pressure to provide a "living" income for those at the lower tail of the distribution. On the other hand, high rates of unemployment in some countries and the premium that more open trade postures put on labor market flexibility has made policy makers wary of introducing new rigidities.

This chapter first provides an overview of the levels of minimum wages in Latin America and their true impact on the distribution of wages using both numerical measures and kernel density plots for eight countries (Argentina, Bolivia, Brazil, Chile, Colombia, Honduras, Mexico, and Uruguay). In particular, it attempts to identify effects higher in the wage distribution and in the unregulated or "informal" sector. The central message is that the minimum wage has impacts on wage setting far beyond those usually contemplated and likely beyond those found in the industrialized countries. The final section then employs panel employment data from Colombia, a country where minimum wages seem high and very binding, to quantify these effects and their impact on employment.

William F. Maloney is lead economist in the World Bank's office of the chief economist (LCRCE) of the Latin America and Caribbean region. Jairo Nuñez Mendez is professor of economics at the Universidad de los Andes, Bogota, Colombia.

Individual country kernel density analysis was done by Wendy Cunningham (Argentina, Mexico), Norbert Fiess (Brazil), Claudio Montenegro and Claudia Sepulveda (Chile), Edmundo Murrugarra (Uruguay), Mauricio Santamaria (Colombia), and Corinne Siaens (Bolivia, Honduras), and we are exceptionally grateful for their efforts. Our thanks for helpful comments to James Heckman, Carmen Pagés, and Guillermo Perry. This work was partially financed by the Regional Studies Program of the office of the chief economist, Latin America and Caribbean region, the World Bank.

1.1 The Importance of the Minimum Wage

The redistributional effects of the minimum wage may have the potential to reduce poverty and even foster growth (see Freeman and Freeman [1992] for a summary of the U.S. debate), but the larger concern in the literature is that the secondary effects through the creation of new rigidities in the labor market and the potential decrease in employment opportunities may offset these gains. The simplest textbook models suggest that putting a wage floor above the equilibrium level will lead to a fall in employment. These effects have traditionally appeared to be weak in the United States, perhaps with the exception of young workers (see, for example, Brown, Gilroy, and Kohen 1982; Card, Katz, and Krueger 1993). Dickens, Machin, and Manning (1999) argue that their finding from the United Kingdom of important impacts on wages, but none on employment, is consistent with the fact that employers generally have some monopsony power in contrast to the usual textbook competitive model.

However, other work does find important adverse effects on employment. Currie and Fallick (1996), Abowd, Kramarz, and Margolis (1999), Neumark, Schweitzer, and Wascher (2000), and Neumark and Wascher (1992) report sharp disemployment effects for those constrained by the minimum wage, with employment elasticities of between 0.4 to 1.6 (in absolute value).[1] Comparing the United States to France, Abowd, Kramarz, and Margoliz (1999) find strong negative impacts on employment in the latter on those workers who earn around the minimum wage. Using a pooled cross-section-time series panel from the Organization for Economic Cooperation and Development (OECD), Neumark and Wascher (1999) find evidence of employment losses for youth, although the magnitude of the impact diminishes where subminimum wages exist for youth and where employers have some discretion in adjusting nonpecuniary characteristics of jobs.

The evidence from Latin America overall suggests large effects. Freeman and Freeman's (1991) analysis of the imposition of U.S. minimum wage norms on Puerto Rico in 1977 leads them to argue that the weak U.S. evidence results primarily from the fact that the minimum wage is so low as to "nibble" rather than "bite" at the wage distribution. When the minimum in Puerto Rico was raised to 63 percent of the average manufacturing wage, the elasticity of employment to the minimum wage became 0.91, and raising the wage led to massive job loss on the island. Card and Krueger (1995),

---

1. They argue that the Card, Katz, and Krueger (1993) findings of no impact results from misspecification both in the omission of a school enrollment effect and lagged dependent variable and incorrect estimation approach that, when corrected, removes the inconsistency in their findings. Card, Katz, and Krueger (1993) take issue with the latter set of findings on several counts, although in addressing these issues Neumark and Wascher (1993) find their original conclusions strengthened.

however, argue that these results are not robust and, in fact, once they correct for the overweighting of very small firms they find that employment *increased* (Card and Krueger 1995, 272). Nonetheless, the presence of adverse employment effects appears to be supported by Bell (1997) in her study using manufacturing panel data from Mexico and Colombia. She finds no impact of the minimum wage in Mexico, where it was not binding. However, in Colombia, she finds an employment elasticity of unskilled workers on the order of 0.15–0.33 and for skilled workers 0.03–0.24, with the effect on workers paid near the minimum wage between 0.55 to 1.22. She concludes that, across the period 1981–1987, the 10 percent rise in the minimum wage from 1981–1987 reduced low-skilled, low-wage Colombia employment in the range of 2 percent–12 percent.

The potentially very high elasticities of those earning near the minimum wage makes the overall impact on poverty potentially ambiguous; an elasticity over 1 implies that total income transfers to the target group *fall* with a rise in the wage. In the United States, the evidence is ambiguous. As examples, Card and Krueger (1995) find weakly significant improvements in poverty, whereas Neumark, Schweitzer, and Wascher (2000) find that earned incomes of low-wage workers decline in response to minimum wage increases, and poverty actually increases.[2] The debate arguably becomes more relevant in less developed countries (LDCs) where enforcement of labor norms is thought not to extend to the "informal" sector. This group of workers is generally found in the unregulated microfirm (usually under five employees) sector, where neither employers nor employees are registered with social protection institutions or authorities more generally. Standard dualistic models ranging from the earliest (Harris and Todaro 1970) to some of the most recent (Agenor and Aizenman 1999) see these unprotected workers as the disadvantaged sector of a labor market segmented by nominal wage rigidities such as the minimum wage. Here, the worker who loses his job has no access to unemployment insurance and instead takes refuge in the informal sector where the wage adjusts to accommodate supply. In this case, a rise in the minimum wage forces some workers into jobs where they earn below what they did before. The available empirical evidence for Latin America is ambiguous. Morely (1995) and de Janvry and Sadoulet (1996) find that poverty falls with a rise in the minimum wage, but only for periods of recovery in the former study and only in periods of recession in the latter. Using worldwide LDC data, Lustig and McLeod (1997) confirm a negative effect on employment and poverty.

The minimum wage also enters strongly into debates about the impacts of mandated nonwage benefit payments and other regulations on labor demand. If, for instance, the worker fully values the health insurance pro-

---

2. Their evidence suggests that the pressure for implementing minimum wages comes from unions seeking to reduce wage competition.

vided by the employer, then, in a market with no rigidities, his or her wage will fall by an equivalent amount. However, in the presence of a wage floor, the mandated benefit raises total costs to the worker and hence reduces total demand. In reality, most regulation can be imagined as a tax on firms whose incidence depends partly on how much workers value it and partly on rigidities in the nominal wage. As an example, restrictions on firing implicitly deprive the firm of an "option" to divest itself of an asset (the worker) and therefore a tax equal to the option value. This could be passed down to the worker as the cost of job security if the worker is risk averse, but not if the minimum wage is binding. The adverse employment effects of poorly designed labor market policies thus can become more extreme in the presence of minimum wages.

A final consideration is how minimum wages may affect how economies adjust to shocks, whether through employment or wages. In the 1994–1995 Tequila crisis, Mexico allowed real wages to be eroded over 25 percent and saw only moderate increases in unemployment. The Colombian Constitution, on the contrary, insists on a *salario minimo movil,* which has been interpreted dictating indexation to past inflation, and this has arguably contributed to the high rates of unemployment experienced in response to the financial crisis of 1998.

1.2   Numerical Measures of the Incidence of Minimum Wages

Raw comparisons of the real minimum wage across countries are of limited use. From both the perspective of improving equity and minimizing labor market distortions, what is of interest is the level of the minimum wage relative to the distribution of remuneration in the individual country. To argue that the minimum is "too low" in Brazil because it is a fraction of that in Argentina is irrelevant if overall labor productivity differs by similar magnitudes.

As a first cut at international comparison, figure 1.1 ranks various Latin American and OECD countries by the minimum wage standardized by the mean wage (SMW).[3] Latin America spans the range with Uruguay, Bolivia, Brazil, Argentina, Chile, and Mexico having the lowest values, and Venezuela, El Salvador, Paraguay, and Honduras having among the highest.[4]

3. The source for countries discussed in detail here are International Bank for Reconstruction and Development (IBRD) staff estimates for the most recent years available. All others come from Inter-American Development Bank (IADB) (1999).
4. The analysis uses the Permanent Household Survey (EPH) from Argentina, the Continuous Household Survey (ECH) from Bolivia, the National Survey from the Sample of Households (PNAD) from Brazil, the Encuesta de Caracterización Socioeconómica Nacional (CASEN) from Chile, the Multipurpose Permanent Survey (EPHM) for Honduras, and the National Urban Employment Survey (ENEU) from Mexico. We restrict the sample to those sixteen–sixty-five, working between thirty and fifty hours a week for informal salaried workers (those working for firms of five employees or below) and formal salaried workers (six workers and above).

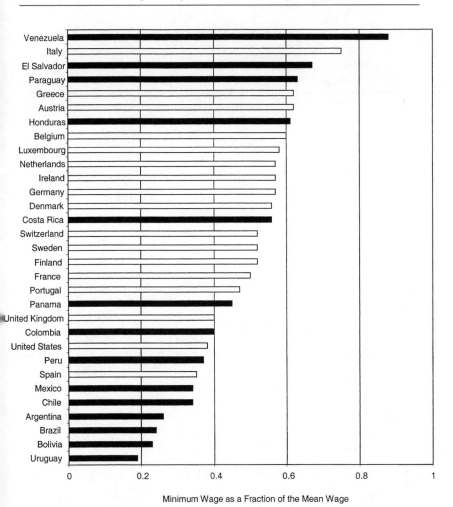

Fig. 1.1   Minimum wage/mean wage in OECD countries and in Latin America

Although informative, standardizing by the first moment is not sufficient to tell us whether the minimum wage is binding for two reasons. First, the number of workers affected will depend on the higher moments of the distribution as well; more disperse endowments of human capital (variance) or a particularly large fraction of poorly endowed workers (skewness) would lead to more workers being affected by a given SMW. Second, if the minimum wage is not enforced, very high SMWs are irrelevant.

As a second cut, table 1.1 offers several additional measures that attempt to provide a more rounded view. The first column presents the SMW, and the second standardizes by the wage at the 50th quantile (median). The median is a better measure of the central tendency because it is less sensitive to extreme values in the upper tail and to compression of the lower tail by

Table 1.1   Summary Statistics on Minimum Wages and Wage Distributions

Country	Date	Minimum Wage			Standard Deviation	Skewness
		Mean	50th	10th		
Argentina[a]	1998	0.26	0.33	0.67	0.67	0.53
Bolivia	1997	0.22	0.34	0.80	0.80	0.51
Brazil	1998	0.24	0.43	1.00	0.86	0.61
Brazil[a]	1998	0.22	0.37	1.00	0.71	0.60
Chile	1996	0.34	0.55	1.09	0.77	0.58
Colombia[a]	1998	0.40	0.68	1.00	0.51	1.16
Honduras	1999	0.62	0.90	2.26	0.80	−0.14
Mexico[a]	1999	0.34	0.48	0.87	0.64	0.83
Uruguay[a]	1998	0.19	0.27	0.64	0.72	0.06

Source: Authors' estimates.

Note: Samples include workers between sixteen–sixty-five years of age working thirty–fifty hours as salaried workers.

[a]Urban areas only.

the minimum wage. Using it to standardize reverses the SMW rankings of Argentina and Brazil. This effect is even more dramatic if we standardize by the wage at the 10th quantile of the distribution, arguably the range that is of more concern than the center.[5] Brazil suddenly appears among the countries with the most potentially binding minimum wage (excluding Honduras), and far above Argentina and Uruguay. This makes sense when it is noted that Brazil shows the highest wage variance among countries overall and among countries for which the sample is purely urban.

1.3   Graphical Analysis–Kernel Density Plots

However revealing theoretically, the 10th quantile, variance and skewness measures are problematic because they describe the distribution *after* the imposition of the minimum wage. A graphic approach, however, can reliably reveal how the distribution is distorted. The first panels of figure 1.2 are kernel estimates of the density function, with a vertical line to mark the location of the minimum wage.[6] Kernel density estimators approximate the density $f(x)$ from observations on x. The estimator calculates the density at the center of the weighted xs found within a rolling interval or "window." They differ from histogram both in allowing the windows to overlap and by the possibility of different weighting schemes on the xs.

5. Ten percent of the sample earns below this wage, and ninety percent earns above this wage.
6. See DiNardo, Fortin, and Lemieux (1996) for a thorough treatment of kernel density estimation and Velez and Santamaria (1999) for an application of the cumulative distribution function (CDF) to Colombia.

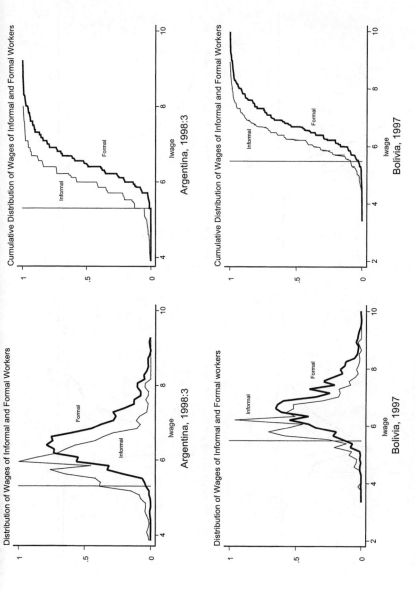

Fig. 1.2 Kernel density plots, cumulative distributions, and minimum wage

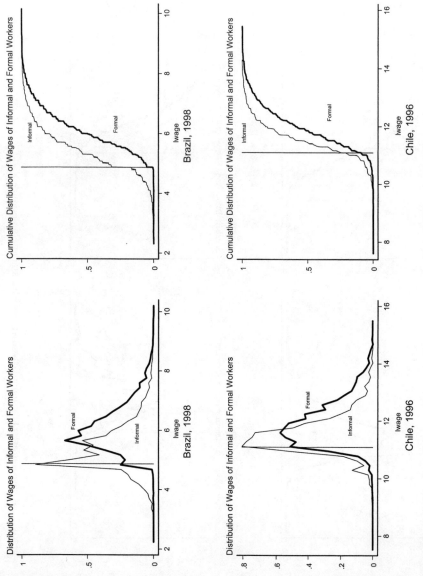

Fig. 1.2. (cont.)

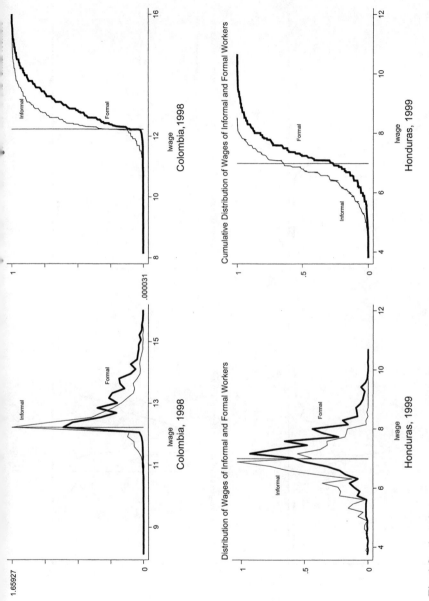

Fig. 1.2 (cont.)

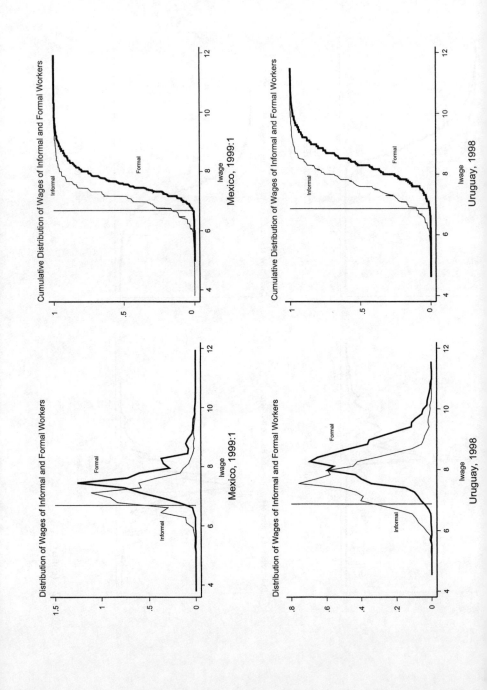

Distribution of Wages of Informal and Formal Workers

Cumulative Distribution of Wages of Informal and Formal Workers

Mexico, 1999:1

Distribution of Wages of Informal and Formal Workers

Cumulative Distribution of Wages of Informal and Formal Workers

Uruguay, 1998

(1)
$$\hat{f}_k = \frac{1}{nh} \sum_{i=1}^{n} K\left(\frac{x - X_i}{h}\right)$$

The function K determines the weights and is termed the "kernel." This estimator has the advantage of giving a clearer idea of the shape of the distribution, but it is sensitive to the bandwidth chosen to smooth. This is particularly important for detecting the impact of minimum wages because an excessively large bandwidth will smooth exactly the "cliff" where the minimum wage is binding. Some adjustments away from the default were necessary to present the most revealing plot.

The second panels are the cumulative distributions of wages. These require no judgements about bandwidths and the vertical "cliffs" indicate where the minimum wage, or multiples, may be influencing. Both the informal and formal wage distributions are plotted in light and dark lines, respectively.[7] In each graph, a "piling up" of the probability mass around the minimum wage, represented in all figures by a vertical line, suggests that the policy has, in effect, forced a change in the distribution.

1.3.1   Interpretation

What is immediately clear is that minimum wages do have the capacity to alter strongly the distribution of wages. Colombia provides an extreme example; the dramatic cliffs in the plots occurring around the minimum wage line, the low standard deviation, and the high skewness (table 1.1) likely reflect the impact of the minimum wage rather than the underlying distribution of human capital, confirming the more detailed findings of Santamaria (1998). Somewhat in contrast to common wisdom, of the Mercosur countries, Brazil and Chile appear to have more binding minimum wages in the formal sector than either the allegedly very rigid Argentina, or Uruguay.

More generally, enforcement varies widely across the region, and SMWs appear to be somewhat deceptive measures of the efficacy of the minimum wage to affect distribution or measures of labor market distortion. Chile and Colombia have SMWs far below that of Honduras, yet the distortion of the wage distributions in the first two seems dramatic in comparison. This suggests that a country's location in the range of SMWs (figure 1.1) is insufficient to indicate the impact of a rise in minimum wage and that empirical work with only the statutory measures may give a misleading picture of what is going on.

---

7. The informal sector is defined in each country either by whether a salaried worker is unaffiliated with social security systems, or works in very small firms (around six workers or less). The Colombian survey, in particular, has only limited data and therefore shows little difference in means between the two.

1.3.2   The Impact on the Informal Sector

In virtually all countries, there is evidence of what has been termed in Brazil the *Efeito Farol* or *lighthouse effect* on the informal distribution.[8] That is, the formal sector minimum wage serves as a reference throughout the economy, including sectors not legally bound by it. In fact, *the influence seems far stronger on the informal sector than the formal* in Brazil, Mexico, Argentina, and Uruguay, countries where the wage appears largely irrelevant to the formal distribution. In each of these cases, the lighter shaded informal wage distribution to the left of the formal sector distribution shows greater distortions around the minimum than is the case in the formal sector. It may be argued that the minimum wage is simply a signal of the wage level in high inflation countries, but the evidence is not supportive: Brazil, Colombia, and Mexico have very moderate rates of inflation in the sample period. Though probably not enforced by law, the minimum wage appears to be an important benchmark for "fair" remuneration.

This would seem to turn conventional conceptions of the relationship between the informal and formal sectors on their heads—the binding wage floor is now in the informal sector—and raises new questions about the *razon de ser* of the informal sector. If it is an inferior unprotected sector, why do workers receive some benefits and not others? Why does some concept of fairness dictate that informal workers should get the minimum wage, but not benefits? One possibility is that forwarded by Maloney (1998) that the sector is as much a way of avoiding the inefficiencies of labor market regulation as the regulations themselves. As discussed earlier, where there is no wage floor in the formal sector, the costs of benefits to employers may be largely passed down to workers in the form of lower wages. If this implicit tax is higher than the perceived benefits, then there is an incentive to evade and seek informal employment. Given that informal workers are, on average, substantially younger than formal workers, it may be that many are still covered by their fathers' health insurance or are recurring to less formal forms of social protection and hence would resist paying the implicit tax again. Further, the often gross inefficiencies in benefits provision drive another wedge between benefits and implicit taxes.

This finding also suggests that the standard dualistic model that sees the flexible informal sector wage as permitting the absorption of workers rationed out from the rigid formal sector is seriously incomplete. It is not clear why we shouldn't also expect a downward sloping demand curve in the informal sector and hence that the binding minimum wage leads to job loss there and reduced capacity to absorb the unemployed. Again, the pres-

8. The original reference of the *Teoria do Farol* is found with reference to Brazil in Souza and Baltar (1979). For more recent references, see Neri, Gonzaga, and Camargo (2000) as well as Amadeo, Gill, and Neri (2000). For recent work on minimum wages in Brazil, see Lemos (2003) and Neumark, Cunningham, and Siga (2003).

ent Colombian situation comes to mind.[9] The historically unprecedented unemployment rates may partially arise from the shock to formal production due to the collapse of the financial sector, but also the jobs lost in the informal sector with the sharp rise in the minimum wage over the last several years.

1.3.3 The Minimum Wage as a Reference for Other Formal Wages

Throughout the region it is common to use the minimum wage as a more general unit of account or *numeraire,* for instance, in quoting wages or monetary contracts in general. In Brazil, for example, Neri, Gonzaga, and Camargo (2000) find strong evidence of this effect throughout the wage distribution, finding that 9 percent of formal sector workers received exactly one minimum wage, but another 6 percent received exactly a multiple. Argentina, Brazil, Mexico, and Uruguay appear to show regular "cliffs" across the distribution that are synchronized between both the formal and informal sectors. The next section will test more explicitly for these effects.

1.4 Econometric Evidence on the Impact of the Minimum Wage from Colombia

In this section, we follow Neumark, Schweitzer, and Wascher (2000) in employing rotating panel data from Colombia to test the impact of a rise in the minimum wage on wages and the probability of becoming unemployed, and for *numeraire* effects in both. The existence of the panel, as well as the impression from the previous section that the minimum wage is high and binding made Colombia an obvious case study.

Since 1997, the National Statistical Agency (DANE) has created a rotating panel by reinterviewing 25 percent of households interviewed in the previous round of the National Household Survey (ENH), yielding a set of two consecutive quarterly observations on the same households. Individuals were identified by household and then on the basis of gender, age, marital status, relation with the head of household, schooling level, and years of education, variables which do not change between quarters. The Euclidian distance from each individual, with respect to the rest of the inhabitants of a house, is calculated and the match accepted if the distance is below a predetermined threshold. Roughly 15 percent of the individuals in a survey can be linked to the past one in eleven rotating surveys. As

9. Fiess, Fugazza, and Maloney (1999), for example, find that the Mexican and, to a lesser degree, the informal and formal sectors behave across the business cycle as if they were integrated sectors-earnings relative to the formal sector rise with share of the workforce in informality. In Colombia, on the other hand, the traditional dualistic view seems more supported with informal self-employment serving as a last resort and unemployment dramatically rising. See also Maloney (2003a,b) and Cunningham and Maloney (2001) for further discussions of the desirability of the informal sector.

Table 1.2   Colombia: Distribution of Sample by Salary Range

Salary in terms of Minimum Wage	Employed in $t = 1$		Unemployed in $t = 1$	
	Workers	Percentage	Workers	Percentage
0.0–0.5	559	6.24	267	15.99
0.5–0.7	574	6.40	229	13.71
0.7–0.9	1,112	12.41	237	14.19
0.9–1.1	1,444	16.11	235	14.07
1.1–1.3	1,095	12.22	145	8.68
1.3–1.5	536	5.98	85	5.09
1.5–2.0	965	10.77	132	7.90
2.0–3.0	1,121	12.51	155	9.28
3.0–4.0	455	5.08	49	2.93
>4.0	1,102	12.29	136	8.14
Total	8,963	100	1,670	100

Note: Sample includes men who work thirty–fifty hours per week.

table 1.2 shows, when we restrict to that used in the kernel density plots—men working thirty–fifty hours per week—we have a total of 10,633 observations who are employed in the first period. Slightly over 19 percent of these will become unemployed in the second period. Of these, 66 percent report being salaried workers, and 34 percent report being self-employed. Although the year chosen to estimate the kernel density plots permitted separating "formal" from "informal" wage earners in every period, this is not the case in other years, and we combine the two in the "salaried" sector. Roughly 25 percent earn below the minimum wage. However, the vast majority of these, as suggested in the kernel density plots, are informal.

We examine the self-employed as a control that can help separate general price indexing effects from "true" minimum wage effects. If the minimum is simply an economywide mechanism for coordinating prices, we might see the self-employed using it to fix their product prices. If this were not the case, we would expect that their incomes would be determined by the profitability of their enterprise, and they would not raise their implicit "wage" at the risk of becoming uncompetitive.

The panel nature of the data permits identifying the impact of the two annual changes in the minimum wage that occurred between 1997 and the end of the available sample in 1999.[10] We estimate the determinants of the percentage change in the real hourly wage worker i receives, (dw) or the probability of becoming unemployed (prob[$z = 1$]) across two quarters as

---

10. This period corresponds to what is widely acknowledged as the country's worst employment crisis in the postwar period.

$$(2) \quad dw, \text{prob}(z = 1) = \sum_{j} \beta_j \mathbf{R}(w_{i1}, mw_1)_j \left(\frac{mw_2 - mw_1}{mw_1} \right) + \sum_{j} \gamma_j \mathbf{R}(w_{i1}, mw_1)_j$$

$$+ \sum_{j} \phi_j \mathbf{R}(w_{i1}, mw_1)_j \left(\frac{w_{i1}}{mw_1} \right) + \delta \mathbf{X}_{i1} + \lambda T_i + \pi A_i + \varepsilon_i,$$

where mw is the real minimum wage, respectively, in the two periods.[11]

Though it is common to examine the impact of the minimum wage on wages and employment at the minimum wage, the kernel density plots suggest that there are *numeraire* effects throughout the distribution. If we are interested in the total effect of the minimum wage on distribution and employment, we need to look for these effects as well. Further, there may be general equilibrium effects at higher wage levels through changes in relative demand. For these reasons, we create j dummy variables, the vector $\mathbf{R}$, that locate individual i's wage in the real hourly wage distribution in year 1 at fractions and multiples of the minimum wage (table 1.2). This allows us to see the impact of a change of minimum wage, not only on those earning one minimum wage, but also those earning, for example, two or three times the minimum wage.

The first term on the right-hand-side of the equation captures this effect of a change in the minimum wage on different regions of the wage distribution. The second term permits the level of wage growth, independent of minimum wage effects, to change by each cohort in the wage distribution. The third term induces more flexibility in the function, allowing the estimation of the implicit spline specification without constraining the lines to join at the knot points.

Finally, $\mathbf{X}$ is a vector with the individual characteristics such as gender, age, education, and so on, T and A are a set of quarterly and regional dummy variables which capture the dependence of observations of the same period (including seasonal effects) and region, respectively.

Previous papers find that low-income families receive a short-run benefit when the minimum wage increases but are negatively affected over the longer term (Neumark, Schweitzer, and Wascher 2000). This is because short-run adjustments are made via prices and long-run adjustments via quantities; firms must follow the law at first, but then, if required, they fire workers. For this reason, the lagged minimum wage gain $(mw_1 - mw_0)/mw_0$ is also introduced. From the point of view of measuring these longer-run impacts, it would be preferable to have, as Neumark, Schweitzer, and Wascher (2000) do, a full year span rather than the two quarter panels the ENH offers. This limitation may not be as serious as appears at first for measuring the impact on wages because the generally higher inflation rates in Latin America erode more quickly any mandated increase in the minimum wage than in the United States. It has also been argued by Brown,

---

11. The deflator used was the consumer price index for each city.

Table 1.3   Colombia: Effect of a 1 Percent Rise in the Minimum Wage on
                 Hourly Salaries

Salary in terms of Minimum Wage	Self-Employed	Lag	Salaried	Lag
0.0–0.5	0.9860***	−0.0653***	1.7411***	−0.1191
0.5–0.7	1.0695**	0.0796	1.2325***	−0.1865**
0.7–0.9	1.1598	0.0486	0.8723***	−0.1576*
0.9–1.1	1.2723	0.0563	0.5971***	−0.1746*
1.1–1.3	0.4563	0.0583	0.6607***	−0.1618*
1.3–1.5	0.1591	0.0652	0.2861**	−0.1806*
1.5–2.0	0.7346	0.0597	0.3896***	−0.1794*
2.0–3.0	0.4508	0.0626	0.3528***	−0.1816*
3.0–4.0	0.1242	0.0680	0.3848**	−0.1654*
>4.0	0.0843	0.0703	0.1611***	−0.1736*
Average			0.6378***	−0.1696***
N		2,744		5,267

Notes: Sample includes men who work thirty–fifty hours per week. N = number of observations.
***Significant at the 1 percent level.
**Significant at the 5 percent level.
*Significant at the 10 percent level.

Gilroy, and Kohen (1982) that the high turnover in low-skilled workers may imply that employment adjustment in the most critical ranges around the minimum wage may be relatively rapid. Further, Maloney (2001) shows that average manufacturing tenure in Latin America is roughly 70 percent of the OECD, so the quantity adjustment might occur more rapidly. Nonetheless, we put less weight in our analysis on the lags and do not follow Neumark, Schweitzer, and Wascher (2000) in generating "representative" worker responses to lagged minimum wages.[12]

1.4.1   Effects on Wages

Table 1.3 reports the effects on real wages of a change in the real minimum wage on salaried workers. The results are broadly consistent with Neumark, Schweitzer, and Wascher (2000). Around the minimum wage, those earning 0.7–0.9 minimum wages, the effect is high for salaried workers; 0.87 of the rise in minimum wages is communicated to wages. Moving

12. Neumark argues that, generally speaking, the lag has the usual interpretation as long as the individual history is not relevant, that is, that the contemporary effect of a change in the minimum wage does not depend on past wages. The problem that he highlights is that a rise in the minimum wage in the previous period may have "swept up" a worker into a different category. Therefore, the correct total effects (contemporaneous plus lagged) needs somehow to compensate for individuals changing classification, which involves generating a set of representative workers in each cell.

up the income scale, the effect remains significant for up to four minimum wages, although with decreasing coefficients and falling to only 0.16 for those earning more than four minimum wages. What is remarkable is that the effect dies off much more slowly than in the United States. Between two and three minimum wages, Neumark, Schweitzer, and Wascher (2000) found an impact of only 0.06 percent, whereas in Colombia at four minimum wages the impact is 0.38. This suggests a far greater *numeraire* effect and hence substantially greater impact of the minimum wage on the overall distribution. As Neumark, Schweitzer, and Wascher (2000) found, very large effects are found below the minimum wage, and we also do not have an obvious explanation for this. The self-employed show a significant effect below the minimum wage, but overall, there appears to be little impact on the distribution above the minimum wage. This suggests that the impact is not through the minimum wage acting as a general signal of price rises throughout the economy.

The effect of a one-quarter lag suggests two interesting effects. First, across the wage distribution there is a significant, and broadly uniform (about 17 percent), erosion of the first period effect, perhaps due to inflation. This suggests that we cannot take the impact effect as the wage rise that firms will use in making employment decisions. Second, again the impact on the self-employed is virtually never significant, and the magnitudes are roughly one-third of those for salaried workers. This suggests that not only do the self-employed not respond strongly to lighthouse effects but that they may update their "wages" frequently to avoid inflation erosion. This, in fact, may be one of the advantages of being self-employed versus salaried in high inflation environments.

1.4.2   Effects on Employment

Table 1.4 shows the consequent effects on employment. Equation (2) is run again, but this time as a logit, where the individual is assigned a value of 1 if he retains his job and a 0 if he is without a job in the second quarter.

The results are consistent with the wage regressions. A rise in the minimum wage has a statistically very significant impact on the probability of becoming unemployed that again decreases with a rising position in the wage distribution. The lags echo this pattern and suggest that, as might be expected, the adjustment does not take place instantaneously. On average, the contemporaneous effect is roughly twice that found by Neumark, Schweitzer, and Wascher (2000) for the United States and, again, extends far higher in the distribution. Corresponding to the apparent impact on the wages of the very lowest ranges of the self-employed distribution, there are negative impacts on employment as well as some impacts higher in the distribution. Figure 1.3 graphs both the impact on wages and unemployment probability by position in the distribution.

The regressions, therefore, suggest statistically very significant effects on

Table 1.4 **Colombia: Effect of a 1 Percent Rise in the Minimum Wage on the Probability of Becoming Unemployed**

Salary in terms of Minimum Wage	Self-Employed	Lag	Salaried	Lag
0.0–0.5	−0.2259***	−0.2205***	−0.3566***	−0.3462***
0.5–0.7	−0.2207***	−0.2160***	−0.3151***	−0.3035***
0.7–0.9	−0.1611**	−0.1541**	−0.2715***	−0.2615***
0.9–1.1	−0.0921	−0.0847	−0.2765***	−0.2595***
1.1–1.3	−0.1182	−0.1206*	−0.2298***	−0.2169***
1.3–1.5	−0.1378*	−0.1327**	−0.2933***	−0.2890***
1.5–2.0	−0.1044	−0.0988	−0.0967	−0.0623
2.0–3.0	−0.0620	−0.0505	−0.1962**	−0.1675**
3.0–4.0	−0.0408	−0.0343	−0.2530***	−0.2204**
>4.0	−0.0695	−0.0653	−0.1969*	−0.1933**
N		3,128		5,835

Notes: Sample includes men who work thirty–fifty hours per week. N = number of observations.

***Significant at the 1 percent level.
**Significant at the 5 percent level.
*Significant at the 10 percent level.

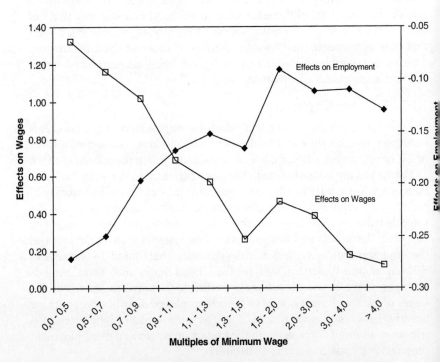

Fig. 1.3   Colombia: Impact of minimum wage on wages and employment

employment and magnitudes of effect far larger than those seen in the United States. However, because they measure the impact on the flow out of employment, they cannot answer the question of what happens to the total stock of jobs. As a very rough first approximation, we run equation (2) again—eliminating the **R** dummies (leaving only the constant) so as to get the "average" effect of the minimum wage rise—effectively integrating under the wage distribution in table 1.3. The average contemporaneous impact is 0.64 and lagged is –0.17, leaving a total effect of 0.47 percent rise in wages. We then multiply this by the Fajnzylber and Maloney (2001) estimate of the long-run own-wage elasticity of blue-collar manufacturing employment of 0.32. If there is no further inflationary erosion, this would imply an elasticity of employment with respect to minimum wage of 0.15. This is quite consistent with Bell's (1997) estimates and suggests that the 9 percent rise in minimum wage in 1999 would have had the effect of reducing employment by 1.4 percent.

1.5   Conclusion

The Colombian case confirms the evidence offered by the kernel density estimates. First, the minimum wage can have an important impact on the wage distribution in the neighborhood of the minimum wage. Second, the effects echo up the wage distribution in a way that suggests important *numeraire* effects. That this effect is far stronger than found by Neumark, Schweitzer, and Wascher (2000) in the United States suggests that the minimum wage induces farther-reaching rigidities in the labor market and that the trade off between any possible effect on poverty and reduced flexibility is likely to be more severe in Latin America. The employment effects are shown to be large as a result. The data did not allow testing of the impacts on informal salaried sector wages, but the kernel density plots speak convincingly about the lighthouse effect and the potentially greater impact on the informal sector. In sum, the minimum wage has impacts both in the higher reaches of the formal distribution and in the informal labor markets that magnify its distortionary effects beyond what was previously thought.

References

Abowd, J., F. Kramarz, and D. Margolis. 1999. High wage workers and high wage firms. *Econometrica* 67:251–333.
Agenor, P., and J. Aizenman. 1999. Macroeconomic adjustment with segmented labor markets. *Journal of Development Economics* 58:277–96.
Amadeo, E. J., I. S. Gill, and M. C. Neri. 2000. Do labor laws matter? The 'pressure points' in Brazil's labor legislation. In *Readdressing Latin America's "forgotten reform": Quantifying labor policy challenges in Argentina, Brazil and Chile,*

ed. I. S. Gill and C. E. Montenegro World Bank, The International Bank for Reconstruction and Development. Unpublished Manuscript.

Bell, L. A. 1997. The impact of minimum wages in Mexico and Colombia. *Journal of Labor Economics* 15 (3): 103–35.

Brown, C. 1996. The old minimum-wage literature and its lessons for the new. In *The effects of the minimum wage on employment,* ed. M. Kosters, 87–98. Washington, D.C.: AEI Press.

Brown, C., C. Gilroy, and A. Kohen. 1982. The effect of the minimum wage on employment and unemployment. *Journal of Economic Literature* 20:487–528.

Card, D., L. F. Katz, and A. B. Krueger. 1993. An evaluation of recent evidence of the federal minimum wage. *Industrial and Labor Relations Review* 46 (1): 38–54.

Card, D., and A. B. Krueger. 1994. Minimum wages and employment: A case study of the fast-food industry in New Jersey and Pennsylvania. *American Economic Review* 84:772–93.

Card, D. and A. B. Krueger. 1995. *Myth and measurement: The economics of the minimum wage.* Princeton, N.J.: Princeton University Press.

Carrasquilla, A. 1999. Reforma laboral en Colombia: ¿Cuáles son los temas? [Main concerns for Colombian labor reform]. *Economía Colombiana y Coyuntura Política* 276:5–12.

Contraloría General de la República. 1993. *Contribución a la discusión sobre el salario mínimo y su impacto en el empleo y la productividad.* [Contribution to the minimum wage debate regarding its impact in employment and productivity]. Bogotá, Colombia: Contraloría General de la República.

Cunningham, W., and W. F. Maloney. 2001. Heterogeneity among Mexico's microenterprises: An application of factor and cluster analysis. *Economic Development and Cultural Change* 50:131–56.

Currie, J., and B. C. Fallick. 1996. The minimum wage and the employment of youth: evidence from the NLSY. *Journal of Human Resources* 31:404–28.

de Janvry, A. and E. Sadoulet. 1996. Household modeling for the design of poverty alleviation strategies. University of California, Berkeley, Department of Agricultural and Resource Economics (CUDARE). Working Paper no. 787.

Dickens, R., S. Machin, and A. Manning. 1999. The effects of minimum wages on employment: Theory and evidence from Britain. *Journal of Labor Economics* 17 (1): 1–22.

DiNardo, J., N. M. Fortin, and T. Lemieux. 1996. Labor market institutions and the distribution of wages, 1973–1992: A semi-parametric approach. *Econometrica* 62:1001–44.

Fajnzylber, P., and W. F. Maloney. 2001. How comparable are labor demand elasticities across countries? The International Bank for Reconstruction and Development (IBRD). Working Paper no. 2658. Washington, D.C.: World Bank.

Fiess, N., M. Fugazza, and W. F. Maloney. 2002. Exchange rate appreciations, labor market rigidities and informality. World Bank Policy Working Paper no. 2771. Washington, D.C.: World Bank.

Freeman, A. C., and R. B. Freeman. 1991. Minimum wages in Puerto Rico: Textbook case of a wage floor? NBER Working Paper no. 3759. Cambridge, Mass.: National Bureau of Economic Research, June.

———. 1992. When the minimum wage really bites: The effect of the U.S.-Level minimum on Puerto Rico. In *Immigration and the work force: Economic consequences for the United States and source areas,* ed. G. J. Borjas and R. B. Freeman, 177–211. Chicago: University of Chicago Press.

Gramlich, E. 1976. Impact of minimum wages on other wages, employment and family incomes. *Brookings Papers on Economic Activity,* Issue no. 2:409–51.

Grossman, J. B. 1983. The impact of the minimum wage on other wages. *Journal of Human Resources* 18 (3): 359–78.

Harris, J. R., and M. P. Todaro. 1970. Migration, unemployment, and development: A two sector analysis. *American Economic Review* 60 (1): 126–42.

Inter-American Development Bank (IADB). 1999. *Facing up to inequality in Latin America.* Baltimore: Johns Hopkins University Press.

Lemos, S. 2003. A menu of minimum wage variables for evaluating wages and employment effects: Evidence from Brazil. University College London. Unpublished Manuscript.

Lora, E. 1993. Macroeconomía del salario mínimo. [Macroeconomics of minimum wages]. *Debates de Coyuntura Económica* 30:21–35.

Maloney, W. F. 1998. Does informality imply segmentation in urban labor markets? Evidence from sectoral transitions in Mexico. *World Bank Economic Review* 13:275–302.

———. 2001. Self-employment and labor turnover in developing countries: Cross-country evidence. In *World Bank economists' forum,* ed. Shanta Devarajan, F. Halsey Rogers, and Lyn Squire, 137–67. Washington, D.C.: World Bank.

———. 2003a. Informality revisited. World Bank Policy Research Working Paper no. 2965. Washington, D.C.: World Bank.

———. 2003b. Informal self-employment: Poverty trap or decent alternative? In *Pathways out of poverty: Private firms and economic mobility in developing countries,* ed. G. Fields and G. Pfefferman. Boston: Kluwer, forthcoming.

Morely, S. 1995. Structural adjustment and the determinants of poverty in Latin America. In *Coping with austerity: Poverty and inequality in Latin America,* ed. N. Lustig, 42–70. Washington, D.C.: The Brookings Institution.

Neri, M., G. Gonzaga, and J. M. Camargo. 2000. Efeitos informais do salário mínimo e pobreza. [The informality sector and its effects on minimum wages and poverty]. *Revista de Economia Política,* forthcoming.

Neumark, D., W. Cunningham, and L. Siga. 2003. The distributional effects of minimum wages in Brazil, 1996–2001. World Bank. Unpublished Manuscript.

Neumark, D., M. Schweitzer, and W. Wascher. 1998. The effects of minimum wages on the distribution of family incomes: A non-parametric analysis. NBER Working Paper no. 6536. Cambridge, Mass.: National Bureau of Economic Research, April.

———. 2000. The effects of minimum wages throughout the wage distribution. NBER Working Paper no. 7519. Cambridge, Mass.: National Bureau of Economic Research, February.

Neumark, David and William Wascher. 1992. Employment effects of minimum and subminimum wages. *Industrial and Labor Relations Review* 46 (1): 55–80.

———. 1993. Employment effects of minimum and subminimum wages: Reply to Card, Katz, and Krueger. NBER Working Paper no. 4570. Cambridge, Mass.: National Bureau of Economic Research, December.

———. 1999. A cross-national analysis of the effects of minimum wages on youth unemployment. NBER Working Paper no. 7299. Cambridge, Mass.: National Bureau of Economic Research, August.

———. 2002. Do minimum wages fight poverty? *Economic Inquiry* 40 (3): 315–33.

Nickell, S. 1997. Unemployment and labor market rigidities: Europe versus North America. *Journal of Economic Perspectives* 11 (3): 55–74.

Santamaria, M. 1998. Nonparametric density estimation and regression: An application to the study of income inequality and poverty in Colombia. Ph.D. diss. Georgetown University, Washington, D.C.

Siebert, H. 1997. Labor market rigidities: At the root of unemployment in Europe. *Journal of Economic Perspectives* 11 (3): 37–54.

Souza, P., and P. Baltar. 1979. Salario minimo e taxa de salarios no Brasil. *Pesquisa e Planejamento Economico* 9:629–60.
Velez, C. E., and M. Santamaria. 1999. Is the minimum wage binding in Colombia?: A short note on empirical evidence for 1998. Latin America and the Caribbean Department, IBRD. Washington, D.C.: World Bank.

2

Labor Market Reforms and Their Impact over Formal Labor Demand and Job Market Turnover
The Case of Peru

Jaime Saavedra and Máximo Torero

2.1 Introduction

After the expansionary phase of the "heterodox" experiment (1986–1987) of the García government, the Peruvian economy fell into a very deep recession. Output fell between 1988 and 1990, in the midst of a hyperinflationary process. The Fujimori government implemented a harsh macroeconomic stabilization program in August 1991, and a few months later a comprehensive set of structural reforms was launched. Peru experienced one of the fastest trade liberalization processes and one of the deepest labor market reforms in Latin America. These reforms were accompanied by a downsizing of the public sector, the start of a privatization process, the abolition of all state-owned monopolies, and a tax reform. In addition, restrictions to capital account transactions were eliminated while the financial sector was deregulated.

The Peruvian Labor Code, developed during the import substitution period, had been termed one of the most restrictive, protectionist, and cumbersome of Latin America (International Labor Organization [ILO] 1994). The code was extremely complex and comprised a collection of overlap-

Jaime Saavedra is executive director and senior researcher at the Grupo de Análisis para el Desarrollo. Máximo Torero is senior researcher at the same institution.

This project was undertaken as part of the IADB Research Network. We thank the staff of the Ministry of Labor of Peru for helping us in handling the data used for the labor demand estimations. We owe a great debt to Daniel Hamermesh, James Heckman, and Carmen Pagés-Serra for numerous helpful comments on the different drafts of this work. Their comments and criticisms improved it substantially. We also received helpful suggestions from participants in the Inter-American Development Bank (IADB) Research Network. We also thank Giuseppe Bertola and two anonymous referees for their comments. We are grateful to Juan Jose Diaz, Eduardo Maruyama, and Erica Field for their extremely valuable assistance in this project.

ping decrees that had undergone many changes over time. The military government of 1969–1975 made firing extremely difficult by sanctioning job stability after a probationary period. In 1985, the García government reduced the probationary period to just three months, during what was the period of most rigid labor market legislation. In 1991, labor market regulations were relaxed through a succession of reforms. Firing costs diminished sharply through the progressive elimination of job stability regulations, the reduction in red tape for the use of temporary contracts, and changes in the severance payment structure. In addition, firms in the formal sector faced high nonwage costs: payroll taxes, social security and health contributions, a tenure bonus, training fund contributions, family allowances, and a long thirty-day vacation period. During the 1990s overall nonwage costs increased slightly.

One first adjustment mechanism to a restrictive labor legislation is the use of informal contracts. In this sense, changes in firing costs expected by the firm and in nonwage labor costs have an impact on the distribution of employment between the formal and informal sectors but not necessarily on overall employment. If firing costs are perceived by firms as a tax imposed on layoffs, a reduction, like the one observed in Peru given the fall in expected severance payments, and the abolition of job stability and the facilities given for the use of temporary contracts will increase the equilibrium employment level. Moreover, reductions in expected firing costs may have an effect on the response pattern of firms to changes in product demand, which may be reflected in larger employment-output elasticities. In this paper, we analyze the impact of changes in expected severance payments and labor costs by estimating labor demand functions for the formal sector. We use data from firm-level surveys for formal firms in Metropolitan Lima. With these data we construct a pseudo-panel data set of ten economic sectors observed bimonthly during the period 1987–1997 and three shorter panels of about 400 firms for the periods 1987–1990, 1991–1994, and 1995–1997, dates dictated by sample changes.

Also, reductions in labor legislation–related firings costs typically accelerate the process of job creation and job destruction, therefore increasing turnover and reducing job duration, particularly in the formal sector. We examine changes in job duration and labor market turnover using data from a series of annual household surveys, with which we analyze changes in mean tenure in both the formal and informal sectors. Informality is conceptualized here as a state chosen by firms and workers depending on a cost-benefit analysis. Many firms, typically smaller ones, operate totally underground, fire and hire at will, and do not pay any kind of socially mandated benefits. In most of the cases, their productivity is too low for them to afford to pay any kind of benefits. To operationalize this we define a worker as working in the formal sector if he or she receives social benefits or belongs to a union. In addition, using the Living Standards Measurement Survey, we construct complete and incomplete employment spells with which we calculate empirical hazards for different subsamples, and we estimate exponential hazard models.

The paper proceeds as follows. In section 2.2 we analyze the legal context regarding the probationary period, severance payments, nonwage costs, and temporary contracts, all factors that affect firm and worker behavior. We also describe changes in employment in Metropolitan Lima during the period of analysis and discuss how informality and temporary contracts have been mechanisms through which firms avoid paying mandated benefits and firing costs. In section 2.3 we present results of labor demand estimations at both the sectoral and firm levels. Finally, in section 2.4, we analyze basic patterns of employment duration. In order to assess possible impacts of labor laws, we compare patterns of the self-employed with those of wage earners in the formal and informal sectors. We present a comparison of job duration among different groups of workers using empirical hazards, and we show the results of exponential hazards functions.

2.2   Changes in the Regulatory Framework during the 1990s

Prior to the reforms, the Peruvian Labor Code was extremely complex and comprised a large collection of overlapping decrees. Formal workers enjoyed several employment stability provisions, payroll taxes and social security contributions were high, and collective bargaining and other regulations gave unions great power. Since 1991, labor market regulations were relaxed through a succession of reforms. In this section we describe the changes in firing costs determined by the severance payment and job stability regulations, the changes in regulations and in the use of temporary contracts, and the evolution of nonwage labor costs.

2.2.1   Severance Payments and Job Stability

The costs of firing in Peru comprised two main elements, mandated severance payments upon dismissal and the costs imposed by job stability regulations. The military government of General Velasco introduced severance payments in 1970, as a fixed value equivalent to three months' wages upon dismissal without "just cause." It was conceived as a compensation to the hardship of dismissal and simultaneously as an unemployment insurance device. In addition to severance payments, Peruvian labor laws had very rigid employment protection clauses, which increased firing costs dramatically. During the period 1971–1991, a worker who completed the probationary period—the length of which was changed a few times—was granted absolute job stability. That meant that if a firm dismissed a worker and could not prove just cause in labor courts, he or she could choose between being reinstated in the job and receiving the severance payment. This made the severance payment the lower bound of the firing cost, as workers

Table 2.1   **Probationary Period and Job Stability Regulations**

	Probationary Period Length	Job Stability Status	Temporary Contracts Availability
Before June 1986	3 years	Granted after 3 years	Low
June 1986–October 1991	3 months	Granted after 3 months	Low
November 1991–July 1995	3 months	In effect only for workers hired before November 1991	High
After July 1995	3 months	Abolished	High

had the incentive to ask to be reinstated in their jobs, and then settling out of court became a larger severance payment. This setting also implied high administrative and litigation costs. Just cause did not include economic reasons, and workers could be fired due only to serious misdemeanor or through complicated collective layoffs. From the employers' perspective, a worker was effectively "owner of his post."

In 1978, the length of the probationary period was increased to three years (see table 2.1). The severance payment schedule was raised, and workers with less than three years in a firm received the equivalent of three months' wages if fired without notice, while workers with longer tenures received twelve months' wages upon dismissal. During the probationary period, the employer had to inform the worker in advance if he wanted to fire him to avoid the severance payment.

Since June 1986, the probationary period was reduced again, to just three months, and a large portion of workers suddenly acquired total job stability. An interesting feature here is that the change was announced in June 1985, about a year before the law was effectively sanctioned. Casual evidence for that year shows that employers did not increase layoffs massively among workers with less than three years of tenure who had not concluded their probationary period. Given that the economy was starting an expansionary period, it is probable that business expectations regarding higher demand were on the rise, which reduced the incentive of employers to fire workers that could potentially receive job stability rights. Still, the announcement of the policy change, ceteris paribus, must have had a positive effect on turnover for these workers. The severance payment was set to the equivalent of three months' wages for those workers who had been employed between three months and one year, six months' wages for those with one to three years of tenure, and twelve months' wages for those with more than three years of tenure (see García schedule in figure 2.1 and table 2.2).

The June 1986 changes in labor laws by the García administration made the 1986–1991 period the one with the highest degree of rigidity, as severance payments were high, the probationary period was short, and job stability rights were still in place. Rigid job protection pushed firms to seek ways to get around these regulations. One way was to lobby for the gener-

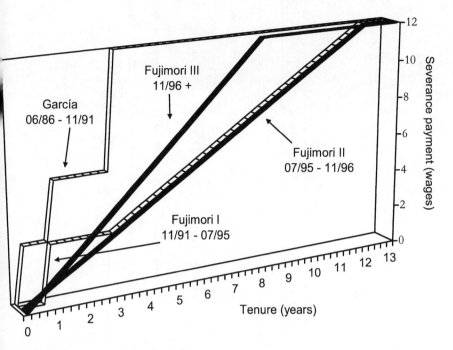

Fig. 2.1   Severance payment regimes

ation of the so-called Emergency Employment Program. The other form was to fire workers a few days before they completed the three-month probationary period and then rehire them. Another form of eluding these regulations was making workers sign an undated letter of resignation at the beginning of the contract period.

In 1991, the government introduced several changes aimed at reducing the extreme rigidity imposed by labor laws. The intention of the drafters of the Law Decree 726 of November 1991 was to abolish job stability. However, the right to job stability was written in the 1979 Constitution, so, in principle, only through a two-year process could the Congress pass a law approving a constitutional change. The outcome was the creation of a dual regime in which workers with contracts signed before November 1991 maintained their job security rights, while new workers would only have protection against unjustified dismissal. This meant that these workers could be dismissed at will upon payment of a severance benefit. In addition, just cause clauses were extended to include issues related to workers' productivity.[1] Also, the severance payment rule was modified in order to reduce firing costs. It was fixed at one months' wage for every year of tenure for workers with more than one year in the firm, with a minimum of three

---

1. In practice, it was very difficult for firms to use these clauses due to administrative problems in proving a reduction of productivity.

Table 2.2   **Severance Payment Legislation: Rules and Examples**

	Rule		Worker's Tenure		
	Tenure	Severance	2 Years	10 Years	20 Years
June 1986–November 1991	3 months–1 year = 1–3 years = More than 3 years =	3 months' wages 6 months' wages 12 months' wages	6 months' wages	12 months' wages	12 months' wages
November 1991–July 1995	3 months–1 year = 1–3 years = 3–12 years = More than 12 years =	0 months' wages 3 months' wages 1 months' wage per year 12 months' wages	3 months' wages	10 months' wages	12 months' wages
July 1995–November 1996	3 months–12 years = More than 12 years =	1 months' wage per year 12 months' wages	2 months' wages	10 months' wages	12 months' wages
November 1996+	3 months–12 years = More than 8 years =	1.5 months' wages per year 12 months' wages	3 months' wages	12 months' wages	12 months' wages

months' wages and a maximum of twelve months' wages, as shown in figure 2.1 (Fujimori I schedule).

In July 1995, with the second wave of labor reforms, the severance payment schedule was simplified to one month per year of work up to a maximum of twelve months (Fujimori II schedule in figure 2.1). As the 1993 Constitution replaced the right to job stability with the right to unjustified dismissal, the 1995 law eliminated job security rules and the two-tier regime. These changes, plus the reduction in severance payments, implied a sharp reduction in firing costs, which may be interpreted as a lower level of the tax on dismissals perceived by firms. This may have the effect of giving formal firms more flexibility to adapt to output changes, of increasing the formal employment level, and also of increasing the output elasticity in labor demand estimations for formal firms. In addition, reductions in firing costs typically accelerate the process of job creation and job destruction, therefore increasing turnover. Finally, in November 1996 the severance payments rule was again modified. Instead of receiving one months' wage for each year in the firm, the employee received one and a half months' wages, an important large increase in the firing costs of low-tenured workers. The maximum cap of twelve months' wages remained unaltered (Fujimori III schedule in figure 2.1).

Quantifying the Severance Payment

The severance payment rule has an effect on the amount of resources firms have to reserve to finance dismissals. Given that in Peru, as in many other Latin American countries, these payments are linked to tenure, these reserves will vary depending on the tenure structure of the workforce of the firm. In turn, the firm's tenure structure may be endogenous to the severance payment rule, as firms will try to avoid hiring workers who will later be relatively more expensive to dismiss. The tenure structure will also depend on technology and other characteristics of the firm and sector.[2]

We calculated the evolution of potential reserves for severance payment as a commodity contingent on a firing (F) or a hiring (H) state of the economy.[3] We may therefore think of a firm as choosing among probability distributions or "prospects" whose uncertain consequences are to be received with respective state probabilities $\pi = (\pi_H, \pi_F)$. Specifically, expected severance payment is calculated by state and sector using the evolution of the tenure structure, an estimate of the firing probability for each tenure group, and the corresponding mandated severance payment. The following formula describes how it is calculated (time subscripts have been eliminated):

---

2. For instance, the share of long-tenure workers will generally be larger in the manufacturing sector, where firm- and sector-specific knowledge is more important than in trade.

3. This is following the expected utility rule of John Von Neumann and Oskar Morgenstern.

$$E(\text{sp})_i = \pi_F \left[\sum_X \lambda(X)_{i,F} \cdot N_X \cdot \text{sp}(X) \right] + \pi_H \left[\sum_X \lambda(X)_{i,H} \cdot N_X \cdot \text{sp}(X) \right]$$

$E(\text{sp})_i$ is the expected severance payment, which is a probability-weighted average for the severance payments in each of the states, hiring and firing, and sector i. The first bracketed portion corresponds to the severance payment for the firing state and the second to that for the hiring states, which are weighted by π_H and π_F, the probabilities of being in a hiring (H) or in a firing (F) state of the economy, respectively. The severance payment in each of the bracketed sections for sector i is calculated by multiplying a time-invariant sector-specific and state-contingent firing probability, $\lambda_{i,\text{state}}(X)$; by the number of workers in a specific tenure group (N_X); and by the mandated severance payment that will have to be paid to employees in that group if they are fired, $\text{sp}(X)$. X denotes the tenure group. To calculate this firing probability we used the average employment reduction by tenure group in each possible state (hiring and firing), and when employment grew we assumed zero variation. Because of this, we obtained a constant probability across the whole period that was different across sectors, tenure groups, and states. Data on the structure of tenure groups and employment changes by sector come directly from the Quarterly Survey of Wages and Salaries (QSWS).[4]

Figure 2.2 shows the evolution of $E(\text{sp})$ for the period 1986–1996 as a percentage of total wages. Note that we are fixing the sector-specific firing probability, so, in this aggregate, changes may only be attributed to changes in the employment share of different sectors and changes in legislation. The first large fall in the index is at the end of 1991, and it reflects the reduction in the mandated severance payment schedule. Further changes are related to increases in the share of short-tenure groups. Changes observed in June 1995 coincide with a further reduction in mandated severance payments, while the increase in August 1998 coincides with an increase in these payments. On average, reserves that firms had to maintain for severance payments were reduced from 16 percent of the wage bill to around 8 percent after the reforms.[5]

4. The survey includes a sample of workers per firm, from which we calculate the firm tenure structure. N_x is calculated with this structure and total firm employment. The characteristics of the QSWS will be described presently.

5. Figure 2.2 also shows an "adjusted" $E(\text{sp})$ for the period 1992–1995. The increase in the calculated $E(\text{sp})$ between 1992 and 1995 is related to an undersampling of newer firms. During those years the sample was not renewed, so only "deaths" were registered. As no new firms entered the sample, older firms, which tend to have older workers, are overrepresented. This implies a tenure structure biased toward older workers, therefore increasing the $E(\text{sp})$. In the calculation of the employment series this problem was tackled through expansion factors that weighted the original data in order to take into account sample changes in the structure of firms by size.

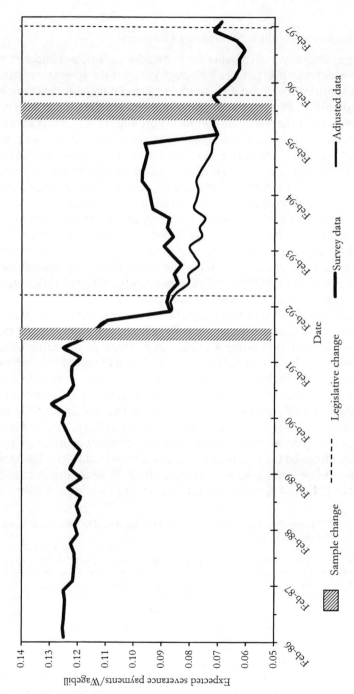

Fig. 2.2 Expected severance payments as a percentage of total wages, 1986–1996

2.2.2   Reducing Rigidities: Temporary Contracts

One possible way of bypassing the large adjustment costs imposed by employment protection policies is through lobbying the government to introduce short-term or temporary contracts. Temporary contracts were introduced in 1970. Firms required prior authorization from the Ministry of Labor in order to use them, and contracts were allowed under very specific circumstances. In practice, the high administrative costs this process implied restricted their use heavily. As shown in table 2.3, between 1986 and 1990, around 20 percent of workers in formal firms were under temporary contracts. Most of them carried full social benefits but had no employment protection clauses (*contratos sujetos a modalidad*), and important proportions of temporary workers were probationary-period workers. During the short-lived populist boom of 1987, in the midst of a period of extreme job protection, firms were allowed to hire using short-term temporary contracts through an emergency employment program (*Programa Ocupacional de Emergencia,* or PROEM). These contracts, which could last up to a year, were used mainly by large formal firms.

In August 1991, with the first wave of labor reforms, red tape for the use of fixed-term contracts was significantly reduced, and the reasons that could be used to justify hiring a worker under this type of contract were increased. The Ministry of Labor confined its role to record keeping and charging a fee for each contract. In general, in contexts of restrictive job protection regulations the output elasticity of temporary contracts is larger than that of permanent contracts, given that usually they do not carry firing costs (Bentolila and Saint-Paul 1992). In Peru, despite the reduction in firing costs for new workers under permanent contract in 1991, firms still preferred the now easier-to-use temporary contracts. The share of workers under these contracts increased from 20 percent in 1991 to 31 percent in 1992, and most of formal private employment growth observed

Table 2.3	Metropolitan Lima: Structure of Total Private Formal Salaried Employment, 1986–1997 (%)									
	1986	1987	1989	1990	1991	1992	1993	1994	1995	199
Total	100.0	100.0	100.0	100.0	100.0	100.0	100.0	100.0	100.0	100.
Permanent	80.7	82.1	82.9	80.8	80.1	68.6	67.9	64.8	59.8	56.
Temporary	19.3	17.9	17.1	19.2	19.9	31.4	32.1	35.2	40.2	44.
Fixed-term contract	19.3	17.7	14.3	19.2	19.6	30.0	29.8	33.3	39.4	39.
Youth contracts	0.0	0.1	0.0	0.0	0.3	0.0	0.4	0.0	0.3	2.
Probationary period	—	—	2.7	—	—	1.4	1.9	1.9	0.5	1.

Source: Encuesta de Hogares del MTPS 1986–1995, Encuesta Nacional de Hogares del INEI 1997.

Note: Not all the surveys between 1986 and 1997 allow the separation between workers under fixed-term contracts and those under probationary periods. Dashes indicate that there was no probationary perio in those years.

during the 1990s was explained by temporary contracts. Moreover, even after the elimination of the two-tier system in 1995 with the elimination of job stability for all workers, as well as an additional reduction in severance payments, temporary contracts continued growing, covering 44 percent of private formal wage employment in 1997.[6] This could be explained by the fact that firing costs for permanent workers, even if smaller than before, are still high or that firms may be reluctant to hire workers as permanent employees because they fear a setback in the progress toward flexibility. In fact, a change in the severance payments schedule in 1997 implied an increase in firing costs.[7] In our estimations we cannot distinguish permanent from temporary contracts; however, the lower administrative costs of using temporary contracts should imply a larger output elasticity after the reforms.

2.2.3   Nonwage Costs

In Peru an important source of public finance is payroll taxation. This burden has been heavily criticized, mainly along the lines that these contributions increase labor costs, reduce competitiveness, and have possible negative effects over employment. Peru has a complicated and unstable structure of nonwage labor costs, a description of which follows.

- *Public and private retirement plan payments.* Between 1986 and 1993, the employer had to pay to the public pension agency, the Instituto Peruano de Seguridad Social (IPSS), a contribution of 6 percent of the employee's wage, while the employee had to pay 3 percent. Poor and corrupt management, increasing numbers of retirees, and inflation led to the near collapse of the pay-as-you-go public system. In 1993, a private pension system was created, with individually held accounts managed by institutions called the Administradoras de Fondos de Pensiones (AFPs). Currently, both pension systems coexist. In 1995, after a few changes, the rate was set at a total of 11 percent in both systems, and the entire contribution had to be paid by the employee.[8]
- *Health plan payments.* The public health plan offered by IPSS is still the only option for workers. The total contribution rate has been fixed at 9 percent during the last few years. However, its composition with respect to employers and employees has changed: Before 1995 the em-

---

6. By 1997, according to Household Survey data, 316,000 private salaried workers in Lima had signed temporary contracts. According to the administrative records of the Ministry of Labor, 434,000 new contracts were signed that year. As a percentage of the total employment in Lima (i.e., including public workers and the informal sector), the share of workers under this type of contract reached 24 percent.

7. A surprisingly large output elasticity of temporary contracts was also observed in Spain in 1986, when the economy picked up and restrictions for the use of temporary contracts had been lifted, and almost all job creation was explained by this type of contract. Between 1987 and 1990, the share of temporary contracts increased from 15 percent to 32 percent.

8. See details in table 2A.1.

ployer had to pay 6 percent and the employee had to pay 3 percent. Currently, the employer must pay the entire contribution fee.

- *Accident insurance.* The employer is required to pay a accident insurance for his blue-collar workers. The amount is calculated as a rate of the employee's salary. This rate varies depending on the level of risk involved in the job and averages around 2 percent.
- *Manufacturing training fund (SENATI).* This is paid by the employers of firms in manufacturing industries. Initially it was set at 1.5 percent of the worker's income. In 1995, it was reduced to 1.25 percent, in 1996 to 1 percent, and in 1997 to 0.75 percent.
- *National Housing Fund (FONAVI).* Originally created as a contribution to workers' housing needs in the late 1970s, the National Housing Fund (FONAVI) rapidly resulted in a costly payroll tax, mainly due to inefficient and faulty management of collected funds.[9] Up to 1988, the FONAVI contribution paid by the employer was 4 percent of the employee's wage, while the employee's rate was 0.5 percent, and the maximum taxable wage was set at eight tax units (UITs). In November of that year, the employer's contribution rate was increased to 5 percent and the employee's rate to 1 percent. In May of 1991 the employer's rate was set at 8 percent, while the employee's rate remained unchanged, raising the total contribution to 9 percent and further widening the gap between the amount paid by the employer and the amount received by the employee. In January 1993 the employer's contribution responsibilities were abolished altogether, and the employee's rate was set at 9 percent. Even though the total contribution rate remained constant (at 9 percent), the maximum effective taxable wage was abolished, which might have increased the effective rate. Ten months later, due to harsh political pressures, the employee's contribution rate was diminished to 3 percent and the employer's rate was increased to 6 percent. In August of 1995 the employee's contribution was abolished and the employer's contribution rate was set at 9 percent. Finally, in January of 1997, the total contribution was reduced to 7 percent (paid completely by the employer), but the Christmas and holiday bonuses of a monthly salary were included in the taxable base.
- *Individual savings account (Compensación por Tiempo de Servicios, or CTS).* This is additional wage paid by the employer to the employee for every year of worker tenure. Prior to January 1991, the employer paid a maximum bonus of ten minimum wages if the employee's wage

9. As a result of this, FONAVI became an important issue in political discussion, as opposition parties used it as justification to attack the government, while the latter constantly shifted the FONAVI rate back and forth between employers or employees and altered its total level, to satisfy political and financing needs. Throughout the document, when talking about the payroll tax, we refer to this contribution.

was higher than that amount. Employers were allowed to keep those funds until an employee left the firm (the only obligation being to register it in the firm's balance sheet as a liability). The system failed due to employers' lack of compliance in actually keeping these bonuses for workers. In actuality, when a worker was fired, the payment of this bonus worked as an additional firing cost. Since January 1991 the employer has had to deposit 50 percent of an employee's monthly salary in an individual account in the worker's name in a commercial bank on May and November of each year.

- *Christmas and national holiday bonuses.* On December 1989, it became obligatory for the employer to pay two additional months' wages to his employees (on July and December of each year). However, this was already a common practice before the law was established, especially in medium-sized and large firms. In the public sector, these bonuses had been paid regularly to employees for several years, since the mid-1980s, but the amount varied.

Figure 2.3 shows the evolution of the effective rate paid by a firm in the case of a blue-collar worker who is affiliated to a public pension plan. To calculate the nonwage costs' effective rate it was necessary to estimate each of the nonwage costs just listed. The main difficulty in the estimation was to combine the effect of the different rates with the maximum and minimum taxable bases, so we calculated each of the nonwage costs separately and then summed them together. Most of the sources of change are related to cap changes in the tenure bonus and changes in the payroll tax rate. In

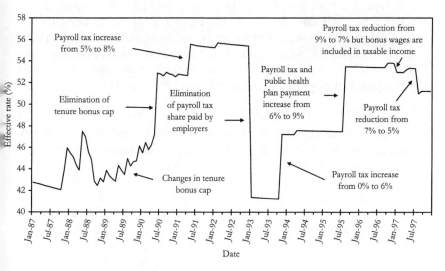

Fig. 2.3   Evolution of nonwage costs paid by employers

addition, on several occasions different rates were changed in such a way that the total employer contribution remained unaltered. This is the variable used later in the labor demand estimations.

2.3   Evidence of the Effect of Labor Laws on Labor Demand

We can identify at least three main changes in labor legislation during the period 1986–1996 that had an effect on labor demand: changes in severance payments and job stability, changes in nonwage costs, and changes in the use of temporary contracts. The difficulty lies in isolating these changes from the effect of the cycle over labor demand. In the Peruvian case in this particular period, even if it is very probable that the legislative changes had a large impact on the level and structure of demand, the economy underwent a very drastic process of structural adjustment (see Saavedra 1996a,b). The purpose of this section is to estimate labor demand functions and assess the effect of changes in two specific regulations in Peru: firing costs and nonwage costs. In 1991, absolute job stability was eliminated for new hires, and in 1995, after the constitutional change of 1993, job stability was totally abolished. Severance payments rules were simplified, and the severance profile was made less steep. This, together with the reduction in red tape for the use of temporary contracts, implied a drastic reduction in firing costs in two steps, one in 1991 and the second in 1995. On the other hand, nonwage costs were increased in 1987 and in 1990, first due to changes in caps and minimums in several contributions, and later through the increase in FONAVI, a plain payroll tax, and the pension contribution. We limit the analysis to labor demand for the formal sector, which is precisely the one affected by regulations. However, being formal (i.e., being in the universe of this study) is endogenous. One of the first consequences of high firing and nonwage costs in a low-productivity economy is informality, so we start the analysis by looking at how informal and formal salaried employment adjusted between 1986 and 1996.

2.3.1   Informality, the First Way to Avoid Regulations

Firms and workers adjust to the labor market regulatory framework through multiple mechanisms. Job protection legislation and severance payments constitute firing costs that increase uncertainty about the actual costs of labor and render labor a quasi-fixed factor. Given the regulatory framework that prevailed until 1991, Peruvian firms devised ways to reduce the costs of adjusting labor to their desired levels. The first adjustment mechanism was—and for many firms still is—the informal sector. Informality is conceptualized here as a state chosen by firms and workers depending on a cost-benefit analysis. Many firms, typically small ones, operate totally underground, fire and hire at will, and do not pay any kind of socially mandated benefits. In most of these cases, their productivity is too

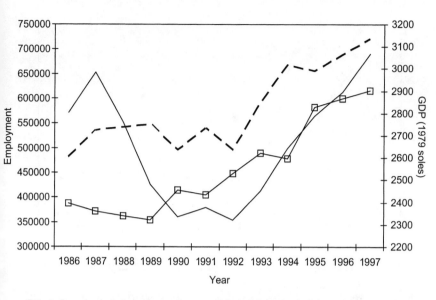

Fig. 2.4   Metropolitan Lima: Private formal and informal salaried employment and GDP, 1986–1997

Source: INEI, Encuesta de Hogares del MTPS 1986–1995, Encuesta Nacional de Hogares del INEI 1997.

low for them to afford to pay any kind of benefits. Both for the firm and for the worker, any kind of mandated benefit is a luxury. However, many firms operate in the gray area. In fact, there is a continuum of firms with different levels of productivity, and there is a cutoff point at which the firm decides that it has to operate formally. The decision to become formal entails a cost-benefit analysis. Firms evaluate the costs and benefits of formality (mandated benefits compliance and a larger volume of business, respectively) against the costs and benefits of informality (fines adjusted by the probability of being caught and savings in mandated benefits and firing costs, respectively).

Given changes in the regulatory framework, the balance in this cost-benefit analysis determines the evolution of formal and informal salaried employment. We used data from household surveys and defined formal salaried workers as those who show signs of working in a firm that complies with regulations.[10] As shown in figure 2.4, salaried informal employment increased since 1987 throughout the period of analysis. However, employ-

---

10. Operationally, formal salaried workers were defined as those who had health insurance, had a retirement plan, or belonged to a union. An application of this definition is found in Saavedra and Chong (1999).

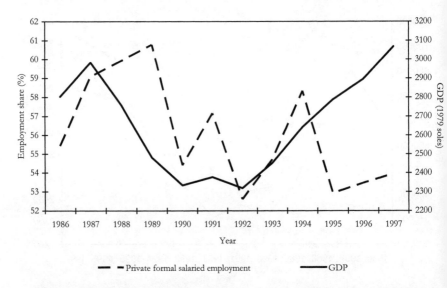

Fig. 2.5   Metropolitan Lima: Share of private formal salaried employment in total private salaried employment and GDP, 1986–1997 (percentage)
Source: INEI, Encuesta de Hogares del MTPS 1986–1995, Encuesta Nacional de Hogares del INEI 1997.

ment among formal salaried workers was more responsive to the business cycle. It fell slightly between 1987 and 1992 and then increased rapidly since 1993. It could be argued that the rigidities in labor legislation in the 1980s prevented formal employment from falling dramatically. Conversely, the more flexible environment of the 1990s allowed for a quick employment expansion. Looking at the shares of formal and informal salaried employment in total private salaried employment (figure 2.5), it is clear that the former fell sharply during the downturn and tended to increase timidly as output bounced back during the 1990s after the launching of the reforms.

2.3.2   Formal Labor Demand Estimations

Using household surveys, we only have annual data for ten years, so a formal analysis of the labor demand is not possible. Notwithstanding, it seems to be clear that, ceteris paribus, as the volume of business falls (as in 1988–1992) the costs of operating formally increase and outweigh the benefits, so more firms go underground, or more new firms decide to launch operations informally rather than formally. As of 1993, output rose again, and so did productivity; consequently, more firms should have found it profitable to operate formally. But to complicate matters, firms' decisions involve increasing or decreasing the share of their payroll that goes underground or not, and other developments also affect this decision. Reductions in firing costs could have had a positive effect on formal labor demand, but at the same time, nonwage labor costs increased, with the opposite effect over this demand.

In what follows, and with the purpose of analyzing formally the effects of these changes, using the quarterly data sets for the formal sector described next, we first perform static estimations of the labor demand at the sector level and at the firm level.[11] We show the results of different specifications, in which we analyze elasticity of wages, payroll contributions—taxes, health insurance, and pension and other contributions—and expected severance payments.

The Data

The main data source used to estimate static and dynamic labor demand functions for formal firms in Lima was the Quarterly Survey of Wages and Salaries (QSWS) conducted by the Ministry of Labor. The QSWS is a quarterly firm survey that collects pooled data on both the firm and individual worker levels. This survey collects approximately 600 private firms of ten or more workers in Metropolitan Lima (composed of the province of Lima and the constitutional province of Callao) and 8,000 workers from the same firms. The survey is divided into two sections. Part A provides firm-specific information that covers the gross wage bill divided into wage and nonwage costs, levels of employment, and presence of collective bargaining, each specified by category of employment (blue collar, white collar, and executive) and standardized international industrial code (SIIC). In Part B, five to twenty-five workers (according to the size of firm) from each firm are surveyed at random, thus providing individual-level information on age, gender, tenure, salary breakdown, and specific occupation, as well as employment category.

In 1986 the method of sample selection changed from a univariate distribution to one stratified across ten categories of economic sector and four categories of firm size.[12] This methodology ensures adequate representation of each cross section of firm sectors and sizes—totaling forty-eight groups of firms, among which a multivariate probability distribution is determined according to number of firms in each group, while minimizing total wage variance per group with standard optimal sampling methods.[13]

---

11. Using only formal firms—registered in the Ministry of Labor data sets—generates a selection bias for which we do not control.

12. The survey has been conducted since 1957, although at several points it has undergone important modifications. Due to the significance of modifications, data prior to 1986 are inappropriate for analytical comparisons with those of later periods. Furthermore, only hard copy tabulations of data from this period have been preserved.

13. Firms are divided into four size categories: 10–49 workers, 50–99, 100–499, and 500 or more. The economic sectors are agriculture, mining, manufacture of consumption goods, manufacture of intermediate and capital goods, utilities, construction, wholesale trade, retail trade, financial activities, insurance and real estate, transportation and communications, and services. Agricultural firms have been dropped from the sample.

Thus, the extent of survey information useful for analysis is restricted to the period 1986–1997, which comprises ten years of bimonthly data and quarterly data since 1996, representing a total of sixty-eight distinct points in time.[14]

During 1986 to 1997 there were three different samplings of firms, from the Ministry of Labor's "*Hoja de Resumen de Planillas*" (HRP) of 1986, 1990, and 1994. The HRPs are summary payroll forms that all private formal firms are legally required to present annually. The degree of compliance is high among large firms, and the probability of compliance increases with size. Total number of sampled firms per period remains around 500, but they were not replaced if the firm died or did not report during that period. Therefore, for the economic-sector estimations, we pool the data of all the firms in each sector and use expansion factors to calculate sector-level aggregates; we also use part B of the survey to calculate tenure structures by sector, which we then use for constructing the expected severance payment variable. With these, we build a pseudo panel at the sector level with fifty-six time points per sector. In addition to this firm database, we constructed time series of gross domestic product (GDP), which varied yearly by economic sector. To make the sector pseudo panel comparable to the firm-level panel described, we divide it into three pseudo subpanels according to the sampling dates, 1987–1990, 1991–1994, and 1995–1997. Although they roughly coincide with three distinct periods in terms of labor legislation (recall that the two main laws were enacted in November 1991 and July 1995) there is variability within periods, particularly regarding payroll contributions.

Figure 2.6 shows the evolution of employment of formal firms in Lima throughout the period. The gray bars show the periods in which the sample changed. Using the same data set, we constructed a sample of workers for each sector in each period. From that sample, we analyzed some basic worker characteristics. The results confirm the trends observed from household survey data. In particular, it is found that in the 1990s the proportion of younger workers increases, there is a slight increase in the share of female employment, and average tenure falls.

Finally, using this 1986–1997 QSWS survey data, we constructed three firm-level panels comprising all firms that remain in the sample set throughout the subperiods. The panels were constructed according to the

---

14. Data from all surveys prior to 1991 were stored only on eight-inch diskettes formatted with the antiquated XENIX system, which required the use of a Radio Shack TRS-16B computer and an eight-inch hard drive. None of those machines in Peru were in operating condition. The data were translated into a readable format by a software company based in Indianapolis, and the information was processed in order to recover the shape of the original databases. Only a few internal documents from the Ministry of Labor prior to 1990 describing the data existed. Fortunately, the survey did not undergo any methodological changes during that period, according to several current and former employers of the Direccion Nacional de Empleo y Formación Profesional (DNEFP) that were interviewed.

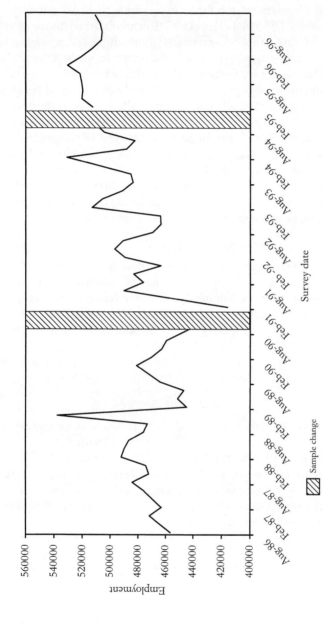

Fig. 2.6 Metropolitan Lima: Total employment in formal firms of more than ten workers

Source: Encuesta de Sueldos y Salarios del MTPS 1986–1996.

sampling periods and identify firms that remained in the survey throughout each subperiod. The first panel is 1987–1990, and all firms were drawn
from the 1985 summary payroll forms of formal firms registered with the
Ministry of Labor. The panel comprises 389 firms observed during twenty
quarters. The second panel goes from 1991 through 1994, comprising 408
firms observed during twenty-four periods, drawn from the 1989 payroll
forms. These two panels are the largest due to the fact that firms were never
resampled from the total population of registered firms during this period.
In other words, the list of panel observations is altered only by the death of
firms that were originally sampled, and thus its size is determined solely by
the mortality rate of those firms. In contrast, between 1995 and 1997, surveyed firms were resampled yearly from an updated sample set. Despite
this greater variation in sampled observations, our third panel is only
slightly smaller than its earlier counterpart (341 firms), largely because
both the population (from payroll forms) and sample populations of surveyed firms have been considerably enlarged in recent years.[15]

Econometric Labor Demand Specifications

The objective here is to specify a static labor demand function from
which the impact of different regulations may be inferred. We are mainly
interested in analyzing the effect of payroll contributions—taxes on wages
and social security payments—and severance payments on labor demand.
With this objective, we will specify a static labor demand function following Hamermesh (1993).

The equations to be estimated will be derived first from a profit-
maximizing framework. Consider the following firm's profit function:

(1) $$\pi = F(K, L) - E(w)L - rK,$$

where K is capital, L is labor, and w and r are the cost of labor and capital,
respectively. $E(w)$, which is the expected cost of labor, is used in order to account for the expected costs the firm would incur in the event of layoffs.
This is important because w in the firm's maximization problem is not fully
represented by the observed salaries, making it necessary to add other factors to appropriately represent the relevant cost per worker (following the
distinction made in Hamermesh 1993).

The problem of the firm is to choose (K, L) such that it maximizes profit.

(2) $$\max[F(K, L) - E(w)L - rK],$$

15. We attempted the construction of a panel of all firms that appeared continuously in the
survey data between 1990 and 1997. This panel spanning both subperiods is by far the smallest, and, given its obvious biases, we will not include it in our estimations. On account of the
fact that in 1995 a new sample of firms was selected (largely at random) from an updated payroll census for the first time since 1991, very few firms from the 1991–1994 period are resampled in 1995 and reappear continuously in the 1995–1997 sample populations.

where

(3) $$E(w) = w + p + E(\text{sp}),$$

where w is the wage paid to the employee, p is all payroll contributions paid by the firm, and $E(\text{sp})$ is a measure of the expected severance payments as described in section 2.2.

A wide variety of functional forms have been developed in the past decade, although the derived factor demand functions are still analyzed under the same optimizing behavior (Merrilees 1982). The question remains as to which flexible production function will best suit our hypothesis testing. Here we use one of the approaches proposed in Hamermesh (1986) and estimate a simple and flexible functional form without any imposition of the restrictions that factor demand must be homogeneous of degree zero in all factor prices:

(4) $$\ln L_i = a + \sum b_j \ln E(w_j)_i + c \ln Y_i + \beta \cdot Z_i,$$

where j indicates the factor, i indicates the sector or the firm, w_j corresponds to two production factor prices, w and r, and Z_i is a vector of other explanatory variables at the sector or firm level. As mentioned by Hamermesh (1993), equation (4) should be viewed as part of a complete system of factor-demand equations, but given that we do not have data on all factors it is not possible to estimate a complete system.

Our initial objective is to see the effect of changes in labor regulations over labor demand in the formal sector of the economy. We analyze how labor cost elasticity changes as we add payroll contributions and the expected severance payment in a marginal productivity condition. We do not attempt to estimate labor supply relationships under the plausible assumption that the labor supply to the formal sector, in an economy with a very large informal sector, tends to be nearly horizontal. We estimate two variants of equation (4) that measure the effects of the different components of labor costs over employment:

(5) $$\ln L_i = a + b_1 \ln w_i + b_2 \ln E(\text{sp})_i + c \ln Y_i + \beta \cdot Z_i$$

(5′) $$\ln L_i = a + b_1 \ln(w_i + p_i) + b_2 \ln E(\text{sp})_i + c \ln Y_i + \beta \cdot Z_i$$

In equation (5) we include the average wage of the sector or firm and the expected severance payment as the two main labor costs. In equation (5′) we add to the average wage the average nonwage costs (public and private pension contributions, health contributions, accident insurance, etc.; see section 2.2.3) mandated by law that the employer had to pay in addition to the wage. These contributions are added to the salary because they are monthly charges paid by the employer, in contrast to the expected severance payment, which depends on the tenure structure of the employees.

Additionally, we estimate labor demand functions with sector-aggregated data and firm-level data with our three panels of the Peruvian firms (1987–1990, 1991–1994, and 1995–1997).[16] Following a modified version of Bentolila and Saint-Paul (1992), the econometric specification of labor demand is

$$(6) \quad \ln L_{i,t} = a + b_1 \ln[w_{i,t} + p_{i,t}] + b_2 \ln E(\text{sp})_{i,t} + c \ln \hat{Y}_{t-L} + d \ln \hat{L}_{i,t-L}$$
$$+ e \ln \hat{L}_{i,t-L} \cdot \ln E(\text{sp})_{i,t} + \delta t + \beta Z_{i,t} + \varepsilon_{i,t},$$

where wages (w) and payroll taxes (p) represent the labor costs, $E(\text{sp})$ represents the expected severance payments, $\hat{Y}$ is the quarterly output by economic sector as a proxy of firm output—instrumentalized with the lag—$\hat{L}_{t-L}$ is the number of workers in the previous period instrumentalized with the rolling regressions technique and using one- to four-period lagged employment, and t is a time trend.

Lagged employment is also included to measure the speed of adjustment to changes in output. The coefficient of this variable can lie between zero and 1; a large value is associated with a slower speed of adjustment, and a small value implies that the adjustment is instantaneous.

Finally, following Burgess and Dolado (1989), we try to measure the adjustment costs of changes in employment by including the interaction between lagged employment and expected severance payment as the main firing costs. The coefficient of this interaction measures whether there are increasing marginal costs of changing employment, and therefore a positive coefficient is expected.

Empirical Results

Using quarterly data for ten economic sectors observed between 1987 and 1997, we estimated the constant output labor demand wage elasticity for equations (5) and (5′).[17] As can be observed in table 2.4, all the components of $E(w)$ from equation (3) are significant and have the expected negative sign when included individually. The estimate of –0.19 for the labor demand wage elasticity (in the model in which labor costs included wages plus payroll contributions [b]) lies within the typical range for static labor demands using sector data (Hamermesh 1986, 1993).[18]

16. As mentioned before, the periods roughly coincide with three different legislation regimes.
17. This estimation is only done for the sector pseudo panel and not for the firms panel because we cannot generate a panel for the whole time period (1987–1997) given the structure of the survey.
18. As a sensitivity test, we also carry out a constant elasticity of substitution (CES) estimation, which included a proxy of the price of capital. The results of the CES specification were an elasticity of –0.13 for the wage and payroll cost variable and a positive elasticity for the price of capital. The latter reflects the positive cross-price elasticity of demand due to substitutability of labor for capital in production. Finally, the coefficient for the expected severance payment was –0.221.

Table 2.4   **Constant Output Labor Demand Estimation: Sector-Level Estimation (1987–1997)**

	Model 6 with Fixed Effects	Model 6' with Fixed Effects
Constant	13.528***	13.701***
	(0.572)	(0.620)
$\ln(w)$	–0.174*	
	(0.096)	
$\ln(w + p)$		–0.191*
		(0.098)
$\ln[E(\text{sp})]$	–0.406***	–0.401**
	(0.060)	(0.060)
$\ln(Y)$	0.047**	0.047**
	(0.022)	(0.022)
Log likelihood	–183.22	–182.97
$\chi^2(9)$	1,083.01***	1,084.59***
No. of observations	504	504

Note: Standard errors in parentheses.
***Significant at the 1 percent level.
**Significant at the 5 percent level.
*Significant at the 10 percent level.

Moreover, as hypothesized, the coefficient of the average wage paid by the employer (b_1) is smaller by two points than the coefficient of the average wage plus all the payroll costs paid by the firm (b_1'). Therefore, as we include payroll taxes, the employment response to changes in labor costs increases. Additionally, we carried out an encompassing test on the model fit to select which specification should be used. We used a nonnested procedure and a Cox test for nonnested hypothesis (Greene 1997), and we were able to choose equation (5') where $\ln(w + p)$ is used as the correct set of regressors. The Cox test, in which the null hypothesis was that equation (5) contained the correct set of regressors, was rejected with a p-value of 0.000 (Cox statistic = 5.27). On the other hand, when the null was that equation (5') contained the correct set of regressors, we could not reject it at any significance level (Cox statistic = 3.56).

On the other hand, the coefficient of the expected severance payment, which varies across sectors and along time, also has the expected negative sign and is significant at the 99 percent level. This gives us evidence that the reduction in firing costs has a positive effect on employment level. Regarding the output elasticity, the coefficient for the whole period is around 0.05. This is a very small coefficient because in the models presented in table 2.4 we are including fixed effects by sector absorbing most of its variation— which is mainly across sectors rather than within. Specifically, when running the regressions without fixed effects the output elasticity is 0.17 and significant at the 99 percent level. We included the log of Y_i lagged six months, because the correlation between the errors and the actual output level that results from measurement error also biases ordinary least squares (OLS) output elasticity toward zero, and output measurement error can also bias the estimates of own-price elasticities. Griliches and Hausman (1986) demonstrate that when panel data are available, lead or lag of a variable subject to measurement error may be an appropriate instrumental variable. On the other hand, we are assuming that firms will not adjust immediately to changes in labor regulation, especially given the preexisting rigidities explained earlier.

Table 2.5 reports the results of equation (6), at both the sector and firm level, for the three subperiods determined by changes in the sample of firms: 1987–1990, 1991–1994, and 1995–1996. The first three columns are the results for the sectoral-level panels, and the last three columns show the results for the three firm-level panels. The variables used are the ones included in equation (5') plus the instrumentalized lagged employment[19] as a measure of adjustment costs, its interaction with the expected severance payment, and a time trend. For the estimations we apply generalized least squares and correct for serial correlation with a correlation coefficient specific for each panel when needed. For the sector panel we include and test for sector fixed effects.[20]

In four out of six cases wage elasticities are negative and significant. Unfortunately, there are two exceptions: first at the sector level, for the first period in which the coefficient is positive and significant, and finally in the second subperiod on the firm-level data. It should be noted that variations in the measured price of labor may be the spurious result of shifts in the distribution of employment among subaggregates with different labor costs, as mentioned by Hamermesh (1986). It is difficult, however, to determine the extent of these potential problems. Regarding the expected severance payment, we found that in the first subperiod this variable had a negative and significant coefficient, –0.89 at the sector level and –0.31 at the firm level. In the last subperiod, the coefficient reduces to –0.31 at the sector level and to –0.14 at the firm level, losing its significance in both cases.[21] This result may be related to the fact that after 1995 there was not enough time variability in firing costs within the subperiod to establish an effect over the employment level, or that the variance of within-firm tenure structures had already fallen, reducing differences in expected severance payments across firms. In the firm panel data set, the interaction of the

19. This variable is instrumentalized using the rolling regressions technique with one- to four-period lagged employment.

20. We did not include fixed effects for the firm-level estimations because both the expected severance payment and the GDP were available only at the sectoral, and not at the firm, level.

21. We were not able to get evidence of statistically significant differences between these and other parameters when comparing different subperiods, using Wald tests. The limitation of these tests is that we assume that they are independent random samples, which is not true, given that large firms are always included in the samples.

Table 2.5   Labor Demand Estimation Results for Panels at the Sector and Firm Level

	Sector Level			Firm Level		
	1987–1990	1991–1994	1995–1997[a]	1987–1990[a]	1991–1994	1995–1997
Constant	8.262***	15.395***	13.657***	0.470***	0.032	1.678***
	(1.570)	(2.217)	(3.688)	(0.166)	(0.085)	(0.507)
$\ln(w + p)$	0.560***	−0.322***	−0.298**	−0.030***	0.028***	−0.053*
	(0.203)	(0.115)	(0.127)	(0.008)	(0.005)	(0.028)
$\ln[E(\text{sp})]$	−0.892**	−0.575	−0.315	−0.310***	−0.041**	−0.140
	(0.363)	(0.422)	(0.632)	(0.034)	(0.017)	(0.101)
$\ln(Y)$[b]	0.014	0.113	0.094*	0.249***	0.008	0.085**
	(0.067)	(0.101)	(0.053)	(0.008)	(0.007)	(0.033)
$\ln(L_{t-1})$[b]	0.070	−0.194	0.077	0.736***	0.942***	0.616***
	(0.147)	(0.215)	(0.310)	(0.027)	(0.016)	(0.088)
$\ln(L_{t-1}) \cdot \ln[E(\text{sp})]$	0.042	0.063	0.015	0.071***	0.006	0.040*
	(0.027)	(0.045)	(0.060)	(0.006)	(0.004)	(0.021)
Log likelihood	210.55	139.45	199.31	2,460.04	2,484.48	−1,389.821
χ^2	12,547.95***	4,537.29***	3,353.03***	230,609.34***	186,386.48***	2,728.07***
No. of observations	189	189	117.000	4,753	6,491	1,722

Notes: Standard errors in parentheses. Sector level includes fixed effects. For firm level, a time trend was included. It was significant for periods 1987–1990 and 1991–1994, but not for 1995–1997.

[a]Corrected for serial correlation when tests for autocorrelation were significant with a correlation coefficient specific for each of the panels because of the presence of lagged dependent variables.

[b]Instrumentalized with lagged values using rolling equations.

***Significant at the 1 percent level.

**Significant at the 5 percent level.

*Significant at the 10 percent level.

expected severance payment with the lag of employment, a measure of the marginal cost of changing employment, has a small but significant and positive coefficient that decreases over time.

In the sector-level estimations, the output elasticity increases from the first to the last subperiod, as shown in table 2.5. During the first subperiod it is 0.014 and not significant, while in the last subperiod it is 0.09 and significant at the 90 percent level.[22] This increase in output elasticity may be related to the fact that labor reforms made it easier for firms to adjust to the desired employment levels given changes in output. Given the lower level of the tax on dismissals generated by the reduction in severance payments and the abolition of job stability rights, and also given the lower administrative costs of using temporary contracts, formal firms enjoyed more flexibility in adapting to output changes. As shown in section 2.2, available evidence suggests that most of the increase in formal employment during the period seems to have been concentrated in temporary contracts. Nevertheless, this fact might also introduce a bias in the estimates, as our data aggregate employment and wages for both permanent and temporary contracts, and the true estimate for each of them might be different. This problem is dragged to the firm-level panel estimations also.[23] Output coefficients in this case are only significant for the first subperiod. It should be noted, however, that the output variable is defined at the sectoral level, so the coefficient cannot be interpreted as firm-level employment elasticity.

The lagged employment was included to measure whether adjustment occurs instantaneously. As shown in table 2.5, the effect of this variable is only significant in the firm-level panels with coefficients ranging between 0.62 and 0.94. The magnitudes of these coefficients are within the range of the coefficients found by Abraham and Houseman (1994). Given that this is bimonthly data, a fall from 0.7 in the late 1980s to 0.6 in the mid-1990s would imply a reduction in the median adjustment—as, for example, from six to four quarters. The smaller coefficient in the last period could suggest an increase in the flexibility of the labor market that made it easier to reduce workforce levels during periods of slack demand as well as making employers more willing to hire during periods of rising demand. The speed of adjustment is, however, much lower than the one observed in the United States as reported by Abraham and Houseman (1994).[24]

22. It is important to mention that the coefficient is small because these models include sector fixed effects, but, despite this, in the last subperiod the coefficient is significant. If we exclude the fixed effects the coefficient is around 0.17.

23. Finally, appendix A tests for the implication that total labor demand should vary over the cycle due to employment composition changes (Bentolila and Saint-Paul 1992). When interacting the regressors with the cycle dummy to capture responses to the business cycles, the effects were not significant in practically all of our regressions, as shown in table 2A.1.

24. These authors report a speed of adjustment for the U.S. manufacturing sector of 0.383. On the other hand, the speeds of adjustment for West Germany, France, and Belgium were similar to our results: 0.837, 0.935, and 0.823, respectively.

2.4   Effects on Duration and Turnover of Changes in Labor Legislation

In this section, we analyze basic patterns of employment duration in Peru. We address the question of how long jobs last in Peru, if their duration is different in the formal and informal sectors and in different occupations, and if there are significant changes related to changes in labor legislation. Reductions in labor legislation–related firings costs—like the ones observed in Peru in the early 1990s through the reduction in severance payments and the abolition of job stability rights—typically accelerate the process of job creation and job destruction, therefore increasing turnover and reducing job duration, particularly in the formal sector. This is consistent with Lindbeck and Snower's (2002) insider-outsider theory, in which they maintain that labor turnover costs are important only in labor markets that are characterized by stringent job security legislation, such as Peru had. Moreover, the Peruvian reforms facilitated the use of temporary contracts. This had the effect of inducing firms to hire more during expansions and also to lay off more workers during downturns, which implies an increase in turnover. Using different data sets, we find a reduction in employment duration that cannot be explained only by cyclical movements of the economy. Using empirical hazards, we compare job duration and employment exit patterns of the self-employed with those of wage earners in the formal and informal sectors, and we also try to analyze the effects of certain regulations over duration patterns and their changes over time.

We first present trends in job duration using the series of ten annual household surveys from the Ministry of Labor. The main shortcoming of this source is that it only provides us with data on incomplete (elapsed) tenures. However, as long as we are precise about what we are measuring, we can exploit the fact that it allows us to analyze some time series and cross-sectional variations. Then we present empirical hazards and the results of exponential hazard models using data from the Living Standards Measurement Survey, which has the advantage of providing us with an (unfortunately) small sample of complete employment durations.

2.4.1   Analysis of Recent Trends Using Censored Data on Job Duration

We first analyze a repeated cross-sectional data set, the Annual Household Survey of the Ministry of Labor for all the years between 1986 and 1997, with the exception of 1988. This survey collects information regarding job characteristics and elapsed tenure in the case of the employed and time in unemployment for the unemployed. In the case of these surveys, the question is "How long have you been in your current job?" The data are recorded in years and months. The answer does not provide information on the length of a particular contract but only on a match between firm and employee. In the case of the self-employed, this question relates to the time performing the same occupation. All elapsed tenures refer to the main job.[25]

The data available from these surveys are reported as incomplete tenures. Following Lancaster (1990), we can assume that, given a probability density function (PDF) of complete tenures for a sample of the stock of employed workers, there is a related PDF for elapsed tenures. Moreover, it is possible to assume that for workers with some labor market history, the PDF of remaining duration is the same as for the elapsed duration. Therefore, the expected value of completed durations is double the expected value of incomplete (elapsed) durations. This will be true as long as the stationarity of the process is assured; that is, it may not be true for young workers starting their careers, women who enter and reenter the labor market, or older workers approaching retirement (Burgess and Rees 1996). Clearly, these data allow the analysis of the distribution of tenures among those employed at the time of the survey, but not the distributions of jobs.

Figures 2.7, 2.8, and 2.9 show mean elapsed tenures for several categories of prime-age workers (twenty-five to fifty-five years old). In general, it is clear that there is a downward trend in mean tenure. The trend is clear enough to dominate any possible cyclical fluctuations in tenure. During the sharp recession of 1988–1992, when an increase in mean tenure could be expected due to high separation rates and low hiring rates, mean tenure actually fell. Tenure rose only in 1991, when the Peruvian economy hit bottom.[26] In 1992–1993, right after the first changes in labor legislation, there was a sharp reduction in mean tenure. During the period 1994–1997 growth was fast, and hiring and separation rates increased, as usually happens in a booming economy, resulting in a further reduction in mean tenure. However, the 1997 figure was much lower than in 1986–1987, when the economy was also on an upswing. This gives an indication that the reduction in tenures may not be only a cyclical fluctuation but that it might be showing a secular trend.

The downward trend is clearer among prime-age males (figure 2.7). Given that the mean value of complete tenures should be about double the elapsed ones, in the mid-1990s mean completed tenure was about twelve years,[27] down from seventeen years in the mid-1980s. There is also a reduction in mean tenure among females (not shown), but it is harder to assume a stationary process in this case. First, because of maternity women enter and reenter the labor market, and second, during this period there is a rapid increase in labor force participation among women (Saavedra 1998).

25. In all surveys and years, the proportion of workers who declare having a second job fluctuates between 12 percent and 15 percent.
26. Tabulations not reported show that there is no clear trend in mean tenure among young workers.
27. Considering that the average schooling for males in Lima in this cohort is 8.5, and assuming retirement at 65, on average, each individual holds three jobs during his lifetime.

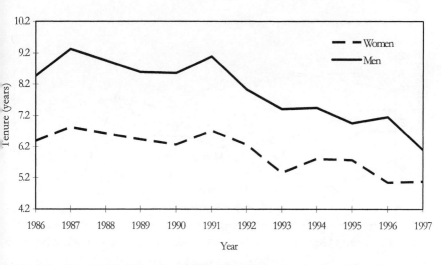

Fig. 2.7   Metropolitan Lima: Incomplete (elapsed) tenure of male and female workers aged twenty-five to fifty-five years, 1986–1997

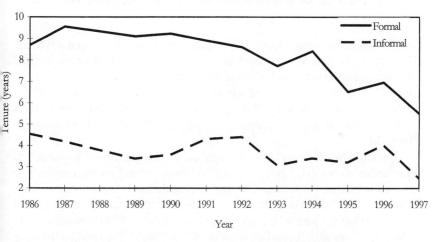

Fig. 2.8   Metropolitan Lima: Incomplete (elapsed) tenure of formal and informal male salaried private workers aged twenty-five to fifty-five years, 1986–1997

The differences in means between 1986 and 1991 and between 1991 and 1997 are statistically significant.

Figure 2.8 shows the evolution of mean elapsed tenures for prime-age male wage earners according to their formal or informal status. To define this status we use a legalistic definition: A worker works formally if he or she has health insurance or a pension plan or belongs to a union. The same definition is used in all the surveys. With this definition, the rate of formal

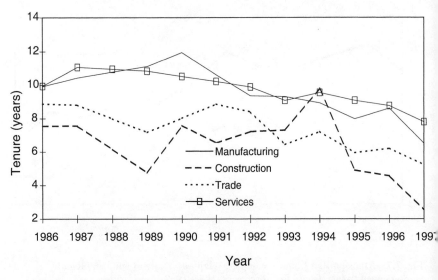

Fig. 2.9   Metropolitan Lima: Incomplete (elapsed) tenure of male formal workers in selected economic sectors aged twenty-five to fifty-five years, 1986–1997

employment fluctuated from 53 percent to 60 percent between 1986 and 1997. Several features are worth mentioning. Differences in mean elapsed tenures are large between formal and informal salaried workers. In fact, for formal salaried workers, mean tenure is between 9 and 6.8 years, while for informal workers, the mean fluctuates around 3. This difference is statistically significant in every year during the period 1986–1997, as shown in table 2.6.

The downward trend is more pronounced among formal workers,[28] in particular after 1991. Table 2.7 (panel A) shows tenure mean comparisons within formal and informal workers pairing different years. Within informal workers there is a significant reduction in mean tenure in the period 1986–1993 and a smaller and less significant reduction in the period 1993–1997. In the case of formal workers the fall is much larger and statistically significant in the postreforms period. From the results shown in panel B of table 2.7, it is clear that the differences in mean tenures between the formal and informal sectors have fallen during the 1990s. As discussed earlier, labor market reforms facilitated formal firms' adjustment to desired employment levels through temporary contracts and by reducing severance payments and eliminating job stability. In addition, unionization rates fell sharply, and union jobs have traditionally been held much longer than nonunion ones.

Figure 2.9 displays elapsed mean tenure calculations for prime-age for-

---

28. Tabulations not reported for self-employed workers show a downward trend among formal self-employed workers, but not among informal self-employed.

Table 2.6   **Tenure Mean Comparison Test**

Year	t-Test
1986	–7.377
1987	–8.400
1989	–10.678
1990	–10.291
1991	–7.715
1992	–7.676
1993	–9.492
1994	–9.416
1995	–7.444
1997	–6.285

Notes: H: (Informal worker tenure in period t – Formal worker tenure in period t) = 0. In all years the p-value was 0.000.

Table 2.7   **Mean Tenure Differences and Differences-in-Difference**

	1986–1993	1993–1997
Difference estimates		
Formal	–0.98	–2.23
	(0.55)	(0.57)
Informal	–1.45	–0.63
	(0.51)	(0.39)
Difference-in-difference estimates		
Formal – Informal	0.48	–1.60
	(0.75)	(0.67)

Notes: Differences of mean elapsed tenure for currently employed wage earners in Metropolitan Lima. Standard errors in parentheses.

mal male salaried workers in selected sectors. In the manufacturing sector, there is a smooth upward trend between 1988 and 1990, as the economy fell into a recession. Afterward, mean tenure falls as the economy picks up. We observe the same trend in services and, to a lesser extent, in trade. We also performed calculations controlling for age structure, and results were similar, which tends to suggest that these changes are not reflecting changes in the type of workers being fired but are an illustration of higher overall turnover.

Several factors may lie behind the reduction in tenure among formal prime-age workers. Before the reforms, high firing costs induced long employment spells among formal workers, but they also induced a lower rate of job creation in the formal sector, which also increased the relative size of the informal sector. The labor market reforms of 1991 facilitated an increase in hiring through temporary contracts and also reduced firing costs through a reduction in the severance payment and the elimination of job stability for new workers. The reforms were followed by an economic expansion that began in 1993 and increased employment, both formal and informal. The increase in net employment suggests that hirings were larger than layoffs. Layoffs in the private sector—also driven by trade liberalization and privatizations—were larger among older workers.[29] On one hand, the relative cost of firing a high-tenured worker fell tremendously with the reforms, in particular with the 1995 changes, when job stability was abolished for all workers. On the other hand, the increase in the demand for labor was larger for younger workers, who could more easily adapt to new technologies. Therefore, layoffs were biased toward older workers, while hirings were biased toward younger ones, with the effect of reducing mean tenures.

Table 2.8 shows mean job durations using elapsed-tenure data from several sources. The first two columns are from the same data sets discussed in the previous paragraphs, the third comes from the firm-level survey used in the labor demand analysis, and the rest are from the Living Standards Measurement Surveys (LSMS) described in the following section. All data sources confirm a reduction in mean tenure for formal workers during the 1990s.

2.4.2   The Duration of Employment Spells

The data used in this part of the analysis come from the LSMS.[30] The employment modules of the LSMS contain information about job characteristics like tenure in the current job, sector of activity, size of firm, whether contract was signed, union membership, type of employment (public/private/self-employed/wage earner), white- or blue-collar job, and so forth.[31] This information is collected regarding the job held in the previous seven days. In addition, individuals who are not working report whether they are looking for a job and number of weeks unemployed. The survey has another module that asks workers—either employed or unemployed—questions regarding their last job in the previous twelve months. If the worker has been unemployed during the last seven days, the survey asks for all the characteristics of the last job held during the previous year. If he or she has been working during the last seven days, the survey inquires if this job is the one held during the last seven days. If the job is different, the survey asks for the characteristics of that job. Two types of job spells are calculated with each survey. We use each survey separately and calculate right-censored spells for the sampled stock of employed workers and complete spells for the unemployed and for those who changed jobs during the last year. The detail of the duration data is as follows:

29. Saavedra (1998) shows that among workers older than 55, the employment-population ratio has not recovered with the employment growth observed in the 1990s and that unemployment has risen for this group of workers.
30. The LSMSs are a series of household surveys developed since 1985 under the technical and financial support of the World Bank and later implemented by Instituto Cuanto.
31. Sample sizes allow for the analysis of all these categories separately. As opposed to what is observed in developed economies, in Peru, as in other Latin American countries, self-employment rates reach 40 percent in urban areas.

Table 2.8   Mean Job Tenure: Comparing Different Data Sources

| | Household Survey | | Firm-Level Survey | LSMS | | | | | | | | |
| | | | | Self-Employed | | | Wage Earner | | | All | | |
	Formal Workers	All		Informal	Formal	All	Informal	Formal	All	Informal	Formal	All
1985	8.87	6.87		8.27	8.58	8.29	3.92	7.53	6.66	7.33	7.58	7.43
1986	8.97	7.28										
1987	9.41	7.00										
1989	9.70	6.97										
1990												
1991	9.45	7.45	10.08			7.64			7.07			7.34
1992	8.98	6.83	10.26									
1993	7.62	5.99	10.46									
1994	8.23	6.39	10.34	7.20	8.70	7.30	4.26	7.08	6.30	6.55	7.21	6.81
1995	7.48	5.85	7.44									
1996	6.11	5.74	6.93									
1997	6.63	5.11		7.14	5.89	7.14	3.6	5.89	5.22	6.3	5.89	6.15

Source: Encuesta de Hogares del MTPS 1986–1995, Encuesta Nacional de Hogares del INEI 1996–1997, Encuesta de Sueldos y Salarios del MTPS 1986–1996, Encuesta Nacional de Hogares sobre Nueles de Vida 1985, 1991, 1994 and 1997.

Notes: Household survey data for Metropolitan Lima, currently employed workers. Firm-level survey data for Metropolitan Lima, currently employed workers. Firm-level survey data for Metropolitan Lima, currently employed workers in firms of ten or more workers. LSMS data for Urban Peru, currently employed workers. Blank cells indicate that information is not available.

- We use right-censored spells for the stock of people currently working, using the question "How long have you been working as [occupation]?" (coded in weeks, months and years).[32]
- For those who declare that they have indeed changed jobs during the last twelve months, we construct two spells, a right-censored spell of less than twelve months and a complete previous spell. These data have two obvious biases. First, we have complete spells only for those who changed jobs during the last twelve months; if the current spell lasts more than that, we have no information about the previous spell. For these movers, we do not have information on possible unemployment periods between the two jobs. Second, for some workers who report a change in job, the change is within a firm. In those cases, we will not count that as a job change. We will isolate those cases by comparing all the job characteristics of the previous and current spells (occupation, sector, size of firm, public or private, etc.).
- We use complete job spell for those who are not currently employed and who answer positively to the question "Have you had a different job during the last twelve months?"[33]

The complete and incomplete employment spells that are constructed in our data sets are summarized in figure 2.10. According to the employment duration data for the years 1985 and 1994 from the LSMS, 78 percent of the job durations of 1985 are incomplete spells, while for the 1994 sample this figure is 86 percent.

We analyze the basic differences in job duration patterns using the LSMS employment duration data for the years 1985 and 1994, including both complete and incomplete employment spells. These spells are to be thought of as independent realizations of a random variable T with survivor function $\bar{F}(t)$. Using the complete and incomplete employment spells from the LSMS data, we use the Kaplan Meier estimator for the survivor function. Following Lancaster (1985), for homogeneous right-censored data the survivor function at t can be estimated by

$$(7) \qquad \hat{\bar{F}}(t) = \prod_{t(j)<t} (1 - \hat{\theta}_j), \qquad t \geq 0,$$

32. The question, as written in the questionnaire, does not look very precise. However, two elements allow us to recognize them as job spells. First, personnel in charge of the fieldwork and of the interviewer's training process maintain that they insisted that the duration reported as an answer to that question should be the length of time working in a specific occupation and in a specific firm. Second, the survey allows for a second check mechanism from a separate question: "What was your main occupation during the last twelve months? Was this the same as your occupation during the last seven days?" In this case, the interviewer manual indicates that even a change in position within a firm should be considered a job change. If the respondent answers that the job was different, then he or she will answer for the characteristics of that previous job.

33. Note that we only have spells for those people—current unemployed or out of the labor force—that had a job during the last twelve months. For those unemployed or inactive for more than that period, we do not have any information.

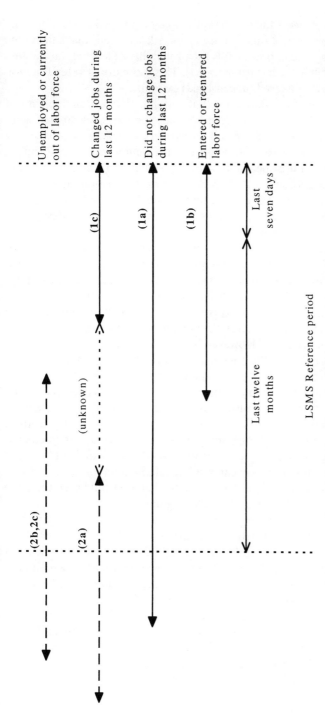

Fig. 2.10   Employment spells using the Peruvian LSMS: *1,* Right-censored job spells: for the currently employed, either (1a) people who didn't change jobs during the last year; (1b) newly employed entrants; (1c) people who changed jobs during the last year. 2, Complete job spells: (2a) currently employed that changed jobs during the last twelve months (this spell is the job held before the current one); (2b) unemployed workers whose unemployment spell is smaller than twelve months and held a job during the last twelve months; (2c) currently out of the labor force, that held a job during the last twelve months.

for $\hat{\theta}_j = n_j/r_j$, where n_j is the number of employment spells—possible only one—observed to end at time t, and r_j is the risk set (spells that end at time t plus those censored at time t). θ_t is the probability of leaving the employment state (i.e., it is the hazard at time t). This estimator is a step function with steps at each observed (uncensored) exit time.

A shortcoming of this data set is that with the observational scheme of the survey complete spells are registered only for workers who are unemployed or out of the labor force and for workers who changed jobs during the year prior to the survey. Therefore, complete employment spell tenures are available only for a specific type of individual. However, as shown in appendix C, there is a similarity between the hazard function calculated using only the complete spells and the hazard function estimated using only the incomplete (censored) spells—as if they were completed despite the possible biases of the censored data.

In addition, the empirical analysis assumes a stationary economic environment. This assumption, which implies that the numbers of jobs created and destroyed are independent of time, allows to use each survey as a photograph of the distribution of their hazards assuming they will not be affected by the passage of time. It is difficult to assume stationarity in the Peruvian case, in particular, given the implementation of a set of structural reforms in the early 1990s. However, if we analyze each survey separately (1985 and 1994), despite the huge macro shocks observed in the Peruvian economy, no clear pattern of steady increase in the rate of job creation has been observed in the years previous to the surveys. In fact, a typical variable that could be used to condition the hazard function to the different environments confronted by different cohorts at their entry to or exit from employment is the rate of unemployment. That variable has fluctuated around a steady mean of 8.5 percent since 1974. Still, it is difficult to assure that a stationarity assumption can hold in volatile economies like Peru, in particular in the case of employment spells when we would need the same data generation process for a relatively long time.

Monthly hazards for a sample of censored and complete spells allow us to investigate duration patterns at the early stages of a job. In most of the cases there are spikes at months three, six, and twelve, which (at least in part) may be a heaping effect. In this sense, it will be important to compare changes through time and between categories. At the time of the fieldwork of the 1985 survey, the probationary period lasted three years, after which workers acquired total job stability. However, the authorities had already announced their intention of giving workers job stability rights after the third month.[34] In fact, the hazard function calculated with 1985 data for spells that started after 1983 and before June 1986 (left panel of figure 2.11) shows a spike at the third month. It is possible that employers in the formal

---

34. The change was actually put into effect in June 1986.

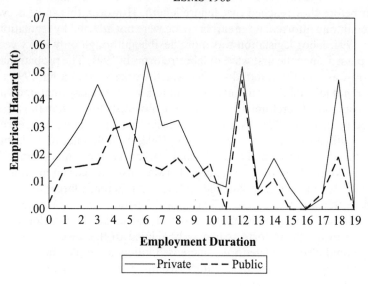

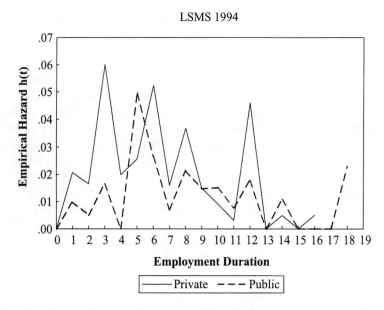

Fig. 2.11   Empirical hazards for formal public and private workers with less than three years of tenure (employment duration in months)

sector had already reacted to the announcement by dismissing workers right before they reached that tenure length. However, this spike is even larger among informal wage earners, who were not affected by regulations.

In 1994, labor legislation was more flexible, although only a few years had passed since the first wave of labor reforms in 1991. The probationary period was still three months, after which workers hired after 1991 obtained not job stability but only the right to a severance payment upon unjust dismissal. Therefore, firing costs were obviously lower than those perceived by firms in 1985. As shown in the right panel of figure 2.12, even if there is still a spike at the third month in 1994, the difference in the hazard functions between formal and informal workers is much smaller until the fourth month. Moreover, for tenures between five and eleven months the probability of leaving the state of employment is actually larger for formal workers than for informal ones. The hazard function for formal wage earners in 1994 is slightly above that for 1985. These higher hazards for formal workers in the postreform year may be related to the lower firing costs. They could also be related to an increased inflow of employment, but, as shown in section 2.2, inflows to informal employment were at least as great as those in the formal sector.

Note that in 1994 there still are large spikes in months 3 and 6. The spike in the third month may be explained by the fact that at that point workers acquired the right to a severance payment upon dismissal.[35] In addition, during this period employers still feared a possible reversal of the legislative changes and a return to a restrictive legislation, so many of them were still reluctant to hire workers under permanent contracts. They relied heavily on temporary contracts for short-term periods, usually three or six months, which in some cases were continually renewed.[36] There is a large spike at the twelfth month that may be related to the increase in the severance payment from zero to three months' wages after completing a year in the firm, so right before finishing that year firms had their last chance to dismiss the worker at zero cost. To summarize, there is an increase in the hazard function for formal wage earners between 1985 and 1994 and an increase in the hazard relative to that in the informal sector for workers with short durations.

An additional piece of evidence comes from the comparison between public and private formal wage earners. As shown in figure 2.11, there is a

35. The severance payment rule in 1994 stated that workers should get the equivalent of one month's salary per year worked if they had more than one year in the firm—with a minimum of three months' wages and a maximum of twelve months' wages. They acquired that right after the three-month probationary period, but the severance payments between the third and twelfth month were zero.

36. The spike in the third month observed in the informal sector may be a rounding effect or may also be some sort of "lighthouse effect."

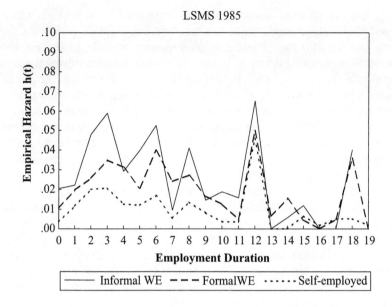

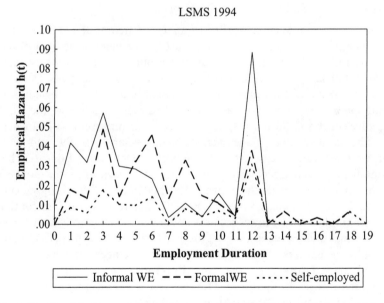

Fig. 2.12   Empirical hazards for wage earners and self-employed workers with less than three years of tenure (employment duration in months)

large spike in the third and sixth month for private formal workers, which is not observed for public workers. This could be consistent with firms' re-hiring workers for two consecutive probationary periods. In general, the probability of exiting the employment state is much higher during the first months in the private sector, something that is not observed in the public sector. Spikes are also observed at one year of tenure, which is consistent with the increase in severance payment at that point in accordance with legislation. In 1994, however, the spike is smaller in the private sector and much lower for the public sector. This is probably related to the reduction in severance payment in the case of the private sector and to the public-sector downsizing that started in 1992.

An interesting change is observed when we compare hazards of blue-collar and white-collar workers. Clearly, during the first ten months of em-ployment, hazards are higher for blue-collar workers, a result consistent with the common view that turnover is higher among those workers (see figure 2.13). In 1985, spikes at the third, sixth, and eighth months are very pronounced for blue-collar workers and are not observed among white-collars. However, after 1991, the spikes are observed in both groups, and, in general, differences in the hazard functions are much smaller.

Parametric Estimation of Hazard Functions

The sample employment spells just analyzed are not drawn from a ho-mogeneous population. In order to adjust for the heterogeneity of obser-vations and analyze patterns for different groups of workers, we estimate exponential hazard models using complete and incomplete spells. Table 2.9 shows the result of the estimation for three different years using employ-ment spells of self-employed and salaried workers. Age shows the usual negative effect over the hazard, suggesting a lower turnover for older work-ers. The negative effect of age over the hazard is larger in 1991 and 1994, consistent with an increase in turnover among older workers. Education has a significant negative coefficient, suggesting lower hazards for the more ed-ucated, particularly after the reforms launched in 1991. Surprisingly, occu-pational training increases hazards in 1991. The results also confirm that the self-employed have lower hazards and much longer employment spells than formal wage earners, and that these in turn have longer spells than in-formal wage earners, the category of control. The negative coefficient for formal salaried workers is larger after the reforms, suggesting a relative in-crease in turnover for this group. However, the standard error is also larger, so the change may not be statistically significant.

Table 2.10 presents an extended model that limits the sample to wage earners. The 1985 estimates show that having a temporary contract in-creases the hazard, suggesting higher turnover among these workers. This effect disappears by 1994, although temporary contracts were intensively used, which may be related to a smaller difference in status within a firm

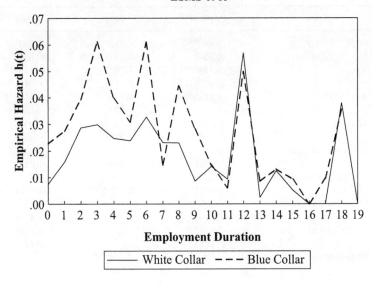

LSMS 1985

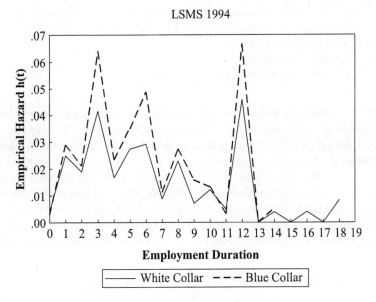

LSMS 1994

Fig. 2.13 Empirical hazards for wage earners (blue-collar and white-collar) with less than three years of tenure (employment duration in months)

Table 2.9   Exponential Hazard Model: Self-Employed and Wage Earners Sample

	1985	1991	1994
Male	−0.462***	−0.212**	−0.293***
	(0.064)	(0.103)	(0.092)
Age	−0.154***	−0.203***	−0.183***
	(0.012)	(0.019)	(0.017)
Age$^2 \cdot 10^{-2}$	0.111***	0.176***	0.143***
	(0.014)	(0.024)	(0.020)
Married	−0.348***	−0.351***	−0.048
	(0.074)	(0.124)	(0.107)
Years of schooling	−0.005	−0.054***	−0.023*
	(0.008)	(0.014)	(0.013)
Occupational training	0.073	0.480***	0.075
	(0.069)	(0.105)	(0.101)
Formal wage earner	−0.360***		−0.433***
	(0.094)		(0.138)
Self-employed	−0.979***		−0.976***
	(0.086)		(0.125)
Wage earner		0.704***	
		(0.114)	
No. of observations	6,144	3,570	4,561
Log likelihood	−4,461.59	−1,788.78	−2,656.25

Note: Standard errors in parentheses.
***Significant at the 1 percent level.
**Significant at the 5 percent level.
*Significant at the 10 percent level.

between temporary and permanent positions.[37] Having social security coverage, a clear indication of formality, reduces the hazard rate, a result consistent with the higher empirical hazards found before for informal workers. Surprisingly, belonging to a private-sector union increases the hazard; however, as the influence of unions vanishes through time, the estimate for this variable is not significant during the 1990s. We also find that married workers tend to have longer employment spells, and hazards are larger for blue-collar workers, as was suggested in the empirical hazard analysis. Limiting the sample only to private workers does not modify the result significantly.

2.5   Concluding Remarks

Peru is one of the countries that made more progress in terms of labor market deregulation in Latin America as part of a package of structural re-

37. Saavedra and Maruyama (1999) show that before the reforms temporary workers tended to be younger, less experienced, and less educated than permanent ones. These differences diminished sharply after the reforms. Also, there was a significant reduction in the earning premia of permanent workers.

Table 2.10   **Exponential Hazard Model: Wage Earners Sample**

	1985	1991	1994
Male	−0.702***	−0.293**	−0.517***
	(0.097)	(0.139)	(0.134)
Age	−0.175***	−0.222***	−0.176***
	(0.019)	(0.030)	(0.032)
Age$^2 \cdot 10^{-2}$	0.146***	0.224***	0.123***
	(0.024)	(0.037)	(0.041)
Married	−0.355***	−0.463***	−0.010
	(0.096)	(0.164)	(0.139)
Years of schooling	0.050***	0.010	0.029
	(0.012)	(0.022)	(0.019)
Occupational training	−0.049	0.544***	−0.068
	(0.088)	(0.139)	(0.145)
Union	0.350**	0.128	−0.303
	(0.137)	(0.197)	(0.272)
Social security	−1.180***	−1.212***	−1.219***
	(0.117)	(0.171)	(0.170)
Temporary contract	0.182*		0.157
	(0.104)		(0.143)
Public worker	−0.362**	−0.188	−0.484**
	(0.157)	(0.274)	(0.221)
Blue collar worker	0.393***	0.269*	0.288**
	(0.103)	(0.156)	(0.146)
Union · public worker	0.019	−0.107	0.535
	(0.200)	(0.338)	(0.376)
No. of observations	3,344	1,945	2,330
Log likelihood	−2,557.92	−1,039.92	−1,481.19
χ^2(df)	1,171.71	517.49	592.49
Prob > χ^2	0.00	0.00	0.00

Note: Standard errors in parentheses.
***Significant at the 1 percent level.
**Significant at the 5 percent level.
*Significant at the 10 percent level.

forms that took place in the 1990s. One of the most important changes in labor legislation was the large reduction in firing costs, through the reduction in the steepness of the tenure-related severance payment profile since 1991, the progressive abolition of job stability, and the facilities given to the use of temporary contracts. To analyze the effect of changes in firing costs we constructed an expected severance payment indicator as a proxy of the monetary resources firms have to reserve in order to cover firing costs. We broke down the data into state-contingent components of firing and hiring states of the economy. Within each state, the severance payment was calculated by sector using the evolution of the tenure structure of workers, an estimate of the firing probability for each tenure group, and the corresponding mandated severance payment structure. These probabilities were allowed to vary only across sectors and were kept constant through time in order to reduce endogeneity. A series of nonwage costs was calculated by simulating the total labor costs paid by the firm as a proportion of the wage for different wage levels. This was necessary because several mandated benefits and the payroll tax had absolute lower and upper bounds that were continuously changed. In many cases, most of the changes in the effective rate paid were due to changes in these limits.

To analyze the effects of changes in labor costs and firing over labor demand, we used a pseudo-panel data set of ten economic sectors observed bimonthly during the period 1987–1997 and three shorter panels of about 400 firms for the periods 1987–1990, 1991–1994, and 1995–1997. There are four main empirical findings. The wage plus payroll elasticity is –0.19 for the whole period of study when using the sectoral-level panel. This price elasticity is larger when the payroll taxes are added as part of the labor costs than in an estimation in which only wages are included, and we were able to test that the latter was the model that should be used. In most of the subperiods, at both the sector and firm levels, labor costs have a negative and significant effect over labor demand. Labor demand elasticities may not be stable as the economy opens up, as happened in Peru with the trade liberalization process that started in 1991. However, Saavedra and Torero (2001) do not find significant changes in elasticities when interacted with proxies for changes in the trade regime.

The second main finding is that the coefficient of our measure of firing costs, the expected severance payment, is negative and significant, showing that job security provisions have a negative effect on employment. We also found that its magnitude decreases after 1995. This result may be related to the fact that after that year there was not enough time variability in firing costs within the subperiod to establish an effect over the employment level, or to the fact that the variance of within-firm tenure structures had already fallen, reducing differences in expected severance payments across firms.

Third, the output elasticity increases in the last subperiod. This may be related to the fact that labor legislation reforms made it easier for firms to adjust to the desired employment levels given changes in output. The reduction in severance payments and the abolition of job stability rights may be interpreted as a lower level of the tax on dismissals. In addition, the lower administrative costs of using temporary contracts made it easier for formal firms to adapt to output changes. Finally, and in line with the previous result, we also find a speedier employment adjustment during the postreform period.

As discussed previously, labor market reforms facilitated formal firms' adjustment to desired employment levels, through temporary contracts and by reducing severance payments and eliminating job stability. This reduction in firing costs may have the effect of increasing turnover, as firms will tend to increase hirings during expansions and firings during contractions. Using censored employment spells from different data sets that span the period 1985–1997, we find evidence that mean tenure fell since 1992, roughly coinciding with the beginning of labor market legislation changes, suggesting an increase in turnover in the Peruvian labor market. The reduction in mean tenure may also be related to the recovery initiated in 1993, when salaried employment was created, both in the formal and informal sector. However, even if mean tenure among informal workers fell, among formal workers the fall is much larger and statistically significant in the post–labor reform period. This is showing, therefore, as mentioned by Lindbeck and Snower (2002), that the smaller a firm's labor turnover costs, the more profitable it is for the firm to stop bargaining with its current employees (insiders) and start bargaining with the new potential hires (outsiders) instead. The differences in mean tenures between the formal and informal sectors also fell significantly during the 1990s.

The LSMSs for 1985 and 1994 allowed us to construct censored employment spells for currently employed workers and complete employment spells for the unemployed and for workers that changed a job during the twelve-month period before each survey. With this data we calculated empirical hazards for several groups of workers. We found spikes at three months of tenure, corresponding to the time at which the probationary period ended among formal workers. However, these spikes are also found in the informal sector. Also, spikes were found at the sixth and twelfth months, probably related to renewal of short-term contracts—as a way to avoid job stability measures—and to avoid discrete jumps in the severance payment. After the reforms, there is an increase in the hazard function for formal wage earners and an increase with respect to the hazard function of informal-sector wage earners. Large hazards in the third and sixth months are observed among private formal workers, and not among public ones, consistent with private firms' using short-term contracts in order to avoid job stability. Hazards are always higher for blue-collar workers, but the difference between blue- and white-collar workers diminishes after the reforms. Finally, we performed parametric estimations of hazard estimations in order to control for demographic characteristics of workers. These confirmed the results of higher hazards for informal, younger, private, and blue-collar workers. Education has a significant negative coefficient, suggesting lower hazards for the more educated, particularly after the reforms launched in 1991. There is evidence of a small relative increase in turnover for formal wage earners after the reforms. Having a temporary contract increases the hazard, suggesting higher turnover among these workers. This effect disappears by 1994, although temporary contracts were intensively used, which may be related to a smaller difference in status between temporary and permanent positions within a firm. Further work is needed, as 1994 is close to the beginning of the labor market reforms.

Appendix A

Table 2A.1   Evolution of Nonwage Costs Paid by Employer and Employee by Item, 1987–1997

	1987	1988	1989	1990	1991	1992	1993		1994		1995		1996		1997	
							IPSS	AFP	IPSS	AFP	IPSS	AFP	IPSS	AFP	IPSS	AFP
Nonwage Costs Paid by Employer																
Tenure bonus	8.33[a]	8.33	8.33	8.33[b]	8.33[c]	8.33	8.33	8.33	8.33	8.33	8.33	8.33	8.33	8.33	8.33	8.33
National Housing Fund	4.00[d]	5.00[e]	5.00	5.00	8.00[f]	8.00	6.00[g]	6.00	6.00	6.00	9.00[h]	9.00	9.00	9.00	9.00[i]	9.00[i]
Holidays bonus	16.67	16.67	16.67[j]	16.67	16.67	16.67	16.67	16.67	16.67	16.67	16.67	16.67	16.67	16.67	16.67	16.67
IPSS payments	6.00[k]	6.00[l]	6.00	6.00[m]	6.00	6.00	6.00		6.00[n]		[h]	[h]				
Public health plan	6.00	6.00[o]	6.00	6.00	6.00	6.00	6.00	6.00	6.00	6.00	9.00[p]	9.00[p]	9.00	9.00	9.00	9.00
Accident insurance	2.00	2.00	2.00	2.00	2.00	2.00	2.00	2.00	2.00	2.00	2.00	2.00	2.00	2.00	2.00	2.00
Industrial Training Fund	1.50	1.50	1.50	1.50	1.50	1.50	1.50	1.50	1.50	1.50	1.25[q]	1.25[q]	1.00	1.00	0.75	0.75
Vacations	8.33	8.33	8.33	8.33	8.33	8.33	8.33	8.33	8.33	8.33	8.33	8.33	8.33	8.33	8.33	8.33
Total	52.83	53.83	53.83	53.83	56.83	56.83	54.83	48.83	54.83	48.83	54.58	54.58	54.33	54.33	54.08	54.08
Nonwage Costs Paid by Employee																
National Housing Fund	0.50[d]	1.00[e]	1.00	1.00	1.00	1.00	3.00[r]	3.00[r]	3.00	3.00	[h]	[h]				
IPSS payments	3.00[k]	3.00[s]	3.00	3.00	3.00	3.00	3.00		3.00		11.00[p]		11.00		13.00	
AFP payments								10.0		10.0		8.00[p]		8.00		8.00
Solidarity payment								1.00		1.00		[p]				
Accident/burial expenses[21]								2.25		2.01		1.17		1.33		1.38
Percentual commission[21]								0.64		2.03		1.98		2.02		2.34
Public health plan	3.00	3.00[o]	3.00	3.00	3.00	3.00	3.00	3.00	3.00	3.00	[p]	[p]				
Total	6.50	7.00	7.00	7.00	7.00	7.00	9.00	19.89	9.00	21.04	11.00	11.15	11.00	11.35	13.00	11.72
Total nonwage costs	59.33	60.83	60.83	60.83	63.83	63.83	63.83	68.72	63.83	69.87	65.58	65.73	65.33	65.68	67.08	65.80

Source: Análisis Laboral (1987–1997).

Notes: IPSS = public retirement plan. AFP = private retirement plan. Blank cells indicate that information is not available.

[a]Last wage for every complete year of tenure. The maximum taxable wage equals ten Minimum Vital Wages.

[b]Since June 1990, the maximum taxable wage is the last wage, including holiday bonuses.

[c]Since January 1991 the employer must deposit the tenure bonus in an authorized financial institution on May and November.

[d]The maximum taxable wage is set at eight tax units.

[e]Changed in November 1988.

[f]Changed in May 1991.

[g]On January 1993 the employer's payment and the maximum taxable wage were abolished. On November 1993 it was set at 6 percent.

[h]Changed in August 1995.

[i]In January 1997 the employer's contribution was reduced to 7 percent, but holiday bonuses were included in the taxable wage. In August 1997 the contribution was reduced to 5 percent.

[j]Officially regulated since December 1989. However, this was already a usual practice long before this date.

[k]The minimum taxable wage equals one Minimum Vital Income, and the maximum equals ten Minimum Legal Incomes.

[l]Since January 1988, the maximum taxable wage was set at twenty Minimum Legal Incomes.

[m]In August 1990 the Minimum Legal Income is replaced by the Minimum Vital Remuneration. In October 1990, the maximum taxable wage is eliminated.

[n]Abolished in August 1995.

[o]The maximum taxable wage, set at ten Minimum Legal Incomes, was eliminated in January 1988.

[p]Changed in August 1995.

[q]The contribution decreases 0.25 percent every year until 1997 (0.75 percent).

[r]In January 1993, the employee's payment was set at 9 percent, and the maximum taxable wage was abolished. In November 1993, it was set at 6 percent.

[s]The maximum taxable wage for the employee was eliminated in January 1988.

[t]In January 1997, the employee's contribution increases to 13 percent.

[u]Market average.

Appendix B
Labor Demand Estimations

To test for cyclical variations of total labor demand due to employment composition changes (Bentolila and Saint-Paul 1992) we estimate the equation

$$\ln L_{i,t} = X_{i,t}\Omega' + d \ln \hat{L}_{i,t-L} + e \ln \hat{L}_{i,t-L} \cdot \ln E(\text{sp})_{i,t} + \delta t + \beta Z_{i,t}$$
$$+ \text{cycle}_t(X_{i,t}\Omega') + \varepsilon_{i,t},$$

where

$$\Omega = (b_1, b_2, c, \delta)$$
$$X_{i,t} = [w + p, Y, E(\text{sp})],$$

where "cycle" is a dummy equal to zero in recessions and equal to 1 in expansions, and is interacted with all the regressors in the equation $(X_{i,t})$. This variable has a value of 1 when sectoral growth is 4 percent or more and zero otherwise. We used generalized least squares and correct for serial correlation with a correlation coefficient specific for each of the panels. The results of the estimations are shown in table 2B.1.

Appendix C
Equality of Empirical Hazard Functions

Graphical Analysis

In order to verify the equality of the hazard functions for complete and incomplete spells we assume that incomplete spells are completed ones and then compute the empirical hazard rates (Kaplan and Meier 1958) for both types of spells. These estimates are shown in the graph; note that the empirical hazard for incomplete spells has the same shape and spikes as the complete ones. Hazard functions for complete spells are above those using incomplete data, a fact that is consistent with lower mean tenures calculated using the former data set. Still, the pattern followed by the hazard function looks similar.

Kolmogorov-Smirnov Test

We use the Kolmogorov-Smirnov (K-S) statistic to formally test the equality of the empirical hazards functions between complete and incomplete spells (defined as uncensored spells). The test evaluates the closeness of the distributions λ^{is} and λ^{cs} (for incomplete and complete spells hazards)

Table 28.1   Labor Demand Estimation Results for Panels at the Sector and Firm Level

	Sector Level			Establishment Level		
	1987–1990	1991–1994	1995–1997	1987–1990	1991–1994	1995–1997
Constant	8.189***	15.511***	14.900***	0.437***	0.027	1.554***
	(1.579)	(2.218)	(3.762)	(0.151)	(0.085)	(0.512)
$\ln(w+p)$	0.574***	−0.316***	−0.353***	−0.031***	0.026***	−0.056*
	(0.204)	(0.118)	(0.137)	(0.009)	(0.006)	(0.033)
$\ln[E(sp)]$	−0.907**	−0.613	−0.443	−0.223***	−0.036*	−0.125
	(0.363)	(0.424)	(0.634)	(0.032)	(0.018)	(0.104)
$\ln(Y)^a$	0.017	0.112	0.094*	0.206***	0.008	0.083**
	(0.067)	(0.102)	(0.054)	(0.009)	(0.008)	(0.035)
$\ln(L_{t-1})^a$	0.074	−0.206	−0.005	0.787***	0.943***	0.613***
	(0.148)	(0.215)	(0.313)	(0.024)	(0.016)	(0.088)
$\ln(L_{t-1}) \cdot \ln[E(sp)]$	0.041	0.066	0.028	0.053***	0.006	0.041*
	(0.027)	(0.045)	(0.060)	(0.005)	(0.004)	(0.021)
cycle dummy $\cdot \ln(w+p)$	−0.035	−0.022	0.018	0.040***	0.005	0.006
	(0.052)	(0.049)	(0.018)	(0.010)	(0.008)	(0.043)
cycle dummy $\cdot \ln(E(sp))$	0.046	0.030	−0.026	−0.009	−0.010	−0.023
	(0.063)	(0.066)	(0.024)	(0.013)	(0.011)	(0.059)
cycle dummy $\cdot \ln(gdp)$	0.017	0.020	−0.013	−0.078***	0.001	0.043
	(0.040)	(0.037)	(0.014)	(0.011)	(0.009)	(0.057)
Log likelihood	210.86	139.94	200.42	2,757.98	2,485.27	−1,388.166
χ^2	12,589.99***	4,561.53***	3,474.32***	100,574.42***	186,433.25***	2,736.63***
No. of observations	189	189	117	4,754	6,491	1,722

Notes: Standard errors in parentheses. Sector level includes fixed effects. For establishment level, a time trend was included. It was significant for the period 1991–1994, but not for 1987–1990 and 1995–1997.

[a]Instrumentalized with lagged values using rolling equations.

***Significant at the 1 percent level.

**Significant at the 5 percent level.

*Significant at the 10 percent level.

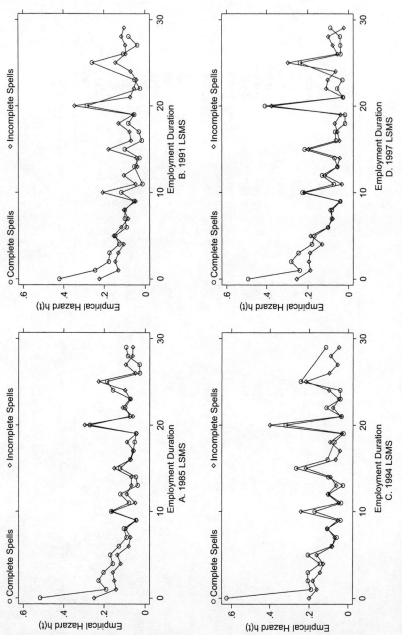

Fig. 2C.1 Empirical hazard functions of complete spells (assuming completeness of incomplete spells)

Table 2C.1   **Kolmogorov-Smirnov D Statistic**

LSMS	D statistic	P Value	Critical Value (95%)
1985	0.2143	0.228	0.22
1991	0.1721	0.661	0.23
1994	0.1884	0.470	0.23
1997	0.1779	0.553	0.22

by computing the least upper bound of all pointwise differences $|\hat{\lambda}^{is}(x) - \hat{\lambda}^{cs}(x)|$. We can write the K-S statistic D as

$$D = \sup_x [\,|\hat{\lambda}^{is}(x) - \hat{\lambda}^{cs}(x)|\,].$$

The null hypothesis ($H_0 : \lambda^{is} = \lambda^{cs}$) is accepted if λ^{is} is sufficiently close to λ^{cs}, in other words if the value of D is sufficiently small or smaller than the critical value at a certain significance level. The results are shown in table 2C.1. At the 95 percent significance level we cannot reject the null hypothesis that the two empirical hazard functions are equally distributed.

References

Abraham, K., and S. Houseman. 1994. Does employment protection inhibit labor market flexibility? Lessons from Germany, France, and Belgium. In *Social protection vs. economic flexibility: Is there a trade-off?* ed. R. Blank, 59–93. Chicago: University of Chicago Press.

Bentolila, S., and G. Saint-Paul. 1992. The macroeconomic impact of flexible contracts, with an application to Spain. *European Economic Review* 36 (5): 1013–53.

Burgess, S., and J. J. Dolado. 1989. Intertemporal rules with variable speed of adjustment: An application to U.K. manufacturing employment. *Economic Journal* 99:347–65.

Burgess, S., and H. Rees. 1996. Job tenure in Britain 1975–92. *Economic Journal* 106 (435): 334–44.

Greene, W. H. 1997. *Econometric analysis.* 4th ed. New York: Macmillan.

Griliches, Z., and J. A. Hausman. 1986. Errors in variable panel data. *Journal of Econometrics* 31:93–118.

Hamermesh, D. 1986. The demand for labor in the long run. In *Handbook of labor economics,* vol. 1, ed. O. Ashenfelter and R. Layard, 429–71. New York: North-Holland.

———. 1993. *Labor demand.* Princeton, N.J.: Princeton University Press.

International Labor Office (ILO). 1994. *Labor overview: Latin America and the Caribbean.* Lima, Peru: ILO.

Kaplan, E. L., and P. Meier. 1958. Non parametric estimation for incomplete observations. *Journal of American Statistical Association* 53:457–81.

Lancaster, T. 1985. Some remarks on wage and duration econometrics. In *Unemployment, search and labor supply,* ed. R. Blundell and I. Walker. Cambridge: Cambridge University Press.

————. 1990. *The econometric analysis of transition data.* New York: Cambridge University Press.

Lindbeck, A., and D. Snower. 2002. The insider-outsider theory: A survey. IZA Discussion Paper. Bonn, Germany: Institute for the Study of Labor.

Merrilees, W. J. 1982. Labour market segmentation in Canada: An econometric approach. *Canadian Journal of Economics* 15 (3): 458–73.

Saavedra, J. 1996a. Perú: Apertura comercial, empleo y salarios. [Peru: Trade liberalization, employment, and wages]. ILO Working Paper no. 40. Lima, Peru: International Labor Office.

————. 1996b. Liberalización comercial e industria manufacturera en el Peru. [Trade liberalization and the manufacturing industry in Peru]. Brief Research Series no. 2. Lima, Peru: Consorcio de Investigación Económica.

————. 1998. Crisis real o crisis de expectativas: El mercado laboral Peruano antes y despues de la reformas. [Real crisis or expectations crisis? Peruvian labor market before and after structural reforms]. IADB Working Paper no. 388. Washington, D.C.: Inter-American Development Bank.

Saavedra, J., and A. Chong. 1999. Structural reforms, institutions and the informal sector in Peru. *Journal of Development Studies* 35 (4): 95–116.

Saavedra, J., and E. Maruyama. 1999. Estabilidad laboral e indemnización por despido: Efectos sobre el funcionamiento del mercado laboral Peruano. [Labor stability and severance pay: Effects of dismissal costs on the Peruvian labor market performance]. GRADE Working Paper no. 28. Lima, Peru: Grupo de Análisis para el Desarrollo.

Saavedra, J., and M. Torero. 2001. Labor demand elasticities and trade liberalization in Peru. World Bank. Mimeograph.

The Effect of Job Security Regulations on Labor Market Flexibility
Evidence from the Colombian Labor Market Reform

Adriana D. Kugler

3.1 Introduction

Job security regulations are usually considered to inhibit labor market flexibility by reducing the ability of firms to hire and fire workers. While severance pay and other job security provisions admittedly protect workers from unjust termination, these laws may also adversely affect workers by reducing their ability to find new jobs. State-mandated severance pay and job security requirements are equivalent to taxes on job destruction that reduce firms' incentives not only to dismiss but also to hire new workers. In fact, it has often been suggested that the elevated severance pay and job security requirements in Europe are in part to blame for the high unemployment levels in this continent.

The perception that reducing firing costs would help to reduce unemployment by enhancing labor market flexibility, through increased worker turnover into and out of unemployment, has driven several European countries to introduce labor market reforms in this direction. In particular, a number of countries, including England, France, Germany, and Spain, introduced temporary contracts during the 1980s as a way of reducing severance payments and payments for unjust dismissals. In contrast, Ameri-

Adriana D. Kugler is an associate professor of economics at the Universitat Pompeu Fabra, an assistant professor of economics at the University of Houston, a research affiliate at the Centre for Economic Policy Research (CEPR), and a research fellow at the Institute for the Study of Labor (IZA).

I am grateful to George Akerlof, Josh Angrist, Giuseppe Bertola, Antonio Cabrales, Hugo Hopenhayn, Bernardo Kugler, David Levine, Ricardo Paes de Barros, and especially Dan Hamermesh, James Heckman, and Carmen Pagés for very helpful comments. I also thank the Inter-American Development Bank for financial support and seminar participants at the various meetings of the Research Network Study on Labor Market Regulation for comments. Jairo Augusto Nuñez provided the National Household Surveys.

can labor markets became more rigid during the 1980s. During this decade, a number of states in the United States introduced indemnities for unjust dismissals, thus creating exceptions to the employment-at-will doctrine.

Although the evidence on the effects of these legislative changes on employment and unemployment in Europe and the United States has been ambiguous, reforms to reduce labor market rigidities have also been advocated and implemented in a number of less-developed countries. In less-developed countries the effects of these reforms are considered to be even greater, as labor market regulations are considered not only to discourage hiring and firing but also to encourage noncompliance with labor legislation and the expansion of the informal sector.

In this paper, I consider the incidence of a substantial reduction of firing costs on flexibility and unemployment in a less-developed country. In particular, this paper studies the impact of the Colombian labor market reform of 1990, which reduced severance payments substantially, on worker flows into and out of unemployment and its implied net effect on unemployment. I use a microlevel data set from Colombia to examine the effects of a reduction in firing costs on worker turnover. The labor market reform introduced in Colombia in 1990 reduced severance payments for all workers hired after 1990 and covered by the legislation (formal-sector workers). Informal workers, who are not covered by the legislation, were not *directly* affected by the reform and, thus, are used as a comparison group in the estimations. The empirical analysis exploits this variability in the coverage of the legislation between formal- and informal-sector workers together with the temporal change in the Colombian legislation to identify the effects of a reduction in firing costs on the exit rates out of employment and out of unemployment. The annual Colombian Household Surveys (conducted in June) provide information about formal- and informal-sector activity and allow estimating hazard rates for formal and informal workers, before and after the reform. The results of the hazard models using a difference-in-differences estimator indicate that hazard rates into and out of unemployment increased after the reform for formal-sector workers (covered by the legislation) relative to informal workers (uncovered). Moreover, the increase in worker turnover was greater among younger, more educated workers employed in larger firms, who are likely to have been affected most by the changes in the legislation.

The rest of the paper proceeds as follows. In section 3.2 I survey the evidence on the effect of firing costs on employment volatility, the speed of employment adjustment, and employment levels, labor market participation, and unemployment for developed countries. In section 3.3 I describe the legislative changes introduced by the Colombian labor market reform of 1990 that led to a reduction in severance pay and other firing costs. In section 3.4 I develop a matching model with endogenous sorting into a formal and an informal sector. The model is useful as it predicts the direct effect of a reduction in severance pay on worker turnover as well as the general equilibrium effects of the reform on turnover in the two sectors. Section 3.5 discusses the identification strategy of the firing cost effects on worker turnover. In section 3.6 I describe the data and present the results on the incidence of firing costs on the exit rates into and out of unemployment. In section 3.7 I use the steady-state condition from the model together with the results in section 3.6 to estimate the net impact of the reform on unemployment. Section 3.8 concludes.

3.2   Review of the Literature

The perception that flexible labor markets promote employment and reduce unemployment is widely accepted. However, the theoretical and empirical evidence on the net effects of firing costs on employment and unemployment is ambiguous.

Past theoretical work on the effects of firing costs shows that while reductions (increases) in firing costs are expected to increase (reduce) hiring and firing as well as employment volatility, the net effects of reductions in firing costs on employment and unemployment are ambiguous. Theoretically, the net effect of firing costs on employment is very sensitive to the assumptions of the model. The net effect of firing costs on employment depends crucially on whether the entry-exit margin is considered and on the stochastic process assumed to be generating the demand shocks. Hopenhayn and Rogerson (1993) simulate the effect of firing costs in a general equilibrium framework with firm entry and exit, and they find that an increase in firing costs reduces employment. In contrast, Bentolila and Bertola (1990) consider a partial equilibrium model with a monopolistic firm and find that employment increases slightly with firing costs, because the firing effect dominates the hiring effect. In addition, Bentolila and Dolado (1994) argue that in an insider-outsider model à la Lindbeck and Snower (1988), firing costs may strengthen the position of insiders and increase their employment while reducing the employment of outsiders.

Similarly, past empirical evidence indicates that lower firing costs are related to greater employment volatility, but the evidence of the net effect of firing costs on employment and unemployment in these studies has been mixed. Bertola (1990) constructs job security indexes for ten countries and finds that job security provisions are negatively correlated with the variance of employment and with unemployment's response to output changes (i.e., Okun's coefficient). Using a panel of retail firms in the United States, Anderson (1993) finds that the seasonal variability in employment is lower in firms facing higher adjustment costs. Moreover, a number of studies have related the speed of employment adjustment to shocks to the level of firing costs. As predicted by the theory, Anderson (1993) finds that the probability of responding to shocks is negatively correlated to the adjustment costs faced by firms. In addition, Hamermesh (1993) finds that the speed of employment adjustment to shocks fell in nonunionized industries over the 1980s in the United States, when exceptions to the employment-at-will doctrine were being introduced. Using British data, Burgess (1988) finds a lower speed of employment in industries subject to higher firing costs. Bentolila and Saint-Paul (1993) also find that employment adjustments over the business cycle increased in Spain after the introduction of temporary contracts in 1984. Thus, these studies provide evidence of the greater employment volatility when firing costs are lower.

The evidence on the impact of firing costs on employment and unemployment, however, appears mixed. Lazear (1990) uses cross-country data from twenty-two developed countries over twenty-nine years and finds evidence that suggests that high severance payments and advance notice requirements reduce employment and labor force participation. Grubb and Wells (1993) construct job security indices for Organization for Economic Cooperation and Development (OECD) countries and also find a negative correlation between job security and employment. Di Tella and MacCulloch (2004) use a measure of flexibility provided by employers, and they find that flexibility is positively correlated with employment and participation and, to a lesser degree, with unemployment. In contrast, Bertola (1990) finds evidence suggesting that job security provisions are unrelated to medium- and long-run employment. Nickell and Layard (1999) find that employment and labor force levels are lower when employment protection legislation (EPL) is stricter, but since they are exploiting cross-country variation they cannot control for the fact that female labor force participation is lower and EPL stricter in Southern European countries. In fact, they find that the results disappear when they consider a sample of adult males. The OECD's *Employment Outlook* (1999) exploits additional temporal variation in EPL and finds no effect of EPL on aggregate employment. However, consistent with the story that EPL protects insiders, the *Employment Outlook* finds that EPL increases the employment of adult men and reduces the employment of young workers and women.

Exploiting the temporal change in the labor legislation across states in the United States, Dertouzos and Karoly (1993) find that employment levels fell in states that introduced more stringent employment protection. In contrast, Miles (2000) finds no effect of the changes in unjust dismissal costs in the United States on aggregate employment. However, both Autor (2003) and Miles (2000) find that stricter employment protection contributed to the rise in temporary employment in the United States over the 1980s. Anderson (1993), instead, exploits the experience-rating feature of the U.S. unemployment insurance system to quantify adjustment costs and finds higher average employment in firms subject to higher adjustment costs. The mixed results observed in the literature are not surprising if one considers that cross-section studies are subject to omitted variable biases, simultaneity problems, and endogeneity of the legislation. The panel studies, while mitigating the concerns of omitted variable biases and simultaneity, are subject to the possibility of endogeneity of the legislation as well as to selection biases. Thus, while the evidence on the effects of firing costs on the volatility of employment appears robust, the net effect of firing costs on employment and unemployment is not as clear.[1]

More recently, a handful of studies have exploited the differential variation in labor legislation for certain groups of workers to set up natural experiments of the impact of firing costs using microdata. While Acemoglu and Angrist (2001) find no effect of the Americans with Disabilities Act on separations of disabled relative to nondisabled employees, Oyer and Schaefer (2000) find substitution of individual dismissals for mass layoffs after the passage of the Civil Rights Act of 1990 for groups covered by the legislation. Kugler and Saint-Paul (2004) and Autor, Donohue, and Schwab (2003) find decreased hires and employment in those states that introduced certain unjust dismissal provisions over the 1980s. Kugler and Pica (2003) also find decreased hires and dismissals of workers in small relative to large firms after the introduction of the 1990 Italian labor market reform, which raised dismissal costs for firms with less than fifteen employees. Finally, Kugler, Jimeno, and Hernanz (2003) find increased hiring of young workers and increased separations of older workers after the introduction of the Spanish labor market reform of 1997, which reduced dismissal costs and payroll taxes for these groups of workers.

While microstudies solve some of the problems faced by studies relying on macrodata, these studies have focused on the impact of firing costs in developed countries. There is little evidence on the impact of firing costs in less-developed countries. In the next section, I describe the legislative change introduced in Colombia in 1990, which allows me to exploit the temporal variability and the variability in coverage of labor legislation in order to estimate the impact of firing costs on turnover and unemployment in a less-developed country.

3.3   Changes in the Colombian Institutional Framework

In 1990, Colombia introduced a labor market reform that substantially reduced the costs of dismissing workers. The Colombian reform reduced severance payments, widened the definition of "just" dismissals, extended the use of temporary contracts, and sped up the process of mass dismissals.

---

1. However, a number of recent studies, including Angrist and Kugler (2003), Bertola, Blau, and Kahn (2002), and Blanchard and Wolfers (2000), find that the negative effects of labor market institutions on employment and unemployment are realized when economies are faced with bad shocks.

All of these policy changes reduced the costs of firing workers covered by the legislation after 1990.[2] The reform thus reduced firing costs for firms in the formal sector but not for informal firms, which did not comply with labor legislation.

Although the reform introduced various legislative changes simultaneously, the one major policy change that decreased the costs of dismissals was the reduction of severance payments.[3] The reform reduced the severance paid for dismissals in three ways. First, prior to the reform, employers were mandated to pay severance of one month per year worked based on the salary at the time of separation. After the reform, employers were instead required to deposit a monthly contribution equivalent to one month of the yearly salary at that moment in time to an individual severance payments savings account (*Fondo de Cesantías*), which would be accessible to workers in the event of separation. Thus, total severance payments were reduced because the monthly payment per year worked was no longer based on the higher salary at the time of separation but, rather, on the salary during each month. Second, prior to the reform, workers could obtain advance payments from their severance to use for investments in education and housing, which would only be credited to the employer in nominal terms in the event of separation. After the reform, although the withdrawal of funds was still permitted, these loans were now credited to the employer in real terms. According to Ocampo (1987) the fact that, prior to the reform, withdrawals were credited to the employer in *nominal* terms implied, on average, a cost of 35 percent of the total severance payments in the manufacturing sector prior to 1990. Finally, the change in the legislation reduced severance pay, because the introduction of guaranteed severance payments essentially turned severance payments into a deferred compensation scheme, allowing workers lower wages in exchange for future severance.[4] Not all workers were, however, affected in the same way by the reduction in severance payments. As indicated previously, workers hired by informal firms are not covered by the legislation and, thus, should not have been affected directly by the reform. Moreover, family workers, temporary workers, and workers employed by firms with five or less employees are not entitled to severance payments, and domestic workers and

2. In addition to the labor market reform of 1990, a social security reform was passed in 1994 and implemented in 1995 and 1996. However, since the social security reform increased payroll taxes, the increase in nonwage recurrent costs of this reform implies different effects on turnover than the reduction in dismissal costs of the labor market reform of 1990. Moreover, the study by Gruber (1997) of a similar reform in Chile finds no effects of payroll taxes on employment because recurrent costs are passed on to wages.

3. Note that both before and after the reform, employers were exempt from the payment of severance in cases when employees were dismissed because of undue care, sabotage, or release of employers' proprietary information.

4. Kugler (2002) studies the impact of a change from a standard severance payments system into a system of severance payments savings accounts.

ble 3.1   **Indemnities for Unjust Dismissal by Tenure**

Pre- and Postreform			Prereform	Postreform
ss Than a Year	≥ 1 and <5 years	≥ 5 and <10 years	≥ 10 years	≥ 10 years
days	45 days and 15 additional days after the first year	45 days and 20 additional days after the first year	45 days and 30 additional days after the first year	45 days and 40 additional days after the first year

workers employed by firms with very little capital are entitled only to a severance payment of fifteen days per year worked.

A second important change introduced by the reform was the change in the legislation with regards to indemnities for "unjust" dismissals. First, the definition of unjust dismissals changed in 1990. Prior to the reform, just-cause dismissals included dismissals of employees because of fraud, violence, undue care, sabotage, discipline problems, deficient performance, and release of proprietary information. After the reform, the definition of just-cause dismissals was extended to include any dismissal for failure to comply with firm regulations and instructions from one's supervisors. The exemptions for the payment of indemnities for unjust dismissals were thus extended after the 1990 reform, reducing firing costs for formal firms. Second, the reform eliminated the ability of workers with more than ten years of tenure to sue for back pay and reinstatement. At the same time, however, the reform increased the cost of "unjustly" dismissing workers with more than ten years of tenure (see table 3.1), and this may have increased the incentives for firms to dismiss workers just before reaching ten years of seniority.[5] Thus, these changes in unjust dismissal legislation can be expected to have the greatest impact on formal workers with intermediate levels of seniority.

Another important change brought about by the reform was the extension of the use of fixed-term contracts.[6] Prior to 1990, fixed-term contracts were allowed for a minimum duration of a year.[7] After the reform, these fixed-term contracts were extended to contracts of less than a year (renewable up to three times). This change in the legislation thus lowered firing costs for firms hiring workers for less than a year and would be expected to

5. Note, however, that employees with more than ten years of experience who were hired before 1990 could also choose to be covered by the new regime with severance payments savings accounts.

6. While temporary contracts are subject to payroll taxes and social security contributions, these contracts are not subject to severance pay and unjust dismissal legislation as long as contracts end by the agreed date.

7. Despite legislation on fixed-term contracts, however, firms could circumvent this restriction by subcontracting workers from temp agencies even prior to the reform.

Table 3.2   Advance Notice Requirements by Firm Size

Firm Size	Threshold for Advance Notification of Collective Dismissals
>10 and <50 employees	30% of the workforce
≥50 and <100 employees	20% of the workforce
≥100 and <200 employees	15% of the workforce
≥200 and <500 employees	9% of the workforce
≥500 and <1,000 employees	7% of the workforce
≥1,000 employees	5% of the workforce

have increased turnover among formal workers with less than a year of tenure after the reform.

An additional change introduced by the reform was a reduction in the advance notice required for mass dismissals. While advance notice requirements for mass layoffs existed prior to the reform (see table 3.2), the reform introduced penalties to bureaucrats who did not process requests for mass layoffs quickly. If such threats to bureaucrats were effective, this change in the legislation should have speeded up the dismissal process for formal firms and lowered their costs of firing.

Finally, the reform also introduced a new type of contract that eliminated severance payments altogether. This type of contract (*Salario Integral*) allowed formal workers who earned more than ten times the minimum wage to opt out of severance payments, indemnities for unjust dismissals, benefits (except paid vacations), social security contributions, and payroll taxes in exchange for a higher salary. The introduction of this type of contract effectively allowed firms to eliminate the cost of dismissing highly paid workers who opted for the *Salario Integral*. Thus, one would expect to find a greater effect of the reform on formal-sector workers with salaries above ten times the minimum wage.[8]

The changes in severance pay legislation, unjust dismissal legislation, temporary contracts, and mandatory advance notice introduced by the Colombian labor market reform should have directly reduced the costs of dismissals for formal firms and increased turnover in the formal sector. Moreover, it is often argued that job security regulations simply encourage the expansion of the informal sector, and one would thus expect for this type of reform to have encouraged greater compliance with the legislation. The next section introduces a matching model with firing costs, which shows the direct effect of a reduction in firing costs on formal turnover as

8. By 1994 only 1.5 percent of all workers in manufacturing and 0.6 percent of workers in commerce had opted for this type of contract (Lora and Henao 1995). Since the surveys used in the analysis do not indicate whether a worker indeed opted for an Integral Salary, we examine whether the impact of the reform was greater on older and highly educated workers who are more likely to earn above ten times the minimum wage.

well as the indirect effects on formal and informal turnover through the compositional changes of firms in each sector. The model shows that a reform that reduces dismissal costs may not only increase turnover but also increase compliance with state-mandated firing costs.

3.4 A Sorting Model of Compliance with Job Security Provisions

This section presents a matching model with a formal sector and an informal sector in which firms sort themselves between the two sectors. Firms producing in the formal sector must comply with labor legislation and have to pay state-mandated severance in the event of a dismissal, while firms in the informal sector do not comply with job security legislation and avoid the severance payment. Productivity in the informal sector is, however, lower overall than in the formal sector, because informal firms must produce at a smaller scale to remain inconspicuous to the authorities. Moreover, the presence of a firm-specific component to productivity in the model implies that, in equilibrium, firms with higher idiosyncratic productivity self-sort into the formal sector while firms with lower idiosyncratic productivity self-sort into the informal sector.

The model predicts that the probability of being dismissed by a formal firm is lower because of the legislated severance payments, but also because formal firms are more productive. Also, a reduction in severance payments increases the probability of dismissals in the formal sector through a direct effect on the firing costs. In addition, however, the reduction in firing costs has effects on the idiosyncratic composition of firms in each sector as well as on the wages paid in each sector. This model thus highlights the potential biases that may arise in empirical studies that attempt to quantify the effects of firing costs.

3.4.1 Assumptions

In this model, heterogeneous firms may choose to produce in a formal sector, in which they must comply with job security provisions, or to produce in the informal sector, without complying but at the cost of lower productivity. Workers are identical ex ante, but they may have different productivity ex post depending on how well they match. After a match, the firm and worker set the wage according to a Nash bargaining solution. Then the firm decides whether to keep or dismiss the worker.

Production in Each Sector

Formal and informal production is a function of a sector-specific component, a_s, of a firm idiosyncratic component, A, and of the match quality component, γ, and firms produce with a technology, $Y_s = a_s \gamma A$, for $s = F, I$. Sector-specific productivity is fixed, and it is assumed, without loss of generality, that $a_F = 1 > a_I = a$. The firm idiosyncratic component comes from a distribution $F(A)$, and the match quality component comes from a distribution $G(\gamma)$.

Timing

Firms, first, observe their firm-specific productivity. Firms then choose a sector given the productivity in the sector and their known firm-specific productivity. Formal and informal firms hire in the same market, and, immediately after hiring, they observe the match-specific productivity. Then firms and workers bargain over wages. At the end of the process firms decide whether to keep or dismiss the worker, and formal firms that do dismiss must provide a severance payment, C. However, workers may still be separated afterward at arrival rates, λ_F and λ_I, due to exogenous reasons, in which case firms do not pay severance.

Matching

All firms and workers search in the same market. The arrival rate of applicants to formal and informal firms is the same, $q(\theta) = m(1/\theta, 1)$, where $\theta = v/u$. The arrival rate of job opportunities is $\theta q(\theta)$, and workers receive offers from formal or informal firms with a given probability that depends on the share of firms in each sector.

Wage Setting

Each firm and worker pair sets the wage based on Nash bargaining. Wages are set after firm-specific and match-specific productivities are observed. In this model, all wages are affected by job security legislation, because the severance pay raises the utility of the unemployed and thus raises the reservation wage of all workers.[9]

3.4.2   Solution to the Model

The model is solved by backward induction. First, the solution for the dismissal choices in each sector is found. Second, the Nash bargaining solution of the wage is determined. Finally, the marginal firm between the two sectors is determined in order to solve for the split of firms between the formal and informal sectors.

Dismissal Decisions

The present discounted profits for a firm with a filled job is J_s, and the present discounted value of a vacant job is V_s, for $s = F, I$ (formal and in-

---

9. As pointed out by Lazear (1990), in a perfectly competitive market, the state-mandated severance pay could be undone given the proper contract. In particular, the worker would have to post a bond for the cost of the severance pay to the firm upon the signing of the contract. However, as in Lazear (1990), it is assumed that the state-mandated severance pay is not completely offset by a private transfer, because workers may be liquidity constrained and because of moral hazard problems on the part of firms.

formal, respectively). Thus, the asset equation of a filled and a vacant job are given by the following equations, respectively:

$$rJ_s = Y_s - w_s + \lambda_s (V_s - J_s)$$
$$rV_s = q(\theta)(J_s - V_s).$$

As there is free entry, and all profit opportunities are exploited, $V_s = 0$. Thus,

$$J_s = \frac{a_s \gamma A - w_s}{r + \lambda_s + q(\theta)}.$$

Once matched, a firm must choose whether to keep or dismiss a worker. A formal firm has to pay a cost, C, if it decides to dismiss, while an informal firm does not have to pay the firing cost. Thus, the minimum match-productivity that triggers a dismissal by a formal firm is given by

$$\overline{\gamma}_F = \frac{w_F - C[r + \lambda_F + q(\theta)]}{A}.$$

For informal firms, the trigger productivity is given by

$$\overline{\gamma}_I = \frac{w_I}{aA}.$$

Given firm-specific productivity and wages, the probability that a formal firm dismisses a worker is less than the probability that an informal firm dismisses; that is, $\overline{\gamma}_F < \overline{\gamma}_I \Leftrightarrow G(\overline{\gamma}_F) < G(\overline{\gamma}_I)$. This is both because formal firms must pay severance payments and because sector productivity is higher if a firm is producing formally.

Determination of Wages

Wages are set by each firm-worker pair before the match quality is realized. Wages are set according to Nash bargaining, and each side has the same bargaining power. Thus, formal and informal firms split their surplus equally with workers, as follows:

$$J_F^e - V_F - G(\overline{\gamma}_F)C = E_F^e - U,$$
$$J_I^e - V_I = E_I^e - U,$$

where J_F^e, J_I^e, E_F^e, and E_I^e are the expected discounted profits of a formal and informal job and the expected lifetime utilities of a formal and an informal worker, respectively, and U is the expected lifetime utility of an unemployed worker. The asset equations of employed and unemployed workers are given by

$$rE_s^e = w_s + \lambda(U - E_s^e),$$
$$rU = \theta q(\theta)(E^e - U),$$

where E^e is the expected lifetime utility of employment for an unemployed job seeker. Since an unemployed worker is uncertain about whether he will be hired in a formal or an informal job, his expected utility of employment is

$$E^e = \text{Pr(formal offer)}\{[1 - G(\overline{\gamma}_F)] E_F^e + G(\overline{\gamma}_F)C\}$$
$$+ \text{Pr(informal offer)} [1 - G(\overline{\gamma}_I)]E_I^e.$$

Solving for $(E_s^e - U)$ in each sector and substituting into the equal split equation just given determines the wages in each sector:

$$w_F = \frac{(r + \lambda_F)[r + \theta q(\theta)]\left[\int \gamma E[\overline{\gamma}_F, \overline{\gamma}]\gamma Ag(\gamma)d\gamma - G(\overline{\gamma}_F)C\right] + r[r + \lambda_F + q(\theta)]\theta q(\theta)E^e}{[2(r + \lambda_F) + q(\theta)][r + \theta q(\theta)]},$$

$$w_I = \frac{(r + \lambda_I)[r + \theta q(\theta)]\int \gamma E[\overline{\gamma}_I, \overline{\gamma}]a\gamma Ag(\gamma)d\gamma + r[r + \lambda_I + q(\theta)]\theta q(\theta)E^e}{[2(r + \lambda_I) + q(\theta)][r + \theta q(\theta)]}.$$

Wages are expected to be higher in the formal sector because of the higher sector productivity in formal jobs. However, as shown, in equilibrium the average match quality is lower in formal-sector firms, as firms in this sector are more likely to keep less productive matches than informal firms. Hence, the lower quality of the matches in the formal sector lowers the expected wage in the formal sector. In addition, wages are affected not only by average productivity but also by the level of the firing cost. Both formal and informal wages are raised by the presence of state-mandated severance pay, because the severance payment raises workers' reservation wages.

Sorting into Sectors

Given dismissal choices and wages, firms choose whether to sort into the formal or the informal sector. The benefit of producing formally is that the productivity of this sector is higher, but the cost of producing in this sector relative to the informal sector is the payment of state-mandated severance in the event of a dismissal. As firms are heterogeneous, firms may split between the two sectors. Firms produce formally if the difference between the expected stream of profits of formal and informal firms is nonnegative—that is, if $(J_F^e - J_I^e \geq 0)$, and they produce informally if it is negative—that is, if $(J_F^e - J_I^e) < 0$. As the firm-specific productivity increases, the output gains in the formal sector relative to the informal sector increase. Thus, the gains from going into the formal sector are greater for more productive firms than for less productive ones:

$$\frac{d(J_F^e - J_I^e)}{dA}$$

$$= \int_{\gamma \in [\overline{\gamma}F, \overline{\gamma}]}\left[\frac{\gamma}{r + \lambda_F + q(\theta)}\right]g(\gamma)d\gamma + \int_{\gamma \in [\overline{\gamma}I, \overline{\gamma}]}\left[\frac{a\gamma}{r + \lambda_I + q(\theta)}\right]g(\gamma)d\gamma > 0.$$

Firms with $A \in [\underline{A}, A_{\text{crit}}]$ produce in the informal sector, while firms with $A \in [A_{\text{crit}}, \overline{A}]$ produce in the formal sector, where A_{crit} is the firm-specific productivity of the firm that is marginal between producing formally and producing informally. Consequently, since formal firms are more productive in equilibrium, they dismiss less often and pay higher wages than informal firms.[10]

3.4.3 Severance Pay and Turnover

The presence of state-mandated costs and higher productivity in the formal sector imply different hazards into and out of unemployment in the two sectors. On the one hand, the probability of endogenous dismissal in the formal sector is likely to be lower than the probability of dismissal in the informal sector—that is, $\theta q(\theta)(1 - F[A_{\text{crit}}])G(\overline{\gamma}_F) < \theta q(\theta)F(A_{\text{crit}})G(\overline{\gamma}_I)$. On the other hand, the hiring probability will be higher or lower in the formal sector relative to the informal sector depending on the share of firms producing in each sector—that is, $\theta q(\theta)(1 - F[A_{\text{crit}}]) > \theta q(\theta)F(A_{\text{crit}})$. As the proportion of firms producing formally increases, then the hiring probability in the formal sector increases relative to the informal sector.

Moreover, the hazards into and out of unemployment are affected directly and indirectly by changes in severance pay legislation. First, a reduction in state-mandated severance pay has a direct effect on formal firms by increasing the threshold match productivity that triggers dismissals. Second, a reduction of severance payments pushes down wages in both sectors due to the fall in the reservation wage. Wages increase, however, due to the greater probability of dismissal in the formal sector, and the net effect on wages in both sectors is positive as well as the effect of wages on turnover. Finally, a reduction of severance payments changes the composition of firms in each sector. In particular, decreasing severance payments increases the incentives to produce in the formal sector and shifts lower-productivity firms that were previously unwilling to produce formally away from the informal sector. The compositional change increases the dismissal and hiring rates in the formal sector due to the greater share of firms producing formally.

The direct and indirect effects of a reduction in firing costs on turnover that emerge in the model illustrate the problems that may arise when trying to estimate the impact of a change in firing costs on turnover. First, the effects of firing costs on wages imply that the effect of firing costs on turnover captures not only the direct effect previously mentioned but also the indirect effect of firing costs on turnover going through wages. This is not problematic insofar as one is interested in measuring the total effect,

---

10. The self-sorting of more productive firms into the formal sector thus makes evident the problems of identifying the effect of legislation on turnover, simply by estimating the effect of firing cost on the hazard rates.

both direct and indirect, of firing costs on turnover. However, the self-sorting of firms into formal and informal sectors according to their firm-specific productivity and the effect of the reduction of firing costs on this self-sorting are likely to introduce selection biases. Finally, if a policy change occurred simultaneously with a change in the distribution of the shocks, then one might attribute to the reform an effect that might indeed be due to a worsening in the distribution of the matches.[11] The following sections discuss an identification strategy to deal with the problem of contemporaneous changes in the distribution of the shocks and discuss inference given the presence of a selection problem.

3.5   Identification Strategy

3.5.1   Differences-in-Differences

The theory I have laid out suggests that firing costs should only have direct effects on the exit rates of workers in the formal sector (covered by the legislation) and not on the exit rates of workers in the informal sector (uncovered by the legislation). Hence, the firing costs should have direct effects only on the tenures of formal sector workers and not on the tenures of workers employed in the informal sector. Similarly, the unemployment duration of workers whose spells end as a result of being hired in the formal sector should be directly affected by firing costs, but not the duration of workers whose spells end as a result of being hired in the informal sector. Comparing the hazards into and out of unemployment (or tenures and unemployment spells) between formal and informal workers (covered and uncovered by the legislation) could then provide an estimate of the effect of firing costs on turnover. The sample counterpart of the firing cost effect on tenure (unemployment spells) using differences would be

$$\Delta \bar{s} = (\bar{s}^{\text{formal}} - \bar{s}^{\text{informal}}),$$

where $\bar{h}^{\text{formal}} = 1/\bar{s}^{\text{formal}}$, $\bar{h}^{\text{informal}} = 1/\bar{s}^{\text{informal}}$, $\bar{s}$ indicates mean tenures (unemployment spells), and $\bar{h}$ indicates mean hazard rates.[12] Considering the simplest possible model of tenure (unemployment duration) with no regressors, tenure (unemployment) depends only on a Formal dummy,

$$s_{it} = \beta + \delta \, \text{formal}_{it} + u_{it}, \qquad E(u_{it} | \text{formal}_{it}) = 0.$$

Given this model, it is easy to see that the difference of the mean tenures in the formal and informal sectors provides an estimate of the firing cost

---

11. In addition, a change in firing costs is also likely to affect turnover in both sectors through its indirect effect on wages.

12. This sample counterpart holds as long as the hazards follow a Poisson process.

effect, δ. This way of estimating the firing cost effect is, however, likely to be biased for three reasons. First, the two groups may have different characteristics and, thus, different turnover behavior and different mean tenures and unemployment spells. Including regressors in the model allows us to control for observable characteristics and helps to solve this problem. Second, the error term could be correlated with the formal dummy if there is self-selection into the groups—that is, $E(u_{it} | \text{formal}_i = 1) \neq E(u_{it} | \text{formal}_i = 0)$. Finally, the two groups may be subject to different shocks, and part of the differences in turnover patterns—and thus tenures and unemployment spells—between the groups may be simply capturing these differences (i.e., $\beta_F \neq \beta_I$).

Exploiting the temporal change in the legislation introduced by the labor market reform of 1990, in addition to the variability in coverage between covered and uncovered workers, allows controlling for self-selection and for the difference in shocks across groups. In the model of tenure (unemployment spells) with no regressors, tenure (unemployment) depends only on a formal dummy, on a postreform dummy, and on an interaction term between the two,

$$s_{it} = \beta + \delta_0 \text{formal}_{it} + \delta_1 \text{Post90}_{it} + \delta_2 \text{formal}_{it} \times \text{Post90}_{it} + u_{it}.$$

First, if self-selection is constant over time—that is, $E(u_{i\text{pre90}} | \text{formal}_i = 1) = E(u_{i\text{post90}} | \text{formal}_i = 1)$ and $E(u_{i\text{pre90}} | \text{formal}_i = 0) = E(u_{i\text{post90}} | \text{formal}_i = 0)$—the firing cost effect can be estimated by simply taking differences-in-differences:

$$\Delta \bar{s}^{gt} = (\bar{s}^{\text{post90}} - \bar{s}^{\text{pre90}})^{\text{formal}} - (\bar{s}^{\text{post90}} - \bar{s}^{\text{pre90}})^{\text{informal}},$$

where $\bar{h}^{gt} = 1/\bar{s}^{gt}$. Taking differences of average tenures (unemployment duration) for formal workers between the pre-1990 and the post-1990 periods provides an estimate of the firing cost effect and allows us to difference out the biases introduced by self-selection when self-selection is constant over time. Taking differences of these differences with respect to informal workers (uncovered by the legislation) allows controlling for common trends that affect both groups, whether it is a constant trend, β, or a changing trend common to both groups, δ_1.

As indicated previously, however, it is possible that the two groups are subject to different shocks (i.e., $\beta_F \neq \beta_I$). In this case, differences-in-differences would work provided that the post-reform shocks can be adjusted using prereform trends. Thus, differences-in-differences would work even if the trends were different in the two groups under two circumstances. First, differences-in-differences would work if the trends are constant over time for each group (i.e., $\beta_{F\text{pre90}} = \beta_{F\text{post90}}$, $\beta_{I\text{pre90}} = \beta_{I\text{post90}}$, and $\delta_1 = 0$). Second, differences-in-differences would also work if the trends change over time for each group but the trends change by a common factor in both groups (i.e., $\beta_{Fpre90} \neq \beta_{Fpost90} = \beta_{Fpre90} + \delta_1$ and $\beta_{Ipre90} \neq \beta_{Ipost90} = \beta_{Ipre90} + \delta_1$).[13]

To estimate the effect of the reform on the hazard rates into and out of unemployment, the analogue of differences-in-differences is estimated using a formal hazard model. I estimate an exponential model that controls for observables and includes the formal dummy, the post-1990 dummy, and the interaction term between the formal and the post-1990 dummy:

$$h(s_{it} \,|\, \mathbf{X}_{it}) = \mathrm{esp}(\beta \mathbf{X}_{it} + \delta_0 \mathrm{formal}_{it} + \delta_1 \mathrm{Post90}_{it} + \delta_2 \mathrm{formal}_{it} \times \mathrm{Post90}_{it}),$$

where $\mathbf{X}_{it}$ is a $1 \times k$ vector of regressors, and β is a $k \times 1$ vector of parameters. The vector of covariates, $\mathbf{X}_{it}$, includes age, education, sex, marital status, number of dependents, the city where the person lives, and industry of employment. The formal variable is included to control for constant differences between the groups. Thus, δ_0 is expected to be negative since the dismissal of formal workers is more costly than that of informal workers, both before and after the reform. The Post90 dummy controls for common shocks affecting the turnover behavior of all workers after 1990. Finally, the interaction term of the formal and Post90 dummies is included to estimate the effect of the reduction in firing costs introduced by the reform on the hazard rates. A test of the impact of the reform is equivalent to a test that the coefficient on the interaction term, δ_2, is different from zero. In particular, the test considers whether workers covered by the legislation changed their turnover behavior relative to uncovered workers after 1990.

3.5.2   Potential Sources of Contamination

The identification strategy provided exploits both the temporal variability and the cross-section variability available in the Colombian context. Nonetheless, these differences-in-differences estimators rely on a number of assumptions that may yield inconsistent estimates of the effects of firing costs on turnover. First, the differences-in-differences estimators ignore the general equilibrium effects of a reduction in firing costs on composition suggested by the model in the previous section. Second, the estimators rely on the assumption that trends did not change differentially across groups over time. In turn, I consider the implications for the identification of the firing cost effect of having these two potential sources of biases.

As highlighted by the model in the previous section, the reduction of firing costs introduced by the reform is likely to have generated general equilibrium effects. In particular, the model given here showed that a reduction in firing costs not only has direct effects on turnover by reducing the costs

---

13. Moreover, even if trends do not change by a common factor in both groups, an unconventional differences-in-differences estimator could be obtained using a method proposed by Heckman and Robb (1985). This method assumes that a prereform model that is stable over time could be fitted for each group and then used to quantify postreform shocks that can be inserted into equations fitted to postreform data.

of dismissals; it also has indirect effects on turnover through its impact on sector selection. As I have described, the differences-in-differences estimator provided is consistent as long as self-selection is constant over time. The model in the previous section showed, however, that a reduction in firing costs changes the incentives to sort into the formal and informal sectors and generates compositional changes that also affect turnover. Thus, a reduction in firing costs may itself generate compositional changes that invalidate the assumption of a constant self-selection rule, before and after the reform. Yet the model does suggest that the bias introduced by differences-in-differences should be negative. In the model, the reduction in firing costs induces firms with low firm-specific productivities to start producing formally, and the reallocation between sectors thus lowers the average firm-specific productivity and increases turnover in both sectors. However, the effect of this change in composition on turnover was shown to be greater in the informal sector. Thus, while the firing cost effect obtained with differences-in-differences is inconsistent, the estimate should be a lower bound of the effect of the reduction in firing costs on turnover. Moreover, the next section shows that the change in the size of the two sectors was small, and this may indicate that the selection bias is unlikely to be large.

The second reason why the differences-in-differences estimators may yield inconsistent estimates of the firing cost effects is the possibility that trends change differently over time for formal and informal workers. As discussed previously, an important assumption that has to be fulfilled for differences-in-differences to yield consistent estimates of the reform is that it eliminates the effect of aggregate shocks or trends on turnover. The effect of aggregate shocks is eliminated if aggregate shocks are common to both groups or if aggregate shocks are specific to each group but either the shocks are constant over time or the shocks change similarly across groups. However, if trends are different across groups and they change differently over time, the firing cost effects obtained from differences-in-differences are likely to be biased. Aside from macroshocks, which are common to both groups, there were two additional shocks occurring during this period that could have affected turnover. First, trade was liberalized during this period, and, second, a social security reform was introduced in the early 1990s.

Colombia's trade liberalization during the early 1990s should be expected to have increased instability for workers employed in tradable sectors after 1990. Nonetheless, trade shocks should have affected formal and informal firms alike, and hence differences-in-differences should control for the effect of these shocks on turnover. If, however, formal firms were more likely to produce in tradable sectors and informal firms in nontradable sectors, then differences-in-differences would yield upwardly biased estimates of the firing cost effect. Hereafter, I estimate differences-in-differences across sectors to identify whether the changes in turnover were greatest in tradable sectors. There are two reasons to believe, however, that the trade shocks did not generate the changes in turnover presented later. First, the next section shows no consistent pattern across sectors in the differences-in-differences estimates. In addition, differences-in-differences for different firm sizes and age groups show that the change in turnover was greatest for large firms and middle-aged workers, who should have been affected most by the changes in job security legislation but not by trade shocks.

The social security reform introduced during the early 1990s affected formal firms but not informal firms. Thus, the social security reform introduced a shock affecting formal and informal firms differentially over time. As I have described, the social security reform increased employers' health and pension contributions and thus increased nonwage labor costs for firms complying with the legislation. The increased variable costs should have reduced hiring and should have had no effect on dismissals in the formal sector relative to the informal sector. This means that the social security reform should have generated very different effects on turnover from those predicted by a reduction in firing costs and from those reported in the next section.[14] Moreover, if firms adjusted to the increased nonwage labor costs by reducing wages, then the social security reform should not have had any turnover effects. There is evidence that employers tend to pass on their nonwage costs to workers as lower wages. For example, Gruber (1997) shows that the sharp reduction in payroll taxes that followed the privatization of Chile's social security system had no employment effects because wages adjusted fully to the change in nonwage costs. Moreover, differences-in-differences across different firm sizes and age groups show that turnover changed most among larger firms and middle-aged workers, who should have been affected most by the changes in job security legislation but not by the social security reform.

3.6   Empirical Analysis

This section examines the impact of the Colombian labor market reform of 1990, which included a substantial reduction in severance payments, on the hazard rates out of employment and out of unemployment of formal-sector workers relative to informal-sector workers.

3.6.1   The Data

Description

The data I use to analyze the effects of the reform on the exit rates out of employment and out of unemployment are drawn from the Colom-

---

14. See Kugler, Jimeno, and Hernanz (2003) for an analysis of the differential effects of firing costs and payroll taxes on turnover and employment.

bian National Household Surveys (NHS) for June of 1988, 1992, and 1996. The June NHSs were administered in seven metropolitan areas: Barranquilla, Bogota, Bucaramanga, Cali, Manizales, Medellin, and Pasto. The benefit of using the June surveys is that these include information on informality that allows us to separate formal-sector workers (covered) and informal-sector workers (uncovered). The June surveys allow us to define workers as covered and uncovered in two ways. First, formal (covered) workers are defined as those workers whose employers make social security contributions, and informal (uncovered) workers are defined as those whose employers do not contribute to the social security system. This definition is a useful one, because whether the employer contributes to social security is a good proxy of whether the employer generally complies with labor legislation. Second, formal (covered) workers are defined as wage earners employed in firms with more than ten employees, and informal (uncovered) workers as family workers, domestic workers, self-employed workers (excluding professionals and technicians), and wage earners employed in firms with less than ten employees. As discussed previously, employers with five or less employees, family workers, and the self-employed are all exempt from severance pay legislation, and domestic workers and workers in firms with low levels of capital are entitled only to half the amount of severance pay received by other employees. These surveys also include information on gender, age, marital status, educational attainment, number of dependents, and city and sector of employment, which allows us to control for differences in turnover due to differences in characteristics across individuals. In addition, the surveys include information about whether the worker is permanent or temporary, which allows us to distinguish the effect that the legislative change on temporary contracts had on turnover.

Table 3.3 presents summary statistics for the covered and uncovered groups (using the two definitions), before and after the reform. Columns (1) and (2) present the characteristics of formal (covered) workers, and columns (3) and (4) present the characteristics of informal (uncovered) workers, before and after the reform, respectively. Under both definitions, covered workers have more education, are slightly younger, have larger families, and are more likely to be married and female and to have a permanent contract than uncovered workers. However, aside from the differences in educational attainment, the differences in characteristics between the two groups are small. In addition, the changes in characteristics of the two groups between the pre-1990 and the post-1990 periods have moved in the same direction and are similar in magnitude. Educational attainment, average age, and the share of married workers increased in both groups after 1990, while the share of men, the size of households, and the share of workers with permanent contracts decreased in both groups after 1990.

These summary statistics suggest that differences in composition be-

Table 3.3   Basic Characteristics of Formal and Informal Workers, Before and After
                   the Reform

	Formal		Informal	
	Prereform (1)	Postreform (2)	Prereform (3)	Postreform (4)
Definition 1 of informality				
Share of total employment	44.84%	15.05%	55.16%	48.95%
Share of permanent workers	90.66%	88.84%	77.64%	74.5%
Share of men	68.69%	64.9%	69.6%	67.56%
Share of married workers	69.79%	73.38%	68.1%	72.17%
Average education	8.9 years	9.74 years	6.1 years	6.67 years
Average age	35.52 years	35.87 years	36.01 years	36.54 years
Average no. of dependents	0.81 persons	0.72 persons	0.80 persons	0.78 person
Definition 2 of informality				
Share of total employment	41.47%	45.22%	58.63%	54.78%
Share of permanent workers	86.6%	84.95%	81.27%	79.24%
Share of men	70.53%	66.8%	68.24%	65.75%
Share of married workers	69.71%	72.43%	68.39%	73.09%
Average education	8.93 years	9.79 years	6.29 years	6.95 years
Average age	34.7 years	35.02 years	36.57 years	37.17 years
Average no. of dependents	0.84 persons	0.77 persons	0.78 persons	0.73 person

Notes: The table reports proportions and means of the variables in the formal and informal sectors be fore and after the reform using two alternative definitions of informality. The proportions and means us ing the first definition are presented first, while those using the second definition are presented secon Under definition 1, workers are defined as those whose employers pay social security taxes and inform workers are those whose employer does not pay social security contributions. Under definition 2, form workers are defined as wage earners employed by firms with more than ten employees and inform workers are family workers, domestic workers, self-employed workers, and wage earners employed ! firms with less than ten employees. In Colombia, family workers, the self-employed, and workers er ployed by firms with less than five employees are completely exempt from severance pay legislation, whi domestic workers and workers employed by firms with little capital are subject to half the severance pa ments of workers completely covered by the legislation.

tween the groups are not substantial. Nonetheless, the differences in characteristics may account for part of the changing turnover patterns, and thus raw differences in turnover between covered and uncovered groups should be interpreted carefully. For this reason, in the analysis that follows I estimate formal hazard models that allow us to control for individual characteristics. The use of these models is thus crucial for identifying the firing cost effect of the labor market reform. Another source of compositional bias may arise if, as highlighted by the model, the composition of firms changes over time. Table 3.3 shows an increase in the size of the formal (covered) sector after 1990, according to both definitions. The percentage of workers in the formal sector increased from 44.84 percent to 51.05 percent, according to definition 1, and from 41.47 percent to 45.22 percent according to definition 2, between the pre- and postreform periods. Thus, the increase in the size of the formal sector indicates the importance of controlling also for firm characteristics, as the composition of formal firms may have also changed. Although the NHS offers little information on firm characteristics, the hazard models that follow do control for industry affiliation. Moreover, the fact that the increase in the size of the formal sector was small and that it cannot be directly attributed to the reform suggests that the selection biases described previously may not be of great concern.

Sampling Plan

The June NHSs include information on tenure on the current job (in years) and on the duration of unemployment (in months) right before entering the current job that allows us to estimate hazard rates. In particular, the survey asks currently employed workers "How long have you been working on your current job?" and "How long were you unemployed between your current job and your previous job?" The data thus provide information on *incomplete* employment spells of currently employed workers, and on *complete* unemployment spells of workers who are currently employed and had a previous job (see figure 3.1).

The stock sampling for the employment spells generates two types of biases. First, the sampled employment spells are too short because of the sampling of *incomplete* employment spells. In particular, Heckman and Singer (1985) show that, under the assumptions of a time homogenous environment, no heterogeneity, and independence between employment and unemployment spells, the completed spells would be on average twice as long. Second, as a consequence of sampling currently employed workers, the incomplete employment spells are *longer* than the completed spells from a sample that follows worker flows from job to job over time. Thus, the sampling of currently employed workers introduces *length bias.* Heckman and Singer (1985) show, however, that under the assumptions stated and, in addition, under the assumption of no duration dependence the two biases exactly cancel out. I will estimate exponential hazard models that impose these assumptions.

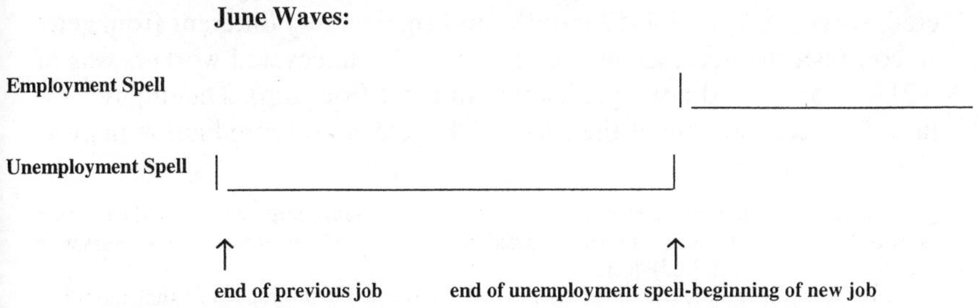

June Waves:

Employment Spell

Unemployment Spell

↑   ↑
end of previous job   end of unemployment spell-beginning of new job

Fig. 3.1   Sampling of employment and unemployment spells in the June surveys

Similarly, the stock sampling of the unemployment spells may also introduce a number of biases. Although the data provide complete unemployment spells, the fact that the spells are drawn from a sample of workers who are currently employed and had a previous job may generate biased estimates. First, sampling currently employed workers introduces length bias. This is because one oversamples workers with short spells relative to long spells. Thus, the mean of the sampled spells would be shorter than the mean of the spells from a flow sample. Second, sampling workers who had a previous job excludes all new entrants into the labor force, and this introduces another type of length bias. By excluding new entrants from the sample, one oversamples workers with long spells relative to short spells, implying that the mean of the sampled spells would be shorter than the mean of the spells from a flow sample. Although the distribution of unemployment spells obtained from this sampling plan is likely to be distorted, the bias due to stock sampling may be small in practice because the two biases have opposite signs and thus may cancel out.

3.6.2   Tenure and Unemployment Spells, Before and After the Reform

Average Tenure

The model I have presented indicates that the direct and indirect effects of the reduction in firing costs introduced by the reform should have increased the exit rates out of employment for formal workers relative to informal workers. Thus, the reform should have reduced the average tenure of workers covered by the reform (formal workers) relative to the tenure of uncovered workers (informal workers).[15]

Table 3.4 presents the average tenure for the covered and uncovered groups (using the first definition) before and after the Colombian labor market reform of 1990.[16] The first row corresponds to the average tenure after the reform, the second row corresponds to the average tenure prior to the reform, and the third row corresponds to the differences. The last row provides the differences-in-differences estimate of the effect of the reform on tenure. The average tenure of covered workers decreased after the reform from 5.6002 to 5.3130 years. The decrease in average tenure for covered workers was of 3.4452 months and significantly different from zero. In contrast, the decrease in average tenure for uncovered workers was of 0.2112 months and not significantly different from zero. The differences-in-differences estimate of the effect of the reform was a reduction in aver-

---

15. In particular, the average tenure of formal workers should decrease because the fraction of workers with short tenures (those just hired) increases and/or the fraction of workers with long tenures (those just fired) decreases.

16. This section and the rest of the analysis rely on the first definitions of formal and informal since the two measures are highly correlated and the results are robust to the definition used.

Table 3.4   **Sample Differences-in-Differences Estimates of the Effect of the Reform on Average Tenure**

	Formal	Informal
Postreform	5.3130	4.5376
	(0.0461)	(0.0496)
Prereform	5.6002	4.5197
	(0.0632)	(0.0588)
Differences	−0.2872***	−0.0176
	(0.0782)	(0.0769)
Differences-in-differences	−0.3051**	
	(0.1098)	

Note: Standard errors in parentheses.
***Significant at the 1 percent level.
**Significant at the 5 percent level.

age tenure of 3.6612 months. The effect is large and significantly different from zero, and, as predicted by the theory, most of the change comes from the reduction in average tenure of covered workers rather than from the increase in average tenures of uncovered workers. Table 3.5 presents the differences-in-differences estimates of the reform on average tenure by gender. This table shows that most of the change in the aggregate figures is driven by the effect of the reform on men's tenures. The differences-in-differences estimate of the effect of the reform was a reduction of 4.1208 months for men and of 2.1012 months for women, although the effect is not significantly different from zero for women.

Tables 3.6 and 3.7 present differences-in-differences estimates of the reform for different age and education groups. Table 3.6 shows that the effect of the reform was greatest for middle-aged workers. The differences-in-differences estimate of the effect was a reduction of 4.0176 months for middle-aged workers, while the estimates for young and older workers were not significantly different from zero. These results are consistent with the change in severance pay legislation and with the change in unjust dismissal legislation that raised the cost of unjustly dismissing workers with more than ten years of tenure. In particular, the change in the legislation should have induced firms to dismiss workers just prior to completing ten years of tenure. This result is confirmed in the next section with the formal hazard analysis. In contrast, table 3.7 shows that the differences-in-differences estimates of the effects of the reform were greatest for employees with primary education and with a university degree or more education. This result, however, inverts itself in the formal hazard analysis that controls for changes in turnover for these groups after the reform.

Table 3.8 shows the differences-in-differences estimates of the effect of the reform by sector, to identify whether the reduction in tenures could have

Table 3.5   Sample Differences-in-Differences Estimates of the Effect of the Reform on Average Tenure, by Gender

	Men		\Women	
	Formal	Informal	Formal	Informal
Postreform	5.57424	4.9987	4.5173	3.5772
	(0.0610)	(0.0636)	(0.0659)	(0.0749)
Prereform	6.1141	5.0270	4.4730	3.3577
	(0.0812)	(0.0753)	(0.0914)	(0.0842)
Differences	−0.3717***	−0.0283	0.0443	0.2194**
	(0.1016)	(0.0986)	(0.1127)	(0.1127)
Differences-in-differences		−0.3434***		−0.1751
		(0.1416)		(0.1594)

Note: Standard errors in parentheses.
***Significant at the 1 percent level.
**Significant at the 5 percent level.

Table 3.6   Sample Differences-in-Differences Estimates of the Effect of the Reform on Averag⟨ Tenure, by Age Group

	Age < 24 years		24–55 years		Age > 55 Years	
	Formal	Informal	Formal	Informal	Formal	Informa⟨
Postreform	1.6480	1.4058	5.3971	4.5180	11.2889	10.1111
	(0.0331)	(0.03030)	(0.0821)	(0.0525)	(0.2860)	(0.2523⟨
Prereform	1.6107	1.3709	5.7419	4.5280	12.3513	10.7321
	(0.0394)	(0.0309)	(0.0663)	(0.0615)	(0.3589)	(0.3008⟨
Differences	0.0372	0.0349	−0.3448***	−0.0100	−1.0624***	−0.6209⟨
	(0.0515)	(0.0433)	(0.0821)	(0.0808)	(0.4589)	(0.3926⟨
Differences-in-differences	0.0023		−0.3348***		−0.4414	
	(0.0684)		(0.1156)		(0.2111)	

Note: Standard errors in parentheses.
***Significant at the 1 percent level.
*Significant at the 10 percent level.

been the result of trade liberalization. This table shows that the differences-in-differences estimates for agriculture, mining, manufacturing, construction, and commerce are not significantly different from zero at conventional levels. Moreover, the differences-in-differences estimate of the reform was a reduction of 6.4836 months in transportation, which was only significant at the 10 percent level; a reduction of 10.7028 months in financial services, only significant at the 5 percent level; and a reduction of 10.236 months in services, significant at the 1 percent level. Thus, the estimates by sector do not show a consistent pattern of changes across tradable and nontradable sectors. These results are confirmed by the formal hazard analysis that will

Table 3.7 Sample Differences-in-Differences Estimates of the Effect of the Reform on Average Tenure, by Education Group

	Primary Education		Secondary Education		High School		University Education		University Degree or More	
	Formal	Informal	Formal	Informal	Formal	Informal	Formal	Informal	Formal	Informal
Postreform	6.0542	5.1540	4.9525	3.8160	4.7533	3.9912	4.6618	3.4520	6.2258	5.2305
	(0.1115)	(0.0816)	(0.0911)	(0.0745)	(0.0785)	(0.1046)	(0.1242)	(0.1714)	(0.1208)	(0.2575)
Prereform	6.6346	5.0796	4.8250	3.6165	4.9365	4.0059	5.0506	3.6039	6.3984	4.9899
	(0.1316)	(0.0862)	(0.1105)	(0.0963)	(0.1222)	(0.1451)	(0.1771)	(0.2505)	(0.1871)	(0.3093)
Differences	−0.5803***	0.0744	0.1275	0.1996**	−0.1832*	−0.0147	−0.3888**	−0.1519	−0.1726	0.2407
	(0.1724)	(0.1187)	(0.1432)	(0.1218)	(0.1453)	(0.1788)	(0.2163)	(0.3035)	(0.2227)	(0.4024)
Differences-in-differences	−0.6547***		−0.0720		−0.1685		−0.2368		−0.4133	
	(0.2111)		(0.1867)		(0.2380)		(0.4018)		(0.4923)	

Note: Standard errors in parentheses.

***Significant at the 1 percent level.

**Significant at the 5 percent level.

*Significant at the 10 percent level.

Table 3.8   **Sample Differences-in-Differences Estimates of the Effect of the Reform on Average Tenure, by Industry**

	Formal	Informal	Formal	Informal	Formal	Informa
	Agriculture		Mining		Manufacturing	
Postreform	5.6232	5.0688	5.8725	4.1875	5.3031	4.2360
	(0.3975)	(0.4503)	(0.4731)	(0.8474)	(0.0915)	(0.1128)
Prereform	5.724	6.0402	4.4010	3.4091	5.0920	4.3843
	(0.6194)	(0.4503)	(0.5431)	(0.7922)	(0.1164)	(0.1438)
Differences	−0.1008	−0.9714	1.4716**	0.7784	0.2112*	−0.1483
	(0.7359)	(0.6947)	(0.7245)	(1.1601)	(0.1481)	(0.1827)
Differences-in-	0.8706		0.6931		0.3595	
differences	(1.0964)		(1.3608)		(0.2341)	
	Utilities		Construction		Commerce	
Postreform	6.8926	—	4.0121	4.2889	4.5763	4.9136
	(0.3778)	—	(0.1859)	(0.1729)	(0.0823)	(0.0862)
Prereform	7.9114	—	4.0532	3.4439	4.6654	4.9855
	(0.4736)	—	(0.2558)	(0.1904)	(0.1217)	(0.1001)
Differences	−1.0188***	—	0.0411	0.8449***	−0.0892	−0.0719
	(0.6059)	—	(0.3163)	(0.2572)	(0.1469)	(0.1321)
Differences-in-	—		−0.8861		−0.0173	
differences	—		(0.4382)		(0.2046)	
	Transportation		Financial Services		Services	
Postreform	5.22	4.5496	4.8835	5.1026	6.2118	4.2454
	(0.1766)	(0.1564)	(0.1364)	(0.2744)	(0.0992)	(0.0985)
Prereform	6.1895	4.9789	5.6848	5.0121	6.8428	4.0234
	(0.2455)	(0.2144)	(0.2072)	(0.3692)	(0.1332)	(0.1053)
Differences	−0.9695***	0.4292**	−0.8013***	0.0905	−0.6310***	0.2220*
	(0.3025)	(0.2654)	(0.2480)	(1.2636)	(0.1661)	(0.1442)
Differences-in-	−0.5403†		−0.8919**		−0.8530***	
differences	(0.4009)		(0.4961)		(0.2189)	

Note: Standard errors in parentheses.
***Significant at the 1 percent level.
**Significant at the 5 percent level.
*Significant at the 10 percent level.

be presented. Moreover, consistent with the changes predicted by the labor market reform, the changes that are significant are driven by reductions in the tenures of covered workers and not by the increase in tenures of uncovered workers.

Table 3.9 shows the differences-in-differences estimates by firm size. The results show that the effects of the reform were greatest for larger firms, as predicted by the changes in the legislation. The differences-in-differences estimates for the self-employed and for workers employed in firms with two to five employees and in firms with five to ten employees are not significantly different from zero. In contrast, the estimate of the effect of the

Table 3.9   Sample Differences-in-Differences Estimates of the Effect of the Reform on Average Tenure, by Firm Size

	Self-Employed		Firms 2–5 Employees		Firms 5–10 Employees		Firms > 10 Employees	
	Formal	Informal	Formal	Informal	Formal	Informal	Formal	Informal
Postreform	6.2577	5.8356	4.9708	4.1192	4.2154	2.8678	5.3992	2.7353
	(0.1868)	(0.1333)	(0.1372)	(0.0804)	(0.1254)	(0.1175)	(0.0542)	(0.0863)
Prereform	6.4868	5.7927	5.0944	4.1052	4.2092	2.9897	5.7947	2.6027
	(0.3235)	(0.1014)	(0.1826)	(0.0931)	(0.1804)	(0.1444)	(0.0736)	(0.1156)
Differences	−0.2291	0.0426	−0.1237	0.0139	0.0063	−0.1219	−0.3955***	0.1326
	(0.3736)	(0.1333)	(0.2284)	(0.1230)	(0.2197)	(0.1862)	(0.0914)	(0.1442)
Differences-in-differences	−0.2718		−0.1377		0.1281		−0.5281***	
	(0.3734)		(0.2514)		(0.2864)		(0.2134)	

Note: Standard errors in parentheses.

***Significant at the 1 percent level.

reform for workers employed in firms with more than ten employees was a reduction of 6.3372 months. The effect of the reform on workers employed by large firms is big, significantly different from zero, and driven mainly by a reduction of tenures of covered workers rather than by an increase of the tenures of uncovered workers. This evidence is strongly consistent with the expected effects of a reduction in firing costs, since the self-employed and workers employed in firms with less than five employees are completely exempt from severance, and workers employed in firms with little capital are only entitled to partial severance payments.

Unemployment Duration

The model predicts that a reduction in dismissal costs should increase the exit rate out of unemployment and into formal jobs relative to the exit rate out of unemployment and into informal jobs. Thus, the reduction in severance payments would be expected to shorten unemployment spells of workers hired into formal jobs relative to those of workers hired into informal jobs.[17]

Table 3.10 presents the differences-in-differences estimates of unemployment spells.[18] The average unemployment spell for workers whose spell ended with a formal-sector job increased. However, the average unemployment spell of workers whose spell ended in an informal-sector job lengthened by even more than that of formal workers. Thus, the differences-in-differences estimate was a reduction in the average unemployment spell of 3.1108 weeks and significantly different from zero.[19] Table 3.11 presents the results for men and women separately. The differences-in-differences estimate for men was not significantly different from zero, but the effect on women was a shortening of the average unemployment spell of 7.9672 weeks and was significant at the 1 percent level. Table 3.12 presents the differences-in-differences estimates for different age groups, and table 3.13 presents the differences-in-differences estimates for different education groups. The results show that unemployment spells decreased most for young and middle-aged workers. This result is consistent with the expectation that a decrease in firing costs should increase hiring, especially for out-

17. In particular, the average unemployment spell of those going into formal jobs should decline because the increased probability of being hired into a formal firm should reduce the fraction of workers with long spells. Moreover, the fraction of workers with short spells (those just fired from formal jobs) increases.

18. Unemployed workers are defined as formal if the job subsequent to their unemployed spell was in the formal sector and as informal if their job subsequent to the unemployed spell was in the informal sector.

19. Contrary to the results for tenure, the differences-in-differences results for unemployment spells are driven mainly by the lengthening of the spells of those exiting into the informal sector. This is, however, consistent with the model previously presented. On the one hand, the model predicts that the probability of being hired in the formal sector should rise after the reform because of the increase in the number of firms producing in this sector. On the other hand, the probability of being hired into the informal sector falls unambiguously.

Table 3.10   **Sample Differences-in-Differences Estimates of the Effect of the Reform on Average Unemployment Duration**

	Formal	Informal
Postreform	7.5985	9.7731
	(0.1187)	(0.1489)
Prereform	7.3328	8.7297
	(0.1489)	(0.1630)
Differences	0.2657*	1.0434***
	(0.1904)	(0.2208)
Differences-in-differences		−0.7777***
		(0.2929)

Note: Standard errors in parentheses.
***Significant at the 1 percent level.
*Significant at the 10 percent level.

Table 3.11   **Sample Differences-in-Differences Estimates of the Effect of the Reform on Average Unemployment Duration, by Gender**

	Men		Women	
	Formal	Informal	Formal	Informal
Postreform	6.6402	7.3753	9.3743	14.7665
	(0.1284)	(0.1420)	(0.2394)	(0.3413)
Prereform	6.3455	6.9092	9.4983	12.8988
	(0.1536)	(0.1569)	(0.3321)	(0.3894)
Differences	0.2947**	0.4660***	−0.1240	1.8678***
	(0.2002)	(0.2116)	(0.4094)	(0.5178)
Differences-in-differences	−0.1713		−1.9918***	
	(0.2925)		(0.6592)	

Note: Standard errors in parentheses.
***Significant at the 1 percent level.
**Significant at the 5 percent level.

siders, and is also confirmed in the formal hazard analysis that follows. Moreover, table 3.13 shows that the differences-in-differences estimates are greatest for workers with incomplete secondary or incomplete university education. Thus, the firing cost effect on hiring appears to be greater on workers that are risky hires. This is also confirmed by the formal hazard analysis.

Table 3.14 presents the differences-in-differences estimates of the effect of the reform on unemployment spells by industry. The differences-in-differences estimates are not significantly different from zero in agriculture, mining, manufacturing, utilities, construction, transportation, and financial services. Only the effects on commerce and services are signifi-

Table 3.12   **Sample Differences-in-Differences Estimates of the Effect of the Reform on Averag Unemployment Duration, by Age Group**

	Age < 24 years		24–55 Years		Age > 55 Years	
	Formal	Informal	Formal	Informal	Formal	Inform
Postreform	5.0951	5.7650	7.6482	10.0925	11.7779	14.7266
	(0.1924)	(0.1940)	(0.1328)	(0.1813)	(0.6590)	(0.6043
Prereform	5.3906	5.2083	7.5569	9.2324	9.0156	12.8679
	(0.2454)	(0.1823)	(0.1729)	(0.2077)	(0.7171)	(0.6642
Differences	−0.2956	0.5567***	0.0914	0.8601***	2.7623***	1.8587
	(0.3118)	(0.2662)	(0.2180)	(0.2757)	(0.9739)	(0.8979
Differences-in-differences	−0.8523**		−0.7688***		0.9037	
	(0.4184)		(0.3481)		(0.1396)	

Note: Standard errors in parentheses.
***Significant at the 1 percent level.
**Significant at the 5 percent level.

cantly different from zero. The differences-in-differences estimate of the effect of the reform was a reduction of 1.2746 weeks of the unemployment spell in commerce, which was only significant at the 5 percent level, and a reduction of 1.3126 weeks of the unemployment spell in services, which was significant at the 1 percent level. Thus, as for tenure, the results do not show a consistent pattern of a differential impact on tradable and non-tradable sectors. In contrast, the differences-in-differences estimates by firm size in table 3.15 provide some evidence that the firing cost effect was greatest among larger firms. In particular, the differences-in-differences estimates of the reform on firms with five to ten employees and on firms with more than ten employees indicate reductions of the average unemployment spell of 0.8038 weeks and of 0.2913 weeks, respectively. Although neither effect is significant at conventional levels, the p-values for the differences-in-differences estimates of larger firms are greater than the p-values for the estimates of the self-employed and of firms with two to five employees.

3.6.3   Employment and Unemployment Survivor Functions, Before and After the Reform

While the previous section presented the implied effects of the reform on tenure and unemployment spells, this section presents evidence on the effects of the reform on the survival probabilities in employment and unemployment. If the reduction of dismissal costs introduced by the reform was indeed important, then the probability of survival in a formal job should have fallen after the reform relative to the probability of survival in an informal job. In addition, if the reduction in dismissal costs generated more hiring, then the probability of survival in unemployment should have fallen after the reform for workers exiting into formal jobs relative to those exiting into informal jobs.

Table 3.13   Sample Differences-in-Differences Estimates of the Effect of the Reform on Average Unemployment Duration, by Education Group

	Primary Education		Secondary Education		High School		University Education		University Degree or More	
	Formal	Informal	Formal	Informal	Formal	Informal	Formal	Informal	Formal	Informal
Postreform	8.8191	9.4874	7.8214	9.6863	7.5593	10.8365	6.7676	10.9950	6.0907	8.9383
	(0.2843)	(0.2115)	(0.2306)	(0.2738)	(0.2248)	(0.4081)	(0.3448)	(0.8242)	(0.2727)	(0.6899)
Prereform	7.4296	8.4493	8.1181	8.5266	7.4414	11.1706	6.9614	8.3146	5.3086	7.8942
	(0.2739)	(0.2166)	(0.2948)	(0.2956)	(0.3164)	(0.5824)	(0.4944)	(0.8936)	(0.3918)	(0.9386)
Differences	1.3894***	1.0381***	−0.3666	1.1597**	0.1179	−0.3341	−0.1938	2.6804***	0.7822**	1.0441
	(0.3948)	(0.3027)	(0.3742)	(0.4029)	(0.3881)	(0.7111)	(0.6027)	(1.2157)	(0.4773)	(1.1648)
Differences-in-differences	0.3513		−0.5263***		0.4520		−2.8742***		−0.2619	
	(0.5224)		(0.5560)		(0.7431)		(1.2379)		(1.1239)	

Note: Standard errors in parentheses.

***Significant at the 1 percent level.

**Significant at the 5 percent level.

Table 3.14   **Sample Differences-in-Differences Estimates of the Effect of the Reform on Avera Unemployment Duration, by Industry**

	Formal	Informal	Formal	Informal	Formal	Inform
	Agriculture		Mining		Manufacturing	
Postreform	6.5332	6.5428	6.0294	6.2292	7.2766	10.2512
	(0.9948)	(0.8265)	(1.1816)	(2.2612)	(0.2177)	(0.3665)
Prereform	7.812	6.3489	5.9455	6.5606	7.4136	9.9015
	(1.3781)	(0.8538)	(1.1462)	(2.0028)	(0.2703)	(0.4279)
Differences	−1.2788	0.1939	0.0839	−0.3314	−0.1370	0.3496
	(1.6995)	(1.1883)	(1.6462)	(3.0207)	(0.3471)	(0.5634)
Differences-in-differences	−1.4728		0.4153		−0.4866	
	(2.0497)		(3.2289)		(0.6275)	
	Utilities		Construction		Commerce	
Postreform	9.8	6.5	5.8669	5.3911	7.4709	11.59
	(1.1168)	(1.6065)	(0.4841)	(0.2734)	(0.2522)	(0.2940)
Prereform	6.4314	3	5.4792	4.8239	7.4513	10.3010
	(0.8747)	(1.5)	(0.5700)	(0.2947)	(0.3427)	(0.3118)
Differences	3.3686***	3.5*	0.3878	0.5671*	0.0197	1.2943
	(1.4186)	(2.1979)	(0.7478)	(0.4019)	(0.4254)	(0.4286)
Differences-in-differences	−0.1314		−0.1794		−1.2746**	
	(6.2663)		(0.7816)		(0.6425)	
	Transportation		Financial Services		Services	
Postreform	6.3961	6.9820	6.9234	9.6664	8.8563	10.1112
	(0.3678)	(0.3759)	(0.3546)	(0.7508)	(0.2602)	(0.3019)
Prereform	6.6343	6.4011	6.6883	10.1782	8.0041	7.9464
	(0.5120)	(0.4580)	(0.4317)	(1.0164)	(0.3233)	(0.2956)
Differences	−0.2381	0.5809	0.2351	0.5119	0.8522**	2.1648*
	(0.6304)	(0.5925)	(0.5586)	(1.2636)	(0.4150)	(0.4226)
Differences-in-differences	−0.8190		−0.7470		−1.3126***	
	(0.8679)		(1.1993)		(0.5924)	

Note: Standard errors in parentheses.
***Significant at the 1 percent level.
**Significant at the 5 percent level.
*Significant at the 10 percent level.

Figure 3.2 presents the Kaplan-Meier survival estimates for employment. This figure includes the probabilities of survival for formal and informal workers before and after the reform. The figure shows that the probability that a formal job lasts more than two years decreased after the reform. For tenures of more than two years, the survivor function of formal workers after the reform (formal/Post90) shifts down with respect to the survivor function of formal workers before the reform (formal/Pre90). However, for tenures of less than two years, the survivor function of formal

Table 3.15 Sample Differences-in-Differences Estimates of the Effect of the Reform on Average Unemployment Duration, by Firm Size

	Self-Employed		Firms 2–5 Employees		Firms 5–10 Employees		Firms > 10 Employees	
	Formal	Informal	Formal	Informal	Formal	Informal	Formal	Informal
Postreform	9.8851	12.0358	8.3693	8.7661	6.7852	6.6247	7.3144	7.3804
	(0.5317)	(0.2641)	(0.3914)	(0.2359)	(0.3668)	(0.3684)	(0.1333)	(0.2880)
Prereform	8.4208	10.3226	7.2331	8.2628	6.6018	5.6375	7.3701	7.1446
	(0.8966)	(0.2876)	(0.4802)	(0.2618)	(0.4255)	(0.3359)	(0.1687)	(0.3545)
Differences	1.4642*	1.7132***	1.1361**	0.5033*	0.1834	0.9872	−0.0556***	0.2358
	(1.0424)	(0.3905)	(0.6195)	(0.3524)	(0.5618)	(0.4986)	(0.2150)	(0.3926)
Differences-in-differences	−0.2490		0.6328		−0.8038		−0.2913	
	(1.0863)		(0.7099)		(0.7486)		(0.5205)	

Note: Standard errors in parentheses.

***Significant at the 1 percent level.

**Significant at the 5 percent level.

*Significant at the 10 percent level.

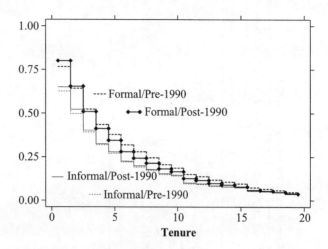

Fig. 3.2   Kaplan-Meier employment survival estimates, by period and coverage

workers after the reform shifted up from what it had been before the reform. That survivor function is greater for formal workers with less than two years of tenure after the reform is surprising, given the extension by the reform of the use of temporary contracts for less than a year. However, this shift in the survivor function for those with less than two years of tenure may simply reflect the greater hiring of new permanent workers after the reform, as will be shown in the estimation of formal hazard models. The downward shift of the survivor function of formal workers after the reform is consistent with the reduction in dismissal costs for formal firms after the reform. In contrast, however, figure 3.2 shows that the probability of survival increased slightly for informal workers after the reform relative to the probability prior to the reform. The survivor function of uncovered workers after the reform (informal/Post90) shifted up slightly from its level before the reform (informal/Pre90). If common shocks to both groups were responsible for the decreased probability of survival of formal jobs, then the figure should also show a downward shift of the survivor function for informal workers. Moreover, consistent with the fact that formal workers are covered by job security regulations while informal workers are not, the survivor functions for formal workers are higher than the survivor functions of informal workers both before and after the reform. The survivor functions for the covered and uncovered groups, as well as the shifts of the survivor functions for each group after the reform, are thus consistent with the predicted effects of firing costs and with the predicted effects of the reform on formal turnover.

Standard Kaplan-Meier survival functions of unemployment show a similar change after the reform. Figure 3.3 shows that the unemployment survival functions of formal hires shifted down between the prereform

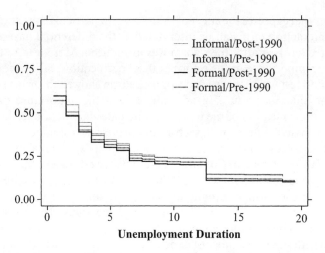

Unemployment Duration

Fig. 3.3   Kaplan-Meier unemployment survival estimates, by period and coverage

(formal/Pre90) and postreform (formal/Post90) periods. Thus, for every unemployment spell of duration t, the probability of remaining unemployed decreased after the reform for those who exited into formal employment. In contrast, figure 3.3 shows that the unemployment survival functions increased slightly for informal workers after the reform. These shifts are consistent with the expected effects of the reform. The reduction of firing costs would have predicted that the probability of remaining unemployed at every time t should have decreased for workers covered by the reform but not for uncovered workers. Moreover, the next section shows that the escape rates into and out of unemployment increased for formal workers relative to informal workers, even after controlling for observable characteristics.

3.6.4   Formal Hazard Models

It is possible that the employment and unemployment spells and the survivor functions presented in the foregoing sections changed after the reform due to changes in the characteristics of workers and jobs after 1990. Thus, I will proceed to estimate formal duration models that allow the effects of changes in worker and job characteristics on exit hazard rates to be controlled for.

As described in section 3.4, I estimate exponential hazard models that control for age, education, marital status, city, industry of employment, and the number of dependents. More important, these formal hazard models can capture the effects of the reform. The models include a formal dummy that controls for differential turnover patterns across groups, a Post90 dummy that captures the differential turnover pattern in turnover after 1990 for all groups, and an interaction term of the formal and Post90 dummies that captures the effect of the reform. In particular, the coefficient of the interaction term can be interpreted as the differential hazard rates of covered workers after the reform was introduced. Moreover, to further probe the importance of the reform, other specifications of the model are included to test whether the effects of the reform showed the expected patterns for different groups. In addition, to test the importance of trade shocks, a specification of the model that includes interaction terms of the formal × Post90 dummy with sector dummies is also estimated.

Table 3.16 shows the results of the estimation of exponential exit hazard rates out of employment. Column (1) presents the estimates obtained from the basic specification of the model that includes the covariates previously mentioned, the formal dummy, the Post90 dummy, and the interaction term of the two. The results show the expected signs. The hazards are higher for younger, more educated, female, and single workers and for workers with smaller number of dependents. The results also show that the hazards out of employment decreased during the post-1990 period for informal workers. Moreover, as expected, formal workers, who are covered by the legislation, have lower hazards out of employment than do informal workers. Most important, the coefficient on the interaction term is positive and significant at the 1 percent level. In particular, the coefficient indicates that after the reform covered workers are 6.17 percent more likely to exit employment than are uncovered workers. This result suggests that the reduction in firing costs introduced by the reform substantially increased the exit rates out of employment. Exit hazards out of employment are likely to have increased after the reform, both because of the increase in dismissals and because of the increase in employees' quitting that results from greater hiring after the reform.

Another essential feature of the reform was the greater flexibility in the use of temporary (fixed-term) contracts, and one may thus suspect that a great deal of the increases in turnover after the reform may simply be the result of increased hiring of temporary workers in the formal sector. The specification in column (2) allows us to distinguish whether the increase in the exit rates out of employment was purely the result of the increase in the use of temporary contracts or if the reduction in the cost of firing permanent workers also played a role. Column (2) in table 3.16 presents the estimates of a model including a permanent dummy, an interaction term of the Post90 dummy and the permanent dummy, an interaction term of the formal dummy and the Permanent dummy, and an interaction of the formal × Post90 dummy with the Permanent dummy.[20] All the coefficients have the same signs as before, and the coefficient on the Permanent dummy is

---

20. The permanent dummy takes the value of 1 if the worker is a permanent worker and zero if the worker is temporary.

le 3.16	Exponential Hazard Model Estimates of Employment Duration			
iable	(1)	(2)	(3)	(4)
mal	−0.2286	0.1354	−0.0853	−0.2409
	(0.0113)	(0.0036)	(0.0027)	(0.0105)
t90	−0.1247	−0.0508	−0.0483	0.0688
	(0.0011)	(0.0022)	(0.0019)	(0.0080)
mal × Post 90	0.0617	0.0673	0.0279	0.0284
	(0.0015)	(0.0042)	(0.0032)	(0.0129)
manent		−0.3939		
		(0.0021)		
mal × Permanent		−0.3401		
		(0.0039)		
t90 × Permanent		0.0268		
		(0.0026)		
mal × Post90 × Permanent		−0.0062		
		(0.0045)		
mal × Post90 × Age 25–55 years			0.0359	
			(0.0029)	
mal × Post90 × Age > 55 years			−0.0222	
			(0.0049)	
mal × Post90 × Secondary Education			0.0124	
			(0.0031)	
mal × Post90 × High School Degree			0.0538	
			(0.0035)	
mal × Post90 × University Education			0.0596	
			(0.0035)	
mal × Post90 × University Degree			−0.0254	
			(0.0054)	
mal × Post90 × Mining				−0.4799
				(0.0281)
mal × Post90 × Manufacturing				−0.0321
				(0.0133)
mal × Post90 × Utilities				1.9788
				(0.0661)
mal × Post90 × Construction				0.0867
				(0.0143)
mal × Post90 × Commerce				−0.0033
				(0.0133)
mal × Post90 × Transportation				0.1178
				(0.0141)
mal × Post90 × Financial Services				0.1339
				(0.0144)
mal × Post90 × Services				0.0367
				(0.0133)
;-likelihood	−12.256,412	−12,131,391	−12,157,990	−12,240,447

es: No. of observations = 55,683. The table reports changes in the employment hazard estimate with onential hazard models. The models include three age dummies, five education dummies, dummies sex and marital status, number of dependents, nine industry dummies, and six city dummies. mptotic standard errors are in parentheses.

negative and significant at the 1 percent level, as expected. The results show that the coefficient on the formal $\times$ Post90 interaction is positive, but the interaction term of the formal $\times$ Post90 dummy with the Permanent dummy is negative and significant at the 1 percent level. The results indicate that, after the reform, the probability of exiting employment was 6.7 percent higher for temporary workers in the formal sector than for temporary workers in the uncovered sector. At the same time, the probability of exiting employment was 6.1 percent higher for permanent workers in the formal sector than for permanent workers in the uncovered sector after the reform. Thus, while the introduction of temporary contracts does appear to explain part of the increased turnover of formal workers, the results also suggest that the reduction of dismissal costs for permanent workers also contributed to increasing turnover.

Column (3) in table 3.16 presents the results of specifications including interaction terms of the reform effect with the age and education variables. This specification of the model allows us to see whether the impact of the reform was greater on the groups that would be expected to be affected most by the changes in the legislation. First, since the reform increased the costs of dismissing workers with more than ten years of tenure, the impact of the reform would be expected to be greater for groups with less than ten years of tenure (i.e., younger workers). Second, the special contracts introduced by the reform, which exempted workers with more than ten times the minimum wage from severance payments, would be expected to affect most the turnover of highly educated workers who are likely to earn more than ten times the minimum wage. Column (3) shows that, indeed, the hazard rates of younger and middle-aged workers increased by more than the hazard rates of older workers. Young workers with secondary education hired in the formal sector were 4.1 percent more likely to exit employment than were younger informal workers with secondary education after the reform. Similarly, middle-aged formal workers with secondary education were 7.9 percent more likely to exit employment than were middle-aged informal workers with secondary education after the reform. The smallest impact of the reform was on older formal workers, who were only 1.8 percent more likely to exit employment than were older informal workers after the reform. These results are thus consistent with lower expected dismissals of workers with more than ten years of tenure. Moreover, the results also indicate that the impact of the reform was greater on more educated workers, who are more likely to have benefited from the use of Integral Salary contracts. The exit rate of middle-aged formal workers with a primary education increased by 6.6 percent after the reform relative to middle-aged informal workers with the same level of education. The exit rate of middle-aged formal workers with secondary education, a high school degree, and university education increased after the reform by 7.9 percent, 12.5 percent, and 13.1 percent, respectively, relative to middle-aged informal workers with the same levels of education. In contrast, the hazard out of employment increased only by 3.8 percent for middle-aged formal workers with more than a university degree after the reform relative to middle-aged informal workers with the highest educational attainment. The impact was thus smallest among the least and the most educated. The small impact on these groups may be due to the fact that these workers have longer tenures and consequently are more likely to have been affected by the increase in the costs of unjust dismissals for tenures of more than ten years.

While these patterns are consistent with the effects of the labor market reform on different groups, it may be that part of the increased turnover is the result of trade shocks that affect various groups differently. Column (4) in table 3.16 presents the results from an exponential hazard model that includes interaction terms of the formal × Post90 dummy with sector dummies. The idea is that if trade liberalization were responsible for the increased turnover after the labor market reform, then the observed impact would be greater on workers employed in tradable sectors than on those employed in nontradable sectors. The results from Column (4) in table 3.16 show that the increase in turnover of covered workers after the reform was greater in utilities, transportation, construction, and services. The probability of exiting formal employment in these sectors after the reform was 640 percent, 15.7 percent, 12.3 percent, and 17.6 percent greater than the probability of exiting informal employment in these sectors. However, if the trade shocks were a main source of the increased turnover, it would be expected that the exit rate out of employment would have increased more for workers hired in trade-intensive sectors such as commerce and manufacturing. In fact, after the reform formal workers in commerce were only 2.5 percent more likely to exit employment than were informal workers in this sector. Moreover, the probability of exiting employment was 1 percent lower after the reform for formal workers relative to informal workers hired in manufacturing. Thus, the results from the exponential hazard model do not provide any reason to believe that trade liberalization increased turnover for covered workers after 1990.

Table 3.17 includes the results of exponential hazards out of unemployment. Given the reduction of mandated firing costs, one would expect greater hiring in the covered sector and a corresponding increase in the escape rate out of unemployment for workers hired into formal-sector jobs. Column (1) shows that, indeed, the exit hazard out of unemployment increased by 5.75 percent for covered workers after the reform relative to uncovered workers.[21] Moreover, while the extension of temporary contracts appears to explain part of the increased hiring, most of the increase in the

---

21. The sign on the formal dummy is positive and significant at the 1 percent level. This could be explained if unsuccessful discouraged workers who get tired of searching for formal work turned to the informal sector as a last resource.

Table 3.17   **Exponential Hazard Models of Unemployment Duration**

Variable	(1)	(2)	(3)	(4)
Formal	0.0575	−0.0070	−0.1752	−0.330
	(0.0016)	(0.0036)	(0.0036)	(0.010
Post90	−0.0450	−0.0255	−0.1202	0.056
	(0.0011)	(0.0023)	(0.0028)	(0.008
Formal × Post 90	0.0575	0.0400	0.0827	0.327
	(0.0016)	(0.0042)	(0.0045)	(0.013
Permanent		0.2676		
		(0.0022)		
Formal × Permanent		0.1335		
		(0.0039)		
Post90 × Permanent		−0.0092		
		(0.0026)		
Formal × Post90 × Permanent		0.0208		
		(0.0046)		
Formal × Post90 × Age 25–55 years			−0.1908	
			(0.0041)	
Formal × Post90 × Age > 55 years			−0.3479	
			(0.0066)	
Formal × Post90 × Secondary Education			0.1468	
			(0.0041)	
Formal × Post90 × High School Degree			0.1195	
			(0.0047)	
Formal × Post90 × University Education			0.4229	
			(0.0072)	
Formal × Post90 × University Degree			0.2184	
			(0.0066)	
Formal × Post90 × Mining				0.049
				(0.028
Formal × Post90 × Manufacturing				−0.299
				(0.013
Formal × Post90 × Utilities				−0.083
				(0.066
Formal × Post90 × Construction				−0.342
				(0.014
Formal × Post90 × Commerce				−0.261
				(0.013
Formal × Post90 × Transportation				−0.287
				(0.014
Formal × Post90 × Financial Services				−0.394
				(0.014
Formal × Post90 × Services				−0.223
				(0.013
Log-likelihood	−17,671,211	−17,613,645	−17,639,878	−17,643

Notes: No. of observations = 55,683. The table reports changes in the unemployment hazard estim
with exponential hazard models. The models include three age dummies, five education dummies, d
mies for sex and marital status, number of dependents, nine industry dummies, and six city dumm
Asymptotic standard errors are in parentheses.

exit hazards out of unemployment is due to the increased hazards into permanent jobs in the formal sector. The results from column (2) in table 3.17 show that the escape rate out of unemployment increased by 4 percent for formal temporary workers after the reform relative to temporary informal workers. However, the exit rate out of unemployment increased by even more for formal permanent workers after the reform, indicating that the reduction in dismissal costs of permanent workers did increase the incentives to hire this type of workers. The results show that the probability of exiting unemployment and entering a formal permanent job increased by 6.1 percent after the reform relative to the probability of entering an informal permanent job.[22]

Column (3) in table 3.17 presents the results of the exponential hazard model, including interaction terms of the reform effect with the age and education variables. The estimates from this model show that, as for the hazards out of employment, the impact of the reform was greater on younger and more educated workers. The reform should have had greater effects on the exit rates out of unemployment for younger workers if the reduction in dismissal costs decreased the power of insiders and induced more hiring of young outsiders. In fact, the exit rate out of unemployment and into formal jobs for young workers increased by 25.8 percent after the reform relative to the exit rate into informal jobs. The exit rate into formal jobs for middle-aged workers also increased after the reform, but not by as much. In particular, the hazard rate out of unemployment and into formal jobs increased by 3.9 percent for middle-aged workers relative to informal workers. In contrast, the hazard rates out of unemployment and into formal jobs decreased by 11.1 percent for older workers after the reform relative to those entering informal jobs. In addition, these results show that the impact of the reform on exit hazard rates out of unemployment was greatest on the more educated. This is to be expected, given that these workers are the ones more likely to opt for the Integral Salary contract that exempts workers from severance and other dismissal costs. In fact, the hazards out of unemployment and into formal jobs decreased after the reform by 10 percent relative to the hazard out of unemployment and into informal jobs for workers with primary education and by 3.9 percent and 1.2 percent for workers with secondary schooling and a high school degree, respectively. In contrast, after the reform, the exit rates out of unemployment and into formal jobs increased by 37 percent for university graduates and by 12 percent for workers with more than a university degree relative to the exit rates into informal jobs.

---

22. The sign on the permanent dummy is positive and significant at the 1 percent level. As in note 21, this is probably due to the possibility that discouraged workers who are unsuccessful in finding a permanent position turn to temporary jobs as a last resource.

Finally, column (4) in table 3.17 shows the results of the hazard model with sector dummy and reform interactions. The results show that the increase in the exit rates out of unemployment after the reform was greater for workers exiting into formal-sector jobs in mining, utilities, and services. The probability of exiting unemployment into formal employment in these sectors after the reform was 45.7 percent, 27.6 percent, and 10.9 percent greater than the probability of exiting unemployment into informal employment in these sectors. However, the probability of exiting unemployment into formal employment in trade-intensive sectors such as commerce and manufacturing was only 2.8 percent and 6.7 percent higher than the probability of exiting unemployment into informal employment in these sectors. Thus, like the results from the employment hazard models, these results from the unemployment hazard model do not provide evidence to indicate the importance of trade liberalization in increasing worker turnover after 1990. Instead, the increased hazards in utilities and services, which are more likely to be public-sector jobs covered by the legislation, indicate the importance of the labor market reform in generating these patterns in turnover.

3.7   Worker Turnover and Unemployment

The previous section showed that the functioning of labor markets changed substantially in Colombia after the introduction of the labor market reform of 1990. In particular, the estimates from the formal hazards show that, after controlling for observable characteristics, the postreform period was characterized by higher exit rates into and out of unemployment in the formal sector relative to the informal sector.

While the results in the previous section indicate that the reform increased labor market flexibility by increasing the flows into and out of unemployment, the net effects of the reform on employment and unemployment are ambiguous. In this section, I use the steady-state condition of the model in section 3.4, together with the hazard rate results obtained in section 3.6, to obtain a rough estimate of the net effect of the reform on unemployment.

In the previous model, a steady-state condition has to be satisfied such that the flow into unemployment from both sectors must equal the flow out of unemployment and into both sectors:

$$\lambda_F e_F + \theta q(\theta)[1 - F(A_{crit})]G(\overline{\gamma}_F)u + \lambda_I e_I + \theta q(\theta)F(A_{crit})G(\overline{\gamma}_I)u$$
$$= \theta q(\theta)[1 - F(A_{crit})]u + \theta q(\theta)F(A_{crit})u$$

Substituting for employment in each sector, $e_F = (1 - F[A_{crit}])e$ and $e_I = F(A_{crit})e$, and for the identity, $e + u = 1$, and solving for u yields the following formula for the unemployment rate:

$$u =$$

$$\frac{[1 - F(A_{\text{crit}})]\lambda_F + F(A_{\text{crit}})\lambda_I}{[1 - F(A_{\text{crit}})]\lambda_F + F(A_{\text{crit}})\lambda_I + [1 - F(A_{\text{crit}})]\theta q(\theta)[1 - G(\bar{\gamma}_F)] + F(A_{\text{crit}})\theta q(\theta)[1 - G(\bar{\gamma}_I)]}$$

The unemployment rate can be estimated from this equation by substituting for the average hazard rates into and out of unemployment during the prereform period and the shares in each sector. The average hazard rates are estimated with the average tenure and unemployment spells in tables 3.4 and 3.10, which indicate an average tenure of 67.2 and 54.2 months in the formal and informal sectors and average unemployment spells of 1.8 and 2.2 months in the formal and informal sectors during the prereform period. The shares of formal and informal employment are reported in table 3.1. Before the reform, the shares of formal and informal employment were 0.45 and 0.55, respectively. After the reform, the shares of formal and informal employment changed to 0.51 and 0.49, respectively. Finally, tables 3.16 and 3.17 show an increase in the hazards into and out of unemployment of 6.17 percent and 5.75 percent.

As the model abstracts from many factors affecting labor markets, the estimated unemployment obtained from the previous formula should not be interpreted as a precise estimate of the unemployment rate but rather as an indication of the magnitude of the changes in unemployment rates between the two periods. For example, taking into account other flows such as retirements, new entries into the labor market, and deaths, the unemployment rate is

$$u =$$

$$\frac{\xi + \psi + \sigma + [1 - F(A_{\text{crit}})]\lambda_F + F(A_{\text{crit}})\lambda_I}{\xi + \psi + \sigma + [1 - F(A_{\text{crit}})]\lambda_F + F(A_{\text{crit}})\lambda_I + [1 - F(A_{\text{crit}})]\theta q(\theta)[1 - G(\bar{\gamma}_F)] + F(A_{\text{crit}})\theta q(\theta)[1 - G(\bar{\gamma}_I)]},$$

where ξ, ψ, and σ are the flows due to retirements, new entries, and deaths, which are estimated assuming a working life of thirty-five years, entry at eighteen years of age, and a life expectancy of sixty years for those who die before retiring.

The unemployment rate for the prereform period obtained with this formula is 4.84 percent, which is lower than the true unemployment rate of 11.8 percent in Colombia in 1988. The postreform unemployment rate estimated with the postreform shares is 4.69 percent, which is also lower than the true unemployment in 1992 and 1996, which was 10.2 percent and 10 percent, respectively. These results suggest a reduction in unemployment of 0.15 percent points between the pre- and postreform periods, compared to the actual reduction in unemployment of 1.6 percent between 1988 and 1992 and of 1.8 percent between 1988 and 1996. These results suggest that the reform contributed to about 10 percent of the reduction in the unemployment rate between the pre- and postreform periods.

3.8   Conclusion

The Colombian labor market reform of 1990 provides an interesting quasi-experiment with which to analyze the effects of a reduction in firing costs. This study exploited the temporal change in the legislation together with the difference in coverage between formal and informal workers to analyze the impact of the reform on worker turnover. The differences-in-differences estimates indicate that the reform increased the dynamism of the Colombian labor market by increasing the exit rates into and out of unemployment. Moreover, aside from contributing to increased mobility in the labor market, the reform is also likely to have contributed to increased compliance with labor legislation by lowering the costs of formal production. The increased churning in the labor market and the greater compliance with the legislation are estimated to have contributed to about 10 percent of the reduction in the unemployment rate from the late 1980s to the early 1990s. At the same time, the reform is likely to explain in part the surge in the unemployment rate during the late 1990s. This is because the greater flexibility in hiring and firing after the reform is likely to translate into increased hiring relative to firing during expansions but in increased firings relative to hiring during recessions.

References

Acemoglu, Daron, and Joshua Angrist. 2001. Consequences of employment protection? The case of the Americans with Disabilities Act. *Journal of Political Economy* 109 (5): 915–57.
Anderson, Patricia. 1993. Linear adjustment costs and seasonal labor demand: Evidence from retail trade firms. *Quarterly Journal of Economics* 108 (4): 1015–42.
Angrist, Joshua, and Adriana Kugler. 2003. Protective or counter-productive? Labor market institutions and the effect of immigration on EU natives. *Economic Journal* 113:F302–F331.
Autor, David. 2003. Outsourcing at will: Unjust dismissal doctrine and the growth of temporary help employment. *Journal of Labor Economics* 21 (1): 1–42.
Autor, David, John J. Donohue, III, and Stewart J. Schwab. 2003. The costs of wrongful-discharge laws. NBER Working Paper no. 9425. Cambridge, Mass.: National Bureau of Economic Research, January.
Bentolila, Samuel, and Giuseppe Bertola. 1990. Firing costs and labor demand: How bad is eurosclerosis. *Review of Economic Studies* 57 (3): 381–402.
Bentolila, Samuel, and Juan J. Dolado. 1994. Labour flexibility and wages: Lessons from Spain. *Economic Policy* 9 (181): 53–99.
Bentolila, Samuel, and Gilles Saint-Paul. 1993. The macroeconomic impact of flexible labor contracts, with an application to Spain. *European Economic Review* 36 (5): 1013–54.
Bertola, Giuseppe. 1990. Job security, employment, and wages. *European Economic Review* 54 (4): 851–79.

Bertola, Giuseppe, Francine Blau, and Lawrence Kahn. 2002. Comparative analysis of labor market outcomes: Lessons for the US from international long-run evidence. In *The roaring nineties: Can full employment be sustained?* ed. Alan Krueger and Robert Solow. New York: Russell Sage and Century Foundations.

Blanchard, Oliver, and Justin Wolfers. 2000. The role of shocks and institutions in the rise of European unemployment. *Economic Journal* 110:C1–C34.

Burgess, Simon. 1988. Employment adjustment in UK manufacturing. *Economic Journal* 98:81–104.

Dertouzos, James N., and Lynn A. Karoly. 1993. Employment effects of worker protection: Evidence from the U.S. In *Employment security and labor market behavior,* ed. C. Beuchtermann, 215–227. Ithaca, N.Y.: ILR Press.

Di Tella, Rafael, and Robert MacCulloch. 2004. The consequences of labour market flexibility: Panel evidence based on survey data. *European Economic Review,* forthcoming.

Grubb, David, and William Wells. 1993. Employment regulations and patterns of work in EC countries. *OECD Economic Studies* 21:7–39.

Gruber, Jonathan. 1997. The incidence of payroll taxation: Evidence from Chile. *Journal of Labor Economics* 15 (3): S72–S101.

Hamermesh, Daniel. 1993. Employment protection: Theoretical implications and some U.S. evidence. In *Employment security and labor market behavior,* ed. C. Buechtemann, 126–143. Ithaca, N.Y.: ILR Press.

Heckman, James, and Richard Robb, Jr. 1985. Alternative methods for evaluating the impact of interventions. In *Longitudinal analysis of labor market data,* ed. J. Heckman and B. Singer, 156–245. Cambridge: Cambridge University Press.

Heckman, James, and Burton Singer. 1985. Social science duration analysis. In *Longitudinal analysis of labor market data,* ed. J. Heckman and B. Singer, 39–110. Cambridge: Cambridge University Press.

Hopenhayn, Hugo, and Richard Rogerson. 1993. Job turnover and policy evaluation: A general equilibrium analysis. *Journal of Political Economy* 101 (5): 915–38.

Kugler, Adriana. 2002. Severance payments savings accounts: Evidence from Colombia. CEPR Discussion Paper no. 3197. London: Centre for Economic Policy Research.

Kugler, Adriana, Juan F. Jimeno, and Virginia Hernanz. 2003. Employment consequences of restrictive permanent contracts: Evidence from Spanish labor market reforms. CEPR Discussion Paper no. 3724. London: Centre for Economic Policy Research.

Kugler, Adriana, and Giovanni Pica. 2003. Effects of employment protection and product market regulations on the Italian labor market. CEPR Working Paper no. 4216. Bonn, Germany: Institute for the Study of Labor.

Kugler, Adriana, and Gilles Saint-Paul. 2004. How do firing costs affect worker flows in a world with adverse selection? *Journal of Labor Economics,* forthcoming.

Lazear, Edward. 1990. Job security provisions and employment. *Quarterly Journal of Economics* 105 (3): 699–726.

Lindbeck, Assar, and Dennis Snower. 1988. Cooperation, harassment, and involuntary unemployment. *American Economic Review* 78 (1): 167–88.

Lora, Eduardo, and Marta Luz Henao. 1995. Efectos económicos y sociales de la legislación laboral. [Economic and social effects of labor legislation]. *Coyuntura Social* 13:47–68.

Miles, Thomas. 2000. Common law exceptions to employment at will and U.S. labor markets. *Journal of Law, Economics, and Organization* 16 (1): 74–101.

Nickell, Stephen, and Richard Layard. 1999. Labour market institutions and economic performance. In *Handbook of labor economics,* vol. 3, ed. O. Ashenfelter and D. Card, 3029–84. Amsterdam: North-Holland.

Ocampo, José Antonio. 1987. El régimen prestacional del sector privado. [The nonwage benefit legislation in the private sector]. In *El problema laboral Colombiano*, ed. José Antonio Ocampo and Manuel Ramírez. Bogotá, Colombia: Departamento Nacional de Planeación.

Organization for Economic Cooperation and Development (OECD). 1999. *Employment outlook.* Paris: OECD.

Oyer, Paul, and Scott Schaefer. 2000. Layoffs and litigation. *RAND Journal of Economics* 31 (2): 345–58.

Determinants of Labor Demand in Colombia 1976–1996

Mauricio Cárdenas and Raquel Bernal

4.1 Introduction

In spite of a labor reform introduced in 1990 as part of a reform package that liberalized the economy in many dimensions,[1] Colombia's urban unemployment reached an unprecedented 20 percent by the end of that decade. The 1990 reform made labor contracts more flexible, including a reduction in job security provisions. The most significant change took place in relation to severance payments, with the introduction of a system of individual accounts managed by specialized private funds. Under the old system, employers managed the funds, and employees were allowed to make partial withdrawals at any time. At the time of separation, those withdrawals were debited in nominal terms, adding to the costs faced by employers. In practice, the new system implied a reduction in the level and uncertainty of severance payments for firms. In fact, the initial effect of the reform was to lower nonwage labor costs to 42.9 percent of the basic wage, down from 47.1 percent during the late 1980s. However, the reform did not deal with other important areas of labor legislation, especially payroll taxation.[2]

Mauricio Cárdenas is executive director of Fedesarrollo in Bogotá, Colombia. Raquel Bernal is assistant professor of economics at Northwestern University.

This chapter was mostly written while the authors were affiliated with Fedesarrollo in Bogotá, Colombia. We are grateful to Daniel Hamermesh, Carmen Pagés, and Juan Mauricio Ramírez for comments and suggestions, and to Jairo Augusto Núñez for his valuable help in processing the data for this project.

1. The reforms of the early 1990s were introduced mainly as a result of low growth during the 1980s, combined with an election turnout that gave President César Gaviria, a convinced reformist, a significant majority in congress.

2. The reform kept a 9 percent payroll tax earmarked for labor training by SENA (2 percent), social welfare programs for the unprotected childhood by ICBF (3 percent), and family subsidies provided by the privately managed *Cajas* (4 percent).

The reform package also included a social security law, enacted in 1993, which raised employers' mandatory contributions for health and pension programs. From the viewpoint of the labor market, this reform had important implications resulting from the significant increase in nonwage labor costs. In fact, by 1996 nonwage labor costs had risen to 52 percent of the basic salary, an increase of nearly 10 percentage points relative to their level in 1991.

This chapter analyzes the combined effect of these two reforms on labor demand.[3] The results indicate that the increase in labor costs resulting from the pension and health reform had a negative impact on labor demand. Thus, the chapter calls for a new generation of labor market reform in Colombia, aimed at reducing nonwage labor costs.

The chapter is structured in the following way. Section 4.2 discusses the institutional and regulatory framework governing the labor market, with special attention to the changes introduced in the 1990 and 1993 reforms. Particular emphasis is placed on measuring the nonwage costs implied by the regulation. Section 4.3 shows the main stylized facts in the labor market between 1976 and 1996. Section 4.4 deals with the incidence of payroll taxation on wages in a framework that analyzes the possible endogeneity of wage and nonwage labor costs. More specifically, the section tests whether higher nonwage costs faced by employers have been transferred to workers in the form of lower basic wages. The results suggest that firms do not lower wages when facing higher nonwage labor costs resulting from the legislation. The chapter then moves to the analysis of labor demand. Section 4.5 estimates standard labor demand equations with the time series data. The emphasis of the estimation is placed on the measurement of the own-wage elasticities, as well as the elasticities of substitution between different factors of production. It also tests for possible changes in the value of those elasticities, associated with the reform package of the early 1990s.[4] Section 4.6 presents the results of estimating the determinants of labor demand in a dynamic framework that considers explicitly the impact of the regulations on the path of employment adjustment. Sections 4.7 and 4.8 present the results of labor demand estimations based on panels of manufacturing establishments and sectors, respectively. Section 4.9 concludes.

The main conclusions of the chapter are the following. First, labor demand elasticities in Colombia are around –0.5, a value that is not low[5] (in absolute terms) by international standards. *Ceteris paribus*, the increase in

3. Kugler (chap. 3 in this volume) analyzes the effects of changes in job security provisions, such as severance payments and other dismissal costs, on labor turnover.
4. Trade liberalization was an essential part of the package. As is well known, trade liberalization can make labor demand more elastic by making output markets more competitive and by making domestic labor more substitutable with foreign factors. Or in the words of Hicks (1963, 242), "the demand for anything is likely to be more elastic, the more elastic is demand for any further thing which it contributes to produce."
5. This is assuming that all the increase in taxes and contributions implied an increase in labor costs.

labor costs, has resulted in a significant reduction in labor demand. The message is that the payoff, in terms of greater employment, of a reduction in payroll taxes is considerable. Second, adjustment costs of changing employment as well as wage elasticities were not affected by changes in the regulations regarding severance payments and dismissal costs. In this sense, structural reforms did have an impact on labor demand through its effect on relative prices alone. Finally, we conclude that the wage elasticity of labor demand increases (in absolute terms) during contractions. Hence, the increase in prices and the beginning of a recession had a significant effect on employment.

4.2 Labor Legislation: Recent Changes

As mentioned in the introduction, the regulation of the labor market in Colombia saw important changes during the 1990s. This section summarizes key aspects of the 1990 labor reform and the reform to the social security system that was enacted in 1993.[6]

- Severance pay was the highest nonwage labor cost under the pre-1990 regime. Employees were entitled to one-month salary per year of work (based on the last salary). Partial withdrawals were allowed and deducted in nominal terms from the final payment, implying a form of "double retroactivity" (with an estimated cost of 4.2 percent of the total wage bill).[7] The new legislation eliminated this extra cost in all new labor contracts and introduced a monthly contribution (9.3 percent of the basic salary) to a capitalized fund in the workers' name, accessible in the event of separation or retirement. Thus, the reform effectively reduced the level and uncertainty of the costs associated with severance payments.
- The reform increased the indemnity paid to workers dismissed without just cause. Workers with less than one year of tenure on the job receive forty-five days' wages. Workers with more than one year of tenure receive forty-five days' wages for the first year plus an additional amount for each extra year, which implied an increase relative to the old regime. For example, in the event of separation, a worker with more than ten years of tenure on the job used to receive thirty days' wages for each extra year (after the first). As can be seen in table 4B.1, the new legislation increased the indemnity to the equivalent of forty days' wages per additional year.[8] Although the legal definition of *just cause* was widened, the reform increased the costs of dismissal.

---

6. See Lora and Henao (1995), Cárdenas and Gutiérrez (1996), Lora and Pagés (1997), and Guash (1997).
7. Apart from tenure, the real cost of termination of employment increased with the frequency of partial withdrawals, uncertain to the employer.
8. Based on the highest salary during the last year of employment.

- However, the right of workers with more than ten years tenure to sue for reinstatement was eliminated. Prior to the reform, successful plaintiffs could oblige firms to rehire workers with back pay.
- Workers earning more than ten minimum wages were allowed to opt for a new contract ("integral salaries") with higher wages instead of severance pay and other mandatory benefits (such as the especial bonus or *prima*). However, in a survey conducted by Fedesarrollo in 1994, manufacturing firms reported that less than 2 percent of the employees had this type of contract.
- Labor contracts for less than one year were allowed (renewable up to three times under the same terms),[9] provided that all benefits are paid in proportion to the duration of the contract.
- Legal restrictions on the creation of labor unions were lifted. In particular, the Ministry of Labor lost discretionary powers in this regard. Also, it became unlawful for employers to discourage the creation of labor unions. A minimum of twenty-five workers is still necessary to form a union.
- The 1993 social security and health reform (Law 100) increased total contributions for health from 7 percent of the basic salary (until 1994) to 8 percent in 1995 and 12 percent afterwards. One-third of the total contribution has to be paid by the employer (the same proportion as in the old system).
- The same law increased pension contributions to 13.5 percent in 1996 (14.5 percent for workers that earn more than four minimum wages) from 8 percent of the basic salary in 1993. The increase was implemented gradually. Contributions were first raised to 11.5 percent in April 1994 and then to 12.5 percent in 1995. Employers currently pay 10.1 percentage points of the total contribution, as opposed to 4.3 before the reform.[10]

Figure 4.1 summarizes the effects of labor and social security reform on nonwage labor costs. Total nonwage labor costs paid by the firm (as a percentage of the basic salary) rose to 52 percent after the 1993 pension reform from 42.9 percent after the 1990 labor reform. For the purpose of the analysis, we divide nonwage costs into three relatively arbitrary categories: (1) deferred wages, which include vacations, extra bonuses, pension, and health contributions. In theory, deferred wages affect the total labor cost but do not have an impact on the path of employment adjustment; (2) severance payments, which, in addition to the direct impact on labor costs,

9. The fourth renovation has to be made for at least one year. See Farné and Nupia (1996).
10. Law 100 (1993) eliminated the monopoly of the Social Security Institute (ISS) in the provision of health and pensions. The coverage of health services was extended to the whole family and to low-income groups that were unattended under the previous system. In relation to the pension system, employees were given the option of choosing between the old pay-as-you-go system or the new fully funded system provided by private pension funds.

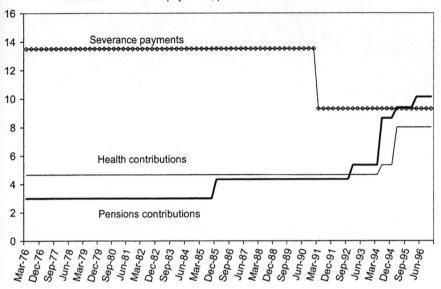

A. Evolution of severance payments, pensions and health contributions

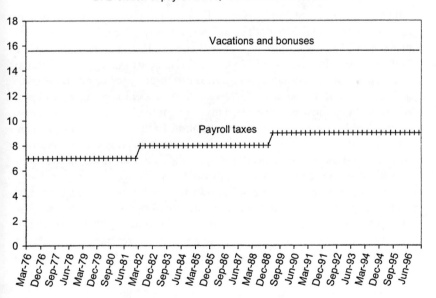

B. Evolution of payroll taxes, vacations and bonuses

Fig. 4.1   Nonwage labor costs (as a percentage of wage)
Source: Ocampo (1987) before 1990 and Regulation Manuals.

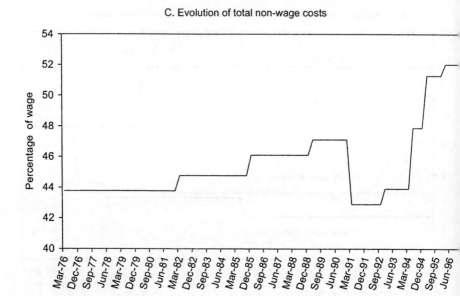

C. Evolution of total non-wage costs

Fig. 4.1   (cont.) Nonwage labor costs (as a percentage of wage)
Source: Ocampo (1987) before 1990 and Regulation Manuals.

affect the dynamics of employment adjustment;[11] and (3) payroll taxes that fund programs with benefits that cannot be fully internalized by the employee (e.g., Instituto Colombiano de Bienestar Familiar (ICBF), Servicio National de Aprendizaje (SENA), and Cajas de Compensacion Familiar (Cajas)).[12] The economic response to these three types of nonwage costs may be different. In the case of deferred wages, the employer can offset part of the cost by adjusting the wage. This may not be the case of payroll taxes earmarked for the provision of public goods. In the fourth section we analyze the possible effect of deferred wages on current wages by estimating a Mincer-type income equation. The hypothesis is that the employer may transfer nonwage costs to workers through lower wages.

The upper panel of figure 4.1 shows the evolution of severance payments, as well as health and pension contributions for an average worker, as a percentage of the basic wage between 1976 and 1996.[13] The middle panel shows the evolution of payroll taxes. These taxes increased by 1 percentage point in 1982 (earmarked to SENA) and again by an equal amount

11. Strictly speaking, severance payments are also deferred wages.
12. Of course, if the linkage between payroll taxes is weak or if the external benefits of social security programs are significant, then partial or complete finance by general revenues may be appropriate. See Kesselman (1995).
13. Workers under "integral salaries" are excluded. After 1991 we ignore workers under pre-1990 contractual terms.

in 1989 (earmarked for ICBF). Vacations and extra bonuses have remained constant throughout the period. The bottom panel adds all these costs together. The cumulative effect shows an increasing trend until 1990. After the 1990 labor reform, nonwage labor costs fell as a result of the changes introduced to the legislation related to severance payments. However, since 1994 these costs have increased sharply as a result of the 1993 health and pension reforms.

4.3 Stylized Facts

Figure 4.2 displays the unemployment rate for the period 1976–1998. After reaching a peak in March 1986 (14.6 percent), unemployment rates declined steadily until 1994 when they were under 8 percent. Unemployment rates have increased sharply since 1995. The figure for September 2000 (20.5 percent) is the highest in the modern Colombian economic history. Although much of the explanation of greater unemployment is related to significant increases in labor supply, this chapter argues that labor demand cannot be ignored. In fact, the increase in the cost of labor—combined with a relatively high own-wage elasticity—had a negative impact on labor demand. However, this is not the only explanation. The 1990 labor reform has also caused greater employment volatility in response to economywide shocks. This has been the result of greater flexibility in the creation and destruction of jobs. Kugler (chap. 3 in this volume) addresses this issue in detail.

This chapter uses mainly data on output, employment (skilled and unskilled), and wages for Colombia's seven largest cities. These variables are available for seven sectors: (1) manufacturing; (2) electricity and gas; (3) construction; (4) retail, restaurants, and hotels; (5) transportation and communications; (6) financial services; and (7) personal and governmental services. The data come from the quarterly National Household Survey (NHS), which has been conducted without interruption since 1976. Output data come from the quarterly gross domestic product (GDP) series processed by Department of National Planning (DNP).

4.3.1 Employment and Production

Table 4.1 displays some basic descriptive statistics on urban employment for the period 1976–1996. Manufacturing and personal and governmental services provide 29 percent and 25 percent of the urban jobs, respectively. We use information only for wage earners, which account for 64 percent of the total urban workers (62 percent before the 1990 labor reform). However, there are sharp differences across sectors. In manufacturing, 76 percent of the workers earn a monetary wage, whereas in retail and restaurants only 50 percent of the workers do.

We use a measure of skill that includes high school graduates plus all of

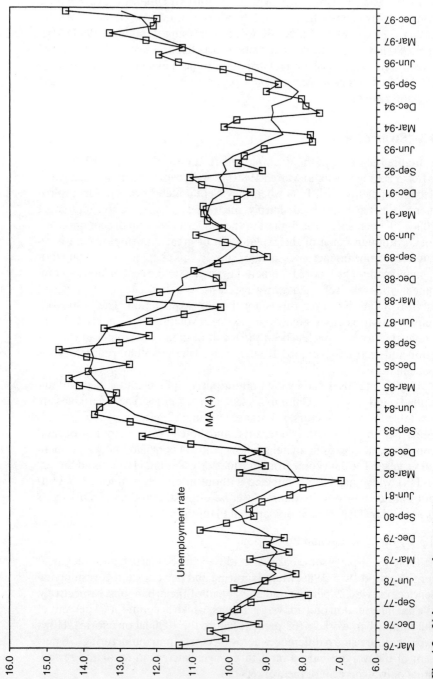

Fig. 4.2 Urban unemployment rate

Table 4.1   Urban Employment Shares

Sector	Share in Total Employment		Share of Wage-Earners in Total Employment		Share of Skilled Workers in Total Employment		Skilled/Unskilled Employment	
	1976–1991	1992–1996	1976–1991	1992–1996	1976–1991	1992–1996	1976–1991	1992–1996
Manufacturing	29.75	27.57	76.10	76.53	10.45	13.96	0.118	0.162
Electricity and gas	1.08	0.97	98.90	98.81	23.87	33.62	0.329	0.514
Construction	6.46	6.31	64.21	58.84	9.46	12.45	0.106	0.143
Retail, restaurants, and hotels	19.65	21.15	50.35	52.80	10.96	15.81	0.126	0.188
Transportation and communications	7.12	7.03	70.03	68.12	11.09	14.69	0.127	0.173
Financial services	8.48	9.47	77.36	79.23	30.10	37.95	0.443	0.615
Personal and government services	25.83	25.73	56.14	59.41	30.17	38.27	0.441	0.622
Total	98.36	98.23	62.66	64.06	17.63	23.28	0.218	0.304

Source: NHS.

those with some tertiary education (all workers with twelve or more years of schooling). By using this definition, the group of more educated workers represented 23 percent of urban employment, on average, between 1992 and 1996. According to figure 4.3, this group's share in total urban employment has increased steadily since 1976, reflecting the greater educational attainment of the population. Indeed, average years of schooling have increased continuously during the past two decades. As can be seen in table 4.1, skilled workers represent more than 30 percent of total employment in public utilities, financial services, and personal and governmental services. These shares have increased significantly since 1992.

Figure 4.4 describes the evolution of employment and production in the Colombian urban sector. It is interesting to note that after 1991 skilled employment has grown faster than unskilled employment in most sectors. This has been particularly true in the case of manufacturing, where employment of unskilled workers has fallen in absolute terms since 1993. The same trend is observed in the construction sector after 1994. These two sectors combined employ approximately 35 percent of the unskilled wage earners in the urban regions.

4.3.2 Factor Prices

Information about labor income received by wage earners (skilled and unskilled) comes from the NHS. Given that this is not necessarily equal to the total labor cost paid by the employer (which is the relevant price in the estimation of labor demand), it is then necessary to quantify nonwage labor costs and construct a measure of the total labor cost. We do that by using the information contained in figure 4.1, which summarizes all nonwage labor costs, expressed as a percentage of the basic salary. This includes severance payments, payroll taxes, and contributions for health and pensions on the part of the employer.

It is not entirely clear whether income reported by the individuals surveyed in the NHS includes benefits such as vacations, mandatory bonuses, and severance payments. Nonetheless, it is probably safe to assume that individuals report their basic pretax salary, without benefits. In order to obtain the total labor cost we add *all* the nonwage labor costs measured in figure 4.1 to the basic salary reported in the NHS. Implicitly, this means assuming the independence of wage and nonwage costs. We do this based on the results of the next section, which support the idea that employees do not transfer higher nonwage costs imposed by the legislation through lower basic salaries. Finally, the overall cost is then deflated using the producer price index. The procedure is identical for skilled and unskilled workers.[14] For completeness, we also report the user cost of capital measured

14. As mentioned in section 4.2, workers with high remuneration (over ten minimum wages) under integral salaries contracts have much lower nonwage costs (33.8 percent of the basic salary versus 52 percent in contracts with full benefits). However, the NHS survey does not provide information on the contract type, so we assume that all workers are paid full benefits.

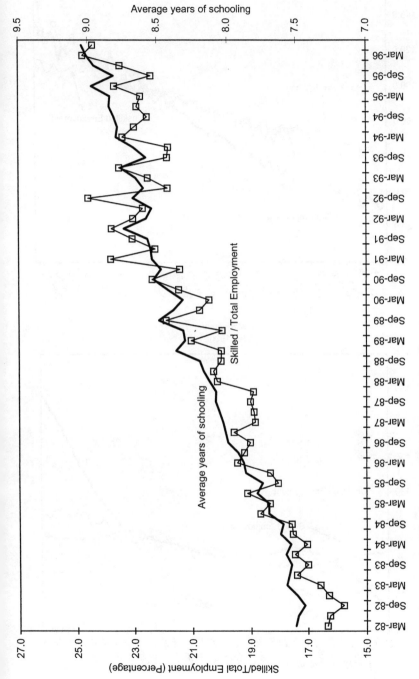

Fig. 4.3 Skilled to total employment ratio and average years of schooling
Source: NHS.

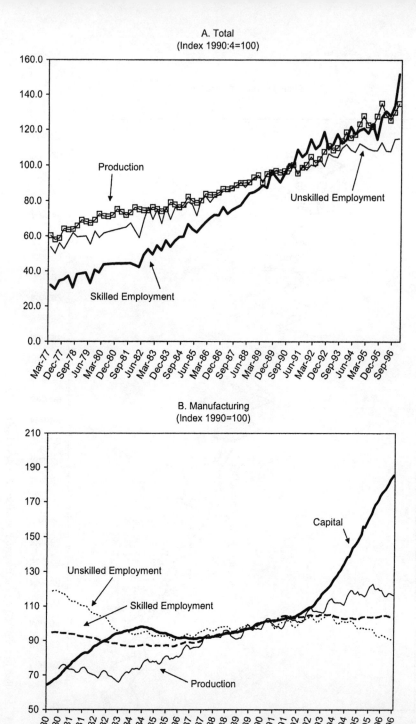

Fig. 4.4   Colombia: Urban employment and production
Source: NHS.

C. Electricity
(Index 1990:4=100)

D. Construction
(Index 1990:4=100)

Fig. 4.4   (cont.)

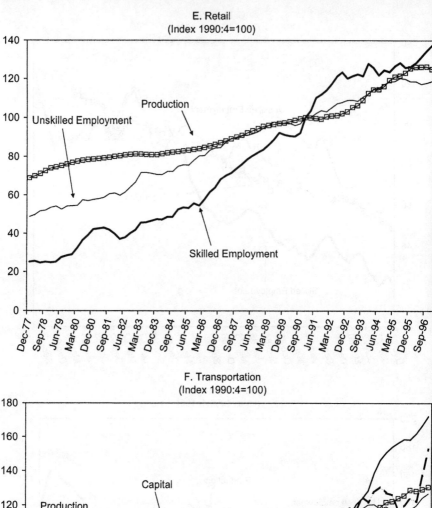

E. Retail
(Index 1990:4=100)

Production

Unskilled Employment

Skilled Employment

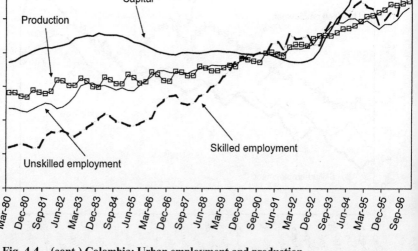

F. Transportation
(Index 1990:4=100)

Capital

Production

Skilled employment

Unskilled employment

Fig. 4.4   (cont.) Colombia: Urban employment and production
Source: NHS.

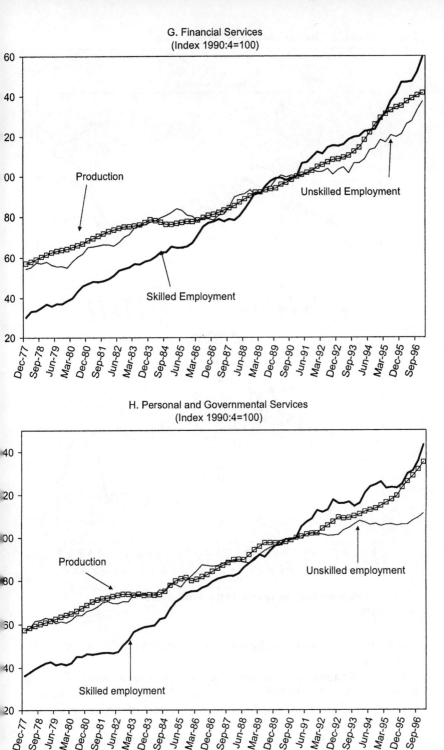

Fig. 4.4 (cont.)

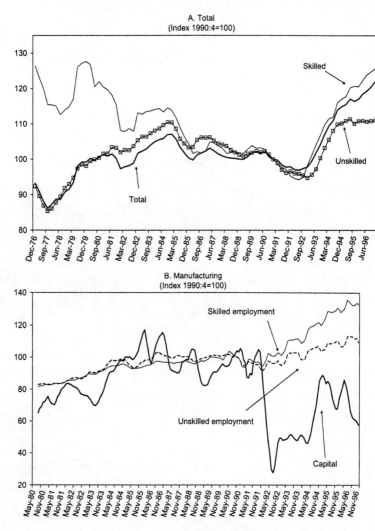

Fig. 4.5   Colombia: Real factor costs in the urban sector
Source: NHS.

according to a standard methodology described in Cárdenas and Gutiér-rez (1996).[15]

Figure 4.5 shows the evolution of real factor costs by sector. There are three key insights for the 1990s: (1) the cost of labor increased significantly; (2) the cost of labor increased faster than the cost of capital; and (3) the

15. Our measure of the user cost of capital is higher than the one obtained by Pombo (1997), who estimates the depreciation rates (and the corresponding tax deductions) for different asset types in the manufacturing sector.

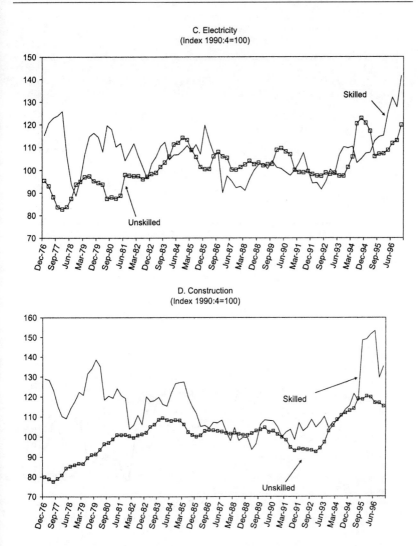

Fig. 4.5   (cont.)

cost of skilled relative to unskilled labor rose during this period. In fact, the user cost of capital decreased considerably during the period 1992–1994 as a result of the reduction in the interest rate and the real currency appreciation. As shown in table 4.2, the average annual growth in real labor costs between 1992 and 1996 was 11.4 percent for skilled workers and 8.4 percent for unskilled workers. These rates are substantially higher than the average for the prereform period. In sum, labor costs increased in an unprecedented way after 1990, especially in the case of skilled workers.

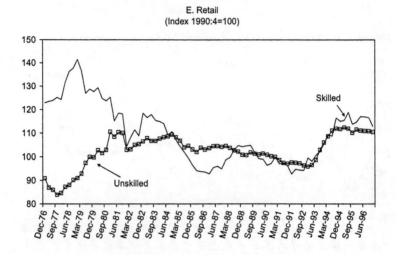

E. Retail
(Index 1990:4=100)

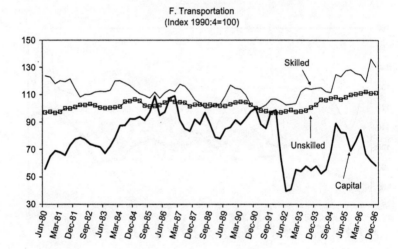

F. Transportation
(Index 1990:4=100)

Fig. 4.5   (cont.)

4.4   Endogeneity of Wage and Nonwage Costs

As mentioned previously, we need to support our assumption that wage and nonwage costs can be added together, ignoring the incidence of payroll taxation on wages. Several authors have warned against this assumption, arguing that wages and nonwage costs are endogenously determined. This is the case in Newell and Symons (1987) for the European context and in Gruber (1995) for Chile. Their view is that ignoring this issue can be misleading when making policy recommendations.

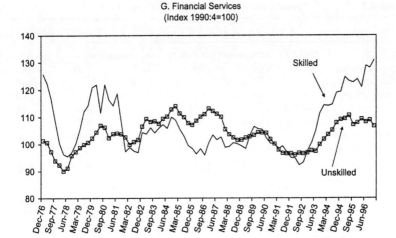

G. Financial Services
(Index 1990:4=100)

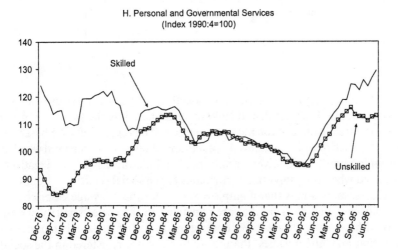

H. Personal and Governmental Services
(Index 1990:4=100)

Fig. 4.5   (cont.)

There are different ways to deal with this potential endogeneity. Some authors estimate an equation of the wage rate as a function of the payroll tax rate and a constant. If the coefficient on the payroll tax rate variable is equal to –1, then they conclude that taxes are fully shifted into wages. This is the procedure used by Gruber (1995).

Here we adopt a somewhat different procedure. We estimate the determinants of wages based on information from the NHS. Every two years (in June) the NHS includes a special module on informality where workers re-

Table 4.2   Annual Average Growth in Total Real Labor Cost (%)

Sector	1977–1985	1986–1991	1992–1996	1977–1996
Unskilled Employment (less than 12 years of education)				
Manufacturing	1.80	−1.45	8.09	2.40
Electricity and gas	1.73	−0.20	10.93	3.45
Construction	3.03	−1.16	9.89	3.49
Retail, restaurants, and hotels	2.03	−1.08	8.08	2.61
Transportation and communications	2.23	−0.97	8.28	2.78
Financial services	1.11	−1.84	7.49	1.82
Personal and government services	1.58	−1.38	8.85	2.51
Total urban	1.65	−1.34	8.36	2.43
Skilled Employment (12 years of education or more)				
Manufacturing	−1.96	−2.78	11.85	1.25
Electricity and gas	3.58	−2.34	15.58	4.81
Construction	−0.32	0.55	13.41	3.37
Retail, restaurants, and hotels	−1.68	−0.59	10.04	1.58
Transportation and communications	0.73	−0.11	10.79	3.00
Financial services	−1.38	−0.56	12.83	2.42
Personal and government services	−1.14	−1.61	11.81	1.95
Total urban	−1.63	−1.71	11.36	1.59

Source: NHS.

port whether they are covered by the social security system. We use the data from the June 1988, 1992, and 1996 surveys (including the special module) to estimate a Mincer-type income equation. The regressions are based on data for each one of the surveyed workers and allow us to understand whether an individual's wage, given certain personal characteristics, is negatively affected when the individual contributes to the social security system.[16]

Our assumption is that if employers transfer the nonwage labor cost to employees, then workers that are registered in the social security system would have lower wages (after controlling for other personal characteristics that may affect wages) than those that are not registered in the social security system.[17] In particular, we estimated the following equation:

$$(1) \quad \ln w_t = \beta_0 + \sum_i \beta_i \textbf{pers} + \beta_5 \text{dumss} + \beta_6 \text{mw} + \beta_7 \text{dumss} \cdot \text{mw}$$

$$+ \sum_i \beta_i \textbf{sec} + \sum_i \beta_i \textbf{city} + \varepsilon_t,$$

where w_t is wage at time t, **pers** is a vector of personal characteristics that include average years of schooling, gender, and experience; dumss is a dummy variable which takes a unitary value when the individual is regis-

16. The percentage of workers with health coverage rose to 60 percent in 1996 from 50 percent in 1988.

17. Ribero and Meza (1997) and Sánchez and Núñez (1998) have estimated Mincer-type income equations for Colombia.

tered in the social security system (i.e., the employer pays social security contributions); mw is a dummy variable that controls for individuals that earn the minimum wage[18] (payroll taxes cannot be transferred to these workers in the form of lower wages); **sec** is a vector of dummy variables that account for 9 economic sectors and **city** is a vector of dummy variables for each of the 7 main cities.

Table 4.3 presents the results of estimating equation (1). The adjustment of the regression is high (R-squares are around 0.55) given the total number of observations (approximately 25,000 depending on the year). The personal characteristics variables appear with the correct sign and are statistically significant. In particular, returns to education are positive (but low) and the coefficient is highly significant. The positive coefficient of the dummy variable for gender indicates that given other personal characteristics, labor income is relatively higher for men. In turn, experience has a positive but decreasing impact on wages. According to the sign of the coefficient, individuals that earn the minimum wage have lower incomes than what would be predicted by their personal characteristics. The dummy variables that account for the economic sectors and the city of location also come out significant.

Turning to the variables of interest for this exercise, for a given set of personal characteristics, workers covered by the social security system have higher wages than uncovered workers. This is of interest because it suggests that employers might not transfer social security contributions to workers in the form of lower wages. However, it is possible that social security contributions are proxying for self-selection and unobserved characteristics of the workers, biasing the results. Thus, it is unclear whether the results of this section provide the necessary support in order to use our measure—total labor costs, which is simply the sum of wage and nonwage costs (self-selection may be hiding the true effect of endogeneity bias). We take a pragmatic approach and estimate the labor demand equations with only wages and compare the results with regressions that include both wages and nonwage costs added together.

4.5   Static Labor Demand

The purpose of this section is to measure the own-wage elasticities of the demand for labor, as well as the elasticities of substitution between different factors of production.[19] The literature is rich in terms of functional forms that can be used for the estimation. If changes in the elasticity of substitution are of interest, the generalized Leontief (GL) function is a

18. For the purpose of this exercise, the minimum wage in 1988 (in Colombian pesos) was $28,000, in 1992 it was $72,000, and in 1996 it was $155,000.

19. The elasticities of substitution between different factors of production is defined as the effect of a change in relative factor prices on relative input use of the two factors, holding output and other factor prices constant.

Table 4.3　　　　Mincer Income Equation

Log (Wages)	1988	1992	1996
Constant	10.0354	11.2707	12.0258
	(576.90)	(624.09)	(670.16)
Education	0.044	0.0182	0.0181
	(52.01)	(30.54)	(31.91)
Gender	0.1671	0.1688	0.1585
	(23.45)	(22.11)	(20.18)
Experience	0.019	0.0185	0.0172
	(24.37)	(21.57)	(20.36)
Experience^2	−0.0002	−0.0003	−0.0002
	(−20.53)	(−21.43)	(−18.80)
Dummy health coverage	0.0628	0.1421	0.1838
	(6.84)	(13.93)	(18.63)
Health coverage · minimum wage	0.2848	0.2342	0.1320
	(20.48)	(15.52)	(8.31)
Minimum wage	−1.0045	−1.1018	−1.0907
	(−107.65)	(−106.29)	(−99.55)
Agriculture	0.1267	0.1114	0.4358
	(5.08)	(3.73)	(1.28)
Mining	0.1865	0.4505	0.2378
	(4.13)	(3.73)	(3.90)
Electricity	0.0547	0.0398	0.1868
	(1.45)	(0.92)	(4.32)
Construction	0.0874	0.0602	0.0733
	(5.73)	(3.64)	(4.48)
Retail	−0.0095	0.0367	0.0449
	(−1.02)	(3.61)	(4.20)
Communications	0.0463	0.0751	0.0742
	(3.14)	(4.65)	(4.66)
Financial services	0.0951	0.1564	0.1545
	(6.28)	(9.78)	(9.85)
Government services	−0.0003	−0.0009	0.0413
	(−0.00)	(−0.09)	(2.38)
Other services	−0.1665	0.1180	0.4188
	(−0.43)	(0.70)	(2.38)
Barranquilla	−0.0083	0.0193	0.0374
	(−0.77)	(1.72)	(3.17)
Bucaramanga	0.0065	−0.0504	−0.0662
	(0.55)	(−4.05)	(−5.23)
Manizales	0.0264	−0.0646	−0.1159
	(1.59)	(−3.67)	(−6.77)
Medellin	0.0594	−0.0256	−0.0018
	(6.63)	(−2.50)	(−0.18)
Cali	0.0508	0.0250	0.0189
	(4.77)	(2.15)	(1.52)
Pasto	−0.1405	−0.1943	−0.0781
	(−9.22)	(−12.38)	(−4.87)
No. of observations	29,476	26,900	25,887
R^2	0.5504	0.5526	0.5269

Sources: NHS and authors' calculations.

common choice. The GL specification is also normally used when information is available for more than two factors of production.[20]

The derived factor demands from a GL cost function (see appendix A) can be written as

$$(2) \qquad \frac{x_{it}}{y_t} = \sum_j b_{ij} \left(\frac{p_{jt}}{p_{it}} \right)^{1/2} + \alpha_i y_t + \gamma_i t,$$

where x_{it} is the quantity of factor i used in period t, y_t is output in period t, p_{it} is the price of input i in period t, and t is a time trend. Changes in the input-output ratio can be the result of: (1) changes in relative factor prices; (2) changes in the scale of production (if the production function is not homothetic); and (3) technological change. Diewert (1971) has shown that the GL cost function corresponds to a fixed coefficients technology (no factor substitution) if $b_{ij} = 0$ for all $i \neq j$. Also, the production function exhibits constant returns to scale if $\alpha_i = 0$ for all i (i.e., the function is homothetic). Clearly, factor-augmenting technological change does not occur if $\gamma_i = 0$ for all i. Based on the estimated b_{ij}, we then calculate the own-wage elasticity for factor i (η_{it}) as

$$(3) \qquad \eta_{ij} = - \frac{y \sum_{j \neq i} b_{ij} \left(\frac{p_j}{p_i} \right)^{1/2}}{2x_i}.$$

In turn, the Hicks-Allen partial elasticities of substitution between input i and input j ($\sigma_{ij} = \sigma_{ji}$) can be easily calculated. The appropriate expressions in the case of the GL technology are (s_j is the cost share of input j)

$$(4) \qquad \sigma_{ij} = \frac{\frac{y}{2x_i} b_{ij} \left(\frac{p_j}{p_i} \right)^{1/2}}{s_j},$$

for all $i \neq j$. In this case, the elasticity of substitution is not constant across time. In fact, as can be observed in equation (4), its value depends on the inputs quantities and prices. Finally, the elasticity of input i with respect to output is given by

$$(5) \qquad \varepsilon_i = 1 + \frac{\alpha_i y^2}{x_i}.$$

Thus, when the technology exhibits constant returns to scale the output elasticity is equal to one.

4.5.1   Results

This section summarizes the main results of the estimation of static labor demand equations with quarterly data from the NHS. The estimation

---

20. See Hamermesh (1986).

is first carried out with data for the manufacturing sector alone, based on a system of two equations for the demand of skilled and unskilled labor. The equations use the number of hours worked as the dependent variable. We then turn to the data for the seven largest metropolitan cities, using a similar framework but dropping capital as a factor of production. In both cases we deal with specifications that use relative input prices (skilled and unskilled labor), so the effects of nonwage labor costs vanish (percentage-wise, their impact is identical for each type of labor).

4.5.2   Manufacturing

Table 4.4 presents the results on the factor demands for skilled and unskilled labor.[21] According to the GL specification, the system of two equations describing the behavior of the input-output ratios was estimated using a (Gauss) Full Information Maximum Likelihood procedure (FIML). In order to correct for first-order serial autocorrelation of the error, the lagged residuals were added to each equation (AR1).

The system was estimated with and without the symmetry restrictions ($b_{ij} = b_{ji}$). Conveniently, Theil has shown that minus twice the log of the likelihood ratio (i.e., the maximum of the likelihood function imposing symmetry over the maximum of the likelihood function in the unconstrained case) has a chi-square (χ^2) distribution (with degrees of freedom equal to the number of restrictions imposed).[22] The test rejected the null hypothesis of symmetry. Also, in the estimations the coefficient γ_i came out not significantly different from zero, rejecting the hypothesis of factor-augmenting technological progress.

The estimated b_{ij} (excluding the trend term from the equations) are significantly different from zero, rejecting the existence of a fixed proportion technology (a Leontief production function). Importantly, the signs of the coefficients indicate that the two types of labor are substitutes. The hypothesis of constant returns to scale is also rejected at high levels of significance. The estimated α_i coefficients are all positive and significant. This implies that both employment and output ratios increase as the scale of production is expanded (i.e., the production function is nonhomothetic).

Based on the estimated b_{ij} we then compute the relevant elasticities that, according to the formulae, are time dependent. We report the elasticities for four periods: 1976–1981, 1982–1985, 1986–1991, and 1992–1996. The two types of labor show a decreasing degree of substitutability. Own-wage elasticities are negative.[23] For the 1992–1996 period their value is around –0.35 for skilled workers and –0.4 for unskilled workers. This means that a

21. In this case, we are using total labor costs as the relevant price, that is, salary plus nonwage costs.
22. See López (1980).
23. The change in the wage elasticities over the four periods of time considered here is statistically significant at 95 percent confidence level.

Table 4.4   **Factor Demands for Skilled and Unskilled Labor in the Manufacturing Sector: GL Specification (1977:1–1996:4)**

Employment	Constant	Relative Prices	Production	R^2	D.W.
Skilled	−0.7736***	0.7984***	1.0133***	0.79	2.04
	(−3.06)	(2.72)	(6.38)		
Unskilled	1.2058***	−0.2495***	0.0670	0.23	1.94
	(8.66)	(−2.24)	(1.15)		

	Price, Income, and Substitution Elasticities			
	1976–1981	1982–1985	1986–1991	1992–1996
Own-wage elasticities				
η_{ee}	−0.593	−0.523	−0.431	−0.350
η_{oo}	−0.487	−0.409	−0.390	−0.400
Elasticity of substitution				
σ_{eo}	3.850	2.876	2.498	1.979
Output elasticities				
ε_{ey}	2.204	2.008	1.986	1.968
ε_{oy}	1.050	1.049	1.060	1.068

Sources: NHS and authors' calculations.

Notes: o = unskilled employment; e = skilled employment; y = production. Employment in number of hours.

***Significant at the 1 percent level.

10 percent reduction in wages is related to a 3.5 percent increase in the demand skilled and a 4 percent increase in the demand for unskilled labor.[24] Output elasticities are positive during the whole period but seem to have decreased with time. In particular a 1 percent increase in production is related to a 2 percent increase in skilled labor demand and a 1 percent increase in unskilled labor demand.[25]

4.5.3   Seven Metropolitan Areas

Table 4.5 shows the results of the estimation in the case of the demand for hours worked by skilled and unskilled labor (without capital) in the seven largest metropolitan areas.[26] Besides changes in relative prices, we

24. The results using a constant elasticity of substitution (CES) function are somewhat different. In this case, a 10 percent decrease in wages is related to a 0.8 percent increase in skilled labor demand and a 1.7 percent increase in unskilled labor demand, respectively. Again, the two types of labor show increasing substitutability, just as in the case of capital and unskilled labor. On the other hand, skilled labor and capital are complements. These results are available upon request.

25. The results when splitting up into two subsamples (after and before the reform) are statistically insignificant.

26. Table 4.5 shows the results in which total labor costs (salary plus nonwage costs) are used as the relevant price. However the same exercise was performed using wages only, that is, excluding nonlabor costs. In this case, results are fairly similar.

Table 4.5   **Factor Demands for Skilled and Unskilled Labor in the Seven Largest Metropoli**
                       Areas: GL Specification (1977:1–1996:4)

Employment	Constant	Relative Prices	Production	Demand Shifter	R^2	D.
Skilled	−0.8864***	0.9243***	0.7152***	0.0882***	0.92	2.
	(−3.41)	(3.80)	(11.57)	(2.68)		
Unskilled	1.3739***	−0.485***	−0.026	0.0665***		
	(8.27)	(−3.43)	(−0.62)	(2.66)		

	Price, Income, and Substitution Elasticities			
	1976–1981	1982–1985	1986–1991	1992–1996
Own-wage elasticities				
η_{ee}	−0.755	−0.642	−0.507	−0.445
η_{oo}	−0.573	−0.497	−0.461	−0.515
Elasticity of substitution				
σ_{eo}	1.147	0.982	0.822	0.798
Output elasticities				
ε_{ey}	1.873	1.772	1.714	1.839
ε_{oy}	0.979	0.978	0.975	0.966

Sources: NHS and authors' calculations.

Notes: o = unskilled employment; e = skilled employment; y = production. Employment in number
hours.

***Significant at the 1 percent level.

added a demand shifter in the equation. In particular, we introduced the
investment rate for the urban economy into equation (2) in order to assess any possible changes in labor demand, holding constant relative
prices.

Again, the Wald test rejected the null hypothesis so we estimated the b_{ij}
without symmetry restrictions. The coefficients turned out significantly
different from zero, rejecting the existence of a fixed proportion technology. The estimated α_i coefficient for skilled employment is positive and significant. This implies that skilled employment and output ratio increases
as the scale of production is expanded (i.e., the production function is nonhomothetic). Based on the estimated b_{ij} we computed the relevant elasticities. The two types of labor show a decreasing degree of substitutability as
can be seen in figure 4.6. On average, the elasticity of substitution between
skilled and unskilled employment was 0.93 between 1976 and 1996.

Own-wage elasticities are higher in this case than in the manufacturing sector. In particular, a 10 percent decrease in wages is related to a 4.5
percent increase in skilled labor demand and a 5.1 percent increase in
unskilled labor demand.[27] In the case of unskilled labor, the own-wage

27. The corresponding own-wage elasticities in the case in which wages (excluding nonwage
costs) are used as the relevant price are 4.3 percent and 5.0 percent.

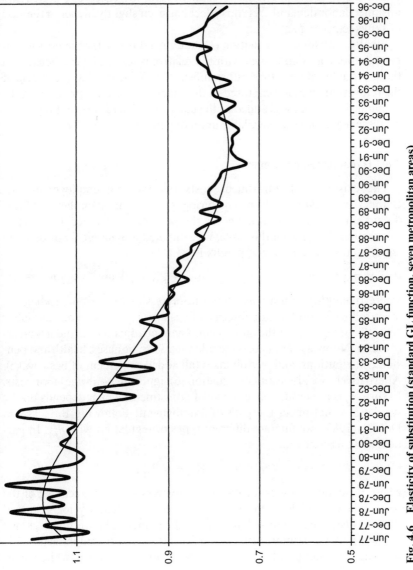

Fig. 4.6 Elasticity of substitution (standard GL function, seven metropolitan areas)
Source: Authors' calculations.

elasticity has increased in absolute value during the postreform period to 0.51 from 0.46 in the prereform period. On the other hand, output elasticities are positive. A one percent increase in output is related to a 1.8 percent increase in skilled labor demand and a one percent increase in unskilled labor demand. Higher investment rates increase both skilled and unskilled labor demand. Yet, this effect has been slightly higher in the case of skilled employment.

Finally, we estimated equation (1), adding a dummy for the postreform period (alone and interacted with the relative prices). The coefficients on these variables did not turn out significant. This means that the effects of the reforms are already captured in the changes in relative prices or in the demand shifter that was added to the equation. The results (not reported) on these regressions are available upon request.

4.6 Dynamic Labor Demand

The existence of adjustment costs of changing employment (net changes) and changes in firing and hiring (gross changes) implies that firms do not adjust instantly to changes in the variables mentioned in the previous section. To capture this issue, we estimated a dynamic labor demand equation that is derived in appendix B:

$$(6) \quad n_t = c + \alpha_0 y_t + \alpha_1 y_{t-1} + \beta_0(w_t + nw_t) + \beta_1(w_{t-1} + nw_{t-1}) + \gamma_t n_{t-1} + u_t,$$

where n is employment, y is a rolling autoregression forecast of production, w is a rolling autoregression forecast of basic wages, nw are nonwage labor costs that do not affect the path of employment adjustment, and u is an error term. Nonwage labor costs include vacations, bonuses, health and pension contributions, and payroll taxes (all added as percent of basic wage). Alternatively, we also estimate equation (6), ignoring nonwage labor costs. In turn, γ_t is a measure of the costs of adjustment, which depends on the regulations that affect the path of employment. Following Burgess and Dolado (1989), we interact different types of regulation with n_{t-1}. In particular, we assume that

$$(7) \qquad\qquad \gamma_t = \gamma_0 + \gamma_1 R1_t + \gamma_2 R2_t,$$

where R1 denotes severance payments (expressed as a percentage of the basic salary), and R2 denotes dismissal costs (indemnity for dismissal without just cause expressed in terms of the number of monthly wages for workers with ten or more years in the firm).[28] As mentioned in section 4.2, severance payments fell as a result of the 1990 labor reform, while the in-

---

28. This variable is taken as a proxy for dismissal costs for all workers. Although desirable, we were unable to redefine the dependent variable in order to measure employment of workers with ten or more years in their current job only.

demnity for unjust dismissal increased.[29] These two changes in the regulation should have had opposite effects on the costs of adjustment. The reduction in severance payments should have reduced the costs of adjustment (a reduction in γ_t), while the increase in dismissal costs should have worked in the opposite direction. Importantly, the 1993 pension and health reform increased labor costs but should not have affected the costs of adjustment.

This formulation is useful in order to assess the impact of a one-unit increase in the costs of regulations on the level of employment (the βs) and that of this increase in the cost per worker on the path of employment adjustment (the γs). In the former case, we can infer the impact or short-run multiplier coefficient (β_0) and the long or equilibrium multiplier ($\beta_0 + \beta_1$)/ ($1 - \gamma_t$). Moreover, we can test whether these multipliers changed as a result of the structural reforms. This can be done as a quasi-natural experiment by including a postreform dummy interacted with wages and the lagged employment measure.

4.6.1 Econometric Results

Table 4.6 presents the results of the estimation of equation (6) with aggregated quarterly data from the NHS. In order to avoid potential endogeneity in the shocking variables, we used rolling-regression (i.e., continuously updated) forecasts of the product demand and wages instead of their actual values. In the case of output, the forecast is based on fourth-order autoregression. Wages are forecasted with a third-order autoregression.[30]

The first three columns show the results of estimating (6) for total urban employment. Unfortunately, we cannot include R1 and R2 in the same regression due to collinearity of the variables. The results are of interest. The first three columns indicate that the product elasticity of employment is 0.57, while the wage elasticity is zero in the short run (impact) but –0.37 in the long run. The same regression was performed ignoring nonwage costs (available upon request). The estimated elasticities are practically identical. The results also suggest that the changes in the regulations did not have an impact on adjustment costs. In fact, the coefficient on lagged employment indicates that quarterly changes in employment are, on average, only 40 percent of the desired adjustment, irrespective of the changes in the regulation.

The remaining regressions separate skilled and unskilled employment. The results suggest that output and price (in absolute value) elasticities are larger for skilled workers (also in the regression without nonwage costs). The costs of adjustment were not affected by changes in the regulations regarding severance payments and dismissal costs for either type of worker.

---

29. However, the elimination of the right to sue for reinstatement with back pay should have reduced the expected firing costs.
30. In both cases we chose the highest order with a significant coefficient.

Table 4.6 Dynamic Labor Demand Estimations (1977:02–1996:04)

	Total Employment			Skilled	Unskilled	Skilled	Unskilled
	(1)	(2)	(3)	(4)	(5)	(6)	(7)
Constant	0.0156 (0.44)	0.0156 (0.44)	0.0156 (0.44)	−0.0364 (−0.36)	0.2143*** (4.18)	−0.1005** (−1.96)	0.2143*** (4.18)
Production$_t$	0.5666*** (2.84)	0.5666*** (2.84)	0.5666*** (2.84)	1.0237*** (4.17)	0.6041*** (2.95)	1.0250*** (4.17)	0.6041*** (2.95)
Production$_{t-1}$	−0.0342 (−0.17)	−0.0342 (−0.17)	−0.0342 (−0.17)	−0.1125 (−0.44)	0.0365 (0.18)	−0.1123 (−0.43)	0.0365 (0.18)
Own Wages$_t$	0.0175 (0.18)	0.0175 (0.18)	0.0175 (0.18)	0.0877 (0.74)	0.1224 (1.22)	0.0880 (0.74)	0.1224 (1.22)
Own Wages$_{t-1}$	−0.1636* (−1.70)	−0.1636* (−1.70)	−0.1636* (−1.70)	−0.2237* (−1.81)	−0.0385 (−0.38)	−0.2254* (−1.81)	−0.0385 (−0.38)
Other type of Employment Wages$_t$				0.1215 (0.98)	0.1222 (1.24)	0.1211 (0.98)	0.1222 (1.24)
Other type of Employment Wages$_{t-1}$			−0.2538 (−1.70)	−0.3684*** (−2.05)	−0.2563** (−3.70)	−0.3684*** (−2.07)	−0.2563** (−3.70)
$R^1_t \cdot E_{t-1}$	0.0334 (0.73)						
$R^2_t \cdot E_{t-1}$		−0.0364 (−0.73)		−0.0680 (−0.92)	0.0089 (0.17)	0.0607 (0.82)	
Dum91 · E_{t-1}			−0.0104 (−0.73)				−0.0097 (−0.17)
E_{t-1}	0.5760*** (4.95)	0.6459*** (5.39)	0.6095*** (5.64)	0.4679*** (4.11)	0.3025*** (2.52)	0.4070*** (2.43)	0.3211*** (2.46)
R^2	0.9790	0.9790	0.9790	0.9847	0.9699	0.9847	0.9699
DW	2.63	2.63	2.63	1.96	2.42	1.98	2.42

Sources: NHS and authors' calculations.

Notes: No. of observations = 75. R^1 indicates severance payments. R^2 indicates dismissal costs, which equals −0.3445755 for col. (1); −0.4125953 for col. (2); −0.3741357 for col. (3); −0.2555911 for col. (4); −0.12028674 for col. (5); −0.2317032 for col. (6); and −0.1235227 for col. (7).

***Significant at the 1 percent level.

Moreover, when a postreform dummy was interacted with the wage variables, the estimated coefficient did not come out significant. This result gives support to the point made in the previous section, suggesting that structural reform did not affect the price elasticity of labor demand. In this sense, structural reforms did have an impact on labor demand through its effect on relative prices alone.[31]

In sum, the results of this section suggest that regulations add to static labor costs rather than to the dynamics of employment adjustment. Therefore, in the next two sections we will revisit the static labor demand estimations, using microdata. Before we move in that direction we present the results of some simulation exercises based on the dynamic labor demand estimation. The simulations are illustrative of the effects of different changes that could be introduced to labor legislation.

4.6.2 Simulations

In this section, we perform a simulation exercise in order to assess how changes in payroll taxes and labor costs affected employment growth in Colombia. For this purpose, we used equations (3), (4), and (5) in table 4.6 to estimate what would have happened to employment had health and pensions contributions not been increased during the 1993 labor reform.

Figure 4.7 shows the fitted value of employment according to the dynamic labor demand specifications presented in table 4.6. Panel A shows the results in terms of total employment, while panels B and C report unskilled and skilled employment, respectively. As employment is in logs, the difference between the two lines represents the percentage change. According to this information, also presented in table 4B.2, during the last quarter of 1996 total employment would have been 1.3 percent higher if health and pensions contributions had not changed during 1993. Similarly, unskilled employment would have been 1.85 percent higher and skilled employment 2.2 percent higher.

Figure 4.8 depicts the results of a similar exercise. In this case we simulate what would have occurred if the 9 percent payroll tax had been eliminated in 1993. In this case, employment would have been 1.3 percent higher during the last quarter of 1996, compared to what actually happened. The figures for unskilled and skilled employment are 1.8 percent and 0.9 percent, respectively.

4.7 Labor Demand in a Panel of Manufacturing Establishments

This section presents some results of the estimation of a homogeneous labor demand equation with a balanced panel of Colombian manufacturing firms. The panel was obtained from the Annual Manufacturing Survey

---

31. Slaughter (1997) has found that labor demand has been growing less elastic over time in the United States.

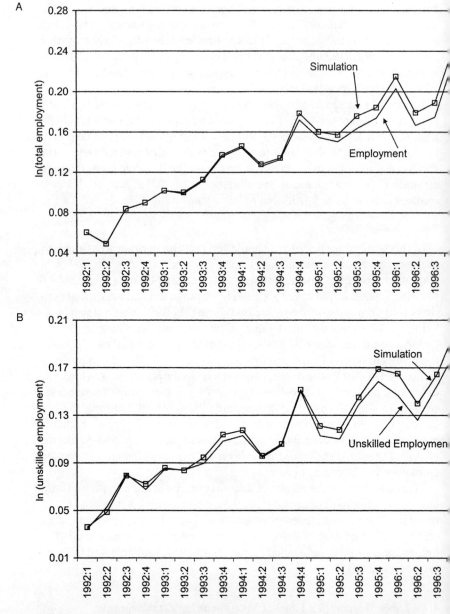

Fig. 4.7 *A,* Total employment and simulation employment assuming no increases in health and pensions contributions; *B,* unskilled employment and simulated unskilled employment assuming no increases in health and pensions contributions; *C,* skilled employment and simulated skilled employment assuming no increases in health and pensions contributions

Sources: NHS and authors' calculations.

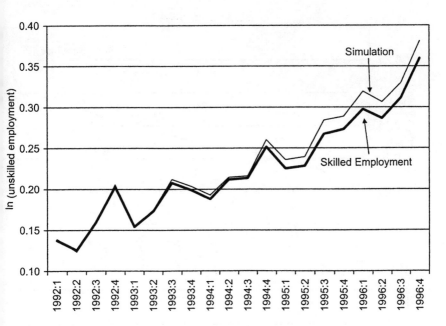

Fig. 4.7   (cont.)

(EAM) and includes 2,570 firms throughout the period 1978–1991.[32] The total labor cost was obtained directly for the surveys by adding wages and other benefits (*prestaciones*). In the specification of the model we follow Bentolila and Saint-Paul (1992). In particular, we estimate

$$(8) \qquad n_{it} = \alpha_0 + \alpha_1 n_{i,t-1} + \alpha_2 w_{it} + \alpha_3 p_{it} + \alpha_4 k_{it} + \alpha_5 dy_{it} + \alpha_6 t + \varepsilon_{it},$$

where n_{it} is the log total employment by firm i at time t, w_{it} is the log of wage paid by the firm (including benefits) deflated by the producer price index (common to all firms), p_{it} is the log of the price of intermediate goods consumed by the firm (also deflated by the producer price index), k_{it} is the log of stock of capital, dy_{it} is the growth rate in gross production by the firm, and t is a time trend.

The results are reported in table 4.7. The first and second columns show the results of the estimation with least squares and instrumental variables, respectively. In the latter, we use the lagged values of employment and intermediate goods' prices as instruments (both at time $t - 2$), as well as the contemporaneous growth rate in government consumption and the stock of capital. The results confirm the negative but low value (in absolute terms) of the short-run wage elasticity of labor demand in the manufacturing sector (around –0.05). However, the long-run value of this elasticity

---

32. The dataset consists of annual observations at the firm level.

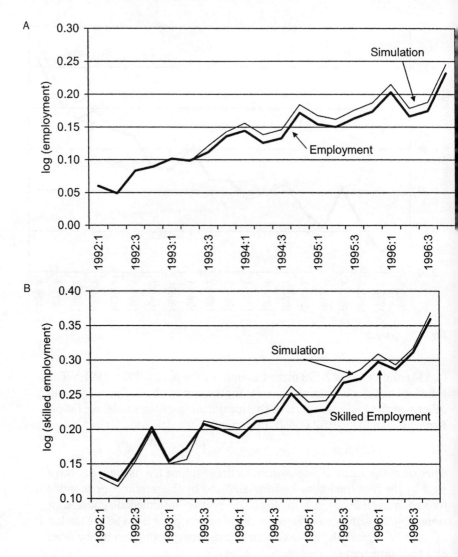

Fig. 4.8 *A*, Total employment and simulated employment assuming elimination of 9 percent payroll tax; *B*, skilled employment and simulated skilled employment assuming elimination of 9 percent payroll tax; *C*, unskilled employment and simulated unskilled employment assuming elimination of 9 percent payroll tax
Sources: NHS and authors' calculations.

is substantially higher in absolute terms (–2.27). The long-run elasticity with respect to other inputs' prices is positive (1.36), suggesting labor and intermediate goods are substitutes in production.

Growth in gross output seems to have a statistically significant effect on employment. Indeed, the results of the estimation indicate that a 1 per-

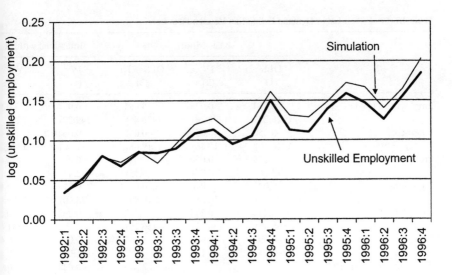

Fig. 4.8   (cont.)

centage point increase in the rate of output growth results in a 0.24 percentage growth in employment. This result is in line with the time series evidence of the previous section. In order to correct heteroskedasticity problems we controlled for fixed effects by adding twenty-eight sectorial dummy variables to the equation. The results remained virtually unchanged.

Finally, we interacted the list of regressors with a dummy variable that captures differential responses to the business cycle. The dummy variable takes a unitary value when output growth for the firm is over 4 percent and zero when growth is below 2 percent. If the growth rate is between 2 percent and 4 percent, the assigned value at time t depends on growth at $t-1$.

The results suggest that the wage elasticity of labor demand decreases (in absolute terms) during expansions, while the elasticity with respect to the price of intermediate inputs increases. Thus, an increase in the cost of intermediate goods induces greater substitutability vis-à-vis labor during expansions than during recessions. Lagged employment shows the expected result, lower inertia in expansion, and the coefficient is highly significant. Last, the results suggest an asymmetric labor demand response to the business cycle conditions. The impact of output growth on employment is larger during recessions than during expansions.

In sum, labor demand elasticities derived from establishment data are lower (in absolute value) than the ones obtained with aggregate data for the manufacturing sector. This is true both in the case of own-wage and output elasticities. The results of this section also indicate that the demand for labor is more elastic in downturns than during expansions. This could ex-

Table 4.7   Labor Demand Estimation Results: Firm Level

	Basic Model			Interacted with BC	
	OLS (1)	IV (2)	OLS + Di (3)	IV (4)	IV + (5)
Employment (t – 1)	0.964	0.978	0.965	0.987	0.9
	(526.20)	(492.76)	(476.46)	(349.27)	(331.
Labor cost	–0.050	–0.051	–0.062	–0.054	–0.0
	(–18.19)	(–17.76)	(–19.08)	(–17.86)	(–20.
Price of materials	0.024	0.030	0.047	0.024	0.0
	(3.78)	(4.27)	(5.15)	(2.43)	(3.
Capital stock	0.025	0.018	0.027	0.015	0.0
	(20.99)	(14.38)	(19.49)	(8.60)	(9.
Growth in production	0.245	0.243	0.242	0.262	0.
	(58.45)	(56.22)	(56.18)	(40.88)	(41.
Year	–0.001	0.000		0.001	0.0
	(–2.24)	(1.19)		(1.91)	(2.
Employment (t – 1) · BC				–0.022	–0.0
				(–5.51)	(–5.
Labor cost · BC				0.003	0.0
				(2.06)	(1.
Price of materials · BC				0.013	0.0
				(0.99)	(0.
Capital stock · BC				0.009	0.0
				(3.29)	(3.
Growth in production · BC				–0.063	–0.0
				(–6.84)	(–7.
Adj. R^2	0.965	0.966	0.966	0.966	0.9

Notes: Di refers to the 28 sectorial dummies; OLS indicates ordinary least squares; IV indicates inst
mental variables; and BC is a business cycle dummy described in the text.

plain why unemployment rates rise very rapidly but take a long time to fall, a pattern that has been found in Colombia.

4.8   Labor Demand in a Panel of Ninety-Two Manufacturing Sectors

This section estimates equation (8) using data from ninety-two industrial sectors (corresponding to the four-digit Clasificación Industrial Internacional Uniforme [CIIU] classification) from 1978 to 1995. In this case, the log of value added replaces the growth rate in gross production. Total labor costs (wages plus nonlabor costs) are used as the relevant price variable.[33] The results are presented in table 4.8, where all the variables are in logs. The first column presents the basic equation estimated by ordinary least squares. The second column corrects fixed effects, and the third column uses instrumental variables, where lagged values of employment,

33. The same exercise was performed using wages only as the relevant price. Results are virtually identical and are available upon request.

	Basic Equation			Structural Change		
	OLS (1)	Fixed Effects (2)	IV (3)	OLS (4)	Fixed Effects (5)	IV (6)
Employment ($t-1$)	0.7476***	0.4417***	0.5767***	0.7791***	0.5165***	0.6119***
	(52.31)	(21.48)	(6.00)	(62.47)	(28.36)	(7.48)
Total wage	−0.2903***	−0.1413***	−0.6056***	−0.2432***	−0.2029***	−0.4746***
	(−11.57)	(−3.57)	(−4.04)	(−11.84)	(−6.02)	(−4.38)
Input prices	−0.2208***	−0.3755***	−0.5197***	−0.3068***	−0.4986***	−0.777***
	(−5.59)	(−7.81)	(−3.90)	(−6.84)	(−9.68)	(−3.69)
Capital stock	0.0289***	0.0212	−0.0198	0.0351***	0.0595***	0.0118
	(2.85)	(0.69)	(−1.58)	(4.52)	(2.55)	(0.93)
Value Added	0.2154***	0.2953***	0.4465***	0.1777***	0.2593***	0.3683***
	(18.94)	(22.12)	(4.52)	(17.77)	(21.45)	(4.71)
Year	−0.0007	−0.0021	0.0001			
	(−0.48)	(−1.25)	(0.07)			
D · Employment ($t-1$)				−0.8045***	−0.6102***	−0.5939***
				(−26.50)	(−20.28)	(−5.77)
D · Total wage				0.1721***	0.1424***	0.4223*
				(5.29)	(4.37)	(1.75)
D · Input prices				0.3620***	0.4321***	0.9379***
				(5.97)	(7.12)	(3.24)
D · Capital stock				0.9964***	0.7764***	1.0687***
				(29.64)	(22.33)	(5.73)
D · Value Added				−0.1720***	−0.1513***	−0.4244**
				(−7.64)	(−6.60)	(−1.94)
R^2	0.9705	0.9763	0.9622	0.9825	0.9833	0.9778

Sources: NHS and authors' calculations.

Notes: No. of observations = 1,502. OLS indicates ordinary least squares; IV indicates instrumental variables; and D is a dummy variable for the period 1992–1995.

***Significant at the 1 percent level.

intermediate goods' prices (both at time $t - 2$), and the stock of capital (at time $t - 1$) as well as the contemporaneous values of the stock of capital and wages are the instruments.

The estimated real-wage elasticity is higher (-0.6)[34] in absolute terms than the value estimated with the firm-level data. Using instrumental variables (IV), the long-run wage elasticity is -1.43. The elasticity with respect to input prices is, on average, -1.2, depending on the method of estimation. Contrary to the firm-level results, the negative sign suggests that labor and intermediate goods are complements in production. Value added has a positive and statistically significant effect on employment. According to these results, a 1 percent increase in value added results in a 0.45 percentage growth in employment.

Finally, the last three columns in table 4.8 show the results when the basic equation is interacted with a dummy variable equal to 1 from 1992 to 1995 (and 0 otherwise) in order to assess for possible changes in the coefficients after the implementation of structural reform. The coefficient on lagged employment indicates that employment has been more flexible since 1992 (lower inertia).

On the other hand, the elasticity with respect to total wage seems to have decreased (in absolute value) after 1991. Similarly, the response of employment to changes in value added virtually disappeared during the postreform period. The elasticity with respect to material prices turns out to be positive during the postreform period, indicating that labor and intermediate goods are substitutes in production. Interestingly, the positive response of employment to the capital stock increased significantly after the new labor regulation was implemented.

4.9 Conclusions

This chapter has analyzed the determinants of the demand for labor in Colombia's urban sector (seven largest metropolitan areas) using different sources of data. The main focus of the chapter is to estimate the own-wage elasticities of labor demand in order to quantify the effects of payroll taxation on employment generation. This is a critical area for policy design, given the abnormal levels of unemployment that the country is facing.

Some have argued that the relevant elasticities are low, discouraging policymakers from undertaking major reforms. The common belief is that the efficiency gains associated with labor reform are relatively weak, while the political costs of changing current labor legislation are very high. This chapter argues that, quite on the contrary, the payoff of reducing labor costs is substantial.

---

34. This elasticity is equal to -0.61 in the case in which nonlabor costs are excluded from labor costs.

ble 4.9   **Labor Demand Elasticities: Summary of Results**

	Own-Wage Elasticity			Output Elasticity		
	Skilled	Unskilled	Total	Skilled	Unskilled	Total
Quarterly Time Series (1976:1–1996:4)						
tatic labor demand						
+Manufacturing	–0.350	–0.400		1.968	1.068	
+7 metropolitan areas	–0.445	–0.515		1.839	0.966	
)ynamic labor demand						
+7 Metropolitan areas						
Estimated with total labor cost	–0.255	n.s.	–0.374	1.024	0.604	0.567
Estimated with wages only	–0.310	n.s.	–0.395	0.999	0.597	0.522
Manufacturing Panel Data (annual)						
2570 establishments (1978–1991)		–0.05/–2.27				0.240
)1 sector (1978–1991)		–0.60/–1.43				0.440

urces: NHS and authors' calculations.
tes: n.s. = not significant. Numbers separated by a solidus indicate short run and long run, respec-
ely.

In order to reach that conclusion, the chapter analyzes the impact of recent changes in the costs of employment and measures their impact on labor demand. The estimated-wage elasticities are summarized in table 4.9.
Using the more reliable quarterly time series obtained from the NHS these
elasticities range from –0.45 to –0.52, depending on the type of labor. However, the elasticities fall (in absolute terms) when the estimation uses a dynamic framework. In this case, the long-run, own-wage elasticity is –0.37.

In the case of the manufacturing sector the elasticities are somewhat
lower. Using the time series data they range between –0.35 (skilled) and
–0.40 (unskilled). In a panel of ninety-two manufacturing sectors the estimated value is –0.6 (in the short run) and –1.43 (in the long run). These results change dramatically in a regression that uses establishment data. In
this case the short-run elasticity is only –0.05, although its long-run counterpart is –2.27.

Output elasticities are larger. In the static labor demand framework the
estimates are close to 2 for skilled workers and 1 for unskilled labor. In the
dynamic specification they are 1 for skilled and 0.6 for unskilled employment. Again, the elasticities fall when panel data is used.

The chapter also analyzes the impact of changes in the regulations on
adjustment costs. The conclusion is that changes in severance payments
and costs of dismissal, associated with the 1990 labor reform, did not affect
the path of employment adjustment. Using this framework, we also conclude that structural reforms did not change the relevant elasticities. This
means that the main effect of regulatory changes affected labor demand
through their direct impact on labor costs. Since these costs have increased

it is likely that the net effect of labor, health, and pension reforms has been a reduction in employment generation. According to the estimated elasticities in the dynamic framework, an elimination of the 9 percent payroll taxes could result in a 1.3 percent increase in employment in the urban areas. Of course, the impact is much greater when the elasticities derived from the static exercise are used. In this case, a 10 percent reduction in labor costs could result in a 5 percent increase in labor demand.

Using a panel of manufacturing establishments, we also concluded that the wage elasticity of labor demand increases (in absolute terms) during contractions. The impact of output growth on employment is also larger during recessions than during expansions. In this sense, we found an asymmetric labor demand response to the business cycle conditions. Last, we did not find evidence of a significant effect of structural reforms (i.e., trade liberalization) on the relevant labor demand elasticities. We conclude that the effects of reforms on labor demand were the result of changes in relative prices alone.

Appendix A

Generalized Leontief (GL) Cost Function

The GL cost function can be written as

$$(A1) \qquad C(P, Q, t) = Q \sum_i \sum_j b_{ij} p_i^{1/2} p_j^{1/2} + Q^2 \sum_i \alpha_i p_i + Qt \sum_i \gamma_i p_i,$$

where Q denotes output and p_i is the price of input i (t is time). The function is homogeneous of degree one in prices and does not impose symmetry, concavity, or homotheticity. Assuming price-taking behavior in factor prices and using Shephard's Lemma, one can derive cost-minimizing input demand functions:

$$(A2) \qquad X_i = \frac{\partial C}{\partial P_i} = \sum_j b_{ij} \left(\frac{p_j}{p_i} \right)^{1/2} Q + \alpha_i Q^2 + \gamma_i Qt,$$

where X_i is the quantity demanded of input i. Factor demands can be expressed in terms of input-output ratios:

$$(A3) \qquad \frac{X_{ti}}{Q_t} = \sum_j b_{ij} \left(\frac{p_{jt}}{p_{it}} \right)^{1/2} + \alpha_i Q_t + \gamma_i t + \mu_{it}$$

Appendix B

Analytical Framework for the Dynamic Labor Demand Estimations

A Cobb-Douglas production function can be written as

(A4) $$Y_t = AL_t^\alpha K_t^{(1-\alpha)},$$

where A denotes a technological parameter, L the level of total employment, K the capital stock, and α the proportion of employment in production.

First-order conditions can be written as

(A5) $$W_t = \frac{\delta Y_t}{\delta N_t} = \alpha A L_t^{*\alpha-1} K_t^{1-\alpha}.$$

Expressing equation (A5) in logarithms, we get

(A6) $$\ln W_t = \ln \alpha A - (1-\alpha)\ln L_t^* + (1-\alpha)\ln K_t.$$

Rearranging terms, we get

(A7) $$\ln W_t = \ln Y_t + \ln \alpha A + \ln A + \alpha \ln L_t^* - (1-\alpha)\ln L_t.$$

If lowercase letters denote logs, then (A7) is equivalent to

(A8) $$l_t^* = \frac{c + y_t + w_t}{(1-\alpha)}$$

(A9) $$l_t^* = c + \alpha y_t + \beta w_t.$$

An adjustment equation satisfies

(A10) $$l_t - l_{t-1} = (1-\lambda)(l_t^* - l_{t-1}) + \varepsilon_{t-1}.$$

Rearranging terms we get

(A11) $$l_t^* = \frac{l_t - l_{t-1}}{(1-\lambda)} + l_{t-1} - \frac{\varepsilon_{t-1}}{(1-\lambda)}.$$

Substituting (A9) into (A11), we get

(A12) $$\frac{l_t - l_{t-1}}{(1-\lambda)} + l_{t-1} - \frac{\varepsilon_t}{(1-\lambda)} = c + \alpha y_t + \beta w_t.$$

Rearranging terms, we get

(A13) $$l_t = (1-\lambda)c + \alpha(1-\lambda)y_t + (1-\lambda)\beta w_t + \lambda l_{t-1} + \varepsilon_t.$$

We now suppose firms have rational expectations and l_t^e satisfying the following condition:

(A14) $$l_t^e = (1-\lambda)l_t + \lambda l_{t-1}^e,$$

Table 4B.1   Dismissal Costs (number of monthly wages)

Years of Tenure	Old Regime	New Regime
5	4.2	4.2
10	10.5	13.5
15	15.5	20.2
20	20.5	26.8

Table 4B.2   Case without Increases in Health and Pension Contributions (%)

	Total Employment	Unskilled Employment	Skilled Employment
1993:2	0.1	0.0	0.1
1993:3	0.1	0.5	0.4
1993:4	0.1	0.6	0.4
1994:1	0.1	0.4	0.5
1994:2	0.2	0.1	0.3
1994:3	0.2	0.1	0.3
1994:4	0.7	0.2	0.9
1995:1	0.6	0.8	1.1
1995:2	0.7	0.8	1.1
1995:3	1.2	0.6	1.7
1995:4	1.1	1.0	1.6
1996:1	1.2	1.9	2.2
1996:2	1.3	1.4	2.0
1996:3	1.4	1.0	1.9
1996:4	1.3	1.8	2.2

Source: Authors' calculations.

Table 4B.3   Case with Elimination of 9 Percent Payroll Taxes (%)

	Total Employment	Unskilled Employment	Skilled Employment
1993:2	0.2	0.2	0.5
1993:3	1.0	0.6	1.0
1993:4	0.7	1.2	0.7
1994:1	1.2	1.4	1.4
1994:2	1.2	1.3	0.9
1994:3	1.3	1.8	1.5
1994:4	1.2	1.1	1.1
1995:1	1.3	1.8	1.5
1995:2	1.2	1.9	1.3
1995:3	1.3	0.9	0.8
1995:4	1.3	1.4	1.4
1996:1	1.2	2.0	1.1
1996:2	1.2	1.4	0.7
1996:3	1.3	0.9	0.6
1996:4	1.3	1.8	0.9

Source: Authors' calculations.
Note: Eliminating mandatory bonuses would be equivalent to eliminating payroll taxes.

where superscript e denotes expectations. Substituting recursively for e^e_{t-s}, we can obtain

(A15) $$l^e_t = \frac{(1 - \lambda)}{(1 - \lambda L)} l_t,$$

where L is the lag operator. Then (A13) can be rewritten as

(A16) $$l_t = (1 - \lambda)c + \alpha y_t - \alpha\lambda y_{t-1} + \beta w_t - \lambda\beta w_{t-1}$$
$$+ \lambda l_{t-1} - \lambda^2 l_{t-2} + \varepsilon_t - \lambda\varepsilon_{t-1},$$

which is the estimated equation.

References

Bentolila, S., and G. Saint-Paul. 1992. The macroeconomic impact of flexible labor contracts, with an application to Spain. *European Economic Review* 36:1013–53.

Burgess, S., and J. Dolado. 1989. Intertemporal rules with variable speed of adjustment: An application to U.K. manufacturing employment. *The Economic Journal* 99:347–65.

Cárdenas, M., and C. Gutiérrez. 1996. Impacto de las reformas estructurales sobre la eficiencia y la equidad: La experiencia colombiana en los noventa. [The effects of the structural reforms on efficiency and equality: The Colombian experience during the nineties]. *Coyuntura Económica* 26 (4): 109–35.

Diewert, W. E. 1971. An application of Shephard duality theorem: A generalized Leontief production function. *Journal of Political Economy* 79:481–507.

Farné, S., and O. A. Nupia. 1996. Reforma laboral, empleo e ingresos de los trabajadores temporales en Colombia. [Labor reform, employment and income of temporal workers in Colombia]. *Coyuntura Social* 15:155–69.

Gruber, J. 1995. The incidence of payroll taxation: Evidence from Chile. NBER Working Paper no. 5053. Cambridge, Mass.: National Bureau of Economic Research, March.

Guash, J. L. 1997. Labor reform and job creation: The unfinished agenda in Latin American and Caribbean countries. The World Bank. Mimeograph.

Hamermesh, D. S. 1986. The demand for labor in the long-run. In *Handbook of labor economics,* vol. 1, ed. O. Ashenfelter and R. Layard. Princeton, N.J.: North-Holland.

Hicks, J. R. 1963. *The theory of wages.* New York: St. Martin's Press.

Kesselman, J. R. 1995. A public finance perspective on payroll taxes. University of British Colombia, Vancouver, Department of Economics. Mimeograph.

Lopez, R. E. 1980. The structure of production and the derived demand for inputs in Canadian agriculture. *American Journal of Agricultural Economics* 62:38–45.

Lora, E., and M. L. Henao. 1995. Efectos económicos y sociales de la legislación laboral. [Economics and social impact of the labor legislation]. *Coyuntura Social* 13:47–68.

Lora, E., and C. Pagés. 1997. La legislación laboral en el proceso de reformas estructurales de América Latina y el Caribe. [Labor legislation in the process of structural reform in Latin America and the Caribbean]. In *Empleo y distribución del ingreso en América Latina: ¿Hemos avanzado?,* ed. M. Cárdenas, forthcoming.

Newell, A., and J. S. V. Symons. 1987. Corporatism, laissez-faire, and the rise in unemployment. *European Economic-Review* 31 (3): 567–601.

Ocampo, J. A. 1987. El regimen prestacional del sector privado. [Severance payments regime in the private sector.] In *El problema laboral Colombiano, Informe de la Misión Chenery,* ed. J. A. Ocampo and Manuel Ramírez. Contraloría General de la República-DNP.

Pombo, C. 1997. How high is the user cost of capital for the Colombian industrial entrepreneur? University of Illinois. Mimeograph.

Ribero, R., and C. Meza. 1997. Ingresos laborales de hombres y mujeres en Colombia: 1976–1995. [Labor income of men and women in Colombia: 1976–1995]. Departamento Nacional de Planeación Working Paper no. 62. Bogota, Colombia: Departamento Nacional de Planeación.

Sánchez, F., and J. Nuñez. 1998. La curva de salarios para Colombia. Una estimación de las relaciones entre el desempleo, la inflación y los ingresos laborales, 1984–1996. [The wage curve in Colombia: An estimation of the relationship between unemployment, inflation, and labor income: 1984–1996]. Departamento Nacional de Planeación Working Paper no. 80. Bogota, Colombia: Departamento Nacional de Planeación.

Slaughter, M. J. 1997. International trade and labor-demand elasticities. NBER Working Paper no. 6262. Cambridge, Mass.: National Bureau of Economic Research, November.

5

The Impact of Regulations on Brazilian Labor Market Performance

Ricardo Paes de Barros and Carlos Henrique Corseuil

5.1 Introduction

Labor market regulations are invariably introduced with two objectives. The first one is to improve the welfare of the labor force, even at the cost of introducing some degree of economic inefficiency. The second consists of improving efficiency, when external factors and/or other labor market imperfections are present.

These regulations may eventually become inadequate due to an unsuitable original design or unexpected changes in the economic environment. This inadequacy may lead to results contrary to the original goals of labor market regulations. Consequently, as a general rule, labor market regulations (as any other market regulation) need to be constantly evaluated and updated if their original goals are to be preserved.

However, any empirical study of the impact of labor market regulations on labor market performance faces three main difficulties. First, it is necessary to face the facts that labor market regulations do not change very often and tend to apply universally to all sectors in the economy. Hence, variations in labor market regulations, which are necessary to identify their

Ricardo Paes de Barros is a researcher at the Institute for Applied Economic Research (IPEA), Brazil. Carlos Henrique Corseuil is a researcher at the Institute for Applied Economic Research (IPEA), Brazil.

This chapter is a compiled version of Barros, Corseuil and Gonzaga (1999) and Barros, Corseuil, and Bahia (1999). The authors would like to thank Wasmália Bivar for valuable information about the PIM database. We also would like to thank Carmen Pagés, James Heckman, Rosane Mendonça, Gustavo Gonzaga, Ricardo Henriques, and Miguel Foguel for comments on previous versions of this chapter. Finally, we cannot forget to mention the extreme dedication of our team in IPEA involved in this project, especially Mônica Bahia, Phillippe Leite, Danielle Milton, Eduardo Lopes, Gabriela Garcia, Viviane Cirillo, and Luis Eduardo Guedes.

impact on labor market performance, are hard to find, both in time series and cross-sections.

Second, even when legislation varies over time, it is difficult to isolate its impact on labor market performance from the impact of other macroeconomic factors. This is particularly important in Brazil, because over the past two decades macroeconomic instability has reached unprecedented levels. Inflation, economic growth, internal and external imbalances, and the degree of openness of the economy have changed considerably. If one opts for using cross-section variations, the drawbacks are not less. In this case, it is necessary to isolate the impact of differences in regulations from all other sector-specific factors that could make performance measures different across sectors.

Finally, measures of labor market performance are needed. The problem here is that performance is a multidimensional aspect of the labor market with no consensus about its precise definition. Hence, there is not a single unidimensional measure for this aspect. The use of the measure for the (supposed) main dimension is usually implemented as a measure of labor market performance.

In respect to the Brazilian labor market, many analysts have been very critical about the benefits of the prevailing labor market regulations.[1] On the whole, these regulations were designed to improve welfare, giving the workers more protection. The analysts claim these regulations have not been wisely designed and, consequently, are failing to reach their objective. Actually their arguments go further, claiming that the regulation worsened not only the welfare of the labor force, but also the efficiency, based on the observation of increasingly poor working conditions and lower wages and a drop in the degree of employability of the Brazilian labor force. They argue that this occurs in a new economic environment that increasingly requires greater labor flexibility. As a consequence, labor market regulation reform has become a central item on the current Congress agenda, particularly after the recent leap in unemployment.[2]

Despite the importance of evaluations of the impact of these regulations on labor market performance, the number of such studies focusing on Brazilian labor markets has been very limited.[3] The three difficulties pointed out are not sufficient to justify the relatively few studies on the subject. First, labor market regulations underwent considerable changes in 1988, when

1. See Jatobá (1994) for a survey of those analyses that consider that a higher nonwage labor cost reduces the job creation. This survey includes the arguments of Bacha, Mata, and Modenesi (1972), Camargo and Amadeo (1990), Almeida (1992), Chahad (1993), Macedo (1993), Pastore (1993), and World Bank (1991).

2. Deseasonalized unemployment in the six main Brazilian metropolitan regions increased from around 5.7 percent in October 1997 to 7.4 percent in June 1998.

3. Some examples are Amadeo et al. (1995), Amadeo and Camargo (1993), Amadeo and Camargo (1996), and Málaga (1992).

a new constitution was enacted, containing most of the prevailing labor market regulations. Moreover, the wealth of information available allows the implementation of promising methodological possibilities for identifying the impact of labor market regulations, based on alternative proxies of labor market performance that can be obtained using the information available.

Hence, the objective of this chapter is to identify whether the prevailing Brazilian labor market regulations, in large extension originated by the 1988 constitutional change, have any impact on labor market performance. To reach this objective we will explore alternative methodologies, sources of information, and measures of labor market performance. The diversification is an attempt on accessing the robustness of our result.

We have two alternatives to measure labor market performance. The first is based on parameters estimated from a labor demand model, and the second is based on turnover rates. Some alternative methodologies for estimation of the effect of the constitutional change are associated to each of these two measures. Regression analysis is the only alternative developed for labor demand parameters estimation. The turnover rates are mainly analyzed through the difference-in-differences methodology, but regressions are also developed as a complement of the difference-in-differences method.

The chapter is organized in five sections, including this introduction. In the next section we briefly describe the 1988 constitutional change, with special emphasis on the topics related to labor costs, which, basically, will be used as the main sources of variation on labor market regulations. The two sections that follow the institutional analysis will focus on the two alternative measures of labor market performance. Section 5.3 is dedicated to the description and implementation of the regression analysis through which we estimate the parameters of labor demand. Section 5.4 contains the description and results achieved when we use turnover rates to measure labor market performance according to difference-in-differences methodology complemented by regression analysis. Finally, section 5.5 summarizes our main findings.

5.2   The Institutional Analysis

5.2.1   The 1988 Constitutional Change

A new Brazilian Constitution was enacted in 1988 as part of the process of redemocratization in Brazil during the second half of the 1980s. Traditionally, Brazilian constitutions are very detailed, stipulating not only general rules, but also many specific legal provisions. Most labor regulations, for instance, are written in the constitution and are, consequently, very difficult to amend. The new constitution of 1988, in particular, considerably affected labor regulations, causing changes in many labor codes that had remained intact since the 1940s.[4] Most of these changes, in tune with the redemocratization environment, increased the degree of the workers' protection.

These changes, shown in table 5.1, affected both individual rights and workers' organizations. The new constitution gave more freedom and autonomy to unions. The possibilities for government intervention in unions were drastically reduced. In fact, many mechanisms of official interference were eliminated (e.g., the right of intervention by the Ministry of Labor and the need to be registered and approved at the same Ministry) as well as many restrictions of an institutional nature used to limit workers' organizations (such as representation scales and diversity of occupational categories). Many regulations on union management were also weakened, ensuring more autonomy to unions during elections of their representatives and in their decisions.

From the point of view of individual rights, we can perceive important changes that increase variable labor costs and the level of dismissal penalties. The increase in protection ensured by the new constitution considerably increased a firm's costs of employment. The maximum number of working hours per week dropped from forty-eight to forty-four hours; the maximum number of hours for a continuous work shift dropped from eight to six hours; the minimum overtime premium increased from 20 percent to 50 percent; maternity leave increased from three to four months; and the value of paid vacations increased from 1 to, at least, 4/3 of the normal monthly wage.

The new constitution also considerably increased the level of dismissal penalties. This change in legislation will be one of the fundamental sources of variation used throughout this study to estimate the impact of regulations on labor market performance.

It is worth mentioning that the changes altered the level of the penalties but not their nature. Traditionally, Brazilian legislation affects the cost of dismissal through two channels. First, employers must give notice to their employees in the case of dismissal. Moreover, between the notice and actual dismissal, workers are granted two hours per day to look for a new job, with no cut in wages. Second, the law states that all workers dismissed for no just cause must receive monetary compensation paid by the employer.

Prior to the 1988 constitution, notice had to be given at least one month in advance. The 1988 constitution states that the period of notice should be given in proportion to the worker's tenure. However, because no specific law has ever regulated this constitutional device, notice continues to be given, as before 1988, one month prior to dismissal for all workers, independent

4. One major exception was the rule regulating dismissals, which suffered major changes in 1966 when the FGTS was created.

Pre-Constitution	Post-Constitution

Individual Rights

Pre-Constitution	Post-Constitution
1. Maximum working hours per week = 48 hours.	1. Maximum working hours per week = 44 hours.
2. Maximum daily journey for continuous work shift = 8 hours.	2. Maximum daily journey for continuous work shift = 6 hours.
3. Minimum over-time remuneration = 1,2 of the normal wage rate.	3. Minimum over-time remuneration = 1,5 of the normal wage rate.
4. Paid vacations = at least the normal monthly wage.	4. Paid vacations = at least 4/3 of the normal monthly wage.
5. Maternity license = 3 months (1 before and 2 after the birth).	5. Maternity license = 120 days.
6. Previous notification of dismissal = one month.	6. Previous notification of dismissal = proportional to seniority (to be regulated by a future law).
7. Fine for nonjustified dismissal = 10% of Fundo de Garantia por Tempo de Serviço (FGTS).	7. Fine for non-justified dismissal = 40% of Fundo de Garantia por Tempo de Serviço (FGTS).
8. Creation of paternity license of 5 days.	
9. Profit-sharing (regulated by a 1996/97 law).	

Unions Organization

Pre-Constitution	Post-Constitution
A) The Ministry of Labor had the right to intervene in the unions and depose their board of directors.	A) The Ministry of Labor is forbidden to intervene in the unions.
B) Every union had to be registered and approved at the Ministry of Labor.	B) Unions do not need to be registered and approved at the Ministry of Labor.
C) National representation of unions was allowed only in exceptional cases.	C) National representation of unions is allowed.
D) Union's representatives were elected by a minimum quorum of 2/3 of the members in the first balloting, 1/2 in the second balloting and 2/5 in the third balloting. In the case of no minimum quorum for the election, the Ministry of Labor could choose union's directors and call another election.	D) Union's representatives are elected following union's own rules.
E) Workers (employers) unions were allowed to be formed by only one type of occupational (economic) category.	E) Workers (employers) unions are allowed to be formed by different types of occupational (economic) categories.
F) Union's decision to go on strike had to be approved by a minimum quorum of 2/3 of union's members in the first calling and 1/3 in the second calling.	F) Union's decision to go on strike follows union's criterias.
G) In case of strike, notification to the employer had to be done 5 days in advance.	G) In case of strike, notification to the employer has to be done 48 hours in advance.
H) Strikes were forbidden in activities considered fundamental (e.g., energy and gas services, hospitals, pharmacies, funeral services); public servants were not allowed to go on strike.	H) There are not any more sectors in which strikes are forbidden: In essential activities, workers and employers are responsible for the provision of minimum services; public servants (excluding military personnel) are allowed to go on strike.

Sources: Camargo and Amadeo (1990) and Nascimento (1993).

of their tenure. Hence, it cannot be used as our source of variation in labor regulations.

Concerning the monetary compensation for dismissed workers, the law states that a fixed percentage of the *Fundo de Garantia por Tempo de Serviço* (FGTS), a sort of job security fund accumulated while the worker was employed by the firm, is to be paid to every worker dismissed for no just cause. There was a fourfold increase in the value of this penalty as a result of the 1988 constitutional change.

The basic characteristics of the FGTS are the following. First, each worker in the formal sector has his own fund; in other words, it is a private fund instead of a single fund for the workers as a group. Second, to build the fund of each individual worker, the employer must contribute, every month, the equivalent of 8 percent of his employee's current monthly wage; consequently, the accumulated FGTS of a worker in any given firm is proportional to the worker's tenure and his or her average wage over his or her stay in the firm. Third, the fund is administrated by the government. Fourth, workers have access to their own fund only if dismissed without just cause or upon retirement.[5] Fifth, if they resign they are *not* granted access to this fund. Sixth, on dismissal, workers have access to their entire fund, including all funds accumulated in previous jobs, plus a penalty in proportion to their accumulated fund in the job from which they are being dismissed.[6]

Before 1988, this compensation was equal to 10 percent of the cumulative contribution of the current employer to the worker's FGTS. After 1988, this penalty was increased to 40 percent of the employer's cumulative contribution to the worker's FGTS. As the monthly rate is 8 percent of the monthly wage, the FGTS accumulates at a rate of approximately one full monthly salary per year in the job. So, quantitatively, the penalty accumulates in a rate equivalent to 40 percent (10 percent prior to 1988) of the worker's current monthly wage per year in the firm. This compensation was certainly very small prior to 1988. In fact, under the former constitution, the worker had to be employed in the firm for at least ten years in order for the compensation to reach the magnitude of one monthly salary. Now it takes 2.5 years in the job for the compensation to reach this value.

Finally, it is worth mentioning that despite the 1988 fourfold increase in the FGTS penalty it is not clear that, even now, this penalty constitutes a major constraint to dismissals or even a major fraction of overall dismissal costs. For instance, the cost of advance notice may be larger than the penalty. In principle, the need for notice would increase the cost of dismissal only to the extent that, for a period of one month, 25 percent of the

---

5. There are a few exceptions. Workers can use their FGTS as a part of the payment for acquiring their home. They also can use it to pay for large health expenses.

6. The FGTS is a fund created by the military regime in 1966 to serve as an alternative to the job security law prevailing at that time. In practice, all new contracts after 1966 adopted the new system because it was preferred by both employees and employers.

hours of the dismissed worker would be paid but not worked. In practice, the productivity of a dismissed worker will drop once he or she has been given notice, implying an overall decline of well over 25 percent in his or her contribution to production. As a result, it is not uncommon for firms to pay a full salary to dismissed workers, without their being required to work a single hour. In other words, the cost of notice is actually between 25 percent and 100 percent of one month's salary, being in practice closer to 100 percent than to 25 percent.

Consequently, the costs of advance notice tend to be higher than the dismissal compensation paid to all workers with tenure of less than 2.5 years. Because most employment relationships in Brazil are short, employers may be more sensitive to the cost of advance notice than to the value of the dismissal compensation.

5.2.2   Dismissal Penalties, Incentives, and Possible Labor Market Outcomes

As far as incentives are concerned, it is worth emphasizing that being fired is the chief mechanism to achieve access and control over their overall FGTS. Furthermore, there are strong incentives for workers to seek access to their FGTS. First, the FGTS has been poorly managed by the government, typically generating negative real returns or returns well below market rates.[7] Second, due to shortsightedness or credit constraints, workers may be heavily discounting the future. The facts that (1) all dismissal penalties are immediately received individually by the dismissed worker, and (2) being dismissed is the chief mechanism for workers to acquire control over their own fund that is poorly managed by the government give them considerable incentives to induce their own dismissal after a certain time in any job. However, those incentives are related to the existence of the FGTS and the amount accumulated in this fund. As we saw in the last section, the constitution did not change those aspects of regulation.

There are other incentives associated with the dismissal penalty that may indeed drive the results estimated on this paper. On one hand this penalty is paid *by the employer to the employee,* as opposed to the employer's paying into a social fund held for all workers as a group. In other words, the dismissed worker (only him) receives the penalty on an individual basis. This characteristic of the law has well-established and major negative effects on the workers' behavior, giving them significant incentives to induce their own dismissal.[8]

On the other hand, firm behavior tends, however, to reduce dismissals when there is an increase on the dismissal's penalties value. Additionally,

---

7. See Almeida and Chautard (1976) for a broad analysis of the FGTS, including topics such as management of the fund and workers' welfare. Carvalho and Pinheiro (1999) provide a more updated analysis, focusing on the role of FGTS on fomenting investments.

8. See Macedo (1985) and Amadeo and Camargo (1996).

as a result of the increase in dismissal penalties, firms become more selective in their hiring procedures, leading to an overall decline even greater in dismissal rates. Hence, the net effect on turnover will depend on the respective responses' intensities of each part (firms and workers) to the magnitude of the penalties. It is worth mentioning that these incentives are associated with employment spells longer than three months because before that employers can fire workers free of any penalty.

Hence, the aggregate effect on turnover will depend also on the firm reaction during the first months of the relation, namely the training period. The firm may become more selective in the first three months because the firing process becomes more expensive later. It means that the turnover may increase during this period as a consequence of an increase on dismissal penalties. So we have to contrast the results related to both periods in order to access the aggregate result on turnover.

According to the incentives described previously, it is not clear that legislation would achieve the original goal of a lower firing level. We can either have an opposite or null result. Additionally, a null net result can also arise from the absence of any reaction. This would be the case if the penalty is not a bidding constraint. In fact, we have some evidence that workers and firms collude to turn voluntary quits into dismissals. Under this circumstance workers can have access to their fund, but firms do not pay any penalty. Barros, Corseuil, and Foguel (2001) show that approximately 2/3 of the workers that voluntarily quit from jobs in the formal sector access their FGTS, which means that these quits were officially registered as dismissals.[9]

5.3   Demand for Labor Estimation

This part of the chapter describes an attempt to estimate the impact of regulations on labor market performance based on the first of the two measures mentioned in the introduction—the labor demand parameters. These parameters constitute our proxy for labor market performance. As we estimate the parameters monthly, we can try to identify whether the evolution of these parameters is associated to the constitutional change or to the evolution of macroeconomic indicators. This exercise constitutes our second step, where we run regressions of the labor demand parameters on an indicator of the constitutional change and on macroeconomic indicators.

This part is organized in five sections. Section 5.3.1 describes a structural model for labor demand on which we base our first step. The estimation procedure of the relation suggested by the theoretical model is described in section 5.3.2. The second step and a data base description are the focus of sections 5.3.3 and 5.3.4, while the results of both steps are commented on in section 5.3.5.

---

9. There are questions about access to the fund in some Brazilian household surveys.

5.3.1 A Structural Model for Labor Demand

In this section we estimate a structural dynamic labor demand model using longitudinal data on establishments. The model, one of the most simple in the literature, assumes labor as a homogeneous input and that labor is the only input undergoing adjustment costs.[10] Moreover, this basic theoretical model assumes that each firm i, at each point in time t, chooses the level of employment, $n_i(t)$, in order to maximize the expected present value of profits; that is, each firm chooses $n_i(t)$ in order to maximize

(1) $\quad E_t\left(\sum_{r=0}^{\infty} \rho^r \{R[n_i(t+r), \mathbf{p}_i(t+r), \boldsymbol{\theta}(t+r), \mu_i(t+r)]\right.$

$$\left. - \delta(t+r)w_i(t+r)n_i(t+r) - C[\Delta n_i(t+r), \eta(t+r)]\}\right),$$

where R is the revenue function and C is the employment adjustment cost function.

Hence, at each point in time the revenue function, R, can be obtained by choosing the level of production and of all nonlabor variable inputs that maximize a current profits condition on a given choice for employment and the state of the technology.[11] As a consequence, the arguments of the revenue function can be divided into three groups: (1) level of employment, $n_i(t)$; (2) price of all other variable inputs relating to the product price, $p_i(t)$; and (3) all factors determining the state of technology. We divide the factors determining the state of technology into two groups: (1) a vector of parameters defining the overall form of technology at each point in time, $\boldsymbol{\theta}(t)$, that is common to all firms; and (2) a certain firm and time-specific technological innovation, $\mu_i(t)$.

The second term in equation (1) is the direct cost of labor. In this equation, $w_i(t)$ is the real wage rate[12] paid by firm i at time t, and $\delta(t)$ is the ratio between the overall variable cost of labor and the wage rate. We are implicitly assuming that all nonwage variable costs are proportional to wages with the proportionality constant and common to all firms but possibly time varying due to changes in the legislation.

Finally, the cost of adjustment (C) is assumed to be a function of the net change in employment, $\Delta n_i(t) = n_i(t) - n_i(t-1)$, and a parameter, $\eta(t)$. This parameter may vary over time to capture changes in the economic environment and in the labor legislation, but it is common to all firms, indicating that all firms face the same adjustment cost.

According to this model, the form of technology and labor costs may vary freely over time. However, idiosyncratic shocks of a firm can only

---

10. See Nickell (1986), Hamermesh (1993), and Hamermesh and Pfann (1996) for surveys of dynamic labor demand models.

11. In the state of the technology, we include the impact of the level of all fixed or exogenously determined inputs.

12. The real wage rate is obtained by dividing the nominal wage rate by the product price.

affect technology. Labor costs are determined by firm-specific wages and a legislation that is common to all firms.

In order to obtain an explicit solution to this problem of maximization, we introduce a series of simplifying assumptions that allow us to write the solution of equation (1) as the following expression defined for the employment level:[13]

$$(2) \quad n_i(t) = \lambda n_i(t-1) + \frac{(1-\lambda)}{\theta^{12}} \left[\theta^{11}(t) + \mu_i(t) + \sum_{s=1}^{m} \varphi_s(t) I_{is} - \delta(t) w_i(t) \right],$$

where λ is implicitly defined by

$$\theta^{12}\lambda = (1-\lambda)(1-\rho\lambda)\eta,$$

and I_{is} indicates whether firm i belongs to sector s, that is, $I_{is} = 1$ if firm i belongs to sector s and $I_{is} = 0$ otherwise. Finally, $\theta^{11}(t)$, $\theta^{12}(t)$ are originated from $\theta(t)$ and correspond to parameters of a quadratic revenue function, the same assumption made for the adjustment cost function.

5.3.2   Econometric Specification

To obtain an empirically feasible econometric specification for the demand for labor, we must be more specific about the firm- and time-specific technological innovation, $\mu_i(t)$. We assume that this innovation consists of three underlying components; that is, we assume that

$$\mu_i(t) = \beta_i + \gamma(t) + U_i(t),$$

where β_i captures a firm-specific, time-invariant technological component, $\gamma(t)$ an aggregated time-specific technological shock, and $U_i(t)$ captures all other technological shocks. The presence of the first two components allows us to assume, without any loss of generality, that the average of $U_i(t)$ over time and across firms is always zero. However, because the econometric model will also include sectorial indicators, I_{is}, we must assume that the average of $U_i(t)$ within each sector is also zero; that is, we assume that for every s,

$$E[U_i(t)\,|\,I_{is} = 1] = 0.$$

To identify the parameters of the model, additional assumptions are required. Probably the simplest route to obtain identification is to assume that $U_i(t)$ is an exogenous moving-average process. Accordingly, we assume that

$$E[U_i(t)n_i(t-p)] = 0$$

for all $p > k^1$. We also assume that although these technological shocks may be correlated with the recent evolution wages, they are uncorrelated with the evolution of wages in the past; that is,

---

13. The complete derivation of the model is reported in appendix A.

$$E[U_i(t)w_i(t - p)] = 0$$

for all $p > k^2$. Notice that if U were an exogenous moving-average process of order

$$k = \max(k^1, k^2),$$

then these two assumptions would be immediately satisfied.

Given this specification for the technological innovation, equation (2) may be rewritten as

$$(3) \quad n_i(t) = \alpha(t) + \beta_i^* + \sum_{s=1}^{m} \varphi_s^*(t)I_{is} - \delta^*(t)w_i(t) + \lambda n_i(t - 1) + U_i^*(t),$$

where

$$\alpha(t) = \frac{1 - \lambda}{\theta^{12}}[\theta^{11}(t) + \gamma(t)],$$

$$\beta_i^*(t) = \frac{1 - \lambda}{\theta^{12}}\beta_i,$$

$$\delta^*(t) = \frac{1 - \lambda}{\theta^{12}}\delta(t),$$

$$\varphi_s^*(t) = \frac{1 - \lambda}{\theta^{12}}(t),$$

$$U_i^*(t) = \frac{1 - \lambda}{\theta^{12}}U_i(t).$$

The presence of $\alpha(t)$ and β_i^* in equation (3) poses some drawbacks for estimation. The presence of $\alpha(t)$ makes estimation of the other parameters unfeasible in a pure time series context, unless some function form for $\alpha(t)$ is imposed.

In a cross-section environment, the difficulty is imposed by the natural correlation between β_i^* and $n_i(t - 1)$. To solve this problem we must rely on longitudinal information. When this type of information is available, we can take first differences to obtain

$$(4) \quad \Delta n_i(t) = \Delta\alpha(t) + \sum_{s=1}^{m} \Delta\varphi_s^*(t)I_{is} - \delta^*(t)\Delta w_i(t) + \lambda\Delta n_i(t - 1) + \Delta U_i^*(t),$$

as long as the ratio between the overall variable cost of labor and the wage rate $\delta(t)$ is time invariant. This equation has the advantage of eliminating the idiosyncratic component β_i^*. Nevertheless, it still cannot be estimated as a multiple regression because

$$E[\Delta n_i(t - 1)\Delta U_i^*(t)] \neq 0.$$

However, it follows from the assumptions made previously about $U_i(t)$ that

$$E[n_i(t - p)\Delta U_i^*(t)] = 0,$$

and

$$E[w_i(t - p)\Delta U_i^*(t)] = 0$$

for all $p > k + 1$. Hence, the model can be estimated by instrumental variable using past values of employment and wages as instruments. Under the assumptions made on $U_i(t)$, all values of employment and wages lagged at least $k + 2$ periods would be valid instruments. However, from a practical point of view it is necessary to limit the number of instruments. In this study we use as instruments 6 lags for employment and 6 lags for wages; that is, we use as instruments employment and wages lagged, $k + 2, \ldots,$ $k + 7$ months. In the estimation we use two alternative values for k (one month and ten months). Hence, to implement this econometric procedure it is necessary to count with panel information at least seventeen months long on firm-specific employment and wages.

Using this econometric model, based on equation (4), it is possible to estimate $\alpha(t)$, λ, δ^*, and $\varphi_s(t)$. Changes on the values of these parameters, especially λ and δ^* after 1988, indicate that the regulation might have impacted on labor market performance.[14] One possibility for investigating these possible changes would be to estimate two sets of parameters, first using data from the years before 1988 and then data from recent years. The available data allows us to obtain monthly estimates of the parameters of the demand function.

This strategy has at least three advantages over the strategy of estimating just two models for a period before and after 1988. First, it is easier to implement because the econometric model is essentially estimated in a cross-section. This feature of the estimation procedure makes estimating the standard errors much easier because in this case it is not necessary to estimate the temporal correlation patterns of the technological shocks.

Second, the estimation of a model for every month has the great advantage of allowing a precise identification of the exact point in time where the parameters have changed. A precise identification of the moment when the parameters changed can provide important insights into the question of whether the constitutional change is the real force behind the changes in the demand for labor. For instance, if the parameters began to change long before or long after 1988, we would become suspicious about the causal

14. At this point it is worthwhile mentioning that, although the demand for labor is estimated for every month, in the estimation procedure the parameters θ^{12}, η, and δ must be at least locally time invariant. The estimated parameters are consistent only if this assumption is valid. If the parameters θ^{12} and η change over time, equation (2) would not be the solution of the Euler equation. Moreover, if δ varies from one month to the next, the first difference made to eliminate the firm-specific time invariant technological component, β_i^*, would still work but would generate a different function form to be estimated because in this case δ^* would not factor out.

link between the 1988 constitutional change and those in the demand for labor.

Third, and more important, monthly estimations of the parameters allow us to identify in which sense their evolutions are determined—by the regulation (1988 constitutional change) or by the evolution of macroeconomic indicators. This is precisely what we do in the second step of this regression analysis.

In the next section we describe this second step in detail. It is worth mentioning that we can also obtain estimated values for coefficients of interest other than the ones mentioned previously. The first of these other coefficients is the long-run impact of changes in wages on employment, ϕ, that can be obtained via

$$\phi = \frac{\delta*}{(1 - \lambda)}.$$

Other parameters of interest are the structural parameters of the production function, θ^{12}, and of the cost function, η. Some additional information is required to obtain estimated values for these parameters. In this study, to recover these original parameters we assume that the discount rate, ρ, and the ratio between the unit cost of labor and the wage, δ, are known and equal to 0.95 and 1.8, respectively. Given the knowledge of these two parameters and estimates for λ and $\delta*$, estimates for the underlying parameters θ^{12} and η can be obtained via

$$\hat{\theta}^{12} = \frac{1 - \hat{\lambda}}{\hat{\delta}*}$$

and

$$\hat{\eta} = \frac{\hat{\lambda}\delta}{\hat{\delta}*(1 - \rho\hat{\lambda})}.$$

5.3.3   Identification Strategy: The Second Step

The monthly estimate of demand functions was just the first step in our econometric strategy. Because the Brazilian economy underwent a process of trade liberalization and was subject to a series of stabilization plans at the same time as the change in the constitution, changes in the parameters of the labor demand function that may have occurred over this period cannot be immediately attributed to the constitutional change.

To isolate the effect of the constitutional change on the parameters of the demand function, we regress our monthly estimates of these parameters on a temporal indicator for the 1988 constitutional change, D_t, controlling for a variety of other macroeconomic indicators, M_t. Because the precision of estimates varies considerably over time, to control for this source of variation we use as our dependent variable the parameter estimate divided by its corresponding standard error. More specifically, we estimate the following regressions

$$\frac{\hat{\lambda}(t)}{s_\lambda(t)} = a_1 + b_1 D(t) + c_1 M(t) + e_1(t)$$

and

$$\frac{\hat{\delta}^*(t)}{s_\delta(t)} = a_2 + b_2 D(t) + c_2 M(t) + e_2(t),$$

where $s_\lambda(t)$ and $s_\delta(t)$ are the standard errors of $\hat{\lambda}(t)$ and $\hat{\delta}^*(t)$, and $D(t) = 0$, if t refers to a period prior to 1988 and $D(t) = 1$ otherwise. We include the following as macroeconomic indicators: (1) the GDP real growth rate; (2) degree of openness measured by the ratio of total trade (exports plus imports) to the GDP; (3) inflation rate; and (4) inflation volatility measured by the inflation standard deviation. Monthly dummies and a linear trend were included in all regressions. These regressions are estimated by ordinary least square method using monthly data covering the period June 1986 to December 1997. Positive and statistically significant estimates for b_1 and b_2 would then be taken as evidence that the 1988 constitutional change had an important effect on the demand for labor and, consequently, on the level of employment and the speed of adjustment.

5.3.4   The Database

In the first step of the regression analysis we estimate the demand for labor using monthly longitudinal information from the Pesquisa Industrial Mensal (PIM). The PIM is a monthly industrial establishment survey conducted by the IBGE (Brazilian Census Bureau), covering the entire country. It is a longitudinal survey of a stratified sample of approximately 5,000 manufacturing establishments employing five workers or more. The panel covers the period from January 1985 to the present.

The survey collects information on labor inputs, labor costs, turnover, the value of production, and so on. The data on labor inputs includes both employment and the total number of hours paid. The survey has three major limitations in terms of measuring labor inputs. First, the information covers the total number of hours paid but not the actual number of hours worked. Second, all data refers only to the personnel directly involved in production. Finally, there is no information on the qualification of the labor force employed.

In relation to labor costs, two types of information are available: (1) total value of contractual wages (that is, value of wages and salaries as specified in labor contracts), and (2) total value of payroll. For the purposes of this study, the payroll data seems to be more informative because it includes, in addition to contractual wages, the payment for overtime, commissions, and other incentive schemes, such as a productivity premium. It also includes all fringe benefits; paid vacations; and any additional payments for hazardous activities, night shifts, and other compensating schemes.[15]

Despite the fact that the payroll data covers a wide variety of labor costs, it does not include all of them. Major exceptions are the employer's contributions to social security, training programs, and other social programs. Fortunately, however, these contributions as fractions of contractual wages have been fairly constant over time, except for a significant change for the occasion of the 1988 constitution.

Hence, for each establishment in the survey we use essentially three pieces of information: (1) employment level, (2) total number of hours paid, and (3) total payroll. Basing our information on these three variables we construct two measures for variable labor cost. These two measures are obtained by dividing total payroll by the level of employment and the total number of hours paid, respectively. For labor input we use both available measures: employment and hours paid. As a result, each demand model is actually estimated twice, depending on whether labor inputs are measured by employment or hours paid. We will refer to the one based on employment level as model 1 and to the one based on hours paid as model 2.

In the first step of the regression analysis we aggregate some macroeconomic indicators mentioned in the last section. The source of the gross domestic product (GDP) data is the IBGE. The data for exports and imports was calculated in joint work by the Fundação Centro de Estudos de Comércio Exterior (FUNCEX) and IPEA. Finally, we used the official inflation index to measure inflation.

Before we move to the labor demand estimates, we present some basic statistics from our sample of establishments. Panels A and B of figure 5.1 present the monthly evolution of the average level of the two measures of labor input used in the study. These figures reveal that firms in our sample employ 200 to 300 workers who are paid a total of 45,000 to 70,000 hours per month during the period analyzed. The average number of hours paid per month per worker in our sample is around 230 hours. Notice that a fraction of the hours paid is not actually worked. For instance, included in the hours paid is at least one day off per week (usually Sunday), which is paid but not worked.

All these figures reveal that, over the 1985–1997 period, employment and hours paid per manufacturing firm declined considerably, with the total decline concentrated in the first two years of the 1990s. The main goal of this study is to determine precisely to what extent this decline can be associated with the 1988 constitutional change or with other macroeconomic

---

15. In this study, all information on contractual wages and payroll has been deflated using the sector's specific wholesale price index, except for the pharmaceutical; plastic; textile; and perfume, soap, and candle sectors. All monetary values referred to constant reais at December 1997.

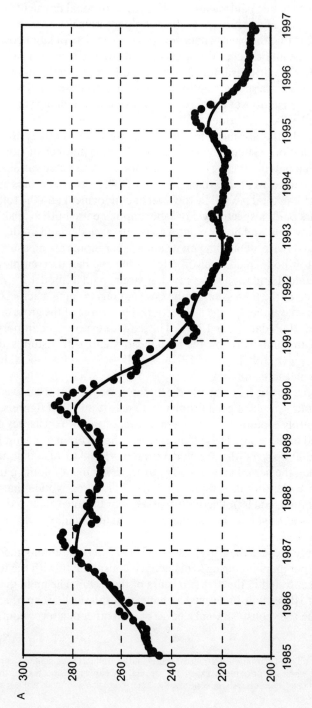

Fig. 5.1   Basic Statistics: *A*, Average employment per establishment; *B*, average number of hours paid per month per establishment; *C*, payroll per production worker; *D*, payroll per hours paid; *E*, evolution of monthly inflation

Sources: A, B, C, and *D,* based on the PIM; *E,* the IBGE.

Note: E, inflation measured by the variation in Índice Nacional de Preço ao Consumidor (INPC-R) from the 15th of one month to the 15th of the subsequent month.

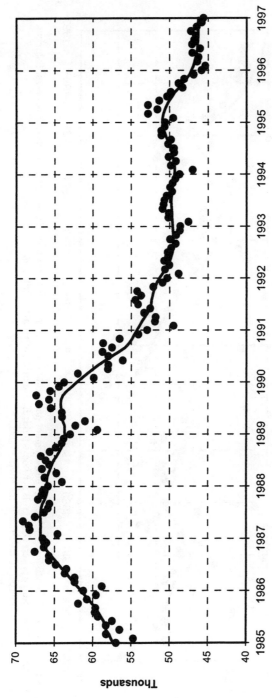

B

Thousands

70 — 65 — 60 — 55 — 50 — 45 — 40

1985 1986 1987 1988 1989 1990 1991 1992 1993 1994 1995 1996 1997

Fig. 5.1 (cont.)

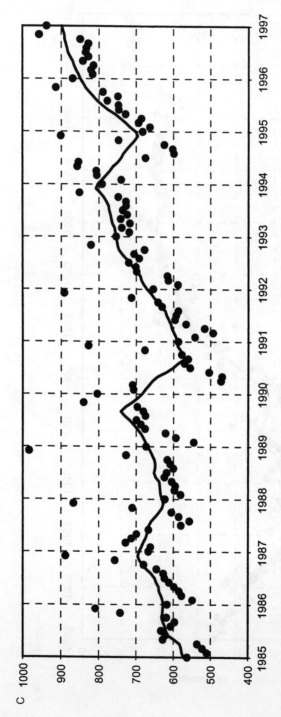

Fig. 5.1 (cont.) **Basic Statistics:** *A*, Average employment per establishment; *B*, average number of hours paid per month per establishment; *C*, payroll per production worker; *D*, payroll per hours paid; *E*, evolution of monthly inflation

Sources: A, B, C, and *D,* based on the PIM; *E,* the IBGE.

Note: E, inflation measured by the variation in Índice National de Preço ao Consumidor (INPC-R) from the 15th of one month to the 15th of the subsequent month.

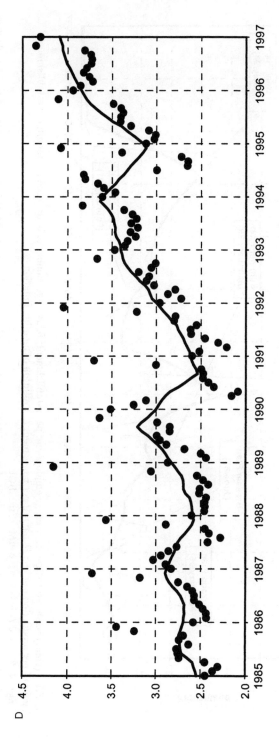

Fig. 5.1 (cont.)

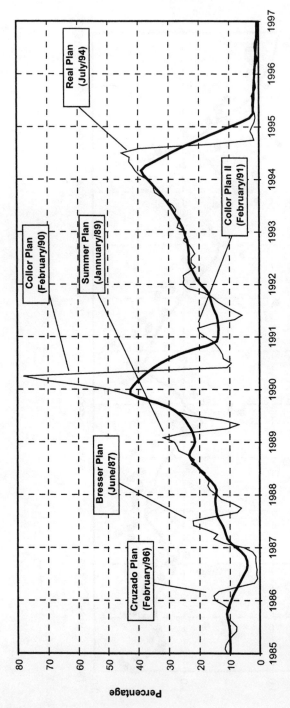

Fig. 5.1 (cont.) Basic Statistics: *A,* average employment per establishment; *B,* average number of hours paid per month per establishment; *C,* payroll per production worker; *D,* payroll per hours paid; *E,* evolution of monthly inflation

Sources: A, B, C, and *D,* based on the PIM; *E,* the IBGE.

Note: E, inflation measured by the variation in Índice Nacional de Preço ao Consumidor (INPC-R) from the 15th of one month to the 15th of the subsequent month.

changes that marked the performance of the Brazilian economy over this period.

Panels C and D of figure 5.1 show the monthly evolution of our two measures for labor costs. These figures reveal that average wages (in Brazilian reais [R]) for production workers in Brazilian manufacturing were, most of the time, between R$600 and R$800 per month, leading to an hourly wage rate between R$2.50 and R$3.50.[16] These figures reveal an overall upward trend in wages over the period, coupled with at least four cyclical fluctuations. These cycles very closely match series of stabilization plans that marked the period 1985–1994; see panel E of figure 5.1.

5.3.5 Empirical Results

The 1988 constitutional change brought an increase in labor costs, firing costs in particular. To the extent that this change was of substantial importance, it would lead to a decline in the response of employment to wages, δ^* and ϕ, and also in the speed of adjustment (i.e., an increase in the coefficient on lag employment, λ).

We estimate labor demand models for each month from June 1986 to December 1997. Although we have information since January 1985, the need for valid instruments determines that parameter estimates could only be obtained from mid-1986, that is, seventeen months after the actual sample information begins.

As already mentioned in the previous sections, two labor demand models were estimated, depending on the choices of measures for labor inputs. Moreover, two estimates are obtained for each model, depending on how far in the past we select the instruments. In total, four estimates for the labor demand function are obtained. In each case we directly estimate two basic parameters: (1) the coefficient on lag employment, λ; and (2) the coefficient on current wages, δ^*. We also obtain estimates for the long-run impact of change in wages on employment (ϕ) and other structural parameters (θ^{12} and η).

Figures 5.2 and 5.3 provide estimates of the monthly evolution of the short-run impact of changes in wages on employment, δ_t^*. Figures 5.4 and 5.5 show corresponding estimates for the coefficient on lag employment, λ_t. Because the estimates vary considerably from month to month, we also compute a trimmed twelve-month moving average. We adopted a two-step procedure to calculate this moving average. First, we eliminate all values in the lowest and highest tenths of the distribution.[17] Second, we calculate the twelve-month moving averages with the remaining estimates. The averages are weighted, using the inverse of the standard errors of each estimate as weights. Basing our information on these moving average estimates for the

---

16. The exchange rate was 1.11 R$/US$ in December of 1997.
17. In each figure, the lowest and highest tenths are indicated by two horizontal lines.

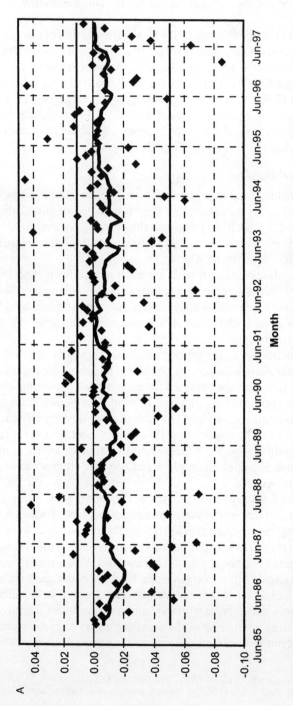

Fig. 5.2 Temporal evolution of the short-run response of employment to labor costs variable ($-\delta^*$), variable in level. Model 1: Employment level: $A, k = 1; B, k = 10$

Source: Based on the PIM.

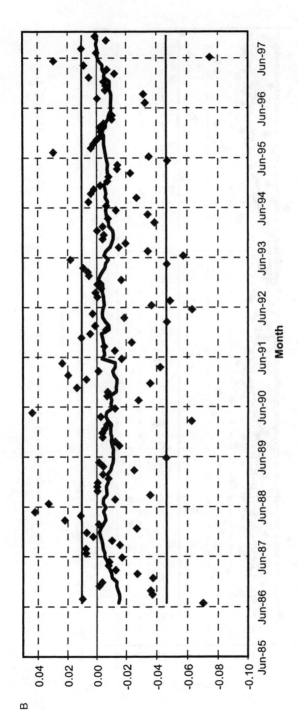

Fig. 5.2 (cont.)

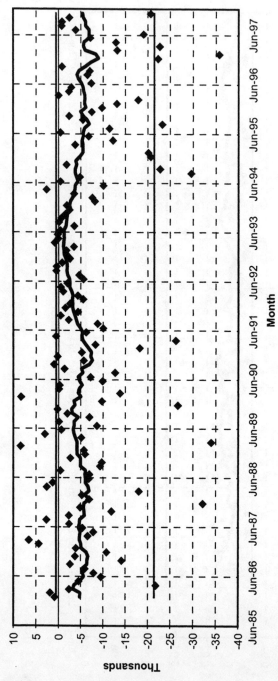

Fig. 5.3   Temporal evolution of the short-run response of employment to labor costs variable (−δ*), variable in level. Model 2: Hours paid: A, k = 1; B, k = 10

Source: Based on the PIM.

B

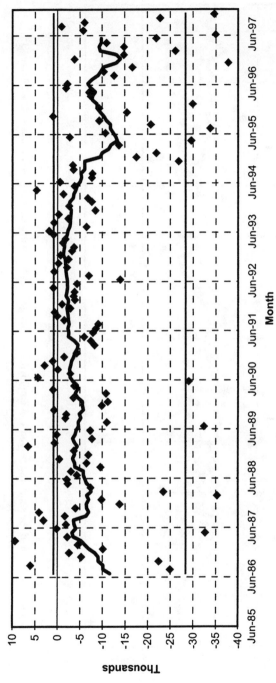

Thousands

10
5
0
-5
-10
-15
-20
-25
-30
-35
-40

Jun-85 Jun-86 Jun-87 Jun-88 Jun-89 Jun-90 Jun-91 Jun-92 Jun-93 Jun-94 Jun-95 Jun-96 Jun-97

Month

Fig. 5.3 (cont.)

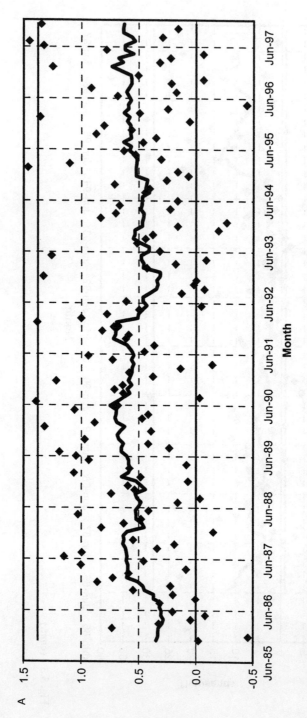

Fig. 5.4 Temporal evolution of the short-run response of employment to lagged employment variable (λ), variable in level. Model 1: Employment level: *A*, *k* = 1; *B*, *k* = 10

Source: Based on the PIM.

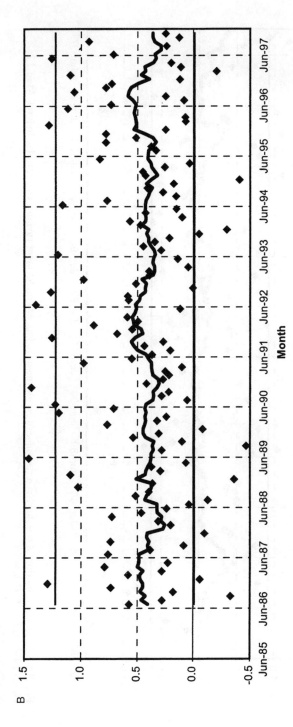

Fig. 5.4 (cont.)

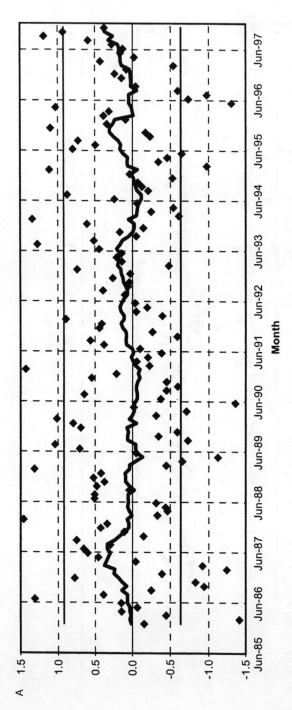

Fig. 5.5 Temporal evolution of the short-run response of employment to lagged employment variable (λ), variable in level. Model 2: Hours paid: *A*, *k* = 1; *B*, *k* = 10

Source: Based on the PIM.

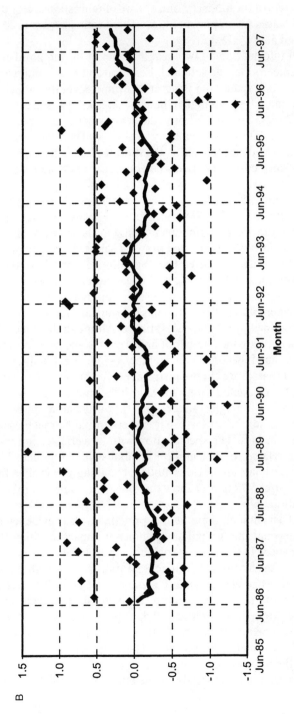

Fig. 5.5 (cont.)

basic parameters of the model (λ_t and δ_t^*), we obtain estimates for the long-run effect of wages on employment, ϕ_t. These estimates are presented in figures 5.6 and 5.7.

Basing our information on two-year averages of the temporal evolution of these parameters and the values chosen for ρ and δ, we obtain estimates for some important remaining structural parameters of the model: θ^{12} and η. These estimates are presented in figures 5.8, 5.9, 5.10, and 5.11.

Figures 5.2, 5.3, 5.6, and 5.7 provide clear evidence that both employment and hours paid decline as labor costs rise. These figures, however, provide no clear evidence that either the short- or long-run response of employment to labor costs increased as a consequence of the 1988 constitutional change.

Figures 5.4 and 5.5 give no evidence that the speed of adjustment was significantly affected by the 1988 constitutional change. In fact, figures 5.4 and 5.5 reveal a modest continuous increase in the speed of adjustment, contrary to what would be expected from a discrete increase in firing costs. It is worth mentioning, however, that the estimates for λ have the correct signed and are statistically significant, at least when we use the number of employed workers as a measure of the labor input. These estimates, however, are considerably smaller (estimates for λ are around 0.5) than what is commonly obtained from time series studies. Although the same pattern is observed when we use the number of hours paid, some point estimates became negative, and it becomes considerably less precise. Finally, figures 5.4 and 5.5 reveal that, as we choose instruments further into the past (i.e., as k increases), the estimated values for λ declines, indicating that serial correlation among technological shocks may seriously bias λ upwards.

The interpretation of the basic parameters would be much easier if all variables were in logs. The specification with all variables in logs is also more similar, related to the tradition in labor demand models. For these reasons, we reestimate all previous models, changing all variables from levels to logs. Figures 5.12 to 5.17 show that the main results are robust to the log specification.

As in the basic model, these figures provide no clear evidence that the 1988 constitutional change had any significant impact on either the magnitude or the speed of the response of labor inputs to labor costs. These figures deserve a few additional comments. First, they show that the short- and long-term wage elasticities are around –0.2 and –0.4, respectively. Second, it is worth mentioning that the estimates for the coefficient on lag of employment remain very close to 0.5, as is the case in the basic model. Third, it should be noted that the further the instruments are in the past, the smaller the estimated coefficients on lag employment, another pattern common to the basic model.

To summarize the evidence about the effect of the 1988 constitutional

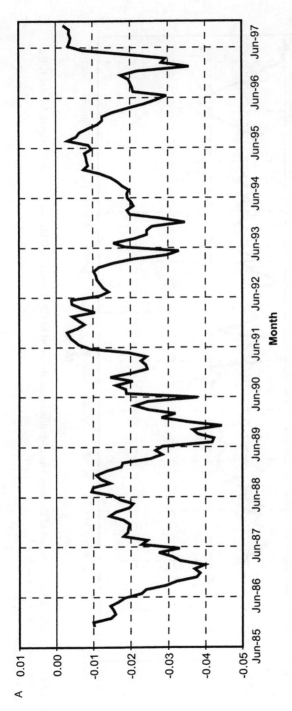

Fig. 5.6 Temporal evolution of the long-run response of employment to labor costs variable (−ϖ), variable in level. Model 1: Employment level: *A*, *k* = 1; *B*, *k* = 10

Source: Based on the PIM.

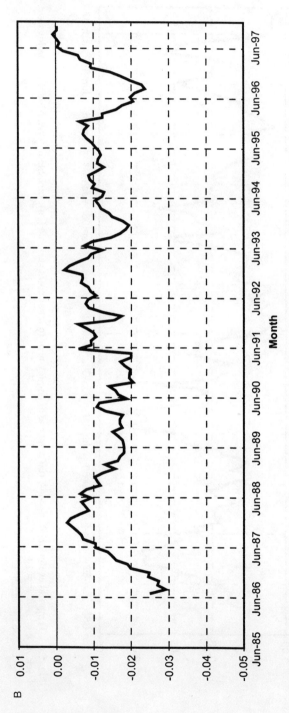

Fig. 5.6 (cont.) Temporal evolution of the long-run response of employment to labor costs variable (—•), variable in level. Model 1: Employment level: *A*, *k* = 1; *B*, *k* = 10
Source: Based on the PIM.

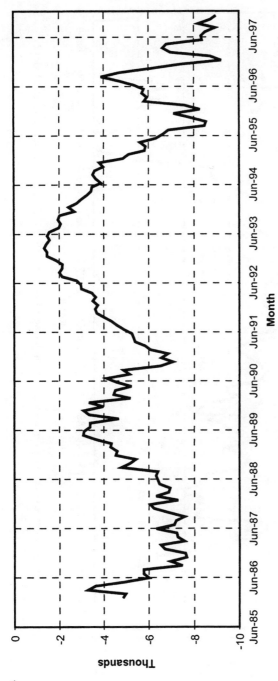

Fig. 5.7 Temporal evolution of the long-run response of employment to labor costs variable (–∘), variable in level. Model 2: Hours paid: A, $k = 1$; B, $k = 10$

Source: Based on the PIM.

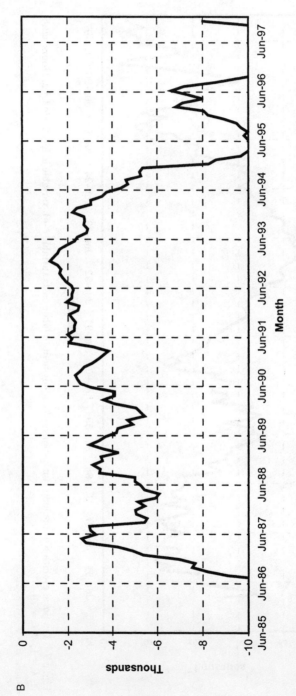

Fig. 5.7 (cont.) Temporal evolution of the long-run response of employment to labor costs variable (–·), variable in level. Model 2: Hours paid: A, $k = 1$; B, $k = 10$

Source: Based on the PIM.

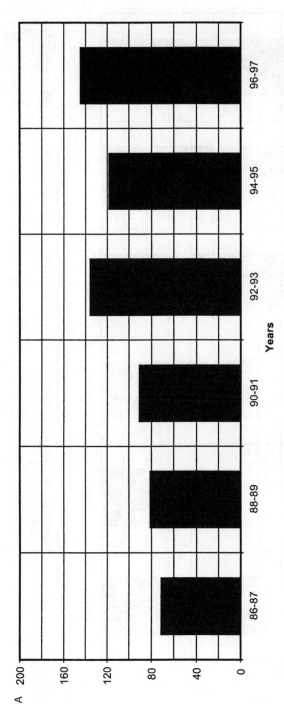

Fig. 5.8 Temporal averages of the short-run evolution of the production function structural parameter (θ^{12}), variable in level. Model 1: Employment level: A, $k = 1$; B, $k = 10$

Source: Based on the PIM.

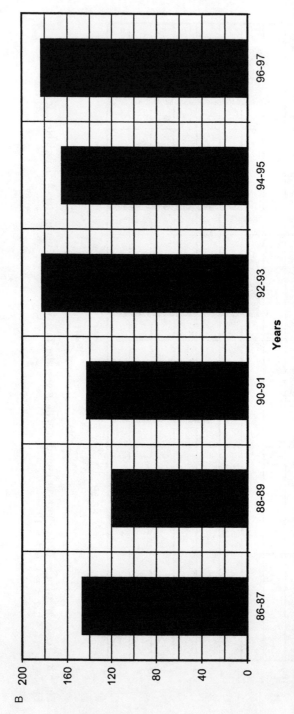

Fig. 5.8 (cont.) Temporal averages of the short-run evolution of the production function structural parameter (θ^{12}), variable in level. Model 1: Employment level: A, $k = 1$; B, $k = 10$

Source: Based on the PIM.

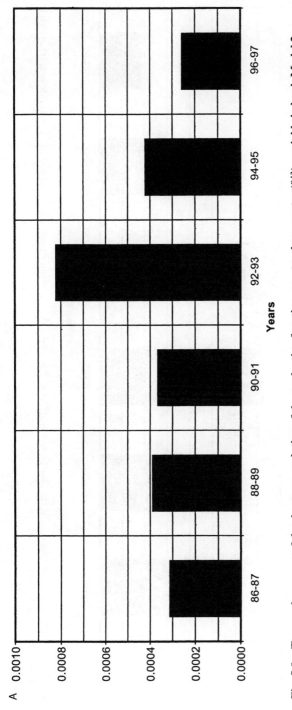

Fig. 5.9 Temporal averages of the short-run evolution of the production function structural parameter (θ^{12}), variable in level. **Model 2: Hours paid:** *A*, $k = 1$; *B*, $k = 10$

Source: Based on the PIM.

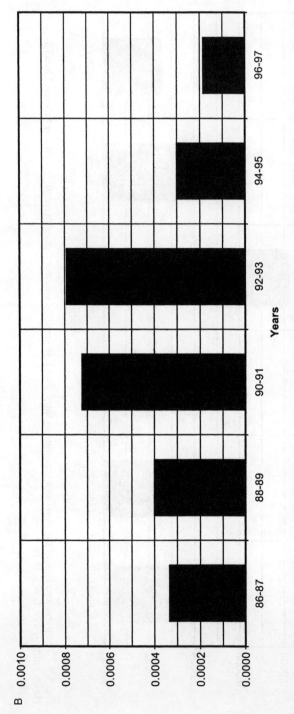

Fig. 5.9 (cont.) Temporal averages of the short-run evolution of the production function structural parameter (θ^{12}), variable in level. Model 2: Hours paid: A, $k = 1$; B, $k = 10$

Source: Based on the PIM.

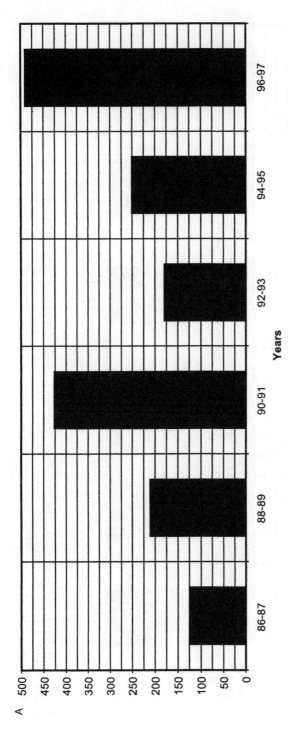

Fig. 5.10 Temporal averages of the short-run evolution of the cost function structural parameter (η), variable in level. Model 1: Employment level: *A*, *k* = 1; *B*, *k* = 10
Source: Based on PIM.

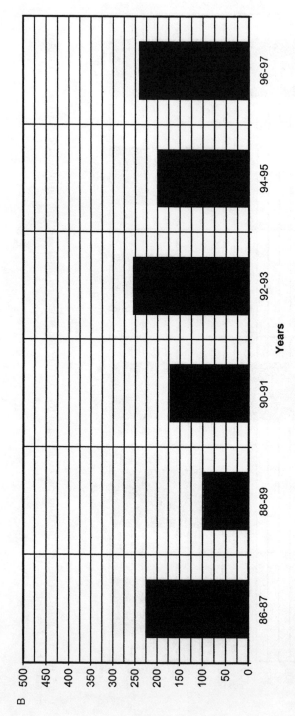

Fig. 5.10 (cont.) Temporal averages of the short-run evolution of the cost function structural parameter (η), variable in level. Model 1: Employment level: *A*, *k* = 1; *B*, *k* = 10

Source: Based on PIM.

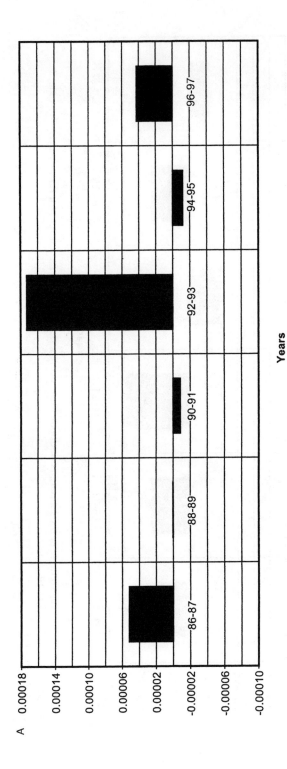

Fig. 5.11 Temporal averages of the short-run evolution of the cost function structural parameter (η), variable in level. Model 2: Hours paid: *A, k* = 1; *B, k* = 10

Source: Based on the PIM.

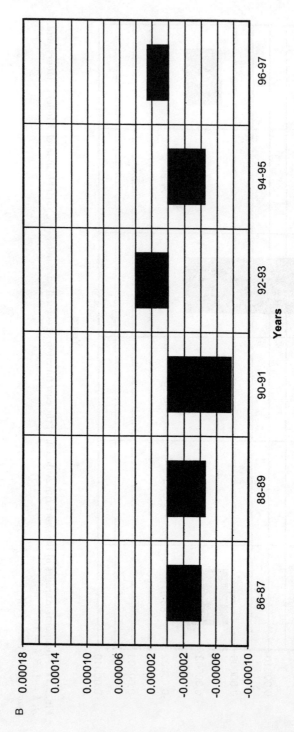

Fig. 5.11 (cont.) Temporal averages of the short-run evolution of the cost function structural parameter (η), variable in level. Model 2: Hours paid: *A*, *k* = 1; *B*, *k* = 10

Source: Based on the PIM.

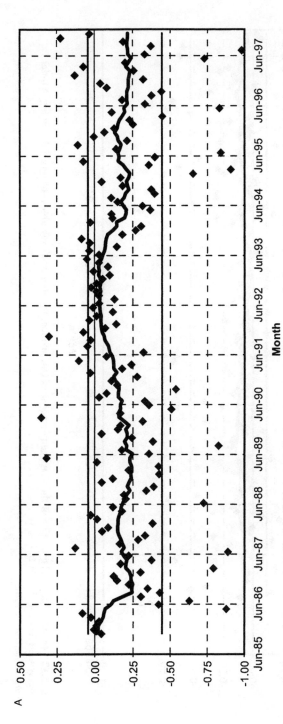

Fig. 5.12 Temporal evolution of the short-run response of employment to labor costs variable (−δ*), variable in log. Model 1: Employment level: *A*, *k* = 1; *B*, *k* = 10

Source: Based on the PIM.

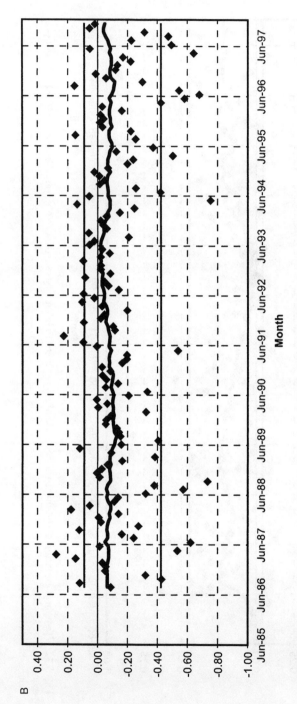

Fig. 5.12 (cont.) Temporal evolution of the short-run response of employment to labor costs variable (−δ*), variable in log. Model 1: Employment level: A, $k = 1$; B, $k = 10$

Source: Based on the PIM.

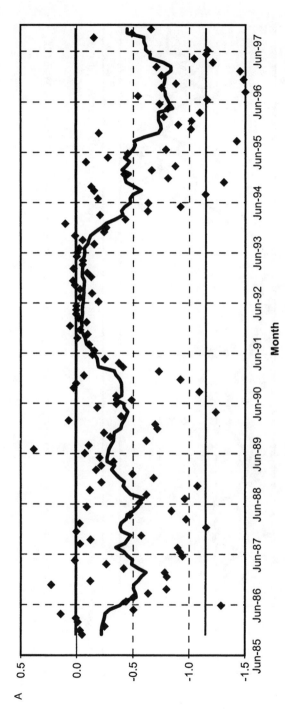

Fig. 5.13 Temporal evolution of the short-run response of employment to labor costs variable ($-\delta^*$), variable in log. Model 2: Hours paid: *A*, *k* = 1; *B*, *k* = 10

Source: Based on the PIM.

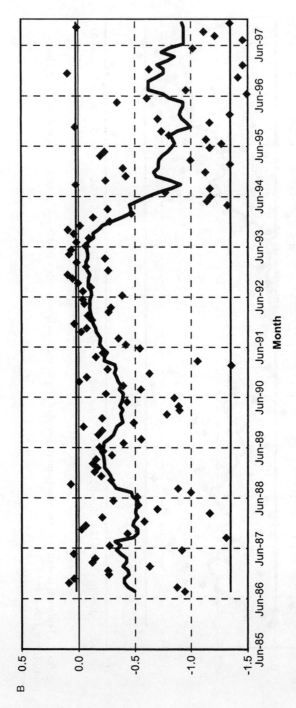

Fig. 5.13 (cont.) Temporal evolution of the short-run response of employment to labor costs variable ($-\delta^*$), variable in log. Model 2: Hours paid: *A*, *k* = 1; *B*, *k* = 10

Source: Based on the PIM.

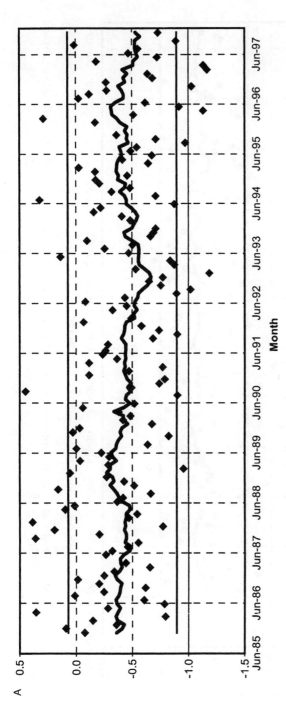

Fig. 5.14 Temporal evolution of the short-run response of employment to lagged employment variable (λ), variable in log. Model 1:
Employment level: *A*, $k = 1$; *B*, $k = 10$

Source: Based on the PIM.

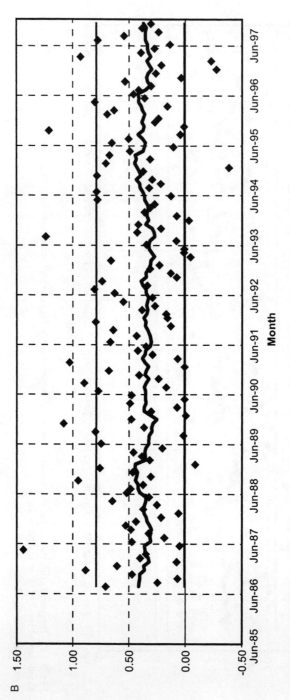

Fig. 5.14 **(cont.) Temporal evolution of the short-run response of employment to lagged employment variable (λ), variable in log. Model 1: Employment level:** *A*, *k* = 1; *B*, *k* = 10

Source: Based on the PIM.

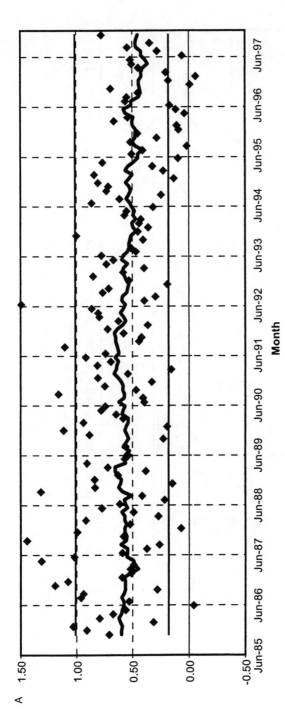

Fig. 5.15 Temporal evolution of the short-run response of employment to lagged employment variable (λ), variable in log. Model 2: **Hours paid:** $A, k = 1; B, k = 10$

Source: Based on the PIM.

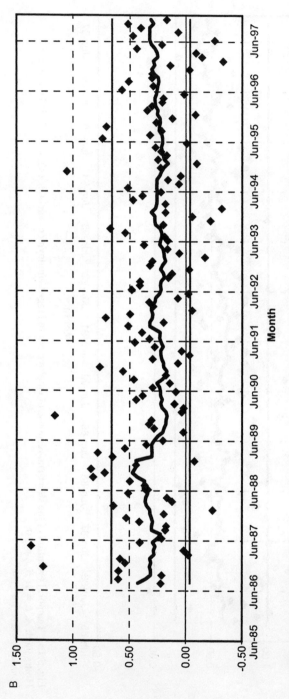

Fig. 5.15 (cont.) Temporal evolution of the short-run response of employment to lagged employment variable (λ), variable in log. Model 2: **Hours paid:** *A*, *k* = 1; *B*, *k* = 10

Source: Based on the PIM.

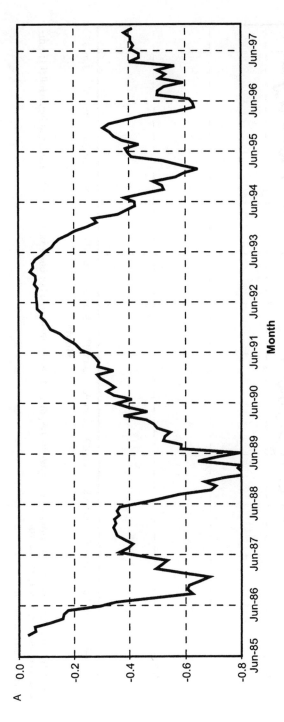

Fig. 5.16 Temporal evolution of the long-run response of employment to labor costs variable (–•), variable in log. Model 1: Employment level: A, $k = 1$; B, $k = 10$

Source: Based on the PIM.

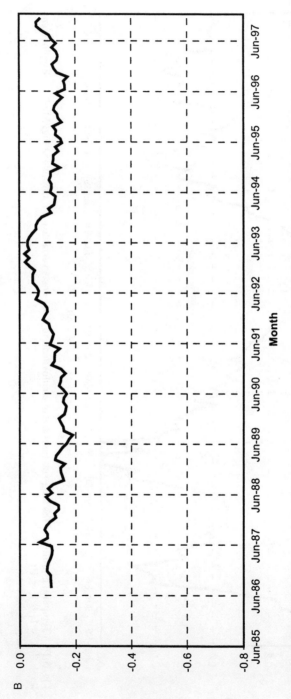

Fig. 5.16 (cont.) Temporal evolution of the long-run response of employment to labor costs variable (–◦), variable in log. Model 1: Employment level: *A*, *k* = 1; *B*, *k* = 10

Source: Based on the PIM.

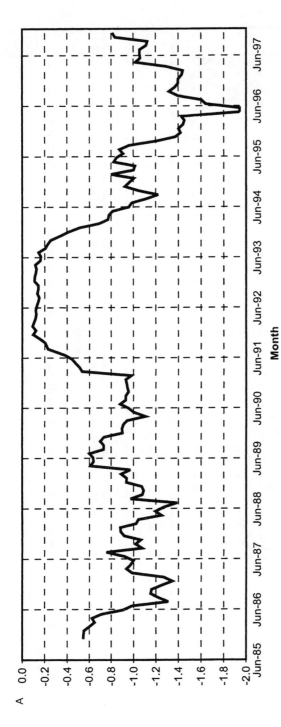

Fig. 5.17 Temporal evolution of the long-run response of employment to labor costs variable (−ω), variable in log. Model 2: Hours paid:
$A, k = 1; B, k = 10$

Source: Based on the PIM.

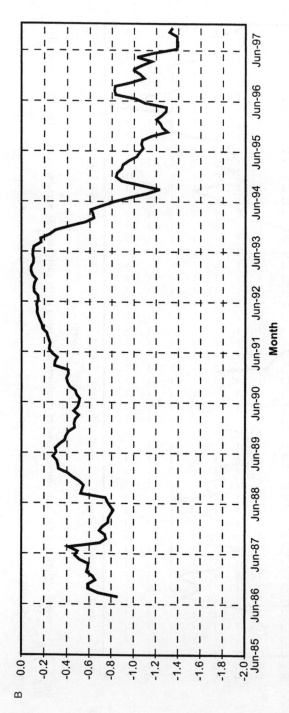

Fig. 5.17 (cont.) Temporal evolution of the long-run response of employment to labor costs variable (−*ø*), variable in log. Model 2: Hours paid: *A*, *k* = 1; *B*, *k* = 10

Source: Based on the PIM.

le 5.2   **Regression Results ($k = 1$)**

	Lagged Employment (λ)		Labor Cost (δ^*)	
	Coefficient	P-value (%)	Coefficient	P-value (%)
del 1				
icator for the constitutional change	−1.542	77.1	−1.861	58.3
)P growth rate	−0.081	84.0	−0.069	78.8
gree of openness	8.617	22.5	−3.998	37.9
ation rate	11.377	29.1	−8.461	22.1
ation volatility	2.491	15.6	1.460	19.4
justed R^2	0.358		0.026	
del 2				
icator for the constitutional change	−5.578	39.3	2.320	43.3
)P growth rate	0.743	13.6	−0.177	43.2
gree of openness	−1.499	86.4	−2.111	59.4
ation rate	20.985	11.5	9.474	11.7
ation volatility	−0.329	87.9	−0.807	41.0
justed R^2	0.135		0.065	

change on labor demand, we regress[18] monthly estimates of the parameters λ and δ^* on an indicator for the constitutional change and control for a set of basic macroeconomic variables. These regressions also include monthly dummies and a linear trend. The results are presented in tables 5.2 and 5.3.

If the constitutional change actually increases labor costs and, as a consequence, has an important effect on the demand for labor, then the estimated coefficients for the indicator of constitutional change would be positive and statistically significant in the regressions involving both parameters. This would be the case because an increase in variable labor costs would increase δ and hence δ^*, whereas an increase in firing costs would increase the cost of adjustment and reduce the speed of adjustment leading to an increase in λ.

Contrary to these expected results, in the regressions presented in tables 5.2 and 5.3 we found no evidence indicating that the 1988 constitution change had any significant effect on the labor demand function. All estimates of the constitution indicator coefficient are not statistically significant, despite the regression R^2 reach values close to 0.4.

18. As demonstrated in section 5.3.3, in these regressions we used as our dependent variable the parameter estimate divided by its corresponding standard error. Our purpose was to reduce the influence of outliers. If the standard error was influenced by the constitutional changes, this procedure would generate biased estimates. But, as this is not the case, estimates extracted from these same regressions, considering only the parameter as a dependent variable, leads us to the same conclusion about the lack of importance of constitutional changes for the level of the parameter.

Table 5.3   **Regression Results ($k = 10$)**

	Dependent Variable			
	Lagged Employment (λ)		Labor Cost (δ^*)	
	Coefficient	P-value (%)	Coefficient	P-value
Model 1				
Indicator for the constitutional change	10.597	77.1	–3.750	58.3
GDP growth rate	0.049	84.0	–0.248	78.8
Degree of openness	–5.272	22.5	1.961	37.9
Inflation rate	–8.950	29.1	–5.417	22.1
Inflation volatility	–2.192	15.6	0.849	19.4
Adjusted R^2	0.213		0.057	
Model 2				
Indicator for the constitutional change	–3.242	39.3	1.526	43.3
GDP growth rate	0.247	13.6	–0.030	43.2
Degree of openness	3.200	86.4	–7.195	59.4
Inflation rate	16.996	11.5	14.988	11.7
Inflation volatility	–0.701	87.9	1.363	41.0
Adjusted R^2	0.194		0.133	

5.4 The Turnover Analysis

This part of the chapter describes an attempt to estimate the impact of regulations on labor market performance based on turnover measures. We first investigate if these measures were affected by the constitution using a difference-in-differences methodology, described in section 5.4.1. The precise definition of the turnover measures that we make use of, as well as the description about how to implement these measures based on the available database, are presented in section 5.4.2. The results are commented on in section 5.4.3. Section 5.4.4 discusses some controversial issues in difference-in-differences methodology that motivates a regression analysis developed in section 5.4.5 with two objectives. These regressions test some hypotheses of the difference-in-differences methodology and access the robustness of the previous results.

5.4.1 The Difference-in-Differences Methodology

According to this methodology, we began by breaking down the overall population into two groups, the so-called treatment and control groups. If this partition attends some conditions, the evolution of the performance for the control group would indicate what would have happened to the treatment group if the 1988 constitutional change had not occurred. Hence, the contrast of the evolution of both performances (that is a difference of the previous differences) correspond to the estimation of the impact of the regulation on the performance of the treatment group.

Ideally, the treatment group would be the group most affected by the change in legislation. The control group, on the other hand, ideally must have two properties. First, contrary to the treatment group, it should not be affected at all by the change in legislation. Second, the impact of the underlying macroeconomic changes on the treatment and control groups must be very similar.

To implement this methodology, we use three alternative ways to break down the population in treatment and control groups.

Quits Versus Layoffs

Data regarding the informal sector is not always available. This is particularly the case when administrative files are used. Hence, it is important to identify other sources of cross-section variation in the legislation. The dichotomy between quits and layoffs is one possibility.

In general, regulations involving quits are totally different from those regulating dismissals. In Brazil, quits remain essentially unregulated, while a considerable amount of legislation was designed to restrict dismissals without just cause. Moreover, the changes brought by the new constitution are entirely related to dismissals. They are silent with respect to quits. Hence, quits and layoffs correspond to our second alternative for the partition between treatment and control groups.

Short Versus Long Employment Spells

According to the new and previous constitutions, the entire regulation on dismissals without just cause only applies to employment spells that have lasted at least three months. Dismissals of workers that have not yet completed three months on the job have been and still are completely unregulated. Hence, an alternative partition in treatment and control groups can be achieved through the contrast between very short spells (control) and other employment spells (treatment), where we consider as very short spells all those that last less than three months.

Formal-Informal Dichotomy

According to the Brazilian labor laws all workers must have a document named *carteira de trabalho*. This document, which resembles a little notebook or passport, acts as a complete record of the main parameters of the worker's current, and all previous, formal labor contracts. In principle, whenever a worker's labor contract is modified, either by moving to a new job or by renegotiating his contract with his current employer, the main parameters of the new contract must be immediately transcribed to the worker's *carteira de trabalho*.

The existence of this document permits an easy empirical separation of workers with formal labor contracts that must comply with the labor laws from workers with informal labor contracts that are not under this legislation. Workers with formal labor contracts are all employees who have the terms of their current labor contract transcribed to their *carteira de trabalho*. Those whose employers have not registered their labor contract in their *carteira de trabalho* should be considered informal.

This clear conceptual dichotomy would be of little practical relevance if the Brazilian employment surveys did not empirically investigate this question. Fortunately, however, essentially all household and employment surveys in Brazil do ask each employee in the sample whether their current labor contract is registered in their *carteira de trabalho*. As a result, it is possible and easy to separate empirically the pool of employees according to whether they have or do not have a formal (registered in their *carteira de trabalho*) labor contract. Moreover, this dichotomy is of the utmost importance, because around 25 percent of the urban occupied labor force is employed without a formal labor contract. So the formal and informal partition of the worker population corresponds to our first alternative of treatment (formal) and control (informal) groups.

5.4.2 Measuring Turnover Rates

Conceptual Preliminaries

As an indicator of turnover we use the probability that the employment spell will be terminated next month, conditional on its current duration. This probability as a function of the current duration of the spell is commonly referred as the *hazard function*. Evidently, in this case the indicator—the hazard function—is inversely related to the duration of employment.

The hazard function is usually preferred to its complement, the probability that it will not be terminated next month, conditional on its current duration. In part, this preference derives from the fact that it can be broken down according to the nature of the separation. In fact, if an employment spell can only be terminated by a quit or dismissal, then the hazard function is equal to the sum of the probability that the employment spell will be terminated by a quit and the corresponding probability that it will be terminated by a dismissal, where both probabilities are conditional on the current duration of the spell. The probability that an employment spell will be terminated by a quit (dismissal), conditional on its current duration, is commonly referred to as the *transition intensity function*. Hence, the property just stated can be summarized by saying that the hazard equals to the sum of the transition intensities.

To define these measures precisely, some symbols must be introduced first. Accordingly, let Ω_t be the universe of all active employment relationships at time t, and for each ω in Ω_t, let $D_t(\omega)$ denote the incomplete duration of the relationship ω up to time t. Moreover, let $S_t(\omega)$ denote an indicator of whether ($S = 1$) or not ($S = 0$) the relationship ω will be terminated in the month beginning at time t. The hazard rate, $h_t(d)$, is then defined as the probability that an active employment relationship, which up to time t has already lasted d months, will be terminated next month, that is,

$$h_t(d) = P(S_t = 1 \mid D_t = d).$$

Moreover, let $Q_t(\omega)$ and $L_t(\omega)$ be indicators of whether the relationship ω will be terminated next month by a quit or a dismissal, respectively. The quit and dismissal transition intensities can be expressed, respectively, by

$$h_t^q(d) = P(Q_t = 1 \mid D_t = d)$$

and

$$h_t^l(d) = P(L_t = 1 \mid D_t = d).$$

If a separation can only occur due to a quit or a dismissal, then

$$h_t(d) = h_t^q(d) + h_t^l(d).$$

These equations refer to the probability of separation for employment spells of a given duration in months. In practice, however, it is more convenient to use the probability of separation for all employment spells with the duration in any given interval.[19] For instance, it may be more convenient to analyze the probability of separations of employment spells that have already lasted six months but have not yet completed one year than the probability of separation of employment spells that have lasted up to now exactly seven months. Fortunately, the above equations can easily be adapted to define the probability of separations for all employment spells with the duration in any given interval. Resuming, we refer to these probabilities as the aggregated hazard and transition intensity rates.

To define them precisely, let $\{a_i : i = 1, \ldots, z\}$ be a partition of $N = \{0, 1, \ldots\}$, so that

$$a_i = \{d_i, \ldots, d_{i+1}\}$$

for all $i = 1, \ldots, z$, $0 = d_1 < d_2 < \ldots < d_z$, and $a_z = \{d_z, d_{z+1}, \ldots\}$. Moreover, let H_{ti} denote the probability that an active employment relationship that up to time t has already lasted between d_i and d_{i+1} months will be terminated next month. Then H_{ti} is given by

$$H_{ti} = P(S_t = 1 \mid d_i \leq D_t < d_{i+1}) = P(S_t = 1 \mid D_t \in a_i).$$

By analogy we can define the corresponding transition intensities, respectively, by

(7) $$H_{ti}^q = P(Q_t = 1 \mid d_i \leq D_t < d_{i+1}) = P(Q_t = 1 \mid D_t \in a_i)$$

---

19. Conceptually, d should refer to an instantaneous measure of time. In this sense the use of month is already a simplification for practical purposes.

and

$$H_{ti}^{l} = P(L_t = 1 \mid d_i \le D_t < d_{i+1}) = P(L_t = 1 \mid D_t \in a_i).$$

In this study we divide employment spells according to their duration in four intervals; that is, we consider the case $n = 5$. These five intervals are determined by choosing $d_1 = 0$, $d_2 = 3$, $d_3 = 6$, $d_4 = 12$, $d_5 = 24$. Hence, spells in the first interval are those that have not yet lasted three months. To simplify the exposition, we refer to them as the very-short spells. The second interval consists of all spells that have already lasted at least three months but have not yet reached six months. Spells in this interval are referred to as the short spells. The third interval is made of all spells that have already lasted at least six months but have not yet reached one year. Spells in this interval are referred to as the not-so-short spells. The fourth interval is made of all spells that have already lasted at least one year but have not yet reached two years. We are going to refer to them as the long spells. Finally, the fifth interval is made of all spells that have already lasted at least two years. We are going to refer to them as the very-long spells.

To obtain estimates for hazard and transition intensities we combine three distinct data sets: the *Relação Annual de Informações Sociais* (RAIS), the *Cadastro Geral de Empregados e Desempregados* (CAGED), and the *Pesquisa Mensal de Emprego* (PME). The PME is a monthly employment survey, while RAIS and CAGED are administrative files.[20] Three alternative empirical procedures are pursued to obtain consistent estimates of the temporal evolution of these probabilities from these data sets. First, two combine data from RAIS and CAGED, while the other relies exclusively on PME data. The data used as well as the nature of the hypothesis necessary to obtain consistent estimators vary considerably between these four procedures. We describe each one of the three empirical procedures in turn in the next subsection.

Measures for Hazard and Transition Intensities

Our first procedure to estimate the transition probabilities consists of using the information from RAIS on the stock of active employment relationships classified by their incomplete duration up to time t, December 31

20. The *Relação Annual de Informações Sociais* (RAIS) is an annual administrative file that provides, at December 31 every year, a complete list of all active employment relationships in the formal sector. The file also includes extensive characteristics of workers and firms. One of the characteristics available for every worker in the file is how long he has been in the current job, that is, the worker's tenure. Hence, based on this information, it is possible to estimate the distribution of active employment relationships according to their incomplete duration up to December 31 of each year. The RAIS is available for all years from 1985 to 1996. The *Cadastro Geral de Empregados e Desempregados* (CAGED) is a monthly administrative file that provides data on the formal sector of all separations that occurred in a given month. This file also includes information about the nature of the separation and basic information on workers and firms. In particular, it is possible to identify in each separation the reason for the separation (quits versus dismissals) and the complete duration of the employment spell.

of a given year, and from CAGED on (1) how many of these active employment relationships are terminated in January of the following year; (2) how many are terminated by quits; and (3) how many are terminated by dismissals. The number of active employment relationships that at time t has already lasted d months is represented by $N_t(d)$, while the number correspondent to those terminated in January by $M_t(d)$. Those terminated by quits are represented by $M_t^q(d)$, and, finally, those terminated by dismissals by $M_t^l(d)$. More specifically, we have

$$N_t(d) = \#(\omega \text{ in } \Omega_t \mid D(\omega) = d)$$

$$M_t(d) = \#(\omega \text{ in } \Omega_t \mid D(\omega) = d \text{ and } S(\omega) = 1)$$

$$M_t^q(d) = \#(\omega \text{ in } \Omega_t \mid D(\omega) = d \text{ and } Q(\omega) = 1)$$

and

$$M_t^l(d) = \#(\omega \text{ in } \Omega_t \mid D(\omega) = d \text{ and } L(\omega) = 1).$$

Basing our information on this, we obtain the hazard and the transition intensity functions for each year via

$$h_t(d) = \frac{M_t(d)}{N_t(d)},$$

$$h_t^q(d) = \frac{M_t^q(d)}{N_t(d)},$$

and

$$h_t^l(d) = \frac{M_t^l(d)}{N_t(d)}.$$

These expressions provide a useful method for estimating the probability of separations of employment spells during some months. Due to the nature of the available data, t is always December 31 for any given year. Consequently, the month beginning at t is always January of the following year. Hence, all estimates will refer to the probability that a separation will occur in January, conditional on the duration of employment spells up to December 31. Therefore, even though we label these estimates by the year associated with time t, they do not reflect the average for this year. Actually, the estimates refer to January of the following years. Estimates for the aggregated hazard and transition intensities can also be obtained by

$$H_{ti} = \frac{\sum_{s=d_i}^{d_{i+1}} M_t(s)}{\sum_{s=d_i}^{d_{i+1}} N_t(s)},$$

$$H_{ti}^q = \frac{\sum_{s=d_i}^{d_{i+1}} M_t^q(s)}{\sum_{s=d_i}^{d_{i+1}} N_t(s)},$$

and

$$(8) \qquad H_{ti}^l = \frac{\sum_{s=d_i}^{d_{i+1}} M_t^l(s)}{\sum_{s=d_i}^{d_{i+1}} N_t(s)}.$$

Combining data from CAGED and RAIS it is possible to estimate all these transition probabilities for each year between 1986 and 1995.

As already mentioned, these estimates described previously refer only to transitions taking place in January. Because these probabilities may follow a seasonal pattern during the year, it is important to verify to what extent our conclusions are sensitive to the choice of a reference month. Unfortunately, we cannot precisely compute these transition probabilities for each month because we only have data for the stock at December 31. Nevertheless, an approximation of the average over the year can be obtained. In fact, because flows are observed for all months, we can combine the average monthly flow for the year with the stock at December 31 in order to obtain an approximation for average monthly transition probabilities for the year. Estimates of the aggregated hazard rate can be obtained by

$$\overline{H}_{ti} = \frac{\frac{1}{12} \sum_{i=0}^{11} \sum_{s=d_i}^{d_{i+1}} M_{t+i}(s)}{\sum_{s=d_i}^{d_{i+1}} N_t(s)}.$$

Once more combining data from CAGED and RAIS, it is possible to estimate all these transition probabilities for each year between 1986 and 1995.

We can also use data from PME to estimate transition probabilities for the formal and informal sectors. PME is a typical employment survey covering the six major Brazilian metropolitan areas. For this study we use monthly data from this survey covering the period 1982–1997. The important feature of this survey is the fact that it has information on the *complete duration of previous employment spells for those currently unemployed.* The survey also has information on whether these employment spells ended as quits or layoffs.

To obtain estimates for the hazard and transition intensities out of employment from this data source, we have to assume, in addition to the steady state hypothesis, that the duration of employment and unemployment spells are stochastically independent. In this case, we can show (see appendix B) that the aggregated hazard rate can be approximated by the following equation:

$$H_{ti} \approx \frac{\frac{1}{(d_{i+1} - d_i)} \sum_{s=d_i}^{d_{i+1}} U_t^l(s)}{\sum_{s=d_i}^{\infty} U_t(s) + \frac{1}{2} \sum_{s=d_i}^{d_{i+1}} U_t(s)},$$

where $U_t(s)$ defines the number of unemployed workers at time t whose previous job lasted a period contained in the interval denoted by s. Similar equations help estimate the aggregated transition intensities.

5.4.3   Empirical Results

To implement the difference-in-differences methodology we must specify a period before and after 1988. For a pre-1988 period we use the years 1986–1987. The choice of a post-1988 period is more difficult. We would like to pick a period as close to 1988 as possible. On one hand, this choice would be useful to isolate the effect of the drastic change in the constitution from the impact of other concomitant macroeconomic changes that occurred spread out over time. In other words, the closer the pre- and post-1988 periods, the better for separating the impact of the constitutional change from the impact of changes in the macroeconomic environment. On the other hand, because the effects of the 1988 constitutional change may also be spread out over time, capturing a significant portion of them would be necessary to use them for a post-1988 period, a time not very close to 1988. In the latter case, however, there would be no guarantee that the effect of changes in the macroeconomic environment was properly separated. By virtue of this trade-off, we choose the years 1991–1992 to represent the post-1988 period.

Estimates of the contrast between the aggregate hazard rates related to these two periods are given in table 5.4. The estimates in this table indicate that the hazard rate, mainly for short spells, dropped considerably just after the constitutional change. The values stay around 2 percentage points for this group.

Because the underlying macroeconomic environment did not remain constant over this period, this finding should be taken with caution. In order to achieve a more precise result, we have to contrast the temporal difference of the hazard rates associated with the treatment and control groups.

To describe the methodology more explicitly, let Y_0^r and Y_1^r be an indicator of the duration of employment for the treatment group before and after the constitutional change, respectively. Moreover, let Y_0^c and Y_1^c be the

Table 5.4   First Differences of Hazard Rates: (1991/92)–(1986/87)

	1/4–1/2 year	1/2–1 year	1–2 years
Administrative files			
Rais and caged (January flows)	–2.7	–0.3	–0.3
Rais and caged (average flows)	–2.0	–0.5	–0.2
Employment survey			
Formal	–1.7	–0.7	–0.1
Informal	–0.8	–0.3	0.0

Sources: Based on the RAIS, CAGED, and PME.

corresponding indicator of the duration of employment for the control group before and after the constitutional change, respectively. In the latter case, the impact of the constitutional change on the treatment group will be estimated by the difference-in-differences estimator, Δ, given by

$$\Delta = (Y_1^r - Y_0^r) - (Y_1^c - Y_0^c).$$

To implement this methodology, we use three alternative ways to breakdown the population in treatment and control groups. First, we use informal workers as the control group and formal workers as the treatment group. Second, we divide job separations into quits and dismissals. In this case, quits form the control group and dismissals the treatment group. Finally, we use the very-short spells as a control group.

The decision about when to use each of these alternative control and treatment groups was finally totally guided by data availability. In fact, we use every alternative that the available data permitted us to use.

When quits are used as controls, the equation for this estimator is simpler. To arrive at this result, we should first notice that the response of quits to macroeconomic changes behaves contrary to dismissals. In fact, as the economy moves into a recession, layoffs will increase while quits fall. Hence, when taking difference-in-differences we should change the sign of the first difference in quits before taking the second difference. More specifically, in this case the difference-in-differences estimator, Δ, is given by

$$\Delta = (Y_1^l - Y_0^l) + (Y_1^q - Y_0^q)$$

or the equivalent

$$\Delta = (Y_1^l + Y_1^q) - (Y_0^l + Y_0^q)$$

because, in general, $Y_1^l + Y_1^q = Y_1$ and $Y_0^l + Y_0^q = Y_0$, where Y_0 and Y_1 are the corresponding indicator for all separations before and after the constitutional change, respectively. It follows that in this case $\Delta = Y_1 - Y_0$, which is the simple difference estimator investigated in the previous section. In other words, all results presented in table 5.4 could be interpreted as being obtained from the difference-in-differences estimator that use quits as a control group.

Table 5.5 presents difference-in-differences estimates for the impact of the constitutional change on employment duration, using the informal sector and very-short spells as control groups.

When the informal sector is used as a control, at least for short spells, the estimated impact of the constitutional change on the duration of employment is still negative and appreciable. The hazard rate for short spells declined in both the formal and informal sector from before to after the constitutional change, but the decline was 1 percentage point larger in the formal sector.

Table 5.5 also presents estimates using very-short spells as a control

ble 5.5   **Differences-in-Differences of Hazard Rates: Treatment–Control**

atabase	Dismissal–Quit	Other Spells–Very Short Spell	Formal–Informal
ais and caged (January flows)			
0–1/4 year	–1.8	—	—
1/4–1/2 year	–2.7	–0.9	—
1/2–1 year	–0.3	1.5	—
1–2 years	–0.3	1.5	—
ais and caged (average flows)			
0–1/4 year	–0.8	—	—
1/4–1/2 year	–2.0	–1.2	—
1/2–1 year	–0.5	0.3	—
1–2 years	–0.2	0.6	—
ME			
0–1/4 year	–1.3	—	0.2
1/4–1/2 year	–1.7	–0.5	–0.9
1/2–1 year	–0.7	0.6	–0.4
1–2 years	–0.1	1.2	0.0

urces: Based on the RAIS, CAGED, and PME.
te: Dashes indicate that no calculations were implemented.

group. The decline in the hazard rate for very-short spells was 0.5 to 1.5 percentage point smaller than for short spells. However, when we compare the evolution of the hazard rates for very-short spells with groups other than the short spells, we have opposite results with similar magnitude; that is, the hazard rates for other spells were .5 to 1.5 percentage point smaller than for very-short spells.

So the results seem to be easier to analyze by employment spell. We have evidence that the hazard rates declined for short spell according to any of the three definitions implemented for the control group. No other employment spells reported such a consistent pattern for hazard rates.

5.4.4   Some Limitations of the Methodology

Although changes in the legislation would not have a *direct* effect on these control groups (one of the necessary conditions that the partition between treatment and control has to attend), it is very likely that they would be indirectly affected by the constitutional change. In section 5.2.2 we mention two mechanisms through which the constitution may affect quitting behavior and the turnover among very-short duration spells. First, it is argued that increases in dismissal penalties are likely to reduce quits as some workers prefer to wait or even to force their dismissal in order to collect the compensation, whereas according to the second argument, firms may increase the dismissal of employees before they complete three months on the job in order to avoid the payment of dismissal penalties later.

In addition to those arguments, there are also arguments that suggest the informal sector may be indirectly affected by the constitution through at least two channels. First, changes in the formal sector tend to affect the informal sector through its effects on overall labor market conditions, for instance, as a result of its effect on the unemployment rate. Second, changes in the legislation may play a role in the bargaining process even in the informal sector through their effect on the notion of fair labor relation.

There also exists another reason why the informal sector quits, and very-short spells may not be an ideal control group. Ideally, it is also necessary that changes in the macroeconomic environment have identical impact on the control and treatment groups. However, there is no theoretical or empirical reason why the response of quits and layoffs, short and long spells, and the formal and informal sectors to macroeconomic shocks should be of the same magnitude. Due to these limitations we decided to analyze results from an alternative methodology.

5.4.5   Regression Analysis

The preceding empirical strategy requires data for only two periods in time: a pre- and a post-1988 period. However, if data is available for a large number of points in time and the macroeconomic changes can be characterized by measurable indicators, then it is possible to obtain estimates of the impact of the constitutional change and macroeconomic factors on hazard rates through a regression analysis.

The procedure would essentially consist of regressing monthly estimates (based on the PME) for the aggregated hazard rate on an indicator for the constitutional change (i.e., an indicator that will have 0 as the value before and 1 as the value after the constitutional change), on another indicator for the group (the treatment group is associated with the 0 value whether the control group is associated with 1), on a set of macroeconomic indicators and interactions between the group indicator and each of the macroeconomic indicators, and also on the constitution indicator.

$$(9) \qquad h_{t,i}(x_1, x_2, c, r) = \beta_0 + \mathbf{x'}_{1t} \cdot \boldsymbol{\beta}_1 + \mathbf{x'}_{2t} \cdot \boldsymbol{\beta}_2 + \beta_3 \cdot c_t + \beta_4 \cdot g_i$$
$$+ \mathbf{x'}_{1t} \cdot \boldsymbol{\beta}_5 \cdot g_i + \beta_6 \cdot g_i \cdot c_t + \mathbf{r'}_i \cdot \boldsymbol{\beta}_7 + \varepsilon_{ti}$$

$\mathbf{x'}_{1t}$ is the transpose vector of values obtained for the four macroeconomic indicators in period t: a) the GDP real growth rate; b) the degree of openness as measured by the ratio between total trade (import plus exports) and the GDP; c) the inflation rate; and d) the volatility of the inflation rate as measured by its temporal standard deviation. $\mathbf{x'}_{2t}$ is a transpose vector of time invariant explanatory variables other than the constitutional indicator (c_t). These variables are a linear time trend and monthly seasonal dummies. Regional indicator ($\mathbf{r'}_i$) and group indicator (g_i) complement our specification. Finally, bold characters represent vector notation.

According to this framework the effect of constitution on the treatment group can be written as β_3. The estimation of this effect through regression (b_3) will be a valid procedure even if the control group is affected by the constitution or there are unbalanced macroeffects. On the other hand, the procedure relies on the assumption that no other factor is related to hazard rates besides those considered in the regression framework.[21]

This procedure was done considering each one of the alternatives for the control group and for each interval in turn, except for the very-short spell (this interval is never supposed to be affected by the constitution, even when it is part of the treatment group). The estimated coefficients are reported on the upper part of tables 5.6, 5.7, and 5.8. The values associated with the constitutional indicator b_3 are an alternative estimation for the impact of the change in legislation on treatment groups' turnover rates. The regression, however, adds an important information namely the confidence of the estimates.

We can see that from the nine alternative estimates of b_3 (three employment spells multiplied by three controls), four are significantly different from zero. These significant coefficients are those associated with short and long employment spells when either very-short spell or quit are used as control. Among these four results we have two negative and two positive estimates. The positive results correspond to those estimated for workers whose employment spell is long, while negative results correspond to those estimated for workers whose employment spell is short. This last result is consistent with findings in the last section.

The next step is the analysis of which control satisfies the necessary conditions stipulated for difference-in-differences estimators. Despite the fact that the test is based on a regression framework, the conditions are not necessary for the regression estimators of the constitutional effects.

As already mentioned, for a control group to be considered valid, it must satisfy two properties. First, it must not be affected by the constitutional change. Second, macroeconomic changes must have the same impact on the treatment and the control groups. As we described in section 5.4.4, those properties may not be valid for the control groups considered in this study. However, both properties are testable under the assumption that we can have explicit control for macroeconomic changes.

If the first property is valid (i.e., the constitutional change had no effect on the control group), then the expected value for the hazard rates associated with the control group should be equal for periods before and after the constitutional change. It can be precisely written as

$$Z = E(h_{t,i} \backslash g_i = 1, c_t = 1) - E(h_{t,i} \backslash g_i = 1, c_t = 0),$$

21. In fact, the regression would still produce valid results if those omitted factors affect in the same way in both groups and the control is not affected by the constitution. In this case our estimator of the effect of the constitution on the treatment group would be $-\beta_6$.

Table 5.6   Pooling Hazard Rates for the Formal and Informal Sectors

	Short Spell		Not-So-Short Spell		Long Spell	
	Coefficient	P-value (%)	Coefficient	P-value (%)	Coefficient	P-value (%)
Variables						
Indicator for the constitutional change (b_3)	0.1	87.5	0.3	82.9	−1.1	48.6
Degree of openness	2.3	1.9	2.0	12.7	3.5	5.0
GDP growth rate	−12.0	0.9	−6.2	29.7	1.7	82.9
Inflation volatility	0.0	19.4	0.0	36.9	0.0	44.9
Inflation rate	1.0	50.9	−0.9	64.5	6.8	1.3
Indicator for informal sector (b_4)	−6.4	0.0	−4.3	1.8	−0.8	74.2
$b_4 \times$ Indicator for the constitutional change (b_6)	−1.3	30.3	0.0	98.5	4.3	5.5
$b_4 \times$ Degree of openness (b_51)	−1.2	36.2	0.8	63.0	−0.4	85.2
$b_4 \times$ GDP growth rate (b_52)	9.8	1.8	8.6	11.5	−0.7	92.9
$b_4 \times$ Inflation volatility (b_53)	0.1	14.1	0.1	13.9	0.0	95.7
$b_4 \times$ Inflation rate (b_54)	−0.3	89.2	3.7	18.6	−1.7	66.4
Tests for the validity of the informal sector as control group						
H1: Informal sector not affected by the constitution ($b_3 + b_6 = 0$)	19.7		80.9		4.6	
H2: Effects of macroeconomic indicators are identical in formal and informal sector ($b_51 = b_52 = b_53 = b_54 = 0$)	5.0		25.4		99.5	

Source: Based on the PME.

Table 5.7   Pooling Hazard Rates for the Very Short and Other Spells

Variables	Short Spell		Not-So-Short Spell		Long Spell	
	Coefficient	P-value (%)	Coefficient	P-value (%)	Coefficient	P-value (%)
Variables						
Indicator for the constitutional change (b_3)	−1.0	2.6	0.3	57.6	3.3	0.0
Degree of openness	2.4	0.0	3.5	0.0	3.3	0.0
GDP growth rate	−2.7	24.2	−1.3	67.1	1.1	78.6
Inflation volatility	0.0	15.9	0.0	4.8	0.0	12.2
Inflation rate	1.2	12.6	3.3	0.2	5.0	0.0
Indicator for very short spell (b_4)	−5.6	0.0	−12.1	0.0	−19.8	0.0
$b_4 \times$ Indicator for the constitutional change (b_6)	0.7	26.4	−0.7	44.6	−3.8	0.1
$b_4 \times$ Degree of openness (b_51)	−0.9	20.5	−1.9	4.1	−2.1	7.0
$b_4 \times$ GDP growth rate (b_52)	−4.3	4.2	−5.1	7.8	−6.8	6.2
$b_4 \times$ Inflation volatility (b_53)	0.0	86.5	0.0	63.9	0.1	5.2
$b_4 \times$ Inflation rate (b_54)	−1.1	31.0	−3.3	3.1	−4.8	1.1
Tests for the validity of the very short spell as control group						
H1: Very short spell not affected by the constitution ($b_3 + b_6 = 0$)	50.8		60.9		53.5	
H2: Effects of macroeconomic indicators are identical in short and very short spells ($b_51 = b_52 = b_53 = b_54 = 0$)	28.4		7.9		0.7	

Source: Based on the PME.

Note: Based on Formal sector.

Table 5.8   Pooling Hazard Rates for the Quit and Dismissals Separations

Variables	Short Spell		Not-So-Short Spell		Long Spell	
	Coefficient	P-value (%)	Coefficient	P-value (%)	Coefficient	P-value (%)
Variables						
Indicator for the constitutional change (b_3)	-1.3	4.5	-0.1	92.7	2.8	3.0
Degree of openness	1.8	1.5	2.8	1.2	2.6	7.2
GDP growth rate	-2.7	41.4	-1.0	83.4	4.2	52.4
Inflation volatility	0.0	27.4	0.0	15.5	0.0	38.0
Inflation rate	1.8	10.3	4.3	1.0	6.6	0.3
Indicator for quit separation (b_4)	-4.4	0.0	-6.2	0.0	-9.3	0.0
$b_4 \times$ Indicator for the constitutional change (b_6)	0.8	36.7	-1.8	18.3	-3.8	3.6
$b_4 \times$ Degree of openness ($b_5 1$)	-3.1	0.2	-6.5	0.0	-8.8	0.0
$b_4 \times$ GDP growth rate ($b_5 2$)	-5.1	9.1	-4.5	31.3	-10.5	8.0
$b_4 \times$ Inflation volatility ($b_5 3$)	-0.1	5.6	0.0	27.0	0.0	93.1
$b_4 \times$ Inflation rate ($b_5 4$)	0.9	55.7	-0.2	91.6	-2.0	51.8
Tests for the validity of the quit separations as control group						
H1: Quit not affected by the constitution ($b_3 + b_6 = 0$)	46.9		5.0		43.3	
H2: Effects of macroeconomic indicators are opposite in quit and dismissals ($-b_1 1 = 2b_5 1$; $-b_1 2 = 2b_5 2$; $-b_1 3 = 2b_5 3$; $-b_1 4 = 2b_5 4$)	0.4		0.2		0.0	

Source: Based on the PME.

where according to (9) we can see that[22]

$$Z = \beta_3 + \beta_6.$$

Our statistic test will be based on the analogous estimated coefficients,

$$b_3 + b_6,$$

where we denoted as b the estimations of the true β coefficients. So we have that if the constitutional change did not affect the control group, the sum of the coefficient on the indicator for the constitutional change and the coefficient on the interaction between the constitution and group indicators must be zero.

If the second property is valid (i.e., macroeconomic changes have the same effect on the control and treatment groups), then the expected value for the effect of the macroeconomic indicators on the hazard rates associated with the treatment and control groups must be equal. It can be precisely written as

$$E\left(\frac{\partial h_{t,i}}{\partial \mathbf{x}'_{1t}}\Big\backslash g_i = 1\right) = E\left(\frac{\partial h_{t,i}}{\partial \mathbf{x}'_{1t}}\Big\backslash g_i = 0\right),$$

which is equivalent to see if $\boldsymbol{\beta}_5 = 0$.[23]

Once more we will base our statistic tests on the analogous vector of estimated coefficients (b_5) to see if each of the elements of this vector is null $(b_5^1 = b_5^2 = b_5^3 = b_5^4 = 0)$. This test is different when we consider quit as the control. In this case we test if the effect of macroeconomic changes for both groups (quit and dismissals) had the same magnitude but opposite signs, that is,

$$E\left(\frac{\partial h_{t,i}}{\partial \mathbf{x}'_{1t}}\Big\backslash g_i = 1\right) = -E\left(\frac{\partial h_{t,i}}{\partial \mathbf{x}'_{1t}}\Big\backslash g_i = 0\right),$$

which is equivalent to see if $-\boldsymbol{\beta}_5 = 2\boldsymbol{\beta}_1$.

The p-value related to both statistics tests mentioned previously, for each of the nine regressions, is shown on the bottom part of tables 5.6, 5.7, and 5.8. The results related to whether the control was affected by the constitution are mostly in accordance with the null hypothesis of a null effect. Only one of the nine alternative combinations of control groups and employment spells considered presents any evidence that it was affected by the constitution—the informal workers whose duration spells are long. So

22. $E(h_{t,i}\backslash g_i = 1, c_t = 1) = \beta_0 + E(\mathbf{x}'_{1t} \cdot \boldsymbol{\beta}_1\backslash g_i = 1, c_t = 1) + E(\mathbf{x}'_{2t} \cdot \boldsymbol{\beta}_2\backslash g_i = 1, c_t = 1) + \beta_3 + \beta_4 + E(\mathbf{x}'_{1t} \cdot \boldsymbol{\beta}_5\backslash g_i = 1, c_t = 1) + \beta_6$ and $E(h_{t,i}\backslash g_i = 1, c_t = 0) = \beta_0 + E(\mathbf{x}'_{1t} \cdot \boldsymbol{\beta}_1\backslash g_i = 1, c_t = 1) + E(\mathbf{x}'_{2t} \cdot \boldsymbol{\beta}_2\backslash g_i = 1, c_t = 1) + \beta_4 + E(\mathbf{x}'_{1t} \cdot \boldsymbol{\beta}_5\backslash g_i = 1, c_t = 1)$.

23. According to equation (9) we have

$$E\left(\frac{\partial h_{t,i}}{x'_{1t}}\backslash g_i = 1\right) = \boldsymbol{\beta}_1 + \boldsymbol{\beta}_5 \text{ and } E\left(\frac{\partial h_{t,i}}{x'_{1t}}\backslash g_i = 0\right) = \boldsymbol{\beta}_1.$$

there is almost no evidence of any effect of the constitution change on the informal sector, the very-short employment spell, or quitting behavior.

However, when we consider whether the groups were equally affected by factors other than the constitution, the results are not so favorable. This hypothesis (considering the sign correction) was rejected among quit and dismissal separations. It was not rejected for the formal and informal partition, and for the very-short and other spells it was rejected only for those workers whose employment spell was long.

So the best alternative to implementing the difference-in-differences methodology requires the use of the very-short spell or the informal sector as control groups restricted to short and not-so-short employment spells.

5.5   Final Considerations

This study is an attempt to estimate the impact on the Brazilian labor market performance due to the 1988 constitutional change. As a result of this change, the compensation for dismissals without just cause increased fourfold. We investigate the impact of these changes on the parameters of the demand for labor and on hazard rates. If the constitutional change had a major impact, we should observe an important change in labor demand parameters and hazard rates around 1988.

Figures 5.2 and 5.3, however, provide no evidence at all that the constitutional change had any effect on labor demand parameters. Nevertheless, these figures reveal considerable temporal fluctuations in the coefficients that could be explained by macroeconomic events. To verify this possibility, we regress our monthly estimates for the parameters of the demand function on an indicator for the constitution change and a series of macroeconomic indicators. The results presented in tables 5.2 and 5.3 reveal that even when taking into account macroeconomic variables, we still found no evidence that the 1988 constitution had any effect on the demand for labor.

Naturally, the fact that we were unable to find significant effects does not necessarily imply that they do not exist. Our results are limited by the richness and quality of our data and economic models. Much further research is still necessary to reach a definite conclusion that labor demand dynamics were not very responsive to this constitutional change.

The estimations using hazard rates show ambiguous results. According to difference-in-differences methodology (applied to appropriated controls), this turnover measure has declined for short employment spells (three to six months) but seems to have increased for not-so-short employment spells (six to twelve months). Regression analysis also provides ambiguous results because it points to a decline for hazard rates associated with short spells and an increase for long spells (twelve to twenty-four months).

Resuming, separation rates have decreased after the constitutional changes for the short employment spell and increased for longer spells, while parameters related to speed of adjustment and wage elasticity of employment have not changed. These facts may be consistent if the movements registered to separations in opposite directions cancel each other, keeping aggregate turnover and, consequently, the parameter mentioned unchanged.

There is a possible explanation for the movements on separation driven by a combination of dismissals and quits movements. On one hand, firms might become more reluctant to fire a worker that did not fit the job offered. They may then give more chances to see the worker perform according to what is expected. On the other hand, the accumulated amount of money on FGTS became more attractive to workers, and this attractiveness increases with the employment spell. Hence, workers may have become more active in proposing a collusion with firms that he quits, pretending a firing and then having access to the fund. So if there is a correspondence between the three- to six-month employment spell and the time at which the firm became reluctant, and between longer employment spells and the time at which worker tries the collusion, the results should be those presented.

Appendix A

The Complete Derivation of the Structural Model for Labor Demand Shown in Section 5.2.1

In order to obtain an explicit solution to this problem of maximization, we mentioned the introduction of a series of simplifying assumptions. These assumptions are described below.

First, we assume that the revenue function is separable in the following sense:

$$R(n_i(t), \mathbf{p}_i(t), \boldsymbol{\theta}(t), \mu_i(t)) = F(n_i(t), \boldsymbol{\theta}^1(t)) + [G(\mathbf{p}_i(t), \boldsymbol{\theta}^2(t)) + \mu_i(t)]n_i(t)$$

Under this assumption, the Euler equation associated with maximizing equation (1) is given by[24]

$$F_n(n_i(t), \boldsymbol{\theta}^1(t)) + G(\mathbf{p}_i(t), \boldsymbol{\theta}^2(t)) + \mu_i(t) - \delta(t)w_i(t) - C_\Delta(\Delta n_i(t), \eta(t))$$
$$+ \rho E_t\{C_\Delta(\Delta n_i(t+1), \eta(t+1))\} = 0.$$

We further simplify this model by assuming that the revenue function is linear-quadratic and the adjustment cost is quadratic; that is, we assume that

$$F(n_i(t), \boldsymbol{\theta}^1(t)) = \boldsymbol{\theta}^{11}(t)n_i(t)\frac{\boldsymbol{\theta}^{12}(t)}{2}n_i(t)^2$$

24. We use F_n and C_Δ to denote the derivatives of the F and c_t functions in relation to their first arguments.

and

$$C(\Delta n_i(t), \eta(t)) = \frac{\eta(t)}{2}(\Delta n_i(t))^2,$$

where

$$\theta^1(t) = (\theta^{11}(t), \theta^{12}(t)).$$

Furthermore, we assume that all firms in the same sector undergo the same price of inputs. As a result,

$$G(\mathbf{p}_i(t), \theta^2(t)) = \sum_{s=1}^{m} \varphi_s(t) I_{is},$$

where I_{is} indicates whether firm i belongs to sector s, that is, $I_{is} = 1$ if firm i belongs to sector s and $I_{is} = 0$ otherwise. Under these additional assumptions the Euler equation becomes

$$\left[\theta^{11}(t) + \mu_i(t) + \sum_{s=1}^{m} \varphi_s(t) I_{is} - \delta(t) w_i(t)\right] - \theta^{12}(t) n_i(t) - \eta(t) \Delta n_i(t)$$

$$+ \rho\eta(t)\{E_t[n_i(t+1)] - n_i(t)\} = 0.$$

Under the assumption that parameters $\theta^{12}(t)$ and $\eta(t)$ are time invariant and that

$$E_t\left[\theta^{11}(t+1) + \mu_i(t+1) + \sum_{s=1}^{m} \varphi_s(t+1) I_{is} - \delta(t+1) w_i(t+1)\right]$$

$$= \left[\theta^{11}(t) + \mu_i(t) + \sum_{s=1}^{m} \varphi_s(t) I_{is} - \delta(t) w_i(t)\right],$$

the solution of this equation is given by

$$n_i(t) = \lambda n_i(t-1) + \frac{(1-\lambda)}{\theta^{12}}\left[\theta^{11}(t) + \mu_i(t) + \sum_{s=1}^{m} \varphi_s(t) I_{is} - \delta(t) w_i(t)\right]$$

as mentioned in section 5.2.1, where λ is implicitly defined by

$$\theta^{12}\lambda = (1-\lambda)(1-\rho\lambda)\eta.$$

Appendix B

Aggregate Hazard Rates and Transition Intensities Based on Employment Surveys, Steady-State Assumption, and Stochastic Independence of Employment and Unemployment Spells

Let $p_t(d, u)$ represent the probability that a worker, whose previous job lasted d months and who is unemployed at time t for u months, will not leave the unemployment pool next month. Then, at each moment in time t, the number of unemployed workers whose previous jobs last d months, $U_t(d)$, is given by

$$U_t(d) = \sum_{s=-\infty}^{t} \left\{ M_s(d) \left(\prod_{r=s}^{t-1} p_r(d, r - s) \right) \right\}.$$

The steady state assumption implies that the time subscripts are not relevant. Thus, in particular, this equation can be rewritten as

$$U(d) = M(d) \sum_{s=-\infty}^{\infty} \left\{ \left(\prod_{r=s}^{\infty} p(d, r - s) \right) \right\}.$$

Moreover, the stochastic independence of the duration of the employment and unemployment spells implies that

$$p(d, r - s) = \lambda(r - s).$$

Therefore,

$$U(d) = M(d) \sum_{s=-\infty}^{\infty} \left\{ \left(\prod_{r=s}^{\infty} \lambda(r - s) \right) \right\} = \Lambda M(d),$$

where

$$\Lambda = \sum_{s=-\infty}^{\infty} \left\{ \left(\prod_{r=s}^{\infty} \lambda(r - s) \right) \right\}.$$

Hence, we have established the useful result that at each moment in time the number of unemployed workers whose previous jobs lasted d months, $U_t(d)$, is proportional to the number of employment spells of duration d ending at time t, $M_t(d)$.

From steady-state assumption it is possible to write the hazard rate as a function of the separations as shown in the following expression:

$$h_t(d) = \frac{M_t(d)}{N_t(d)} = \frac{M_t(d)}{\left\{ N_t(0) - \sum_{s=0}^{d-1} M_t(s) \right\}} = \frac{M_t(d)}{\sum_{s=d}^{\infty} M_t(s)},$$

where we used the assumption that all employment spells have finite duration to obtain that $\lim_{d \to \infty} N_t(d) = 0$, which implies in

$$N_t(0) = \sum_{s=0}^{\infty} M_t(s).$$

Therefore, the hazard rate can be obtained from the data on unemployed workers by

$$h_t(d) = \frac{M_t(d)}{\sum_{s=d}^{\infty} M_t(s)} = \frac{U_t(d)}{\sum_{s=d}^{\infty} U_t(s)}.$$

If it is also assumed that the duration of the unemployment spell is independent of whether the previous employment spell ended by a quit or dismissal, then the transition intensities could also be obtained from data on unemployment workers by

$$q_t(d) = \frac{U_t^q(d)}{\sum_{s=d}^{\infty} U_t^q(s)}$$

and

$$l_t(d) = \frac{U_t^1(d)}{\sum_{s=d}^{\infty} U_t^1(s)},$$

where $U_t^q(d)$ is the number of unemployed workers at time t whose previous job lasted d months and ended in a quit, and $U_t^1(d)$ is the number of unemployed workers at time t whose previous jobs lasted d months and ended in a dismissal.

We take similar steps to write the aggregate hazard rates that can be written as

$$H_{ti} = \frac{\sum_{s=d_i}^{d_{i+1}} M_t(s)}{\sum_{s=d_i}^{d_{i+1}} \sum_{r=s}^{\infty} M_t(r)}$$

to the extent that

$$\frac{\sum_{s=d_i}^{d_{i+1}} M_t(s)}{\sum_{s=d_i}^{\infty} M_t(s)}$$

is very small.

$$\sum_{s=d_i}^{d_{i+1}} \sum_{r=1}^{\infty} M_t(r) \approx (d_{i+1} - d_i) \left[\sum_{s=d_{i+1}}^{\infty} M_t(s) + \frac{1}{2} \sum_{s=d_i}^{d_{i+1}} M_t(s) \right]$$

That allows us to simplify the expression for the aggregates hazard rate to

$$H_{ti} \approx \frac{\dfrac{1}{(d_{i+1} - d_i)} \sum_{s=d_i}^{d_i} M_t(s)}{\sum_{s=d_{i+1}}^{\infty} M_t(s) + \dfrac{1}{2} \sum_{s=d_i}^{d_{i+1}} M_t(s)}.$$

Considering that

$$U_t(d) = \Lambda M(d),$$

the aggregated hazard rate can be approximated by the following equation:

$$H_{ti} \approx \frac{\dfrac{1}{(d_{i+1} - d_i)} \sum_{s=d_i}^{d_{i+1}} U_t^l(s)}{\sum_{s=d_i}^{\infty} U_t(s) + \dfrac{1}{2} \sum_{s=d_i}^{d_{i+1}} U_t(s)}$$

References

Almeida, Sandra Cristina. 1992. As contribuições sociais de empregadores e trabalhadores: Repercussões sobre o mercado de trabalho e grau de evasão. IPEA Policy Document no. 8. Rio de Janeiro, Brazil: Institute for Applied Economic Research.

Almeida, Wanderly J. M. de, and José Luiz Chautard. 1976. FGTS: Uma política de bemestar social. IPEA/INPES Research Report no. 30. Rio de Janeiro, Brazil: Institute for Applied Economic Research.

Amadeo, Edward, Ricardo Paes de Barros, José Márcio Camargo, and Rosane Mendonça. 1995. Brazil. In *Reforming the labor market in a liberalized economy,* ed. Gustavo Márquez, 35–78. Washington, D.C.: Inter-American Development Bank.

Amadeo, Edward, and José Márcio Camargo. 1993. Labour legislation and institutional aspects of the Brazilian labour market. *Labour* 7 (1): 321–54.

———. 1996. Instituições e o mercado de trabalho brasileiro. In *Flexibilidade do mercado de trabalho no Brasil,* ed. José Márcio Camargo, 47–94. Rio de Janeiro, Brazil: FGV.

Bacha, Edmar Lisboa, Milton da Mata, and Ruy Lyrio Modenesi. 1972. Encargos trabalhistas e absorção de mão-de-obra: Uma interpretação do problema e seu debate. IPEA Research Report no. 12. Rio de Janeiro, Brazil: Institute for Applied Economic Research.

Barros, Ricardo Paes de, Carlos H. Corseuil, and Mônica Bahia. 1999. Labor market regulation and the duration of employment in Brazil. Rio de Janeiro, Brazil: IPEA Discussion Paper no. 676. Rio de Janeiro, Brazil: Institute for Applied Economic Research.

Barros, Ricardo Paes de, Carlos H. Corseuil, and Miguel Foguel. 2001. Os incentivos adversos e a focalização dos programas de proteção ao trabalhador no Brasil. IPEA Discussion Paper no. 784. Rio de Janeiro, Brazil: Institute for Applied Economic Research.

Barros, Ricardo Paes de, Carlos H. Corseuil, and Gustavo Gonzaga. 1999. Labor market regulation and the demand for labor in Brazil. Rio de Janeiro, Brazil: IPEA Discussion Paper no. 656. Rio de Janeiro, Brazil: Institute for Applied Economic Research.

Camargo, José Márcio, and Edward Amadeo. 1990. Labour legislation and institutional aspects of the Brazilian labour market. Discussion Paper no. 252. Rio de Janeiro, Brazil: Pontificia Universidade Catolica.

Carvalho, Carlos Eduardo, and Maurício Mota Saboya Pinheiro. 1999. FGTS: Avaliação das propostas de reforma e extinção. Rio de Janeiro: IPEA Discussion Paper no. 671. Rio de Janeiro, Brazil: Institute for Applied Economic Research.

Chadad, José Paulo Zeetano. 1993. Encargos sociais e emprego no Brasil. Discussion Paper. São Paulo, Brazil: FIPE, USP.

Hamermesh, Daniel. 1993. Labor demand. Princeton, N.J.: Princeton University Press.

Hamermesh, Daniel, and Gerard A. Pfann. 1996. Adjustment costs in factor demand. *Journal of Economic Literature* 34:1264–92.

Jatobá, Jorge. 1994. Encargos sociais, custos da mão de obra e flexibilidade do mercado de trabalho no Brasil. In *Conferência sobre regulamentação do mercado de trabalho no Brasil,* ed. IPEA, 1–36. Rio de Janeiro, Brazil: Institute for Applied Economic Research.

Macedo, Roberto Bras Matos. 1985. Diferenciais de salários entre empresas privadas e estatais no Brasil. *Revista Brasileira de Economia* 39 (4): 448–73.

———. 1993. Reforma da previdência social: Resenha e consolidação. In *A previdência social e a reforma constitucional,* ed. Brasil, Ministério da Previdência Social, 4–47. Brasília, Brazil: CEPAL.

Malaga, Guillermo Tomás. 1992. Dynamic labor demands: Cases of interest for Brazil. In Anais XV. Encontro Brasileiro de Econometria, 1992, Campos do Jordão (SP). São Paulo: SBE.

Nascimento, Amauri Mascaro. 1993. *Iniciação ao direito do trabalho,* ed. SBE, 409–30. São Paulo, Brazil: Sociedade Brasileira de Econometria.

Nickell, S. J. 1986. Dynamic models of labour demand. In *Handbook of labor economics,* vol. 1, ed. Orley Ashenfelter and Richard Layard, 437–522. Amsterdam: Elsevier.

Pastore, José. 1994. Encargos sociais no Brasil e no exterior: uma avaliacao critica. São Paulo, Brazil: SEBRAE.

World Bank. 1991. *Brazil: The Brazilian labor market in the 1980s.* World Bank Report no. 9693-BR. Washington, D.C.: World Bank.

6

The Effects of Labor Market Regulations on Employment Decisions by Firms
Empirical Evidence for Argentina

Guillermo Mondino and Silvia Montoya

6.1 Introduction

The 1990s saw vast structural transformations in Argentina. After half a century of low growth, high and volatile inflation, and stagnating living standards, Argentina introduced many reforms that yielded remarkably strong growth while inflation dwindled. The change of "economic paradigm" led to a number of behavioral changes that were reflected in other areas. But perhaps the most striking change took place in the labor market. There, where reforms were moderate, the most noticeable difference appeared. High open unemployment was the outcome. Could it be that the lack of ambitious reforms in labor market practices was behind this unfortunate outcome?

Historically, Argentina's labor market had been characterized by the relative scarcity of unskilled labor. This was reflected in moderate open urban unemployment and in the need to resort, periodically, to foreign labor to cover labor shortages. Wages and other hiring conditions were in keeping with the greater bargaining power that stemmed from excess labor demand. In particular, the dominant economic model limited the need for the economy to reallocate resources. The result was a depressed rate of job creation and, especially, destruction. This made a number of union- and government-sponsored demands compatible with the opportunities faced by firms. However, low growth and high and accelerating inflation ended up pushing the

Guillermo Mondino is an economist at IERAL de Fundación Mediterránea. Silvia Montoya is an economist at IERAL de Fundación Mediterránea.

We would like to acknowledge the tremendous effort put into this research project by Roger Aliaga. Manuel Willington and Marcos Delprato provided helpful research assistance at different stages of the project. Any remaining errors are our responsibility.

Table 6.1   Macroeconomics Indicators: 1974–1998

	GDP per Capita (1)	Jobs per Capita (2)	GDP/Jobs (3) = (1)/(2)	Unemployment[a] (4)	Inflation Rate[b] (5)	Lal Fo» (f
1974	91.9	100.9	91.1	3.3	24.2	10:
1980	100.0	100.0	100.0	2.6	100.8	10(
1985	83.9	95.6	87.8	6.1	672.2	9»
1988	86.7	98.2	88.3	6.3	343.0	10:
1989	79.4	97.2	81.7	7.6	3,079.5	10:
1990	77.0	96.3	80.0	7.5	2,314.0	10:
1991	84.1	98.4	85.5	6.5	171.7	10:
1992	90.9	99.2	91.6	7.0	24.9	10:
1993	95.0	98.5	96.5	9.6	10.6	10»
1994	101.3	96.3	105.2	11.5	4.2	10»
1995	96.1	91.9	104.6	17.5	3.4	11.
1997	106.6	95.1	112.1	14.9	0.5	11»
1998	109.8	97.6	112.5	12.8	0.9	11»

Source: IERAL database.
Note: Index 1980 = 100.
[a]Gran Buenos Aires (GBA).
[b]Annual rate.
[c]GBA. Index 1980 = 100.

economy into a deep crisis. The far-reaching reforms that followed in the 1990s took place mainly in monetary affairs and in goods and service market behavior, not labor markets. This asymmetry in changes has been cited by many as an underlying factor in the appearance of high unemployment.

Argentina evidenced remarkably stable growth in employment during the 1980s (at 1.1 percent annual rate, barely enough to accommodate population growth) while gross domestic product (GDP) was shrinking (–0.9 percent annually). Conversely, during much of the 1990s GDP growth was not only strong but also quite sustained (on average, 5.2 percent per year during 1990–1998). The behavior of employment, once again, did not match that of GDP (0.9 percent per year; see table 6.1).

Unemployment in the 1990s reached record levels (18.6 percent in 1995) and scored in the double digits after 1994. Movements in demand or supply could explain changes in the rate of unemployment. If labor market regulations were to seriously hinder job creation, they would have to operate on the demand side.

Labor demand dynamics could arise from a number of factors. In particular, given our interest in the potential effect of regulations, it appears crucial to evaluate how movements in labor costs could influence job creation dynamics. The question of whether labor market regulations reduce flexibility is a matter of substantial controversy. Critics claim that strong job rights prevent employers from adjusting to economic fluctuations (Lucas and Fallon 1991; Oi 1962). It is also alleged that, by inhibiting layoffs during downturns, strong job rights reduce the employer's willingness to hire people during recoveries, thus contributing to unemployment. Supporters of strong workers' rights argue that job security provisions have no observable effects.

In Argentina, workers have historically enjoyed strong job rights (including a right to advanced layoff notice and to severance payments). During the 1990s, and following the rapid growth in unemployment, these regulations came under attack. Many argued that the cost equivalent of these provisions had become an increasing nuisance. Figure 6.1 shows an approximation to the cost burden implied by job security provisions split into its three main components: (1) average tenure of formal sector employees; (2) layoffs over labor force; and (3) average wages in the formal sector.[1] The three panels suggest significant changes in all three components of firms' expected costs. As the economy went deeper into restructuring and reform (1991–1997), regulations became increasingly binding. As mean real wage earnings grew, the probability that a worker would be laid off (approximated by the fraction of layoffs) tripled, while average tenure was cut by 20 percent.[2]

It is possible that increases in regulatory costs had a substantive impact on labor demand. The puzzling increase in output per worker, presented in table 6.1, could be the result of optimizing behavior by firms that attempted to increase output without new hires and looked to save on the (anticipated) growing costs of severance. Output per worker may have grown in part from an increased use of overtime workers.

In this paper we provide some evidence on these issues. We exploit, for the first time, a panel data set that covers over 1,300 manufacturing firms for the period 1990–1996. The panel provides information on employment and hours worked, as well as overtime, wages, and physical production. The data, however, are constrained to a limited sector (manufacturing) and, most important, to a relatively short period of time. Unfortunately, most sizable changes in labor market regulations occurred by the end of 1995, only a year before the panel was discontinued, making it harder to identify the effects on labor demand. We nevertheless exploit the hours worked/jobs relation to shed some light on labor market dynamics.

We structure the rest of the paper by presenting, in section 6.2, some selected institutional features of Argentina's labor market that focus on job security regulations and payroll taxes. Section 6.3 considers two important descriptive issues: Who benefits from regulations, and how much do they

---

1. The fourth component is the legal provision that mandates the number of salaries per years of tenure. Over the two decades, legislative changes focused only on changing the maximum number of salaries that might be paid. Since these changes were minor and are hard to identify for the aggregate labor force, the pattern observed in figure 6.1 should appropriately proxy for severance payments cost.

2. It is very difficult to construct an aggregate proxy for the average severance costs because of the nonlinearity of the severance compensation scheme.

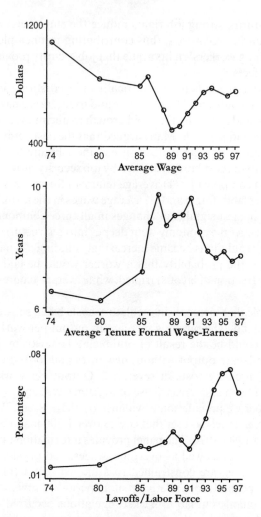

Fig. 6.1   Expected severance payment—Gran Buenos Aires, 1974–1997
Source: IERAL database.

cost? The evidence is based on Permanent Household Survey (PHS) microdata and identifies the effects on individuals' labor market outcomes stemming from varying regulations. We turn to firm-level dynamic labor demand estimation in section 6.4. We document the dynamic responsiveness of employment and hours to changes in output and labor costs at the firm level. Section 6.5 concludes.

6.2   Institutional Background

Argentina's labor market, like those of many developing nations, differs in important ways from those operating in industrial countries. Perhaps the most symptomatic differences are the relative importance of self-employment and informal work practices (defined as those not covered by regulations or contributing to social security). These observations have often been taken as evidence of asphyxiating regulations and steep taxation. Furthermore, and as a natural extension, it is argued that wage formation depends critically on labor market institutions and government regulations such as trade unions, minimum wage laws, job security provisions, and so forth.

There are three layers of binding legal regulations that govern worker-firm relations. They are, in terms of decreasing importance,[3] (1) the Workers' Statute (Ley de Contrato de Trabajo—20.744) and other general legislation such as superior rank laws, which establish many labor relations rules and the framework for collective bargaining; (2) centralized collective bargaining at the sector level, which operates as a second tier; and (3) firm-level contracts, which, if they exist, can only build upon the previous two.[4]

Labor regulations also introduce other distortions. Workers' statutes introduce specific job security provisions in the form of expensive firing costs. The statute also restricts hiring by limiting tryout periods. Sick leave, vacations, and pregnancy provisions are also quite generously provided at the most general level. A thirteenth wage is also mandatory and must be paid in halves at midyear and year-end. Similarly, contributions to union-sponsored health programs are required (regardless of whether the services are being used).[5]

6.2.1 Employment Legislation

Nonwage labor costs include a number of items other than the usual social security contributions. A number of these costs that arise from different regulations have been the subject of changes over the last few years. A basic characterization of labor regulations and taxes appears in the following sections.

Legal Framework for Individual Contracts

The most important provisions are types of contracts; job security provisions; and working hours, holidays, and sick leave.

Of the types of contracts, the most prevalent is the indeterminate duration type, or lifetime contract, which enjoys the highest degree of protection. Dismissal, if it occurs, is always presumed to be unfair. Some types of temporary contracts were allowed and used previous to 1995, but they were

---

3. That is, if contracts are signed taking into consideration agreements at level (3) they cannot be in disagreement with terms established at level (2), much less with those at level (1). In other words, level (1) sets a minimum standard.

4. Some areas are outside the scope of the general laws. In those cases the collective agreement is set up as a statute with rank of law. Examples are the rural sector worker statute, the journalist statute, and others.

5. An additional source of cost is the contribution of active workers to the pensioners' health program (PAMI).

considered exceptional, while permanent arrangements were the rule. In December 1995 some reforms were introduced that added new types of fixed-term contracts. Their main features were lower severance payments, an extended tryout period with reduced social security contributions, and other benefits to make them more attractive for employers. This regulatory change added a new dimension to an already complex labor market. Starting in 1999 those contracts were made illegal.[6]

Job security provisions include mandatory written advance notice before a firing and severance payments. Costs increase with tenure (see figure 6A.1).

There are limited opportunities for micro-level decisions concerning the distribution of hours worked, overtime, night work, and vacation periods. There is generous maternity and sick leave.[7]

Collective Labor Laws

The basic laws are union (called professional associations) laws; sector wage bargaining has been the predominant mode of bargaining in Argentina, framed as collective agreements. As previously mentioned, collective agreements often set floors, which can only be built upon, at lower levels of negotiations.

The interaction of the two laws defines a sticky situation (see figure 6.2). On the one hand, collective agreements delimit the basic features of contracts. On the other hand, union law identifies those participants in any collective bargain and defines conditions under which anyone else other than the sectoral/regional level (third grade) association could sign a collective agreement.[8] Together they have important implications for the functioning of markets and industrial relations. For instance, regional shocks cannot be easily accommodated since they cut across many sectors but, not being widespread enough, will not trigger renegotiations at sector-specific levels.

6. The changes introduced in 1995 were introduced "at the margin" and were aimed at solving the increasingly complicated employment outlook as well as adding some flexibility to a very sclerotic market. In particular, the choice was to enhance the flexibility of hirings for new cohorts of workers that entered the market from 1995 onward. The number of fixed-term contracts rose from less than 1 percent of formal wage earners in 1995 to almost 5 percent by the end of 1998. The steep increase in short-term employment contrasted with moderate growth in total dependent employment. The share of short-run employment (fixed-term plus trial period contracts) reached about 10 percent of total formal employment.

7. Sometimes the restrictions arise from the law; others arise from the collective agreements. The problem is that many of these agreements date from a period of extensive government presence in the economy. It is one thing for sectorial-level unions to negotiate with private firms subject to strict budget constraints and quite another to do it with a government-owned corporation with soft budget constraints. The banking-sector contract is an example of this problem, among many others.

8. The *Ley de Asociaciones Profesionales* defines the structure of the union sector. The third grade association of national range, the most forceful ones, are the only ones who can sign a collective agreement and who, eventually, can give authorization for decentralized negotiations.

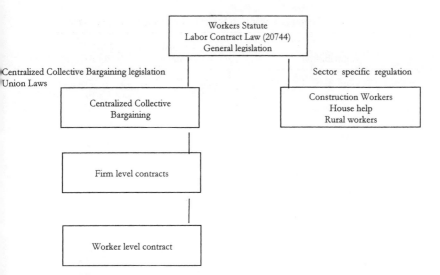

Fig. 6.2   Labor law mechanism
Source: IERAL database.

That is, in spite of individual firms' and workers' having strong incentives to revise their contracts, regulations make such revisions illegal. Business participants report that this has, effectively, been one of the greatest restrictions to renegotiations of contracts, affecting mostly smaller and remote firms and workers with the least say in centralized negotiations.

The problem is compounded because of the automatic renewal clause, called *ultractividad.* This clause automatically extends the terms of an earlier collective agreement if the parties do not reach a new one, which occurs if any one party is in disagreement.

Social Security

Social security consists of pension law, family allowances, workers' compensation laws, health care funds ("obras sociales"), unemployment insurance, and the pensioners' health care scheme (PAMI).[9]

Table 6.2 shows the current picture of labor costs in Argentina for a lifetime contract.[10]

In the 1990s reforms concentrated on two basic aspects: social security

9. Workers' compensation was reformed in July 1996, when a new system was introduced with costs that averaged 2.5 percent of gross wages. The previous scheme was highly unfair and arbitrarily opened up opportunities for expensive litigation and corruption. The reformed system introduced mandatory insurance, the organization of a market, and specific limits on the magnitude of compensations. It is widely regarded as a massive improvement over the previous legislation.

10. Since 1995 employers' contributions have been subject to deductions according to region and branch of activity of the firm.

Table 6.2   Nonwage Labor Cost Structure (percentage over gross wage)

Contributions	Normal Contract	Share Over Total Cost
Pension fund	27	47.4
Employee	11	19.3
Employer	16	28.1
PAMI	5	8.8
Employee	3	5.3
Employer	2	3.5
Family allowances[b]	7.5	13.2
Unemployment fund[b]	1.5	2.6
Health care scheme	9	15.8
Employee	3	5.3
Employer	5	8.8
Workers' comp[b]	2.5	4.4
Social security overall cost	52.5	92.0
Severance payment[a]	5	8.8
Advance notice[a]	0.5	0.9
Employee's cost	17	29.8
Employer's cost	40	70.2
Nonwage labor cost	57	100

Source: IERAL database.
[a]Estimates: employer's cost.
[b]Employer's cost.

and its financing, and the introduction of fixed-term contracts. General dissatisfaction with the costs of the social security scheme triggered a significant reform that became operational in 1994. Workers and firms regard social security contributions as a tax, not deferred compensation. As such, many undertake elusive actions that end up generating inequalities and inefficiencies, favoring a precarious system of labor relationships.[11]

The pension reform was aimed at all workers in the market place. It spurred a transfer of individuals from the pay-as-you-go system onto a newly created fully funded one. The two systems would coexist. Most workers adopted the new system.[12]

11. Figure 6A.2 shows the evolution of social security financing from 1960, the starting period of a more structural social security system. Until 1990 the different programs functioned with great difficulty because of the existence of different institutions performing the same role.

12. Over 60 percent of all covered workers and over 90 percent of new hires belong to the fully funded scheme. A significant difficulty with the original design was finding financing for the transitional phase. Current retirees must be supported via contributions from those who remain in the pay-as-you-go system and through taxes on those in the fully funded one. The high rate of taxation necessary to balance the system became a serious policy issue as it clashed with employment needs. For this reason, in 1994 a system of graduated labor tax reductions was put into place. The reductions were moderated in 1995, because of high fiscal needs, and brought back more aggressively in 1996.

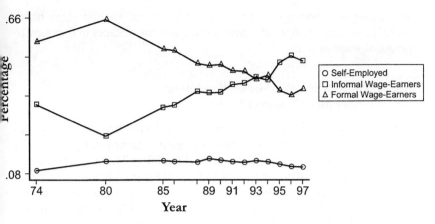

Fig. 6.3   Labor force composition—Gran Buenos Aires, 1974–1997
Source: IERAL database.

6.2.2   Informality

A traditional view regards informality as the disadvantaged workers in a dual labor market who are segmented by rules or legal rigidities that introduce high costs in the formal sector.[13] Only wage earners declare their social security standing and whether they are protected by labor legislation. As it turns out, the correlation between regulatory coverage and social security is close to one. All wage earners registered in the social security system enjoy that protection. The converse is not necessarily true. We define as informal a wage earner who declares himself or herself as not registered in the social security system.

Figure 6.3 shows the breakdown of employment and its evolution for the largest urban center in Argentina: the Greater Buenos Aires area. The graph illustrates a segmentation of the labor market in three basic components:[14] self-employment, formal wage earners, and informal wage earners. Previous work shows that self-employment constitutes a desirable alternative in itself to formal employment.[15] PHS data illustrate that the share of

13. An interesting feature of this segment is that it is hard to establish the most important reason why firms opt to operate there. While regulations may be suffocating, the opportunities for tax evasion are also important. Indeed, if the firm holds informal labor contracts, it cannot contribute to social security, but then it must have a source of unreported revenue to pay those wages. This revenue could stem from tax evasion in the goods market. The decision to operate informally may be associated with a complex set of opportunities.

14. The idea of segmentation is used loosely here. We do not mean two completely separate markets but rather two segments of a market that present different prices and somewhat different properties. Because of the nature of many choices in the labor markets (i.e., large fixed costs and/or irreversibility of some decisions), often the pattern of response is different according to whether we are considering wage earners or self-employed people. What we imply by segmentation in such a case is that the rate of transformation between them is limited.

15. The same evidence is available for Mexico. See Maloney (1997, 1998) for details.

self-employed workers remains relatively constant. On the other hand, there is a significant upward trend over the last two decades in the share of informal wage earners.

6.3 The Effects of Labor Market Regulations: Evidence from Household Microdata

Job security provisions are, in general, regulatory measures enacted as social protection to mitigate the risk of unemployment among workers by forcing firms to provide subsidies during downturns. The main mechanism is large severance payments that prevent workers from being laid off during downturns. In Argentina it also implies lengthy and expensive procedures that inhibit layoffs by driving up firing costs. It is sometimes argued that the macroeconomic adjustment is further shifted toward the informal sector. Hence, many perceive job security provisions as inequitable for unprotected workers (Riveros and Paredes 1990; Rosenweig 1988).[16]

Those who support regulations in the job market claim that they are commendable to the extent that their objective is the protection of workers against unsafe work practices and unjustified dismissals. They also state that regulations protect the weakest members of society, that they help to redistribute income, and that they stabilize earnings for those people subject to greater risks.

Job security is one form of nonwage compensation. Besides inducing greater immobility, job security increases labor costs to the firm. The increase in labor costs depends on how workers value job security and, specifically, whether it is a substitute for or a complement to wage compensation.

Who benefits from these types of regulations? Do they cost something, at least in terms of forgone earnings? Could we predict which individuals are the most likely to profit from deregulation? These questions have no simple answer but deserve serious consideration before any action is taken to alter the current regulatory standing.

6.3.1 Who "Benefits" from Regulations?

The probability of holding a job that is covered by regulations varies across individuals. We analyze a pooled sample of wage earners from the Buenos Aires metropolitan area for the 1975–1997 period. We divide the sample between males and females. The model we estimate is a simple probit equation in which the dependent variable is a dummy distinguishing workers that can claim severance payments in case of dismissal (see table 6A.1 for description of the variables). The correlates included follow.

---

16. In studies that deal with segmented labor markets, an increase in job security leads to greater labor spillover to informal activities, causing a decline in labor earnings and a higher rate of quasi-voluntary unemployment.

Educational level: Higher educational level implies higher productivity and should increase the probability of being in the formal sector. Lower-educational-level workers could be pushed to the informal sector because their low productivity may not be enough to counter the added costs of minimum wage laws and other mandatory costs.

Experience: As with any Mincer equation, experience increases general human capital and, hence, productivity.

Tenure on the job: Longer tenure must reflect a better match and greater job-specific human capital. If a firm could choose the type of jobs for which it offered job security, it would provide it to workers that have accumulated a high level of firm-specific human capital. Workers would in turn pay back in the form of higher productivity.

Branch of activity: This consists of a purely empirical set of correlates to account for sector-specific differences in the enforcement capabilities of control agencies, the degree of monopsony power, unionization, and instability of activities.

The size of the company: These characteristics are similar to those of the previous correlate.

Regulatory status of another family member: It is quite possible that workers become increasingly prone to accept job offers without regulatory coverage when a household has diversified risks—in particular, when the spouse or another family member enjoys regulatory coverage. Moreover, the regulatory framework favors precarious insertion for the so-called secondary workers. There is no incentive to register since health and other benefits will not recognize more than one contribution per household.

Marital status: This variable is introduced in the female regression, bearing in mind the gender-biased features of the legislation. We should anticipate a negative sign.

Children under 6: These characteristics are similar to those of the previous correlate.

Table 6.3 reports the results for females and males of the derivatives of a probit model where the dependent variable is the possibility of claiming severance payment compensation if the worker is laid off.[17]

The results indicate that regulations are increasingly prevalent the higher the human capital of the individual. The chances that regulations are present grow with the educational level. Males show, however, that for those with a college education the probability decreases a bit. Those with a university-level education select themselves out of wage-earning jobs and into self-employment to avoid the impact of high taxation.[18]

---

17. Raw results of probit regressions are reported in table 6A.2.
18. Women, because of their specialization (teaching, nursing, medicine), have a higher probability of being covered than their male counterparts. The reason is that their employer is the government.

Table 6.3   Probit Estimation: Jobs with Severance Payment Rights (Gran Buenos Aires 1975–1997, wage earners subsample)

Variable	Women			Men		
	dF/dx	Z	X-bar	dF/dx	Z	X-ba
Primary	0.0466	2.14	0.3911	−0.008	−0.07	0.55
High school	0.2134	9.24	0.3572	0.0979	7.73	0.25
College	0.2565	10.59	0.1720	0.0773	4.43	0.08
Experience	0.0207	11.82	20.1224	0.0164	13.48	22.31
Experience**2	−0.0003	−8.75	577.0800	−0.003	−11.85	670.01
Tenure	0.0016	3.58	6.8277	0.0025	7.07	7.91
Construction/House help	−0.4622	−20.98	0.1645	−0.2952	−18.93	0.06
Manufacturing	0.2169	2.15	0.0035	0.1213	3.44	0.01
Retail	0.0679	4.16	0.1399	−0.0436	−4.32	0.16
Transport	0.1367	4.28	0.0277	−0.0680	−5.89	0.12
Finance	0.1299	6.86	0.1017	0.0156	1.12	0.08
Private and Social Services	0.1732	11.25	0.5452	−0.0057	−0.58	0.21
Size <25	0.1755	13.54	0.2025	0.1251	16.59	0.23
Size <100	0.3035	21.91	0.1781	0.2284	28.37	0.17
Largest	0.3052	21.26	0.1827	0.2730	33.9	0.23
Family_reg	0.4455	39.67	0.3276	0.3280	41.86	0.26
Ptime	−0.2022	−16.55	0.3532	−0.1992	−17.31	0.11
Household Head	0.0082	0.49	0.1787	0.1422	14.8	0.67
Child <6	−0.0054	−0.5	0.1948			
Married	−0.0504	−3.58	0.4727			
No. of observations		13,202			21,618	

Source: IERAL database.

Notes: dF/dx is for discrete change of dummy variable from 0 to 1. z is the test of the underlying coef ficient being 0. See table 6A.1 for description of the variables.

As with most Mincer equations, experience shows the normal concavity. Here it increases the probability of having regulatory coverage. Tenure also shows a positive coefficient that is significantly different from zero.

Family status is also important. Mothers with young children tend to be less protected. Legislation intends to provide coverage for women (maternity leave, special leaves), yet it ends up with a strong market outcome biased against them.

We also find that if another family member happens to enjoy the coverage of regulations, it is more likely that the worker in question has a regulated match. A plausible explanation is that couples are formed with individuals of equivalent condition.

Part-time activities are less protected. The regulatory framework does not favor registration for part-time contracts. Moreover, there are no incentives for it to do so. Contributions to social security (the biggest component of nonwage labor cost) were calculated, up until late 1996, as if the worker was employed on a full-time basis. Growth in part-time employment plays an important role in the expansion of nonregistered employment.

Finally, we find that larger firms are more likely to offer regulated jobs.

To summarize, the probit analysis confirms that the regulations tend to segment the market and provide protection to those workers with greater human capital. In other words, the regulatory structure is regressive, and whatever protection it might provide does not appear to benefit those people who are objectively worse off. At the same time, the results show the natural response one would anticipate from rational private decision making. Sectors more exposed to supervision and control (namely, larger firms) are more compliant with regulations.

6.3.2   Effects on Earnings

The previous section established that labor market regulations unequivocally affect labor market outcomes in nonrandom ways. It is clear that some groups of workers have a greater chance of having jobs that are under legally enforced regulations. What we have not established, though, is whether workers and firms with those jobs sacrifice something. That is, could it be that a regulated job pays less than a nonregulated one?

One should expect employment protection practices to affect both sides of the labor market: workers and employers. Costs to employers depend not only on the wages paid and the benefit package included but also on labor productivity. Employers should be indifferent to the composition of the total compensation between money wages and benefits.

Employees have preferences between wages and benefits. A crucial parameter when analyzing the size and composition of employer-provided benefits is the wage workers are willing to forgo to obtain benefits. The market value of these trade-offs between wages and fringe benefits is an old research question. This is a difficult empirical issue that, in the literature, does not appear to be resolved. The theoretically predicted negative trade-off has been difficult to uncover.[19]

In this section we present some estimates of a hedonic wage function. We expect a negative relationship between wages and benefits if productivity is effectively held constant. The problem, of course, is to hold productivity constant in practice. If there are unobserved factors affecting productivity, the negative trade-off is no longer true, since benefits may be related to the unobserved productivity factors.

Econometric Problems

The worker's decision to accept a job depends on his or her subjective evaluation of the characteristics of the package. In equilibrium, this inter-

---

19. For a discussion see Smith and Ehrenberg (1983), Leibowitz (1983), and Oi (1983).

action of workers and employers should yield a locus of job matches that trace out the rate at which the market trades off wages and benefits. In our empirical formulation, we use an extended Mincerian framework.

The regression model we estimate is

(1) $$\mathrm{Ln}\ Y_{i,t} = \alpha_t + \beta_t X_{i,t} + \theta \mathrm{Regs} + \mu_{i,t},$$

where Ln $Y_{i,t}$ is the natural log of monthly individual (i) earnings at time t. $X_{i,t}$ is a vector of individual and firm characteristics that encompasses variables such as education, experience, firm size, sector of employment, and so on. Regulations (Regs) reports the legally enforced fringe benefits that characterize the match. The theoretical arguments suggested θ should be negative.[20]

There are several econometric problems that must be handled. The first one is the typical Heckman sample selection bias: We observe wages only for those employed, not for those that decided not to join the labor force. The result is that the conditional mean for the subsample exceeds the mean for the whole distribution. In this situation a straightforward ordinary least squares (OLS) estimate, not corrected for selectivity bias, would be inconsistent. Our estimation strategy takes this problem into consideration and implements a multilayered decision process.

An important issue in Mincer-type equations is that of unobserved heterogeneity. This comes from the fact that people differ in their ability and capacity to acquire human capital. This misspecification error typically results in inconsistent estimates of parameters. To somewhat mitigate this problem we will condition on tenure on the job. Hopefully, an individual with longer tenure is one who evidences greater abilities, at least in regard to his current position.[21]

---

20. To empirically prove the rather simple theory, we need data that do not normally exist in standard household surveys. In the case of Argentina the PHS is the only source. Workers report whether they get regulatory coverage. Unfortunately some fringe benefits can only be found in firm-level data sets. High-ability workers (highly motivated, dependable, aggressive) oftentimes receive higher wages and higher fringe benefits. These benefits, which are not proportional to wages, are very difficult to measure.

21. An additional problem springs out of measurement error. It is very likely that those workers that are not covered by regulations underreport their true earnings. If this source of measurement error was present we could get reverse signs in our estimated coefficients on regulations. Now, regulatory benefits could misleadingly turn out greater reported earnings, even though true returns are lower. One could interpret the coefficient on pensions as controlling for this bias and focus the analysis on the coefficients for the other variables. The problem, however, remains in that pensions and the other regulations are highly correlated. Furthermore, regulations could be a last recourse to remain competitive. The wages inefficient firms pay are lower than those of the high-productivity, law-abiding firms. The observed "black" matches could then report lower wages. To introduce some controls for firm efficiency we use the only two pieces of information in the household survey relating to firms: firm size and sector. Of course, many other sources of unobserved productivity differences remain.

Since our estimates are conducted on an artificial panel (stacked cross sections), another serious problem threatens the reliability of the estimates. If the economy has been subject to large structural shocks, as indeed it has, then the returns to human capital or the wage bar-

Econometric Specification

The regression model we estimate follows, to a great extent, Heckman's (1979) suggestions. We further take into account the difference between the decision to participate in a job search and that of accepting a job offer. This difference takes particular importance in an environment with high unemployment, such as that observed in the 1990s. Formally, we estimate the likelihood of the individual's reporting income as arising from a bivariate probit considering the individual's decision to join the labor force as well as his or her probability of finding a job.

The Model

To estimate the rates of return of the different educational levels, a linear version of equation (1) is estimated:

$$(2) \qquad \text{Ln } Y^* = \alpha + \beta'\mathbf{X} + \theta\text{Regs} + \mu,$$

where $\mathbf{X}$ is the matrix of independent variables affecting the individual's income level and μ is the vector of disturbances. The coefficients of education in equation (2) are the average returns to education.

This equation, if estimated by OLS—ignoring the two sources of selectivity bias—can lead to biased parameters. To deal with that problem Heckman (1979) proposed estimating a model of two simultaneous equations, with the endogenous variables being the income and the unobservable reservation wage. In a context of high unemployment, the probability of finding a job and reporting income need not be random or identical to the decision to participate. For this reason, a second-stage Heckman correction was introduced. Details of the model can be found in Tunalli (1982).

The likelihood of the individual's reporting income is estimated from a bivariate probit considering both the individual's decision to join the labor force and his likelihood of getting a job.

Thus, it is assumed that

$$(3) \qquad I^*_{1i} = \delta'Z_i + \mu_{1i}$$

and

$$(4) \qquad I^*_{2i} = \eta'W_i + \mu_{2i},$$

where Z_i and W_i are independent variables and I^*_{1i} and I^*_{2i} are nonobservable variables associated with an individual's decision to participate and

gaining conditions are likely to have changed drastically over time. We introduced a year fixed effect to absorb some of those changes. Pessino (1995) argues that these changes have considerably affected outcomes in the labor market. Garcia (1996) has shown that the Argentine skill premium has moved remarkably over the last few years. He finds that large changes in relative prices (associated to trade reform and deregulation) and technological change explain the large demand shifts necessary to explain the skill premium movements.

Table 6.4   **Two-Step Selectivity Bias Process: Individual**

Decision Process	Labor Force Status	Decision Process	Job Status	Income
I_1	0 Nonparticipant			Unobserv
	1 Participant	I_2	0 Unemployed	Unobserv
			1 Employed	Observed

Source: IREAL database.

his success in obtaining employment, respectively. What we observe are those individuals that participate and those that obtained employment.

To summarize, the two-step decision process appears in table 6.4. The equations to be estimated are

$$(5) \qquad\qquad I^*_{1i,t} = \delta' Z_{it} + \mu_{1i}$$

$$(6) \qquad\qquad I^*_{2i,t} = \eta' W_{it} + \mu_{2i}$$

$$(7) \qquad\qquad \text{Ln } Y_{it^*} = \beta_{it'} X_{it} + \theta \text{Regs} + \mu_{3i}$$

$$\text{Corr}(\mu_{1i}, \mu_{3i}) = \rho_{13}$$

$$\text{Corr}(\mu_{2i}, \mu_{3i}) = \rho_{23}$$

$$\text{Corr}(\mu_{1i}, \mu_{2i}) = \rho_{12}$$

Following Heckman's two-step procedure, we estimate equation

$$(8) \qquad \text{Ln } Y^*_{it} = \beta'_{it} X_{i,t} + \theta \text{Regs} + \gamma_1 \lambda_{1i} + \gamma_2 \lambda_{2i} + v_{1i},$$

where $\lambda_1 y \lambda_2$ are the well-known inverse Mill's ratios

$$(9) \qquad\qquad \lambda_1 = f(\rho_{12}, \delta' Z_{it}, \eta' W_{it}) \text{ and } \gamma_1 = \rho_{13}\sigma_3,$$

$$(10) \qquad\qquad \lambda_2 = f(\rho_{12}, \eta' W_{it}, \delta' Z_{it}) \text{ and } \gamma_2 = \rho_{23}\sigma_3.$$

The Data

Again, we use pooled PHS data for 1975–1997. Workers report their regulatory status there. The questions are quite specific and focus mainly on legally enforced benefits with details for each of them: severance payments, paid holidays, sick leave, social security, and so on. The possible combinations are sixty-four. However, coverage is highly correlated: Workers who are registered in the social security system typically have the right to severance payments as well as the rest of legal benefits. Otherwise they don't have any benefits. For this reason, we define the Regs variable as 1/0. Voluntary fringe benefits provided by employers are not reported to the PHS.[22] We included the following variables.

---

22. It is likely that these benefits are most valuable to the highest-wage employees. This could result in a bias arising from the omission of some kind of fringe benefits.

X: Human capital (educational level, Mincerian experience) + current job tenure

Job status: category, occupation (self-employed, wage earner), firm size, branch of activity

Regs: 1 if the person is covered by labor legislation, 0 otherwise

Z: including marital status, head of household, number of children, children under six years (0 or 1).

W: including Z plus job status

Table 6.5 reports the results for females and males separately. We chose to report here the estimates for two-step and OLS regressions.[23] We introduced year fixed effects.

As can be seen in the tables, the estimates show an economically and statistically significant effect of regulations on earnings. Males appear to sacrifice about 8 percent of their earnings when regulations are present. Females, on the other hand, sacrifice less, though still a significant amount: 2.8 percent of their earnings. It is intuitive that females present lower coefficients. Since the reduction in earnings will come out of the equilibrium match, and since both the demand and the supply sides are likely to shift down with regulations, one would anticipate that the movement would be smaller as the supply side becomes more elastic. There is considerable evidence that the female labor supply is more elastic than that for men.

Results in table 6.5 show estimated returns to schooling and experience, as well as those to tenure, to be rather strong and consistent with the literature. The size of the corporation where the individual works is also quite important. Large corporations appear to be more productive and accordingly pay higher wages (conditional on regulatory benefits).

In summary, our results indicate that regulations do have an important impact on earnings. While we cannot say that they are welfare reducing, it is quite obvious that a job with regulatory coverage does not come for free. One must sacrifice earnings in order to have access to this coverage. At this point it is very important to emphasize that we have estimated reduced forms. Hence, no inference on the elasticity of labor demand or on the marginal rate of substitution in welfare can be made. Yet the result is quite illuminating, particularly when paired with those of the previous subsection.

Regulations are not distributed fairly. They tend to benefit those with higher earning potential and do segment the market. Those that do get some coverage, however, must sacrifice a portion of their earnings. Still, as we just mentioned, we have not connected the potential impact of regulations to labor demand. For this reason, it is difficult to make any structural inferences as to how the market would clear once these regulations are

---

23. Tables 6A.3 and 6A.4 report results of the selection process.

Table 6.5 **Regression Results: Trade-Off Wages–Fringe Benefits (pooled PHS data 1975–1997; dependent variable: Lnyh)**

	Females		Males	
Variable	2 Step	OLS	2 Step	OLS
Lamp	−.2343		−.1815	
	(−6.558)***		(−3.378)***	
Lame	.9478		−.5816	
	(1.612)		(−4.421)***	
Primary	.1199	.3343	.2210	.2475
	(5.191)***	(8.184)***	(14.131)***	(18.039)***
High school	.5649	.886	.6799	.7589
	(21.62)***	(18.349)***	(31.033)***	(47.85)***
College	1.0448	1.3646	1.264	1.3857
	(12.315)***	(24.691)***	(44.595)***	(69.289)***
Experience	.0256	.0371	.013	.0312
	(7.216)***	(11.856)***	(4.448)***	(24.885)***
Experience**2	−.003	−.005	−.008	−.004
	(−4.515)***	(−8.293)***	(−1.463)	(−17.420)***
Tenure	.0064	.0056	.0072	.0071
	(7.956)***	(4.161)***	(16.579)***	(16.351)***
Manufacturing	−.1085	.0368	.0458	.0479
	(5.100)***	(.912)	(3.212)***	(3.352)***
Public Services	.1212	.1299	.1402	.1428
	(1.477)	(.617)	(3.241)***	(3.294)***
Construction/Maids	.1587	.3129	.0088	.0116
	(6.401)***	(6.797)***	(.503)	(.664)
Retail	−.1800	−.0401	−.003	−.0033
	(−.7329)	(−.922)	(−.198)	(−.213)
Private Services	.1307	.2563	.0632	.0648
	(5.937)***	(6.113)***	(4.367)***	(4.47)***
Public Administration	.0119	.1052	−.0094	−.0105
	(.583)	(2.621)***	(−.489)	(−.542)
Social Services	.1666	.3116	.0089	.0061
	(3.226)***	(3.963)***	(.336)	(.23)
Size5	.0063	.2158	.008	.0018
	(.238)	(4.335)***	(.049)	(.112)
Size <25	.0682	.2875	.0785	.0811
	(2.685)***	(5.850)***	(4.801)***	(4.954)***
Size <100	0.0984	.3072	.1346	.1384
	(3.804)***	(6.037)***	(7.697)***	(7.900)***
Largest	.1654	.3953	.2222	.2278
	(2.89)***	(7.739)***	(13.236)***	(13.553)***
Self	.0762	.0682	.0474	.0538
	(3.996)***	(2.047)***	(3.605)***	(4.091)***
Regs	−.0284	−.0039	−0.0826	−.0757
	(−1.687)	(−.123)	(−7.363)***	(−.6744)***
Constant	1.7757	1.0312	10.7873	10.435
	(10.561)***	(13.262)***	(221.212)***	(345.769)***
Adjusted R^2		.8709		0.9612

Source: IERAL database.

Note: See table 6A.1 for description of the variables. Absolute value of *t*-statistics in parentheses.

***Significant at the 1 percent level.

eliminated. In the next section, we turn to a different exercise and estimate labor demand for a large number of manufacturing firms in Argentina.

6.4   Labor Demand Estimation

We argued previously that most of the regulatory impact would operate through the demand for labor. Theoretical arguments suggest that regulations in the form of taxes will have a negative impact on employment and/ or wages. Contributions to social security are typically thought to affect negatively the demand for labor as well, since the effects through labor supply are probably modest (in countries like Argentina, where workers do not perceive the contributions as deferred or indirect wages, this effect is likely to be very small). Theory, however, provides relatively less guidance over the effects of severance payments on employment. While they are likely to change the ease with which payroll is managed, it is not clear that they reduce the aggregate demand for labor. It appears crucial to have an empirical estimate of how firms respond, in their labor demand decisions, to the presence of regulations.

Hamermesh (1986), summarizing the literature, provides empirical estimates of the employment/labor cost elasticities for various industrial countries. He found the parameter to be low in the sample (.1 to .5), suggesting that policies that increase the fixed cost of employment may reduce the employment-hours ratio only slightly. However, these elasticities could be biased downward as they may reflect the effect of prevailing job security, since these regulations would have induced a substitution away from labor. Less controversial than the effect of job security on the adjustment process is its effect on employment. An increase in job security increases the cost of hiring due to changes in expected future severance payments and the cost of forgone output due to potential mismatches. In the context of shocks to output, firms must strike a balance between hiring more workers and waiting a few periods to forgo the high potential future severance payment.

This section presents the results of estimating a homogeneous labor demand equation with a previously unexploited balanced panel of Argentine manufacturing firms. Our empirical analysis considers the adjustment of employment and hours over the 1990–1996 period.

One of the rich features of the data set is the availability of employment and hours worked. Since some of the effects of stiffening regulations are likely to be a more intense use of hours, we are likely to uncover features here that papers with more aggregate data sources cannot. Of particular interest is the adjustment in the intensive margin (hours) that can follow an increase in the perceived cost of severance. For instance, increases in the demand for goods accompanied by higher severance costs are likely to lead to a reasonably constant level of employment but a more intense use of overtime.

Panel data estimations such as those pursued here present some drawbacks. To begin with, the relatively short period of time covered restricts the variability of regulations. In particular, as mentioned before, there were relatively few changes in the period under consideration, and those that took place happened toward the end of the sample. In any event, as we will see, the effects of regulations come out strongly and highly significant. A second limitation is that the period was one of extraordinary change in a number of dimensions: a large number of firm deaths and births (unfortunately not adequately captured by the sampling technique used to create the panel) and, most remarkably, a period of such strenuous firm reengineering that it casts some concerns over the values of long-run elasticities. On the other hand, the high variance in some of the forcing variables allows a more efficient estimation of the parameters.

6.4.1   The Model

Our empirical approach models labor demand through a fairly general setting. We characterize employment choices as the dynamic interaction of employment and hours adjusting to fluctuations in output, factor prices, and regulations. While the system that will be estimated is unconstrained, the specifications for the demand system correspond to a substantial number of production structures.[24] The system is summarized by the following two equations:

$$(11) \qquad \mathrm{Ln}\, E_t = \alpha_1 + \alpha_2\, \mathrm{Ln}\, E_{t-k} + \alpha_3\, \mathrm{Ln}\, \mathrm{Regs} + \alpha_4\, \mathrm{Ln}\, H_{t-k}$$
$$+ \beta\, \mathrm{Ln}\, \mathrm{Sat} + \gamma \mathrm{Lin} P_t + \varepsilon_{1t}$$

$$(12) \qquad \mathrm{Ln}\, H_t = \alpha_1 + \alpha_2\, \mathrm{Ln}\, H_{t-k} + \alpha_3\, \mathrm{Ln}\, \mathrm{Regs} + \alpha_4\, \mathrm{Ln}\, E_{t-k}$$
$$+ \beta\, \mathrm{Ln}\, \mathrm{Sat} + \gamma \mathrm{Lin} P_t + \varepsilon_{2t},$$

where E_t is employment, H_t are production hours, P_t is industrial production. Regs measures the cost equivalence of regulations, which presumably affect not just the level of demand but also the dynamics. Finally, Sat captures the product wage.

The model assumes that employers seek to maximize the expected value of current and future profit and that the cost of adjusting labor input is a quadratic function of the size of the adjustment made.

The specification is quite flexible. It is consistent with a number of production structures with smooth substitution between workers and hours, including varying degrees of returns to scale or what is even more likely, the presence of imperfect competition in goods markets. In other words, the model does not restrict the source of curvature of the profit function.[25]

---

24. The corresponding derivations may be consulted in Varian (1984), MasCollel, Whinston, and Green (1995), Chambers (1988), and Hamermesh (1986, 1993).

25. For instance, the model is consistent with a setting where firms are imperfectly competitive and face constant marginal costs as well as with one where firms face a competitive market with decreasing returns to labor.

Given this generality, care must be taken to make explicit the maintained hypotheses if the coefficients are to be identified as technology parameters.

It is important to consider the theoretical model on which the specification is based so as to understand the true significance of the parameters. If the production process is assumed to have the features of a Cobb-Douglas production function, labor costs and production parameters are interpreted as labor and return-to-scale parameters, respectively. If, on the other hand, it is assumed that a constant elasticity of substitution (CES) production function explains the model better, the corresponding coefficients represent the capital-labor substitution elasticity and the scale parameter, respectively. In any case, in the estimations presented herein, no restrictions on production function or underlying cost structure will be imposed.

6.4.2 Econometric Specification

The system represented by equations (11) and (12) presents a number of econometric problems that must be addressed.

First, the model, being based on a panel, will be estimated with fixed effects to control for firm idiosyncratic factors. We will also introduce a quarter dummy to correct for any seasonality in the unadjusted data.[26]

Under most reasonable assumptions (local returns to scale, imperfect competition, bargaining structures, and so on) firm output and shocks to the demand decision are likely to be correlated. The same can be said about real wage determination. This, of course, requires the estimation through instrumental variables. At a micro level, the choice of instruments becomes a bit easier than in aggregate models. However, finding firm-specific instruments proved to be very difficult as the data set did not include truly exogenous variables. For this reason, we used a number of aggregate variables and estimated different correlations for each firm.[27] The instruments used are aggregate GDP, the specific branch openness indicator (export plus imports over output), aggregate unemployment rate, price of capital equipment index, log of ratio of wholesale prices to consumer prices, and lagged values of all variables. We report results from OLS and instrumental variables (IV) estimations. Following Bentolila and Saint-Paul (1992), we did not expect labor demand to be stable over the firm's cycle.[28] To partially account for this we defined a dummy variable to capture recessions and expansions when instrumenting. We defined both states as occurring when the real output (log) growth reached a threshold arbitrarily imposed (see table 6A.5 for details).

---

26. Theory indicates that when estimating labor demand conditioned on production (not value added) we should include other factor prices. Nonlabor inputs were unavailable for the estimation.

27. The instruments, while the same for each firm, did vary in that they were not restricted to share the same first-stage coefficients for all firms.

28. Bentolila and Saint-Paul (1992) argue that a lowering in firing cost affects more firing decisions than hiring ones.

The model specification introduces an unrestricted dynamic adjustment. This is motivated via a cost of adjustment technology that depends in part on the hurdles imposed by regulations. The specification we chose was to introduce up to three lags to capture all seasonal as well as inertial factors. To allow for a richer interaction with hours, we also introduced lagged terms of hours in the employment equation and vice versa. As for adjustment costs, we also introduced as an explanatory variable the price of overtime hours. Presumably, an increase in the number of (relative) overtime hours should induce an increase in the level of employment next period. The fact that overtime hours are being used at all is probably a good indicator of significant adjustment costs.[29]

6.4.3 The Data

The data set includes a sample of 1,398 manufacturing private firms. The panel does not provide much information on the type of firms included. For instance, we have no knowledge of whether the employment relations are informal. The panel presents other problems, too. Not all firms systematically answer all questions. Similarly, many firms drop out of the sample, and the replacement criterion is not clear. The panel does not include newly created firms. We report results from estimating a restricted balanced panel and an unbalanced one. The balanced panel drops all those firms that do not answer the relevant questions or that have dropped out of the sample, leaving 200 firms in the data set with all the complete answers for the whole period. Clearly, this decision could create a selectivity bias problem.[30] The unbalanced panel, on the other hand, clears out those firms that do not answer the relevant questions in all quarters. The number of remaining firms was 549 out of the original 1,398.[31] Sources and additional details concerning the data are explained in appendix B.

The available data are in index number format. The definition of each variable has its own complexities. We defined employment as the total number of workers within the firm (white and blue collar). Production is measured via physical production as reported by firms. Multiproduct firms aggregate it up according to a set of fixed weights. There is no control for changes in product design. Wages were defined by dividing payroll ex-

29. When estimating the interaction between hours and employment, it is clear that both respond to a correlated set of innovations. In this paper we estimated them separately. A refinement would estimate them jointly, allowing for a free correlation between both residuals.

30. The problem is complex. First, the methodology claims to replace small firms in the sample but not large ones. Second, we cannot distinguish between firms that did not answer because they decided not to do so (perhaps out of taxation fears) and the ones that were closed. Finally, there is no information in the data to allow us to identify firms that are likely to be dropped out of the sample to attempt a solution to the selectivity bias (i.e., we have no way in which to identify if a firm is large or small).

31. We considered the possibility of reweighting the panel, but it proved impossible because in the balanced panel entire branches were lost. Therefore, we did not have any criteria for expanding the sample.

Table 6.6   **Descriptive Statistics of Firms in the Sample: Annual Average Growth Rate**

Index	(1)	(2)
Employment	–3.0	–2.7
Hours	3.2	1.1
Total wage	10.9	10.6
Hourly wage	7.5	9.9
Regulation cost	–1.3	4.0
Output	8.0	5.7

Source: IERAL database.

Notes: Column (1) is based on extremes values on the series; column (2) is based on the slope of the trend line.

penses by the number of employees. Since we have data on expenses due to overtime hours, we netted them out to compute regular wages. The survey does not include product price information. We estimated the real wage as the ratio of wages to wholesale prices for the sector. For description of the variables see table 6A.5.

Table 6.6 shows some features of the firms in our sample. The table presents average growth rates for a few variables. LnReg is the variable that encompasses labor regulation costs. We included payroll taxes: pensions, family allowances, health care system, and PAMI (see table 6.2 for details). We also introduced a measure of expected severance payments (ESP). We did not include other labor regulations due to the difficulties involved in imputing costs. This was the case with paid holidays, sick leave, and specific collective agreement provisions.

The Index of Regulations Construction

LnReg is estimated every period for each *branch of activity*. LnReg has two main components: taxes and ESP. Expected severance payment is calculated as percentage of normal wage through the following formula:

(13) $$ESP_{it} = U_{it} \cdot F_{it} \cdot T_{it} \cdot P_{it},$$

where i refers to firm's branch of activity and t refers to time (quarter and year); U is the unemployment rate, F is the percentage of fired people over unemployment; T is average tenure, and P is the probability of having the right to severance (the fraction of formal wage earners over total wage earners). Each period we have as many ESPs as branches of activities aggregated at two digits of the third revision of the Clasificación Industrial International Uniforme (CIIU). Because the PHS is gathered twice a year and we have quarterly data, we use the same figure for every two quarters of the Manufacturing Industrial Survey.

We add the taxes to ESP to obtain the full cost of regulation as a proportion of wages.

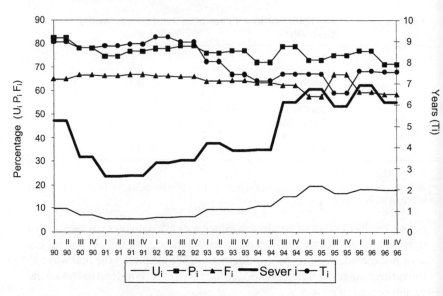

Fig. 6.4   Decomposition of expected severance payment
Source: IERAL database.

(14) $Regs_{it} = ESP_{it} + Taxes_{it}$

The variable is expressed as an index base 1990 = 100 and expressed in logarithm for the regressions. The behavior of the different components of the index is illustrated in figure 6.4.

6.4.4   Results

Table 6.7 presents some OLS results. Our first specification treats output as exogenous. Estimates for jobs and hours are reported for the unbalanced and the balanced panel, respectively. We estimated introducing individual firm fixed effects, correcting for serial correlation. The reported z-score is heteroskedasticity consistent.

The results show that all variables are statistically significant. A 1 percent increase in real wages decreases the level of employment 0.15 percent while hours go down 0.20 percent. A common pattern in our results and the literature is that hours appear more responsive to changes in costs or scale factors. This is probably the effect of costs of adjustment. Theory indicates that with costly changes in manpower a firm is much more likely to rely on adjustments in hours per worker than on the number of jobs offered.[32]

As we mentioned in the introduction, eyeballing the data leads to the im-

---

32. It must be remembered, however, that overtime hours are costlier, and thus firms have to take this into account.

ble 6.7   **Manufacturing Survey: OLS Results**

	Unbalanced Panel		Balanced Panel	
	Employment (1)	Hours per Worker (2)	Employment (3)	Hours per Worker (4)
ormal Wage	−0.151	−0.197	−0.119	−0.180
	(21.23)***	(41.78)***	(14.40)***	(29.63)***
ıtput	0.117	0.061	0.103	0.071
	(33.22)***	(24.22)***	(20.01)***	(17.08)***
ıtput_1	−0.048	−0.023	−0.049	−0.035
	(12.50)***	(8.23)***	(8.94)***	(7.95)***
vertime Wage	0.015	0.063	0.018	0.062
	(8.21)***	(49.52)***	(7.03)***	(31.46)***
nployment_1	0.815	−0.059	0.878	−0.077
	(88.69)***	(9.06)***	(64.26)***	(7.13)***
ınployment_2	−0.239	0.026	−0.277	0.051
	(21.48)***	(3.28)***	(15.67)***	(3.64)***
nployment_3	0.275	−0.030	0.270	−0.023
	(31.17)***	(4.72)***	(20.41)***	(2.19)**
ours per Worker_1	0.022	0.172	0.037	0.251
	(2.00)**	(21.57)***	(2.42)***	(20.37)***
ours per Worker_2	0.073	0.001	0.007	0.015
	(6.56)***	(0.16)	(0.50)	(1.30)
ours per Worker_3	0.042	0.014	0.084	0.033
	(4.13)***	(1.87)**	(6.46)***	(3.18)***
cond quarter	−0.033	0.100	−0.040	0.100
	(7.89)***	(33.32)***	(8.57)***	(25.99)***
ıird quarter	−0.032	0.099	−0.032	0.089
	(7.39)***	(31.49)***	(6.44)***	(22.32)***
ırth quarter	−0.018	0.085	−0.015	0.075
	(4.59)***	(29.42)***	(3.29)***	(20.59)***
ıgulation	−0.013	0.031	−0.009	0.028
	(2.04)**	(6.80)***	(1.22)	(4.82)***
ınstant	0.441	4.322	0.277	3.689
	(5.20)***	(70.69)***	(2.63)***	(42.81)***
djusted R^2	.89	.70	.86	.67
ɔ. of observations	11,061		4,997	

urce: IERAL database.
ɔtes: Absolute value of z-statistics in parentheses. See table 6A.5 for description of the variables.
*Significant at the 1 percent level.
Significant at the 5 percent level.

pression that Argentina's job market showed apparent low responsiveness of employment to output. Our OLS estimates show that, in manufacturing, when output grows 1 percent, hours increase 6–7 percent and workers 10–12 percent on impact.

A feature of the results is that output and wage elasticities are higher in the unbalanced panel than in the balanced one. Unfortunately, the selection rule to stay in the panel is unclear. Firms could die or simply not answer in some periods. Thus, while the results are suggestive, there is no real basis to conclude that regulations do have an impact in pushing firms into bankruptcy.

The model reported in table 6.7 shows, in both panels, fairly similar results. Employment and hours appear sensitive to wages. Remarkably, the cost of regulations (severance costs and taxes) always affects significantly the demand for workers. The results, however, assumed that physical volume of production as well as wages could be treated as exogenous, ignoring questions of simultaneity in the determination of output, employment, and prices.

When using microdata the simultaneous problems of output determination and employment are typically avoided. The reason is simple: Under perfect competition, demand is given and hence firms only choose how many workers to hire. Unfortunately, in the case at hand, the assumption of competitive markets may be a bit strict—at least for the first few years of the sample, when the economy was quite closed and few firms disputed the local market. Under imperfect competition the decisions to hire workers and sell goods are closely intertwined, and disturbances that affect one will probably affect the other. For this reason we should instrument for movements in final goods demand.[33]

As for wages, firms have a limited say in the wage offer. The institutional setting in Argentina limits that discretion. Centralized bargaining restricts the choices for a firm, and only upward deviations in wages are allowed. Furthermore, the price deflator used to construct the real wage, just as the level of output, is endogenous under imperfect competition. For this reason, in table 6.8 we report instrumental variable estimations assuming both wage costs and output as jointly determined with employment.

The instrumental variable estimation makes little change in the short-run output elasticities in the employment equations. The elasticity for the hours equation, on the other hand, doubles. Interestingly, it appears that the endogeneity problem was more serious for the hours equation—the margin where most changes would take place when in the presence of adjustment costs. This pattern is present in both tables and is most remarkable in the unbalanced panel estimates.

The responsiveness of employment to changes in wage costs is a bit more of a concern. When we only instrument for output, the elasticity remains stable at a 0.15–0.20 level (in the unbalanced panel case). However, when we instrument for the potential endogeneity of wages, the cost elasticity

33. Table 6A.6 shows the results of instrumenting the level of output assuming wages to be exogenous.

Manufacturing Survey, IV-Endogenous: Wages and Product

	Unbalanced Panel		Balanced Panel	
	Employment (1)	Hours per Worker (2)	Employment (3)	Hours per Worker (4)
t. Normal Wage	−0.118	−0.022	−0.041	−0.038
	(10.27)***	(2.61)***	(3.09)***	(3.61)***
t. Output	0.110	0.103	0.050	0.124
	(9.72)***	(12.11)***	(3.68)***	(10.75)***
tput_1	−0.042	−0.045	−0.030	−0.065
	(6.61)***	(9.30)***	(3.58)***	(9.04)***
vertime Wage	0.016	0.062	0.022	0.055
	(6.29)***	(32.96)***	(6.61)***	(20.37)***
mployment_1	0.825	−0.056	0.910	−0.071
	(76.24)***	(6.94)***	(59.58)***	(5.50)***
mployment_2	−0.260	0.042	−0.317	0.063
	(19.16)***	(4.00)***	(16.03)***	(3.64)***
mployment_3	0.310	−0.051	0.294	−0.032
	(28.22)***	(6.29)***	(20.14)***	(2.66)***
urs per Worker_1	0.038	0.202	0.015	0.279
	(2.90)***	(20.70)***	(0.85)	(19.08)***
urs per Worker_2	0.076	−0.015	0.001	0.021
	(5.99)***	(1.51)	(0.05)	(1.47)
urs per Worker_3	0.036	0.013	0.051	0.026
	(2.95)***	(1.42)	(3.34)***	(2.05)**
cond quarter	−0.028	0.123	−0.033	0.112
	(5.97)***	(33.08)***	(6.24)***	(24.36)***
ird quarter	−0.029	0.122	−0.021	0.105
	(5.74)***	(31.44)***	(3.87)***	(22.08)***
urth quarter	−0.020	0.100	−0.013	0.084
	(4.11)***	(27.50)***	(2.40)***	(18.95)***
gulation	−0.022	−0.012	−0.021	−0.003
	(3.04)***	(2.15)**	(2.59)***	(0.45)
onstant	0.159	3.548	0.310	2.989
	(1.53)	(43.68)***	(2.54)***	(27.35)***
ljusted R^2	.89	.72	.86	.69
o. of observations		10,532		4,997

urce: IERAL database.

otes: Absolute value of z-statistics in parentheses. Instruments are normal wage_1; output_2; out-
t_3; output_4, consumer price index, capital services price index, wholesale price index, aggregate un-
ployment index, dce; dca. See table 6A.5 for description of the variables.

*Significant at the 1 percent level.

Significant at the 5 percent level.

drops substantially in both equations, with a more dramatic impact on the hours one. Since we measure wages by dividing the wage bill by employment we could have introduced an upward bias in the least square estimates of the labor cost elasticity.

Hours appear less responsive than jobs to fluctuations in costs or scale factors. Theory indicates that with costly changes in manpower, a firm is much more likely to rely on adjustment in hours than on the number of jobs offered. We failed to find support to these arguments, as other studies using quarterly data had previously done (Hamermesh 1993, chap. 7).

When we consider the regulatory burden the results change. To begin with, as regulations get stiffer, employment drops more than hours. That is, firms substitute away from both types of labor: workers and hours. Workers and hours thus appear to be *p-complements*. An increase of 1 percent in the estimated regulatory burden produces a short-run drop in employment of around 0.02 percent, while hours would drop by 0.01 or 0.003 percent (unbalanced and balanced, respectively). This is exactly what we would have expected. As regulations get tighter, firms are more likely to get rid of workers. It is quite remarkable that regulations do have this effect, which is completely counter to that sought by regulators. Job security provisions are typically introduced to protect workers, yet they tend to reduce the number of jobs and increase only in the margin the effort demanded from those who can preserve theirs.

To summarize, upon impact, the presence of regulations seems disturbing for the behavior of the labor market. Theoretically, in the presence of high fixed costs firms could substitute away from labor into capital or other inputs. Yet, while firms have to pay the additional hours at the overtime rate ($+50$ percent/$+100$ percent) plus proportional payroll taxes,[34] the expected severance payments are invariant since the regulation recognizes the straight-time rate as the severance cost. Hence, the theoretical elasticity prediction is ambiguous.[35] Our results suggest that an increase in the regulatory burden reduces the employment-hours ratio somewhat. But the negative effect on total workers and hours employment indicates substitution away from labor.

Robustness

The cost of severance was calculated using sector-specific data. It is possible, however, that some sectors with low employment levels might also show high turnover rates. Under those circumstances, the cost of severance would be high and a spurious negative correlation might develop. The less

34. Table 6.2 showed that 92 percent of nonwage labor costs are social security contributions proportional to wages.
35. The long-run trade-off between jobs and standard hours has been difficult to find in the literature. See Hamermesh (1993).

time variability the index of regulations shows, the more severe the problem could be. That is, when most of the regulation variability comes from the between component across sectors, other unobserved components could explain the sign and size of the estimated coefficient.

To check for the existence of spurious correlation we run our labor demand equations on an aggregate index of regulations. That is, we recalculated the index of regulation for the whole of manufacturing. Now the index becomes

(15) $$\text{Regs}_t = \text{Taxes}_t + \text{ESP}_t = U_t \cdot F_t \cdot T_t \cdot P_t,$$

where U is aggregate unemployment rate, F is the fraction of the unemployed that were laid off, T is average tenure, and P is the probability of having severance payment (the percentage of formal wage earners over total wage earners). The results are reported in table 6.9.

Little changes from the results previously reported. The wage elasticity is somewhat lower but roughly equivalent. The output elasticity remains the same. Lagged terms remain invariant as well, insuring that the dynamics will look the same. Finally, the impact of regulations on employment is even stronger than the one previously reported. Now the impact elasticity climbs to 0.09, a level equivalent to that of wages. The effect on hours appears to dwindle away. The coefficient is now economically and statistically indistinguishable from zero (and the sign becomes positive). Overall, the specification appears robust to this source of spurious correlation.

It would seem appealing to evaluate the differential impact that the different components of the regulatory index have on employment. In table 6.10 we report the results of conducting three exercises. All of them limit the time variability and focus on the cross-sectional factors. The first, which we call option A, holds unemployment and the probability of having been laid off fixed at the mean for the period. Option B assumes that the tenure structure has remained constant over time. Option C holds unemployment, the fraction of those laid off, and the probability of access to severance payments constant.

Somewhat limiting the time variability of the index of regulations has a very modest effect on our estimates. In all cases, the job elasticity increases. At the same time, hours respond less, turning economically and statistically insignificant. All other parameters remain largely unaffected.

The deleterious effects of regulations on employment seem robust to alternative specifications. Neither restricting the cross section nor restricting the time series variability appears capable of reducing the size or significance of the estimates. In fact, in all cases the impact elasticity increases, sometimes making them equivalent to the wage cost. Conversely, in the case for hours, the effects are weakened.

Table 6.9   Manufacturing Survey, IV-Endogenous: Wages and Product, Unbalanced
                   Panel (aggregated regulation index)

	Employment (1)	Hours per Worker (2)
Est. Normal Wage	-0.097	-0.032
	(-7.834)	(-3.628)
Est. Output	0.115	0.096
	(10.164)	(11.319)
Output_1	-0.042	-0.046
	(-6.634)	(-9.616)
Overtime Wage index	0.014	0.063
	(5.019)	(33.478)
Employment_1	0.821	-0.050
	(75.662)	(-6.292)
Employment_2	-0.260	0.032
	(-19.187)	(3.213)
Employment_3	0.306	-0.048
	(27.847)	(-5.846)
Employment_1	0.036	0.204
	(2.763)	(20.923)
Hours per Worker_2	0.075	-0.028
	(5.935)	(-2.951)
Hours per Worker_3	0.037	0.013
	(2.979)	(1.471)
Second quarter	-0.026	0.123
	(-5.553)	(32.769)
Third quarter	-0.027	0.121
	(-5.508)	(30.734)
Fourth quarter	-0.020	0.099
	(-4.074)	(27.156)
Regulation	-0.091	0.004
	(-5.545)	(0.291)
Constant	0.059	3.570
	(0.580)	(45.026)
Adjusted R^2	0.86	0.68
No. of observations	10,532	10,532

Source: IERAL database.

Notes: Absolute value of z-statistics in parentheses. Regulation index = Uit × Fit × Tit × Pit + taxes, with i = sectors and t = quarters. Instruments are normal wage_1; output_2; output_3; output_4, consumer price index, capital services price index, wholesale price index, aggregate unemployment index, dce; dca. See table 6A.5 for description of the variables.

6.4.5   Dynamics: The Speed of Adjustment

So far we have discussed the static, short-run response of employment and hours to changes in wage costs, output, and labor regulations. Next we turn to the adjustment process that firms will follow when one of these variables is shocked. We next present a set of graphs of the dynamic response of firms to 10 percent changes in output, wages, or the costs of regulations.

Table 6.10   Manufacturing Survey, Alternative Regulation Index (IV-endogenous: wages and product, unbalanced panel)

	Regulation Index, Option A		Regulation Index, Option B		Regulation Index, Option C	
	Employment (1)	Hours per Worker (2)	Employment (1)	Hours per Worker (2)	Employment (1)	Hours per Worker (2)
Est. Normal Wage	-0.105	-0.028	-0.114	-0.029	-0.095	-0.029
	(-8.636)	(-3.195)	(-9.846)	(-3.466)	(-7.649)	(-3.284)
Est. Output	0.113	0.097	0.109	0.096	0.116	0.096
	(9.939)	(11.477)	(9.651)	(11.545)	(10.187)	(11.361)
Output_1	-0.042	-0.046	-0.041	-0.046	-0.042	-0.046
	(-6.571)	(-9.669)	(-6.395)	(-9.673)	(-6.667)	(-9.633)
Overtime Wage index	0.015	0.063	0.016	0.063	0.014	0.063
	(5.643)	(33.529)	(6.155)	(33.680)	(5.134)	(33.458)
Employment_1	0.823	-0.051	0.824	-0.051	0.821	-0.051
	(75.960)	(-6.407)	(76.088)	(-6.400)	(75.745)	(-6.368)
Employment_2	-0.260	0.032	-0.261	0.032	-0.260	0.032
	(-19.176)	(3.209)	(-19.182)	(3.207)	(-19.166)	(3.213)
Employment_3	0.308	-0.048	0.309	-0.048	0.306	-0.048
	(28.057)	(-5.938)	(28.185)	(-5.933)	(27.876)	(-5.904)
Employment_1	0.036	0.204	0.037	0.204	0.036	0.204
	(2.751)	(20.958)	(2.786)	(20.957)	(2.701)	(20.942)
Hours per Worker_2	0.075	-0.028	0.075	-0.028	0.075	-0.028
	(5.884)	(-2.952)	(5.854)	(-2.955)	(5.913)	(-2.950)
Hours per Worker_3	0.037	0.014	0.036	0.014	0.037	0.014
	(2.984)	(1.505)	(2.944)	(1.494)	(3.014)	(1.494)

(continued)

Table 6.10   (continued)

	Regulation Index, Option A		Regulation Index, Option B		Regulation Index, Option C	
	Employment (1)	Hours per Worker (2)	Employment (1)	Hours per Worker (2)	Employment (1)	Hours per Worker (2)
Second quarter	−0.028	0.123	−0.028	0.123	−0.028	0.123
	(−5.880)	(33.269)	(−5.826)	(33.352)	(−5.901)	(33.156)
Third quarter	−0.028	0.121	−0.028	0.121	−0.028	0.121
	(−5.726)	(31.127)	(−5.655)	(31.194)	(−5.722)	(31.015)
Fourth quarter	−0.021	0.099	−0.020	0.099	−0.021	0.099
	(−4.234)	(27.408)	(−4.095)	(27.399)	(−4.364)	(27.381)
Regulation	−0.062	−0.008	−0.039	−0.006	−0.084	−0.004
	(−4.361)	(−0.788)	(−3.911)	(−0.766)	(−5.431)	(−0.373)
Constant	0.064	3.560	0.088	3.563	0.044	3.564
	(0.628)	(44.836)	(0.869)	(45.174)	(0.436)	(44.735)
Adjusted R^2	0.86	0.68	0.86	0.68	0.86	0.68
No. of observations	10,532		10,532		10,532	

Source: IERAL database.

Notes: Absolute value of z-statistics in parentheses. Regulation index = $Uit \times Fit \times Tit \times Pit$ + taxes, with i = sectors and t = quarters. Option A: Uit and Fit fixed to the mean of the period. Option B: Tit fixed to the mean of the period. Option C: Uit, Fit, and Pit fixed to the mean of the period. Instruments are product: linsat_1; linpf_2; linpf_3; linpf_4, lipc, lipk, lipm, lni_uag, dce; dca; wages: linsat_1; linpf_2; linpf_3; linpf_4, lipc, lipk, lipm, lni_uag, dce; dca. See table 6A.5 for description of the variables.

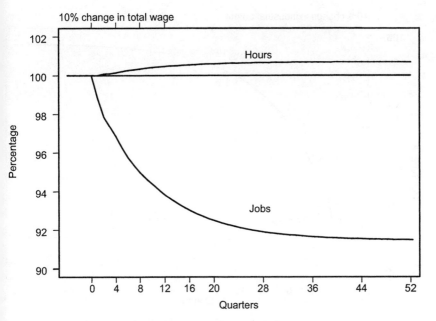

Fig. 6.5 Impulse-response function—change in total wage
Source: IERAL database and table 6.9.

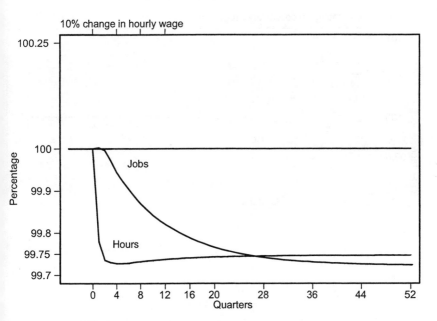

Fig. 6.6 Impulse-response function—change in hourly wage
Source: IERAL database and table 6.9.

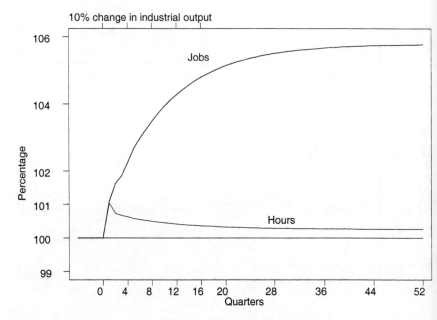

Fig. 6.7 Impulse-response function—change in industrial output
Source: IERAL database and table 6.9.

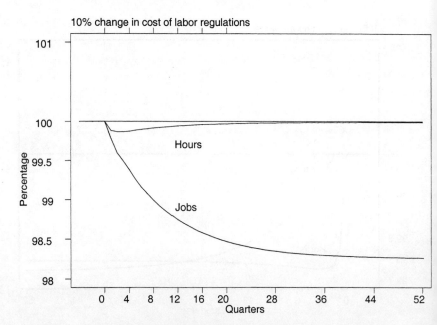

Fig. 6.8 Impulse-response function—change in regulations
Source: IERAL database and table 6.9.

The exercise is conducted based on the regressions previously presented in table 6.8. We selected the unbalanced panel estimates. We allow for the interaction between hours and employment as we shock both equations simultaneously. Figures 6.5 and 6.6 show the response to a 10 percent change in total wages and in hourly wages. Figures 6.7 and 6.8 illustrate the response to a 10 percent increase in output and in regulatory costs.

The median lags are 1.5 and 2.5 years for output and wage shocks. They also illustrate that the response is always greater in employment than in hours. There we observe again the damaging effect of regulations on labor demand. This can only be the case when firms substitute workers in the extensive margin for hours in the intensive one. Firms increase almost 1 percent the hours per worker, while an equivalent increase in wages would have reduced employment 8 percent. The bivariate hours-workers microdata estimation allows us to draw some important conclusions: Regulations do have a negative impact on labor demand, and the impact grows over time.

Another interesting finding is that when we allow for dynamics we find that the response of employment to output is substantially higher than the short-run estimate. While the short-run elasticity is fairly low, the long-run response appears more respectable and close to 0.57.

Tables 6.11 and 6.12 present the estimated coefficients and long-run responses of hours and employment. For comparison purposes we first reproduce the coefficients from the labor demand model under different assumptions.

Table 6.11 presents estimates of the labor demand elasticity under the different models reported in tables 6.7 and 6.8 and IV-product reported in table 6A.6. The median speed adjustment is among the values reported in

Table 6.11   **Labor Demand Coefficients under Difference Alternatives**

| | Wage | | | | | |
	Total	Hourly	Regs	Output[a]	λ_{EH}[b]	λ_{HE}[b]
OLS						
Hours	—	−0.197	0.031	0.038	—	−0.063
Jobs	−0.151	—	−0.013	0.069	0.137	—
IV: product						
Hours	—	−0.193	0.021	0.077	—	−0.076
Jobs	−0.173	—	0.000	0.076	0.163	—
IV: product and wages						
Hours	—	−0.022	−0.012	0.058	—	−0.065
Jobs	−0.118	—	−0.022	0.068	0.150	—

Source: IERAL database and tables 6.7, 6.8, and 6A.6.

Note: Dashes indicate data not available.

[a]Includes one lag.

[b]Includes three lags.

Table 6.12   Long-Run Labor Demand Elasticities under Different Alternatives

| | Wage | | | |
	Total	Hours	Regs	Output
OLS				
Hours	0.073	−0.226	0.042	−0.031
Jobs	−0.946	−0.208	−0.049	0.603
IV: product				
Hours	0.115	−0.219	0.030	0.037
Jobs	−1.187	−0.274	−0.039	0.631
IV: product and wages				
Hours	0.070	−0.025	−0.001	0.026
Median lags	9	1[a]	1[a]	1[a]
Jobs	−0.860	−0.030	−0.177	0.575
Median lags	7	10	7	6

Source: IERAL database and tables 6.7, 6.8, and 6A.6.
[a]Less than 1 quarter.

the literature for estimates using quarterly data: 5.5 quarters for jobs and a quicker adjustment for hours. The median for hours adjustment implies a lag on the order of one quarter.

We consider the terms that describe the simultaneous adjustment of employment and hours. We found $\lambda_{EH} > 0$ in our specifications suggesting workers and hours to be dynamic p-complements. The estimate of $\lambda_{HE} < 0$, statistically significant, with absolute values smaller than λ_{EH} in our specifications suggesting workers and hours to be dynamic p-complements. Results suggest that for a 10 percent long-run decrease in employment there is a 4 percent increase in the demand of hours per worker. The net effect is still a substitution away from labor.

Finally, table 6.12 provides long-run elasticities that can be benchmarked with those previously found with aggregate data (see Montoya and Navarro 1996; Pessino 1995). We found higher values for long-run elasticities. Our results show an output elasticity in the long run of 0.575 percent and 0.03 percent for workers and hours, respectively. The response to wages is also important in the long run, with an estimated employment elasticity of −0.86 percent.

6.5   Concluding Remarks

Argentina's experience in the 1990s raises serious questions about the adjustment of the labor market. While output was growing strongly, employment was lagging behind. Many policy observers argued that as the economy demanded greater flexibility to adjust to a more competitive business environment, labor regulations were becoming ever more binding.

We have shown that Argentina's regulations do not quite do what they are intended to do. They reverse discriminate provision of protection to those workers with greater human capital. Regulations appeared regressive, limiting the opportunities of those worse off and protecting the jobs of those endowed with higher human capital. We also found that, other things being equal, those who do have regulatory coverage get lower incomes. That is, there is a trade-off between this fringe "benefit" and earnings. The cost, while relatively small, was still significant.

Regulations, and in particular severance payments, represent a cost for business. Firms rationally respond to them by lowering their demand for labor. Indeed, both in the short run and (mostly) in the long run, there is a strong negative effect of regulations on the level of labor demand. This downward shift of labor demand is at least partially responsible for the drop in earnings that is found to be associated with regulatory coverage. Similarly, any downward shift of a demand curve increases the potential for employment reduction.

To compound the problem, our estimates indicate that when regulations become stricter, firms rationally alter their labor allocations. They substitute workers for hours. Indeed, we find that individually worked hours go up with an increased regulatory burden at the same time that the number of workers is reduced. Regulations do not appear to be helpful in creating employment.

Appendix A

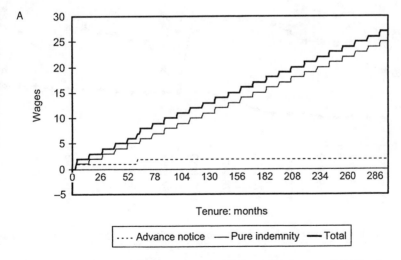

Fig. 6A.1   Labor regulations regulatory costs: *A*, **severance payment;** *B*, **holiday leave**
Source: IERAL database, based on legislation enforced in each period.

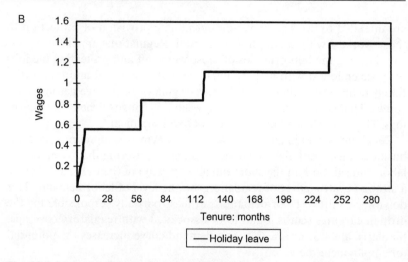

Fig. 6A.1   (cont.) Labor regulations regulatory costs: *A*, severance payment; *B*, holiday leave

Source: IERAL database, based on legislation enforced in each period.

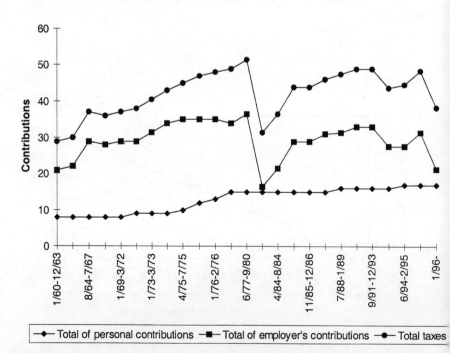

Fig. 6A.2   Evolution of the personal and employer contributions to social security as percentage of gross wage

Appendix B
Permanent Household Survey

The microdata data set available to track down the evolution of employment is the Permanent Household Survey (PHS). The PHS survey is a random sample of households that contains an array of personal, demographic, and economic information on individual household members. They are conducted twice a year (in May and October) since 1974 in the main urban centers of Argentina.[36] The files record information on each respondent's labor market status and living arrangements during the survey week as well as the retrospective data on labor market activity during the previous month.

In terms of personal, demographic, and economic information on individual household members, the following information is available: labor market status (employed, unemployed, or nonlabor force), relation to household head, age, sex, marital status, hours worked in the survey week, occupation, firm size and sector of activity, nonlabor income, schooling, number of children, hourly wage, and number of hours worked. Wage earners declare fringe benefits, making it possible to detect covered and uncovered people. It is not difficult to join personal and household files and to create from these joined databases variables related to households than can influence individual behavior toward the labor market.

The PHS has a rotating sample design, with households (addresses, strictly speaking) in the survey for four waves (two years), with the sample renewed for each wave.

---

36. Considering the total sample is about 80 percent of Argentina's urban population. It must be remembered that about 15 percent of Argentina's population lives in rural areas (defined as villages of less than 5,000 persons).

Table 6B.1   Description of the Variables

Variable Definition	Name	Measurement Issues
Family status		
Marital Status	Married	Dummy variable. 1 if the person is married.
Household Position	Household Head	Dummy variable. 1 if the person is the household head.
Number of Children	Children	Quantity of children.
	Child < 6	Quantity of children younger than 6 years old.
Nonlabor Income	Nonlabor	Log of the difference between household income and person's income divided by the quantity of household members but the referred person.
Activity status		
	Participant	Dummy variable. 1 if a person is a labor force participant.
	Employed	Dummy variable. 1 if the person is employed given the person is in the labor force. It is set to missing when the person is not in the labor force.
	Wage	Hourly wage or earnings corresponding to the last month for reporting unit. Wage after social security deductions in wage earner's case.
	Lnyh	Natural logarithm of hourly wages. It is set to missing if the person is not part of the labor force or if he or she is unemployed.
	Ptime	Dummy variable. 1 if the person works less than 35 hours per week.
Human capital		
Schooling		Maximum educational attainment. Defined as dichotomous in all cases.
	Illiterate	1 if the person has incomplete (including illiterates) elementary level.
	Primary	1 if the person has complete primary level or incomplete secondary level.
	High school	1 if the person has complete secondary level or incomplete university level.
	College	1 if the person has complete university level.
Experience	Experience	Mincerian experience calculated as (years of schooling – age – 6).
	Exper**2	Describes the age-earnings profile.
Tenure	Tenure	Continuous variable. Years of tenure in the same job. It tries to measure specific on-the-job training.

Branch of activity		Sector of activity of the main occupation at the week of reference, classified under CIIU Rev. 3rd. Defined as dichotomous in all cases.
	Manufacturing	1 if the person works in manufacturing sector.
	Construction	1 if the person works in construction sector.
	Retail	1 if the person works in retailing sector.
	Private services	1 if the person works in restaurants, hotels.
	Elect/Public Services	1 if the person works in utility companies.
	Finance	1 if the person works in financial services or insurance companies.
	Transport	1 if the person works in transportation services.
	Public Administration	1 if the person works in public sector or defense.
	Social Services	1 if the person works in health, education, or other social services.
	House help	1 if the person works as household aid.
Firm size		Size of the employee's main occupation firm at the week of reference. Defined as dichotomous in all cases.
	Size5	1 if the person works in a firm with up to 5 employees.
	Size <25	1 if the person works in a firm with between 6 and 25 employees.
	Size <100	1 if the person works in a firm with between 26 and 100 employees.
	Largest	1 if the person works in a firm with more than 100 employees.
Job status		Main occupation category of the person at the week of reference.
	Self	Dummy variable. 1 if the person is self-employed in his or her main occupation.
Labor regulations		
	Registered	1 if the person is registered in the social security system.
	Family_reg	1 if any other family member has a job covered by labor regulations.

Source: IREAL database.

Table 6B.2   **Probit: Right to Severance Payment**

	Wage Earners	
	Women (1)	Men (2)
Primary	0.127	−0.002
	(2.14)**	(0.07)
High school	0.609	0.330
	(9.24)***	(7.73)***
College	0.814	0.266
	(10.59)***	(4.43)***
Experience	0.056	0.052
	(11.82)***	(13.48)***
Experience**2	−0.001	−0.001
	(8.75)***	(11.85)***
Tenure	0.004	0.008
	(3.58)***	(7.07)***
Elect	0.734	0.461
	(2.15)**	(3.44)***
Retail	0.190	−0.134
	(4.16)***	(4.32)***
Transport	0.410	−0.205
	(4.28)***	(5.89)***
Finance	0.380	0.050
	(6.86)***	(1.12)
Service	0.470	−0.018
	(11.25)***	(0.58)
Size25	0.516	0.433
	(13.54)***	(16.59)***
Size100	1.008	0.938
	(21.91)***	(28.37)***
Largest	1.011	1.113
	(21.26)***	(33.90)***
Family_reg	1.448	1.364
	(39.67)***	(41.86)***
Household Head	0.022	0.432
	(0.49)	(14.80)***
Ptime	−0.539	−0.563
	(16.55)***	(17.31)***
Married	−0.137	
	(3.58)***	
Child <6	−0.015	
	(0.50)	
Constant	−1.388	−1.003
	(15.55)***	(15.74)***
No. of observations	13,202	21,618

Source: IERAL database.

Note: Robust *z*-statistics in parentheses.

***Significant at the 1 percent level.

**Significant at the 5 percent level.

Table 6B.3   Probit Model with Sample Selection: Women

	Coefficient	Standard Error	Z	P > z
Employed				
Primary	−0.079102	0.0419559	−1.885	0.059
High school	0.0753084	0.0486756	1.547	0.122
College	0.4914512	0.0753675	6.521	0
Experience	0.0177675	0.0051296	3.464	0.001
Experience**2	−0.0001513	0.0001033	−1.466	0.143
Children	0.0107576	0.0137898	0.78	0.435
Child <6	−0.035998	0.0240721	−1.495	0.135
Constant	1.063247	0.1024139	10.382	0
Probability of participation				
Primary	−0.1724532	0.0177661	−9.707	0
High school	0.1627323	0.0202538	8.035	0
College	0.9491935	0.0301072	31.527	0
Experience	0.059959	0.0017564	34.138	0
Experience**2	−0.0014007	0.0000328	−42.723	0
Children	−0.1488518	0.0050678	−29.372	0
Household Head	0.8155764	0.0198255	41.138	0
Nonlabor	−0.0000649	0.0019907	−0.033	0.974
Constant	−0.4423268	0.0261064	−16.943	0
/athrho	−0.0956706	0.0812272	−1.178	0.239
Rho	−0.0953798	0.0804883		
Log likelihood	−3.61e + 07			
Censored observations	34,291			
Uncensored observations	24,235			
Wald $\chi^2(7)$	208.54			
Prob > χ^2	.0000			

Source: IERAL database.

Table 6B.4   **Probit Model with Sample Selection: Males**

	Coefficient	Standard Error	Z	P > z
Employed				
Primary	0.1316827	0.0291969	4.51	0
High school	0.3709243	0.0366284	10.127	0
College	0.6478144	0.0576389	11.239	0
Experience	0.0185666	0.0036929	5.028	0
Experience**2	−0.0001938	0.0000677	−2.861	0.004
Children	0.0075412	0.0094311	0.8	0.424
Child <6	0.0625686	0.019189	3.261	0.001
Constant	0.9992917	0.0478594	20.88	0
Probability of participation				
Primary	−0.0951961	0.0286152	−3.327	0.001
High school	0.1236844	0.0349269	3.541	0
College	0.3313181	0.0650153	5.096	0
Experience	0.1497022	0.0028334	52.836	0
Experience**2	−0.0030261	0.0000478	−63.361	0
Children	0.0727816	0.0098712	7.373	0
Household Head	0.717768	0.027059	26.526	0
Nonlabor	−0.005561	0.0027943	−1.99	0.047
Constant	−0.3758164	0.0383718	−9.794	0
/athrho	−0.5661471	0.067164	−8.429	0
Rho	−.5125241	.0495213	−0.6029607	−0.4090819
Log likelihood	−2.26e+07			
Number of observations	49,152			
Censored observations	7,994			
Uncensored observations	41,158			
Wald χ²(7)	273.54			
Prob > χ²	0.0000			

Source: IERAL database.

Appendix C
INDEC Industrial Survey: Methodology

The source of data for the preparation of the indexes of physical volume, workers employed, hours worked, and wages per worker is the Monthly Industrial Survey carried out by INDEC on a total of 1,271 industrial establishments. It is a countrywide sample selected from the third stage of the 1985 National Economic Census. The universe consists of establishments employing more than ten workers and covers all of manufacturing. Complementary data are also provided for public and private institutions.

The survey consists of two questionnaires (A and F), which are answered by the same group of establishments. Questionnaire (A) registers data on jobs, timetables, and wages, while (F) registers product information—phys-

Table 6C.1   Description of Variables Used in Manufacturing Survey Analysis (INDEC Industrial Survey)

Variable Definition	Name	Measurement Issues
Employment and hours	Employment	Log of manufacturing employment index.
	Employment_k	"Linem" lagged k periods.
	Hours per Worker	Log of hours per worker index.
	Hours per Worker_k	"Linhe" lagged k periods.
	Linhag	Log of agency hours personnel index.
Wage and labor cost	Normal Wage	Log of normal wage index (without overtime hours).
	Overtime Wage	Log of overtime hours wage index.
	Hourly Wage	Log of hourly wage index.
	Regulation	Log of labor regulations index. The index is based on severance payment (sector average tenure · sector average lay-offs) plus payroll taxes.
Product and production	Output	Log of production index.
	Output_k	"Linpf" lagged k periods.
Instrumental variables	Linpbi	Log of GDP index.
	Unemployment Aggregate Index	Log of aggregate unemployment index.
	Lni_gram	Log of economic openness index ([import + export]/GDP) by sector.
	Physical Capital Price Index	Log of physical capital price index.
	Consumer Price Index	Log of consumer price index.
	Wholesale Price Index	Log of wholesale price index.
	Dcb	Dummy equal to 1 if output growth was less than 2.7% by quarter.
	Dce	Dummy equal to 1 if output growth was between 2.7% and 4% by quarter.
	Dca	Dummy equal to 1 if output growth was greater than 4% by quarter.

Source: IERAL database.

ical amounts produced with own and third-party raw materials and dispatches in physical and monetary units—with a specifically designed questionnaire per establishment. Both questionnaires are submitted monthly.

The bulk of the forms are collected by surveyors from INDEC or from the Provincial Statistics Departments according to agreements with INDEC.

Once the survey forms are collected, they are subjected to routine editing and registry in the database; a team of analysts assesses their consistency, missing items are allocated, and then indicators are calculated.

Since the Monthly Industrial Survey began to be taken in January 1990, it was decided to publish the new series with the average of the 1990 indexes as a basis for comparison and to call this year the base year for the sake of simplicity.

Table 6C.2   **Manufacturing Survey IV-Endogenous: Product**

	Unbalanced Panel		Balanced Panel	
	Linem (1)	Linhe (2)	Linem (3)	Linhe (4)
Linsat	−0.173	−0.193	−0.121	−0.173
	(21.79)***	(36.54)***	(13.51)***	(26.51)***
Prodh	0.119	0.129	0.064	0.136
	(10.59)***	(17.58)***	(4.85)***	(13.74)***
Linpf_1	−0.043	−0.052	−0.030	−0.066
	(6.86)***	(12.26)***	(3.67)***	(10.39)***
Linsae	0.018	0.054	0.026	0.053
	(7.01)***	(32.56)***	(8.09)***	(22.07)***
Linem_1	0.815	−0.079	0.888	−0.093
	(77.04)***	(11.07)***	(59.86)***	(8.24)***
Linem_2	−0.252	0.059	−0.297	0.080
	(18.90)***	(6.52)***	(15.36)***	(5.41)***
Linem_3	0.307	−0.056	0.288	−0.038
	(28.38)***	(7.60)***	(20.13)***	(3.45)***
Linhe_1	0.047	0.208	0.027	0.270
	(3.65)***	(23.56)***	(1.57)	(20.54)***
Linhe_2	0.078	−0.013	0.007	0.017
	(6.20)***	(1.48)	(0.44)	(1.39)
Linhe_3	0.038	0.017	0.055	0.025
	(3.18)***	(2.02)**	(3.68)***	(2.18)**
t2	−0.031	0.093	−0.036	0.092
	(6.70)***	(29.15)***	(6.90)***	(23.26)***
t3	−0.032	0.087	−0.026	0.081
	(6.53)***	(26.06)***	(4.83)***	(19.67)***
t4	−0.020	0.082	−0.013	0.071
	(4.24)***	(25.73)***	(2.47)***	(17.94)***
Lnreg	−0.010	0.021	−0.008	0.017
	(1.40)	(4.48)***	(1.04)	(2.83)***
Constant	0.279	4.051	0.479	3.512
	(2.81)***	(56.12)***	(4.06)***	(37.12)***
Adjusted R^2	.90	.72	.87	.71
No. of observations	10,532			

Source: IERAL database.

Notes: Instruments are product: linsat_1; linpf_2; linpf_3; linpf_4, lipc, lipk, lipm, lni_uag, dce; dca; wages: linsat_1; linpf_2; linpf_3; linpf_4, lipc, lipk, lipm, lni_uag, dce; dca. See table 6A.5 for description of the variables. Absolute value of z-statistics in parentheses.

***Significant at the 1 percent level.

**Significant at the 5 percent level.

Table 6C.3   **Variables in the Industrial Survey**

Index	Weighting Factor
Physical production	Volume value added
Workers employed	Workers employed
Hours worked	Hours worked
Wages per worker	Total wages

Source: IREAL database.

Notes: Value added was calculated as the difference between the values of production and intermediate consumption, excluding value added tax (VAT). Workers, hours worked, and total wages correspond to paid staff employed in production processes of categories no higher than that of supervisor.

ble 6C.4   **Base Year Weights**

General Level: Total and Subdivision Wages	Value Added	Workers Employed	Hours Worked	
General level for industry	100.00	100.00	100.00	100.00
Foodstuffs, beverages, and tobacco	22.76	24.03	24.60	21.26
Textiles and leather products	9.57	16.45	16.20	13.89
Wood, wooden products, and furniture	1.65	4.97	4.71	2.20
Paper, printers, and publishers	5.04	5.10	5.26	6.00
Chemicals and petroleum-based products	29.75	10.19	10.43	12.44
Cement, glass, ceramics, and other nonmetallic minerals	3.59	5.64	5.74	5.57
Basic metals industry	4.01	7.83	7.59	10.98
Metal products, machinery, and equipment	22.81	25.11	24.82	27.19
Other manufacturing industries	0.82	0.66	0.64	0.47

urce: IREAL database.

In the sampling design, a stratified method of optimal allocation was used, making the selection probability for any given establishment vary according to branch of activity and strata.[37] The indicators for different aggregation levels up to division and general levels are obtained from the most disaggregated results, weighting them according to the percentage share in year 1986 of the variable chosen for each indicator (see table 6C.3).

The percentage share of each division during 1986[38] in the aforementioned indicators is detailed in table 6C.4.

37. The denomination of activity branch is applied to a subgroup of the third revision of the CIIU, or a body of subgroups generally coinciding with the four-digit subgroups of the third revision of the CIIU and, in a few cases, with the three-digit subgroups of the third revision of the CIIU. The strata are two: (1) establishments with between 10 and 200 paid staff, and (2) establishments with more than 200 paid staff.

38. This corresponds to the third stage of the 1985 Economic Census and refers to the universe of establishments with paid staff.

The Index of Physical Volume of Production (IVF) provides, with quarterly frequency, an approximation to the development of value added at constant prices. It is worth noting that this last measurement cannot be carried out for each year concerned, let alone each quarter, since in order to obtain it one would have to measure its components (production and intermediate consumption values) at current prices and measure the corresponding deflators. This is why the IVF is usually considered to be the best substitute.

However, it is necessary to add the caution that the relationship between value added and production is not constant. As an illustration it may be mentioned that, as from the census data, a drop in this relationship was noticed during the 1986–1993 period. This was basically due to the economy's externalization process, which stemmed from the deep structural change taking place from 1990.

Calculation Procedure

The main source of data is Form F of the Monthly Industrial Survey. This contains data on the product basket for each establishment surveyed.

In each establishment, the index of physical volume is calculated monthly, relating the value of its monthly production basket at 1986 figures to the value of the same for that year. For establishment e this would give

$$\text{IVF}_e = \left(\frac{\sum_i p_i^0 q_i^t}{\sum_i p_i^0 q_i^0} \right) \cdot 100,$$

in which sigma covers all products i selected for the establishment, and

$\mathbf{p}^0$ = the 1986 price vector

q_t^0 = the vector of monthly amounts for 1986

$\mathbf{q}_t$ = the amounts in month t

It should be mentioned that vectors $\mathbf{p}$ for prices and $\mathbf{q}$ for amounts correspond to a product basket that represents at least 80 percent of the value of production in each establishment.

In other words, the basic expression of the calculation corresponds to a Laspeyres quantity index. When new products appear, they are incorporated into the calculation, assigning them a zero amount in 1986 and establishing a $\mathbf{p}^0$ emerging from the analysis of current prices based on similar products of other establishments—or, if this is not possible, respecting the relative current price relationship for that year. Quarterly indexes are obtained as simple averages of monthly indexes.

References

Bentolila, S., and G. Saint-Paul. 1992. The macroeconomic impact of flexible labor contracts, with an application to Spain. *European Economic Research* 36: 1013–53.

Chambers, J. 1988. *Applied production analysis.* Cambridge, U.K.: Cambridge University Press.

Garcia, D. 1996. Hyperinflation, stabilization, and structure of wages in Argentina, 1989–1992. University of Chicago, Department of Economics. Mimeograph.

Hamermesh, D. 1986. The demand for workers and hours and the effects of job security policies: Theory and evidence. NBER Working Paper no. 2056. Cambridge, Mass.: National Bureau of Economic Research, October.

———. 1993. *Labor demand.* Princeton, N.J.: Princeton University Press.

Heckman, J. 1979. Sample selection bias as a specification error. *Econometrica* 47:153–61.

Leibowitz, A. 1983. Fringe benefits in employee compensation. In *The measurement of labor cost,* ed. J. Triplett. Chicago: University of Chicago Press.

Lucas, R., and P. Fallon. 1991. The impact of changes in job security regulations in India and Zimbabwe. *The World Bank Economic Review* 5 (3): 395–413.

Maloney, W. 1997. Labor market structure in LDC: Time series evidence on competing views. World Bank. Mimeograph.

———. 1998. Are LDC labor markets dualistic? World Bank. Mimeograph.

Mascollel, A., M. Whinston, and J. Green. 1995. *Microeconomic theory.* Oxford, U.K.: Oxford University Press.

Montoya, S., and L. Navarro. 1996. La demanda de trabajo en Argentina: Teoría, aplicación y evaluación de una política [Labor demand in Argentina: Theory, application, and policy evaluation]. IERAL *Estudios* 19, no. 78.

Oi, W. 1962. Labor as a quasi-fixed factor. *Journal of Political Economy* 70:538–55.

———.1983. The fixed employment costs of specialized labor. In *The measurement of labor cost,* ed. J. Triplett, 63–116. Chicago: University of Chicago Press.

Pessino, C. 1995. Determinants of labor demand in Argentina: Estimating the benefit of labor policy reform. CEMA Working Paper no. 114. Buenos Aires, Argentina: Centro de Estudios Macroeconomicos de la Argentina.

Riveros, L., and R. Paredes. 1990. Political transition and labor market reform in Chile. Santiago de Chile: World Bank. Mimeograph.

Rosenzweig, M. 1988. Labor markets in low income countries. In *Handbook of development economics,* vol. 1, ed. H. Chenery and T. N. Srinivasan, 713–62. Amsterdam: North-Holland.

Smith, R., and R. Ehrenberg. 1983. Estimating wage-fringe trade-off: Some data problems. In *The measurement of labor cost,* ed. J. Triplett, 347–67. Chicago: University of Chicago Press.

Tunalli, I. 1982. A common structure for models of double selection. Social Research Institute. University of Wisconsin, Social Research Institute. Mimeograph.

Varian, H. 1984. *Microeconomic analysis.* New York: W. W. Norton.

7

Who Benefits from Labor Market Regulations? Chile, 1960–1998

Claudio E. Montenegro and Carmen Pagés

Introduction

The economic literature has devoted considerable attention to studying the impact of labor market regulations on labor market outcomes. However, the issue of whether some subgroups of workers bear the brunt or enjoy the benefits of such regulations has been much less studied.[1] One notable exception has been the burgeoning literature studying the effect of statutory minimum wages on youth employment. Although this subject remains controversial, many studies have found negative effects of minimum wages on teenagers and young workers.[2] Less attention has been paid to the issue of whether minimum wages particularly affect women versus men or unskilled versus skilled workers. One exception is the study by Lang and Kahn (1998) for the United States, which finds that a rise in the minimum wage shifts the composition of employment in the eating and drinking sector from adults to teenagers and students. Neumark, Schweitzer, and Wascher (2000) also examine the effect of minimum wages across

Claudio E. Montenegro is an economist and statistician at the World Bank. Carmen Pagés is a senior research economist in the research department of the Inter-American Development Bank.

We thank the University of Chile for giving us permission to use their data. The views expressed in this paper are those of the authors and do not represent the opinions of the World Bank, the IADB, or their respective boards of directors.

1. One reference in this literature is the paper by Bertola, Blau, and Kahn (2002) on the effect of unions' involvement in wage setting on the relative employment of youth, women, and older individuals.

2. Among the most recent studies, Williams and Mills (2001), Partridge and Partridge (1998), and Bazen and Skourias (1997) find a negative relation between minimum wages and youth employment, while Katz and Krueger (1992), Card, Katz, and Krueger (1994), and Card and Krueger (2000) find no evidence of such an effect.

different individuals by focusing on differential impacts of workers at different points in the wage distribution. They find that although wages of low-wage workers increase, hours worked and employment levels decline, reducing earnings for these workers.

Similarly, relatively little attention has been paid to the effect that job security provisions may have on particular subgroups of the labor force. Two recent exceptions are the Organization for Economic Cooperation and Development (OECD) (1999) and Bertola, Blau, and Kahn (2002). The OECD (1999) reports negative, but not statistically significant, effects of job security provisions on youth and prime-age females. Bertola, Blau, and Kahn (2002) find evidence that job security provisions increase the employment rates of male prime-age workers relative to the employment rates of male older workers. They also find evidence that job security provisions are associated with higher employment rates for prime-age women relative to women aged fifteen to twenty-four. Instead, they do not find statistically significant effects on youth relative to prime-age employment rates for male workers or in the distribution of employment across women and men.

In this chapter, we take advantage of the unusual variance in labor market policies in Chile to examine how minimum wages and job security provisions affect different types of workers. We look at the effects of regulations on the distribution of employment by age, and also, by skill, which to our knowledge has not been examined before. To this effect, we use a sample of repeated household surveys spanning the period 1960–1998 and several measures of labor market regulations across time. We make use of cross-section and time series methods to estimate the effect that these policies have on the distribution of employment and on particular subgroups' employment rates. We are able to control for time effects that affect all workers in a similar manner, as well as demographic groups-specific effects of business cycles and labor market institutions. In addition, to assess whether our estimates are reflecting the effect of regulations instead of the effect of some unobservable correlates, we also estimate the effect of labor policy on sectors not covered by regulations. We find large and statistically significant effects on the covered sectors and no effects, or effects going in the opposite direction, on the uncovered sectors.

Our results indicate that labor market regulations are far from neutral. We find that job security provisions and minimum wages reduce the employment rates of youth and the unskilled at the benefit of older and skilled workers. We also find opposite effects of these policies on women's and men's employment shares and rates. Job security provisions tend to benefit men at the expense of women, while the reverse seems to be true for an increase in the minimum wage.

We then explore some explanations for these regularities and, while we cannot fully discriminate among all of them, we are at least able to reject some hypotheses. There is little evidence that the differential effects of job security are driven by differences in labor supply elasticities or wage adjustments across subgroups. Instead, our findings suggest that job security regulations produce unequal shifts in labor demand across groups of workers. Regarding minimum wages, our results tend to fit the predictions of the competitive model for age and skill but not for gender. Contrary to our results, the competitive model predicts higher effects of minimum wages for women because they tend to earn lower wages than men.

The rest of the chapter is organized as follows. Section 7.1 reviews the arguments that predict nonneutral effects of regulations. Section 7.2 describes the evolution of job security and minimum wage regulations in Chile. Section 7.3 describes the data used in our empirical section. Section 7.4 describes the methodology implemented to estimate the effects of regulations on the distribution of employment. Section 7.5 describes our results for both the distribution of employment and the overall effect on employment rates. Finally, section 7.6 concludes.

7.1 Why Regulations May Affect Some Workers Differently

There are a number of reasons to suspect that labor market regulations alter the distribution of employment across subgroups. In the next two subsections, we review the theoretical arguments that predict differential effects of job security provisions and minimum wages across workers of different age, skill level, and gender.

7.1.1 Job Security

Job security provisions are introduced to discourage firms from adjusting their labor forces in the face of adverse economic conditions. However, job security provisions also alter hiring decisions. In good times, firms hire fewer workers because they take into account that these workers may have to be laid off in the future, and that is costly. The overall impact of job security provisions on employment rates is undetermined because it depends on whether the negative effect on layoffs is offset by the reduction in hiring rates.[3]

Job security provisions will have differential effects across subgroups of workers if changes in legislation bring changes in hiring and layoff rates that have a larger impact on some subpopulations than on others. Lazear (1990) conjectured that an increase in job security might act as a barrier, preventing the entry of young workers into the labor market. This is because job security reduces job creation, and entry rates are especially high among youth. This argument, however, does not consider that the effect of

---

3. See Bertola (1990), Bentolila and Bertola (1990), Bertola (1991), Bentolila and Saint-Paul (1994), Hopenhayn and Rogerson (1993), and Risager and Sorensen (1997), among others, for a theoretical discussion of the effects of job security on employment rates.

lower job creation rates can be offset by lower job destruction rates—which also tend to be large among youth. Pagés and Montenegro (1999) suggest an argument whereby job security provisions may actually *increase* young workers' layoff rates. Their argument is related to the regularity that, across countries, job security is positively related with a worker's tenure. Mandatory severance payments that increase with tenure change the cost of dismissing workers with short tenures relative to workers with more seniority at the firm. In this context, it is expected that job security concentrates layoffs among youth because, other things being equal, young workers tend to have lower average tenures than older workers. If severance pay increases substantially with tenure, and this effect is important, job security simultaneously reduces entry and increases layoffs among youth, resulting in a lower employment share and lower employment rates for this group of workers. Instead, the share of older workers in employment tends to increase due to their relatively lower layoff rates.

Similar reasoning can be used to predict the effect of job security provisions across gender. To the extent that women experience higher rotation and, therefore, have lower average tenure than males at every age, high job security will tend to concentrate layoffs among women. This effect will tend to reduce their employment share relative to men. However, higher turnover rates also imply that stringent job security may be less of an issue when hiring female workers because employers expect them to quit prior to attaining high job security.[4] In this case, employers might be more willing to hire women relative to men, but also more likely to lay them off should bad times arise. The overall effect on female versus male employment rates is undetermined and remains an empirical issue.

It is tempting to extend the former argument to unskilled and skilled workers. If unskilled workers have higher rotation and lower tenures than skilled workers, the same reasoning applies. However, while higher female turnover rates may be motivated by life-cycle decisions exogenous to the employer, such exogeneity is more difficult to claim when explaining the higher rotation of unskilled workers.

The insider-outsider literature provides further arguments for why job security may have a differential effect on the employment rates of different subpopulations.[5] According to this literature, more stringent job security reduces the elasticity of wages to changes in the unemployment rate. When employed workers know their jobs are insured against demand fluctuations, they may be less willing to accept the wage adjustments necessary to reduce unemployment rates. This situation may help to create two kinds of workers: insiders, who hold their jobs and have high wages; and outsiders,

---

4. See Pagés and Montenegro (1999) for a more formal development of this argument in the context of a partial equilibrium model.
5. See, for instance, Lindbeck and Snower (1988).

who either are unemployed or hold temporary, part-time or fixed-terms jobs without job security.[6] If women, the young, and the unskilled are more likely to be outsiders, then job security (through this wage effect) will bias employment against these groups.

Finally, differences in labor supply elasticity may contribute to differential effects across subpopulations, even if job security brings a uniform change in labor demand across groups. Let us assume that an increase in job security reduces labor demand. If women, the young, and the unskilled have higher labor supply elasticity than the average worker, higher job security would bring a higher decline in employment for these workers than for other groups with a lower elasticity of labor supply.[7]

In summary, the arguments put forth in this section suggest that youth, and possibly women and the unskilled, bear the brunt of job security regulations.

7.1.2   Minimum Wages

The effect of minimum wages on employment remains a controversial topic. In the competitive model, workers are paid their marginal product, and any artificial increase in the price of labor above the marginal product therefore prices the worker out of the labor market. Conversely, models that allow for employers' monopsony power predict wages lower than the marginal product, and, thus, an increase in minimum wages can increase wages without reducing employment rates.[8] In the Lang and Kahn (1998) model of bilateral search, the effects of minimum wages also differ from the expected effects in the competitive model. In their model, minimum wages affect the quality of the pool of applicants to jobs. Higher minimum wages allow firms to get better applicants for jobs, while reducing the employment prospects of less-productive workers.

On average, youth, women, and the unskilled tend to have lower wages than older, male, or skilled workers. Therefore, because minimum wages are more likely to be binding among these workers, the competitive model predicts larger unemployment effects for the first group. In the imperfect competition model, however, the effects are less clear-cut. In principle, the magnitude and sign of the minimum wage effect will depend on how far wages are from their respective marginal products in each subpopulation. If that gap is larger in some groups than in others, an increase in minimum wages may have "competitive" effects on some groups and "noncompeti-

---

6. The insider-outsider argument requires a strong union fixing wages for new entrants. Otherwise, firms could always pay very low wages at the beginning of the employment relationship to compensate for higher wages in the future. See Bertola (1990) for an analytical study of this issue.

7. See Hamermesh (1993).

8. There are many situations that give rise to imperfect competition in the labor market, such as monopolistic power on the part of employees, incomplete information, or imperfectly mobile workers.

tive" effects on others. Given this ambiguity, the sign and magnitude of the effects become an empirical question.

7.2   Labor Market Regulations in Chile

Chile has experienced a very wide range in labor market policies, providing a privileged case scenario for analyzing the impact of regulations on labor market outcomes. We distinguish between job security provisions and statutory minimum wages.[9]

7.2.1   Job Security Provisions

Among the most interesting aspects of the Chilean experience is that, in the thirty-nine years covered by our sample, Chile has gone from a situation of dismissal at will to a rigid labor market by OECD standards (Heckman and Pagés 2000). Since their inception in 1966, job security provisions have favored full-time indefinite employment over part-time, fixed-term, or temporary contractual relationships. To this end, in case of a firm-initiated separation, labor codes regulate the following: (1) compulsory advance notice periods; (2) the causes for which a dismissal is considered justified or unjustified; and (3) severance pay related to the tenure of a worker and the cause of dismissal. While the minimum period of advance notice has always been kept constant and equal to one month, the formula for computing severance pay and the causes for just or unjust dismissal have varied widely over the years. This is the variance that we exploit in our empirical work.

Table 7.1 summarizes the changes in legislation that took place in the 1960–1998 period. From 1960 to mid-1966, firms had to provide a one-month advance notice (or pay the equivalent of one month of salary), but, otherwise, "employment at will" was the norm. In 1966, the congress approved a new law under which firms had to pay compensation equal to one month's wage per year of work to all workers dismissed without just cause. The economic needs of the firm were considered a just cause in the law, and, therefore, a worker dismissed for this reason would not qualify for severance pay. In practice, however, workers would appeal to courts, and judges tended to consider these dismissals unjustified (Romaguera, Echevarría, and González 1995). In that event, the employer could choose between paying the mandatory compensation—plus wages foregone during trial— or reinstate the worker in his or her old post. This reform substantially increased the difficulty and the cost of labor force adjustments.

After 1973, a violent change in political regime brought about a de facto liberalization. Although job security provisions were not modified in the

9. See Edwards and Cox-Edwards (2000) for an excellent summary of labor market reforms in Chile during the 1960–2000 period.

Table 7.1   **Employment Protection Provisions in Chile: 1960–1998**

Period	Prior Notice Period	Economic reasons just cause for dismissal on the law? In the courts?	Compensation for Dismissal in Case of Just Cause	Compensation for Dismissal in Case of Unjust Cause	To whom do changes apply?
1960–1966	1 month	Dismissals at will	Dismissals at will	Dismissals at will	Dismissals at will
1966–1973 Firms could not dismiss workers without a just cause	1 month	Economic reasons were just cause in the law. In practice labor courts considered most dismissals unjustified.	The law does not mandate any compensation in this case.	One month's pay per year of work at the firm plus forgone wages during trial. Trials could last at most 6 months. There is no maximum in the amount to be awarded.	All workers
1973–1978	1 month	Labor courts were much more pro-firm. Workers' claims were weaker.	Same as previous period	Same as previous period	All workers
1978–1980 (June 15, 1978): Decree 2,200	1 month	Economic needs were considered just cause.	zero	1 month per year of work, without maximum limit	Only workers hired after June 1978
1981–1984 (August 14, 1981): Law 18,018	1 month	Economic needs were considered just cause.	zero	1 month's wage per year of work with a maximum of 150 days	Only workers hired after August 1981
1984–1990 (Dec. 1984): Law 18,372	1 month	Economic needs were no longer considered just cause for dismissal.	zero	1 month's wage per year of work with a maximum of 150 days	All workers
1990–today (Nov. 1990): Firms need to justify dismissals	1 month	Firms have to justify dismissals, but economic needs are considered just cause for dismissal.	Economic reasons: 1 month's wage per year of work with a maximum of 11 months' pay	1.2–1.5 months per year of work	All workers hired after August 1981

Source: Pagés and Montenegro (1999).

law, in practice, it was more likely that judges ruled against workers, effectively reducing dismissal costs. In 1989 and 1981, successive modifications reduced the cost of dismissal under the law. In 1981, the maximum amount to be awarded to a worker dismissed without just cause was reduced to the equivalent of five months' pay. This reform substantially reduced the cost of dismissal, particularly for workers with long tenures, although it only applied to newly hired workers.

After 1984, the tide shifted and job security provisions became progressively stricter. In December of that year, the law was modified to exclude economic needs of the firm as a justified cause of dismissal. However, the maximum amount payable to a worker was kept at five months of pay. In 1990, after the return of democracy, a new labor reform still in force further increased the cost of dismissal. This law considers dismissals motivated by the economic needs of the firm justified, but employers are still liable to pay compensation equal to one month's pay per year of work, with a maximum amount of eleven months of pay. It is the responsibility of the firm to prove just cause. If such causality cannot be demonstrated, there is a 20 percent surcharge in the amount of compensation.

We summarize this variance in law and court practice by means of a job security measure derived in Pagés and Montenegro (1999).[10] This measure is computed as follows:

$$JS_t = \sum_{i=1}^{T} \beta^i \delta^{i-1}(1 - \delta)[b_{t+i} + a_t SP^{jc}_{t+i} + (1 - a_t)SP^{uc}_{t+i}],$$

where δ is the probability of remaining in a job, β is the discount factor, T is the maximum tenure that a worker can attain in a firm, b_{t+i} is the advance notice to a worker that has been i years with a firm, a_t is the probability that the economic difficulties of the firm are considered a justified cause of dismissal, SP^{jc}_{t+1} is the mandated severance pay in that event to a worker that has been i years at the firm, and finally, SP^{uc}_{t+1} denotes the payment to be awarded to a worker with tenure i in case of unjustified dismissal.

This measure computes the expected cost, at the time a worker is hired, of dismissing this worker in the future. This cost is measured in terms of monthly wages. The advantage of this measure in respect to other measures that compute the cost conditional on having achieved a certain tenure is that our job security measure captures the whole profile of severance pay at each level of tenure. The assumption is that firms evaluate future dismissal costs based on current law. Higher values of this variable indicate periods of relatively high job security, whereas lower values characterize periods in which dismissals were less costly.

---

10. See the mentioned paper and Heckman and Pagés (2000) for a complete description of the methodology used, how it is applied across time and countries, and the relative advantages and costs of using this measure versus other measures of job security.

Table 7.2   **Parameters Used to Compute the Job Security Index**

	β	δ	b	a	SP^{fc}	SP^{uc}
1960–1965	0.92	0.88	1	1	0	0
1966–1973	0.92	0.88	1	0.2	0	(1)
1974–1977	0.92	0.88	1	0.5	0	(2)
1978–1980	0.92	0.88	1	0.8	0	(2)
1981–1984	0.92	0.88	1	0.8	0	(3)
1985–1990	0.92	0.88	1	0	0	(3)
1991–	0.92	0.88	1	0.9	(4)	(5)

Notes: To compute β we use the fact that the average real interest from 1960–1998 was 8.4 percent. To compute δ we assume that the average Chilean turnover rate *without* employment protection would be similar to the U.S. rate. According to Davis and Haltiwanger (1995), average turnover rates average 12 percent a year in the United States. (1) corresponds to one month's pay per year of work augmented by three months to capture the average payments in forgone wages during trial. (2) = one month's pay per year of work without upper limit. (3) = one month's pay per year of work with an upper limit of five months' pay. (4) = one month's pay per year of work with an upper limit of eleven months' pay. (5) = 1.2 months of pay per year of work with eleven months upper limit. We assume the maximum tenure a worker can attain at a firm is twenty-five years.

Based on the legal information summarized in table 7.1 and assumptions regarding β, δ, *a*, and *T*, we obtain a measure of job security (JS). We take β to be a constant value such that the average real interest is equal to 8.4 percent, which corresponds to the average real interest rate in Chile during the 1960–1998 period. The discount rate is computed based on the assumption that without job security, turnover rates in Chile would be comparable to those observed in the United States.[11] Davis and Haltiwanger (1992) report an average annual turnover rate of 12 percent. The probability that a dismissal originated by the economic needs of the firm will be considered just depends on whether the law says so and whether labor judges rule so if workers take firms to court. For the period 1966–1984, although economic needs of the firm were considered just cause in the law, we assume *a* to be larger than zero and determined by the position taken by labor courts. Finally, we assume *T* = 25. See table 7.2 for a complete description of the parameters used in the computation of the job security measure.

The evolution of this variable over time is depicted in figure 7.1. After some years of relatively low employment protection, job security increases eightfold after the introduction of compulsory severance pay in the law. Expected dismissal costs decline markedly in 1973 and then successively in 1978 and 1981. Subsequently, employment protection increases again, but without reaching the levels attained during the late 1960s.

---

11. Although turnover rates can be measured, this measure is itself affected by labor law. Given this endogeneity, we choose instead to use the U.S. turnover rate, because it is well established that dismissal costs in the United States are very small.

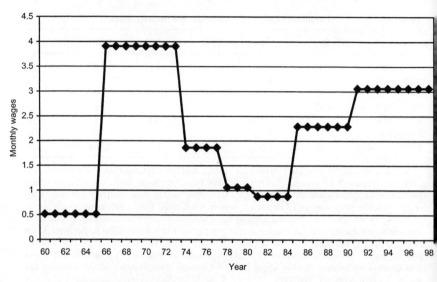

Fig. 7.1   Job security (in monthly wages)
Source: Pagés and Montenegro (1999).

7.2.2   Minimum Wages

Columns (2) and (3) in table 7.3 present the hourly real minimum wage in 1998 pesos; these indices were constructed using Chile's Central Bank Bulletins.[12] It is interesting to note that since 1989 there has been a lower minimum wage for workers eighteen years old or younger. This wage has been fixed at a level between 15 and 20 percent of the adult wage. Figure 7.2 summarizes the evolution of the minimum wage in relation to the average wage for teen and adult workers. The figure shows that minimum wages are much higher, relative to each group average rate, for teens than for adult workers. It also shows that the level of teen minimum wages has been quite volatile relative to the average wage.

Between 1960 and 1998, adult real minimum wages increased by 186 percent and teen minimum wages by 104 percent. However, because average ages rose more than the increase in the minimum wages, minimum wages lost ground in relation to the average wage. Despite this long-term secular trend, Chile experienced a wide range of fluctuations in minimum wages, both in its rate of growth (in real terms) and in its level in relation to the average wage. During the 1960s, the real value of minimum wages was held constant, but since real wages increased, the ratio of the minimum to the average real wage declined. In the early 1970s, minimum wages increased

12. Per hour minimum wages are constructed as monthly minimum wages divided by 4.2 · 40 hours.

Table 7.3　　**Basic Statistics of the Sample**

Year	Job Security Index (1)	Minimum Wage Age Under 18 (2)	Minimum Wage Age Over 18 (3)	Bargaining Index Original (4)	Bargaining Index Smoothed (5)	By Sex Male (6)	By Sex Female (7)	By Skill Level Low (8)	By Skill Level High (9)	By Age Group 15–24 (10)	By Age Group 25–49 (11)	By Age Group 50–65 (12)	GDP Deviation from Trend (%) (13)	Employment Rate (%) (14)	Wage Employment Rate (%) (15)	Self-Employment Rate (%) (16)
1960	0.5199	119	119	3.3333	3.3333	302	152	157	475	133	283	306	-0.86	52.5	39.8	12.7
1961	0.5199	114	114	3.3333	3.3333	370	179	171	554	164	331	435	-1.41	52.2	41.1	11.1
1962	0.5199	126	126	3.3333	3.3333	373	203	181	615	162	361	418	-1.37	53.2	41.2	11.9
1963	0.5199	109	109	3.3333	3.3333	376	206	n.a.	311	219	342	395	0.20	53.0	41.4	11.5
1964	0.5199	107	107	3.3333	3.3333	268	160	n.a.	230	133	272	296	-2.15	52.9	42.3	10.6
1965	0.5199	114	114	3.3333	3.3333	n.a.	n.a.	n.a.	n.a.	n.a.	n.a.	n.a.	-5.23	54.4	43.3	11.2
1966	3.9090	118	118	3.3333	3.3333	380	211	187	591	179	376	434	1.50	53.0	42.2	10.8
1967	3.9090	116	116	3.3333	3.34724	427	268	222	648	217	420	539	1.50	54.0	43.2	10.8
1968	3.9090	111	111	3.3333	3.39543	466	278	224	699	251	450	502	1.79	53.2	41.9	11.4
1969	3.9090	107	107	3.3333	3.46403	475	279	231	709	218	470	560	2.79	52.4	41.2	11.2
1970	3.9090	133	133	3.66667	3.53596	549	351	256	804	248	536	693	2.97	52.3	41.4	10.9
1971	3.9090	183	183	3.66667	3.57675	689	437	302	957	307	660	779	9.67	53.7	42.1	11.5
1972	3.9090	195	195	3.66667	3.52856	712	457	342	929	359	698	729	7.28	52.7	41.3	11.4
1973	3.9090	108	108	3.66667	3.40525	525	332	279	671	280	512	553	0.37	51.4	39.6	11.8
1974	1.8642	204	204	3	3.26140	435	310	275	561	255	436	496	0.12	49.0	37.1	11.8
1975	1.8642	245	245	3	3.12419	376	277	225	483	214	376	420	-14.58	45.0	34.7	10.4
1976	1.8642	259	259	3	3.01390	486	352	249	635	280	474	542	-12.67	45.5	34.5	11.2
1977	1.8642	269	269	3	2.88227	692	512	320	953	357	696	786	-5.01	48.3	38.1	10.1
1978	1.0599	346	346		2.62090	868	517	360	1,090	400	799	1,072	0.87	48.0	37.1	10.9
1979	1.0599	345	345	2.66667	2.27455	913	640	432	1,150	496	904	1,009	6.66	47.8	36.8	10.9
1980	1.0599	354	354	1.33333	1.90434	890	611	424	1,120	476	881	932	11.83	47.4	36.6	10.7
1981	0.8772	334	334	1.33333	1.53353	1,057	799	510	1,338	590	1,099	1,016	15.64	50.9	39.3	11.6
1982	0.8772	365	365	1.33333	1.25825	1,235	852	508	1,499	618	1,206	1,295	-1.15	41.8	33.0	8.8
1983	0.8772	276	276	1	1.13070	842	622	345	1,056	416	872	721	-6.79	43.5	34.4	9.1
1984	0.8772	243	243	1	1.06209	843	573	355	1,028	371	845	780	-4.19	46.1	35.8	10.3

(continued)

Table 7.3 (continued)

Year	Minimum Wage Job Security Index (1)	Age Under 18 (2)	Age Over 18 (3)	Bargaining Index Original (4)	Smoothed (5)	Average Wage By Sex Male (6)	Female (7)	By Skill Level Low (8)	High (9)	By Age Group 15–24 (10)	25–49 (11)	50–65 (12)	GDP Deviation from Trend (%) (13)	Employment Rate (%) (14)	Wage Employment Rate (%) (15)	Self-Employment Rate (%) (16)
1985	2.2915	220	220	1	1.01390	699	480	312	808	323	683	725	-6.19	46.4	36.6	9.8
1986	2.2915	215	215	1	1	653	471	301	742	314	634	731	-5.35	47.0	37.3	9.7
1987	2.2915	199	199	1	1	796	539	288	932	355	764	907	-4.05	50.1	39.5	10.5
1988	2.2915	222	222	1	1.02781	766	542	316	902	376	751	799	-2.93	50.9	38.6	12.2
1989	2.2915	293	340	1	1.12419	869	679	376	981	434	868	973	0.41	53.1	41.6	11.5
1990	2.2915	298	346	1	1.26140	1,003	682	390	1,074	462	960	1,011	-2.83	52.0	40.5	11.4
1991	3.0598	278	327	1.66667	1.40525	971	694	401	1,046	470	951	949	-2.47	53.2	41.2	11.9
1992	3.0598	293	340	1.66667	1.54247	904	726	455	998	503	914	900	1.47	55.7	43.6	12.1
1993	3.0598	294	341	1.66667	1.63885	1,072	832	496	1,158	627	1,054	1,093	0.98	55.9	44.0	11.9
1994	3.0598	294	342	1.66667	1.66667	1,141	840	535	1,194	624	1,101	1,163	-1.22	55.4	42.5	12.9
1995	3.0598	302	351	1.66667	1.66667	1,230	919	566	1,310	657	1,215	1,199	0.81	55.5	42.8	12.7
1996	3.0598	279	324	1.66667	1.66667	1,329	1,047	621	1,412	725	1,283	1,465	1.59	55.8	43.7	12.0
1997	3.0598	248	333	1.66667	1.66667	1,392	1,100	613	1,505	775	1,380	1,335	2.79	56.7	44.1	12.6
1998	3.0598	243	341	1.66667	1.66667	1,356	1,136	759	1,427	792	1,325	1,500	0.70	56.8	43.6	13.2

Source: Authors' calculations (see data section) and Banco Central de Chile (2001).

Note: n.a. = not available.

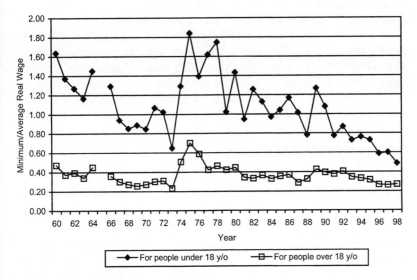

Fig. 7.2   Minimum to average real wages
Source: Authors' calculations (see data section).

substantially, surpassing the growth rate of average wages. In consequence, the ratio of the minimum to the average real wage increased sharply in that period. From 1975 to 1980, minimum wages lost ground relative to the average wage. After the return to democracy in 1990, real minimum wages increased steadily, but they continued declining relative to the average wage. The decline was particularly sharp for the teen group, whose minimum to average real wage rate fell from 1.80 in 1975 to 0.50 in 1998. It is interesting to note that while there are several studies in the Chilean case that suggest that the minimum wage is binding, others such as Bravo and Vial (1997) suggest that it is not.[13]

7.3   Data

The household surveys used in this study were obtained from the University of Chile's economics department. The economics department's survey monitors the employment-unemployment status in the metropolitan area of Santiago, Chile four times a year. Unfortunately, only the surveys taken in June of each year contain information about wages and other employment status variables. Therefore, these are the surveys used in this study. The format of the survey and the definition of the variables have been kept constant since 1957, when the survey started, and so the infor-

13. See, for instance, Castañeda (1983), Paredes and Riveros (1989), Montenegro (2002), and Cowan et al. (2003). An excellent review of the impact of minimum wages in the case of the United States can be found in Kosters (1996). A more recent survey on the international evidence of minimum wages can be found in Dowrick and Quiggin (2003).

mation contained in them is comparable across years.[14] During the period from 1960 to 1998, the surveys interviewed between 10,000 and 16,000 people and around 3,700 and 5,400 active labor force participants each year. During this period, the metropolitan area of Santiago, Chile represented about one-third of Chile's total population and a higher proportion of gross domestic product (GDP).[15] The data set is formed by stacked cross-sectional data sets, which means that individuals are not followed over time. The only restriction applied to our sample is that the people included in the estimates must be at least fifteen years old and no older than sixty-five.

We merge labor policy and macrovariables taken at the annual frequency with our individual-level annual data. We include the job security index and the minimum wage data described in Section 2. We also include a measure of wage bargaining to control for changes in union activity that can be correlated to our variables and to employment. While perhaps the best measure of the influence of unions on wage determination is union coverage, that is, the share of workers whose wages are affected by collective bargaining, a time series of this nature does not exist in Chile. Because union membership is also not available for all years covered in our sample, we measure unions' bargaining power by means of an index that reflects the degree of centralization of collective bargaining constructed by Edwards and Cox-Edwards (2000). This variable takes values from 1 (total decentralization) to 4 (total centralization). The use of this measure is based on the observation that union coverage tends to be larger in countries where collective bargaining is centralized. Finally, we include as a measure of economic activity deviations, with respect to potential GDP. To obtain this variable, we use GDP data from the World Bank and apply a Hodrick-Prescott filter to obtain trend GDP.

Table 7.3 summarizes some basic statistics of our sample, by year. The first three columns display the value of the job security index and the real minimum wage for people eighteen or younger and for adult workers. The next two columns summarize the index of bargaining (column [4] presents the original index, and column [5] presents the smoothed index). The evolution of these variables over time is depicted in figure 7.3. Higher values of this measure, like those registered from 1960 to 1970, reflect periods of higher union centralization.[16] The next seven columns summarize the average hourly wage broken down by sex (columns [6] and [7]); skill level (col-

14. In this study we use data from 1960 on, because the previous years (1957–1959) do not have reliable data.
15. According to the 1992 census, the metropolitan area accounted for 39 percent of the total population.
16. Although not shown in the results, we checked the robustness of our results using the strikes index constructed by Edwards and Cox-Edwards (2000) instead of the centralization index. The results were invariant to different specifications.

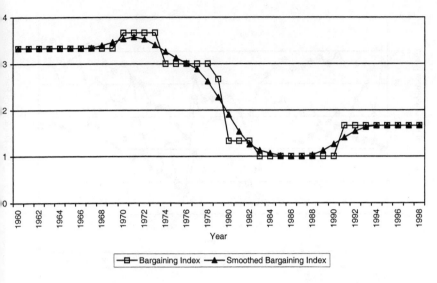

Fig. 7.3   Bargaining index
Source: Edwards and Cox-Edwards (2000).
Notes: Bargaining index measures the degree of centralization of wage bargaining. It takes values from 1 to 4. Higher values indicate higher centralization of collective bargaining.

umns [8] and [9]); and age group (columns [10], [11] and [12]). Column (13) summarizes the deviation of the GDP from its potential or trend value. Finally, columns (14), (15), and (16) present the percentage of total people employed, the percentage of people that work for someone else (wage employment), and the percentage of people self-employed as a proportion of total population between fifteen and sixty-five years old. These three rates are also depicted in figure 7.4, which, jointly with figure 7.5 (which shows GDP deviations from its trend), illustrates the violent swings experienced by the Chilean economy during the 1960–1998 period, and, in particular, between 1970 and 1985.[17] Some additional indicators describing the performance of the Chilean economy are summarized in table 7.4.

7.4   Methodology

To estimate the differential impact of labor market regulations across subpopulations we assume that the employment status of an individual is characterized by

17. Chilean economic performance has been extensively documented by Edwards and Cox-Edwards (1991, 2000), de la Cuadra and Hachette (1992), Wisecarver (1992), Bosworth, Dornbusch, and Laban (1994), Hudson (1994), Soto (1995), and Cortazar and Vial (1998).

Fig. 7.4   Employment and dependent rates
Source: Authors' calculations (see data section).

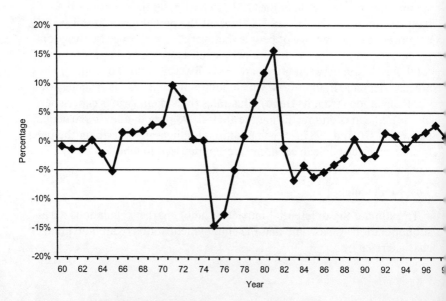

Fig. 7.5   GDP deviation from trend
Source: Authors' calculations (see data section).

Table 7.4   General Economic Indicators: Chile 1960–1998

Series Name	GDP per Capita Growth (annual %)	Inflation, Consumer Prices (annual %)	National Unemployment, Total (% of total labor force)	National Unemployment, Female (% of female labor force)	National Unemployment, Youth Total (% of total labor force ages 15–24)	Gran Santiago Unemployment, total (% of total labor force)	Gini Coefficient
1960	n.a.	n.a.	n.a.	n.a.	n.a.	8.0	42.5
1961	1.5	7.7	n.a.	n.a.	n.a.	7.1	45.2
1962	2.7	14.0	n.a.	n.a.	n.a.	5.7	45.5
1963	3.6	44.1	n.a.	n.a.	n.a.	5.2	n.a.
1964	0.3	46.0	n.a.	n.a.	n.a.	4.9	n.a.
1965	-1.8	28.8	n.a.	n.a.	n.a.	5.0	n.a.
1966	7.6	23.1	n.a.	n.a.	n.a.	6.0	45.2
1967	1.5	18.8	n.a.	n.a.	n.a.	5.9	45.8
1968	1.6	26.3	n.a.	n.a.	n.a.	6.4	48.1
1969	1.5	30.4	n.a.	n.a.	n.a.	7.1	48.0
1970	0.2	32.5	n.a.	n.a.	n.a.	7.0	47.5
1971	7.1	20.0	n.a.	n.a.	n.a.	5.2	47.7
1972	-2.5	74.8	n.a.	n.a.	n.a.	3.7	43.1
1973	-6.5	361.5	n.a.	n.a.	n.a.	3.1	44.1
1974	0.8	504.7	n.a.	n.a.	n.a.	10.3	40.7
1975	-12.8	374.7	n.a.	n.a.	n.a.	16.1	41.1
1976	1.8	211.8	n.a.	n.a.	n.a.	18.0	47.2
1977	7.1	91.9	n.a.	n.a.	n.a.	13.0	48.4
1978	5.9	40.1	n.a.	n.a.	n.a.	12.8	49.8
1979	7.1	33.4	n.a.	n.a.	n.a.	12.5	49.4

(*continued*)

Table 7.4   (continued)

Series Name	GDP per Capita Growth (annual %)	Inflation, Consumer Prices (annual %)	National Unemployment, Total (% of total labor force)	National Unemployment, Female (% of female labor force)	National Unemployment, Youth Total (% of total labor force ages 15–24)	Gran Santiago Unemployment, total (% of total labor force)	Gini Coefficient
1980	6.5	35.1	10.4	10.0	20.8	11.7	49.1
1981	3.2	19.7	11.3	9.9	21.5	9.0	47.3
1982	–11.7	9.9	19.6	18.3	30.5	23.2	51.2
1983	–5.3	27.3	14.6	14.7	24.7	22.7	52.7
1984	6.3	19.9	13.9	n.a.	25.2	18.4	54.2
1985	5.4	29.5	12.1	13.4	22.7	16.2	51.5
1986	3.9	20.6	8.8	9.7	17.3	15.4	48.7
1987	4.9	19.9	7.9	9.3	n.a.	13.5	57.6
1988	5.5	14.7	6.3	7.8	14.3	11.2	53.7
1989	8.7	17.0	5.3	6.1	13.2	9.3	50.8
1990	1.9	26.0	5.7	5.7	13.1	9.7	53.9
1991	6.2	21.8	5.3	5.8	12.7	8.3	52.4
1992	10.4	15.4	4.4	5.6	10.9	6.0	47.4
1993	5.2	12.7	4.5	5.1	11.0	6.4	45.4
1994	4.0	11.4	5.9	6.8	13.2	6.3	45.9
1995	8.9	8.2	4.7	5.3	11.5	6.1	46.3
1996	5.7	7.4	5.4	6.7	12.8	7.2	45.4
1997	6.0	6.1	5.3	6.6	13.0	6.7	n.a.
1998	2.5	5.1	7.2	7.6	16.7	6.9	n.a.

Sources: World Bank World Development Indicators Data Base and Gini coefficient from background data, Montenegro (1998).

Note: n.a. = not available.

(1) $$y^*_{ijt} = \mathbf{X}_{it} \cdot \boldsymbol{\beta}_1 + \mathbf{X}'_{it} \cdot \mathbf{Z}_t \cdot \boldsymbol{\beta}_2 + \gamma_t + \varepsilon_{ijt},$$

where

$$y_{ijt} = 1 \text{ if } y^*_{ijt} > 0$$

$$y_{ijt} = 0 \text{ otherwise,}$$

and y^*_{ijt} is an unobservable variable that determines whether an individual i, in subpopulation j at time t will be employed or not, and y_{ijt} is the observable employment status of this individual. This variable takes a value of 1 if the individual is employed and zero if it is not. In some specifications, we focus only on wage employment (self-employment), and, therefore, this variable takes the value of 1 if an individual is wage (self-) employed and zero otherwise. The sample corresponds to the whole population between fifteen and sixty-five years old. In addition, $\mathbf{X}_{it}$ is a vector of variables that summarizes the personal characteristics of the individual i at time t, $\mathbf{Z}_t$ is a vector of variables that vary with t, γ_t is a year fixed effect, and ε_{ijt} is an error term. Among the personal characteristics, we include age, gender, skill level, number of children, and number of children interacted with gender. In some specifications, we also include age interacted with gender and age interacted with skill to capture differential effects of age across gender and skill groups. Given the number of observations available, we divided the data into three age groups (fifteen–twenty-four, twenty-five–fifty, and fifty-one–sixty-five) and two skill levels (nine years of education or less and more than nine years). Adding the skill and the age groups to the gender division, we have twelve different subpopulations, $j = 1, \ldots 12$

In the vector of aggregate variables, $\mathbf{Z}_t$, we include the index of job security, deviations from GDP trend, and the union centralization variable (all in logarithms). We also include the minimum wage index (also in logarithms), but we let it change for individuals eighteen and younger. By construction, the vector of coefficients on the interaction of $\mathbf{X}_{it}$ and $\mathbf{Z}_t$, $\boldsymbol{\beta}_2$, gives the sign of the *differential* effect. In addition, assuming that the Prob($y^*_{ijt} > 0$) is distributed as a standard normal distribution, the size of the marginal differential effect is given by $\phi(\cdot)\mathbf{X}_{it}\boldsymbol{\beta}_2$, where $\phi(\cdot)$ is the normal density function.

Although specification (1) is a reduced form equation, in some cases it will be useful to add a measure of wages. To construct this variable, w_{ijt}, we assign to all workers $i \in j, j = 1, \ldots, 12$, at period t, the average wage of all employed workers in group j at period t.

Our original intention was to estimate

(1') $$y^*_{ijt} = \mathbf{X}_{it} \cdot \boldsymbol{\beta}_1 + \mathbf{X}'_{it} \cdot \mathbf{Z}_t \cdot \boldsymbol{\beta}_2 + \mathbf{Z}_t \cdot \boldsymbol{\beta}_3 + \varepsilon_{ijt}.$$

With such a specification we could recover the *total* marginal effect of a labor policy on subpopulation j as $\phi(\cdot)(\mathbf{X}_{it}\boldsymbol{\beta}_2 + \boldsymbol{\beta}_3)$. However, despite finding robust estimates for the differential effects, our estimates for the level effect (β_3) proved to be extremely sensitive to the set of variables included in Z_t, suggesting that our time variables did not properly account for the time variation of the series. In view of these results, we opted for estimating specification (1). This estimation still allows us to compute marginal effects, but the total effects are now absorbed by the constant term. Therefore, we can measure the impact of labor market regulations on the *distribution* but not on the *level* of employment. Nonetheless, estimating equation (1) instead of (1′) offers substantial advantages from an econometrics point of view. It allows controlling for macroeconomic trends and cycles as well as policy changes and other unobservable variables that are common to all individuals and that could be correlated to employment and labor market regulations and bias the estimation. In addition to the inclusion of time variables, we minimize the risk of omitted variable biases and spurious correlations in four additional ways.

First, by using individual data from a series of stacked household surveys to estimate specification (1), we can control for changes in the relative size of the population of each group and changes in fertility, which, if omitted, could bias our estimates. Second, by controlling for effects of changes in the business cycle (using GDP deviations from its trend) across individuals (that is, including $X'_{it} \cdot Z_t$, where Z_t contains the business-cycle variable), we can partially control for changes in policy and institutions that are endogenous to changes in relative employment. This is because such movements are likely to be correlated with changes in the business cycle. Third, by estimating the differential effect of policy while including contemporary labor market policies and institutions, we make sure that our measured effects are not biased by the correlation between these variables and the distribution of employment. Finally, by comparing the estimated effects on the probability of wage employment (which is covered by labor policy) with the results on self-employment (which is not covered) once appropriate pull-push factors from and to self-employment are accounted for, we assess whether we are capturing the effect of policy, or, instead, the effect of some unobservable correlate with group-specific employment.

7.5   Empirical Results

7.5.1   The Effect of Job Security on the Distribution of Employment

Our results indicate that job security provisions have a differential impact across demographic subgroups. In table 7.5, we report the results of estimating our empirical specification (1) assuming normality in the distribution of errors. The reported numbers correspond to the coefficients of the probit model, while the marginal effects for selected subpopulations of workers are reported in table 7.6. The t-tests, reported next to the coefficients, are robust to the presence of heteroskedasticity of unknown kind

Table 7.5   The Effect of Job Security and Minimum Wages, Probit Results

Dependent Variable	(1) Employed β	t-test	(2) Employed β	t-test	(3) Wage Employment β	t-test	(4) Self-Employment β	t-test	(5) Employed β	t-test	(6) Employed β	t-test	(7) Employed β	t-test
Dummy young	-0.8954	-104.2	0.4921	2.6	0.9189	5.0	-0.4202	-1.4	-1.1703	-6.1	-0.9651	-4.9	1.2757	9.1
Dummy old	-0.6709	-66.8	-1.6509	-7.3	-1.6967	-7.5	0.4176	1.7	-2.0996	-9.1	-2.1226	-9.0	-1.4101	-8.6
Dummy women	-0.5461	-66.7	-2.0260	-12.2	-1.8595	-11.6	-0.3632	-1.7	-2.4413	-14.2	-1.9622	-11.3	-2.7873	-22.7
Dummy unskilled	0.0007	0.1	1.8635	10.9	1.8843	11.2	-0.3281	-1.5	1.4867	8.6	1.8356	10.3	2.2867	18.1
Children per father	0.1570	45.0	0.1569	44.6	0.0594	25.7	0.0273	11.3	0.1152	32.0	0.1152	31.5	0.1562	44.6
Children per mother	-0.3931	-93.9	-0.3921	-92.7	-0.3147	-86.9	-0.0196	-5.4	-0.3179	-70.1	-0.3160	-68.5	-0.3919	-93.1
Interacted with logarithm of job security														
Dummy young	-0.0935	-10.8	-0.1112	-12.7	-0.0826	-9.7	-0.0161	-1.2	-0.0913	-5.6	-0.1163	-6.7		
Dummy old	0.0124	1.2	0.0196	1.8	0.0292	2.7	0.0173	1.5	0.0253	1.2	0.0123	0.6		
Dummy women	-0.0468	-6.1	-0.0266	-3.4	-0.0021	-0.3	0.0267	2.7	-0.546	-4.5	-0.0873	-6.8		
Dummy unskilled	-0.0334	-4.2	-0.0563	-7.0	-0.0733	-9.3	0.0344	3.4	-0.0382	-3.3	-0.0596	-4.8		
Dummy young · dummy women									0.0835	4.7	0.1033	5.4		
Dummy old · dummy women									-0.0035	-0.2	0.0064	0.3		
Dummy young · dummy unskilled									-0.0381	-2.2	-0.0164	-0.9		
Dummy old · dummy unskilled									0.0033	0.2	0.0146	0.6		
Interacted with logarithm of minimum wage														
Dummy young			-0.1406	-8.2	-0.1557	-9.3	-0.0366	-1.3	-0.0111	-0.6	-0.0215	-1.2	-0.2129	-16.0
Dummy old			0.0913	4.4	0.0911	4.4	-0.0286	-1.3	0.1301	6.2	0.1301	6.1	0.0715	4.6
Dummy women			0.1455	9.6	0.1551	10.7	-0.0299	-1.5	0.1677	10.8	0.1303	8.2	0.2097	18.0
Dummy unskilled			-0.1811	-11.6	-0.1811	-11.9	0.0304	1.5	-0.1587	-10.1	-0.1810	-11.2	-0.2196	-18.3
Dummy young · dummy women									0.0248	11.0	0.0223	9.8		
Dummy old · dummy women									-0.0035	-1.3	-0.0019	-0.7		
Dummy young · dummy unskilled									0.0393	17.4	0.0346	15.2		
Dummy old · dummy unskilled									0.0133	4.9	0.0145	5.3		

(continued)

Table 7.5 (continued)

Dependent Variable	(1) Employed β	(1) t-test	(2) Employed β	(2) t-test	(3) Wage Employment β	(3) t-test	(4) Self-Employment β	(4) t-test	(5) Employed β	(5) t-test	(6) Employed β	(6) t-test	(7) Employed β	(7) t-test
Interacted with union centralization														
Dummy young			0.1320	8.2	0.1422	9.2	0.0800	3.0	−0.3006	−13.1	−0.2785	−11.9		
Dummy old			0.0272	1.4	0.0241	1.2	0.0152	0.7	−0.0966	−3.2	−0.0854	−2.8		
Dummy women			−0.0968	−6.8	−0.1222	−8.9	0.0802	4.2	−0.2494	−13.5	−0.2177	−11.6		
Dummy unskilled			0.0756	5.2	0.0480	3.4	0.0358	1.9	−0.0843	−4.6	−0.0599	−3.3		
Dummy young · dummy women							0.2957	12.3	0.2712	10.9				
Dummy old · dummy women							0.1530	5.2	0.1359	4.5				
Dummy young · dummy unskilled									0.3485	14.1	0.3306	13.0		
Dummy old · dummy unskilled									0.0265	0.9	0.0249	0.8		
Interacted with GDP deviation from path														
Dummy young			−0.0852	−0.9	0.2102	2.2	0.0208	0.1	−0.2928	−1.7	−0.3618	−2.1		
Dummy old			−0.3872	−3.1	−0.2161	−1.7	−0.0041	0.0	−0.7902	−3.4	−0.8027	−3.4		
Dummy women			−0.4917	−5.5	−0.3108	−3.6	0.3153	2.7	−0.8047	−6.0	−0.8958	−6.7		
Dummy unskilled			0.4345	4.8	0.3467	3.9	0.0777	0.7	0.4079	3.2	0.4152	3.2		
Dummy young · dummy women									0.3973	2.0	0.5022	2.5		
Dummy old · dummy women									0.3863	1.6	0.4749	1.9		
Dummy young · dummy unskilled									−0.2455	−1.3	−0.1571	−0.8		
Dummy old · dummy unskilled									0.1912	0.8	0.1761	0.7		
Logarithm of hourly wage											0.1520	16.9		
No. of observations	303,945		303,945		303,945		303,945		303,945		295,318		303,945	
Pseudo R^2	0.196		0.168		0.11		0.08		0.211		0.210		0.197	

Notes: Besides the control variables mentioned in the table, all specifications include yearly dummies (not reported). Standard errors are robust to the presence of heteroskedasticity. The employed dummy variable is defined as 1 if the person is employed and zero otherwise (unemployed or inactive). The wage employment dummy variable is defined as 1 if the person is a dependent employee and zero otherwise (independent, unemployed, or inactive). The self-employed dummy variable is defined as 1 if the person works as an independent worker and zero otherwise (dependent, unemployed, or inactive).

Table 7.6   Marginal and Total Effects of Labor Market Regulations

	Marginal Effects		Total Effects	
	Job Security (1)	Minimum Wage (2)	Job Security (3)	Minimum Wage (4)
Men, 15–25, unskilled	−0.066 [0.000]	−0.0516 [0.000]	−0.049	−0.0516
Men, 15–25, skilled	−0.0351 [0.000]	−0.004 [0.52]	−0.0181	−0.004
Men, 26–50, unskilled	−0.008 [0.001]	−0.036 [0.000]	0.009	−0.036
Men, 51–65, unskilled	−0.0035 [0.620]	−0.005 [0.54]	0.0135	−0.005
Men, 51–65, skilled	0.008 [0.22]	0.045 [0.000]	0.025	0.045
Unskilled	−0.0343 [0.000]	−0.012 [0.09]	−0.0173	−0.012
Skilled	−0.015 [0.000]	0.044 [0.000]	0.002	0.044
Women	−0.0278 [0.000]	0.0463 [0.000]	−0.0108	0.0463
Men	−0.0151 [0.000]	−0.017 [0.000]	0.0019	−0.017
Young	−0.0394 [0.000]	0.0134 [0.08]	−0.0224	0.0134
Older	−0.008 [0.14]	0.0596 [0.0000]	0.009	0.0596

Note: P-values of the test that the marginal effects are equal to zero are reported in square brackets.

using the White (1980) method. Most coefficients on the individual characteristic variables exhibit the expected patterns: Female and older workers are less likely to be employed than prime-age (twenty-six–fifty) men. Additionally, the number of children per father increases the probability of being employed, and the number of children per mother decreases the probability of being employed. Instead, the coefficients on the variable young and unskilled change signs across specifications.

In column (1) we report the results of interacting the job security measure with dummies for age (young and older), gender (women), and skill level. A negative (positive) sign indicates that periods of more stringent job security provisions are associated with a decline (increase) in the probability of employment of a particular subpopulation, relative to the omitted category. We find strong age effects. The coefficient on the young-job security interaction is negative and statistically significant, while the coefficient on the older-job security interaction is positive although not statistically significant. Our results suggest that high job security tends to bias the distribution of employment against younger workers. We also find significant effects across the skill divide. The coefficient on the unskilled-job security interaction is negative and statistically significant, suggesting that job security provisions reduce the probability of employment of unskilled workers relative to skilled ones. Last, the coefficient on the female-job security interaction suggests a negative effect of job security on the probability of employment of women relative to men.

Column (2) shows the results once we control for the evolution of the minimum wage, union activity, and deviations of GDP with respect to its trend, as well as interaction of these variables with age, gender, and skill dummies. The only difference with respect to column (2) is that the coefficient on the dummy for older workers is now somewhat larger and statistically significant at the 10 percent level, suggesting that job security provisions benefit the employment prospects of older workers relative to prime-age ones. In columns (3) and (4) we report the coefficients resulting from estimating the same specification for wage employment and self-employment separately. Our results are encouraging because they suggest that our findings are driven by policy changes instead of by some unobservable factors correlated with labor policy and employment. The signs and magnitudes of the coefficients for total and wage employment are very similar, except for the coefficients on women. Instead, for self-employment, the coefficients are either not statistically different from zero or going in the opposite direction than for wage employment. This is the case with the coefficients on the gender and unskilled variables, which suggests that more stringent job security regulations increase the probability that women and the unskilled are employed in the self-employment sector relative to men and the skilled.

Column (5) exhibits the results once we allow for further interactions between age, skill, and gender groups. With this finer level of disaggregation we can examine whether the impact of job security is the same across young men and young women, or across young skilled and unskilled workers. These additional variables not only provide a more complete description of the effects of job security on the distribution of employment, but also help to infer the channels through which job security affects that distribution. The coefficients for these additional interaction variables are all statistically significant, and a test for their joint significance strongly rejects the null hypothesis of all the coefficients being zero.

The estimates in column (5) contain some interesting additional information relative to the estimates in columns (1) to (4). We find that an increase in job security tends to reduce the employment probabilities of young men relative to those of young women. However, we also find that this effect is reversed at older ages. Thus, job security provisions seemingly reduce the probabilities of employment of middle-aged and older women relative to those of men in that same age group. Our estimates also suggest that an increase in job security provisions reduces the probability of employment of both skilled and unskilled youth, but the effect is larger for unskilled youth.

Finally, column (6) reports the results of estimating the same specification as in column (5), but in addition controls by the average wage of each subpopulation group in period t. Controlling for the wage level of each group allows us to assess whether some of the observed effects are driven by differences in wage adjustment across subpopulations. Yet the results should be taken with caution because some wage movements may be endogenous to the probability of employment. Overall we find that holding wages constant does not affect our main results. The only coefficient that changes size and significance is the interaction between the young unskilled and job security. Holding wages constant reduces the coefficient and the significance of the effect on unskilled youth (relative to more skilled youth). Instead, most of the other coefficients become larger (in absolute value) than the ones reported in column (5). This suggests that more stringent regulations are partly paid by workers in the form of lower wages.

The marginal effects reported in table 7.6 correspond to the specification reported in column (5) of table 7.5. They are computed for different combinations of the dummies for gender, age, and skill.

The results indicate that the largest adverse effects are on unskilled youth. However, the effects on skilled youth are also substantial; an increase of 100 percent in job security reduces the probability of employment by 0.066 points (or 6.6 percentage points) for unskilled youth and by 0.0351 for skilled youth workers, relative to prime-age skilled workers. The results in table 7.6 suggest that skilled prime age male workers gain relative to all other groups with the exception of older workers. In addition, the marginal effects suggest that job security policies tend to have more adverse effects on women than on men.

In light of the different theories described in section 7.2, how do we explain the results presented previously? Although we cannot totally discriminate among different theories, we are at least able to reject some hypotheses. The fact that most of our results remain unchanged when wages are included suggests that the differential effects presented previously cannot be explained by differences in the elasticity of labor supply across demographic groups. The only exception is the larger effect on young unskilled workers, which seems to be driven by a higher labor supply elasticity of this group.[18] Our results also suggest that these differential effects cannot be explained by insider-outsider theories, because in that case the effect would also be through wages. Instead, our results suggest that the differ-

18. Cowan et al. (2003) find that, in Chile, seemingly high transitions between schooling and the labor market lead to a very elastic labor supply for the young unskilled.

ential effects on employment are demand driven: Changes in job security provisions bring about changes in hiring and firing rates that selectively affect different types of workers.

A barrier-of-entry effect can explain the negative impact of job security on the employment rates of young workers relative to other demographic groups. However, it cannot account for the estimated differences in impact between young women and young men. One possible way to explain these findings is to consider differences in turnover rates across groups. As discussed in section 7.2, a higher exogenous turnover rate can bring about two effects. On the one hand, workers with a higher propensity to rotate have lower average tenures and, therefore, are more likely to be laid off in bad times. On the other hand, higher rotation reduces expected severance payments and, therefore, increases the incentives to hire these workers. Consequently, higher rotation among women can explain why job security provisions affect young women less than young men. It can also explain why middle-aged and older women benefit less from job security than men of the same age.

Differences among turnover rates could also partially explain the results for skilled and unskilled workers. Higher rotation among the unskilled would imply lower tenure rates and higher probabilities of dismissal for middle-aged and older unskilled workers, relative to more skilled ones. This is consistent with the deleterious effect of job security on the employment rates of middle-aged and older unskilled workers, relative to skilled ones. Of course, the higher turnover rates among unskilled workers are less likely to be exogenous to the decisions of employers than female turnover rates. In consequence, a complete discussion of this effect requires a model that explains why turnover rates are different in the first place. This model does not seem to be able to explain why the effect on employment appears more negative on the unskilled than on skilled youth, but as we have seen, this effect seems to be driven by a relatively more inelastic labor supply of the latter.

7.5.2   Distribution of the Effect of Minimum Wages

Table 7.5 also reports the results of interacting personal characteristic dummies with the evolution of minimum wages over time. An increase in the statutory wage has qualitative effects on the distribution of employment across age and skill that are similar to the qualitative effects of stricter job security provisions. To account for contemporary employment policies and economic conditions, we include measures of union activity, job security provisions, and GDP deviations, interacted with demographic dummies in all specifications in columns (2) to (6), but not in column (7). As in other studies for developed countries, the results in column (7) suggest that an increase in the minimum wage reduces the employment prospects of young workers relative to older ones. We also find a negative effect on the unskilled. Instead, our results also indicate that minimum wage hikes may increase the probability of employment for women relative to men.

Controlling for the subgroup effects of contemporary changes in policy and the business cycle does not alter the results reported in column (7).[19] The comparison between the results obtained from the wage employment and the self-employment specifications (columns [3] and [4]) is also encouraging. As with the coefficients associated with job security provisions, we find that the coefficients on wage employment are very similar to the ones obtained for total employment, while the coefficients on self-employment are not statistically significant. All in all, these results suggest that the effects we are capturing are indeed associated with changes in policy rather than with some unobservable correlate of employment across demographic groups.

In column (5) we present our results once we allow for differential effects across age-skill and age-gender categories and control for contemporaneous changes in policy and economic conditions. As in column (7), we find a negative effect of minimum wages on the employment probabilities of unskilled workers. The effect of minimum wages is negative for young unskilled workers and not statistically significant for young skilled ones. Instead, higher minimum wages tend to shift employment toward older workers. Finally, we find that women, and in particular the young, tend to benefit from minimum wage policies.

The former specification assumes that the effect of raising the minimum wage is unrelated to the level of the going wage. However, it is plausible that the effect may be positively related to the distance between the statutory and the going wage. To account for this possibility, we include average wages, computed as described in section 7.5.[20] The results reported in column (6) indicate that controlling for the time evolution of the average wage of subpopulation $j = 1, \ldots, 12$ does not alter the results reported in columns (3) to (5).

Column (2) in table 7.6 summarizes the marginal effects, which give an estimate of the magnitude of the effects on different demographic groups. A 10 percent rise in the minimum wage reduces the employment probability of young unskilled workers by 0.005 (0.5 percentage points). While the effects on youth skilled workers are insignificant, the results indicate an adverse effect on prime-age unskilled workers. This is an interesting result in the context of a literature that almost exclusively focuses on the effects on youth workers.

While most of our findings are consistent with the competitive model,

---

19. See column (3) as well.

20. Including such variables is tantamount to including a set of noncoverage adjusted, demographic group-specific Kaitz ratios. However, we are not imposing the constraint that the coefficient on the minimum wage is the same as the coefficient on the group-specific average wage.

some are difficult to explain with this paradigm. For instance, this model cannot explain why minimum wages tend to shift employment toward women. One possible interpretation is that while men are able to obtain wages that are close to the competitive ones, women's wages are below their marginal products. This would be consistent with the systematic wage gaps found between observationally identical men and women and with the asymmetric gender effects of minimum wages. If wage gaps are explained by imperfect competition in female labor markets, employers are supply constrained when hiring women. Therefore, an increase in minimum wages reduces the demand for male workers and increases the supply of labor for women.

7.5.3   Total Effects

In our previous results, all the estimated coefficients measured the effects of labor regulations on each particular subpopulation *relative* to the omitted category, but they did not provide information on whether the employment probabilities of the different subgroups increased or declined in absolute terms after changes in policy. In this section, we attempt to gauge the total effects of labor market policies on the probability of employment by estimating their effect on the aggregate employment rates of prime-age skilled men (the omitted category in the specifications reported in table 7.5). To do so, we estimate the following error correction specification:

$$(2) \quad \Delta N_t = c - \lambda(N_{t-1} - N^*) + B_1(y_t - y_t^*) + B_2 \Delta \log(W_t) + B_{3\Lambda} \Delta N_{\tau - L} + \varepsilon_t,$$

$$(3) \quad \text{where } N_\tau^* = \gamma_0 + \gamma_1 \log(\mathrm{JS}_t) + \gamma_2 \log(\mathrm{MW}_t) + \gamma_3 \log(\mathrm{Union}_t),$$

and where N_t denotes the employment rate—that is, the employment to population ratio—of prime-age male skilled workers in period t, N^* denotes long-run equilibrium employment, $y_t - y_t^*$ denotes GDP deviations from its trend (in logs), W_t denotes average wages for prime-age skilled male workers, JS_t denotes the measure of job security, MW_t denotes minimum wages, Union_t denotes the index of wage bargaining, and L is the length of the maximum lag. In expression (2), employment changes in function of previous period deviations from long-run equilibrium employment, GDP deviations from its trend, and changes in wages and short-run dynamics. Expression (3) assumes that, in the long run, employment rates are a function of labor market policies and the structure of wage bargaining.

Using aggregate time series techniques to estimate the effect of policies on the reference group allows us to model short- and long-run employment dynamics. The first step in the estimation of expression (2) and (3) is to test whether the variables are stationary. The first panel in table 7.7 reports the results of testing for the presence of unit roots using the Augmented Dickey-Fuller test (ADF). The tests are specified with three lags. In those cases in which the plot of the series indicated the presence of a time trend,

ble 7.7   **Unit Root and Cointegration Tests**

ames of the Series	Symbol	Specification	ADF Test Statistic	5% Critical Value
DP deviation from its trend	$y - y^*$	Constant	–4.8412	–2.9472
age growth	$\Delta(\log W)$	Constant	–3.8514	–2.9705
garithm minimum wage	L(Minwage)	Trend	–1.4709	–3.5426
garithm job security	L(JS)	Constant	–2.43	–2.9472
garithm union centralization	L(Union)	Trend	–2.7568	–3.5426
gged employment rate	N_{t-1}	Constant	–1.6736	–2.9472
rst diff. lagged emp. rate	ΔN_{t-1}	Constant	–3.0433	–2.9499
ange in log minimum wage	ΔL(Minwage)	Constant	–2.5591	–2.9499
ange in log job security	ΔL(Index)	Constant	–2.655	–2.9499
ange in log union	ΔL(Union)	Constant	–2.3443	–2.9499

kelihood Ratio	5% Critical Value	Hypothesized Number of Cointegrating Equations
Johansen Cointegration Test: Series: N_{t-1} *L(Minwage) L(JS) L(Union)*		
8.64	53.12	None***
.35	34.91	At most 1***
.64	19.96	At most 2**
6	9.24	At most 3

*Denotes rejection of the hypothesis at the 1 percent significance level.
Denotes rejection of the hypothesis at the 5 percent significance level.

we included a constant and a time trend in the specification; in the other cases, we included only a constant. While we can reject the unit root hypothesis for GDP deviations from its trend and for changes in hourly wages, we cannot reject nonstationarity for the lagged employment rate, the logarithm of minimum wages, the logarithm of the job security index, and the logarithm of union centralization. However, ADF tests on the first differences of these four series indicate that the hypothesis that these series are integrated of order one, $I(1)$, is not rejected.

Given the nonstationarity of the employment rate, expression (2) is well defined only if lagged employment deviations, with respect to the long-run equilibrium rate, are stationary. This is equivalent to saying that the series N_t^* has to cointegrate with N_{t-1}. The second panel in table 7.7 reports the results of the Johansen cointegration test between N^* and N_{t-1}. The likelihood ratio test indicates the presence of three cointegrating equations, indicating that the error correction model is well defined.

Table 7.8 presents the results of estimating the error correction model (ECM) once expression (3) has been substituted into expression (2). We use the results of the Akaike's Information Criteria (AIC) test to determine the optimal length of the lagged endogenous variable and determine that

Table 7.8   Level Effects on Male Prime-Age Employment

Independent Variable	(1)	(2)
N_{t-1}	−0.63	−0.66
	(−3.05)	(−3.24)
Deviations GDP$_t$	0.08	0.10
	(1.21)	(1.48)
$\Delta \log Wt$	—	0.018
		(0.84)
Log(JS)	0.011	0.015
	(1.80)	(2.23)
Log(Minwage)	−0.01	−0.014
	(−0.93)	(−1.13)
Log(Union)	0.03	0.029
	(1.54)	(1.45)
Constant	0.61	0.651
	(3.55)	(3.92)
ΔN_{t-1}	0.277	0.239
	(1.48)	(1.30)
No. of observations	37	35
Adj. R^2	0.16	0.23
Long-term effect of JS	0.017	0.023
Long-term effect of Minwage	0	0

Note: *t*-statistics shown in parentheses.

$L = 1$. We estimate the ECM with and without wages to see whether introducing wages alters our results, and we find the results to be very similar in both cases. Essentially, we find that job security provisions increase the long-run equilibrium rate of prime-age skilled male employment. This is not totally surprising. As mentioned in section 7.2, job security provisions increase the cost of dismissing workers with long tenure relative to the costs of dismissing less-tenured workers, reducing the layoff rate of the first relative to the layoff rate of the latter. Because prime-age skilled workers tend to have longer tenures than other, younger, less-skilled workers, job security provisions reduce the layoff rates of prime-age skilled workers relative to the layoff rate of other demographic groups. The positive sign in the ECM suggests that this effect on the layoff rate more than compensates for the negative effect of job security on employment creation. Instead, we do not reject the hypothesis that an increase in the minimum wage does not affect the employment rate of prime-age, skilled male workers, regardless of whether we control for the evolution of wages.

The estimated effect of job security provisions and minimum wages on the employment rate can be used to infer the total effect of these regulations on the employment probabilities of other demographic groups. In order to do so, the coefficients on job security provisions and minimum wages, reported in table 7.8, should be divided by (minus) the coefficient on the lagged employment variable to obtain the coefficients in expression (3). They reflect the magnitude of the long-run effect of regulations on prime-age skilled male employment. The third and fourth columns of table 7.6 present our estimates for the total effects. They are obtained by adding the marginal effect reported in the first and second columns of table 7.6 to the long-run elasticities obtained from specification (1) in table 7.8.[21]

The total effects reported in columns (3) and (4) suggest that job security provisions not only shift the distribution of employment toward older and skilled workers, but also increase their employment rates. Instead, more stringent job security provisions reduce the employment rates of young workers. Moreover, job security provisions reduce employment opportunities for women while increasing those of men. The magnitudes of these estimated effects are substantial. According to them, the 1990 labor reform, which increased our measure of job security by about one-third, reduced the employment rates of young unskilled male workers by 1.6 percentage points of the population.

We also find nonneutral effects of minimum wage spikes. Our estimates suggest that a 10 percent increase in minimum wages reduces the probability of employment for young unskilled male workers by 0.51 percentage points. Lastly, we find that a 10 percent increase in the minimum wage raises the employment rates of women by 0.46 percentage points.

7.6 Conclusions

The effect of regulations on employment is far from neutral across demographic subgroups. Paradoxically, job security and minimum wage regulations appear to be detrimental to the very workers that they are supposed to help. Our results suggest that both minimum wages and job security regulations reduce the employment opportunities of the young and the unskilled—and particularly unskilled youth—while promoting the employment rates of skilled and older workers. We have also found indications that job security regulations may force some workers, particularly women and the unskilled, out of wage employment and into self-employment. This paper has only examined the effects on employment. A complete analysis of who benefits and who loses from regulations would require examining the effects of regulations on the distribution of wages and benefits as well.

There is an ongoing debate on whether raising minimum wages and job security provisions have any effects on aggregate employment rates. However, even if researchers concluded that job security provisions or minimum wages do not have an effect in the aggregate, it is important to care-

---

21. The long-run effect of job security on the employment rates of middle-age skilled workers is computed as 0.011 divided by 0.63, which is equal to 0.017.

fully consider these distributional effects when evaluating their desirability. At best, these policies will help some disadvantaged workers, although perhaps at the expense of other poor workers. At worse, they distribute jobs from less advantaged to better-off workers.

References

Banco Central de Chile. 2001. *Indicadores económicos y sociales de Chile: 1960–2000*. [*Chile: Economic and social indicators, 1960–2000*]. Santiago, Chile: Banco Central de Chile.

Bazen, S., and N. Skourias. 1997. Is there a negative effect of minimum wages on youth unemployment in France? *European Economic Review* 41 (3–5): 723–32.

Bentolila, S., and G. Bertola. 1990. Firing costs and labour demand: How bad is eurosclerosis? *Review of Economic Studies* 57:381–402.

Bentolila, S., and G. Saint-Paul. 1994. A model of labor demand with linear adjustment costs. *Labour Economics* (1):303–26.

Bertola, G. 1990. Job security, employment and wages. *European Economic Review* 34:851–86.

———. 1991. Labor turnover costs and average labor demand. NBER Working Paper no. 3866. Cambridge, Mass.: National Bureau of Economic Research, October.

Bertola, G., F. Blau, and L. Kahn. 2002. Labor market institutions and demographic employment patterns. NBER Working Paper no. 9043. Cambridge, Mass.: National Bureau of Economic Research, July.

Bosworth, B., R. Dornbusch, and R. Laban, eds. 1994. *The Chilean economy, policy lessons and challenges*. Washington, D.C.: Brookings Institution.

Bravo, D., and J. Vial. 1997. La fijación del salario mínimo en Chile: Elementos para una discusión. [The minimum wage setting in Chile: Topics for a discussion]. *Colección de Estudios CIEPLAN* 43:117–51.

Card, D., L. F. Katz, and A. B. Krueger. 1994. Employment effects of minimum wages: Panel data on state minimum wages laws; Comment. *Industrial and Labor Relations Review* 47 (3): 487–97.

Card, D., and A. B. Krueger. 2000. Minimum wages and employment: A case study of the fast food industry in New Jersey and Pennsylvania; Reply. *American Economic Review* 90:1397–420.

Castañeda, T. 1983. Salarios mínimos y empleo en el Gran Santiago: 1978 y 1981. [Minimum wages and employment in Great Santiago: 1978 and 1981]. *Cuadernos de Economía* 20 (61): 279–93.

Cortazar, R., and J. Vial. 1998. *Construyendo opciones: Propuestas economicas y sociales para el cambio de siglo.* [*Building options: Economic and social proposals for the new century*]. Santiago, Chile: CIEPLAN and DOMEN.

Cowan, K., A. Micco, A. Mizala, C. Pagés, and P. Romaguera. 2003. Un diagnóstico del desempleo en Chile. [An analysis of the Chilean unemployment]. Inter-American Development Bank and la Universidad de Chile, Departamento Ingeniería Aplicada. Mimeograph.

Davis, S., and J. Haltiwanger. 1992. Gross job creation, gross job destruction, and employment reallocation. *Quarterly Journal of Economics* 107 (3): 819–63.

de la Cuadra, S., and D. Hachette. 1992. The Chilean trade liberalization experience. Editorial de Econômia y Administracion. Santiago, Chile: Universidad de Chile.

Dowrick, S., and J. Quiggin. 2003. A survey of the literature on minimum wages. Australian National University and the University of Queensland. Mimeograph.

Edwards, S., and A. Cox-Edwards. 1991. *Monetarism and liberalization: The Chilean experiment,* 2nd ed. Chicago: University of Chicago Press.

———. 2000. Economic reforms and labour markets: Policy issues and lessons from Chile. *Economic Policy* 15 (30): 181–230.

Hamermesh, D. S. 1993. *Labor demand.* Princeton, N.J.: Princeton University Press.

Heckman, J., and C. Pagés. 2000. The cost of job security regulation: Evidence from Latin American labor markets. *Economía* 1 (1): 147–51.

Hopenhayn, H., and R. Rogerson. 1993. Job turnover and policy evaluation: A general equilibrium analysis. *Journal of Political Economy* 101 (5): 915–38.

Hudson, R. 1994. *Chile: A country study.* Washington, D.C.: Library of Congress.

Katz, L., and A. B. Krueger. 1992. The effect of the minimum wage on the fast-food industry. *Industrial and Labor Relations Review* 46 (1): 6–21.

Kosters, M. H., ed. 1996. *Effects of the minimum wage on employment.* Washington, D.C.: AEI Press.

Lang, K., and S. Kahn. 1998. The effect of minimum-wage laws on the distribution of employment: Theory and evidence. *Journal of Public Economics* 69:67–82.

Lazear, E. 1990. Job security provisions and employment. *Quarterly Journal of Economics* 105 (3): 699–726.

Lindbeck, A., and D. J. Snower. 1988. *The insider-outsider theory of employment and unemployment.* Cambridge: MIT Press.

Montenegro, C. E. 1998. The structure of wages in Chile, 1960–1996: An application of quantile regression. *Estudios de Economía* 25 (1): 71–98.

———. 2002. Unemployment, job security, and minimum wages in Chile: 1960–2001. World Bank. Mimeograph.

Newmark, D., M. Schweitzer, and W. Wascher. 2000. The effects of minimum wages throughout the wage distribution. NBER Working Paper no. 7519. Cambridge, Mass.: National Bureau of Economic Research, February.

Organization for Economic Cooperation and Development. 1999. Employment protection and labour market performance. *Economic Outlook* 65 (1): 49–132. Paris: OECD.

Pagés, C., and C. E. Montenegro. 1999. Job security and the age composition of employment: Evidence from Chile. IADB Research Department Working Paper no. 398. Washington, D.C.: Inter-American Development Bank.

Paredes, R., and L. Riveros. 1989. Sesgo de selección y el efecto de los salarios mínimos. [Selection bias and the effect of minimum wages]. *Cuadernos de Economía* 26 (79): 367–83.

Partridge, M., and J. Partridge. 1998. Are teen unemployment rates influenced by state minimum wage laws? *Growth and Change* 29 (4): 359–82.

Risager, O., and J. R. Sorensen. 1997. On the effects of firing costs when investment is endogenous: An extension of a model by Bertola. *European Economic Review* 41 (7): 1343–53.

Romaguera, P., C. Echevarría, and P. González. 1995. Chile. In *Reforming the labor market in a liberalized economy,* ed. G. Márquez, 79–135. Washington, D.C.: Inter-American Development Bank; Baltimore, Md.: Johns Hopkins University Press.

Soto, R. 1995. Trade liberalization in Chile: Lessons for hemispheric integration. In *NAFTA and trade liberalization in the Americas,* ed. E. L. Echeverri-Carroll,

231–60. Austin, Tex.: University of Texas, Graduate School of Business, Bureau of Business Research.

White, H. 1980. A heteroskedasticity-consistent covariance matrix estimator and a direct test for heteroskedasticity. *Econometrica* 48:817–38.

Williams, N., and J. Mills. 2001. The minimum wage and teenage employment: Evidence from time series. *Applied Economics* 33 (3): 285–300.

Wisecarver, D. ed. 1992. *El modelo económico Chileno. [The Chilean economic model]*. Santiago, Chile: Centro Internacional para el Desarrollo Económico (CINDE), Instituto de Economía de la Pontificia Universidad Católica de Chile.

Unions and Employment in Uruguay

Adriana Cassoni, Steven G. Allen, and
Gaston J. Labadie

8.1 Introduction

The subject of how unions affect employment adjustment generates strong opinions. The prevailing view among many economists and policy analysts is that unions prevent labor market forces from operating effectively. Unions take a hard line in bargaining that prevents wages from falling, no matter how high unemployment has gotten. They resist attempts by management to streamline production and introduce new technology. They stand in the way of team-based production by clinging to outdated job descriptions and occupational jurisdictions. They insist on advance notice and severance pay arrangements that make it extremely costly to reduce employment.

Au contraire, say union supporters. Centralized negotiations provide a framework for wage adjustments to take place more rapidly than they would in a world where all bargaining is one-on-one. Unions see the handwriting of technological change on the wall as clearly as management and also see that management does not think about implementation of new technology in the workplace until installation time. Joint committees provide a framework to make changes more productive by getting full input from employees on how to redesign jobs and processes. Rules on job security admittedly make downsizing more difficult, but other parts of union agreements make labor markets more effective by encouraging long-term employment relationships and investments in firm-specific skills.

Adriana Cassoni is professor of economics at the University of Uruguay. Steven G. Allen is professor of economics and business management at North Carolina State University, and a research associate of the National Bureau of Economic Research. Gaston J. Labadie is dean of the faculty of administration and social sciences at the Universidad ORT Uruguay.

In Latin America, the prevailing wisdom is that the former view is closest to the truth. Even though most markets have been liberalized, the labor market has been what Sebastian Edwards, the former chief economist for Latin America and the Caribbean at the World Bank, calls "the forgotten sector" (1995, 277). Welfare losses come from three main sources: (1) wages set above market clearing levels, (2) lost output and wages from strikes, and (3) rent-seeking activities such as support for protectionism and state ownership of industry. Edwards (1995, 286) argues

> Reforming legislation governing labor-management relations in Latin America is an important unfinished part of the recent structural reforms. In general, a modern and flexible legislation is characterized by incentives to resolve conflicts quickly and fairly. This requires clear rules of the game, modern institutions, an efficient judiciary, and a system in which both parties incur costs if the conflict becomes protracted. In most countries, however, the current situation is far from that: there are asymmetric costs for unions and employers that, in fact, do not penalize delaying agreements.

Given these very strong views, one would think that there would be a massive research literature on how unions affect employment adjustment to changes in wages and output. Think again. Globally this subject has received little attention, and in Latin America it has received virtually no attention. In the case of Uruguay, some theoretical work has been developed by Rama (1993a,b, 1994), while there is some recent empirical research (Allen, Cassoni, and Labadie 1994, 1996; Cassoni, Labadie, and Allen 1995). Although there are numerous studies making union-nonunion comparisons for particular countries at particular time periods, they have generally concentrated on wage gains and wage gaps (Blanchflower 1984; Freeman and Medoff 1984; Hirsch and Addison 1986; Lewis 1986, 1990) while employment differentials have been somehow neglected.[1] Regarding elasticities of substitution between labor and capital and among different types of labor, research has been even less prolific. In the United States, it has been found that they are much lower in union than nonunion establishments (Allen 1986; Freeman and Medoff 1982). Further, Boal and Pencavel (1994) found some evidence suggesting the underlying production function is different, depending on the sector's being unionized or not. In the United Kingdom, Blanchflower, Millward, and Oswald (1991) analyzed the impact of unionism on the path of employment growth, finding significant differences, although their result has been criticized for not being robust (Machin and Wadhwani 1991).

Another line of research that has been followed is that related to the influence of unions on the costs of adjusting the level of employment (Burgess 1988, 1989; Burgess and Dolado 1989; Hamermesh 1993; and Lockwood and Manning 1989 are examples). Finally, it has been found that

1. An extensive survey can be found in Pencavel (1991) and Booth (1995).

workers in the United States have lower quit rates (Freeman 1980), higher layoff rates in the private sector (Medoff 1979), and lower layoff rates in the public sector (Allen 1988), relative to nonunion workers.

Although all of the previous papers do illuminate one component or another of the effects of unions on wages and/or employment, they do not address the bottom-line questions. For the same establishment or individual with and without union status, does employment adjustment to changes in wages and output vary when the firm is unionized and when it is not? How long does it take to complete the adjustment in these two settings?

This chapter examines these issues directly, using evidence from manufacturing industries in Uruguay from 1975 through 1997. Uruguay is well suited for such a study because the economy has gone through a series of regime changes. A military government took over in 1973 and stayed in power through 1984. During and after this regime, there were significant changes in labor and trade policy that will allow us to identify the impact of these policies on labor demand parameters.

Collective bargaining was proscribed during the military regime, but labor unions regained the right to bargain collectively with the return of democracy in 1985. As part of its anti-inflation policy, the national government played a significant role in negotiations. Since then, legal regulations of work—which constitute public-order individual rights and therefore cannot be resigned under any circumstance—can be superseded by collective agreements. They can go beyond these restrictions, increasing (but not decreasing) the benefits that workers have in the area of minimum wages, working conditions, job security, and employee benefits. Tripartite negotiations took place at the industry level through "Wage Councils," allowing wage adjustment to vary by industry. If an agreement met the government's anti-inflation targets, then it would apply to all firms in the industry—even those with nonunion work forces—once the agreement was officially endorsed.

The government stopped participating in this system in 1991. Some bargaining is still conducted through industry-wide Wage Councils, but increasingly it is being done at the company level. As a result there are three different bargaining regimes that can be examined in this study: (1) before 1985, when bargaining was banned; (2) 1985–1991, when there was tripartite bargaining; and (3) 1992 to the present, when the government did not participate in bargaining.

Although the primary focus of this study is on the impact of these regime changes, the role of changes in trade policy cannot be ignored. Taxes on traditional exports were substantially cut in the mid-1970s, and some initial steps were taken toward lowering import barriers, steps that halted during the global recession of 1982. After a temporary increase in 1985, tariffs were gradually decreased starting in 1986. By the end of 1993, the highest tariff was 20 percent. At the same time, there were reductions in nontariff barriers, elimination of some sectoral privileges, and reductions of export subsidies. Accompanying these unilateral policy changes was the creation of the Southern Cone Common Market (MERCOSUR) in 1991. By 1995 a great number of Uruguayan products could be exchanged with MERCOSUR members (Argentina, Brazil, and Paraguay) without any tariff. As a consequence, there was a sizable increase in the volume of both exports and imports that, as will be shown in the following, had a significant impact on union behavior.

This study looks at two types of evidence. The primary focus is on estimating labor demand parameters under different bargaining regimes. Using standard techniques, the elasticity of employment to wages and output is estimated and compared across policy regimes. The model is then extended to examine the dynamics of the adjustment process. A dynamic labor demand model is estimated, letting the length of the lag vary with the extent of openness and with the percentage of workers covered by collective bargaining. Additionally, the odds of layoffs and turnover resulting in unemployment are examined to further understand the microprocesses by which unions have an effect on the adjustment process.

The chapter begins with background on the economy, the labor market, and collective bargaining in Uruguay (section 8.2), followed by a brief theoretical overview on unions and labor demand (section 8.3) and a description of the data (section 8.4). The labor demand results (section 8.5) indicate that a structural shift in the labor demand function occurred at about the same time as the return of collective bargaining. Wages are weakly exogenous to employment through 1984, but weak exogeneity is rejected afterward. The elasticity of employment to wages and output fell by more than 50 percent after 1984. There is no change in the amount of time needed for the market to adjust, as indicated by the coefficient of lagged employment. Results from a bargaining model show that union wage demands are highly sensitive to the openness of the economy. These patterns are further analyzed in the dynamic and in the mobility and unemployment results (section 8.6). The concluding section summarizes and assesses these findings.

8.2 Background on Uruguay

8.2.1 Macroeconomic and Labor Market Conditions

Traditionally, the Uruguayan economy has been subjected to a series of global and regional shocks, particularly those coming from Argentina (Favaro and Sapelli 1986), and this has continued during the last twenty-five years. At the beginning of the sample period (1975), the Uruguayan economy was still recovering from the oil shock of 1973 and the ensuing global recession. These conditions were exacerbated by the European Community's decision in 1974 to stop importing beef. Unemployment was above 10 percent in 1976–1978 (see figure 8.1).

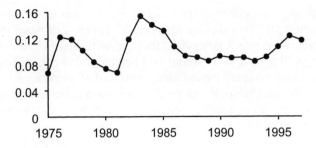

Fig. 8.1   Unemployment rate

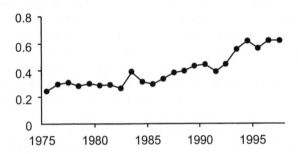

Fig. 8.2   Openness

The economy recovered in the late 1970s in response to a series of steps to liberalize financial markets and promote exports. Growth accelerated when the government adopted a preannounced schedule of monthly devaluations, with the rate of devaluation declining gradually over time. Global economic conditions, however, were not kind to this schedule; by the early 1980s, the net result was a highly overvalued currency that had to be devalued in the global recession of 1982. Unemployment had fallen to 7 percent by 1980–1981 but increased to 15 percent in 1983 and stayed above 10 percent through 1986. The gross domestic product (GDP) decreased by 15.9 percent in three years.

By 1988 Uruguay had successfully recovered from this deep recession. The economy grew 8.9 percent in 1986 and 7.9 percent in 1987, supported by an increase in demand from Brazil, which was implementing a stabilization plan (Plan Cruzado). Exports grew and the public deficit decreased to 4.2 percent of GDP in 1987. In 1989, however, the favorable regional environment changed, the public sector deficit grew to 7 percent, and a stabilization plan was implemented by the new government (elected in 1990). These policies have resulted in a sustained, steady decline in inflation from 129 percent in 1991 to 15 percent in 1997.

During the 1990s, together with the regional shocks, a domestic stabilization plan and an increase in the openness of the economy had significant effects on macro and industry performance (as shown in figure 8.2, where openness is defined as the ratio of imports plus exports to GDP). The Argentinian "Plan de Convertibilidad," imposed in April 1991, improved relative competitiveness for Uruguay, with exports to that country increasing 130 percent in 1991 and 74.3 percent in 1992. Expanded trade with Argentina, no small part of which consisted of tourism, and a deterioration of the real exchange rate meant that growth in the service sector far outstripped growth in goods production. Within the latter, the actual impact depended upon exposure to external competition.

Besides the domestic stabilization plan, during the period 1990–1992 a series of trade policy measures consolidated the opening of the economy that had started in the mid-1970s during the military regime, but that was discontinued in the early 1980s. In 1982, the highest tariff was 55 percent and after a temporary increase in 1985, a gradual decrease started in 1986, which ended with a maximum tariff of 40 percent in 1989. The pace of these changes accelerated in 1991–1993. By 1993 the highest tariff was 20 percent. Together with these reductions, many nontariff barriers and sectoral privileges (like those given to the automotive industry) were removed, and export subsidies were reduced (de Brun and Labadie 1997).

These unilateral trade policy changes were accompanied by a series of regional tariff reductions as a consequence of the creation of the MERCOSUR. By 1995 a great number of Uruguayan products could circulate among its members, Argentina, Brazil, Paraguay, and Uruguay, without any tariff. The exceptions to the Common External Tariff are subject to a calendar that was established in December 1994. Economic conditions deteriorated after 1994, largely in response to high unemployment generated by the "tequila effect" in Argentina. Unemployment increased to 11 percent in 1995 and 12 percent in 1996–1997. Unemployment held steady at around 9 percent between 1987 and 1994.

The manufacturing sector has been severely affected by all of these factors. Its share in total output has gone down from 25–27 percent at the beginning of the period to 18 percent in 1997. Employment in manufacturing grew until 1989, but it has decreased significantly since then, to unprecedented levels. This decrease reflects the impact of trade liberalization as some establishments cut back production, whereas others raised productivity to compete.

8.2.2 Collective Bargaining

When Parliament was closed by the military in June 1973, the union confederation Convención National de Trabajadores (CNT) launched a general strike. The government reacted by banning union activity and giving employers the right to dismiss anyone who did not return to work. Many union leaders were jailed; the others went into hiding or exile. The union movement began a political comeback in the early 1980s, with a series of demonstrations and general strikes organized by a new confederation, but there was no bargaining until the return of democracy in 1985.[2]

In the absence of unions, employers were relatively free to adjust wages and employment. Wage increases were limited to lagged inflation. This policy, along with high unemployment, was accompanied by a 49 percent decrease in real wages from 1973 through 1984. Employment adjustment also became more flexible. Interview evidence compiled by Handelman (1981) indicates that after the ban on unions, many employers used the opportunity to get rid of trade union officials and excess employees. Dismissals of public-sector workers also were permitted by law between 1977 and 1984 (Gillespie 1991). On the supply side, there was a surge in emigration precipitated by political repression and high unemployment. Taking into account all of these factors, it is clear that the Uruguayan labor market was exposed to strong competitive forces during the ban on unions.

Starting in 1985, Uruguay's unique system of Wage Councils was reinstituted. Collective bargaining in the private sector in Uruguay had traditionally operated mainly through a system of trilateral Wage Councils that set minimum wages by industry and labor category. Wage levels were adjusted three times per year through 1990; since then, accumulated inflation since the last adjustment had to pass a specific threshold for wages to be adjusted. Often, the Wage Councils agreed to a formula that would be in effect for sixteen to twenty-four months, allowing adjustment to take place without a formal meeting. If the government delegates gave their consent to the wage agreement, it applied to the entire sector, not just to the firms and unions involved in the bargaining. Government approval usually required keeping wage increases in line with official inflation targets. Direct negotiation between the union and the firm was also practiced, especially in manufacturing. In 1991 there was a significant change in the structure of negotiations. The government stopped participating in bargaining, and the terms of the contract became binding only on those firms and unions that were actually represented in the negotiation. Currently, Wage Councils meet in only a few sectors and the result, to be shown in the following, has been a sharp drop in union density in the private sector.

Much bargaining now takes place at the company level. Membership is not compulsory and union dues are voluntary in most cases. In 1988, only three years after unions were legal again, the single National Central Union reported a total of 188,000 members and five years later, in 1993, 177,000 members, belonging to seventeen federations and 359 unions. In 1996, there were 164,000 members in the National Central Union, but some unions are not members of it. By 1993, 54 percent of the membership

---

2. For a general description of labor market institutions in Uruguay, see Cassoni, Labadie, and Allen (1995).

belonged to the public sector, which has had the smallest drop in its number of affiliates.

The role that collective agreements play in introducing rigidities could be very significant, varying in degree depending on union density and the specific clauses of the contracts, which include wage adjustments, minimum wages by job categories, length of work day, holidays, job rotation and stability, recognition of union officers, "peace clauses" that preclude strikes under certain circumstances, and other work-related conditions. Although there are no explicit clauses regarding severance pay or restrictions to hiring new workers, unions have generally imposed extra costs to employment adjustment. In some sectors, additional compensation beyond that dictated by the labor contract has been a common practice, while in others strikes have worked as a means of getting additional severance pay. Government intervention in collective bargaining is only provided in the case of Wage Councils, and there is no other regulation of the bargaining process, not even in the case of conflict and strikes (for a more detailed description, see Cassoni, Labadie, and Allen 1995, 167–70). No database up to this date has actually evaluated the impact of the contents of collective agreements. Recently, Cedrola, Raso, and Perez Tabó (1998) have examined qualitatively the contents of collective agreements for the period 1985–1995. For this study, a database that covers all collective agreements registered at the Ministry of Labor between 1985 and 1997 has been developed, and the contents of its clauses have been quantified to determine the actual nonwage costs resulting from the bargaining process at the industry level.

Using these data it is possible to analyze quantitatively a period in which union behavior was absent (through 1984); a period in which we know the union density of the sector as well as the amount of nonwage costs imposed on all firms in an industry, a consequence of a bargaining structure in place from 1985 through 1991; and a more recent period in which we know union density, but the collective agreements are exclusively binding for those firms and those workers that participated in the negotiation and signed the agreement. The completeness of data for this final period is less clear, because many of these agreements did not have to be registered at the Ministry of Labor (precisely because they did not have to be endorsed by the public authority in order to be binding among the contracting parties).

This study focuses on manufacturing, where there are pronounced changes in union density during the last decade, with no small amount of variation across individual industries. Upon the return of unions in 1985, 60 percent of production workers were covered by collective-bargaining agreements (see figure 8.3).

This initial level probably reflects political support for the role unions played in the return to democracy. Union sustainability hinges on both worker support for collective, as opposed to individual, agreements, and

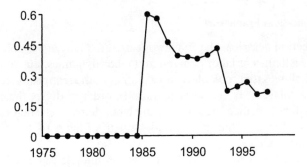

Fig. 8.3   Percentage union

Table 8.1   Percentage Union and Openness Ratio, by Year and Industry

Industry	Union				Open		
	1985	1988	1992	1997	1985	1992	1997
Food products	59	54	55	27	24	24	28
Textiles and apparel	77	54	46	16	49	54	83
Paper products	70	52	44	39	19	19	45
Chemicals	100	87	100	94	16	44	60
Nonmetallic	48	21	11	10	12	22	36
Metal products	100	43	43	19	76	146	350

on the ability of unionized employers to survive economically. Union density gradually dropped to 40 percent by 1988 and stayed near that level through 1992. By this point the contracts signed under the old Wage Council system had expired, and the impact of trade liberalization was beginning to be felt. The openness ratio jumped from 44 percent in 1992 to 55 percent in 1993 and was above 60 percent for most of 1994–1997. Union density dropped from 42 percent in 1992 to 22 percent in 1993 and has stayed at about that level since. The pattern of union growth and decline has varied considerably across industries, as shown in table 8.1.

Union strength remained near 100 percent throughout the sample period in the chemical and oil industries, which not coincidentally consist largely of state-owned enterprises. In fact, union density dropped in all industries after 1992, except in chemicals and oil products. The most dramatic decline took place in metal products and nonmetallic industries, where union coverage in the period dropped to 20 percent of its original level. At the same time, and particularly in metal products, imports plus exports increased sharply. There also was a considerable drop in union coverage in textiles and apparel and, to a lesser extent, in the paper industry. With the exception of food products, all industries experienced an increase in openness after 1992.

8.3   Theoretical Framework

This section describes the framework used to analyze possible changes in both elasticities of labor demand and labor dynamics, due to the institutional changes that took place in 1985, that is, the reappearance of trade unions as "players" in the labor market. In order to do so, the estimable models will be specified so as to measure labor demand elasticities for production workers and the speed of adjustment of labor to its equilibrium level in both regimes.

Through 1984, a competitive model seems suitable to describe the behavior of the labor market. Wage increases were set by the government from 1968 up to 1979, although from 1977 onward there were extra shifts in some sectors. The government concerns in this process were focused on stopping the huge increase in inflation rates so that it decided to "freeze" all prices and wages in the economy, not taking into account labor demand conditions. Hence, they were exogenous to the firm. Since 1985, it might be possible to approximate the observed employment and wage pairs using the same model, but the institutional framework actually changed. Since that date, the wage level has been the result of a bargaining process that has, itself, evolved all along the decade. Before 1992, bargaining was a synchronized process, taking place at the industrial-sector level through Wage Councils. After that date, it became more heterogeneous as negotiations at the firm level have become quite common, while synchronization has deteriorated.

Given the previously mentioned institutional changes, the following research strategy was developed: First, a model of labor demand derived from a pure neoclassical static framework was estimated. The wage variable is a cost of labor proxy, including wage plus nonwage costs—such as health insurance and payroll taxes—as well as other benefits bargained between firms and unions from 1985 onward.

As will be shown in more detail in the following, the model was estimated for the whole period and the stability of the parameters was tested. The econometric analysis supported the specification of a different model for the post-1984 period. This model was derived from a bargaining framework. A first implication is that wages are not exogenous as in the previous specification, as they are determined jointly by unions and firms through a bargaining process, where firms attempt to maximize profits and unions maximize their members' utility function. Second, other variables could enter the model as alternative wages or fallback positions of the parties.

8.3.1   Labor Demand: Theoretical Framework

We begin with a standard specification for a labor demand equation in a static framework. Assuming a generalized constant elasticity of substitution (CES) production function with three inputs (capital and labor divided in production and nonproduction workers), maximization of profits would yield a three-equations system of derived demands for each input. The equation describing the demand for production workers would be

$$(1) \qquad \ln N_t = \alpha_0 + \alpha_1 \ln\left(\frac{w}{p}\right)_t + \alpha_2 \ln Q_t,$$

where N = employment of production workers, w = wage, p = product price, and Q = output.

Hence, the elasticity of substitution between capital and employment (σ) is equal to $-\alpha_1$, while the wage elasticity of labor demand is $-\alpha_1 \cdot (1 - s_L)$, with s_L denoting labor share in value added.

In order to estimate the model, some methodological issues have to be resolved. If variables are not stationary, a possible strategy is to estimate the model in differences. A second approach would be to test if the variables involved are cointegrated and, if so, if the estimation can be carried out in levels. Because the estimators in equation (1) are biased in finite samples, it might be preferable to estimate a dynamic version of the model based on Engle and Granger's representation theorem (Engle and Granger 1987):

$$(2) \qquad \alpha(L)(1 - L)\mathbf{Z}_t = -\gamma\beta\mathbf{Z}_{t-1} \, d(L)\varepsilon_t,$$

where $\alpha(L)$ is a polynomial matrix in the lag operator; $\mathbf{Z}$ denotes the vector of variables involved (N, w/p, Q); $d(L)$ is a polynomial; and ε_t is a stationary process.

The model can be linearly transformed as an autoregressive-distributed lag model:

$$(3) \qquad \alpha_1(L)y_t = \alpha_2(L)\mathbf{X}_t + \varepsilon_t,$$

where $\alpha_1(L) = 1 - \Sigma_{i=1}^{m} \alpha_{1i}L_i$; $\alpha_2(L) = \Sigma_{i=0}^{m} \alpha_{2i}L_i$ and $(y,\mathbf{X}) = \mathbf{Z}$.

The econometric analysis of the model will determine its final dynamic structure. It has been shown that the lag structure of each variable need not be the same (for an extensive discussion of all the above methodological issues, see Banerjee et al. 1993).

The fact that variables are nonstationary means that at least some shocks have permanent effects on them. In particular, shocks related to productivity and accumulated knowledge have been generally found to be nontransitory so that they have long-lasting effects on output and employment (Aghion and Saint-Paul 1993; Blanchard and Quah 1989; and references therein). Thus, variables would have a stochastic trend, but, if cointegrated, the equilibrium relationship among them would still be stationary and hence stable. The dynamics are the result of agents not being able to adjust instantaneously to equilibrium because of factors such as adjustment costs, price rigidities, and so on. Adjustment costs have been extensively discussed in the literature (Hamermesh 1993, 1995; Hamermesh and Pfann 1996) as the source of the observed lags in adjusting employment. They would explain why actual employment (N) differs from its equilibrium level (N^e). If firms maximize expected profits, expectations are static and costs are quadratic, the optimum path of employment would be

(4) $$N_t = g(N^e - N_t),$$

yielding a demand for labor equation like

(5) $$N_t = \lambda N_{t-1} + \beta \mathbf{X}_t,$$

with $\mathbf{X}_t$ being a vector of variables determining long run labor demand and λ a parameter measuring the speed of adjustment to equilibrium, which is thus assumed to be constant.

8.3.2 Bargaining Models

Since 1985 unions started playing a role in the determination of wages, working conditions, and employment. Their role has varied over time, as well as the issues they bargained over. After analyzing all the collective agreements that have been signed since then, it is clear that there have always been negotiations over wages but rarely over employment. Agreements have covered a wide range of other benefits, increasing the annual wage a worker receives; linking the wage to different variables, such as productivity or tenure; and increasing fringe benefits. Working conditions have also been in the bargaining agenda, as well as the length of the working week and year. Although at first glance negotiations looked as if done in stages, this turned out to be false. The procedure followed has generally been one by which at some point unions and firms have bargained over the wage, other benefits, and working conditions. Regarding every issue but the wage, agreements have worked as long-term contracts (one year minimum, three years on average). Regarding the wage, however, they were quite short, covering a time period of three or four months, so that most of the contracts were agreements only over the wage.

The foregoing suggests that the most suitable benchmark to analyze the Uruguayan bargaining process is that of a right-to-manage model (for a discussion on this topic, see Pencavel 1991). The model will be considered as a maintained hypothesis, based on the analysis of all collective agreements. No tests against an efficient contract model will be carried out as it has been extensively proven by now that those tests cannot support one specification against the other (Booth 1995; Pencavel 1991).[3] Thus, the following specification is used:

---

3. For example, the alternative income would enter the employment equation only in the efficient contract model. However, some utility functions can yield a solution to the efficient bargain that excludes the alternative income from the specification. Further, the empirical distinction between both models is not straightforward, as the contract curve may lie on the labor demand curve (Carruth and Oswald 1987). Given the model proposed, we are explicitly assuming that unions have no direct impact on employment. However, we did perform the exercise of adding union variables to the employment equation, and the estimation results supported the model specified. The output of these regressions is available upon request.

First Stage: Unions and Firms Bargain over the Cost of Labor

$\Gamma(w, w_a, N)$ is the union's utility function, where w is the real wage, w_a is the alternative income, and N is employment. It is assumed that membership status is lost if unemployed; that all members of the union are equally considered by union leaders; and that members care about the real wage surplus over the alternative income they would earn working elsewhere or being unemployed (de Menil 1971). A standard specification is then

$$\Gamma(w, w_a, N, M) = (w - w_a)N^\phi,$$

where ϕ is a parameter denoting how much weight the union gives to employment in its utility function. If ϕ equals 1, then the model is the rent-maximization model (Pencavel 1991).

$\Pi(p, Q, K, N, p_c, w)$ is the firm's profit function, where K = capital and p_c = price of K. It is assumed that managers maximize revenue minus costs, so that

$$\Pi(p, Q, K, N, p_c, w) = pQ - wN - p_cK.$$

A well known solution to the bargaining problem is given by the maximization over the wage of the generalized Nash bargain, subject to the optimum labor demand that will be set in a second stage:

(6) $$\underset{w}{\text{Max }} Y = (\Gamma - \Gamma_0)^\beta (\Pi - \Pi_0)^{1-\beta}$$

s.t.

$$N = N^*$$

Γ_0 and Π_0 are the fallback positions of each player. They refer to what the union and the firm would get in the event of no agreement (Binmore, Rubinstein, and Wolinski 1986). If we assume that under this circumstance there will be a strike, then the firm will have zero operating profits, and union members will have zero earnings.[4]

Second Stage: Firms Maximize Profits

(7) $$\underset{N,K}{\text{Max }} \Pi = pQ - wN - p_cK$$

Subject to quite restrictive assumptions, the solution for (6) and (7) is

(8) $$N^* = N(w/p; Q)$$

$$w^* = \eta w_a.$$

The first equation is just the result of profit maximization by firms, under a CES production function, for example. However, to get the equation

---

4. There are no legal provisions assuring any income to strikers in Uruguay. They generally ask people for contributions, but this cannot be measured.

for the wage level, it has to be assumed that, when bargaining, firms take capital as given; that is, they have already made decisions on the capital level. Thus, the profit function depends solely on employment. The parameter η is a markup over the alternative income. This parameter is a function of sector characteristics, such as the degree of competitiveness and the affiliation rate (Layard, Nickell, and Jackman 1991).

Finally, the alternative-income workers consider as a comparison wage is a weighted average of what they would earn if they got a job in any manufacturing industry, what they would get if they decided to become self-employed, and what they would receive as unemployment benefits in the event of losing their jobs. Weights are given by the probability of being in each of the mentioned states, calculated as the annual frequency of each category.

The estimable model proposed is a multivariate model, in which wages are not exogenous but set subject to the determination of the level of employment. Unionism is treated as an exogenous variable because the major changes in this variable during our sample period were driven by social and political processes.

8.3.3   Union Impact

In a static framework, unions have an incentive to take whatever steps they can to reduce the wage elasticity of labor demand so that they can bargain for increased wages with less severe consequences for employment. Unions can make product demand less elastic by making fewer options available to consumers through various rent-seeking activities. One way of doing this is to create entry barriers, such as state ownership or regulated entry into markets where establishments are unionized. Tariffs, quotas, and other barriers to free trade also can be used to reduce consumer choice.

The elasticity of substitution between union labor and other inputs can be reduced through collective bargaining. Contracts with unions often spell out the conditions under which work is to be performed, including dictates on minimum crew sizes, limitations on substituting nonunion personnel for work that "belongs" to the union, and limits on technologies that reduce labor hours.

Empirically, it is well known (at least since Marshall) that unions should try to organize the sectors of the economy with the most inelastic demand. In this study we look at the same sectors of manufacturing before and after reunionization, so this allows us to control for this self-selection into rent-seeking opportunities. Instead, this study will be able to establish in a before-and-after framework whether unions are actually able to reduce labor demand elasticities.

The impact of unions on adjustment lags and the elasticity of labor demand to output hinge on a variety of factors. Ignoring adjustment costs for the moment, keep in mind that firms can adjust labor hours to a change in output by changing employment or by changing hours per person. The impact of unions on this tradeoff is not clear ex ante. Unions often negotiate for premium rates for overtime that are well above those required by labor legislation, which would by itself lead unionized firms to increase employment more for a given increase in output. However, unions also negotiate for employee benefits that make increasing employment expensive relative to increasing hours. Lower turnover in unionized establishments encourages greater investments in employee training, which in turn increase the cost of hiring an additional person. In a frictionless world, the effect of unions on the employment-hours balance would be an empirical question that would hinge on whether the marginal cost of an extra hour per person is the overtime rate dictated by labor laws or the superovertime rates from the union contract. If it is the standard overtime rate, then the dominating effect of unions would be through increased costs of hiring an extra person, and we would expect a smaller elasticity of employment to output.

A final channel for union influence is the speed at which labor adjustments are made. Unions have numerous methods at their disposal to change the cost of making changes in employment. This can be done with formal contract provisions dictating advance notice or severance pay in case of layoffs or through informal threats of slowdowns or strikes. Another factor leading to slower adjustment of employment to output in unionized establishments is the low rate of voluntary turnover. When attrition is sufficiently high, employment can adjust very quickly through a simple hiring freeze.

The expected duration of layoffs often plays an important role. If the expected duration of a drop in output is expected to be short, unions will not hesitate to opt for layoffs rather than hours reductions so that workers can take full advantage of unemployment insurance. The prevailing wisdom is that unions create longer adjustment lags through their impact on advance notice and severance pay.

8.4   Data

Before describing the actual definition of variables, some aggregation issues are worth stating. First, the units of observation considered will be manufacturing industries at the two-digit level of aggregation. Six of them can be observed during the period 1975 to 1997: food, beverage and tobacco; textiles and apparel; paper; chemicals and oil products; nonmetallic minerals; and metal products. It is well known that the optimum unit of observation is the establishment, as adding up technologies never guarantees that the parameters obtained for the aggregate are what they are sought to be. However, working with industries is not the worst of the alternatives. In a small country like Uruguay, most of the year-to-year variation in industry data is driven by a small number of firms; hence, problems related to aggregate data should be fewer than in a large country. Nevertheless, it should be taken into account that this might bias the estimates (Hamermesh 1993). Second, temporal aggregation does not seem a problem here as quarterly data will be used so that the lag structure should not understate the true lag structure.

8.4.1   Cost of Labor: W

The measure to be used in the model has to approximate the total cost of labor for the firm so that it has to include not only the wage but also nonwage costs. The latter include labor taxes; social security contributions; and bargained costs since 1985. We are omitting, however, all costs related to hiring and firing workers. In order to account for these costs, the labor demand function should be specified, contingent on different states of nature that would imply firing or hiring workers, and a distribution of these states should be also proposed. It can be shown that not specifying a state-contingent labor demand might bias the estimates of the elasticities downward due to the omission of relevant variables. We will not address this issue empirically as data needed to calculate marginal firing and hiring costs are not available.[5]

Data on wages are obtained from the Quarterly and Annual Industrial Surveys carried out by the National Institute of Statistics (INE).[6] Annual data for production workers are available from 1975 up to 1997. Quarterly

5. The law relative to severance pay has not changed in the sample period, and the compensation a worker is entitled to is the same for all industries and depends on his/her tenure (none if tenure is less than three months; one wage per year for those working for more than three months, up to a maximum of six). Average tenure for those employed in 1991–1997 (the only years for which the data is available) is between seven and ten years, not varying much between industries. Hence, the expected average severance pay does not change, being between 3.7 and 4.2 wages, depending on the industry. As it is not possible (due to the number of observations) to calculate the probability of a worker being laid off for each tenure, this should be calculated as the overall frequency of layoffs and will thus be negatively correlated with employment by definition. Finally, even if we included a tentative measure of average severance pay based on tenure of employees instead of on that of laid off workers, we would be introducing biases which need not be of the same sign along the period. They would depend on the prevailing rules of firing workers, and these have been probably different during 1975–1997. The only evidence available was especially collected for the last quarter of 1997. Manufacturing workers who were laid off in the month prior to the survey had an average tenure of 1.5 years, while the average for all unemployed manufacturing workers was six years. This suggests that a rule of last in–first out was in place. However, during periods of restructuring, as were the late 1970s and the early 1990s, firms might have gotten rid of more senior workers, that is, workers with higher wages and who were not easily retrainable. Given all these issues, we will omit these costs from the analysis, although they might be reflected in the estimated effect of unions on the labor demand model.

6. These surveys are carried out using a sample of firms employing five workers and more that stems from the previous industrial census. Data collected refer to many variables related to production, employment, and inputs. The Quarterly Industrial Survey reports indexes while the Annual Industrial Survey publications report values. The Wage Survey is carried out on a monthly basis at establishments belonging to all economic sectors.

data, however, are not published (nor processed by the INE) after 1991. Hence, for 1992–1997, the within-year evolution of wages was assumed to follow the same pattern as that stemming from the Wage Survey (INE) for manufacturing workers.[7]

Data on nonwage costs were taken from Picardo, Daude, and Ferre (1997) and from Cassoni and Ferre (1997). All costs related to health insurance and social security as well as payroll taxes were used to build a factor by which to increase wages for each two-digit industrial sector. Social security and health insurance contributions are a fixed percentage of wages that has varied over time. On the other side, payroll taxes, first imposed in 1982, have generally varied, depending on the level of earnings. Hence, information from the Household Survey (INE) was used to calculate the distribution of workers in the different relevant segments, yearly, for each manufacturing sector. Apart from these factors increasing wages, employers face an annual extra payment of one monthly salary plus twenty days that must be paid before the worker starts his/her annual holidays before the end of the year. Both were also included in the cost of labor. There are several issues over which unions have bargained since 1985. Among them, supplemental end-of-year bonuses, either related to tenure, productivity, or simply on a general basis; shorter length of the working day; and extra holidays. These negotiations took place at the industrial two-digit level so that they vary by industry. Annual premia applying to all workers was directly used to increase the factor built upon the legal rates. Information on extra holidays was used to calculate the percentage increase in costs due to nonworking days. If paid vacations were twelve days more per year over the legal standard, the actual monthly wage would be 25/24 times w, instead of w. Where agreements were reached shortening the legal length of the working day or week, the cost of labor was increased by the proportion of legal to bargained hours in the same way as paid vacations.

All the information described above, stemming from the manufacturing collective agreements signed between 1985 and 1997, was used to build an index increasing the legal cost of labor. This index varied in time and among industries, with an average value for the whole manufacturing sector of 12 percent. Industries with the lowest extraordinary bargaining costs were paper; metallic industries; and nonmetallic minerals, for which the increase was around 1 percent on average. Sectors related to food, beverage and tobacco, and chemicals have negotiated increases of 12 percent over the legal costs, while those related to textiles have an average percentage premia of 21 percent during the period. Given all the foregoing, the cost of labor variable was defined as

---

7. The Wage Survey is carried out on a monthly basis at establishments belonging to all economic sectors.

Cost of Labor = CL = Wage*(1 + legal nonwage costs

+ bargained nonwage costs).

8.4.2   Variable Definitions

Employment (N) refers to total number of production workers obtained from the Quarterly and Annual Industrial Surveys at the two-digit level. An index of production (Q) is available on a quarterly basis (INE). The index was then transformed to monetary values using the 1988 Industrial Census and the Annual Industrial Survey (INE). Data on product prices (p) refer to the producer price index (PPI) at the two-digit level (INE). All data refer to monthly values calculated as an average on a quarterly basis.

8.4.3   Some Corrections to the Official Data

In Uruguay, the industrial census is performed every 10 years. Each time a census is done, annual and quarterly surveys update their samples based on the new information. These samples are such that those establishments with more than 50 or 100 workers (depending on their share on the industry value added) are always surveyed (hence, death and births are accounted for), while smaller plants are sampled at the beginning of the period and remain in the sample until the new industrial census is carried out. In 1988, the last national industrial census was performed and its results showed that the samples that were being used in the industrial surveys—stemming from the 1978 census—were severely misrepresenting the different sectors. Annual surveys started including the new information in 1989, while quarterly surveys did so in 1993. However, no correction to the data was done before those dates. The differences in the samples meant that the estimated levels of employment and output for the whole manufacturing sector differed by about 25 percent depending on the sample used. At the two-digit level there were even broader differences. It was thus decided to correct the official data, discussing and taking advice from those in charge of the surveys at the INE. Given that the 1982–1983 economic recession had major and different effects, depending on the industrial sector, the assumption used to calculate the new data was that the lack of representativeness of the 1978 sample went back to 1984. As other sources showed that the evolution of the variables stemming from the surveys along the post-1984 period was quite correct, the differences in the levels according to both samples were geometrically distributed along those years (1984–1988 for the annual survey; 1984–1993 for the quarterly survey).

8.4.4   Degree of Openness: OPEN

The index was calculated as total exports plus total imports divided by value added, *per* manufacturing industry. Data came from the Republic

Bank of Uruguay (BROU), which was the authority in charge of collecting the data.

8.4.5   Alternative Wages: AW

Alternative wages were calculated using the information of wages in manufacturing as described in 8.4.1 and that of average income of self-employed individuals according to the Household Survey. The alternative income for a worker in industry j was defined as the weighted average of the wage in the rest of the manufacturing industries; the income the worker would receive if he/she becomes unemployed and collects unemployment benefits (50 percent of his/her current wage); and the average income of self-employed individuals. Weights were defined as the annual frequency of each category as stemming from the Household Survey.

8.4.6   Union Density: UNION

Union density was calculated using annual number of production workers as stemming from the Industrial Surveys and total membership reported by the National Union Federation after each congress. Congresses took place in 1985, 1987, 1990, 1993, and 1996–1997. In intervening years, union membership is estimated through simple interpolation.

Descriptive statistics for the above variables are summarized in table 8.2, differentiating between the pre- and postreunionization subperiods (1975–1984 and 1985–1997). Data for the entire manufacturing sector are reported to indicate overall trends; data for manufacturing industries indicate the diversity of conditions across different markets. Note that with the return of collective bargaining, the market trends are toward greater production, reduced employment, higher wages, and increased openness.

To preview the dynamic patterns of the key variables, the quarterly change in employment for the manufacturing sector is plotted along with the quarterly changes in production and employment (all in logs) in figures 8.4 and 8.5. Employment varied less on a quarterly basis with the return of unionization; the standard deviation of the log change in employment fell from 0.036 in 1975–1984 to 0.028 in 1985–1997. At the same time production became more variable, with the standard deviation of log change rising from 0.063 to 0.095 for the same two periods. This would indicate a strong likelihood that employment-output elasticity fell after 1985. The story for wages is less clear-cut. The standard deviation of the log change in wages decreased from 0.124 to 0.063.[8] Proportionally speaking, the quarterly variation in wages fell by more than the quarterly variation in employment, indicating a possible increase in the wage elasticity of labor de-

---

8. The null hypothesis of no change in the variance is rejected at the 5 percent level for all three variables and at the 1 percent level for wages and output, with $F(38,51) = 3.85$ for log wages, $F(38,51) = 2.27$ for log output and $F(38,51) = 1.65$ for log employment.

Table 8.2   **Descriptive Statistics**

Variable	1975.1–1984.4 (Obs. = 40)				1985.1–1997.4 (Obs. = 52)			
	Mean	SD	Max.	Min.	Mean	SD	Max.	Min.
	Manufacturing Sector							
W	82.02	13.97	103.6	56.81	90.02	21.64	133.3	52.38
LNWC	1.336	0.071	1.426	1.243	1.332	0.031	1.375	1.290
BNWC	1.000	0.000	1.000	1.000	1.123	0.038	1.156	1.000
TLC	109.7	18.6	143.54	72.56	136.2	36.34	203.7	67.79
AW	0.000	0.000	0.000	0.000	42.95	11.67	62.59	24.87
UNION	0.000	0.000	0.000	0.000	0.365	0.129	0.601	0.200
OPEN	0.298	0.036	0.388	0.242	0.468	0.109	0.620	0.295
Q	57.00	6.740	70.00	44.60	60.16	5.097	71.04	49.16
N	108,143	14,496	129,491	86,010	104,782	19,727	129,995	71,735

	1975.1–1984.4 (Obs. = 240)				1985.1–1997.4 (Obs. = 312)			
	Mean	SD	Max.	Min.	Mean	SD	Max.	Min.
	Manufacturing Industries							
W	86.93	28.84	202.9	41.90	104.8	40.96	246.3	41.25
LNWC	1.337	0.071	1.433	1.238	1.328	0.038	1.383	1.232
BNWC	1.000	0.000	1.000	1.000	1.076	0.096	1.265	1.000
TLC	115.3	35.31	255.6	58.65	151.4	68.23	405.8	53.23
AW	0.000	0.000	0.000	0.000	69.88	21.27	136.7	30.79
UNION	0.000	0.000	0.000	0.000	0.507	0.285	1.000	0.083
OPEN	0.338	0.257	1.149	0.096	0.575	0.657	3.500	0.102
Q	9.431	6.971	27.42	1.598	9.804	6.784	26.69	1.296
N	17,661	12,763	49,715	4,167	16,543	12,292	42,150	3,897

Notes: W is monthly real wage per production worker in 1988 pesos; LNWC is 1 + percentage increase in wages due to legal nonwage costs; BNWC is 1 + percentage increase in wages due to bargained nonwage costs; TLC are monthly total real labor costs in 1988 pesos; AW is the monthly real alternative wage in 1988 pesos; UNION is percentage union; OPEN is degree of openness; Q is production in 1988 million pesos; N is number of production workers; Obs. is the number of observations; and SD represents standard deviation.

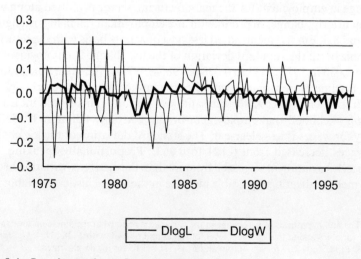

Fig. 8.4   Log changes in employment and wages

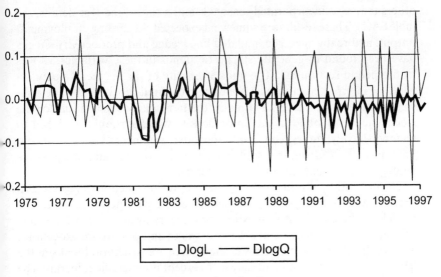

Fig. 8.5   **Log changes in employment and production**

mand. However, between 1975 and 1980 there are six nearly consecutive
episodes of a sharp (0.1 or larger) increase in wages followed one or two
quarters later by an equally sharp decrease in wages. It is doubtful that employers reacted very much to such short-term wage shocks.

8.5   Labor Demand: Empirical Results

8.5.1   Specifying a Model for the Whole Period

To determine whether and how much elasticities and adjustment lags of
labor demand in the manufacturing sector changed after the return of collective bargaining, we must first establish the appropriate specification of
the empirical model.[9] The quarterly data on the six manufacturing industries described in previous sections was used. To estimate equation (1) as it
stands, the stationarity of the variables must first be established, which we
did by estimating the order of integration of employment, labor costs, and
output for each manufacturing industry in the 1975–1997 period. All variables are nonstationary, but their first differences are stationary so that
they are integrated of first order—I(1). The unit root tests used to perform
the analyses were those proposed by Fuller (1976), known as Augmented
Dickey-Fuller tests (ADF). The models over which the tests were performed were different depending on the variable and industry, including
only a constant and lags of the dependent variable in some cases, while in

9. We are grateful to John E. Driffill for his useful comments as well as to Fernando Lorenzo
for his econometric advice.

others they also incorporated seasonals and a time trend (for details, see table 8A.1). These results are somewhat expected. Regarding employment, output, and real wages, accumulated knowledge and productivity shocks have been found to generate stochastic trends in these variables, as was mentioned in section 8.3. The nonstationarity of the degree of openness could be interpreted in similar terms, with external shocks and trade policies at the root of the result. Finally, the most likely explanation for the stochastic trend found in the union density variable should be linked to membership dynamics and insider-outsider arguments (Blanchard and Summers 1986). Given the statistical properties of the data, one possible strategy is to estimate the model in differences.

The institutional framework depicted in previous sections suggests, as a second step, the analysis of the stability of the parameters in time. The model in differences was thus estimated industry by industry, using recursive least squares (RLS) and assuming wages and output are exogenous. The results, depicted in figure 8.6, show there are structural breaks in the labor demand equation in all industries except nonmetallic minerals. The timing of the breaks is not identical in each industry, but breaks can be identified at some point in the early 1980s as well as at another point around 1991–1993. These dates can be clearly related to the major economic crisis in 1982–1984; the end of the military regime in 1985; and the end of government participation in the Wage Councils.

A third stage of the analysis involved using the pooled cross-section time series data set. Given the nonstationarity of the variables and the instability of the parameters, the model was specified in differences with the parameters shifting in various combinations of 1983, 1985, and 1993 and estimated by ordinary least squares (OLS). Elasticities were imposed to be the same for all six industries, while wages and output were taken as exogenous variables. These results are reported in table 8.3.

The first three columns test for a single break in 1983, 1985, and 1993. The null hypothesis of no shifts cannot be rejected for 1983 and 1993, but it is rejected for 1985. The output coefficient falls from 0.141 in 1975–1984 to 0.073 in 1985–1997. The wage coefficient becomes smaller in absolute value terms, going from –0.103 to –0.047. The sum of the two lagged employment coefficients falls from 0.196 to 0.022. The models in the last two columns test for multiple break points. Having established a shift in the early 1980s, these results examine whether there was an additional shift in 1993. In the fourth column, breaks in 1983 and 1993 are included, while in the fifth column the shifts take place in 1985 and 1993. The joint null hypothesis of no breaks is rejected in both cases.

Finally, cointegration techniques were also applied. When variables are nonstationary, the estimation of the model in levels has been proven to be misleading, unless the variables are jointly stationary; that is, they are cointegrated. Hence, cointegration (CI) tests were then done to see if an equi-

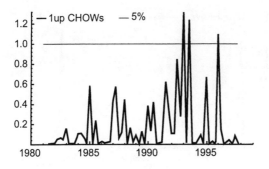

Food, beverage & tobacco: breaks in 1992–93

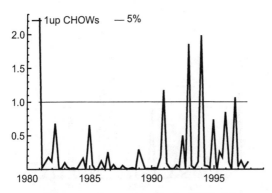

Paper products: breaks in 1991–92

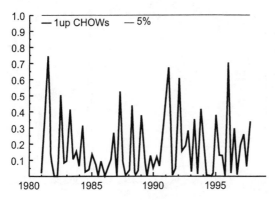

Nonmetallic minerals: no breaks

Fig. 8.6   Recursive residuals, by industry

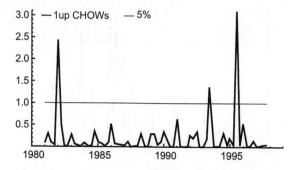

Textiles & apparel: breaks in 1982–95

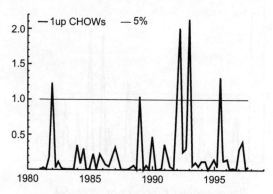

Chemicals: breaks in 1982–93

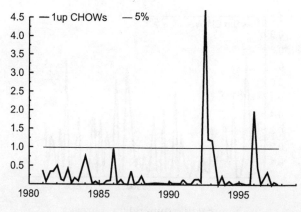

Metallic products: break in 1992

Fig. 8.6 (cont.)

able 8.3	Estimation in Differences, Manufacturing Industries, 1975–1997				
	Structural Breaks				
ariable	1983	1985	1993	1983 and 1993	1985 and 1993
mployment$_{t-1}$	0.01256	0.04312	0.02399	0.01316	0.03833
	(0.0604)	(0.0564)	(0.0468)	(0.0593)	(0.0557)
mployment$_{t-2}$	0.16010	0.15278	0.09722	0.16832	0.15082
	(0.0605)	(0.0564)	(0.0469)	(0.0594)	(0.0559)
roduct$_t$	0.15244	0.14078	0.12545	0.15180	0.14259
	(0.0306)	(0.0263)	(0.0203)	(0.0300)	(0.0260)
age$_t$	−0.08480	−0.10309	−0.09007	−0.08364	−0.10675
	(0.0296)	(0.0234)	(0.0224)	(0.0291)	(0.0264)
mployment$_{t-1}$ · dummy Year 1	−0.01144	−0.07197	−0.08663	0.01955	−0.06430
	(0.0833)	(0.0835)	(0.1043)	(0.0943)	(0.0995)
mployment$_{t-2}$ · dummy Year 1	−0.11730	−0.10185	0.03228	−0.21630	−0.20982
	(0.0837)	(0.0839)	(0.1051)	(0.0950)	(0.1002)
roduct$_t$ · dummy Year 1	−0.05929	−0.0679	−0.05994	−0.04599	−0.04991
	(0.0374)	(0.0349)	(0.0388)	(0.0410)	(0.0430)
age$_t$ · dummy Year 1	0.01234	0.05570	0.09638	−0.01371	0.04344
	(0.0424)	(0.0244)	(0.0704)	(0.0449)	(0.0507)
mployment$_{t-1}$ · dummy Year 2				−0.24582	−0.18643
				(0.1233)	(0.1293)
mployment$_{t-2}$ · dummy Year 2				0.03721	0.04908
				(0.1213)	(0.1273)
roduct$_t$ · dummy Year 2				−0.03598	−0.02352
				(0.0430)	(0.0473)
age$_t$ · dummy Year 2				0.13014	0.09706
				(0.0747)	(0.0793)
2	0.0930	0.1028	0.0922	0.1398	0.1344

otes: Dependent variable: ΔEmployment$_t$ = Employment$_t$ − Employment$_{t-1}$. Variables are in first ifferences; Employment is number of production workers; Wage is the real labor cost of a production orker; dummy Year 1 is a dummy variable that is equal to 1 in the subperiod starting in 1983, 1985, or 93 according to the column; dummy Year 2 is a dummy variable that is equal to 1 in the subperiod arting in 1993. Standard errors are in parentheses below each estimated coefficient. No. of observa- ons = 534.

librium relationship could be sustained for the whole period. Both Engle and Granger (EGM) and Johansen (JM) methods were used, specifying various models that differ in the number of lags included, as well as in the in- clusion of seasonal dummies or a constant. Cointegration between employ- ment, production, and labor costs was rejected for all industries according to at least some of the tests performed (table 8A.2). In those cases in which CI cannot be rejected, the graph of the CI relation shows it is not stationary so that it is probably spurious, as is the existence of a structural break in the relation that makes the statistics significant (see figures 8A.1 to 8A.4).

In summary, all the previous analyses suggest 1985 stands out on both institutional and statistical grounds as the date at which a structural change in labor demand behavior took place. There is also some evidence of a further shift in the 1990s. These break points will be used in the remainder of the chapter.

8.5.2   Specifying a Model for Each Subperiod

Once we determined 1985 as the breaking point, we first repeated the analysis of order of integration and cointegration of variables for each subsample and each industry. For 1975–1984 and 1985–1997, every variable is I(1) within each subperiod. Details are reported in tables 8A.3 and 8A.4. Second, for 1975–1984, the tests using EGM and/or JM report a CI relation for at least one model (see table 8A.5).[10] For 1985–1997, no CI among employment, labor costs, and production can be found in any industry for any model using EGM. However, CI is not rejected in any industry once variables that would reflect a bargaining framework—alternative wages, bargained costs, degree of openness, and union density—are included. The existence of an equilibrium relation between the variables—according to the nonrejection of CI—would state that shocks, having a long-lasting effect on each of the individual variables, alter equilibrium only in a transitory way. In the first subperiod, the result is consistent with a standard neoclassical labor demand framework. In 1985–1997, however, the need to include other variables to achieve CI suggests that the framework in which labor demand has been determined actually changed. One possibility is to link the existence of a stochastic trend in the residuals to not having modeled technical change. One might argue that this is partially captured when adding the degree of openness: Increases in openness would force the different industries to invest in new technology once they face greater competitive pressures, or it would force firms with older technologies to close so that, on average, technical progress would be observed. However, as not only openness but variables accounting for bargaining are included in the CI relation, there is also evidence supporting the premise that a bargaining framework is in place to analyze the labor demand schedule in 1985–1997.

To further establish whether the return of collective bargaining was a likely cause of the observed change in parameters, we then performed exogeneity tests on wages. In the competitive model, wages are assumed to be exogenous to the firm and industry, while in the bargaining model, they are not. In the latter case they would be set either simultaneously or subject to the determination of employment. Using a Hausman test (1978) in which the OLS estimate of the wage parameter is compared to a seemingly unrelated regressions estimate (SUR), weak exogeneity of wages cannot be rejected in the first subperiod while it is rejected in the second.[11] The SUR es-

---

10. The EGM was preferred due to the number of observations available. The JM was used for paper and chemicals to check if a CI relation could be found.

11. The Hausman statistic is $T(b\text{OLS} - b\text{SUR})2\text{Var}(b\text{OLS} - b\text{SUR}) - 1$, where b is the estimator, by OLS or SUR, and T is the number of observations. It is distributed as a χ^2 with 1 degree of freedom.

Table 8.4   **Weak Exogeneity Tests for Wages, 1975–1984 and 1985–1997**

	1975–1984	1985–1997
Model 1	3.02	5.9
Model 2	—	90.4
Model 3	—	294.2
Model 4	—	226.6
Hausman Statistic 95% confidence	3.84	

Notes: Each model contains 5 industry dummies and a constant. In models 1 and 2 labor demand is specified as a function of wages and output, using 4 lags of every variable. In models 3 and 4 a dummy variable for 1993 is also included in both the labor demand and the wage equations. In models 1 and 3, instruments used for the wage are just its lags while in models 2 and 4 instruments for the wage include bargaining variables.

timator is calculated using lags of the wage as instruments in both subperiods. For 1985–1997, however, the test was also performed including bargaining variables (degree of openness and union density). Further, given the evidence on the existence of instability in the 1990s, the statistics were also calculated, including a dummy variable in the equations, which takes the value 0 before 1993 and 1 after that date. The values of the statistics for the different models are reported in table 8.4. The results provide further support for estimating a standard neoclassical labor demand model for 1975–1984 and a bargaining model for 1985–1997. Given all the previous results, the estimated models are as follows:

$$1975-1984: \ln N_t = \alpha_0 + \alpha_1(L)\ln\left(\frac{w}{p}\right)_t + \alpha_2(L)\ln Q_t + \alpha_3(L)\ln N_{t-1}$$

$$1985-1997: \ln N_t = \beta_0 + \beta_1(L)\ln\left(\frac{w}{p}\right)_t + \beta_2(L)\ln Q_t + \beta_3(L)\ln N_{t-1}$$

$$\ln\left(\frac{w}{p}\right)_t = \gamma_0 + \gamma_1(L)\text{UNION} + \gamma_2(L)\text{OPEN} + \gamma_3(L)\ln(w_a)_t$$

$$+ \gamma_4(L)\ln\left(\frac{w}{p}\right)_{t-1},$$

where N refers to number of production workers; w/p are real labor costs (which after 1985 include bargained costs); Q is production; union is union density; open is degree of openness; and w_a is the alternative wage. The order of the polynomials in the lag operator will be tested empirically, starting with polynomials of order four. The bargaining model is a recursive, two-equation model, so gains in efficiency can be achieved through simultaneous estimation. To avoid possible endogeneity bias due to the non-modeling of output, lag values of Q (up to two lags), seasonals, and industry dummies were used as instruments for this variable in the estimation for both subperiods. Hence, estimation was done using instrumental variables

(IVE) in the first subsample and three-stage least squares (3SLS) in the second, using PCGive and PCFiml 9.0 software (1996). The data set is the pooled cross-section time series described previously. Fixed effects per industry are always allowed for. Elasticities are imposed to be equal for all industries so that the estimates reflect the average elasticities for the whole manufacturing sector.

8.5.3   Main Results

For both subperiods, table 8.5 reports three simple versions of the labor demand model. Starting with a model including up to four lags for every variable, sequential reductions were performed. Further, the different coefficients were allowed to vary in 1993 in order to check for possible shifts. We only report the last two steps including the shifts that were significant as well as two lags of employment in column (1) and only previous-quarter employment in column (2). Column (3) includes the variable OPEN in the labor demand equation, so as to test if increased openness was affecting the estimates. The wage equation for the bargaining model allows the wage bargain to vary by industry after 1993. This was done to test whether the change in the bargaining structure has had an overall impact on wage demands and whether the effect varies by industry. Residuals are not autocorrelated, but they are heteroskedastic. Thus, standard errors were calculated according to White (1980). Although normality is rejected, hypothesis testing results should be robust to nonnormality given the sample size (Spanos 1986).

As can be seen by comparing columns (1) and (2) of the labor demand results within each subperiod, employment from one quarter ago has an effect on employment in the current quarter, but employment from two quarters ago has no impact. Further, the degree of openness is not only statistically nonsignificant, but does not alter the estimates of the relevant elasticities. Accordingly, our attention will focus on the results for column (2). These show three major results:

1. The output coefficient falls from 0.093 in 1975–1984 to 0.040 in 1985–1997.
2. The wage coefficient falls (in absolute value) from –0.102 in 1975–1984 to –0.039 in 1985–1997.
3. There is no significant change in the impact of lagged employment between these two periods.

The wage equation results show that the effect of union density on wages decreased significantly after 1992, although the extent of this change varies per industry.[12] A key finding in the wage equation results is that bargained

---

12. The negative effect of unions on wages should be taken just as an indicator of changes in the bargaining regime by the mid-1990s. The available number of temporal observations is not enough to estimate different models for the subperiods, so structural breaks in this case are used to capture possible shifts and not as a quantitative assessment.

Table 8.5   **Estimates of Labor Demand and Wage Equations: Manufacturing Industries**

Variable	Sample: 1975–1984			Sample: 1985–1997		
	(1)	(2)	(3)	(1)	(2)	(3)
	Labor Demand Equation: dependent variable: N_t					
Constant	1.4969	1.3840	1.5638	1.3403	1.3630	1.3526
	(0.2980)	(0.3012)	(0.3338)	(0.2333)	(0.2187)	(0.2186)
N_{t-1}	0.90382	0.88844	0.87473	0.79468	0.86921	0.87186
	(0.1299)	(0.0315)	(0.0330)	(0.0625)	(0.0218)	(0.0202)
N_{t-2}	−0.01477			0.07809		
	(0.1181)			(0.0588)		
Q_t	0.09074	0.0930	0.09092	0.03912	0.04024	0.03309
	(0.0261)	(0.0244)	(0.0239)	(0.0244)	(0.0245)	(0.0173)
W_t	−0.10000	−0.10180	−0.09865	−0.04098	−0.03886	−0.03882
	(0.0227)	(0.0182)	(0.0174)	(0.0178)	(0.0184)	(0.0172)
DUMMY93				−0.03957	−0.04019	−0.0393
				(0.0123)	(0.0126)	(0.0122)
IND.31	−0.04217	−0.04499	−0.07533	0.08076	0.08336	0.08755
	(0.0285)	(0.0271)	(0.0357)	(0.0287)	(0.0287)	(0.0250)
IND.32	0.03857	0.03757	0.02439	0.08019	0.08335	0.08357
	(0.0247)	(0.0267)	(0.0296)	(0.0206)	(0.0206)	(0.0202)
IND.34	0.02271	0.02498	−0.03521	−0.05909	−0.06096	−0.06533
	(0.0276)	(0.0273)	(0.0442)	(0.0209)	(0.0214)	(0.0238)
IND.35	−0.10358	−0.10557	−0.15528	−0.04310	−0.04563	−0.04006
	(0.0242)	(0.0221)	(0.0409)	(0.0246)	(0.0249)	(0.0201)
IND.36	−0.04382	−0.04285	−0.10538	−0.07504	−0.07684	−0.08307
	(0.0243)	(0.0233)	(0.0460)	(0.0279)	(0.0283)	(0.0279)
Qr.1	−0.01536	−0.01524	−0.01451	0.00098	−0.00019	−0.00111
	(0.0127)	(0.0127)	(0.0127)	(0.0081)	(0.0080)	(0.0080)
Qr.2	0.00815	0.00783	0.00846	0.01122	0.01031	0.00996
	(0.0079)	(0.0082)	(0.0082)	(0.0059)	(0.0058)	(0.0053)
Qr.3	−0.01340	−0.01323	−0.01286	−0.01589	−0.01778	−0.01793
	(0.0069)	(0.0067)	(0.0068)	(0.0072)	(0.0069)	(0.0067)
OPEN			−0.07185			−0.00090
			(0.0532)			(0.0092)
No. of observations	228	228	228	300	300	300
R^2	0.9946	0.9947	0.9947	0.9967	0.9967	0.9967
AR 1-4	3.3058	3.5757	3.9374	1.2294	1.7403	1.7430
	[0.5080]	[0.4665]	[0.4145]	[0.8732]	[0.7834]	[0.7829]
Normality	143.0	138.0	131.7	60.4	56.6	56.7
	[0.0000]**	[0.0000]**	[0.0000]**	[0.0000]**	[0.0000]**	[0.0000]**
χ^2	2.9151	2.272	2.309	1.5052	1.7656	1.5585
	[0.0002]**	[0.0067]**	[0.0039]**	[0.0353]*	[0.0074]**	[0.0247]**

	Sample: 1985–1997		
	(1)	(2)	(3)
	Wage Equation: dependent variable: W_t		
Constant	−0.29674	−0.27408	−0.27471
	(0.1068)	(0.1041)	(0.1041)
W_{t-1}	0.36874	0.43003	0.43033
	(0.0563)	(0.0401)	(0.0402)

(*continued*)

Table 8.5 (continued)

	Sample: 1985–1997		
	(1)	(2)	(3)
W_{t-2}	0.07493		
	(0.0433)		
AW$_t$	0.71198	0.72145	0.72126
	(0.0523)	(0.0540)	(0.0540)
OPEN$_t$	–0.02471	–0.02426	–0.02424
	(0.0107)	(0.0107)	(0.0107)
UNION$_t$	0.15515	0.15477	0.15470
	(0.0227)	(0.0229)	(0.0229)
UNION93$_t$	–0.23953	–0.23432	–0.23437
	(0.0693)	(0.0703)	(0.0703)
UNION93$_t$ · Ind.31	0.05711	0.06146	0.06161
	(0.0846)	(0.0862)	(0.0862)
UNION93$_t$ · Ind.32	–0.14993	–0.14841	–0.14815
	(0.0784)	(0.0809)	(0.0809)
UNION93$_t$ · Ind.34	–0.04242	–0.03842	–0.03838
	(0.0745)	(0.0763)	(0.0762)
UNION93$_t$ · Ind.35	0.17082	0.17512	0.17504
	(0.0616)	(0.0627)	(0.0626)
UNION93$_t$ · Ind.36	–0.89888	–0.89890	–0.89809
	(0.2909)	(0.2934)	(0.2935)
DUMMY93	0.10029	0.10001	0.09997
	(0.0332)	(0.0331)	(0.0331)
Qr.1	–0.04555	–0.04357	–0.04358
	(0.0107)	(0.0109)	(0.0109)
Qr.2	0.01220	0.02054	0.02056
	(0.0091)	(0.0086)	(0.0086)
Qr.3	0.01208	0.00984	0.00985
	(0.0085)	(0.0083)	(0.0083)
No. of observations	300	300	300
R^2	0.9780	0.9782	0.9782
AR 1-4	1.9425	1.6430	1.6429
	[0.7530]	[0.7928]	[0.7927]
Normality	7.74	7.85	7.85
	[0.0209]*	[0.0198]*	[0.0198]**
χ^2	1.9445	2.0968	1.9892
	[0.0014]**	[0.0006]**	[0.0010]**

Notes: N is number of production workers; *W* is the real labor cost of a production worker; *Q* is production; AW is the alternative wage; UNION is union density; OPEN is the degree of openness; Qr.*j* is a dummy variable for quarter *j*; Ind.*i* is a dummy variable for industry *i*; DUMMY93 is a dummy variable equal to 1 in 1993–1997; UNION93 is UNION multiplied by DUMMY93. Industries reported are: food, beverage, and tobacco (31); textiles and apparel (32); paper (34); chemicals (36); nonmetallic minerals (36); metal products (38). Models (1) and (2) differ in that the former includes 2 lags of the dependent variable, while the latter only includes 1. Model 3 includes the variable OPEN in the labor demand equation. Variables are in logs, except for UNION; OPEN and binary variables. Corrected (according to White, 1980) standard errors are in parentheses below each estimated coefficient. AR 1-4 is a test of autocorrelation of order 4 in the residuals; Normality is Jarque-Bera's test; χ^2 is a test for heteroskedasticity of the residuals, using all variables and their squared value in the model for the variance.

Table 8.6   Labor Demand Parameters: Manufacturing Industries, 1975–1997

	1975–1984		1985–1997	
Variable	Estimate	Confidence Interval	Estimate	Confidence Interval
	Short Run Estimates			
Production	0.09304	(0.045, 0.141)	0.040243	(0.007, 0.087)
Labor costs	–0.10180	(–0.137, –0.066)	–0.03886	(–0.075, –0.003)
Lagged employment	0.88844	(0.827, 0.950)	0.86921	(0.826, 0.912)
	Long Run Estimates			
Production	0.8339	(0.525, 1.143)	0.3077	(0.080, 0.536)
Labor costs	–0.9125	(–1.368, –0.457)	–0.2971	(–0.534, –0.060)
Labor share (s_L)	0.248		0.257	
Wage elasticity of labor demand	0.69		0.22	

Notes: s_L is equal to the wage bill (all wage and nonwage costs included) divided by value added. The wage elasticity of labor demand is equal to $-(1 - s_L) \cdot \sigma$, where σ is the elasticity of substitution between capital and labor and is given by the estimated coefficient of the wage in the labor demand equation.

wages fall with increased openness. The effect is rather small, however—a 50 point change in openness being associated with a 1.5 percent change in the bargained wage.

Because of the different approaches taken to estimating the IVE labor demand and the 3SLS bargaining model, one might wonder if these findings are sensitive to the choice of estimation method or to the inclusion/exclusion of variables in the model. To put the two subperiods on an equal footing, both models were nested in a two-equation system and estimated by 3SLS. In order to do so, each variable was multiplied by two binary variables—one for 1975–1984, another for 1985–97—so that $X75$ equals X in 1975–1984 and 0 after that date, and $X85$ is equal to X in 1985–1997 and 0 before that date. Tests of significance of coefficients and tests of coefficients being equal before and after 1985 were performed, and they all reinforce the previous results (see table 8A.5).

In tables 8.6 and 8.7, labor demand elasticities and results for other relevant parameters are summarized, using models (2) of the previous table. Confidence intervals are also reported. These results show that the wage elasticity of labor demand dropped from 0.69 in 1975–1984 to 0.22 in 1985–1997. The employment-output elasticity fell by more than 50 percent, from 0.83 to 0.31.

The estimated speed of adjustment is the same in both periods, about five quarters, so that there is no evidence that the return of bargaining lengthened the amount of time needed for employment to adjust, which is contrary to what one might generally expect.[13]

13. An exception is the paper by Lockwood and Manning (1989) in which the opposite result is found.

Table 8.7   Impact of Key Variables on Real Labor Costs: Manufacturing Industries, 1985–1997

| | Short Run | | Long Run | |
Variable	Estimate	Confidence Interval	Estimate	Confidence Interval
Openness	−0.02426	(−0.045, −0.003)	−0.04256	(−0.075, −0.010)
Alternative wage	0.72145	(0.616, 0.827)	1.26580	(1.175, 1.356)
Lagged wage	0.43003	(0.351, 0.509)		
Union 1985/92	0.15477	(0.110, 0.200)	0.27154	(0.215, 0.328)
Union 1993/97				
Ind.31	−0.01809	(−0.176, 0.140)	−0.03174	(−0.328, 0.265)
Ind.32	−0.22796	(−0.384, −0.072)	−0.39995	(−0.722, −0.078)
Ind.34	−0.11797	(−0.246, 0.010)	−0.20698	(−0.451, 0.037)
Ind.35	0.09557	(0.031, 0.159)	0.16767	(0.062, 0.273)
Ind.36	−0.97846	(−1.585, −0.372)	−1.71670	(−2.756, −0.677)
Ind.38	−0.07955	(−0.215, 0.056)	−0.13957	(−0.387, 0.108)

Note: Industries are food, beverage, and tobacco (31); textiles and apparel (32); paper (34); chemica (36); nonmetallic minerals (36); metal products (38).

Although the estimates might be biased downward due to the omission of hiring and firing costs, the evidence of a decline between both subperiods is quite robust. The smaller responses of employment to changes in output and wages are consistent with collective bargaining restricting the options available to employers. Once unions reappeared and started playing a role in wage setting, the rules of the game changed. Costs of hiring and firing workers were expected to increase because of union resistance. Employment would not adjust to changing output demand as before because of increased uncertainty on the reaction of unions. Hence, there would have been more labor hoarding during slowdowns and increased use of overtime work during upswings than when unions were not active.

After 1992 the structure of bargaining changed, so that firm-level negotiations became quite common in some industries. The effect of this institutional change is captured in both the labor demand and the wage equations, but in different ways. In 1993 the labor demand equation has shifted in, while the other estimated coefficients are stable. Regarding the wage, the estimated effect is an overall increase in wages but with a reduction of the impact of union power on the markup that is different per industry. Industries that have experienced a greater reduction of this positive effect are those in which firm-level negotiations have become more common. Hence, while no significant change is detected in chemicals (35)—a concentrated industry in which public firms are present—in nonmetallic minerals (36), union power has become less effective in increasing the markup over alternative income. The estimated long-run effect of unions is to increase wages by 1.5 percent per each 10 percent increase in coverage in 1985–1992. Given the changes that took place in the 1990s, the average effect is almost

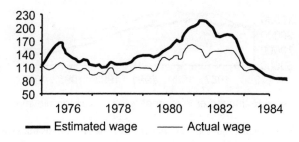

Fig. 8.7   Labor costs 1975–1984 assuming the existence of unions

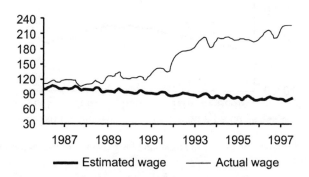

Fig. 8.8   Labor costs 1986–1997 assuming there were no unions

null for the whole period.[14] The indirect effect of unions over employment via wages is such that an increase in coverage of 10 percentage points is associated with a 0.8 percent decline in labor demand before 1993.

As almost every parameter changed, a simulation was done using both models in order to capture all possible effects. First, the wage was calculated for the period 1985–1997 using an ARIMA(4,1,0) model estimated using data for 1975–1984. Comparing the average value of the estimated wage with the actual average value, the result is that wages were 46 percent higher than what they would have been had no changes occurred. For 1975–1984, the same exercise shows that actual wages in the period were 18 percent lower than what they would have been if there had been bargaining over wages and a union density equal to its average value in 1985–1997 (see figures 8.7 and 8.8).

Second, using actual wages and the two specifications of the labor demand equation, the estimated effect of the different regimes on labor demand is that the employment level in 1985–1997 was 9 percent higher than what it would have been according to the 1975–1984 model. This is the combined effect of the decrease in the output and wage parameters. Ac-

14. These effects are calculated at the mean value of UNION.

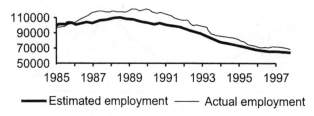

Fig. 8.9   Employment 1986–1997 assuming there were no unions but using actual wages

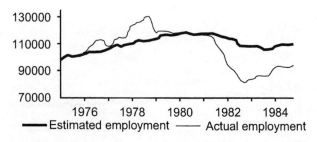

Fig. 8.10   Employment 1975–1984 assuming the existence of unions but using actual wages

cordingly, in 1975–1984, employment would have been 5 percent higher than its observed level if elasticities had been those stemming from the bargaining model (see figures 8.9 and 8.10).

Finally, considering both the estimated wage level and the change in elasticities, the employment level in 1985–1997 was 24 percent lower than what it would have been if wages had followed the 1975–1984 ARIMA(4,1,0) model and elasticities had been those according to the 1975–1984 labor demand equation. In 1975–1984, on the contrary, if wages had been those predicted by the bargaining model and elasticities had had the values estimated with this same model, then the employment level would have been 1 percent lower than what it actually was (see figures 8.11 and 8.12). In summary, unions could have prevented wages from falling as much as they did before 1985 at the cost of a 1 percent employment loss while, if unions had not been reinstated, employment would have been 24 percent higher, but at the cost of a much lower level of earnings.

These figures should be considered only as rough indicators. The ARIMA(4,1,0) model for wages, as well as the 1975–1984 model for employment, do not take into account the 1993 estimated shifts and the role that variables such as output and terms of trade would have played after 1985 in the absence of a regime change. These might be linked to structural reforms and productivity gains brought about by increased openness. Hence, the simulated paths in 1985–1997 are overestimated in the former

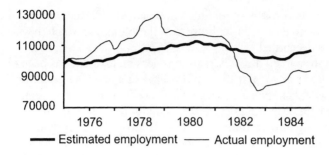

Fig. 8.11   Employment 1975–1984 assuming the existence of unions

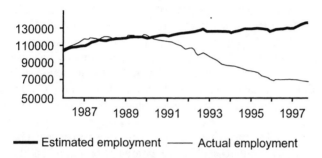

Fig. 8.12   Employment 1986–1997 assuming there were no unions

case, while they are underestimated in the latter using the 1975–1984 models (simulated wage gains and employment losses are smaller than simulated).

All the results discussed above stem from a model for the whole manufacturing sector using industry data in which output and wage elasticities of labor demand were assumed to be the same for all industries. A natural question is if this last assumption holds and, if not, if it is biasing the results significantly. To address the issue, all the coefficients were allowed to vary per industry in both subperiods and the restriction imposed was tested. In 1975–1984, the hypothesis of common elasticities and speed of adjustment was not rejected. For 1985–1997 the wage elasticity and the lagged employment coefficient were statistically equal among industries, while a unique output elasticity was rejected. Paper and chemicals have a significantly smaller elasticity. However, the average elasticity for the manufacturing sector estimated using this model is only slightly higher, while the wage elasticity and the parameter accounting for the speed of adjustment do not show important biases.[15]

Although such similarity between industries is not expected to hold a priori, the statistical result supports the estimation procedure followed us-

15. Results are available upon request.

ing the pooled cross-section time series data set. Further, the decline in the elasticities holds, no matter how much the amount in which they decreased might be overstated.

Even though no direct bargaining over employment has been observed, all our findings suggest that unions have had an effect on labor demand. This has taken place through two mechanisms. First, reunionization changed the way wages were set. Bargaining over wage levels has been done, taking into account the likely effects on the labor demand schedule and outside opportunities for those that would eventually be unemployed. Industries that have been most exposed to competition have registered lower markups than the rest. Union membership, which has declined systematically all along the period, raised the markup during the 1980s. At the beginning of the 1990s, and probably as a consequence of the progressive decentralization of bargaining and nonenforcement of contracts, this effect has vanished in some industries, while in others it has even become negative. Increased openness also has tempered wage demands by unions.

Second, unions have effectively altered the labor demand choice set for employers. Output and wage elasticities have gone down, and union resistance is one of the probable causes. As unions forced wages up and more limits were posed to pass that increase onto prices, firms have been forced to adjust employment to cyclical variations of demand less than before. Further, expected union resistance has probably been at the root of a smaller adjustment of employment to wage increases. As a result of all these changes, wages are higher and employment is lower today than what they would have been if no institutional changes had taken place.

8.6   The Effect of Unions on Employment Adjustment: Other Evidence

Two lines of research were followed in order to further analyze the impact of unions on the labor market, focusing on how they affect employment adjustment. A first approach to the study of labor dynamics was carried out, looking for evidence on the impact of unions on the employment path to equilibrium. Second, the effect of unions on layoff rates was examined, performing the analysis for the whole economy and not just for the manufacturing sector.

8.6.1   Dynamic Labor Demand

Although the conventional wisdom is that unions lengthen the time needed for labor demand adjustment, the estimates in table 8.5 show no change between 1975–1984 and 1985–1997. It is possible that a simple before-after comparison fails to yield an accurate assessment of union impact because of other changes that were taking place in 1985–1997. In particular, the opening of the Uruguayan economy could have shortened adjustment lags at the same time that unionization was lengthening them.

A useful approach to test for this is to consider that the speed of adjustment is itself a function of some variables related to changing the level of employment. This would imply that in equation (5), $\lambda = \lambda(\mathbf{ac}_t)$, with $\mathbf{ac}$ a vector of variables accounting for adjustment costs, that would hence interact with lagged employment (Burgess, 1988, 1989; Burgess and Dolado 1989). Variables that will be included are union density and the openness ratio. Union density should reflect implicit costs of firing workers as well as potential restrictions on the hiring of new workers. On the other hand, when there is more openness, it is quite likely that employers are subject to greater competitive pressure to compete both abroad and domestically, leading to shorter adjustment lags.

Three models are considered in table 8.8: (1) percentage union interacts with lagged employment; (2) openness interacts with lagged employment, and (3) complete interactions among percentage union, openness, and lagged employment. Linear effects are included (and interacted in the third model); otherwise, the interaction coefficients could be interpreted as proxies for linear effects omitted from the model. As shown in columns (1) and (2), the simple interactions with percentage union and openness are positive and negative, respectively, as expected, but estimated with little precision. In the model with complete interactions in column (3), the coefficient for lagged employment decreases with openness but also with percentage

Table 8.8   **Estimates of Dynamic Labor Demand Equations, 1985–1997**

Variable	(1)	(2)	(3)
N_{t-1}	0.876	0.889	0.902
	(0.028)	(0.025)	(0.038)
Q_t	0.056	0.055	0.073
	(0.016)	(0.017)	(0.019)
W_t	−0.034	−0.032	−0.060
	(0.015)	(0.016)	(0.018)
$N_{t-1} \cdot$ UNION	0.001		−0.065
	(0.028)		(0.059)
UNION	0.005		0.522
	(0.266)		(0.532)
$N_{t-1} \cdot$ OPEN		−0.027	−0.102
		(0.024)	(0.052)
OPEN		0.248	0.908
		(0.222)	(0.474)
OPEN $\cdot$ UNION			−0.882
			(1.226)
$N_{t-1} \cdot$ OPEN $\cdot$ UNION			0.108
			(0.134)
SEE	0.044	0.044	0.043

Notes: Each equation also contains three seasonal dummies, five industry dummies, a shift parameter for the 1993–1997 period, and a constant. Each equation is estimated by 3SLS along with a wage equation that includes the same variables as in column (2) of table 8.5.

union. In any case, neither coefficient is estimated with an acceptable degree of precision. Openness also was included in the wage-bargaining equation and consistently had a negative effect on the negotiated wage. An increase in openness from 30 to 60 percent is associated with a 1.7 percent reduction in wages.

These results are not as robust as those related to the static labor demand. However, as a first approach to employment dynamics, they do suggest that low openness in 1985–1992 led to longer lags for employment adjustment, compared to 1975–1984. However, with the increase in openness in the 1990s, the lags quickly shortened and by 1997 were shorter than they were in 1984. The overall effect for the entire 1985–1997 period is an average lag similar to that prevailing for 1975–1984, which is what we reported in table 8.5. Regarding the union effect, no conclusions can be drawn at this stage. A more complex specification for the λ parameter might be needed, possibly accounting for different effects per industry from 1993 onward, but this is beyond the scope of this chapter.

8.6.2   Labor Mobility

The results in section 8.5 showed that labor demand became less responsive to changes in output and wages after the return of collective bargaining in 1985. What we do not know is if unions affect employment adjustment, given that the results in section 8.6.1 were not robust. This is an important question because the success of any policy designed to make the Uruguayan labor market more flexible will hinge on the precise mechanisms through which unions influence employment.

Unionization could be correlated with slower employment adjustment because higher wages for union members virtually eliminate all voluntary turnover. In this case, policy would have to be directed toward the bargaining power of unions. Another possibility is that union threats of wildcat strikes are sufficient to prevent management from ever conducting layoffs. In this case, policy would need to be targeted at strike behavior.

We do not have data on flows in and out of the firm that would allow us to decompose employment changes into changes in hiring, layoffs, and quits (including retirement) and get more meaningful insights into union influence. As a second-best strategy, this section examines household survey data on unemployment, quits, and layoffs. If unionization has resulted in smaller responses of employment to changes in wages or output, this effect should be echoed by some combination of a lower hiring rate, a lower quit rate, and a lower layoff rate. The emphasis here will be on the effect of unions on layoff rates.[16] The analysis will be done using data for all economic sectors, not just manufacturing. Because of possible ambiguity in the responses

---

16. Data on new hires are only available since 1991, and quits are only observed if they result in unemployment.

to questions about events initiating unemployment, we report results not just on layoffs, but also for all unemployment and quits resulting in unemployment. In addition to gaining insights into how unions influence employment adjustment, these results will help determine whether the conclusions for manufacturing industries are generalizable for the entire economy.

Further, there is a sizable literature on how unions affect various forms of turnover, which provides some insights into models of union behavior. It has been well established since Freeman (1980) that unionization is associated with much lower quit rates. The reasons for this correlation remain unsettled. Freeman argues that if unions provide employees with a constructive channel for settling disagreements at the workplace, they will be less likely to quit. Pay compression within unionized workplaces further reduces the quits of employees who receive the largest relative benefits— the least skilled and the youngest. Others have argued that the correlation simply reflects the fact that the wage level is an inadequate measure for the rents received by union members; with a better measure of such rents, the impact of unions would vanish.

The impact of unions on layoff rates is more difficult to predict. In a framework where the welfare of each union member gets equal weight in the aggregate union preference function, one would expect the union to push for job security for all members. Today, however, most models presuppose the existence of politically dominant coalitions of workers within the union, usually the most senior members. In such a setting, only members of the dominant group are sheltered from layoffs. A further complicating factor is the availability and level of unemployment benefits. In the United States, unions have traditionally used layoffs by seniority and unemployment benefits to buffer their most senior members from economic fluctuations. Medoff (1979) found that layoff rates are actually higher for union members than nonunion workers. However, in the public sector in the United States, Allen (1988) found that union members were less likely to be laid off than nonunion workers. The unemployment insurance system in Uruguay provides a much lower replacement rate of income (50 percent–75 percent of the previous monthly wage, capped up to seven minimum wages) than comparable systems in the United States and the European Community, so one might expect Uruguayan unions to place a higher priority on avoiding layoffs at all costs. Unions can significantly increase the transactions costs associated with layoffs. The obligations of a nonunion employer are limited to severance pay. Unions can create additional costs, including work stoppages and slowdowns.[17]

---

17. Initially we planned to include union contract data on severance payments beyond those required by national regulations as part of this exercise. Upon studying the contracts, however, we learned that such payments are negotiated on an as-needed basis, rather than being part of an explicit contractual arrangement. These arranged payments can be quite substantial, as shown in our case study of the banking sector in Cassoni, Labadie, and Allen (1995).

Due to the changes that have taken place, it is important to allow the effect of unions on layoffs to vary within the 1985–1997 period.

Models and Data

To estimate the impact of collective bargaining on labor mobility, ideally one would estimate hazard rates for employment, both overall and separately for quits and layoffs. There are no panel surveys of households in Uruguay and no repeated cross sections with data on completed spells of employment (or unemployment for that matter). The monthly household survey can be used to identify experienced workers who are unemployed, the sector and industry of their last job, and the reason for leaving their last job. Workers are defined as laid off if they say they lost their last job because they were "fired" or the "plant or company closed." Workers who say they were suspended from work or who are receiving unemployment insurance are excluded from this definition because of the ambiguity of whether a separation has occurred. All other separations leading to unemployment (including those who gave a reason for leaving their last job that was coded as "other") are defined as quits.

A new questionnaire was adopted for the household survey in 1991. The survey items used to identify layoffs were not changed, but the wording and number of options for quits were substantially altered. This makes it impossible to estimate models of specific types of quit behavior, such as quits for low pay or quits to return to school. As long as quits are defined broadly, there does not seem to be any significant break in the series between 1990 and 1991 (see table 8.9).

The quit-layoff distinction can be problematic empirically. Interviews with employers about the reasons for a separation would no doubt yield different answers than the household survey. In addition, the timing of the decision and the stated rationale can conceal as well as reveal, for example, workers may quit so as to avoid any stigma associated with dismissal. Accordingly, this study also examines the odds that an experienced worker is unemployed, ignoring the stated reason. This latter measure includes individuals who have been suspended or who are receiving unemployment benefits.

A clear limitation of this approach is that we do not observe cases where persons leave their job without an intervening spell of unemployment. This is unlikely to be too much of a problem with the analysis of layoffs—even with advance notice (which is not required in Uruguay); very few job losers are able to find a new position before their old one ends. Difficulties are more likely in interpreting the results on quits. Simple errors in measurement make this study less likely to reject any null hypothesis. Nonetheless, we must emphasize that the results here deal with only one dimension of quit behavior—quits followed by unemployment—and may not be generalizable to all quits.

Table 8.9   **Means and Standard Deviations of Variables Used in Labor Mobility Analysis**

	1981	1982	1984	1986	1990	1991	1992	1993	1994	1995	1996
Unemployed (yes = 1)	0.068	0.124	0.118	0.090	0.081	0.077	0.082	0.074	0.080	0.104	0.121
	(0.251)	(0.329)	(0.322)	(0.287)	(0.273)	(0.267)	(0.275)	(0.262)	(0.272)	(0.305)	(0.326)
Laid off (yes = 1)	0.009	0.026	0.028	0.017	0.015	0.021	0.023	0.019	0.024	0.036	0.049
	(0.097)	(0.158)	(0.166)	(0.128)	(0.121)	(0.143)	(0.150)	(0.136)	(0.154)	(0.185)	(0.216)
Quit and unemployed (yes = 1)	0.045	0.066	0.077	0.066	0.054	0.054	0.058	0.054	0.055	0.068	0.071
	(0.208)	(0.248)	(0.267)	(0.248)	(0.227)	(0.227)	(0.235)	(0.226)	(0.227)	(0.252)	(0.256)
Percentage union	0.340	0.326	0.324	0.299	0.261	0.248	0.235	0.222	0.216	0.208	0.168
	(0.244)	(0.218)	(0.211)	(0.176)	(0.158)	(0.157)	(0.151)	(0.146)	(0.154)	(0.158)	(0.142)
No. of observations	5,385	5,329	10,196	10,088	9,233	10,794	10,668	10,822	10,944	11,354	11,475

Note: Numbers in parentheses indicate standard deviations.

Probit equations for unemployment, quits, and layoffs are estimated over all experienced wage and salary workers in the household survey for 1981, 1982, 1984, 1986, 1990, and 1991–1996. Data for 1981 and 1982 are available only for the second half of the year. Union membership is not measured in the household survey. It was calculated as stated in section 8.4.

Other variables included in the analysis include employment in the public sector, age, age squared, sex, years of schooling, percentage informal in the last industry of employment (as indicated by lack of health coverage),[18] marital status (one variable indicating married, spouse present), industry (two variables flagging manufacturing and construction—the industries with the most layoffs and unemployment), and quarter (three variables).

Means and Trends

Descriptive statistics for the main dependent and explanatory variables are reported in table 8.9.

Unemployment ranges between 7 and 12 percent over the sample period. These figures are lower than reported unemployment rates, mainly because first-time job seekers are not included in our sample (we also exclude self-employed and unpaid workers). The peak periods of unemployment are the global recession of 1982–1984 and 1995–1996, when Argentina was experiencing very high unemployment. Quit unemployment tracks the overall unemployment rate fairly closely.

The percentage of the labor force on layoff is much higher in the 1990s than in the 1980s, reaching a maximum of 5 percent in 1996. This is almost twice as large as the layoff percentage in 1982, even though the overall unemployment rates for experienced workers in the two years are both around 12 percent. Layoff percentages in 1992 and 1994 averaged 2.4 percent, despite low overall unemployment near 8 percent. In comparison, the layoff percentage in 1982 was 2.6 percent, although the unemployment rate was 12.4 percent.

Union density varies significantly through the sample period. Keep in mind that there was no collective bargaining through 1984; the values reported in table 8.9 for 1981–1986 are based on 1987 data. They are used to control for unobserved industry effects that are correlated with union density. (They vary from year to year because of changing industry composition of employment.) The mean value of percentage unionized dropped from 30 percent in 1986 to 17 percent in 1996. The decline is fairly gradual, except for a sharp four-point drop between 1995 and 1996. Union density declined by 10 or more percentage points in food and beverages, textiles and clothing, transportation and communication, and financial services in the 1990s.

---

18. There is legal mandatory health coverage by social security for those who work in the private sector. The Household Survey poses questions that refer specifically to health. Hence, those that report not having the mandatory coverage are defined as informal workers for the purposes of this study.

Probit Results

The impact of unions varies markedly over the time period (see table 8.10). It is no surprise that in 1981 and 1982 the percentage union variable (which is acting in those years as a proxy for union sentiment or conditions making a sector conducive to union organization) is uncorrelated with layoff, quit, or unemployment odds.

By 1984, unions had become a powerful political force, organizing strikes and demonstrations in an effort to pressure the military government to step down. Percentage union is associated with lower odds of unemployment in 1984, all of which results from fewer quits into unemployment in unionized industries. This behavior probably reflects anticipation of a return to democracy and the restoration of collective bargaining. There is also some indication that layoff rates in sectors of the economy that were to become unionized had already become slightly lower than layoff rates in sectors that were to stay nonunion. The union coefficient in the layoff pro-

Table 8.10   **Transformed Coefficients and Standard Errors of Union Coefficient in Probit Estimates**

Year	Unemployed (yes = 1)	Laid Off (yes = 1)	Quit and Unemployed (yes = 1)
1981	0.008	−0.006	0.011
	(0.024)	(0.006)	(0.020)
1982	0.059	−0.005	0.029
	(0.032)	(0.013)	(0.024)
1984	−0.109	−0.016	−0.066
	(0.026)	(0.010)	(0.021)
1986	−0.065	−0.027	−0.025
	(0.025)	(0.009)	(0.021)
1990	−0.065	−0.011	−0.018
	(0.021)	(0.006)	(0.016)
1991	−0.032	−0.008	−0.023
	(0.019)	(0.008)	(0.016)
1992	−0.053	−0.016	−0.034
	(0.021)	(0.009)	(0.018)
1993	−0.054	-0.014	−0.035
	(0.019)	(0.007)	(0.016)
1994	−0.040	−0.021	−0.004
	(0.019)	(0.008)	(0.016)
1995	−0.088	−0.033	−0.047
	(0.026)	(0.013)	(0.021)
1996	−0.135	−0.084	−0.041
	(0.027)	(0.016)	(0.020)

Notes: Coefficients indicate change in probability resulting from a change in fraction unionized; standard errors appear in parentheses. Control variables include fraction employed in informal sector (as proxied by health insurance coverage), employment in public sector (yes = 1), age, age squared, male, years of schooling, married, industry (dummies for manufacturing and construction), and quarter.

bit increased from –0.005 in 1982 to –0.016 in 1984 (although the latter effect is not estimated with a high degree of precision).

The picture changes further by 1986, when percentage union (based on 1987 data, as in 1981–1982 and 1984) is now strongly associated with lower layoff odds. Unionization is associated with a 1 to 2 percentage point reduction in layoff odds in most years between 1986 and 1994. This may seem modest in absolute terms, but keep in mind that the mean layoff rate varies between 1.5 and 2.4 percent over this period. Assuming a mean unionization of 25 percent, a mean layoff rate of 2 percent, and a union-nonunion difference in layoff rates of 1.5 percent, this implies that the odds of layoff for a union worker are 0.9 percent versus 2.4 percent for a nonunion worker.

Even though union density was declining and unionized companies were more exposed to global competition, the estimated effect of unions on layoffs actually stayed quite strong in 1995 and 1996. The aggregate layoff rate increased to 3.6 percent in 1995 and 4.9 percent in 1996. The impact of unions increased to 3.3 percent in 1995. Based on this coefficient and the means of the key variables, this result implies that the layoff odds for a union worker were 1.0 percent versus 4.3 percent for a nonunion worker. Compared to previous years, all of the increase in layoff risk was borne by nonunion workers. The results for 1996 are too strong; the union coefficient in the layoff and unemployment probits is larger than the mean layoff and unemployment rate.

The increase in the union-nonunion gap in layoff rates might seem puzzling in light of the decline in union density. One might argue that union members are self-selecting into firms with lower turnover, but the model controls for the odds that a worker is in the informal sector, where mobility would be greatest. Another possibility is that the remaining union workers have higher tenure (relative to nonunion workers) in 1995 and 1996 than in previous years, but the data show that this difference (1.2 years) is the same in 1995 and 1996 as in 1991–1994. The most logical possibility is that the unions that did survive until 1995–1996 were the most powerful ones. Layoff rates in those firms stayed at 1 percent, while those in the nonunion sector increased dramatically.

The overall implication of these results is that the layoff odds of a worker in a unionized sector were less than 1 percent from 1986 through 1996. Any fluctuation in aggregate layoff rates reflected adjustments by nonunion employers.

Even with near-zero layoff rates, unionized employers still have some freedom to make changes in employment if the quit rate is sufficiently high. This is not the case in Uruguay. Instead, employer flexibility in unionized enterprises is especially hampered by very low quit rates. The size of the effect varies from year to year between 1984 and 1994, but in most years it is close to a 3 percentage point difference in the odds of quitting and becoming unemployed between workers in a fully unionized and a fully nonunion industry. The impact of unions on quits resulting in unemployment rises in 1995 and 1996.

In summary, the change in labor demand elasticities observed at the industry level of aggregation is no optical illusion. What we see at the micro, individual-worker level matches what we see at the industry level—employment now adjusts less than it would have in the absence of unions. What makes these results all the more convincing is that the same measure of union density used for 1986–1996 has no effect on unemployment, quits, or layoffs when applied retrospectively to 1981–1982. Effects on quits (and a weak effect on layoffs) begin to appear in 1984 as unions became more active, but the full effect on layoffs is not present until bargaining had officially resumed.

8.7   Conclusions

This study has examined a unique situation in Uruguay where before-after comparisons about the impact of collective bargaining can be made. During the period under study there were three distinct regimes: (1) 1975–1984, when bargaining was banned, (2) 1985–1991, when there was tripartite bargaining, and (3) 1992–1997, when there was bargaining without government involvement. During the third regime, the economy became much more open, which would presumably also have an effect on bargaining results.

We have reported strong evidence of a change in economic behavior after 1985. Recursive residuals show structural shifts in five of six industries, with the shifts coming at about the same time as the regime changes. These breaks are also significant in a model specified in differences. Cointegration of employment, output, and labor costs is rejected for the whole period. Wages are exogenous to employment before 1985, but not afterwards.

Based on this evidence we estimated a standard IVE labor demand model for 1975–1984 and a right-to-manage bargaining model for 1985–1997. The results showed that the long-run wage elasticity of labor demand and the employment-output elasticity fell sharply. Although there was no overall change in the amount of time needed for employment adjustment, a detailed examination of the 1985–1997 period suggested that the increased lag created by collective bargaining may have been offset by a shorter lag created by greater openness.

The bargaining model results indicated that unions significantly raised wages in 1985–1992. Afterward, the change in bargaining structure and increased openness had a pronounced effect on bargaining outcomes. Labor demand shifted to the left from 1993 onward. The union wage differential vanished in 1993 in four industries where there were sharp increases in openness and sharp declines in percentage union. Wages in the chemical and oil industry were not affected very much. Although that industry became more open, it has remained heavily unionized, which is no doubt a consequence of state ownership.

What would have happened to wages and employment had the ban on unions been maintained? To build a counterfactual, we estimated an ARIMA(4,1,0) model of wages for 1975–1984, which was used to project a wage path through 1997. Actual wages have been significantly higher than the simulated "nonunion" wage, based on average values for 1985–1997. Taking into account the higher wage level and the reduced elasticities, employment in 1985–1997 was lower than it would have been if unions had not returned.

Because of possible skepticism regarding the use of industry rather than establishment data, we also examined the effect of unionization on turnover, using household survey data. These results showed that workers in unionized industries were much less likely to be laid off starting in 1985 than workers in nonunion industries. Before 1985, no such pattern is present, indicating that unionization is not acting as a proxy for other industry characteristics associated with high layoff odds.

The following picture emerges from these results. Unions returned on the scene as a political and economic force in 1985, and for two years more than half of Uruguay's workers were union members. Union density settled down to about 40 percent in 1987–1992, and unions were able to successfully negotiate higher wages and were able to protect against job loss by reducing employment elasticities. It would be useful to know the precise mechanisms through which unions reduced employment adjustment. It is doubtful that unions had much effect on consumer choices, because no steps were made to expand state ownership or deliberalize trade when unions returned. The most likely channels through which unions had an impact were restrictive work practices and the threat of strikes or slowdowns in situations where layoffs were thought possible.

In the 1990s, the end of tripartite bargaining, trade liberalization, and the recession in Argentina forced unions to make compromises at the bargaining table. Faced with an adverse shift in labor demand, unions reduced their wage demands to preserve jobs. Percentage union declined to 20 percent, as many unionized establishments were no longer economically competitive and others were forced to increase productivity to survive. When a few more years of data become available, it would be fruitful to determine if elasticities had returned to their 1975–1984 values.

This study has focused on wage and employment effects of unions. To get a more complete view of the overall impact of unions on the Uruguayan economy, further study of strikes would be necessary to get a lower-bound estimate of work hours lost to strikes. These would include not only strikes against employers in the context of bargaining over wages, but also strikes—including employer-specific, sector-specific, and general strikes—that take place when a bargaining agreement is in effect.

Finally, this study has not discussed the benefits that result from successful union-management cooperation. Future work should carefully examine this matter, not only because of a need to focus as carefully as possible on labor demand and bargaining, but also because the structure of the system of labor relations has become increasingly decentralized in Uruguay, and unions are apparently changing their utility function when they bargain at the firm level under competitive pressures.

Appendix

Table 8A.1   **Tests of Order of Integration per Manufacturing Industry, 1975–1997**

Lag	Ind.31	Ind.32	Ind.34	Ind.35	Ind.36	Ind.38
			Employment: level (N)[a]			
2	–1.1390	–0.76966	–0.76308	–0.90884	–1.2061	–1.1304
1	–1.3592	–0.37021	–0.62265	–0.44888	–1.1309	–1.0459
0	–1.4418	0.065646	–0.41783	–0.61987	–1.5025	–0.71382
			Employment: first differences (ΔN)[b]			
2	–6.2857**	–3.9358**	–4.5668	–4.6456**	–5.3364**	–3.9579**
1	–7.9173**	–4.8130**	–5.9609**	–5.1050**	–6.8421**	–5.8053**
0	–9.8103**	–7.5615**	–8.5221**	–10.638**	–11.078**	–7.9268**

	Model 1		Model 2		Model 1	
	Ind.31	Ind.32	Ind.34	Ind.35	Ind.36	Ind.38
			Production: level (Q)[c]			
2	–1.3540	–2.5795	–1.9669	–2.5885	–2.1739	–2.5012
1	–2.1006	–2.6076	–2.1029	–2.7678	–2.0751	–2.2671
0	–3.3231	–2.5531	–2.4932	–3.4557	–2.5633	–2.2659

	Ind.31	Ind.32	Ind.34	Ind.35	Ind.36	Ind.38
			Production: first differences (ΔQ)[d]			
2	–12.875**	–9.3050**	–6.6666**	–5.6461**	–6.9455**	–7.3525**
1	–9.9075**	–9.3008**	–8.4027**	–8.7462**	–8.6921**	–8.2238**
0	–15.957**	–11.736**	–11.903**	–11.808**	–11.269**	–11.540**
			Real Labor Costs: level (W)[e]			
2	–1.6274	–1.4101	–1.1787	–0.66944	–1.6212	–0.80691
1	–1.0999	–1.4270	–1.5039	–0.77055	–1.6527	–1.4528
0	–1.5100	–2.1114	–1.5233	–1.1714	–1.9015	–2.0100
			Real Labor Costs: first differences (ΔW)[f]			
2	–6.3493**	–7.1240**	–7.2240**	–7.2307**	–6.4613**	–9.2235**
1	–5.7181**	–7.6787**	–7.7919**	–7.6088**	–7.1191**	–10.307**
0	–11.331**	–12.536**	–9.5372**	–11.935**	–10.601**	–12.048**

Note: Industries reported are: food, beverage, and tobacco (31); textiles and apparel (32); paper (34); chemicals (35); nonmetallic minerals (36); and metal products (38).

[a]Unit-root tests 1975 (4) to 1997 (4) Augmented Dickey-Fuller statistic (t-adf). Critical values: 5% = –2.894; 1% = –3.505; Constant included.

[b]Unit-root tests 1976 (1) to 1997 (4) Augmented Dickey-Fuller statistic (t-adf). Critical values: 5% = –2.894; 1% = –3.505; Constant included.

[c]Unit-root tests 1975 (4) to 1997 (4) Augmented Dickey-Fuller statistic (t-adf). Critical values Model 1: 5% = –3.46; 1% = –4.064; Constant and Trend and Seasonals included. Critical values Model 2: 5% = –2.894; 1% = –3.505; Constant included.

[d]Unit-root tests 1976 (1) to 1997 (4) Augmented Dickey-Fuller statistic (t-adf). Critical values: 5% = –2.894; 1% = –3.505; Constant included.

[e]Unit-root tests 1975 (4) to 1997 (4) Augmented Dickey-Fuller statistic (t-adf). Critical values: 5% = –2.894; 1% = –3.505; Constant included.

[f]Unit-root tests 1976 (1) to 1997 (4) Augmented Dickey-Fuller statistic (t-adf). Critical values: 5% = –2.894; 1% = –3.505; Constant included.

Table 8A.2   CI Tests per Manufacturing Industry, 1975–1997

Johansen's Method

H_0: Rank = p	M1		M2		M3		M4		M5		M6	
	λ-max	Trace	λ-max	Trace	λ-max	Trace	λ-max	Trace	λ-max	Trace	λ-max	Trace
	Industry 31: Food, beverage, and tobacco											
p = 0	26.5**	37.0**	19.8	29.1	19.3*	22.7	12.4	21.2	17.6	29.3	21.0*	26*
p ≤ 1	7.2	9.6	7.3	9.3	3.5	3.5	8.3	8.9	10.5	11.7	5.1	5.3
p ≤ 2	2.2	2.2	2.0	2.0	0.0	0.0	0.6	0.6	1.3	1.2	0.1	0.1

Engle & Granger's Method[a]

	t-adf	beta Y_1	\sigma	Lag	t-DY_lag	t-prob	F-prob
RES31	−2.3634	0.86425	0.052712	2	0.40579	0.6859	0.1390
RES31	−2.3397	0.86806	0.052456	1	−1.9782	0.0511	
RES31	−2.8569	0.84108	0.053326	0			

Johansen's Method

H_0: Rank = p	M1		M2		M3		M4		M5		M6	
	λ-max	Trace	λ-max	Trace	λ-max	Trace	λ-max	Trace	λ-max	Trace	λ-max	Trace
	Industry 32: Textiles and apparel											
p = 0	29.4**	46.1**	15.2	26.5	29.3*	37.3**	20.6	28.5	14.7	22.3	16.6	21.9
p ≤ 1	15.1	15.6	11.2	11.3	7.1	8.0	7.7	7.9	7.6	7.6	4.5	5.3
p ≤ 2	0.0	0.0	0.1	0.1	0.9	0.9	0.2	0.2	0.0	0.0	0.8	0.8

Engle & Granger's Method[a]

	t-adf	beta Y_1	\sigma	Lag	t-DY_lag	t-prob	F-prob
RES32	−1.5819	0.90187	0.081372	2	−3.9343	0.0002	0.0002
RES32	−2.8267	0.82114	0.087956	1	0.78533	0.4344	0.0006
RES32	−2.7237	0.83683	0.087762	0			

Johansen's Method

Industry 34: Paper

	M1		M2		M3		M4		M5		M6	
	λ-max	Trace	λ-max	Trace	λ-max	Trace	λ-max	Trace	λ-max	Trace	λ-max	Trace
p = 0	17.0	26.0	16.3	24.8	9.5	18.6	10.5	15.9	10.9	16.0	6.7	13.3
p ≤ 1	7.8	8.4	6.9	7.7	7.8	9.0	5.0	5.3	4.8	5.1	4.9	6.5
p ≤ 2	0.6	3.8	0.8	0.8	1.2	1.2	0.3	0.3	0.3	0.3	1.6	1.6

Engle & Granger's Method[a]

	t-adf	beta Y_1	\sigma	Lag	t-DY_lag	t-prob	F-prob
RES34	-1.3420	0.93107	0.052093	2	0.34664	0.7297	0.7297
RES34	-1.3032	0.93579	0.051826	1	-0.34372	0.7319	0.8884
RES34	-1.4554	0.93126	0.051563	0			

Johansen's Method

Industry 35: Chemicals

	M1		M2		M3		M4		M5		M6	
	λ-max	Trace	λ-max	Trace	λ-max	Trace	λ-max	Trace	λ-max	Trace	λ-max	Trace
p = 0	17.1	25.7	17.0	24.0	17.2	24.2	18.2	27.3	16.5	27.0	18.6*	27*
p ≤ 1	8.6	8.6	6.9	6.9	5.3	7.0	9.1	9.1	10.5	10.5	7.0	8.2
p ≤ 2	0.0	0.0	0.0	0.0	1.7	1.7	0.0	0.0	0.0	0.0	1.1	1.1

Engle & Granger's Method[a]

	t-adf	beta Y_1	\sigma	Lag	t-DY_lag	t-prob	F-prob
RES35	-1.9601	0.91697	0.052822	2	2.7837	0.0066	0.0066
RES35	-1.4932	0.93509	0.054856	1	-1.6864	0.0954	0.0062
RES35	-1.8562	0.92017	0.055434	0			

(continued)

Table 8A.2   (continued)

Johansen's Method

Industry 36: Nonmetallic minerals

	M1		M2		M3		M4		M5		M6	
	λ-max	Trace	λ-max	Trace	λ-max	Trace	λ-max	Trace	λ-max	Trace	λ-max	Trace
p = 0	25.0*	34.7*	24.4*	32.6*	9.3	15.7	16.9	26.0	16.9	25.2	7.6	15.5
p ≤ 1	6.7	9.6	5.1	8.2	5.6	6.4	6.8	9.1	5.8	8.6	6.6	7.8
p ≤ 2	2.9	2.9	3.0	3.0	0.8	0.8	2.3	2.3	2.4	2.4	1.2	1.2

Engle & Granger's Method[a]

	t-adf	beta Y_1	σ	Lag	t-DY_lag	t-prob	F-prob
RES36	−2.4155	0.75575	0.078311	2	−0.51098	0.6107	0.6107
RES36	−2.7520	0.73861	0.077974	1	−2.5504	0.0125	0.0396
RES36	−4.2689**	0.62802	0.080403	0			

Johansen's Method

	M1		M2		M3		M4		M5		M6	
	λ-max	Trace	λ-max	Trace	λ-max	Trace	λ-max	Trace	λ-max	Trace	λ-max	Trace
					Industry 38: Metallic products							
p = 0	32.1**	52.0**	22.6*	37.8**	23.8**	31.7**	23.1*	34.6*	18.8	29.2	12.3	16.5
p ≤ 1	17.8*	20.0**	12.4	15.2	7.1	7.9	9.7	11.5	9.1	10.4	3.5	4.2
p ≤ 2	2.2	2.2	2.8	2.8	0.8	0.8	1.8	1.8	1.3	1.3	0.7	0.7

Engle & Granger's Method[a]

	t-adf	beta Y_1	\sigma	Lag	t-DY_lag	t-prob	F-prob
RES38	-2.4862	0.75854	0.09377	2	-2.4572	0.0160	0.0160
RES38	-3.6267**	0.66597	0.09648	1	-0.0800	0.9364	0.0539
RES38	-4.1070**	0.66271	0.09593	0			

Notes: The values reported of the λ-max and trace statistics are those for small samples. M1 to M6 refer to different models: M1 is a model with one lag and a constant; M2 includes seasonals; M3 excludes constant and seasonals. M4 to M6 are the same as M1 to M3 but with 2 lags. Critical values for M1; M2; M4 and M5 for the λ-max statistic are 21.0, 14.1, 3.8 for p = 0, p ≤ 1, p ≤ 2, respectively. Those for the trace statistic are 29.7, 15.4, and 3.8. The figures for M3 and M6 are 17.9, 11.4, 3.8, 24.3, 12.5, and 3.8. RES$_j$ are the residuals of the static regression of the log of employment on the log of real labor costs and output.

[a] Unit-root tests 1975 (4) to 1997 (4) Augmented Dickey-Fuller statistic (t-adf). Critical values: 5% = −2.894; 1% = −3.505; Constant included.

**Significant at the 99 percent level.

*Significant at the 95 percent level.

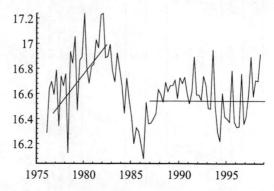

Fig. 8A.1   CI relation 1975–1997: Food, beverage, and tobacco

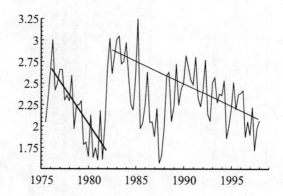

Fig. 8A.2   CI relation 1975–1997: Textiles and apparel

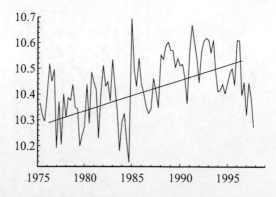

Fig. 8A.3   CI relation 1975–1997: Nonmetallic minerals

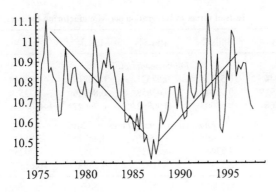

Fig. 8A.4   CI relation 1975–1997: Metal products

Table 8A.3   Tests of Order of Integration per Manufacturing Industry, 1975–1984

Lag	Ind.31	Ind.32	Ind.34	Ind.35	Ind.36	Ind.38
			Employment: level (N)[a]			
2	−2.5950	−1.6086	−1.2078	−1.2582	−0.83448	−1.2016
1	−2.7889	−1.3369	−1.1917	−1.1657	−0.85303	−1.0131
0	−2.7786	−0.87525	−1.2005	−1.1396	−1.2904	−0.40892
			Employment: first differences (ΔN)[a]			
2	−3.5006*	−2.3858	−3.1008*	−2.7929	−3.3449*	−2.2757
1	−4.7977**	−2.7784	−4.0736**	−3.3230*	−4.7078**	−2.9124
0	−5.9422**	−3.9935**	−5.9520**	−5.3326**	−7.8115**	−3.8907**
			Production: level (Q)[a]			
2	−1.3551	−1.5597	−1.0378	−1.5105	−1.2428	−1.3483
1	−1.5006	−1.7065	−1.0796	−1.9170	−1.1518	−1.1211
0	−3.5859*	−1.8756	−1.3054	−2.1261	−1.3826	−1.4192
			Production: first differences (ΔQ)[a]			
2	−7.0006**	−4.5957**	−3.1842**	−3.6610**	−4.1848**	−3.8934**
1	−5.8296**	−4.8931**	−4.4946**	−5.3628**	−4.1581**	−3.9342**
0	−11.328**	−6.5990**	−6.8692**	−6.5669**	−6.7829**	−7.2999**
			Real Labor Costs: level (W)[a]			
2	−1.9026	−1.5492	−1.2954	−1.2465	−1.6269	−1.2547
1	−1.4888	−1.0608	−1.6641	−1.2532	−1.3242	−1.5461
0	−1.7139	−1.7121	−1.5443	−1.7968	−1.4835	−1.8132
			Real Labor Costs: first differences (ΔW)[a]			
2	−4.1317**	4.5866**	−5.2300**	−4.6311**	−3.4348*	−5.0862**
1	−3.7696**	−4.3153**	−5.0854**	−4.8072**	−3.6439**	−5.5376**
0	−6.6798**	−8.0047**	−5.5840**	−8.1063**	−6.5290**	−7.1038**

Note: Industries reported are: food, beverage, and tobacco (31); textiles and apparel (32); paper (34); chemicals (35); nonmetallic minerals (36); and metal products (38).
[a]Unit-root tests 1976 (1) to 1984 (4). Augmented Dickey-Fuller statistic (t-adf). Critical values: 5% = −2.945; 1% = −3.623; Constant included.

Table 8A.4   **Tests of Order of Integration per Manufacturing Industry, 1985–1997**

Lag	Ind.31	Ind.32	Ind.34	Ind.35	Ind.36	Ind.38
			Employment: level (N)[a]			
2	0.46044	0.52536	0.52631	0.23815	−0.85312	−0.19819
1	0.071919	0.73045	0.47858	0.84976	−0.72559	−0.35062
0	−0.15768	0.56007	0.90892	0.26647	−0.68648	0.43073
			Employment: first differences (ΔN)[b]			
2	−5.4181**	−3.1749*	−3.1094*	−3.4679*	−3.8123**	−3.3249*
1	−6.4158**	−4.3344**	−4.2772**	−3.8352**	−4.2025**	−5.3928**
0	−7.8121**	−7.3548**	−5.5190**	−9.3899**	−6.6537**	−7.1566**

	Model 1	Model 2		Model 3		Model 2
	Ind.31	Ind.32	Ind.34	Ind.35	Ind.36	Ind.38
			Production: level (Q)[b]			
2	−0.75192	−1.2447	−2.9285	−1.9864	−4.2071**	−2.1404
1	−1.5892	−1.5003	−2.6061	−1.9425	−3.9310*	−2.1935
0	−2.6469	−1.6600	−3.3922	−2.6681	−4.1709**	−2.3594

Lag	Ind.31	Ind.32	Ind.34	Ind.35	Ind.36	Ind.38
			Production: first differences (ΔQ)[c]			
2	−13.804**	−8.5948**	−5.3499**	−3.9875**	−5.6954**	
1	−8.6737**	−7.4293**	−6.0758**	−6.3471**	−7.0047**	
0	−10.568**	−9.2444**	−8.7901**	−8.9858**	−8.4481**	

Lag	Ind.31	Ind.32	Ind.34	Ind.35	Ind.36	Ind.38
			Real Labor Costs: level (W)[a]			
2	−0.91189	−0.79368	−0.28570	−1.2903	−0.39377	−0.16091
1	−1.0367	−0.87610	−0.27960	−1.3079	−0.75799	−0.63152
0	−1.1111	−1.1709	−0.37651	−1.3448	−1.0533	−1.2518
			Real Labor Costs: first differences (ΔW)[a]			
2	−4.8027**	−5.8573**	−3.5825**	−4.7689**	−6.4608**	−9.4354**
1	−4.5204**	−6.6026**	−5.0680**	−5.3096**	−6.8041**	−9.1931**
0	−11.318**	−9.6385**	−7.2193**	−7.5302**	−8.0805**	−9.8846**
			Alternative Income: level (AW)[a]			
2	−1.0622	−0.26599	−0.68071	−1.5105	−1.2264	−0.31812
1	−1.0977	−0.27479	−0.70182	−1.5243	−1.2636	−0.50304
0	−1.3744	−0.53359	−0.58792	−1.5418	−1.3169	−0.75351
			Alternative Income: first differences (ΔAW)[a]			
2	−5.3632**	−5.0075**	−3.6446**	−4.2448**	−5.0124**	−6.1520**
1	−5.1457**	−5.5917**	−4.6648**	−4.8143**	−5.3230**	−6.6413**
0	−11.588**	−8.8841**	−6.2868**	−6.7643**	−7.3100**	−8.3432**

Table 8A.4 (continued)

Lag	Ind.31	Ind.32	Ind.34	Ind.35	Ind.36	Ind.38
			Open: level (OPEN)[a]			
2	–1.9511	–0.71192	–0.40513	–2.6096	–0.83810	0.037784
1	–1.8791	–0.75411	–0.42541	–2.6449	–0.90096	–0.074127
0	–1.8177	–0.79349	–0.44497	–2.6798	–0.95574	–0.16839
			Open: first differences (ΔOPEN)[a]			
2	–3.8378**	–4.0946**	–3.9638**	–4.0242**	–4.6335**	–4.5125**
1	–4.7509**	–4.9832**	–4.8664**	–4.9206**	–5.4326**	–5.3361**
0	–6.7895**	–7.0051**	–6.8980**	–6.9481**	–7.3932**	–7.3130**
			Union: level (UNION)[a]			
2	–0.40374	–1.6373	–2.8522	–2.1880	–2.9658*	–2.7446
1	–1.0067	–1.8707	–2.8877	–2.2243	–3.0142*	–2.7748
0	–0.87189	–1.9477	–2.9067	–2.1657	–3.2859*	–2.7978
			Union: first differences (ΔUNION)[a]			
2	–4.6465**	–4.3718**	–4.2272**	–3.3584*	–3.6973**	–3.3502*
1	–6.4368**	–6.2137**	–4.7436**	–5.0175**	–3.9382**	–4.7011**
0	–6.3998**	–7.2938**	–6.5521**	–6.8383**	–5.2671**	–7.1536**

Note: See table 8A.3.

[a]Unit-root tests 1986 (1) to 1997 (4) Augmented Dickey-Fuller statistic (t-adf). Critical values: 5% = –2.923; 1% = –3.571; Constant included.

[b]Unit-root tests 1986 (1) to 1997 (4) Augmented Dickey-Fuller statistic (t-adf). Critical values Model 1: 5% = –2.923; 1% = –3.571; Constant included. Critical values Model 2: 5% = –2.923; 1% = –3.571; Constant and Seasonals included. Critical values Model 3: 5% = –3.504; 1% = –4.158; Constant and Trend and Seasonals included.

[c]Unit-root tests 1986 (1) to 1997 (4) Augmented Dickey-Fuller statistic (t-adf). Critical values Model 1: 5% = –2.923; 1% = –3.571; Constant included.

**Significant at the 99 percent level.

*Significant at the 95 percent level.

Table 8A.5   CI Tests per Manufacturing Industry, 1975–1984 and 1985–1997

Industry 31: Food, beverage, and tobacco

Residual	t-adf
	1975–1984[a]
RES31	−2.6059
RES31	−2.6875
RES31	−3.0998*

	M1 (t-adf)	M2 (t-adf)	M3 (t-adf)
	1985–1997		
RES31	−2.2252	−2.7936	−2.2839
RES31	−2.2789	−2.8361	−2.2479
RES31	−2.6317	−3.1671	−2.2749

	t-adf
	1985–1997: bargaining variables added[b]
RES31	−2.8864
RES31	−4.2126**
RES31	−3.6730**

Industry 32: Textiles and apparel

	t-adf
	1975–1984[c]
RES32	−3.8745*
RES32	−4.4456**
RES32	−4.9328**

	M1 (t-adf)	M2 (t-adf)	M3 (t-adf)
	1985–1997		
RES32	−3.1211*	−3.2543	−3.0265
RES32	−2.8752	−3.1210	−2.7955
RES32	−2.9059	−3.1968	−2.8656

	t-adf
	1985–1997: bargaining variables added[b]
RES32	−2.3054**
RES32	−3.0523*
RES32	−3.5752**

Industry 34: Paper

H_0: Rank = p	λ-max	95%	Trace	95%
	1975–1984			
p = 0	23.1*	21.0	26.22	29.7
p ≤ 1	3.11	14.1	3.113	15.4
p ≤ 2	0.003218	3.8	0.00321	3.8

	M1 (t-adf)	M2 (t-adf)	M3 (t-adf)
	1985–1997		
RES34	−1.3382	−1.4095	−1.3407
RES34	−1.7062	−1.6750	−1.7311
RES34	−1.5440	−1.4807	−1.6605

	λ-max	95%	Trace	95%
	1985–1997: bargaining variables added			
p = 0	73.1**	21.0	95.88	29.7
p ≤ 1	13.95	14.1	22.78**	15.4
p ≤ 2	.818	3.8	8.828	3.8

Industry 35: Chemicals

H_0: Rank = p	λ-max	95%	Trace	95%
	1975–1984			
p = 0	21.45*	21.0	25.64	29.
p ≤ 1	7.315	14.1	8.189	15.4
p ≤ 2	0.8738	3.8	0.8738	3.8

	M1 (t-adf)	M2 (t-adf)	M3 (t-adf)
	1985–1997		
RES35	−1.9685	−3.1844	−3.1820
RES35	−1.8963	−3.2570	−3.2627
RES35	−2.2876	−3.4259	−3.2335

	t-adf
	1985–1997: bargaining variables added[b]
RES35	−3.1295*
RES35	−2.9980*
RES35	−2.9394*

Industry 36: Nonmetallic minerals			Industry 38: Metal products		
Residual	t-adf		Residual	t-adf	
	1975–1984[a]			*1975–1984*[a]	
RES36	–2.7816		RES38	–2.2774	
RES36	–2.6459		RES38	–2.8069	
RES36	–4.7583**		RES38	–3.2082*	
	M1 (t-adf)	M2 (t-adf)	M3 (t-adf)	M1 (t-adf)	M2 (t-adf)	M3 (t-adf)

	M1 (t-adf)	M2 (t-adf)	M3 (t-adf)		M1 (t-adf)	M2 (t-adf)	M3 (t-adf)
	1985–1997				*1985–1997*		
RES36	–2.1903	–2.1938	–1.8111	RES38	–1.7686	–1.4230	–1.6327
RES36	–2.6522	–2.5122	–2.2906	RES38	–2.7850	–2.6151	–2.3922
RES36	–3.1145*	–2.9676	–2.7709	RES38	–3.0954*	–2.9954	–2.6557

	t-adf		t-adf	
	1985–1997: bargaining variables added[d]		*1985–1997: bargaining variables added*[b]	
RES36	–2.6123	RES38	–2.7060	
RES36	–2.6298	RES38	–3.3316*	
RES36	–3.2504*	RES38	–4.4244	

Notes: RES*j* are the residuals of the static regression of employment on output and real labor costs for industry *j*. In 1975–1984 and 1985–1997, the regression was done by OLS. When bargaining variables are added, the residual refers to the same model but real labor costs include bargained costs and the method of estimation is 3SLS, so that wages and output are endogenous. Variables explaining the wages are real alternative income, union density and degree of openness. For industries 31 and 35, a dummy variable with value 1 after 1992 is also included. Instruments for output are own lags and seasonals. For industry 34, results using Johansen method are reported. M1 refers to a model with constant; M2 includes also a trend; and M3 further includes seasonal variables. Critical values at 5% are –2.921 for M1; –3.502 for M2 and M3.

[a] Unit-root tests 1975 (4) to 1984 (4). Critical values: 5% = –2.942; 1% = –3.617; Constant included.

[b] Unit-root tests 1986 (1) to 1997 (4). Critical values: 5% = –2.923; 1% = –3.571; Constant included.

[c] Unit-root tests 1975 (4) to 1984 (4). Critical values: 5% = –3.535; 1% = –4.224; Constant and Trend included.

[d] Unit-root tests 1986 (1) to 1997 (4). Critical values: 5% = –2.923; 1% = –3.568; Constant included.

*Significant at the 99 percent level.

*Significant at the 95 percent level.

Table 8A.6   **Nesting the Models: Manufacturing Industries, 1975–1997**

Variable	Coefficient	Standard Error	t-value	t-prob
		Equation 1 for LBLUES		
DUMMY75	1.5171	0.16578	9.151	0.0000
DUMMY85	1.2348	0.18315	6.742	0.0000
DUMMY93	−0.042049	0.011321	−3.714	0.0002
Ind3175	−0.051645	0.023671	−2.182	0.0296
Ind3275	0.043068	0.018266	2.358	0.0188
Ind3475	0.029696	0.020280	1.464	0.1437
Ind3575	−0.11854	0.017924	−6.613	0.0000
Ind3675	−0.044275	0.017602	−2.515	0.0122
Ind3185	0.058061	0.024076	2.412	0.0162
Ind3285	0.070982	0.017312	4.100	0.0000
Ind3485	−0.042266	0.016816	−2.513	0.0123
Ind3585	−0.064253	0.020555	−3.126	0.0019
Ind3685	−0.051673	0.021734	−2.378	0.0178
Qr175	−0.014015	0.0092678	−1.512	0.1311
Qr275	0.0078926	0.0089734	0.880	0.3795
Qr375	−0.013270	0.0090311	−1.469	0.1423
Qr185	0.0028249	0.0085712	0.330	0.7418
Qr285	0.0093799	0.008029	1.168	0.2433
Qr385	−0.017306	0.007874	−2.198	0.0284
Q75	0.10918	0.017011	6.418	0.0000
Q85	0.061004	0.017210	3.535	0.0004
W5	−0.10453	0.015246	−6.856	0.0000
W85	−0.029461	0.017607	−1.673	0.0949
N75_1	0.87269	0.017045	51.198	0.0000
N85_1	0.87360	0.016696	52.323	0.0000

\sigma = 0.0490045

Variable	Coefficient	Standard Error	t-value	t-prob
		Equation 2 for W5		
DUMMY85	−0.25003	0.090993	−2.748	0.0062
DUMMY93	0.17669	0.029745	5.940	0.0000
Qr185	−0.0016989	0.0088961	−0.191	0.8486
Qr285	−0.0053882	0.0085706	−0.629	0.5298
Qr385	0.0015368	0.0084766	0.181	0.8562
AW85	1.1983	0.025099	47.742	0.0000
UNION	0.23724	0.014423	16.449	0.0000
UNION93	−0.37267	0.070938	−5.253	0.0000
UN3193	0.11571	0.074984	1.543	0.1234
UN3293	−0.25977	0.075826	−3.426	0.0007
UN3493	−0.033919	0.067072	−0.506	0.6133
UN3593	0.33136	0.058549	5.659	0.0000
UN3693	−1.6041	0.25859	−6.203	0.0000

Table 8A.6   (continued)

Variable	Coefficient	Standard Error	t-value	t-prob
OPEN85	–0.044855	0.0089277	–5.024	0.0000
W85_1	0.0088766	0.0053193	1.669	0.0958

\sigma = 0.0528143

loglik = 3,274.5936 $\log|\backslash\text{Omega}| = -11.9948$
$|\backslash\text{Omega}| = 6.17595\text{e-}006$ T = 546
LR test of over-identifying restrictions: $\chi^2(28) = 249.677\ [0.0000]^{**}$

Notes: N is number of production workers; W is the real labor cost of a production worker; Q is production; AW is the alternative wage; UNION is union density; OPEN is the degree of openness; Qrj is a dummy variable for quarter j; Ind.i is a dummy variable for industry i. Industries included are: food, beverage, and tobacco (31); textiles and apparel (32); paper (34); chemicals (35); nonmetallic minerals (36); and metal products (38). "_1" attached to a variable indicates the variable is lagged one period. Variables with "75" have the actual values from 1975 up to 1984 and zero elsewhere. Those ending in "85" have a value of zero in 1975–1984 and the actual value from that date on. DUMMY75 is a dummy variable equal to 1 in 1975–1984; DUMMY85 is a dummy variable equal to 1 in 1985–1997; DUMMY93 is a dummy variable equal to 1 in 1993–1997. UNION93 is UNION multiplied by DUMMY93; UNj 93 is UNION93 multiplied by Ind.j. The method of estimation is 3SLS. The present sample is 7 to 552.
Tests of hypothesis: (1) $Q75 = Q85$: &19-&20 = 0; Wald test for general restrictions: Gen-Res $\chi^2(1) = 4.6104\ [0.0318]^*$.
  (2) $W75 = W85$: &21-&22 = 0; Wald test for general restrictions: GenRes $\chi^2(1) = 10.469$ [0.0012]**.
  (3) *LAGGED N75 = LAGGED N85:* &23-&24 = 0; Wald test for general restrictions: Gen-Res $\chi^2(1) = 0.15229\ [0.6964]$.

References

Aghion, P., and G. Saint-Paul. 1993. Uncovering some causal relationships between productivity growth and the structure of economic fluctuations: A tentative survey. NBER Working Paper no. 4603. Cambridge, Mass.: National Bureau of Economic Research, December.
Allen, S. 1986. Union work rules and efficiency in the building trades. *Journal of Labor Economics* 4 (2): 212–42.
———. 1988. Unions and job security in the public sector. In *When public sector workers unionize,* ed. R. B. Freeman and C. Ichniowski, 271–96. Chicago: University of Chicago Press.
Allen, S., A. Cassoni, and G. J. Labadie. 1994. Labor market flexibility and unemployment in Chile and Uruguay. *Estudios de Economía* 21 (special number): 129–46.
———. 1996. Wages and employment after reunionization in Uruguay. *Cuadernos de Economía* 33 (99): 277–39.
Banerjee, A., J. Dolado, D. Hendry, and J. W. Galbraith. 1993. *Co-integration, error-correction, and the econometric analysis of non-stationary data.* New York: Oxford University Press.
Binmore, K., A. Rubinstein, and A. Wolinsky. 1986. The nash bargaining solution in economic modelling. *Rand Journal of Economics* 17:176–88.

Blanchard, O. J., and D. Quah. 1989. The dynamic effects of aggregate demand and supply disturbances. *The American Economic Review* 79 (4): 655–73.

Blanchard, O. J., and L. H. Summers. 1986. Hysteresis and the European unemployment problem. In *NBER macroeconomic annual 1986,* ed. S. Fischer, 15–78. Cambridge, Mass.: MIT Press.

Blanchflower, D. G. 1984. Union relative wage effects: A cross-section analysis using establishment data. *British Journal of Industrial Relations* 22:311–32.

Blanchflower, D. G., N. Millward, and A. J. Oswald. 1991. Unionism and employment behaviour. *Economic Journal* 101:815–34.

Boal, W. M., and J. H. Pencavel. 1994. The effects of labor unions on employment, wages and days of operation: Coal mining in West Virginia. *Quarterly Journal of Economics* 109:267–98.

Booth, A. L. 1995. *The economics of the trade unions.* New York: Cambridge University Press.

Burgess, S. M. 1988. Employment adjustment in UK manufacturing. *Economic Journal* 98:81–93.

———. 1989. Employment and turnover in UK manufacturing industries, 1963–1982. *Oxford Bulletin of Economics and Statistics* 51 (2): 163–92.

Burgess, S. M., and J. Dolado. 1989. Intertemporal rules with variable speed of adjustment: An application to UK manufacturing employment. *Economic Journal* 99:347–365.

Carruth, A., and A. Oswald. 1987. On union preferences and labour market models: Insiders and outsiders. *Economic Journal* 97:431–45.

Cassoni, A., and Z. Ferre. 1997. Costos no salariales en el mercado de trabajo del Uruguay. [Nonwage costs in the Uruguayan labor market]. Working Paper no. 8/97. Montevideo, Uruguay: Departamento de Economía, Facultad de Ciencias Sociales, Universidad de la República.

Cassoni, A., G. J. Labadie, and S. Allen. 1995. Uruguay. In *Reforming the labor market in a liberalized economy,* ed. G. Márquez, 137–91. Washington, D.C.: Inter-American Development Bank, Centers for Research in Applied Economics.

Cedrola, G., J. Raso, and F. Perez Tabó. 1998. *La negociación colectiva en el Uruguay, 1996–1997.* Santiago, Chile: I.L.O., forthcoming.

de Brun, J., and G. J. Labadie. 1997. Mercado laboral, apertura y recesión: La experiencia uruguaya de los noventa. [Labor market, openness, and economic crisis: The Uruguayan experience in the nineties]. In *Mercados laborales en los 90: Cinco ejemplos de América Latina,* ed. CIEDLA, 283–353. Buenos Aires, Argentina: Konrad Adenauer Stiftung.

de Menil, G. 1971. *Bargaining: Monopoly power versus union power.* Cambridge, Mass.: MIT Press.

Edwards, S. 1995. *Crisis and reform in Latin America.* New York: Oxford University Press.

Engle, R. F., and C. W. J. Granger. 1987. Cointegration and error correction: Representation, estimation and testing. *Econometrica* 55:251–76.

Favaro, E., and C. Sapelli. 1986. *Shocks externos, Grado de apertura y política doméstica.* [External shocks, degree of openness, and domestic economic policy]. Montevideo, Uruguay: Banco Central del Uruguay.

Freeman, R. 1980. The exit-voice tradeoff in the labor market: Unionism, job tenure, quits, and separations. *Quarterly Journal of Economics* 94 (4): 643–74.

Freeman, R., and J. L. Medoff. 1982. Substitution between production labor and other inputs in unionized and nonunionized manufacturing. *Review of Economics and Statistics* 64 (2): 220–33.

———. 1984. *What do unions do?* New York: Basic Books.

Fuller, W. A. 1976. *Introduction to statistical time series.* New York: John Wiley and Sons.

Gillespie, C. G. 1991. *Negotiating democracy.* Cambridge, U.K.: Cambridge University Press.

Hamermesh, D. S. 1993. *Labor demand.* Princeton, N.J.: Princeton University Press.

————. 1995. Labour demand and the source of adjustment costs. *The Economic Journal* 105:620–34.

Hamermesh, D. S., and G. A. Pfann. 1996. Adjustment costs in factor demand. *Journal of Economic Literature* 34 (3): 1264–92.

Handelman, H. 1981. Labor-industrial conflict and the collapse of Uruguayan democracy. *Journal of Interamerican Studies and World Affairs* 28 (4): 371–94.

Hausman, J. A. 1978. Specification tests in econometrics. *Econometrica* 46: 1251–71.

Hirsch, B. T., and J. T. Addison. 1986. *The economic analysis of unions: New approaches and evidence.* Boston: Allen and Unwin.

Layard, R., S. Nickell, and R. Jackman. 1991. *Unemployment: Macroeconomic performance and the labor market.* New York: Oxford University Press.

Lewis, H. G. 1986. *Union relative wage effects: A survey.* Chicago: University of Chicago Press.

————. 1990. Union/nonunion wage gaps in the public sector. *Journal of Labour Economics* 8 (1): S260–S328.

Lockwood, B., and A. Manning. 1989. Dynamic wage-employment bargaining with employment adjustment costs. *Economic Journal* 99:1143–58.

Machin, S., and S. Wadhwani. 1991. The effects of unions on organisational change and employment. *Economic Journal* 101:835–54.

Medoff, J. L. 1979. Layoffs and alternatives under trade unions in U.S. manufacturing. *American Economic Review* 69 (3): 380–95.

Pencavel, J. 1991. *Labor markets under trade unionism: Employment, wages and hours.* London: Basil Blackwell.

Picardo, S., C. Daude, and Z. Ferre. 1997. Indice del costo de la mano de obra: 1982–1995. [Index of labor costs: 1982–1995]. Working Paper no. 1/97. Montevideo, Uruguay: Universidad de la República, Departamento de Economía, Facultad de Ciencias Sociales.

Rama, M. 1993a. Organized labor and the political economy of product market distortions. Washington, D.C.: World Bank/CINVE.

————. 1993b. Institucionalidad laboral y crecimiento económico en el Uruguay. Academia Nacional de Economía. Mimeograph.

————. 1994. Bargaining structure and economic performance in the open economy. *European Economic Review* 38:403–15.

Spanos, A. 1986. *Statistical foundations of econometric modelling.* New York: Cambridge University Press.

White, H. 1980. A heteroskedasticity-consistent covariance matrix estimator and a direct test for heteroskedasticity. *Econometrica* 48:817–38.

9

Labor Market Policies and Employment Duration
The Effects of Labor Market Reform in Argentina

Hugo A. Hopenhayn

Introduction

Over the last few years, the debate on labor market reform has been at the center of economic policy debate in Argentina. This debate has been fueled by the sustained growth in the unemployment rate observed during the decade. One of the major targets of the attack on labor market regulation has been high dismissal costs.[1]

Attempts to reduce dismissal costs for all existing jobs have faced strong opposition. As a compromise, and to stimulate job creation, employment promotion contracts for new jobs were introduced in 1995. These contracts are limited to a fixed term ranging from three months to two years.

It is a standard view that the reform stimulated the creation of a large number of these temporary contracts, which currently dominate the flow of new jobs. However, there is now a growing concern about the volatility of these temporary jobs, referred to as *junk contracts,* and a predominant view that they tend to generate excessive turnover. This chapter studies the effect of this reform on job duration.[2]

Our main findings are that the reform generated an overall increase in the hazard rate, and particularly so for the first three months of employment. During this period, the average hazard rate increased by almost 40

Hugo A. Hopenhayn is professor of economics at the University of California, Los Angeles.

1. For an analysis of the effects of job security provisions on employment and reallocation, see Blanchard and Portugal (2001), Hopenhayn and Rogerson (1993), Nickell (1997), and Pagés and Montenegro (1999).

2. Blanchard and Landier (2001) find that temporary contracts in the French labor market increased turnover but not employment. Similar results for Spain are reported in Saint-Paul (2000).

percent. For tenure above three months, the increase was on the order of 10 percent.

9.1 Recent Changes in Labor Market Legislation

During the 1990–1999 decade, there were two major changes in labor market legislation. These have not been major reforms, but rather they introduced flexibility *at the margin* by creating fixed-term and temporary contracts that eliminate or reduce dismissal costs and labor taxes.

The original law (1976) specified mandated severance payments equivalent to one month of salary per year of seniority. Changes were introduced in December 1991 and March 1995.

9.1.1 The 1991 Reform

This reform introduced fixed-term contracts and special-training contracts for young workers. Fixed-term contracts to promote employment were subject to the following terms:

- Applicability is restricted to workers who are registered in the national employment office as unemployed or laid off as a consequence of government employment cutbacks.
- The minimum duration is six months. The minimum renewal period is six months. The maximum total duration is eighteen months.
- Severance payment is determined in two ways. If the contract expires, the payment consists of half one month's salary. If the contract is terminated before expiration, the previous law applies.
- A reduction in labor taxes means that employer contributions are reduced from 33 percent to less than 20 percent.

Fixed-term contracts for new activity involved a somewhat different set of conditions.

- Applicability is restricted to new establishments or new lines of production or services in existing establishments.
- The minimum duration is six months. The minimum renewal period is six months. The maximum total duration is twenty-four months.
- Severance payment is determined in the same ways as for fixed-term contracts to promote employment.
- The same reduction in labor taxes applies as for fixed-term contracts to promote employment.

The most distinct category consisted of training-promotion contracts, which featured the following conditions:

- Applicability is limited to workers less than twenty-four years old.
- Duration varies from a minimum of four months to a maximum of twenty-four months.

- There is no severance payment.
- There are no labor taxes.

It appears that this reform did not have a great impact. The law required approval by trade unions in order for these contracts to apply. The monthly flow of new employment promotion contracts registered at the employment office (which was a requirement) totaled less than 5,000 for the whole country.

9.1.2   The 1995 Reform

This reform introduced a trial period for all contracts, special contracts to promote the employment of certain age groups, and a special regime for small firms. The trial period provision introduced the following conditions:

- Applicability to all new contracts
- Duration of three months
- No severance payments for terminations within this period
- Tax reduction for employee from 20 percent to less than 8 percent, and tax reduction for employer from 33 percent to approximately 10 percent

Special employment promotion contracts:

- They are applicable to workers more than forty years old, who are not required to register in government employment offices.
- The minimum duration is six months; the minimum renewal period is six months; the maximum duration is twenty-four months.
- There is no severance payment at termination of contract. Standard severance payment applies for early termination.
- For labor taxes, employer contributions are reduced from 33 percent to less than 20 percent.

Training contract conditions are similar to previous law for unemployed workers between fourteen and twenty-five years of age.

In the case of small firms, the law establishes that these firms can use the employment promotion contracts from the previous law (described previously) with the following added advantages:

- No previous approval of the trade unions is required.
- There is no need to register the contract in the government employment agency.
- There is no severance payment.

9.2   General Trends during the Period

The period considered has been marked by a sizable increase in unemployment rates, starting at 7.5 percent in the beginning of the decade,

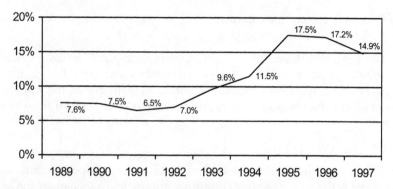

Fig. 9.1   Unemployment rate: Greater Buenos Aires region
Source: Ministerio de Economía, INDEC—May surveys.

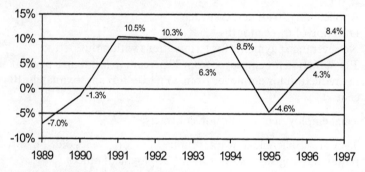

Fig. 9.2   GNP growth: Constant prices 1986
Source: Ministerio de Economía, INDEC.

peaking in May 1995 at 20 percent, and staying around 17 percent in the most recent surveys. Although part of this increase is explained by an upward trend in participation, most is accounted for by unemployment of existing labor market participants. Figure 9.1 gives an account of this evolution since 1993. As far as the business cycle is concerned, fluctuations have been large in the period, averaging out to a 3.7 percent growth rate. As seen in figure 9.2, the first two years of our study correspond to a big recession that is followed by three years of high growth rates. A new sharp recession occurs in 1995, also followed by a period of high growth.

Figures 9.3 and 9.4 provide standard estimates of creation and destruction flows for job matches. The rate of match creation is measured by the ratio of employed workers with less than one month (or six months) of tenure to the stock of employed workers. The rate of destruction is measured by taking the ratio of unemployed workers with less than one month (or six months) duration to the stock of employed workers.

These flows are fairly constant up to 1994. The severe recession in 1995

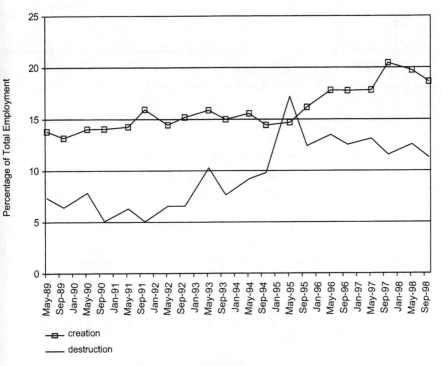

Fig. 9.3   Match creation and destruction: Six months

results in a large shock to match destruction, which is then followed by a steady increase in creation. After 1995, both flows stay at values at least 50 percent larger than those experienced during the first part of this decade. The breakpoint (1995) is a recession year, but also the beginning of the new labor market regime. In what follows, we attempt to identify the impact of this regime change.

9.3   The Sample

We use a linked panel of household survey data for the area of the Federal District and surroundings (Gran Buenos Aires), which amounts to approximately 60 percent of total Argentinean employment. The survey is conducted every six months (April/May and October) with a 25 percent rotation of the panel. As a consequence, each household can—in principle—be followed for two years at intervals of six months. Our sample consists of the linked panels from May 1989 to October 1998. There are a total of approximately 64,000 individuals in the sample, evenly distributed throughout the years, of whom over 44,000 have multiple observations. Based on these observations, our sample comprises a total of over 93,000 transition

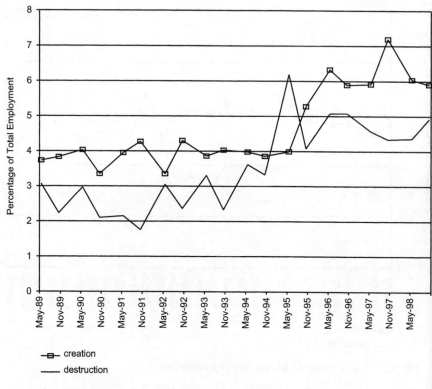

Fig. 9.4   Match creation and destruction: One month

pairs. After restricting the sample to those individuals between twenty-one and sixty-five years old, we are left with a total of approximately 71,000 transition pairs. Our conditional likelihood estimates consider only those individuals with initial tenure under five years who are still in the labor force the following period. This leaves a total of 14,854 transitions.

9.3.1   Variables Used

The variables considered were the following:[3]

- Personal characteristics such as sex, age, and education
- Job characteristics, including

  - type of employment (salaried worker or self-employed)
  - size of firm
  - benefits received (social security contributions, paid vacations, extra month supplement, severance payment, and unemployment insurance)

3. For a list of variables included in this survey, see INDEC (2001).

- duration of current job (if employed) or duration of unemployment spell (if unemployed)

We restrict our analysis to salaried employment, thus excluding the self-employed, entrepreneurs, or family workers, who are not subject to the above regulations.

9.4   Measuring the Effect of Regulation on Employment Duration

The 1995 reform provides a natural experiment that can be used to evaluate the impact of changes in regulation. Overall, one might expect an increase in the flows into and out of employment, as a consequence of the availability of short-term contracts, which we quantify in the following. Given the three-month limit to temporary contracts, one might also expect to see a peak in the hazard rates at this term. The special regime for small firms provides another source for a natural experiment. In particular, one might expect a peak in the hazard rates for employment termination to appear at the point of expiration of the employment promotion contracts (twenty-four months), as well as at times of renewal (every six months).

9.5   Methodological Considerations

9.5.1   Stock Sampling versus Flow Sampling

Our panel data allow us to compute conditional probabilities for transitions out of employment, thus avoiding the problem of stock sampling. Correspondingly, our specification of hazard rates allows for duration dependence.

9.5.2   Interval Censoring

The panel's sampling plan presents the problem of interval censoring. Consider two consecutive surveys, which take place at time t and $t + \Delta$, where Δ corresponds to the six months interval. The survey provides information on the agent's state of employment for each of these two periods and the elapsed duration in that state. Let s_{it} and $s_{it+\Delta}$ denote the states and d_{it} and $d_{it+\Delta}$ the corresponding elapsed durations. Take a worker who is employed in the first survey with elapsed duration d_0. Three things may happen in the following interval: (1) the worker is employed in the same job with duration $d_1 = d_0 + \Delta$; (2) the worker is in a new job with duration $d_1 < \Delta$; and (3) the worker is unemployed where $d_1 < \Delta$ is the length of the current spell.

In cases (2) and (3), where a transition has occurred, it is impossible to determine exactly when the initial job was terminated, because there could have been multiple transitions. However, an upper bound for the duration

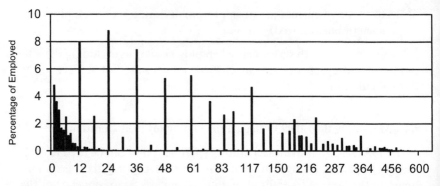

Fig. 9.5   Reported job tenure (in months)

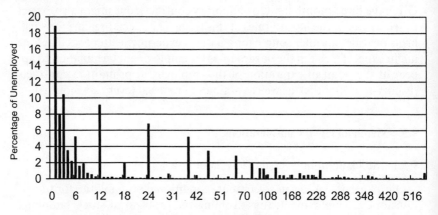

Fig. 9.6   Reported retrospective tenure (in months)

of the first job is given by $d_0 + \Delta - d_1$, which would be exact if only one transition had taken place. The sample variation in d_1 for these workers is thus informative and contributes to identifying the underlying hazard rates. As usual, the observations from workers in case (1) can be treated as right-censored observations.[4]

9.5.3   Measurement Error in Duration Data

As is well known, retrospective questions typically lead to significant reporting errors. In recalling the length of a current or past spell, individuals typically round off their elapsed duration. This gives rise to a common heaping problem where reports get concentrated at particular duration lengths, such as six months, one year, five years, ten years, and so on. This is illustrated in figures 9.5 and 9.6, which give, respectively, reported elapsed job tenure for employed workers and completed tenure in the last

4. For an excellent discussion on interval censoring, see Magnac and Robin (1994).

job for those unemployed, corresponding to all salaried workers in our sample. Unfortunately, some of these heaping times correspond to termination dates of certain contracts, making inference problematic. However, assuming that the distribution for reporting errors has not changed over time, the effect of changes in the duration of specific contracts can still be analyzed by looking at differences in hazard rates before and after the reform.

A second source of problems comes from the ambiguity in the question used to calculate job tenure for employed workers. The survey asks "How long have you been in this occupation?" Some respondents may interpret the occupation as a job description and not a particular match. Measurement error of this type is quite dramatic in our data. If we define a worker who has not changed jobs as one for which job tenure in the second interview exceeds six months, and if reports are correct in both intervals, job tenure should have increased by six months between the two surveys. Table 9.1 gives a distribution of the change in tenure for all workers, those with tenure less than one year, and those with tenure less than six months. As seen, only 5.6 percent of all matches (13.6 percent of those less than one year and 16 percent of those less than one month) satisfy this criteria. Notice that almost 24 percent of all reported changes in job tenure are negative (recall that we are excluding new jobs) and a similar amount report changes in tenure of over one year. The degree of inconsistency is less for workers with lower duration. Furthermore, for workers in this class, a large fraction hold new jobs (less than six months of tenure).

Measurement error is probably less of a problem for identifying when an individual has changed from one state to another (employment to unem-

ble 9.1   **Changes in Reported Tenure**

	All Workers		Tenure < 1 Year		Tenure < 6 Months	
ange in Tenure	%	Cumulative %	%	Cumulative %	%	Cumulative %
ss than 0	23.7	23.7	1.7	1.7	0	0
	22.7	46.4	8.0	9.7	0	0
	0.2	46.6	0.8	10.5	0.5	0.5
	0.5	47.1	1.9	12.5	1.1	1.6
	0.6	47.7	2.3	14.8	1.5	3.1
	1.2	48.8	4.8	19.6	4.6	7.7
	1.3	50.1	6.1	25.7	7.1	14.8
	5.6	55.7	13.6	39.4	16.0	30.9
	1.1	56.8	5.1	44.5	8.8	39.7
	0.9	57.6	3.8	48.3	6.3	46.0
	0.8	58.4	3.6	51.9	6.5	52.4
	0.7	59.1	2.8	54.7	4.5	56.9
	0.5	59.6	2.4	57.1	4.2	61.1
	16.3	75.9	10.7	67.9	1.7	62.8

ployment or vice versa), for which there is a specific question in the survey. The measurement error is more critical in attempting to identify transitions within the same state, times of transition, and elapsed duration. Unless there has been a change of state, we adopt the convention of defining as a new spell one where tenure or unemployment duration in the second survey is less than or equal to six months. If the survey indicates a change of state and elapsed duration in the second state exceeds six months, we consider this a change of state with censored time of change.

9.6   Flows in and out of Employment

The panel data can be used to estimate total flows in and out of employment. The flows are calculated by considering all employed workers in a given survey and observing their state in the following survey period. The flow data thus constructed is pooled across all samples to compute the mean transition probabilities. All calculations were done for salaried workers. Figure 9.7 gives estimates corresponding to all transitions of employed workers into unemployment or a new job. Total flows out of em-

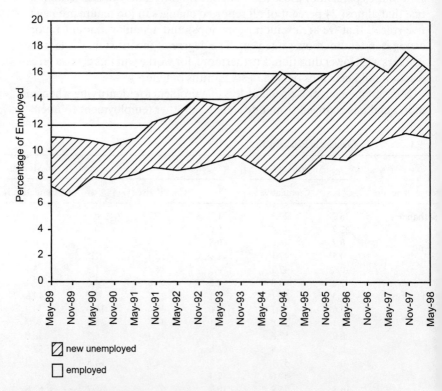

Fig. 9.7   **Transitions from employment**

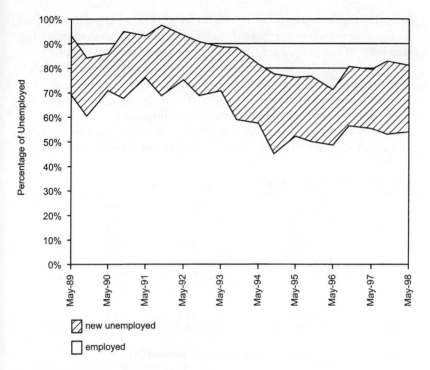

Fig. 9.8   Transitions from unemployment

ployment increased from approximately 10 percent at the beginning of our sample period to over 15 percent at the end. Both components of the out-flow have increased, though in the last few years the growth comes mostly from changes to new jobs.[5] Similar conclusions follow when considering transition flows for workers with short initial job tenure.

Figure 9.8 considers the flows out of unemployment. These have de-creased during the sample period, particularly dominated by lower proba-bilities of being employed after the six month interval between surveys.

Table 9.2 gives hazard rates for total separation, classified by initial job tenure and for years prior to and after the 1995 reform. Most remarkably, these hazard rates exhibit a sharp increase for workers in low tenure brack-ets. In contrast, for workers with initial tenure over six months, there is no detectable change. This table also indicates that total separation rates are initially very high and decrease rapidly with tenure.

Table 9.3 gives the fraction of employed workers in each tenure bracket that ended unemployed in the following survey. The patterns are quite sim-

---

5. It is worth recalling that, due to interval censoring, a transition to a new job may have involved a passage through unemployment.

ilar, with large increases after the reform for workers with initial tenure under three months. It is worth recalling that this duration corresponds to the time limit of temporary contracts. Overall, the transitions to unemployment are a small, but increasing, fraction of total separations. This could be the consequence of either high quits into new jobs or high rates of escape from unemployment. Estimates of the multiple-cycles model studied in the following indicate that the latter effect dominates.

Tables 9.4 through 9.9 provide decompositions of the previous two tables by age, benefits, and firm size. The following specific conclusions emerge:

Table 9.2   Hazard Rates for Total Separations (%)

Years	Before	After
0–1 month	52.8	66.1
1–3 months	37.3	45.6
3–6 months	25.3	32.6
6 months–1 years	21.2	22.3
1–2 years	13.5	13.5
2–5 years	9.1	9.9
Total	13.1	15.7

Table 9.3   Hazard Rates of Involuntary Separations (%)

Years	Before	After
0–1 month	12.9	22.7
1–3 months	9.9	12.8
3–6 months	6.4	8.1
6 months–1 year	5.8	6.8
1–2 years	3.2	4.1
2–5 years	2.5	3.4
Total	3.5	5.0

Table 9.4   Hazard Rates for Total Separations, by Age (%)

	Younger than 25		25–40		Older than 40	
Years	Before	After	Before	After	Before	After
0–1 month	64.0	78.2	48.0	60.0	40.3	60.5
1–3 months	46.1	50.8	35.4	42.9	23.2	41.6
3–6 months	31.9	31.9	22.0	38.9	22.4	23.6
6 months–1 year	27.4	26.6	19.5	20.0	15.9	19.8
1–2 years	16.9	14.8	11.5	13.6	13.1	11.8
2–5 years	11.3	15.6	8.5	8.9	8.4	7.5
Total	25.1	28.3	12.6	15.4	8.5	10.5

Table 9.5   **Hazard Rates of Involuntary Separations, by Age (%)**

	Younger than 25		25–40		Older than 40	
Years	Before	After	Before	After	Before	After
0–1 month	14.4	30.7	11.2	16.9	12.9	20.9
1–3 months	15.0	14.2	5.7	12.9	7.1	10.8
3–6 months	6.9	6.6	5.6	10.6	6.7	6.4
6 months–1 year	8.2	6.0	4.3	5.6	4.8	9.6
1–2 years	2.3	5.0	2.2	4.0	5.4	3.3
2–5 years	2.8	4.7	2.4	3.2	2.3	2.9
Total	4.7	5.4	3.0	4.6	2.6	3.7

Table 9.6   **Hazard Rates of Total Separations, by Social Benefits (%)**

	No Benefits		All Benefits	
Years	Before	After	Before	After
0–1 month	53.3	68.7	46.9	48.3
1–3 months	44.4	48.9	25.4	38.2
3–6 months	27.1	39.5	23.5	20.9
6 months–1 year	24.3	27.3	16.1	16.5
1–2 years	16.7	19.9	10.0	7.3
2–5 years	11.2	12.3	8.3	7.8
Total	17.0	22.9	9.2	8.6

Table 9.7   **Hazard Rates of Total Separations, by Firm Size (%)**

	Small Firms		Large Firms	
Years	Before	After	Before	After
0–1 month	51.0	66.3	58.7	65.3
1–3 months	39.0	47.8	31.5	38.3
3–6 months	24.4	34.0	28.0	28.5
6 months–1 year	21.7	22.8	19.4	20.7
1–2 years	14.5	14.8	10.8	10.1
2–5 years	9.4	11.2	8.3	6.7
Total	13.9	17.7	11.2	11.0

1. The increase in the hazard rate is larger for employees with no benefits. This may actually be explained by the fact that workers on employment promotion contracts—such as the trial period—do not get benefits. Indeed, as we will see later, the share of the flow out of employment due to termination of temporary contracts increased significantly after the reform.

Table 9.8   Hazard Rates of Involuntary Separations, by Social Benefits (%)

	No Benefits		All Benefits	
Years	Before	After	Before	After
0–1 month	12.7	24.4	10.2	12.1
1–3 months	10.9	13.9	8.5	11.6
3–6 months	7.1	8.7	5.9	7.1
6 months–1 year	6.6	8.3	4.3	5.5
1–2 years	4.1	5.8	1.8	2.3
2–5 years	2.5	3.8	2.8	3.0
Total	2.1	2.8	2.6	3.0

Table 9.9   Hazard Rates of Involuntary Separations, by Firm Size (%)

	Small Firms		Large Firms	
Years	Before	After	Before	After
0–1 month	13.0	23.2	12.7	20.4
1–3 months	10.4	12.8	8.1	13.0
3–6 months	6.3	8.8	6.5	6.0
6 months–1 year	5.4	6.5	6.9	8.0
1–2 years	3.4	4.7	2.5	2.8
2–5 years	2.5	4.2	2.4	1.7
Total	3.5	5.6	3.4	3.4

2. The hazard rates separations in low-duration brackets increase more for the treatment groups (small firms, workers less than twenty-five and over forty). The difference is somewhat less pronounced when considering flows into unemployment. This suggests that workers in these targeted groups may be experiencing a fast turnaround from unemployment.

9.7   Hazard Rate Estimation

This section gives details on the methodology used to estimate hazard rates.[6]

9.7.1   Estimation

We construct a piecewise constant-baseline hazard function. Consider a grid of durations $\{0 = t_0 < t_1 < \ldots < t_J\}$, and for $j = 1, \ldots, J$ let $\Delta_j = t_j -$

6. Hazard function models have been extensively used in the economic literature over the last two decades (compare, e.g., Lancaster [1990] and Heckman and Singer [1984]).

t_{j-1}, denote the length of each of the corresponding J intervals. Hazard rates are assumed constant within each interval. Let $J(t) = \max\{j \mid t_j < t\}$, so that $t_{J(t)} \leq t < t_{J(t)+1}$.

Given vectors of covariates $\mathbf{x} = (\mathbf{x}_1, \mathbf{x}_2)$ and parameters $\boldsymbol{\beta} = (\boldsymbol{\beta}_0, \{\boldsymbol{\beta}_j\}_{j=1,\ldots,J})$, the hazard rate is given by

$$h(t; \mathbf{x}, \boldsymbol{\beta}) = g(\mathbf{x}_1, \boldsymbol{\beta}_0)h_{J(t)}(\mathbf{x}_2, \boldsymbol{\beta}_{J(t)}).$$

This is a hybrid model, where some covariates ($\mathbf{x}_1$) affect the hazard rate proportionately, while the remaining covariates ($\mathbf{x}_2$) affect each segment separately. As an example, taking one of the dummy variables to be the indicator of the years with temporary contracts, this formulation allows us to study the effect these contracts had on different segments of the hazard rate.

Given the above specification, the survival function $S(t)$ satisfies

$$S(t; \mathbf{x}, \boldsymbol{\beta}) = \exp\left\{-g(\mathbf{x}_1, \boldsymbol{\beta}_1)\left[\sum_{1 \leq j \leq J(t)-1} h_j(\mathbf{x}_2, \boldsymbol{\beta}_{2j1})\Delta_j + h_{J(t)}(\mathbf{x}_2, \boldsymbol{\beta}_{2j1})(t - t_{J(t)})\right]\right\}.$$

Our data consists of employment spells that may have been completed or continued between two consecutive interviews. For both types of spells, we have information on elapsed duration at the time of the first interview, which we denote by t_0 months. In case of incomplete spells, elapsed duration in the second interval, t_1, is given by $t_1 = t_0 + 6$ because the survey takes place every six months. In case of complete spells, the information is limited due to interval censoring. Letting δ denote the duration of the new spell (either a new job or unemployment), all we know is that $t_1 \in [t_0, t_0 + 6 - \delta]$.

The conditional probability of a continuing spell is given by $S(t_0 + 6)/S(t_0)$, and the conditional probability of a completed spell is given by $(S[t_0] - S[t_0 + 6 - \delta])/S(t_0)$. Letting I_0 denote the set of individuals with continuing spells and I_1 those with completed spells, the likelihood function is given by

$$\ln L(\mathbf{x}, \boldsymbol{\beta}) = \sum_{i \in I_0}[\ln S(t_i + 6; \mathbf{x}_i, \boldsymbol{\beta}) - \ln S(t_i; \mathbf{x}_i, \boldsymbol{\beta})]$$

$$+ \sum_{i \in I_1}\{\ln[S(t_i; \mathbf{x}_i, \boldsymbol{\beta}) - S(t_i + 6 - \delta; \mathbf{x}_i, \boldsymbol{\beta})]\ln S(t_i; \mathbf{x}_i, \boldsymbol{\beta})\}.$$

Note that by restricting our estimates to conditional probabilities, we circumvent the problems associated to length bias sampling and nonstationarity of flows. This is also the reason why we have not included in our estimates the information of the elapsed length of the *second* spell for those individuals that completed the initial spell and were employed in a new job at the time of the second interview.

The specification used for the hazard functions is log-linear, so $g(\mathbf{x}, \boldsymbol{\beta}) = \exp(\boldsymbol{\beta}'\mathbf{x})$ and $h_j(\mathbf{x}, \boldsymbol{\beta}_j) = \exp(\boldsymbol{\beta}_j'\mathbf{x})$.

9.8   Results

The following variables were included in the estimates:

Age	Measured in Years
Sex	0 = female; 1 = male
Sch1	Complete elementary school
Sch2	Incomplete high school
Sch3	Complete high school
Sch4	Incomplete college
Sch5	Completed college
Large firm	Dummy for more than 50 employees
Benefits	0 = no benefits; 1 = some or all benefits
95–98	Dummy for years 95–98

Table 9.10 gives the mean hazard rates and survival function implied by our estimates. Note that hazard rates are quite large during the first few months and fall rapidly thereafter. Almost half of the jobs are terminated before three months, and approximately one-third reach one year. At that point, hazard rates are very low.

Table 9.11 gives the maximum likelihood estimates. For each set of regressions, there are three columns giving, respectively, the parameter estimates, the standard errors, and the risk ratios. Naturally, the latter are only given for dummy variables. The demographic covariates are highly significant and have similar values across the three specifications. Age decreases the hazard rate at a rate of 1.3 percent per year. Male workers face a 20 percent higher risk of termination. Higher schooling reduces the risk of job termination. In particular, college graduates have half the risk of those workers with no complete elementary education. Employment in a large firm results in a mild (but significant) reduction in this risk. Finally, workers with informal labor contracts (those perceiving no benefits) have twice as high a risk of employment termination.

The first three columns correspond to estimates of a hazard function

Table 9.10   Survival Function and Hazard Rate

Years	Survival Function	Hazard Rate[a]
1 month[b]	1	0.326
3 months	0.542	0.158
6 months	0.361	0.023
1 year	0.323	0.023
2 years	0.258	0.016
5 years	0.162	

[a]Hazard rates are monthly and constant in the interval defined by the given row and the following one.

[b]Duration is reported by months, so the minimum reported in the sample is one month.

Table 9.11   Maximum Likelihood Estimates

Parameters	Estimate	Standard Error	Risk Ratio	Estimate	Standard Error	Risk Ratio	Estimate	Standard Error	Risk Ratio
Age	-0.0128***	0.00		-0.0121***	0.0019		-0.0125***	0.0019	
Sex	0.146***	0.05	1.157	0.2066***	0.0451	1.230	0.2038***	0.0451	1.226
Sch1	-0.108*	0.07	0.898	-0.1292**	0.0684	0.879	-0.1295**	0.0685	0.879
Sch2	-0.215**	0.08	0.807	-0.2029***	0.0731	0.816	-0.2057***	0.0733	0.814
Sch3	-0.324***	0.08	0.724	-0.3456***	0.0782	0.708	-0.346***	0.0783	0.708
Sch4	-0.375***	0.09	0.687	-0.457***	0.0859	0.633	-0.4614***	0.0858	0.63
Sch5	-0.702***	0.01	0.496	-0.7324***	0.0972	0.481	-0.7345***	0.0972	0.48
Size	-0.104***	0.04	0.902	-0.128***	0.0423	0.880			
Benefits	-0.608***	0.04	0.544	-0.528***	0.0423	0.589	-0.5288***	0.0425	0.589
1-3 months									
Constant	-0.033	0.12		-0.4523***	0.1294		-1.0716	0.3723	
95-98	0.327***	0.07	1.386	0.3794***	0.1048	1.461	0.4159	0.1272	1.516
Large firm							-0.0616	0.1705	0.94
Large firm · 95-98							-0.1086	0.2272	0.897
3-60 months									
Constant	-3.007***	0.11							
95-98	0.107**	0.05	1.112						
3-6 months									
Constant				-1.0602***	0.1225		-1.6054	0.3734	
95-98				0.1542*	0.0978	1.167	0.1376	0.1162	1.148
Large firm							-0.2542	0.1505	0.776
Large firm · 95-98							0.014	0.2162	1.014

(*continued*)

Table 9.11 (continued)

Parameters	Estimate	Standard Error	Risk Ratio	Estimate	Standard Error	Risk Ratio	Estimate	Standard Error	Risk Ratio
6–12 months									
Constant				-3.1055***	0.1324		-3.676	0.3763	
95–98				0.3312***	0.1175	1.393	0.2278	0.146	1.256
Large firm							-0.1929	0.176	0.825
Large firm · 95–98							0.3311	0.2465	1.393
12–24 months									
Constant				-2.9423***	0.1173		-3.5802	0.3703	
95–98				0.0578	0.086	1.060	0.1272	0.105	1.136
Large firm							-0.0094	0.119	0.991
Large firm · 95–98							-0.1926	0.1858	0.825
24–60 months									
Constant				-3.3049***	0.1175		-3.9331	0.371	
95–98				0.0908	0.0784	1.095	0.1487	0.098	1.16
Large firm							-0.0328	0.1105	0.968
Large firm · 95–98							-0.1549	0.1644	0.857
N	14,854			14,854			14,854		
Mean log-likelihood	-0.5258			-0.4722			-0.4720		

***Significant at the 1 percent level.
**Significant at the 5 percent level.
*Significant at the 10 percent level.

with two segments: elapsed duration of less than three months and elapsed duration of more than three months. Though it is plausible that policy changes affect all of the hazard function, the introduction of temporary contracts in 1995 is more likely to impact the first segment. Indeed, our estimates show this pattern: Hazard rates for the first three months rise by almost 40 percent after 1995, while the overall increase for jobs with longer tenure is around 10 percent. These parameters are estimated quite precisely, so this difference is significant.

The second specification provides a larger set of duration intervals. After 1995, hazard rates in the one- to three-month interval increase by more than 40 percent. For longer tenure brackets, the increase is not monotonic. Most remarkably, in the six- to twelve-month segment, the increase is also close to 40 percent. However, this increase applies to a much lower base: For the average individual in the sample, after 1995 hazard rates in the one- to three-month interval increase by 23 percentage points (33 percent to 46 percent), while for the six- to twelve-month interval, the increase represents less than 1 percentage point (2.3 percent to 3.2 percent).

The increase in hazard rates for jobs exceeding the three-month limit may seem perplexing. However, there is an explanation. Temporary contracts have two effects. On the one hand, it allows firms to terminate bad matches more rapidly. This selection effect leads to a decrease in hazard rates for the period following the end of a temporary contract. On the other hand, temporary contracts reduce the cost of turnover and thus the cost of experimenting with new matches. This can have a positive impact on overall hazard rates.

The third specification allows for the dummies of firm size and its interaction with 1995–1998 to affect selectively each segment of the hazard rate. This specification allows us to test the impact of the special regime for small firms introduced in 1995. None of the coefficients for these added variables turns out to be significant. Similar results were obtained when including dummy variables for age groups interacted with 1995–1998 in each of the segments. Thus, the evidence does not detect a significant impact of the special regimes for small firms and young workers.

9.9   Final Remarks

This chapter analyzes the impact of the 1995 labor market in Argentina. Our results show that this reform had a very strong impact on labor turnover, increasing hazard rates during the trial period by 40 percent, without a compensating decrease for longer tenure. In contrast, the special regimes for small firms and young workers show no sizable effects.

What is the economic significance of this response? The policies implied lower taxes for workers with temporary contracts, inducing an increase in hiring but also a substitution away from longer-term employment. Evaluating the costs of this type of distortion is obviously an important question. In addition, by reducing the cost of experiencing new matches, this policy may have contributed to a better allocation of workers to firms. As indicated by the increase in hazard rates for tenures beyond the limit of temporary contracts, firms seem to have reacted positively to this incentive.

A complete evaluation of the costs and benefits of these policies would require formulating and estimating a structural model of job matching. The results presented in this chapter suggest that research efforts in this direction can prove substantial.

References

Blanchard, O., and A. Landier. 2001. The perverse effects of partial labor market reform: Fixed duration contracts in France. NBER Working Paper no. 8219. Cambridge, Mass.: National Bureau of Economic Research, April.

Blanchard, O., and P. Portugal. 2001. What hides behind an unemployment rate: Comparing U.S. and Portuguese labor markets. *American Economic Review* 91 (1): 187–207.

Heckman, J., and B. Singer. 1984. Econometric duration analysis. *Journal of Econometrics* 24:63–112.

Hopenhayn, H., and R. Rogerson. 1993. Job turnover and policy evaluation: A general equilibrium analysis. *Journal of Political Economy* 101 (5): 915–38.

INDEC. 2001. Encuesta permanent de hogares: Base usuaria ampliada. Available at [http://www.indec.mecon.gov.ar.eph/May2001/Docs/Buadoc2.doc].

Lancaster, T. 1990. *The econometric analysis of transition data.* Econometric Society Monograph Series. Cambridge: Cambridge University Press.

Magnac, T., and J.-M. Robin. 1994. An econometric analysis of labour market transitions using discrete tenure data. *Labour Economics* 1:327–46.

Nickell, S. 1997. Unemployment and labor market rigidities: Europe versus North America. *Journal of Economic Perspectives* 11 (3): 55–74.

Pagés, C., and C. Montenegro. 1999. Job security and the age-composition of employment: Evidence from Chile. IADB Working Paper no. 398. Washington, D.C.: Inter-American Development Bank.

Saint-Paul, G. 2000. Flexibility vs. rigidity: Does Spain have the worst of both worlds? Universitat Pompeu Fabra Discussion Paper no. 144. Barcelona, Spain: Universitat Pompeu Fabra.

Labor Market Regulation and Employment in the Caribbean

Andrew S. Downes, Nlandu Mamingi, and
Rose-Marie Belle Antoine

10.1 Introduction

One of the major economic challenges facing the Caribbean is the generation of employment opportunities to reduce the high levels of unemployment experienced primarily among the young and female segments of the workforce. Although several reasons have been suggested for the high levels of unemployment in the region, little attempt has been made to rigorously assess the underlying causes of unemployment. An analysis of unemployment requires an examination of both the supply and demand sides of the labor market.

This research project focuses on the demand side of the labor market by examining the impact that labor market regulations have had on employment creation in the English-speaking Caribbean countries of Barbados, Jamaica, and Trinidad and Tobago. Although a recent Inter-American Development Bank (IADB) report on labor market reform in Latin America and the Caribbean indicates that the English-speaking Caribbean countries

Andrew S. Downes is professor and director of the Sir Arthur Lewis Institute of Social and Economic Studies, University of the West Indies. Nlandu Mamingi is senior lecturer in the Department of Economics, University of the West Indies. Rose-Marie Belle Antoine is a senior lecturer in law in the Faculty of Law, University of the West Indies.

We would like to thank Professors Daniel Hamermesh, Jim Heckman, and Giussepe Bertola and Carmen Pagés for their comments on various drafts of this paper. We are also grateful to the referees for constructive comments on the last draft of this paper. The participants at the various seminars organized by the office of the Chief Economist of the Inter-American Development Bank provided useful suggestions and a stimulating environment. Research assistants Cyrlene Odle and Adrian Carter provided valuable statistical assistance at different stages of the project. A number of law students of the Cave Hill Campus, University of the West Indies, assisted with the identification of labor legislation. Doris Downes ably typed and edited the paper.

have a lower level of labor market inflexibility than Latin American countries, the regulatory environment in both the labor and commodity markets has had some adverse impact on employment creation in the region (IADB 1996). Results from a study of the operations of the labor market in the Caribbean Group for Cooperation in Economic Development (CGCED) suggest that these regulatory measures do have some effect on the operation of businesses in the region (see Abt Associates 1998).

Labor market regulation generally refers to the range of economic, social, and judicial measures and mechanisms that affect labor market outcomes and behavior. Such regulation emerges from the legislative machinery of the government, case or common law, and the collective bargaining process between labor unions and employers. Labor market regulatory measures cover such areas as the following:

- The establishment and protection of workers' rights
- The protection of the vulnerable
- The establishment of minimum compensation for work
- The assurance of decent working conditions
- The provision of income security (see table 10.1)

Regulatory measures may be direct (i.e., via the legislative machinery or government intervention) or indirect (i.e., via the voluntaristic collective-bargaining process or custom and tradition). While such measures protect

Table 10.1   Labor Market Regulation Measures

Type of Intervention	Guarantees and Policies
Establishment and protection of workers' rights	Right to associate and organize, right to bargain collectively, right to engage in industrial action, right to contest dismissals, job protection during strikes, conciliation and arbitration to resolve conflict
Protection for the vulnerable	Minimum working age to avoid child labor; equality of wages and employment opportunities; antidiscrimination policies covering race, sex, age, disability; special provision for women (such as maternity leave with pay); restriction on temporary contracts with respect to contingent workers; paternity leave; occupational licensing; immigration laws
Establishment of minimum compensation for work	Minimum wages, minimum nonwage benefits, overtime pay, bonus payments, night work
Assurance of decent working conditions	Minimum occupational health and safety conditions, maximum hours of work with break periods, holiday with pay
Provisions of income security	Social security provisions (disability, layoff, old age, sickness), job security and severance pay, wage and price controls, pension regulations, gratuity, advance notice with pay, unemployment insurance, temporary provisions

Source: Adapted from World Bank (1995, 71).

workers from exploitation and poor working conditions, they represent additional costs to employers. The challenge for policymakers is to design a regulatory system that minimizes the additional labor (i.e., adjustment) costs to employers while protecting the socioeconomic welfare of workers in the labor market. By minimizing such labor costs, employers would be in a better position to hire more workers given other favourable economic conditions. It should be noted that labor market regulation represents only one variable that affects the employment of persons in the labor market.

The main objectives of this research project are these:

1. To document the range of labor market regulations existing in the three English-speaking members of the IADB
2. To identify the cost implications of such regulations
3. To empirically determine the impact that such measures have on employment determination using econometric methods

This report documents the findings of research undertaken to determine the impact of labor market regulation on employment in the English-speaking Caribbean countries. Given data availability, the empirical section only deals with Barbados, Jamaica, and Trinidad and Tobago. The structure of the presentation is as follows: In section 10.2, the institutional framework governing the operation of the labor market is outlined. The nonwage cost implications of this framework are examined in section 10.3. An attempt is made to develop indexes of labor market regulation based on the various provisions in labor regulation and, to a lesser extent, in collective bargaining agreements. The incorporation of nonwage labor costs into labor demand function is examined in section 10.4. The statistical data used in the estimation process are examined in section 10.5, while the empirical results are presented in section 10.6. The possible policy implications of the research are given in a closing section.

10.2 Institutional Framework

One aspect of the institutional framework governing the operation of the labor market is the judicial or legislative (direct) aspect of the labor market regulation. The main areas covered by this form of labor market regulation in the Caribbean include freedom of association and industrial action in the form of trade union activity; statutory regulation of dispute settlement (via conciliation or arbitration); the enforceability of collective-bargaining agreements; the recognition of unions; alternative contracts of employment; national insurance and social security; occupational health and safety; maternity and sick leave; overtime and holidays with pay; termination of employment; redundancy and severance; minimum wages; gender equality; equal remuneration; and regulations governing the employment of children. In addition to these legislative measures, labor unions and employers negotiate collective-bargaining agreements that contain measures covering hours of work; shift work; the payment of allowances such as uniform, entertainment, laundry, and hazard allowances; leave arrangements; manning levels; dismissal rules (LIFO); training of workers; and grievance procedures. The nature and extent of these regulations vary from country to country in the region (see table 10.2). Labor law in the Caribbean is characterized by a mixture of legislation, common law doctrines, custom and policy.

The institutional framework governing industrial relations in the region varies from a model of statutory intervention, as observed in Trinidad and Tobago, to the voluntaristic model followed in Barbados. The differences in the institutional framework within the region have emerged from the culture of trade unionism and the need to maintain labor and economic stability in order to propel economic development. For example, Jamaica and Trinidad and Tobago are known to have much more militant trade union movements than Barbados and Belize. In Guyana, Trinidad and Tobago, and the Bahamas, there are statutory provisions making all collective agreements legally enforceable, while in Barbados there is no such provision. There are no legal provisions for the recognition of a trade union in Barbados, Belize, and Guyana. The degree of unionization of labor varies from 13 percent of the labor force in Belize to 32 percent in Guyana (see Rama 1995). Although the degree of unionization appears to be low, the labor unions still have significant membership in strategic sectors of the economy (e.g., the public sector, ports, public utilities).

However, in all of the countries of the region, the original approach was based on the common law—that is, the voluntaristic model, which is still observed in certain countries. This is an important factor in attempting to explain the relative lack of movement in labor law regulatory indexes. The common law, unlike the civil law systems of Latin America, is based on case law and is characterized by ad hoc formulation of legal rules and regulations. In contrast, in the civil law systems, law is characterized by legal legislation and the code, which are deliberate forms of legal policy making. This has had ramifications for labor law regulation in common-law countries because the defining characteristic in common law is nonintervention by government. Labor regulation is therefore dependent on market forces and the strength of the bargaining parties. Legislation is usually relatively late in coming, and even where it occurs it is often distorted by case law.

Key concepts such as redundancy, the recognition of unions, the obligation to pay wages, and holidays with pay were left to the courts to determine. This explains why before the relatively late coming of legislation in the region, mainly in the late 1960s, the economic value of these key concepts stood at zero because the common law had made no provision for them.

In this study we focus on three main areas of labor market regulation in the Caribbean, namely, national insurance payments, severance payments, and minimum wages.

	Bahamas	Barbados	Belize	Guyana	Jamaica	Trinidad and Tobago
Period of prior notice	1/2 to 1 month	Negotiable	1/2 to 1 month	1/2 month	2 to 12 weeks	2 months
Payment for dismissal with just cause	0	0	0	0	0	0
Payment for dismissal without just cause	Negotiable collectively	2 1/2 weeks for service between 1 and 10 years; 3 weeks for service between 10 and 20 years; 3 1/2 weeks for more than 20 years	1 week's pay per year of service after 5 years of service	negotiable collectively		1/2 times period of service for 1 to 4 years of service; 3/4 times period of service for more than 5 years
Payment for dismissal for economic reason	Negotiable collectively	2 1/2 weeks for service between 1 and 10 years; 3 weeks for service between 10 and 20 years; 3 1/2 weeks for more than 20 years	1 week's pay per year of service after 5 years of service	negotiable collectively		1/2 times period of service for 1 to 4 years of service; 3/4 times period of service for more than 5 years
Limit to payment for dismissal	No	Maximum limit to monthly salary	Maximum of 42 weeks	No	No	No
Compensation for termination by worker	None	None	For 10 years of service, 1/4 times the number of years of service	None	None	None
Unemployment insurance	No	Yes	No	No	No	No
Probationary period	3 months to 1 year	Negotiable	2 weeks	None	3 months	Negotiable
Duration of temporary contracts	Without restrictions	Without restrictions	Without restrictions	Without restrictions	Without restrictions	Without restrictions, but in practice it is 6 months
Maximum workday (hrs/wk)	48	40	45	48		
Charges for added hours	50	50	50	50		
Charges for night work	Nothing if ordinary workday	Nothing	Nothing if ordinary workday	Nothing if ordinary workday		
Charges for work on holidays (%)	100 for Sundays; 150 for holidays	100	Nothing if ordinary workday	100		

National insurance and social security benefits are provided in all countries. Benefits cover such areas as medical care, sickness, unemployment, old age/pension/retirement, employment injury, maternity, invalidity, and survival. Although there are differences in the range of benefits provided, all the countries satisfy the minimum standards set by the International Labour Organization. Both employers and employees contribute to the national insurance and social security schemes, which can be considered as payroll taxes. The contribution rates for employees and employers to social insurance schemes are given in table 10.3. The payment of such contributions by employers can represent a significant part of their labor costs, and several employers have been delinquent in their payments to the national insurance scheme. In Barbados, several employers find such contributions relatively high and become delinquent with respect to their payments into the national insurance fund.

The most contentious area of labor law in the region relates to the termination of workers and calculation of associated firing costs to employers (see Antoine [1998] for a full discussion). Employment is usually governed by a mixture of contract and law. Pure contract law principles, which do not usually consider the peculiar relationship of the worker to his or her employment, may also govern the labor law environment. For example, by common law, termination is generally regarded as an essentially contractual concept. This means that A contracts to work for B, and if he does not perform adequately for any reason, such as poor performance, strike, or even serious illness, he has breached the fundamental term of the contract and may be lawfully dismissed. "Summary dismissal" is termination without notice for such actions as misconduct and breaches of confidentiality. The common-law presumption of "dismissal at will" still operates in the region with regard to the termination of employment. By common law, a contract of employment can be terminated at will provided "reasonable notice" is given. If there is no notice, the terminated employee gets payment in lieu of notice (e.g., one week's wage or one month's salary). Wrongful dismissal

Table 10.3   Contribution Rates to Social Insurance Schemes (1991)

Country	Contribution Rates (%)		
	Employer	Employee	Self-Employed
Bahamas	5.4	1.7–3.4	6.8–8.8
Barbados	4.9–6.8	4.65–6.55	8
Guyana	7.2	4.8	10.5
Jamaica	2.5	2.5	5.0
Trinidad and Tobago	5.6	2.8	n.a.

Source: La Foucade (1995, 32–33).
Note: n.a. = not available.

occurs where there is no evidence for termination without notice (i.e., no contractual breach). The issue of notice is therefore fundamental to the concept of the lawful termination of employment in common law.

Although industrial courts and tribunals place some degree of constraint on the freedom of employers to dismiss at will, Caribbean governments are considering the formal introduction of "unfair dismissal," which means that the employer must demonstrate that there is good reason for dismissing an employee. This clearly has implications for the future hiring and firing decisions of employers. Trinidad and Tobago, through its Industrial Court, specifies the concept of unfair industrial relations practice, while Jamaica has provision for "justifiable dismissal." In both cases, reasons for dismissal must be given. In Barbados, where an employee has been dismissed without notice, the concept of "just cause" has been employed to determine if the dismissal is wrongful (see Antoine 1992; Cumberbatch 1995a,b). Damages for such dismissal are paid via provisions in the severance payment legislation. It should be noted that workers taking strike action in Belize, Barbados, Guyana, and Jamaica can be dismissed. Good industrial relations practice, however, reduces the occurrence of such cases, since firms seek to maintain a reputation for being good employers in order to attract high-quality workers who can expect some degree of job security.

In terms of payment for involuntary termination of employment, labor law provides for severance pay (i.e., compensation for termination of employment for whatever reason) and redundancy pay (i.e., compensation for termination due to the existence of economic or technological difficulties; see table 10.4). The redundancy pay concept is more widely used in the region. Redundancy or severance pay is treated as payment for past service; hence, low-tenured workers are severed first on cost-minimizing grounds. Employers in some countries (e.g., Barbados) are responsible for paying severance to employees when they are terminated and then recovering part of the payment from a Severance Payment Fund. In Barbados, the Severance Payments Fund is administered by the National Insurance Board. Employers must make severance fund contributions on behalf of their employees based on their insurable earnings. Employers are required to pay employees their severance and then claim a rebate, which is determined by the minister responsible for the fund's administration. In cases where the employers are unable to make payments to employees, the fund makes the payments to the employees and then seeks to recover the amount from the employers. The severance payments system is not experience rated; hence, employers do not pay a reduced contribution to the fund if they have a long history of nonseverance. In Jamaica and Trinidad and Tobago, there is no fund, so the employer pays the employee the full cost of termination without receiving a refund.

The countries under study in this project have enacted minimum-wage legislation in the form of either a national minimum wage (e.g., Jamaica)

Table 10.4   Severance Pay in Caribbean Countries in the 1990s

Country	Qualifying Service	Rate of Benefit
Antigua and Barbuda	1 year	12 days per year at latest basic wage
Barbados	2 years	12.5 days per year for first 9 years
Belize	5 years	5 days per year with 42 weeks maximum
Dominica	3 years	5 days for first 3 years + 10 days per year for 3 to 5 years; 45 days for next 5 years + 10 days per year for 6 to 10 years; 95 days for over 10 years + 15 days per year for over 10 years; maximum is 52 weeks
Jamaica	2 years	10 days per year for first 5 years; 15 days per year for first 2 years
St. Kitts and Nevis	1 year	10 days per year for first 4 years; 15 days per year for 5 to 10 years; 20 days per year for over 10 years; maximum is 52 weeks 10 days per year
St. Lucia	2 years	5 days per year for first 2 years; 10 days per year for 3 to 7 years; 15 days per year for over 7 years; weekly wage limited to EC$100
St. Vincent and the Grenadines	2 years	10 days per year up to 52 weeks
Trinidad and Tobago	1 year	10 days per year for first 5 years; 15 days for over 5 years

Source: Baker (1997).

or specific minimum wages for selected occupations (e.g., Barbados). In Jamaica, a national minimum wage was introduced in 1975 as part of the government's poverty alleviation program and in recognition that several workers in the nonunionized sectors were low paid. The most recent increase in the national minimum wage took place in January 2002, when it was set at J$1800 per forty-hour week. Barbados, Belize, Guyana, and Trinidad and Tobago (up to 1998) have minimum wages to cover selected workers (e.g., shop assistants, domestic workers, and agricultural workers). These rates are updated on an irregular basis. In June 1998, Trinidad and Tobago introduced the Minimum Wage Act, which specified a national minimum wage of TT$7 (US$1.10) per hour.

Antoine (1998) also discusses other aspects of labor law in the region, namely, sick leave with pay, holiday with pay, temporary employees, the protection of wages, truck acts and other benefits, the employment of child labor, gender equality, and equal remuneration. These regulatory measures form the general background against which firms have to operate in the labor market. Little change has taken place in these legislative measures over the years, so firms have adjusted to their existence.

In summary, the institutional framework governing the operation of the labor market in the Caribbean consists of a set of legislative measures, common-law provisions (case law), customs, and traditions. This range of regulations reflects the existence of two types of models of industrial relations and dispute regulation in the region, namely, statutory intervention and voluntarism. Trade unions are particularly active in the labor market and are recognized in the various labor laws. The state maintains an oversight on the operations of the labor market in the region in the form of legislative provisions and the operation of labor departments. While individual regulatory measures may affect companies (e.g., employers) differently, the overall framework within which companies can hire and fire workers provides the basis on which employment decision making is made. Changes in labor legislation have not been undertaken regularly.

The change in employment depends on the hiring and firing process. If we let L_0 and L_t represent the initial and current levels of employment (i.e., number of persons employed), then we have the relationship

(1) $$L_t = L_0 + H(\cdot) - F(\cdot) - R,$$

where $H(\cdot)$ represents the hiring function and $F(\cdot)$ is the firing function. R represents the number of voluntary resignations and retirements. Mandatory retirement laws will affect the R variable. The discrete change in employment over the time period is given by

(2) $$\Delta L_t = L_t - L_0 = H(\cdot) - F(\cdot) - R.$$

The change in employment therefore depends on the factors that affect the hiring and firing processes. Regulatory measures can either impose additional costs of hiring and firing (e.g., severance, national insurance contributions, and other payroll taxes) or condition the processes (i.e., no discrimination in the hiring process, no child labor, LIFO, or inverse seniority in the firing process). Understanding the factors that affect the H and F functions becomes important in determining changes in employment over time.

10.3 Nonwage Labor Cost Indexes

Labor market regulations give rise to a set of labor costs that employers must take into consideration. Labor costs can be classified into (direct) wage costs and (indirect) nonwage costs. *Direct* wages and salaries relate to remuneration for work performed and include pay for normal time worked, premium pay for overtime and public holiday work, premium pay for shift work and night work, incentive or bonus pay, and cost-of-living allowances. Indirect or nonwage labor costs consist of payment for days not worked (paid holidays and compensation for holidays not taken), social welfare costs (contributions to social welfare and family allowances paid by the firm), statutory social welfare costs (e.g., contributions to national insurance and social security schemes), customary contractual or voluntary costs (e.g., supplementary retirement and provident schemes, supplementary redundancy insurance schemes), benefits in kind (e.g., housing, payment of utility bills), vocational training, and special taxes and subsidies (e.g., employment tax).

In addition to giving rise to these wage and nonwage labor costs, labor market regulations (LMRs) also condition the environment within which companies must operate in the labor market. For example, legislation governing gender equality and equal remuneration and the recognition of a trade union may not affect labor costs directly but may affect the decision to hire and fire workers. The existence of the gamut of legislative measures therefore gives rise to the nature and structure of adjustment costs and makes the labor input a quasi-fixed factor in the production process.

The wide range of regulatory measures makes it difficult to properly analyze their effects on employment and other labor market variables. In some cases, many of the regulations hardly change over a long period and therefore have no intertemporal analytical significance. In other cases, some regulatory measures are changed on a regular basis and therefore provide a "natural experiment" for empirical analysis. Differences in regulation across countries also provide a basis for empirical analysis. In order to manage the range of regulatory measures, analysts have attempted to develop indexes of LMR (see Downes [2002] for a full discussion). Two basic approaches have been employed by labor economists. First, important regulatory measures are identified and specific indexes are developed for each measure (e.g., severance pay, minimum wage [i.e., Kaitz index], national insurance contribution, or payroll taxes). Second, composite indexes are constructed using either the specific indexes or the natural units of the regulatory measures. These composite indexes tend to be unweighted and do not reflect the relative importance of the different measures in the employment decision. The technical solution to this problem is the use of principal components or factor analysis for both qualitative and quantitative variables.

Authors have referred to LMR by different names. For example, Rama (1995) refers to LMR as an index of "labour market rigidity," while Márquez and Pagés (1998) refer to them as an index of "employment protection." Loayza and Palacios (1997) have used a similar procedure to obtain an indicator of labor market reform.

In Rama's (1995) study of thirty-one Latin American and Caribbean countries, the range of his "index of labour market rigidity" was 0.182 (Belize) to 0.654 (Brazil). The indexes for the English-speaking Caribbean are given in table 10.5. Although missing values for some of the variables can affect the overall value of the index, the values of the index of labor market rigidity in the English-speaking Caribbean indicate that Barbados has the highest degree of labor rigidity in the subregion, while Belize has the lowest.

Table 10.5 Labor Market Policies and Institutions in the Caribbean

Country	ILO Conventions Ratified	Annual Leave with Pay (days)	Maternity Leave (days)	Social Security Contributions (wage %)	Government Employment (labor force %)	Minimum Wage (average wage %)	Severance Pay (monthly wages)	Unionization (labor force %)	Labour Market Rigidity (index)	Rank (1 = highest value)
Antigua and Barbuda	15	12	55	10.6	—	49.6	—	24	0.380	4
Barbados	35	15	84	12.0	23	—	—	31	0.580	1
Belize	27	6	50	7.0	—	—	—	13	0.182	11
Dominica	20	10	50	8.9	—	0.0	—	25	0.223	10
Grenada	25	—	50	8.0	—	0.0	—	47	0.328	6
Guyana	—	12	59	12.5	—	—	—	32	0.415	3
Jamaica	25	10	56	5.0	7	21.9	—	24	0.278	8
St. Kitts and Nevis	—	—	64	10.5	—	—	—	34	0.476	2
St. Lucia	25	—	57	10.0	—	—	—	20	0.306	7
St. Vincent and the Grenadines	—	—	55	7.8	—	—	—	12	0.251	9
Trinidad and Tobago	13	14	55	8.4	—	30.8	—	28	0.354	5

Source: Rama (1995).

Márquez and Pagés's (1998) index of employment protection for the six countries in this study also show how levels of protection compared with Latin America. The range of their index goes from 1 (little protection, e.g., the United States) to 35.5 (high degree of protection, e.g., Bolivia and Nicaragua). Four of the six countries in this study record values less than 10 (see table 10.6). Loayza and Palacios's (1997) study of labor market liberalization in Latin America and the Caribbean also comes to the conclusion that low level of labor market distortion exist in the Caribbean compared with Latin America. They state that with a "common law tradition, the English-speaking countries of the Caribbean, especially the Bahamas, Belize and Guyana, are the least rigid in the region, particularly in regard to monetary compensation for dismissal, constraints on temporary contracts and the rate of payroll taxes" (17).

Although these composite indexes provide some indication of the degree of labor market rigidity, distortion, or protection afforded by various regulatory measures, they do not provide an indication of how specific measures affect employment. As indicated earlier, specific indexes can be constructed to determine the impact of LMR on other labor market variables.

In this study, specific indexes are used to examine the effects of labor regulations on employment in the Caribbean. In the case of minimum wage legislation, a Kaitz-type index (KE) is used for Jamaica, which has a national minimum wage. The index is given by

$$(3) \qquad KE = \frac{\text{Minimum Wage Index}}{\text{Average Compensation Index}} = \frac{MW}{AC},$$

where the coverage ratio is unity (see Brown, Gilroy, and Kohen 1982, 499). The traditional Kaitz index is the ratio of the nominal legal minimum wage to average hourly earnings weighted by coverage. For Jamaica, average compensation is used as a proxy for average earnings. In the case of Trinidad and Tobago, where the minimum wage legislation covers a selected number of workers, an "effective minimum wage index" is used. This index is given as the ratio of the minimum wage index for those covered by the legislation to the average earning index. Data on the degree of coverage are unavailable.

Simple unweighted indexes are used to measure the impact of national insurance contributions made by employers and employees in Barbados (because of the unavailability of data for weighting purposes). These contributions cover payments for severance pay, national insurance, and special levies. The overall contribution rates are converted to index number form using 1980 as a base. Simple unweighted indexes are also employed to capture the effect of the payment of wage-related contributions to the national insurance scheme in Jamaica. In the case of Trinidad and Tobago, a dummy variable is used to capture changes in the National Insurance Scheme (NIS) contributions, which started in 1971, and changed in 1980 and 1982.

Table 10.6   Employment Protection Index for the Caribbean

| Country | Definition of Just Cause | Tenure-Related Severance Payment | | | Probationary Period | Severance at 20 Years | Reinstatement | Employment Protection Index |
		1 Year	3 Years	10 Years				
Bahamas	6.5	7	4.5	2.5	13.5	1	14	2
Barbados	6.5	14.5	7	4	35	2	14	8
Belize	6.5	7	4.5	11	33	3	14	5
Guyana	27	14.5	13	19	35	12	14	16
Jamaica	6.5	7	15.5	8	13.5	—	14	4
Trinidad and Tobago	6.5	27	22	23	29.5	16	14	17

Source: Márquez and Pagés (1998).
Note: Dash indicates missing data.

Severance payment legislation has not changed significantly over the study period. The severance payments scheme in Trinidad and Tobago started in 1985 and has not changed since that year. In the case of Barbados, the scheme started in 1978, and some amendments were made in 1991. The scheme in Jamaica began in 1974, and slight amendments were made in 1986 and 1988. With the exception of Barbados, where rates of contribution were changed, the amendments have been administrative.

In this study, therefore, the analysis of the effects of labor market regulations on employment will focus on minimum wage legislation, national insurance contributions, and severance payments.

10.4   Dynamic Labor Demand Functions

The employment of a person by a company involves various costs: (direct) wage costs and (indirect) nonwage costs. Direct wages and salaries relate to remuneration for work performed and include payment for normal time worked, overtime and holiday work, shift and night work, incentive pay, and family allowances. While the payment for some of these items is determined by legislation (e.g., holiday-with-pay legislation), the quantum of the payment is determined by the collective-bargaining process, in which unions are dominant.

The existence of nonwage labor costs, which make labor a quasi-fixed factor of production, has implications for the specification of labor demand (employment) functions and the employer's choice between the number of workers and the number of hours worked per employee. There are also implications for the incidence of layoffs by skill level since differences in such turnover costs by skill level can result in firms' being more reluctant to lay off skilled than unskilled workers in response to a decline in demand for goods and services (i.e., skilled labor is hoarded).

The impact of LMRs on employment, as reflected in wage and nonwage labor costs, has been approached from two directions:

- The estimation of dynamic labor (employment) adjustment models whereby the role of LMR is *implicitly* captured in an adjustment cost function (see, for example, Hamermesh 1993; Hamermesh and Pfann 1996)
- The estimation of labor (employment) demand functions *explicitly* using specific or composite indexes of LMR as explanatory variables (see, for example, Lazear 1990; Erickson and Mitchell 1995)

Dynamic labor demand functions can be motivated via the existence of adjustment costs or the role of expectations. These two factors suggest that there are several specifications of the dynamic labor demand function depending on the nature of adjustment costs and expectations. For example, labor adjustment costs may be symmetric or asymmetric with respect to the hiring or firing of employees, or linear or nonlinear (e.g., quadratic) with respect to the rate of increase in hiring or firing costs. Expectations can also take various forms—adaptive or rational.

In addition to adjustment costs and expectations, alternative labor demand models can be specified according to the assumptions made about the production technology used by the firm, the vintage of the capital stock, the structure of commodity and labor markets, and the institutional framework governing labor market behavior (e.g., the existence of trade unions and their bargaining power). Recent literature on the economics of the collective-bargaining and trade union behavior indicates several models that govern the negotiations process. The two main models are the labor demand and the efficient bargain. There are two variants of the labor demand model: first, the monopoly union model, in which the wage rate is set unilaterally by the union and the firm determines the appropriate level of labor demanded (i.e., employment); and second, the right-to-manage model, wherein the firm determines the demand for labor after the wage rate is determined by the bargaining process. In the efficiency bargain model, the union and the employer bargain over both the wage rate and the level of employment (see Sapsford and Tzannatos [1993] for an overview). The choice of a particular formulation has implications for the specification and estimation of wage and employment functions. Attempts have been made to develop dynamic wage and employment bargaining models in the context of adjustment costs (see Lockwood and Manning 1989; Modesto 1994). The specification of a dynamic labor demand function must therefore reflect the institutional features of the labor market and the behavior of firms in both the product and labor markets.

The standard formulation of the dynamic labor demand model emerges from the solution of an intertemporal constrained optimization problem. Assume that the representative firm has a level of employment at the beginning of a time period, L_0, and is faced with a cost of adjusting the level of employment over time while seeking to maximize profit or minimize costs. The cost of adjustment may be due to legislative, technological, or institutional factors. If the level of employment at some time period, t, is given as L_t, then the problem facing the firm is selecting the speed of adjustment to L_t faced with an adjustment cost function and also the level of employment L_t.

The optimization problem can be solved by using the calculus of variation whereby the firm seeks to find the optimal path of employment over time (see Intriligator 1971). If we assume that adjustment costs are quadratic and symmetric—that is, firing costs are equal to hiring costs for all changes in employment—then we can generate one form of the dynamic labor demand function based on minimizing the intertemporal costs of production subject to a production function constraint (see Downes and Mamingi 1997) given as

(4)
$$L_t^d = L_t^d \left[\frac{W_t}{m_t}, q_t^*, D(L_t) \right],$$

where the optimal demand for labor is a function of the price of labor relative to the rental price of capital (W_t/m_t), planned or expected output (q_t^*), and a distributed lag function of labor demand, $D(L_t)$. The specific form of equation (4) depends on the specification of the production function. As indicated earlier, alternative assumptions about firm behavior (e.g., profit maximization), the adjustment costs function (e.g., nonquadratic and non-symmetric), institutional arrangements (e.g., right-to-manage bargaining model), and production technology can generate different dynamic labor demand functions.

One of the limitations of using equation (4) to determine the impact of LMRs on employment is that *all* sources of adjustment costs are subsumed in the $D(L_t)$ variable. One solution to this problem is to examine the nature and characteristics of LMR and specify regulatory measures related to the wage rate (e.g., payroll taxes) and nonwage regulatory measures (e.g., no child labor, right to join a trade union, no sex discrimination).

If indexes are specified for these regulatory adjusted measures, then a log-linear specification of the equation can be given as

(5) $$\ln L_t^d = \alpha_0 + \alpha_1 \ln\left(\frac{W_t}{m_t}\right) + \alpha_2 \ln \text{REG}(W_t) + \alpha_3 \ln \text{REG}(NW_t)$$
$$+ \alpha_4 \ln q_t + \alpha_5 \ln L_{t-1},$$

where REG(W) and REG(NW) are regulatory indexes associated with the wage rate (W) and nonwage (NW) factors. Equation (5) indicates that the demand for labor depends on the basic wage rate relative to the price of capital services; wage-related regulatory measures (e.g., payroll taxes); nonwage regulatory measures, which are the main factors that make labor a quasi-fixed factor; planned output; and previous level labor demand (which is a proxy for factors other than labor market regulations that affect the adjustment process). In a truly dynamic context, we would expect some interaction between these explanatory variables.

As stated before, composite regulatory measures (indexes) are not particularly useful for specific policy analysis (e.g., whether government should reduce the minimum wage or cut severance pay to boost employment). In order to handle this issue, we need to examine the regulatory environment of a country to determine the main regulations that are likely to affect employment over time (see Zank 1996). In time series analysis, significant variation in regulatory measures can have an impact on employment determination. Across countries, significant variation can also have an impact on employment generation across these countries and explain differences in relative employment growth. Lazear (1990) approached the study of the impact of labor market regulation on employment by specifying the important measures that determine employment across a set of developed countries. An expanded version of his model can be given as

$$(6) \qquad L_t^d = L^d\left(\frac{W_t}{m_t}, q_t^*, r_1, r_2 \ldots \ldots \ldots r_k\right),$$

where r_i ($i = 1, \ldots k$) are alternate regulatory measures (e.g., severance payment, NIS payments). To the extent that there are still residual adjustment costs, a lagged function of L_t, can be incorporated into equation (6), that is,

$$(7) \qquad L_t^d = L^d\left[\frac{W_t}{m_t}, q_t^*, r_1, r_2 \ldots r_k, D^*(L)\right].$$

$D^*(L)$ reflects residual adjustment costs.

The latter approach is more useful for policy analysis than the earlier specifications of the dynamic labor demand functions in that specific labor regulations can be highlighted. While some of the labor market regulatory variables can affect the basic wage rate (e.g., payroll taxes), the focus in this study is on the effects of the regulatory measures on labor demand. The possible endogeneity of the wage rate in the labor demand equation can be handled by an appropriate choice of instrumental variables.

10.5   Statistical Data

One of the major problems associated with labor market analysis in the Caribbean is the unavailability of data on many labor market variables. The authors of a recent study of workers and labor markets in the Caribbean lamented the unavailability of data with which to undertake a detailed analysis of the labor market (Abt Associates 1998). Some countries in the region have undertaken periodic labor force surveys to assess the performance of the labor market in terms of employment, unemployment, and labor force participation. Many of these countries rely, however, on population census data, which are collected on a decennial basis, in order to get a comprehensive picture of important labor market features.

Ideally, a specially designed survey would provide data to undertake a proper analysis of the impact of labor market regulation on employment at the different levels of aggregation.

The absence of the ideal situation means that we must use the available information from different sources. Such a situation makes the results of the exercise somewhat tentative since the databases may not be congruent. A typical situation in the Caribbean relates to the data available on wages and employment. Wage rate data are usually collected from the administrative records of the Labour Department and based on collective-bargaining agreements, while employment data are collected from labor force (continuous household) surveys.

In terms of the database used in this study, only annual data are available for real gross domestic product (GDP) for all the countries. Data at the aggregate level are used in this study, although annual sectoral-level data for real GDP (constant price GDP) are available. The data series for real GDP are as follows: Barbados, 1970–2001; Trinidad and Tobago, 1970–1999; and Jamaica, 1975–2001.

Wage rate and average earnings data are available for only three countries on a continuous basis: Barbados, Jamaica, and Trinidad and Tobago. In the case of Barbados, the Central Bank has constructed a wage rate index using data from collective-bargaining agreements lodged in the Labour Department. This annual Wages Index is based on selected areas of economic activity and is available for the period 1970–2001.

In the case of Jamaica, the Statistical Institute of Jamaica conducts a quarterly Employment and Earnings Survey of large establishments (i.e., employing ten or more persons). Data are available on both a quarterly and annual basis for the average earnings of workers in large establishments for the periods 1976–1979 and 1986–2001. Because of this large gap in the establishment survey data, researchers have had to use the ratio of employees' compensation in the national income accounts to total employees as a proxy for average annual compensation in Jamaica.

The Central Statistical Office in Trinidad and Tobago publishes an index of average weekly earnings. This index was started in 1971 and rebased in 1977 with a wider coverage of employees in sugar, manufacturing, oil refining, and electricity. Data are collected from surveys conducted biannually.

Employment data are collected on a quarterly basis from labor force surveys in the Bahamas, Barbados, Belize, Jamaica, and Trinidad and Tobago. No ongoing survey exists in Guyana. Annual data on employment (and unemployment) in the Bahamas are available for 1973, 1975, 1977, 1979, 1986, 1988–1989, and 1991–1999. No quarterly estimates exist for the Bahamas. Barbados has conducted a quarterly Continuous Household Sample Survey to collect information on employment and other labor force data since 1975. In the case of Belize, a one-off labor force survey was conducted in 1983–1984, but since 1993 labor force data have been collected on an annual basis. Employment (and unemployment) data are available on a biannual basis (April and October) only for 1993 and 1994. Labor force surveys have been undertaken in Jamaica on a continuous basis since 1968. Between 1968 and 1987, six-monthly labor force surveys were conducted (April and October). Since 1988, quarterly data on the labor force have been collected. Labor force surveys began in 1963 in Trinidad and Tobago on a biannual basis (January–June and July–December), but there were no surveys in 1972 and 1976.

An assessment of basic data series for the six Caribbean countries covered in this study indicates that continuous annual data are available for

Barbados (1970–2001), Jamaica (1975–2001), and Trinidad and Tobago (1970–1999).

The absence of wage/earnings data and a continuous employment series for the Bahamas, Belize, and Guyana means that they are excluded from the empirical aspect of this study. Given the low level of distortion caused by LMR in these countries, their exclusion would not affect the results of the study (see Loayza and Palacios 1997).

In terms of LMRs, we have sought to identify the main regulatory measures that are likely to affect employment in the three countries (Barbados, Jamaica, and Trinidad and Tobago). In several instances, there has been little change in LMRs in these countries. Indeed, a recent survey of companies in Barbados, Belize, Jamaica, and Trinidad and Tobago indicated that LMR was not an important labor market issue affecting their operations. There was, however, some concern expressed in Barbados and Trinidad and Tobago about the high level of employer contributions to the social security fund (see Abt Associates 1998, 26). The Severance Pay Act was also a concern to Barbadian employers. In this study, we have therefore focused on the impact of minimum wage legislation in Jamaica and Trinidad and Tobago and social security payments and severance payments in the three countries. Data are available on the national minimum wage introduced in Jamaica in 1975, while a minimum wage index covering selected occupations is available for Trinidad and Tobago. Barbados's minimum wage legislation only covers three categories of workers (shop assistants, domestics, and agricultural workers) who generally tend to receive more than the minimum wage.

Payroll taxes in the form of national insurance contributions are available for Barbados since 1967. The contribution rates for regular employees and employers are available along with the range of taxes paid. The employer is responsible for the partial payment of national insurance, noncontributory old age pension, employment injury, severance pay, and unemployment insurance. Special levies introduced since 1981 are shared by both employers and employees. The limits of insurance earnings have been adjusted periodically to ensure that the National Insurance Fund maintains an equality between income and expenditure. Changes were made in 1974, 1978, 1982, 1984, 1987, 1991, and 1994. Unweighted indexes of the rates for the different contributors (employers and employees) are used in this study. For Jamaica, data are available for the maximum wage-related contributions to the national insurance scheme for the period 1966–2001. In the case of Trinidad and Tobago, the contribution rates have not changed since the introduction of the national insurance scheme in 1971. The maximum insurable earnings were, however, increased in 1980, 1983, and 1999. Severance payment legislation was introduced in Jamaica in 1974 and in Trinidad and Tobago in 1985. No changes have been made with respect to the payment of employees since these periods. A severance payment scheme was introduced in Barbados in 1973. The contribution rate payable by employees into the severance payment fund was raised from 0.25 percent to 1 percent of insurable earnings in April 1991. The maximum on insurable earnings was also raised from $2,600 to $3,100 in October 1991.

In summary, the impact of minimum wage on employment is assessed for Jamaica and Trinidad and Tobago and on payroll taxes (national insurance contributions) and severance payments for all three countries using annual data. Little change has taken place in other LMRs over the study period (1970–2001) in these countries.

10.6   Empirical Results

In this section an empirical examination of the impact of selected LMRs on employment is undertaken using variants of equations (6) or (7). While annual data are used for the three countries (Barbados, Jamaica, and Trinidad and Tobago), the period of investigation varies from country to country according to the availability of data: Barbados, 1970–2001); Trinidad and Tobago, 1970–1999; and Jamaica, 1975–2001. The variables used in the exercise also vary from country to country according to the data availability. They are as follows: total number of persons employed (L); average earnings index (Trinidad and Tobago); average compensation index (Jamaica) and average wage index (Barbados; W); GDP at factor cost at 1990 prices (GDP); real wage rate or earnings/compensation (RW), defined as W divided by the retail or consumer price index (P); minimum wage index (MW); the contribution of employers to the national insurance scheme (NISCOR); severance payment schemes (SEV); effective minimum wage (EMV), given as the minimum wage index divided by an average earnings index (Trinidad and Tobago); and the Kaitz index, defined as the ratio of the minimum wage index to an average compensation index (Jamaica; see the appendix for a discussion of the labor regulation variables).

Table 10.7 gives summary statistics of the data. At least three important features emerge from the reading of coefficients of variation. First, data variability is the rule rather than the exception. The highest variability is recorded by the average compensation index in Jamaica. The smallest variability is registered by the real wage in Barbados. Second, across countries, employment variabilities are statistically the same, and so are GDP variabilities. Third, overall, Jamaica data are more volatile than those of the two other countries.

As the study deals with the relationship between employment and a set of explanatory variables (including regulatory variables), at the very least an examination of correlations between the two sets of variables is warranted. Table 10.8 contains pairwise correlations between variables. The major observation is that correlations between employment and other variables are very high and positive, with the exception of real wage and

Table 10.7   Summary Statistics of Data

	Barbados		Jamaica		Trinidad-Tobago	
	Mean	C.V.%	Mean	C.V.%	Mean	C.V.%
L	101.42	13.54	832.64	12.61	388.65	11.54
P	142.26	49.44	396.02	122.02	157.50	72.52
W	136.47	47.94	705.95	134.79	299.04	64.82
RW	0.98	9.18	1.75	40.00	1.94	20.62
MW			572.29	123.11	329.10	57.96
EMV (KAITZ)			0.93	18.28	1.17	15.38
GDP	790.39	13.45	2,171.75	11.49	17,297.00	14.42
NISCOR	196.46	39.91	136.18	46.72	2.23	46.64
SEV	1.09	71.56	2.11	45.97	0.50	102.00
Period	1970–2001	1970–2001	1975–2001	1975–2001	1970–1999	1970–1999

Notes: Mean is data average; C.V. stands for coefficient of variation; L represents total employment (in 00); P stands for consumer (retail) price index; RW stands for real wage (ratio of nominal wage/earning/compensation index [W] to consumer [retail] price index); GDP stands for gross domestic product at factor cost at some year prices; NISCOR is total employer contribution to national insurance; it is an unweighted simple index of the maximum wage-related payment for Jamaica, an unweighted index of rates (for employers and employees) for Barbados, and a count data variable (with a value of zero in 1970, a value of 1 in 1971–1979, a value of 2 in 1980–1982, a value of 3 in 1983–1998, and a value of 4 in 1999) for Trinidad and Tobago; EMV (effective minimum wage) is the minimum wage index divided by average earnings index for Trinidad and Tobago, and KAITZ index is defined as EMV for Jamaica; SEV represents severance payments; it is a count data variable capturing the change in regimes; for Barbados, takes on a value of zero prior to 1978, 1 in 1978–1990, and 2 in 1991–2001; for Jamaica, it takes on a value of 1 in 1974–1985, 2 in 1986–1987, and 3 in 1988–2001; for Trinidad and Tobago, it is a dummy variable with a value of zero prior to 1985 and 1 in 1985–1999.

effective minimum wage. Of particular significance is the positive relationships between employment and regulatory variables. Moreover, explanatory variables are in general highly and positively correlated. These results must, however, be interpreted with caution because (1) simple correlation does not imply causality, (2) correlation may be spurious, and (3) simple correlation does not necessary capture multivariate relationships (i.e., multicollinearity problem).

It is worth pointing out two major problems encountered in this study. First, the exercise is hampered by the relative shortness of time series, which, in general, can result in the low power of test statistics as well as the invalidation of asymptotic tests. Second, as outlined earlier, the data used do not always capture adequately the concepts used in the theoretical analysis.

The estimation procedure proceeds as follows:

1. Investigate the temporal properties of the series using the augmented Dickey-Fuller (ADF) unit root test (and other unit root tests when appropriate).

2. Check for the existence of meaningful long-run economic relationships via the Johansen tests for cointegration.

Table 10.8   Correlation Coefficient Matrices

	L	P	W	RW	GDP	NISCOR	SEV
			Barbados				
L	1.00						
P	0.90	1.00					
W	0.92	0.99	1.00				
RW	-0.36	-0.51	-0.44	1.00			
GDP	0.95	0.92	0.95	-0.33	1.00		
NISCOR	0.72	0.91	0.91	-0.38	0.78	1.00	
SEV	0.82	0.94	0.92	-0.51	0.84	0.83	1.00

	L	MW	W	KAITZ	GDP	NISCOR	SEV
			Jamaica				
L	1.00						
MW	0.78	1.00					
W	0.72	0.99	1.00				
KAITZ	0.38	0.01	-0.11	1.00			
GDP	0.80	0.83	0.76	0.23	1.00		
NISCOR	0.90	0.80	0.72	0.44	0.82	1.00	
SEV	0.94	0.69	0.62	0.43	0.85	0.81	1.00

	L	MW	W	EMV	GDP	NISCOR	SEV
			Trinidad and Tobago				
L	1.00						
MW	0.81	1.00					
W	0.86	0.97	1.00				
EMV	-0.56	-0.45	-0.57	1.00			
GDP	0.68	0.39	0.37	-0.23	1.00		
NISCOR	0.75	0.96	0.93	-0.51	0.40	1.00	
SEV	0.57	0.87	0.87	-0.46	0.002	0.81	1.00

Note: Variables are as defined in table 10.7.

3. Estimate, if cointegration holds, a long-run relationship between employment and a set of variables using the Phillips-Loretan nonlinear error correction model.

4. Use diagnostic criteria to evaluate the estimated model.

All results are derived from the Eviews computer program. The stationarity/nonstationarity of the series is determined with the ADF t-test. The following equation is used to derive the ADF t-test:

$$(8) \qquad \Delta y_t = c + \rho y_{t-1} + \sum_{i=1}^{m} \lambda_i \Delta y_{t-i} + e_t,$$

where y_t is the variable of interest (any variable explained in the note to table 10.9), Δ stands for the first difference, c is a constant term, ρ and λ_i are parameters, and e_t is a white noise series. The optimal lag length m is ob-

Table 10.9   Augmented Dickey-Fuller Unit Root Test Results

		L	WR	GDP	NISCOR	EMV or KAITZ	SEV
Barbados	Level	0.746	-1.592[a]	-1.590	-1.267		-1.072
1970–2001		(5, 0.991)	(6, 0.427)	(1, 0.473)	(0, 0.632)		(0, 0.714)
	1st diff.	-2.835	-3.184	-3.170	-4.028		-5.385
		(0, 0.006)	(5, 0.003)	(0, 0.032)	(0, 0.000)		(0, 0.000)
Jamaica	Level	-1.318	-9.991	-0.715	-1.313	-1.232	-0.801
1975–2001		(0, 0.606)	(0, 0.000)	(1, 0.827)	(0, 0.609)	(3, 0.642)	(2, 0.803)
	1st diff.	-4.171	-13.318	-3.331	-3.743	-6.761	-3.162
		(0, 0.000)	(0, 0.000)	(0, 0.002)	(0, 0.000)	(0, 0.000)	(1, 0.003)
Trinidad and	Level	-0.116	-4.031	-2.458	-24.872	-4.278	-0.965
Tobago		(0, 0.939)	(8, 0.059)	(2, 0.136)	(8, 0.000)	(0, 0.002)	(0, 0.752)
1970–1999	1st diff.	-2.964	-2.319	-1.417	-7.845	-10.849	-5.196
		(0, 0.004)	(3, 0.022)	(1, 0.142)	(8, 0.000)	(0, 0.000)	(0, 0.000)

Notes: L represents the logarithm of total employment; WR stands for the logarithm of real wage (ratio of nominal wage/earning/compensation index to consumer (retail) price index); GDP stands for the logarithm of gross domestic product at factor cost at 1990 prices; NISCOR is total employer contribution to national insurance; it is the logarithm of an unweighted simple index of the maximum wage-related payment for Jamaica, the logarithm of an unweighted index of rates (for employers and employees) for Barbados, and a count data variable (with a value of zero in 1970, a value of 1 in 1971–1979, a value of 2 in 1980–1982, a value of 3 in 1983–1996, and a value of 4 in 1999 for Trinidad and Tobago; EMV (effective minimum wage) is the logarithm of minimum wage index divided by average earnings index for Trinidad and Tobago and KAITZ index is defined as EMV for Jamaica; SEV represents severance payments and is a count data variable capturing the change in regimes; for Barbados, it takes on a value of zero prior to 1978, 1 in 1978–1990, and 2 in 1991–2001; for Jamaica, it takes on a value of 1 in 1974–1985, 2 in 1986–1987, and 3 in 1988–2001; for Trinidad and Tobago, it is a dummy variable with a value of zero prior to 1985 and 1 in 1985–1999. For figures, the first entries are the ADF test values. The first figures in parentheses are the optimal lags from SIC, and the second figures are the one-sided *p*-values. Regressions in first differences have no constant term. Lag search: maximum values: 9, 8, 8, for Barbados, Jamaica, and Trinidad and Tobago, respectively.

[a] The lag is not optimal. With the optimal lag (3), the series is stationary (ADF: -4.567, *p*-value: 0.001). Nevertheless, the ADF test is invalid given the presence of structural breaks (in 1975 and in 1990). The PP test seems to reveal nonstationarity.

tained by Schwartz Information Criterion (SIC) over a maximum number of lags. The null hypothesis of $\rho = 0$ (unit root) against the alternative hypothesis $\rho < 0$ (stationarity) is tested using the $t_{\hat{\rho}}$ statistic, that is, the ADF *t*-statistic that follows a Dickey-Fuller (DF) distribution. The one-sided *p*-values associated with the *t*-statistic values are compared with the level of significance (10 percent, 5 percent, 1 percent) to decide on stationarity or nonstationarity of variables. When $\rho = 0$, nonstationarity (unit root) is accepted with a drift *c*; that is, y_t is nonstationary with a trend for $c \neq 0$; otherwise it is stationary around a constant mean but has no trend. The ADF *t*-values and their associated *p*-values for variables in levels (y_t) as well as for variables in first differences (Δy_t) are reported in table 10.9. Since the ADF *t*-test has low power in some situations (i.e., in the presence of structural break), the Phillips-Perron Z_t and the Kwiatkowski-Phillips-

Schmidt-Shin (KPSS) tests are also used when the ADF test results look unsatisfactory or suspicious. Note that the Phillips-Perron Z_t—a more powerful test than the ADF test, which also follows a DF distribution— uses a nonparametric correction to approximate autocorrelation in the error term of the DF regression (the ADF regression without lagged left-hand-side variables), unlike the ADF test. The KPSS test has stationarity as the null hypothesis and nonstationarity as the alternative hypothesis.

For Barbados, the results presented in table 10.9 indicate that all variables are nonstationary, that is, integrated of order one. Indeed, the *p*-values of the ADF tests for level variables are greater than the common levels of significance, while those for first-differenced variables are smaller than the levels of significance. For Jamaica, all variables are integrated of order one with the exception of real wage. For Trinidad and Tobago, while the cases of labor and severance are clear cut in the sense that they are integrated of order one, the cases of other variables need further investigation. Using the Phillips-Perron test, GDP (with a structural break in 1982) was found I(1) instead of I(2) as the ADF test indicates. Contribution to national insurance was found I(1) by Phillips-Perron and KPSS tests, and effective minimum wage was also found I(1) by KPSS test.

Since the variables are nonstationary, regression equations involving these variables are only valid if they produce stationary linear combination(s)—that is, if they are cointegrated. Several tests for cointegration are available. The Johansen trace and maximum eigenvalue tests are used here (see Maddala and Kim 1998, chap. 6). The trace test deals with the hypothesis that there are at most $r < n$ (number of variables) cointegrated relationships (vectors). The maximum eigenvalue test deals with the null hypothesis of $r + 1$ cointegrating vectors versus r cointegrating vectors. Although these tests are large sample tests, they are preferred over the Engle-Granger cointegration test since they can reveal the presence of more than one cointegrating relationship when we are dealing with more than two variables.

Given a cointegrating relationship between the variables of interest, we need to use robust methods to obtain unbiased and efficient estimates at least asymptotically. In this study, we adopt the Phillips-Loretan nonlinear error correction model (see Phillips and Loretan 1991). The basic idea behind this procedure is to obtain the long-run (static) estimates of the parameters of an equation by incorporating one or several lagged error (equilibrium) correction mechanisms and current first-differenced explanatory variables as well as their lags and leads. The following equation can be specified as follows:

$$(9)\ l_t = c + X_t\beta + \Gamma(B)(l_t - c - X_t\beta) + \sum_{i=0}^{\infty} \alpha_i \Delta X_{t-i} + \sum_{i=1}^{\infty} \delta_i \Delta X_{t+i} + u_t,$$

where l_t stands for the logarithm of the number of persons employed, X_t is a matrix of explanatory variables (i.e., real wage, real gross domestic product, severance, minimum wage, and contribution to national insurance), $\Delta X_t = X_t - X_{t-1}$, u_t is a well-behaved error term, $\beta = (\beta_1, \beta_2, \ldots)$ is a vector of parameters associated with explanatory variables, α and δ are also vectors of parameters, and $\Gamma(B) = \Sigma_{j=1}^{\infty} \gamma_{1j} B^j$ with B as the backward shift operator.

The nonlinear error correction model in equation (9) achieves full efficiency "in the limit by working to estimate (and eliminate) the effects of long-run feedback between the errors on the long-run equilibrium relationship and the errors that drive the regressors" (Phillips and Loretan 1991, 426). In this connection, the leads of ΔX_t have an important role to play as their inclusion allows us to obtain errors that form a martingale difference sequence with respect to the errors that drive the long-run equilibrium and the errors that drive the explanatory variables. This is useful for estimator efficiency, unbiasedness, and inference (see Phillips and Loretan [1992, 426] for advantages of this method over other cointegration techniques). Maddala and Kim (1998) also corroborate Phillips and Loretan's views on the usefulness of the presence of lags and leads in the estimation of a cointegration equation, precisely when there is a unique cointegrating vector. As can be inferred, this method is an appropriate method for dealing with endogeneity of right-hand-side variables.

In reality equation (9) cannot directly be used as it stands; there is a need for truncation to make it operational. Given the small sample size, one lag and one lead of ΔX_t and $\Gamma(B) = \gamma_{11} B$ are used. Thus, equation (9) now reads

$$(10) \quad l_t = c + X_t \beta + \gamma_{11}(l_{t-1} - c - X_{t-1} \beta) + \sum_{i=0}^{1} \alpha_i \Delta X_{t-i} + \delta_1 \Delta X_{t+1} + u_t.$$

Equation (10) states that employment is affected by three components: the long-run relationship with explanatory variables through the parameter $\beta = (\beta_1, \beta_2, \ldots)$, the short-run relationships with explanatory variables through the parameters α_i and δ_1, and the lagged equilibrium correction mechanism, $(l_{t-1} - c - X_{t-1} \beta)$, through the parameter γ_{11}. The equilibrium correction mechanism—that is, the correction for the deviation from the steady-state equilibrium—may be justified on two grounds. It represents not only an adjustment to the past due to technological and institutional rigidities but also an equilibrium error resulting from agents' expectations or forecasts of changes in employment. The latter stem from the possibility that agents may have more information about the employment variable they are trying to forecast than is contained in the history of the variable alone (see Campbell and Shiller 1988, 507).

Economizing on the number of degrees of freedom, differenced variables in lag or lead forms are progressively eliminated if they do not contribute to the overall fit. Cointegration results are reported on a country-by-country basis.

10.6.1   Barbados

The following variables in levels are of interest here: logarithm of number of employees (L), logarithm of real wage index (WR), logarithm of real GDP (GDP), logarithm of contributions to NIS (NISCOR), and severance payments variable (SEV). Other details concerning these variables are provided in the appendix.

The Johansen trace and maximum eigenvalue tests in table 10.10 reveal the presence of one cointegrated vector among the set of variables just mentioned at the 5 percent level (and presumably at the 10 percent level). Indeed, the trace statistic value for no cointegration (85.31) is greater than the critical value (68.52) at the 5 percent level of significance while the statistic value for at most one cointegrated relationship (46.77) is less than the

Table 10.10   Johansen Cointegration Tests: Barbados

Period: 1970–2001
Trend assumption: Linear deterministic trend
Series: L, W_r, GDP, NISCOR, SEV
Lags interval (in first differences): 1 to 1
Unrestricted Cointegration Rank Test

| Hypothesized | Trace | Critical Value | |
No. of CE(s)	Statistic	5 Percent	1 Percent
None**	85.31158	68.52	76.07
At most 1	46.77154	47.21	54.46
At most 2	24.86835	29.68	35.65
At most 3	11.70971	15.41	20.04
At most 4	1.576054	3.76	6.65

| | Maximum | Critical Value | |
	Eigenvalue Statistic	5 Percent	1 Percent
None*	38.54003	33.46	38.77
At most 1	21.90319	27.07	32.24
At most 2	13.15864	20.97	25.52
At most 3	10.13366	14.07	18.63
At most 4	1.576054	3.76	6.65

Notes: Variables are defined in table 10.9. Hypothesized no. of CE(s) stands for the number of cointegrating equation(s). Trace statistic and maximum eigenvalue statistic are the statistics of interest here for testing cointegration.

**Significant at the 5 percent level.

*Significant at the 10 percent level.

Table 10.11   **Long-Run Estimates from a Variant of Equation (10) using the Phillips-Loretan Nonlinear Least Squares: Barbados, 1970–2001**

Constant	WR	GDP	NISCOR	SEV
–3.197	–0.328	1.104	0.077	–0.018
(–1.828)	(–2.662)	(5.088)	(1.220)	(–0.877)

$R^2 = 0.986$
$\bar{R}^2 = 0.974$
LM(F-statistic) = 0.718 $p = 0.555$
ARCH (F-statistic) = 0.227 $p = 0.799$
Jarque-Bera = 0.236 $p = 0.889$
Wald (F-statistic) = 1.362 $p = 0.281$

Notes: Variables are defined as in table 10.9. Short-run estimates are not reported here. Numbers in parentheses are t-statistics. LM test is the Breusch-Godfrey test for serial correlation using the F-test version because of the small sample size. ARCH test is the autoregressive conditional heteroskedasticity test. Jarque-Bera is the test for normality. p-value is the p-value associated with the respective test. Wald tests for the overall restriction that regulations do not matter, that is, impact NISCOR = impact SEV = 0.

critical value (47.21). Similarly, for the maximum eigenvalue statistic, the value for no cointegration (38.54) is greater than the 5 percent critical value (33.46), while at the same time the value for at most one cointegration (21.90) is less than the 5 percent critical value (27.07).

A parsimonious form of equation (10) with the variables previously indicated is used to estimate the long-run parameters. For reasons of space and also because the focus is on the long-run parameters, the coefficients of the lags and the leads of differenced variables are not reported here. Table 10.11 contains the results of the preferred model. The latter passes the diagnostic tests of interest here. Indeed, at the 5 percent level of significance, there is no autocorrelation of errors as the LM test in its F version with a p-value of 0.56 indicates. Autoregressive conditional heteroskedasticity (ARCH) effects are also absent in this model, as the associated p-value (0.80) implies. The model also passes the test of normality as indicated by the p-value of the Jarque-Bera test. As far as impacts of variables are concerned, real wage and real GDP significantly affect labor demand. The constant term that captures omitted variables is also significant at the 5 percent level. A 1 percent increase in real wage depresses demand for labor by 0.33 percent, at least in the long run. A 1 percent increase in the real GDP brings about a 1.10 percent increase in employment. Severance payments have a negative but insignificant effect on employment. Contributions to national insurance do not affect employment. Results from the Wald test for restrictions indicate that regulations taken as a whole (contribution to NIS and severance payments) do not affect the path of employment in Barbados.

10.6.2   Jamaica

The variables of interest are logarithm of number of employees (l), logarithm of the Kaitz index (KAITZ), logarithm of real GDP (GDP), logarithm of contributions to NIS (NISCOR) and severance payments variable (SEV).

The Johansen trace and maximum eigenvalue statistic tests in table 10.12 indicate the existence of two cointegrated vectors at the 5 percent level and one cointegrated vector at the 1 percent level. Given the nature of the exercise, the emphasis is on the existence of a single cointegrated vector.

Table 10.13 contains the estimation results of a variant of equation (10). The results indicate that there is no autocorrelation of errors as implied by the size of p-value (0.321) of the LM test in its F version. Moreover, there are no ARCH effects as the associated p-value (0.766) indicates. The model also passes the Jarque-Bera test of normality. As for Barbados, in Jamaica real GDP has a significant impact on employment, at least in the long run. A 1 percent increase in real GDP brings about a 0.39 percent increase in employment levels. The impact of minimum wage through the Kaitz index

Table 10.12   **Johansen Cointegration Test: Jamaica**

Period: 1975–2001
Trend assumption: Linear deterministic trend
Series: L, KAITZ, GDP, NISCOR, SEV
Lags interval (in first differences): 1 to 1
Unrestricted Cointegration Rank Test

Hypothesized No. of CE(s)	Trace Statistic	Critical Value 5 Percent	Critical Value 1 Percent
None**	100.3251	68.52	76.07
At most 1*	53.81603	47.21	54.46
At most 2	27.47777	29.68	35.65
At most 3	11.95671	15.41	20.04
At most 4	2.539234	3.76	6.65

Hypothesized No. of CE(s)	Maximum Eigenvalue Statistic	Critical Value 5 Percent	Critical Value 1 Percent
None**	46.50906	33.46	38.77
At most 1	26.33827	27.07	32.24
At most 2	15.52105	20.97	25.52
At most 3	9.417478	14.07	18.63
At most 4	2.539234	3.76	6.65

Notes: See table 10.10.
**Significant at the 5 percent level.
*Significant at the 10 percent level.

Table 10.13   **Long-Run Estimates from a Variant of Equation (10) using the Phillips-Loretan Nonlinear Least Squares: Jamaica, 1975–2001**

Constant	KAITZ	GDP	NISCOR	SEV
3.515	−0.177	0.389	0.023	0.048
(2.505)	(−2.112)	(2.013)	(0.661)	(1.803)

$R^2 = 0.985$
$\bar{R}^2 = 0.965$
LM(F-statistic) = 1.381 $p = 0.321$
ARCH (F-statistic) = 0.271 $p = 0.766$
Jarque-Bera = 0.631 $p = 0.730$
Wald (F-statistic) = 2.727 $p = 0.114$

Notes: See table 10.11.

is worth noting. Indeed, a 1 percent increase in the Kaitz index depresses employment by about 0.18 percent. Contributions to NIS do not seem to have an impact on employment. Severance payments do not affect employment at the 5 percent level. Overall, regulations taken as a whole do not have a significant impact on employment, as the Wald test on restrictions suggests with a p-value of 0.114.

10.6.3   Trinidad and Tobago

The variables of interest are logarithm of number of employees (l), logarithm of effective minimum wage index (EMV), logarithm of real GDP (GDP), contributions to NIS in dummy variable (NISCOR), and severance schemes captured by a dummy variable (SEV). NISCOR and SEV are quantified as explained in the appendix.

The Johansen trace and maximum eigenvalue test values in table 10.14 indicate the presence of one cointegrated vector at the 1 percent and 5 percent and consequently 10 percent levels of significance.

Table 10.15 contains the estimation results of a variant of equation (10). The results indicate that there is no autocorrelation of errors as implied by the size of p-value (0.75) of the LM test in its F version. There are no ARCH effects, as the associated p-value (0.38) indicates. The model also passes the Jarque-Bera test of normality. As for Barbados and Jamaica, real GDP has a significant impact on labor demand, at least in the long run. A 1 percent increase in real GDP brings about a 0.22 percent increase in employment levels. Regulation variables, although having the right signs, are nevertheless not significant at the 5 percent level. The Wald test for the overall impact of regulations indicates that regulations do not affect employment levels in Trinidad and Tobago.

The empirical analysis of the impact of labor regulations on employment in Barbados and Jamaica as well as in Trinidad and Tobago indicates that changes in contributions to NIS (payroll taxes) and severance pay-

Table 10.14   Johansen Cointegration Test: Trinidad and Tobago

Period: 1970–1999
Included observations: 28 after adjusting endpoints
Trend assumption: No deterministic trend (restricted constant)
Series: L, EMV, GDP, NISCOR, SEV
Lags interval (in first differences): 1 to 1
Unrestricted Cointegration Rank Test

Hypothesized No. of CE(s)	Trace Statistic	Critical Value	
		5 Percent	1 Percent
None**	101.4524	76.07	84.45
At most 1	47.59449	53.12	60.16
At most 2	29.97064	34.91	41.07
At most 3	15.28983	19.96	24.60
At most 4	6.240594	9.24	12.97

	Maximum Eigenvalue Statistic	Critical Value	
		5 Percent	1 Percent
None**	53.85791	34.40	39.79
At most 1	17.62385	28.14	33.24
At most 2	14.68081	22.00	26.81
At most 3	9.049235	15.67	20.20
At most 4	6.240594	9.24	12.97

Notes: See table 10.10.
**Significant at the 5 percent level.

ments do not have an impact on the level of employment. With the exception of Jamaica, minimum wage does not affect the level of employment either. To a large degree, these different results are by and large explained by a lack of significant change in LMR over the period of the study. The key factor driving employment in the three countries is output growth.

Despite the reservations put forward at the beginning of this section (shortness of samples—for Jamaica, in particular—reliance on large sample tests, and poor-quality data), there are two reasons that point to some reliability of results. First, the econometric results in this study corroborate, to a large extent, the results of a survey of employers in five Caribbean countries (see Abt Associates 1998). The study indicates that "most companies reported that legislation was not an important labour market issue affecting their company" (26). The low values on the various indexes of labor market rigidity, employment protection, or labor market distortion also suggest that LMR is not a major factor in employment determination in the region. The key to employment generation lies in output growth. Second, the results derived from annual data are by and large concordant with those with quarterly data (not reported here) generated from

Table 10.15   **Long-Run Estimates from a Variant of Equation (10) using the Phillips-Loretan Nonlinear Least Squares: Trinidad and Tobago, 1970–1999**

Constant	EMV	GDP	NISCOR	SEV
3.576	–0.009	0.222	–0.025	–0.028
(3.273)	(–0.125)	(1.932)	(–1.344)	(–1.058)

$R^2 = 0.955$
$\bar{R}^2 = 0.938$
LM (F-statistic) = 0.400 $p = 0.753$
ARCH = 1.018 $p = 0.378$
Jarque-Bera = 0.568 $p = 0.753$
Wald (F-statistic) = 0.963 $p = 0.431$

Notes: See table 10.11.

annual data. Yet with large sample sizes, quarterly data results do not suffer from the problem of "reliance on asymptotic tests."

10.7   Conclusion

Employment creation has been a major economic challenge in the Caribbean. The existence of a range of regulatory measures has been identified by some commentators as a source of labor market rigidity in the region. This research study has examined the range of direct and indirect LMRs in the region. Although several regulations exist in the countries under study, the overall level of labor market distortion caused by these regulations has been small compared with Latin American countries. Furthermore, the adoption of the voluntaristic model of industrial relations by a number of countries has meant that there has been little change in the labor laws in the region over time. For example, the severance payment acts in Trinidad and Tobago and Jamaica have not changed significantly since their introduction. The econometric analysis of the impact of selected regulations (that is, the minimum wage, contributions to the NIS, and severance payments) on employment indicates that these measures have had little statistical significance. Output growth has been identified as a key factor in generating employment in the region.

This study was limited by the small sample size, in particular for Jamaica. One solution might have been to pool data. However, pooling the data from the three countries is not advisable here for at least two reasons. First, there is a lack of homogeneity in the measurements or definitions of variables in some instances: For example, wage is defined as average earnings in Trinidad and Tobago, average compensation in Jamaica, and average wage rate in Barbados; contributions to the NIS are unweighted index of rates in Barbados, unweighted simple index of the maximum wage related payment in Jamaica, and a dummy variable in Trinidad and Tobago.

Consequently, interpreting the results from a pooled model becomes very hazardous. Second, a good or relevant panel data implies that the country dimension is much larger than the time dimension. This is not the case with our data. Another solution is to generate quarterly data from annual data to enlarge the sample size. The problem is that while data aggregation rests on a sound theoretical framework, data disaggregation when only aggregated data exist, in contrast, reposes generally on a dubious theoretical ground. Hence, given the nonexistence of quarterly data and the pooling problems noted here, the way out is to enlarge the data span by collecting more annual data to obtain reliable estimates.

Appendix

Statistical Measurement of Labor Market Regulations

Barbados

Severance payments	1970–1977	0	(scheme introduced in 1973)
(dummy variable)	1978–1990	1	(scheme changed in 1978)
	1991–2001	2	(change in scheme in 1991)

National insurance payments: simple unweighted index of the rates of contribution by employees and employers (1970–2001)

Jamaica

Severance payments	1975–1985	1	(scheme introduced in 1974)
(dummy variable)	1986–1987	2	(change in scheme in 1986)
	1988–2001	3	(change in scheme in 1988)

National insurance payments: simple unweighted index of the maximum wage-related payments (1975–2001)

National minimum wage: simple unweighted index of the minimum wage (started in 1975–2001)

Kaitz index: ratio of the national minimum index to the average compensation index (1975–1996)

Trinidad and Tobago

Severance payments	1970–1985	0	(no scheme)
	1986–1999	1	(introduced in 1971)
National insurance	1970	0	(no scheme)
payments	1971–1979	1	(introduced in 1971)
	1980–1982	2	(changed in 1980)
	1983–1998	3	(changed in 1983)
	1999–		(changed in 1999)

Minimum wage index: simple unweighted index of selected minimum wage rates (1970–1999)

Sources: of minimum wage data is Central Bank of Trinidad and Tobago, various years and Central Statistical Office, various years-a,b.

Statistical Measurement of Wages/Earnings

Barbados

The Wage Rate Index (1970–2001) is a Laspeyres index and is the arithmetic mean of wages and salaries indices for hourly-paid skilled laborers in selected sectors using a forty-hour week as the basis of calculation. Weights are based on the percentage of total employment provided by each sector.

Sources: Central Bank of Barbados, various years; International Monetary Fund, various years; Ministry of Finance and Planning, various years.

Jamaica

In the Average Compensation Index (1975–2001), the ratio of total employees' compensation in the national accounts to total number of persons employed is used as a measure of average annual compensation. The dollar values are converted to simple unweighted index number form using 1985 as the base year.

Sources: International Monetary Fund, various years-b; National Insurance Scheme, various years; Planning Institute of Jamaica, various years; Statistical Institute of Jamaica, various years.

Trinidad and Tobago

The Average Weekly Earnings Index (1976–1999) covers average weekly earnings of employees in the manufacturing, oil, sugar, and electricity sectors.

Sources: Central Bank of Trinidad and Tobago, various years; Central Statistical Office, various years-a,b.

Note: In all cases the real values were obtained by deflating by the retail price index.

Statistical Measurement of GDP and Employment

Data on GDP at constant prices were obtained from the national accounts of the three countries, while employment data were obtained from labor force surveys. In the case of Barbados, estimates of employment for the period 1970–1974 were obtained from Downes and McClean (1988).

References

Abt Associates. 1998. Workers and labour markets in the Caribbean. IADB Background Document, vol. 2. Washington, D.C.: Inter-American Development Bank, May.

Antoine, R. 1992. The CARICOM labour law harmonization report. Cave Hill, Barbados: University of the West Indies, Faculty of Law.

————. 1998. The economic implications of labour law in the IDB CARICOM countries. University of the West Indies. Working Paper.

Baker, J. L. 1997. Poverty reduction and human development in the Caribbean: A cross-country study. World Bank Discussion Paper no. 366. Washington, D.C.: World Bank.

Brown, C., C. Gilroy, and A. Kohen. 1982. The effect of minimum wage on employment and unemployment. *Journal of Economic Literature* 20 (2): 487–528.

Campbell, J. Y., and R. J. Shiller. 1988. Interpreting cointegrated models. *Journal of Economic Dynamics and Control* 12 (2/3): 505–22.

Central Bank of Barbados. Various years. *Annual statistical digest.* Bridgetown, Barbados: Central Bank of Barbados.

Central Bank of Trinidad and Tobago. Various years. *Handbook of key economic statistics.* Port of Spain, Trinidad and Tobago: Central Bank of Trinidad and Tobago.

Central Statistical Office. Various years-a. *Annual statistical digest.* Port of Spain, Trinidad and Tobago: Central Statistical Office.

————. Various years-b. *Labour digest.* Port of Spain, Trinidad and Tobago: Central Statistical Office.

Cumberbatch, J. 1995a. Wrongful dismissal and the "retreat" from Barbados Plastics. *Anglo-American Law Review* 24:213–35.

————. 1995b. Plastic surgery—wrongful dismissal in Barbados after Grosvenor v. the Advocate Co. Ltd.: A comment. *Caribbean Law Review* 5 (1): 314–35.

Downes, A. S. 2002. Indices of labour market regulation: Principles and cases. *Indian Journal of Labour Economics* 45 (1): 117–26.

Downes, A. S., and N. Mamingi. 1997. Dynamic labour demand functions with non-wage labour costs: Theory and estimation techniques. Institute of Social and Economic Research Working Paper no. 5. Cave Hill, Barbados: Institute of Social and Economic Research.

Downes, A. S., and W. McClean. 1998. The estimation of missing values of employment in Barbados. *Research Papers* (Central Statistical Office, Trinidad and Tobago) 13:115–36.

Erickson, C. L., and D. J. B. Mitchell. 1995. Labour market regulation, flexibility and employment. *Labour* 9 (3): 443–62.

Hamermesh, D. S. 1993. *Labour demand.* Princeton, N.J.: Princeton University Press.

Hamermesh, D. S., and G. A. Pfann. 1996. Adjustment costs in factor demand. *Journal of Economic Literature* 34 (3): 1264–92.

Inter-American Development Bank (IADB). 1996. *Economic and social progress in Latin America report.* Washington, D.C.: Inter-American Development Bank.

International Monetary Fund. Various years-a. *Barbados: Recent economic developments.* Washington, D.C.: International Monetary Fund.

————. Various years-b. *International financial statistics handbook.* Washington, D.C.: International Monetary Fund.

Intriligator, M. D. 1971. *Mathematical optimization and economic theory.* Englewood Cliffs, N.J.: Prentice Hall.

La Foucade, A. 1995. *A review of the evaluation and performance of social security schemes in the English-speaking Caribbean.* Port of Spain, Trinidad and Tobago: Inter-American Conference on Social Security/National Insurance Board of Trinidad and Tobago.

Lazear, E. P. 1990. Job security provisions and employment. *Quarterly Journal of Economics* 105 (3): 699–726.

Loayza, N., and L. Palacios. 1997. Economic reform and progress in Latin America and the Caribbean. World Bank Working Paper no. 1829. Washington, D.C.: World Bank.

Lockwood, B., and A. Manning. 1989. Dynamic wage-employment bargaining with employment adjustment costs. *Economic Journal* 99 (398): 1143–58.

Maddala, G. S., and I. M. Kim. 1998. *Unit roots, cointegration and structural change.* Cambridge, U.K.: Cambridge University Press.

Márquez, G., and C. Pagés. 1998. Ties that bind: Employment protection and labour market outcomes in Latin America. Inter-American Development Bank. Mimeograph.

Ministry of Finance and Planning. Various years. *Barbados economic report.* Bridgetown, Barbados: Government of Barbados.

Modesto, L. 1994. Dynamic behaviour of wages and employment: A bargaining model introducing adjustment costs. CEPR Discussion Paper no. 893. London: Centre for Economic Policy Research.

National Insurance Scheme. Various years. *Annual report.* Kingston, Jamaica: National Insurance Scheme.

Phillips, P. C. B., and M. Loretan. 1991. Estimating long run economic equilibria. *Review of Economic Studies* 58 (195): 407–36.

Planning Institute of Jamaica. Various years. *Economic and social survey of Jamaica.* Kingston, Jamaica: Planning Institute of Jamaica.

Rama, M. 1995. Do labour market policies and institutions matter? The adjustment experience in Latin America and the Caribbean. *Labour* 9:S243–S268.

Sapsford, D., and Z. Tzannatos. 1993. *The economics of the labour market.* London: MacMillan.

Statistical Institute of Jamaica. Various years. *Labour market information newsletter of Jamaica.* Kingston, Jamaica: Statistical Institute of Jamaica.

World Bank. 1995. *World development report.* Washington, D.C.: World Bank.

Zank, N. S. 1996. *Measuring the employment effects of regulation: Where did the jobs go?* London: Quorum Books.

Labor Demand in Latin America and the Caribbean
What Does It Tell Us?

Daniel S. Hamermesh

11.1 Introduction

The central questions in labor demand deal with the responsiveness of employers' use of various components of their inputs of labor to changes in their costs. This general rubric includes employment-wage elasticities for labor as a whole and for various labor subaggregates: elasticities of relative employment in different groups in response to changes in their relative costs; the patterns of employment change as scale expands and as capital deepens or improves in quality; the paths of employment as old equilibria are shocked and new ones are approached; and these same things for measures of labor utilization, such as hours per time period.

All of these have been very extensively studied, and the existing literature would seem to give a convincing degree of agreement on at least some of the central issues (see Hamermesh 1993). Nonetheless, not everyone is convinced about how much we really know on even the simplest question—the constant-output own-price elasticity of demand for aggregate labor (Topel 1998). Because this parameter is fundamentally important for understanding the impacts of such diverse policies as payroll taxation, subsidies for employment growth, and others, one wonders whether there is any hope of convincing skeptics that something can be known. Part of the reason for the skepticism may be the fact that most empirical research is based on labor markets in industrialized countries. Such studies suffer from the problem that exogenous changes in labor costs or restrictions on employ-

Daniel S. Hamermesh is Edward Everett Hale Centennial Professor of Economics at the University of Texas, Austin; a research associate of the National Bureau of Economic Research; and program director, Forschungsinstitut zur Zukunft der Arbeit.

I thank several anonymous referees for their comments.

ment demand are very rare in those countries, and when they do occur they are typically small. This means that researchers trying to identify structural parameters using these data must either rely on models that go to great lengths to establish the exogeneity of the labor cost measures, or they must search for tiny changes in employment and/or hours in response to the few tiny exogenous changes in labor costs. Neither approach is particularly satisfying.

So long as one believes that the underlying technologies are the same in developed and developing economies, data from the latter provide an ideal way to infer the sizes of important structural parameters. Broad swings in the political viewpoints of succeeding governments often lead to broad changes in labor market policy in developing countries. The major vicissitudes in policy can be exploited to allow inferences about these parameters that are based on large exogenous changes in labor costs. It is true that in many cases the data on labor markets in developing countries are not as complete as in developed economies, but in some cases they are, and in those instances the availability of good data that cover periods of widespread and substantial policy changes allows us to make inferences about labor demand that should be useful for students of labor market behavior generally.

In some instances Latin America and the Caribbean meet both criteria: Some of the policy changes are much larger, in terms of the size of the shocks, than we typically see in developed economies, and in many cases the data, especially establishment data, are very well suited to studying labor demand. The majority of these studies do meet these criteria. In particular, the Saavedra and Torero (2000) study of Peru and the Barros and Corseuil (2000) study of Brazil meet both of these criteria perfectly, while the others all at least cover periods in which the shocks are much greater than typically seen in industrialized economies. In what follows I examine what we can learn about these central issues in labor demand from recent studies of the economies of this region.

11.2 Evidence on the Overall Demand for Labor

The central parameter in the study of labor demand is the constant-output own-wage elasticity of employment demand. Hundreds of estimates of this parameter have been produced using a variety of methods and types of data (Hamermesh 1993). A large number of the recent Latin American and Caribbean studies generate estimates of this parameter. Moreover, while most of the studies in the literature use aggregate or industry data, many of the studies in this recent group produce their estimates using firm-level data, thus avoiding the aggregation biases that are likely to be severe in what are surely nonlinear economic relationships. Assuming measurement errors in these microdata are not a serious problem,

Table 11.1   **Latin American and Caribbean Estimates of Constant-Output Own-Wage Labor Demand Elasticities**

			Estimated Elasticity		
Country/Study	Data	Frequency/Time Period	Blue-Collar	All	White-Collar
Barbados/Downes et al.	Aggregate	Annual/1970–96		–.17	
Brazil/Paes de Barros & Corseuil	Establishments	Monthly/1986–97		–.40	
Chile/Fajnzylber & Maloney	Firms	Annual/1981–86	–.32		–.48
Colombia/Fajnzylber & Maloney	Firms	Annual/1980–91	–1.37		–.59
Mexico/Fajnzylber & Maloney	Firms	Annual/1986–90	–.42		–.44
Peru/Saavedra & Torero	Sectors	Quarterly/1987–97		–.19	
Uruguay/Cassoni et al.	2-digit industries	Quarterly/1975–84		–.69	
		Quarterly/1985–97		–.22	

even apart from the greater exogenous variation in labor costs that is likely in developing countries, the spatial disaggregation of the data gives these studies an advantage over most earlier studies.

In table 11.1 I summarize estimates of these elasticities from a number of recent Latin American and Caribbean studies. The methodologies of the studies are fairly closely comparable: All estimate equations describing the logarithm of employment as a function of wages and output, thus providing a direct estimate of this crucial parameter. All except the Barbadian study include at least one lag in employment as an additional regressor. Clearly and necessarily the results differ across the studies. In part, these differences arise from slight variations in the methods of estimation and in the data (their frequency, their level of spatial aggregation, and their definitions of the measures of labor costs). These differences may also be due to true differences in the nature of the technologies used in the different countries, perhaps differences in the output mix, perhaps true differences in the available means of producing the same product.

Despite the obvious differences, the results are remarkable for their apparent consistency. Taking the results for the four countries—Barbados, Brazil, Peru, and Uruguay—for which the estimates have been produced covering all employment, the average constant-output own-wage elasticity is –0.30. The estimates by Fajnzylber and Maloney (2000) are somewhat larger than the other estimates, but one must remember that they are based on employment disaggregated by a measure of skill, so it is unsurprising that they are bigger (more in the following). There is clearly a range of estimates presented here so that, as always with any group of empirical studies, no one particular estimate can be inferred as being "the truth." But taking all the estimated elasticities together, one must infer that they reinforce the consensus estimate, –0.30, that I identified (Hamermesh 1993) from the many studies covering mainly industrialized economies and based mainly on more highly aggregated data. That we obtain a set of estimates whose central tendency is around –0.30 is also consistent with the observation that labor's share of output is around 2/3 in a Cobb-Douglas two-factor world.

That the estimates replicate the previous literature should in part lay to rest concerns that our knowledge of the size of this crucial parameter is too uncertain to allow us to make predictions about the likely impact of imposed changes in labor costs on the level of employment. The sizes of the shocks to labor costs in these countries, and their source in the sharp political changes that have swept over the region, suggest that concerns about identification that have led critics to question studies based on developed economies should be less severe here. As in Angrist's (1996) study of the West Bank/Gaza Strip, these additional estimates for developing economies suggest that our inferences from developed economies may be broadly applicable elsewhere.

Although estimates of the constant-output own-wage elasticity for homogeneous labor are the most common in the set of recent Latin American and Caribbean studies, these studies contain a variety of other implications for the analysis of long-run labor demand that merit attention. The Argentine study (Mondino and Montoya 2000) estimates the demand for employment and hours separately, including as regressors lagged values of each component of the labor input. The long-run wage elasticities generated in the study are thus measures of the responsiveness of the employment-hours ratio to changes in payroll costs (and are thus not included in the tabulation of labor demand elasticities in table 11.1). The long-run constant-output elasticity of employment to a change in labor costs, holding hours constant, is –0.94. This implies a substantial degree of worker-hours substitution and indicates that a rise in wages induces employers to work a smaller labor force more intensely each hour. Because the same elasticity based on the equation for hours is only –0.03, by inference a rise in labor costs does not alter the length of the workweek.

Because it disaggregates employment by a broad measure of skill, the three-country study by Fajnzylber and Maloney (2000) allows us to examine whether there are differences by level of skill in the long-run responsiveness to shocks to labor demand. This depends on the nature of the underlying possibilities for multifactor substitution among the types of labor and capital, but past studies suggest that there is an inverse relationship between the amount of skill embodied in a group of workers and the absolute value of the elasticity of demand for their labor. Except for the estimates for Colombia, this is not the case in this study. This apparent inconsistency with the literature may not be as disturbing as it seems at first glance, however. The level of skill in even the lower-skilled groups examined in studies of developed economies may be as high as the average in the white-collar groups summarized in table 11.1. Because the definition of skill is so fluid, the results here simply may not be comparable to those found elsewhere in the literature.

In their estimates for the Caribbean, Downes, Mamingi, and Antoine (2000) recognize that a well-enforced minimum wage that bites high into the distribution of earnings will have major negative effects on employment. Indeed, even though their estimates are based on aggregate data and thus include many workers whose wage and employment are unlikely to be affected by changes in minimum wages, they find this negative effect for Jamaica, where they specify a coverage-weighted minimum wage index (although not for Trinidad and Tobago, where a less complex index is used). The exact sizes of the estimated elasticities tell us nothing about the underlying structure of demand, because they depend on both the labor demand elasticity and the fraction of the workforce affected by the minimum, so I do not include them in table 11.1. Nonetheless, the results for Jamaica are consistent with standard inferences about long-run labor demand elasticities.

While I do not summarize their impacts in table 11.1, most of the studies other than that by Fajnzylber and Maloney (2000) include measures of the costs of employment regulations in addition to the direct measure of labor cost. Most specify these as representing the effect of the changing stringency of administrative regulations rather than the impact of endogenous changes in the actual costs of the programs. Indeed, perhaps the strongest point in some of these studies and their biggest innovation is the careful construction of these measures in an area where the literature is fairly sparse (Hamermesh 1993, chap. 8), and most studies simply look at before-after changes. That in their study of Peru Saavedra and Torero find significant reductions of employment in response to increases in the generosity of severance pay suggests that, as with the wage-cost measures that are included in standard labor demand equations, so too do other exogenous cost increases reduce employment demand. Mondino and Montoya (2000), who also carefully constructed a measure of the cost of employment regulations, find a similar result for Argentina.

Taken together, the Latin American evidence should add considerably to economists' and policy advisors' assurance in emphasizing the long-run economic costs of so-called job protection policies—their impacts on average levels of employment. They should underline the essential irrelevance of a spate of mathematically clever theoretical models based essentially on arguments about market imperfections that claim that such policies may actually increase employment (e.g., Bertola 1992). They should also make one very dubious about empirical results from cross-country comparisons that claim that such policies have no impact on employment levels, based on examinations of the estimated impacts of quickly constructed indexes of regulatory stringency in the labor market (e.g., OECD 1999).

11.3   Dynamic Labor Demand in Latin America and the Caribbean

Most of the recent Latin American and Caribbean studies allow us to examine the path of employment as the labor market moves between old and new equilibria in response to cost or output shocks. All of the studies specify smooth symmetric adjustment by including one or two lagged dependent variables in the labor demand equations. Thus, while they ignore the innovations in the study of the dynamics of factor demand that were pointed out in the 1990s (see Hamermesh and Pfann [1996] for a summary), their firm rooting in the standard literature on factor demand allows for ready comparisons.

Table 11.2 summarizes the speeds of adjustment of labor demand that have been estimated in the recent Latin studies. In each case I have calculated the speed as the number of time periods, t^*, for half the gap between old and new equilibria to be traversed. In these equations with a single lagged dependent variable the calculation is

$$(1) \qquad t^* = \frac{\ln(.5)}{\ln \lambda},$$

where λ is the coefficient on the lagged dependent variable. To facilitate comparisons across studies the table expresses t^* in quarters. That there may be temporal aggregation biases is well known and may explain why the estimates here and in the literature generally indicate slower adjustment the more highly temporally aggregated are the underlying data. Acknowledging this, however, except for the Brazilian study by Barros and Corseuil (2000), all of the estimated speeds of adjustment are slow relative to the typical estimates for developed economies. In the literature, generally, the best estimate is that the half-life of the lag in the adjustment of employment demand is around two-quarters (Hamermesh 1993, chap. 7), below all but the one exception listed in table 11.2.

We cannot determine whether the striking difference between these Latin estimates and the estimates in the general literature arises because adjustment is truly slower in Latin America, or because the dynamic specifications of the estimating equations are incorrect. For example, it may be that the assumption of smooth symmetric adjustment is incorrect, and any one of a large variety of alternative specifications would describe the dynamics in the data sets better. These would include lumpy adjustment, linear adjustment costs, and any kind of asymmetry. Perhaps the problem is especially severe in the context of a developing economy.

Findings in the literature for developed economies have also established some regularities in the estimated relative speeds of adjustment of the demand for different components of the labor aggregate and for different groups of workers. Mondino and Montoya's (2000) finding for Argentina that the demand for hours adjusts more rapidly than the demand for em-

Table 11.2   **Latin American and Caribbean Estimates of Speed of Adjustment of Labor Demand (in quarters)**

Country/Study	Data	Frequency/ Time Period	Half-life of Adjustment		
			Employment	Worker Hours	Hours
Argentina/Mondino & Montoya	Firms	Annual/1970–96	5.4		0.4
Brazil/Paes de Barros & Corseuil	Establishments	Monthly/1986–97		1.0	

	Data	Frequency/ Time Period	Half-life of Adjustment		
			Blue-Collar	All	White-Collar
Chile/Fajnzylber & Maloney	Firms	Annual/1981–86	8.8		4.0
Colombia/Fajnzylber & Maloney	Firms	Annual/1980–91	20.8		5.6
Mexico/Fajnzylber & Maloney	Firms	Annual/1986–90	14.4		19.2
Peru/Saavedra & Torero	Establishments	Quarterly/1987–97		5.1	
Uruguay/Cassoni et al.	2-digit industries	Quarterly/1975–84		5.9	
		Quarterly/1985–97		5.0	

ployees is consistent with both the large empirical literature for developed economies and with the observation that adjusting hours initially in response to what may be perceived as a temporary shock allows employers to avoid incurring the fixed costs of hiring and firing workers.

A comparison of the relative speeds of adjustment of the demand for blue- and white-collar employees in the Fajnzylber and Maloney (2000) estimates is less encouraging. In estimates for two of the three countries that they examine, adjustment is slower for blue- than for white-collar employees. This result is inconsistent with the widespread finding in developed countries' labor markets that adjustment speeds decrease with the skill of the work group (presumably because the fixed costs of hiring and firing are greater among more skilled workers). Why the results should be opposite this is unclear. Perhaps unions and other institutional arrangements restrict the adjustment of blue-collar employment more than that of white-collar employment; perhaps misspecification of the dynamics due to the temporal aggregation of the data is more serious in the equations describing blue-collar employment.

Beginning with Nadiri and Rosen (1969), a small literature has developed examining the linkages among the adjustment paths of several factors. The issue is whether greater speed in the adjustment of one productive input raises the rate at which another adjusts—whether the inputs are dynamic complements or not. There is no consensus in the literature on this point for any pair of inputs, and the results in the one Latin study that provides evidence on this issue do not help to pin down the answer to this question. Mondino and Montoya (2000) do include lags in hours per worker (employment) in the dynamic equations describing employment (hours). Unfortunately, the coefficients on lagged hours in the employment equation sum to 0.15, while those on lagged employment in the equation describing hours sum to –0.06. Perhaps the best conclusion is that there is little evidence for or against the dynamic complementarity of employment and hours per worker.

Increased product-market competition, such as would arise from greater openness to international trade, might be expected to spur employers to adjust more rapidly in response to shocks to costs or output. With competitors from other countries introducing new products and technologies, domestic producers become increasingly uncompetitive if they maintain antiquated staffing structures. Evidence for Mexico based on monthly data covering 1987–1995 (Robertson and Dutkowsky 2002) supports this hypothesis. Cassoni, Allen, and Labadie (1999) provide some weak evidence in favor of it too, because there was a slight rise in the speed of adjustment of employment demand as the Uruguayan economy became more open.

One of the central purposes of the recent group of Latin American and Caribbean studies was to examine how changing employment regulation, particularly job security laws such as those governing severance pay, affected the speed of adjustment of employment demand. (Heckman and Pagés [2000] discuss this at length.) The evidence on this issue in the literature (Hamermesh 1993, chap. 8) is sparse and conflicting. Much of it, like Barros and Corseuil's (2000) study for Brazil, is based on comparing speeds of adjustment pre- and postregulatory change and is inconclusive. Like the few other studies (e.g., Burgess and Dolado 1989) that actually try to measure the severity of regulations, Saavedra and Torero (2000) find in their panel of establishments that increases in a carefully constructed measure of the cost of severance pay slow the speed of adjustment of employment. Their results suggest that, if we hope to uncover their dynamic effects, there is a large payoff in empirical research on labor demand to specifying the details of labor market regulations.

11.4   Conclusions and Implications

No single study of an economic phenomenon, or even several studies, is ever highly convincing, because one can worry about the representativeness of the example and particular problems with the research design. The results of recent Latin American and Caribbean studies, however, based as they are on labor markets that have not been thoroughly examined using modern econometric techniques and that have been characterized by relatively large shocks, should reinforce our confidence about the negative impact on employment of higher labor costs, both payroll costs and job market regulations. They should remind policymakers that in developing economies, as in developed ones, policies that may be socially desirable, but that raise labor costs or increase labor market rigidity, have negative consequences for the level of employment.

In many ways the strengths and weakness of these Latin American and Caribbean studies mirror those of the vast literature of labor demand. The estimates of static labor demand parameters seem generally reasonable—reasonably tightly estimated and consistent with an underlying theory that is fairly closely linked to the estimating equations. The estimates of the dynamics of adjustment are much less convincing, both in these studies and in the larger literature. This may be because the dynamic specifications are much less loosely linked to theory than are the static estimates. This difference suggests that further work on Latin America and the Caribbean should focus on more careful specification of labor market dynamics if we are to be able to draw inferences about the impact of shocks and labor market regulations on fluctuations in the demand for workers and hours.

References

Angrist, Joshua. 1996. Short-run demand for Palestinian labor. *Journal of Labor Economics* 14 (July): 425–53.
Barros, Ricardo Paes de, and Carlos Henrique Corseuil. 2000. The impact of regulations on Brazilian labor market performance. Institute of Applied Economic Research (IPEA). Unpublished Manuscript.
Bertola, Giuseppe. 1992. Labor turnover costs and average labor demand. *Journal of Labor Economics* 10 (October): 389–411.
Burgess, Simon, and Juan Dolado. 1989. Intertemporal rules with variable speed of adjustment: An application to U.K. manufacturing employment. *Economic Journal* 99 (June): 347–365.
Cassoni, Adriana, Steven Allen, and Gaston Labadie. 1999. Unions and employment in Uruguay. Group for the Study of Organization and Social Policy (GEOPS). Unpublished Manuscript.
Downes, Andrew, Nlandu Mamingi, and Rose-Marie Belle Antoine. 2000. Labor market regulation and employment in the Caribbean. IADB Research Network Working Paper no. R-388. Washington, D.C.: Inter-American Development Bank.
Fajnzylber, Pablo, and William Maloney. 2000. Labor demand in Colombia, Chile and Mexico. World Bank. Unpublished Manuscript.
Hamermesh, Daniel. 1993. *Labor demand.* Princeton, N.J.: Princeton University Press.
Hamermesh, Daniel, and Gerard Pfann. 1996. Adjustment costs in factor demand. *Journal of Economic Literature* 34 (September): 1264–92.

Heckman, James, and Carmen Pagés. 2000. The cost of job security regulation: Evidence from Latin American labor markets. NBER Working Paper no. 7773. Cambridge, Mass.: National Bureau of Economic Research, June.

Mondino, Guillermo, and Silvia Montoya. 2000. The effects of labor market regulations on employment decisions by firms: Empirical evidence for Argentina. IADB Research Network Working Paper no. R-391. Washington, D.C.: Inter-American Development Bank.

Nadiri, M. Ishaq, and Sherwin Rosen. 1969. Interrelated factor demand functions. *American Economic Review* 59 (September): 457–71.

Organization for Economic Cooperation and Development (OECD). 1999. *OECD Employment Outlook.* Paris: OECD.

Robertson, Raymond, and Donald Dutkowsky. 2002. Labor adjustment costs in a destination country: The case of Mexico. *Journal of Development Economics* 67 (February): 29–54.

Saavedra, Jaime, and Maximo Torero. 2000. Labor market reforms and their impact over formal labor demand and job market turnover: The case of Peru. IADB Research Network Working Paper no. R-394. Washington, D.C.: Inter-American Development Bank.

Topel, Robert. 1998. Analytical needs and empirical knowledge in labor economics. In *Labor statistics measurement issues,* ed. John Haltiwanger, Marilyn Manser, and Robert Topel, 51–74. Chicago: University of Chicago Press.

Contributors

Steven G. Allen
Departments of Economics and
  Business Management
Box 7229
North Carolina State University
Raleigh, NC 27695-7229

Rose-Marie Belle Antoine
Faculty of Law
University of the West Indies,
  Cave Hill Campus
PO Box 64
Bridgetown, Barbados

Ricardo Paes de Barros
Institute for Applied Economic
  Research (IPEA)
Avenida Nilo Peçanha, no. 50/609
Rio de Janeiro, Cep. 20044-900
Brazil

Raquel Bernal
Department of Economics
Northwestern University
2001 Sheridan Road
Evanston, IL 60208

Mauricio Cárdenas
Fedesarrollo
Calle 78 No. 9-91
Bogota, Colombia

Adriana Cassoni
Departamento de Economía
Universidad de la República
J. E. Rodò 1854
Montevideo, Uruguay

Carlos Henrique Corseuil
Instituto de Pesquisa Economica
  Aplicada (IPEA)
Av. Presidente Antonio Carlos 51
Rio de Janeiro, 20020-010, RJ, Brazil

Andrew S. Downes
Sir Arthur Lewis Institute of Social
  and Economic Studies
University of the West Indies,
  Cave Hill Campus
PO Box 64
Bridgetown, Barbados

Daniel S. Hamermesh
Department of Economics
University of Texas
Austin, TX 78712-1173

James J. Heckman
Department of Economics
The University of Chicago
1126 E. 59th Street
Chicago, IL 60637

Hugo A. Hopenhayn
Department of Economics
Bunche Hall 9353
University of California, Los Angeles
Box 951477
Los Angeles, CA 90095-1477

Adriana D. Kugler
Department of Economics
University of Houston
204 McElhinney Hall 209C
Houston, TX 77204-5019

Gaston J. Labadie
Universidad ORT Uruguay
Facultad de Administración y Ciencias
    Sociales
Cuareim 1451, Uruguay

William F. Maloney
Office of the Chief Economist
The World Bank
1818 H Street, NW
Washington, DC 20433

Nlandu Mamingi
Department of Economics
University of the West Indies,
    Cave Hill Campus
PO Box 64
Bridgetown, Barbados

Jairo Nuñez Mendez
Facultad de Economía
Universidad de los Andes
Cra. 1 No. 18a-10
Santa Fe de Bogotá, D.C. Colombia
Bogotá, Colombia

Guillermo Mondino
Alicia Moreau de Justo 740-Of 321
Puerto Madero-Dock 5
Capital Federal
C1107AAP Buenos Aires, Argentina

Claudio E. Montenegro
The World Bank
1818 H Street, NW
Washington, DC 20433

Silvia Montoya
IERAL de Fundación Mediterránea
Esmeralda 1320, 5° A
C1007ABT Buenos Aires, Argentina

Carmen Pagés
Research Department
Inter-American Development Bank
1300 New York Avenue
Washington, DC 20577

Jaime Saavedra
Grupo de Análisis para el Desarrollo
    (GRADE)
Av. del Ejército #1870
Lima 27, Peru

Máximo Torero
Grupo de Análisis para el Desarrollo
    (GRADE)
Av. del Ejército #1870
Lima 27, Peru

Author Index

Subject Index